Walter Olthoff (Ed.)

ECOOP '95 — Object-Oriented Programming

9th European Conference
Åarhus, Denmark, August 7-11, 1995
Proceedings

Springer

Series Editors

Gerhard Goos
Universität Karlsruhe
Vincenz-Priessnitz-Straße 3, D-76128 Karlsruhe, Germany

Juris Hartmanis
Department of Computer Science, Cornell University
4130 Upson Hall, Ithaca, NY 14853, USA

Jan van Leeuwen
Department of Computer Science, Utrecht University
Padualaan 14, 3584 CH Utrecht, The Netherlands

Volume Editor

Walter Olthoff
Deutsches Forschungszentrum für Künstliche Intelligenz
Postfach 20 80, D-67608 Kaiserslautern, Germany

Cataloging-in-Publication Data applied for

Die Deutsche Bibliothek - CIP-Einheitsaufnahme

Object oriented programming : 9th European conference ; proceedings / ECOOP '95, Århus, Denmark, August 7 - 11, 1995. Walter Olthoff (ed.). - Berlin ; Heidelberg ; New York : Springer, 1995
(Lecture notes in computer science ; Vol. 952)
ISBN 3-540-60160-0 (Berlin ...)
NE: Olthoff, Walter [Hrsg.]; ECOOP <9, 1995, Århus>; GT

CR Subject Classification (1991): D.1-3, H.2, J.1

ISBN 3-540-60160-0 Springer-Verlag Berlin Heidelberg New York

Typesetting: Camera-ready by author
SPIN 10486478 06/3142 - 5 4 3 2 1 0 Printed on acid-free paper

Preface

For the ninth time now, the European Conference on Object-Oriented Programming provides a mid-summer gathering place for researchers, practitioners, students and newcomers in the field of object technology. Despite fierce competition from an increasing number of attractive conferences on object-related topics, ECOOP has successfully positioned itself as the premier European object technology conference. One reason is without doubt the composition of the conference week and the nature of its events. Running in parallel on the first two days, a comprehensive tutorial program and a very selective workshop program are offered to attendees. This is followed by a three-day technical program organized in a single track providing a highly communicative atmosphere of scientific exchange and learning. Overlapping with these events are a two-day industrial exhibition and a two-day opportunity for non-industrial system developers to demonstrate their software. Thus, ECOOP is not just a conference on programming but an event touching on the full spectrum of object technology.

This volume constitutes the proceedings of the Ninth European Conference on Object-Oriented Programming, ECOOP, held in Åarhus, Denmark, August 7-11, 1995. Previous ECOOP conferences were held in Paris (France), Oslo (Norway), Nottingham (England), Ottawa (Canada, jointly with OOPSLA), Geneva (Switzerland), Utrecht (the Netherlands), Kaiserslautern (Germany), and Bologna (Italy).

Object technology continues to increase its impact on the corporate world. Leading companies devote more and more resources to object-oriented development of new software or the gradual adaptation of legacy systems to the object perspective. This results in constant demand for excellent research results, improved development environment concepts and more sophisticated methods for analysis and design. Driven by these forces, ECOOP both benefits and suffers from the fluctuation of economic parameters.

This year, 90 papers were submitted from 19 countries around the world, with significant North American representation. The latter fact probably reflects a kind of load sharing ECOOP has established with the OOPSLA conference series. Jointly they provide a biannual forum for publication of original high-quality object technology research. The selection of papers was carried out during a two-day program committee meeting in Kaiserslautern. Papers were judged according to their originality, relevance and presentation quality, and acceptance was based purely on their own merits, independently of other submissions. The 18 selected papers are of remarkable quality, and range in topic from more theoretical areas like type theory and verification to implementation aspects of programming paradigms, including concurrency, distribution, reflection, specification and interfaces. Although the presentation of the selected papers will constitute the kernel of the technical program, the keynote address and the two invited talks will address essential experiences, visions and research overviews related to the theory and practice of object technology. A paper related to each of the invited talks is included in this volume.

ECOOP95 is the result of considerable effort on the part of a number of people. It has been a pleasure to work together with the members of the program committee and the referees, who each devoted much time in reviewing and discussing the submitted papers. The collaboration with Ole Madsen (Conference Chair) and Jørgen Knudsen (Organizing Chair) was excellent and very effective, despite the hinderances of differing time zones. Thanks must also go to those responsible for the organization of the various ECOOP events: Birger Møller-Pedersen, Eric Jul, Boris Magnusson, Kurt Nørmark, Elmer Sandvad, and to those who helped in the local organization in Åarhus and Kaiserslautern: Susanne Brøndberg, Janne Damgaard, Marianne Iversen and Cornelia Wanders. Finally, ECOOP95 has greatly benefitted from the support of sponsoring organizations whose support and cooperation are gratefully acknowledged. DFKI GmbH graciously provided me with the time and support necessary to serve as Program Chair.

Ultimately, the success of ECOOP95 will be determined by the number of attendees who leave Åarhus with the memory of time well spent. Knowing details of the prepared events I am confident that we will receive a very good rating on this scale. Enjoy the conference and this book!

April 1995

Walter Olthoff
Program Chair
ECOOP'95

Organization

ECOOP'95 is organized by the Department of Computer Science, University of Århus and AITO (Association Internationale pour les Technologies Objets) in cooperation with ACM/SIGPLAN.

Executive Committee

Conference Chair:	Ole Lehrmann Madsen (Århus University, DK)
Program Chair:	Walter Olthoff (DFKI GmbH, Germany)
Organizing Chair:	Jørgen Lindskov Knudsen (Århus University, DK)
Tutorials:	Birger Møller-Pedersen (Norwegian Computing Center, Norway)
Workshops:	Eric Jul (University of Kopenhagen, Denmark)
Panels:	Boris Magnusson (Lund University, Sweden)
Exhibition:	Elmer Sandvad (Århus University, Denmark)
Demonstrations:	Kurt Nørmark (Ålborg University, Denmark)

Program Committee

Mehmet Aksit	University of Twente, Netherlands
Pierre America	Philips, Netherlands
Jean Bezivin	Université de Nantes, France
Pierre Cointe	Ecoles des Mines de Nantes, France
Bjørn Freeman-Benson	Carleton University, Canada
Yutaka Ishikawa	RWCP, Japan
Eric Jul	University of Kopenhagen, Denmark
Gerti Kappel	University of Linz, Austria
Mary Loomis	Hewlett-Packard, USA
Boris Magnusson	Lund University, Sweden
Paola Mello	Università di Bologna, Italy
José Meseguer	SRI International, USA
Bertrand Meyer	ISE, USA/France
Oscar Nierstrasz	University of Bern, Switzerland
Walter Olthoff	DFKI GmbH, Germany
Andreas Paepcke	Stanford University, USA
Jens Palsberg	Århus University, Denmark
Remo Pareschi	Rank Xerox, France
Markku Sakkinen	University of Jyväskylä, Finland
Alan Snyder	SunSoft, Inc., USA
Dave Thomas	Object Technology International, Canada
Mario Tokoro	Keio University / Sony CSL, Japan
Peter Wegner	Brown University, USA
Roberto Zicari	Johann-Wolfgang-von-Goethe-Universität, D

Referees

Birger Andersen
Peter Bichler
Uwe Borghoff
Philippe Brèche
Kim Bruce
Frank Buddrus
Michele Bugliesi
Luca Cardelli
Giuseppe Castagna
Anna Ciampolini
Antonio Corradi
Enrico Denti
Christophe Dony
Gregor Engels
Kathleen Fischer
Steve Freeman
Yasuhisa Fujinami
Natalie Glance
Roberto Gorrieri
Kari Granö
Jørgen Greve
Karl Guggisberg
Görel Hedin
Yasuaki Honda
Juhani Iivari
Christian Jensen
Niels Christian Juul
Gregor Kiczales
Kai Koskimies
Evelina Lamma
John Lamping
Sven-Eric Lautemann
Ulrike Lechner
Thomas Ledoux
Letizia Leonardi
Patrick Lincoln
Frank van der Linden
Markus Lumpe
Munenori Maeda
Jacques Malenfant
Francesco Marcelloni
Narciso Marti-Oliet
Satoshi Matsuoka
Michael Moustgaard
Theo Dirk Meijler
Martin Müller
Philippe Mulet
Piero Mussio
Jörg Nolte
Jens Cornelius Olsen
Andrea Omicini
Jukka Paakki
Lars Jarnbo Pedersen
Wolfgang Pree
Sigi Reich
Philippe Reitz
Werner Retschitzegger
Tamar Richner
Fred Rivard
Jorma Sajaniemi
Ichiroh Satoh
Jean-Guy Schneider
Michael Schwartzbach
Cesare Stefanelli
Antero Taivalsaari
Bedir Tekinerdogan
Patrick Varone
Juha Vihavainen
Mario Wolczko
Franco Zambonelli
Eddy Zondag

Sponsoring Institutions

ACM/SIGPLAN: Association of Computing Machinery - Special Interest Group in Programming Languages
AITO: Association Internationale pour les Technologies Objets
CINCOM Systems, Denmark
DAIMI: Department of Computer Science, University of Åarhus, Denmark
Den Danske Bank, Denmark
DEVISE: Centre for Experimental System Development, Univ. of Åarhus, DK
Faculty of Science, University of Åarhus, Denmark
Sun Division, ICL Data A/S, Denmark

Contents

Keynote Address (Abstract)

Types

Programming Languages

Invited Talk

Reflective Programming / Verification

Implementation

Invited Talk

Concurrency / Specification

Distribution / Interfaces

Keynote Address

Experiences on The Road to Object Utopia

Dave Thomas (Object Technology International)

The talk will present lessons from nearly a decade of experience in making object technologies real in the industrial world. It is also the story of ten years of opportunities for object-oriented research and development activities. From this starting point a critical look is given at where we have been and where we are going to with object technology research and practice.

Dave Thomas has 30 years of experience in the computer industry as an architect, project manager and director.

Dave holds an adjunct research professorship at Carleton University where he previously held the position of Director of Object-Oriented Research Group. During the last 12 years Dave has specialized in the design and implementation of object-oriented systems. Projects have included the successful development and implementation of systems for client-server, embedded systems, manufacturing, networking systems, electronic publishing, integrated circuit testing, defence and instrumentation. Dave is widely published in object-oriented literature. He has served on the program committees for the OOPSLA and ECOOP conferences for the past 8 years.

Dave is founder and CEO of Object Technology International, Inc. (OTI). OTI is an advanced software technology company and a world leader in object-oriented technology. The company's primary business is joint product development and technology licensing. OTI's ENVY portfolio of software components, tools, technology and processes enable OTI alliance partners to develop and deploy innovative tools and products. Over the last 10 years, OTI's products and technology have been key in the commercialization of the Smalltalk language.

The Cartesian Product Algorithm

Simple and Precise Type Inference Of Parametric Polymorphism

Ole Agesen
Computer Science Department, Stanford University
Stanford, CA 94305
agesen@cs.stanford.edu

Abstract. Concrete types and abstract types are different and serve different purposes. Concrete types, the focus of this paper, are essential to support compilation, application delivery, and debugging in object-oriented environments. Concrete types should not be obtained from explicit type declarations because their presence limits polymorphism unacceptably. This leaves us with type inference. Unfortunately, while polymorphism demands the use of type inference, it has also been the hardest challenge for type inference.

We review previous type inference algorithms that analyze code with parametric polymorphism and then present a new one: the cartesian product algorithm. It improves precision and efficiency over previous algorithms and deals directly with inheritance, rather than relying on a preprocessor to expand it away. Last, but not least, it is conceptually simple.

The cartesian product algorithm has been used in the Self system since late 1993. We present measurements to document its performance and compare it against several previous algorithms.

Keywords: concrete types, abstract types, type inference, polymorphism, inheritance, Self.

1 Introduction

1.1 Concrete versus Abstract Types

Concrete types (a.k.a. implementation types or representation types) are sets of classes. For example, an expression that returns instances of class `ListStack` has concrete type `{ListStack}`, and an expression that returns instances of either class `ArrayStack` or `ListStack` has concrete type `{ArrayStack, ListStack}`. Concrete types provide detailed information since they distinguish even different implementations of the same abstract data type.

In contrast, *abstract* types (a.k.a. interface types or principal types) capture abstract properties of objects. They may not distinguish between different implementations of the same abstract data type: both list-based and array-based stacks may have an abstract type like `[push:elmType→void; pop:void→elmType]`. Probably the best known inference algorithm for abstract types is Milner's [16].

Concrete and abstract types are extremes in a spectrum of type systems. Class-types, as found in BETA, C++, and Eiffel, are neither fully abstract (it is impossible to express the type of *any* object that has a push and a pop operation), nor fully concrete (declaring an object with class type `Stack`, does not reveal the specific subclass of which it is an instance).

Concrete types are the focus of this paper. Previous publications have argued that they directly support solutions to several important problems in object-oriented programming environments:

- *Compilation.* Concrete types support important optimizations such as elimination of dynamic dispatch and method inlining [17, 21].
- *Extraction.* Concrete types support delivery of compact applications by enabling an extractor to sift through an image of objects, selecting those that are essential to run a given application [4].
- *Browsing/debugging.* Concrete types help a programmer understand programs by allowing a browser to track control flow (and thereby data flow) through dynamically dispatched message sends [3].

The need for concrete type information may be greater in object-oriented environments than in "conventional" (C-like) environments: object-oriented programs consist of many small methods (hence, inlining is important); emphasis on code reuse yields large and general class libraries (hence, extraction is important); and understanding object-oriented programs is harder because control- and data-flow are coupled (hence, browsers should assist).

Even statically-typed languages like C++ can use concrete type information since the above three problems are not supported well by class types. For instance, knowing that an object is an instance of class `Stack`, is generally not sufficient to inline operations on it (the program may contain several subclasses of `Stack` and from the static type declaration we cannot tell which specific one occurs — but concrete type inference may tell) [13].

1.2 Polymorphism

Polymorphism, the ability of a piece of code to work on several kinds of objects, is a central part of object-oriented programming. Polymorphism is desirable because it enables more code reuse. We distinguish between two kinds. *Parametric polymorphism* is the ability of routines to be invoked on arguments of several types. A length function that works on both singly-linked and doubly-linked lists exhibits parametric polymorphism. *Data polymorphism* is the ability to store objects of different types in a variable or slot[1]. "Link" objects forming a heterogeneous list of integers, floats, and strings, exhibit data polymorphism because their "contents" slots contain objects of several types.

Explicit (programmer-inserted) *concrete* type declarations are undesirable because they limit polymorphism and code reuse. For example, adding the type declaration {Int, Float} to the formal arguments of a `max` routine makes it less reusable, because it can no longer be used to find the larger of two strings. Given that explicit concrete type declarations are undesirable, the considerable interest in *inference* algorithms is not surprising [3, 11, 17, 18, 19, 20, 25]. Ironically, while the desire to maximize polymor-

1. Slots in Self provide the functionality of instance variables, parents, formal arguments, and local variables.

phism demands type inference, polymorphism is also the hardest challenge for inference algorithms. To illustrate this, we applied a simple inference algorithm ("the basic algorithm," see Section 2.2) to the Self expression `30 factorial`, where the `factorial` method for an integer receiver is defined by

```
factorial = (
  self<=1 ifTrue: [1] False: [self * predecessor factorial].
).
```

Rather than {smallInt, bigInt}, this very polymorphic and imprecise type was reported:

{smallInt, bigInt, collector, memory, memoryState, byteVector, mutableString, immutableString, float, link, list, primitiveFailedError, userError, time, false, true, nil, [blk_1], [blk_2], ..., [blk_{13}]}.

In fairness, the situation is more complex than just analyzing `factorial`. All methods invoked by `factorial`, and methods they in turn invoke, etc., must be analyzed. Furthermore, arithmetic overflows cannot be ruled out, forcing analysis of the bigInt implementation which uses lists, byte vectors, etc. In total, approximately a thousand lines of code must be analyzed to find the type of `factorial`. While some of this complexity is peculiar to the Self system and better results may be obtained on other systems, the example clearly demonstrates the insufficient precision of the basic algorithm when analyzing polymorphic code.

To address the imprecision, more accurate algorithms were developed; see [1] for a survey. Some of these can infer the precise type {smallInt, bigInt} for the factorial example. The improved precision came at a cost, though. Type inference got less efficient and more complex to understand. For instance, Phillips and Shepard implemented one of the more precise algorithms and found that it took 10 hours to infer types for the expression `3+4` in ParcPlace Smalltalk [19].

1.3 Contributions

In this paper we propose a new algorithm for analyzing *parametric* polymorphism. The algorithm applies the cartesian product to break the analysis of each send into a case analysis (each case represents a monomorphic combination of actual arguments). This way it simultaneously achieves precision and efficiency, e.g., for `30 factorial` it infers the type {smallInt, bigInt} in 9 seconds; see Section 4. More specifically, the cartesian product algorithm offers these advantages:

- it is precise — in some cases more than all previously published algorithms.
- it is efficient since it simultaneously avoids redundant analysis and iteration, the major performance limitations of previous algorithms.
- it is general; instead of applying the traditional stopgap of expanding away inheritance, the new algorithm handles it directly, permitting precise analysis of any combination of single/multiple/static/dynamic inheritance, inheritance of state (often found in prototype-based languages), and multiple dispatch.
- it is conceptually simple since it involves no expansions or iteration.
- it has been validated on real programs and used in the Self system since late 1993.

We do not consider data polymorphism in this paper, except briefly in the conclusions. For succinctness, from now on we will refer to "parametric polymorphism" as simply "polymorphism" and "concrete type" as "type."

The rest of this paper is organized as follows. Section 2 presents background material, including an overview of previous algorithms. Section 3 presents in detail the new algorithm and compares it against previous algorithms. Section 4 compares the algorithms using measurements obtained on the Self system. Section 5 offers our conclusions and outlines possible directions for future work. Finally, an appendix briefly lists a number of issues that lack of space prevents us from discussing in detail.

2 Background

The algorithms we describe are language independent, but we use Self as a source for examples and measurements [2, 24]. Detailed knowledge of Self is not required, although basic familiarity with Self or Smalltalk syntax and programming style is helpful.

This section reviews background material. Section 2.1 defines concrete types in a prototype-based context. Section 2.2 describes the basic type inference algorithm as a flow analysis. Section 2.3 introduces templates, a high-level way to understand the algorithms. Templates are used both to review previous algorithms and present the new algorithm. Section 2.4 pinpoints why polymorphism is hard to analyze. Finally, Section 2.5 reviews how previous algorithms deal with polymorphism. A more detailed and complete version of this background material is found in [1].

2.1 Definition of Type

In the introduction we informally presented types as sets of classes, following Suzuki and Johnson [23, 15]. Since Self is prototype-based and has no classes we need to modify the definition of type slightly. A Self *program* is a finite set of objects ("prototypes") $\{\omega_1, \omega_2, ..., \omega_n\}$. For example, ω_7 may be `true` and ω_9 may be `point`. A *program execution* is the computation that results from sending a designated message, say `main`, to a particular object, the *main object*. The message invokes the *main method* which in turn may invoke other methods. The main method is equivalent to the function `main()` in a C program.

Conceptually, the prototypes are created before program execution starts. All other objects participating in an execution are created by cloning a prototype or another object which has been recursively cloned from a prototype. The transitive closure of the relation "cloned-from" partitions objects into n *clone families*, one per prototype. We write $\overline{\omega_i}$ for ω_i's clone family. A *concrete type* T is an arbitrary subset of $U = \{\overline{\omega_1}, \overline{\omega_2}, ..., \overline{\omega_n}\}$, i.e., it is a set of clone families. We take the standard interpretation that an expression (slot) *has* type T if it only evaluates to (holds) objects belonging to one of the clone families in T. Examples of types are:

- type(`x<y`) = $\{\overline{\texttt{true}}, \overline{\texttt{false}}\}$
- type(`30 factorial`) = $\{\overline{\texttt{smallInt}}, \overline{\texttt{bigInt}}\}$. Without range analysis or constant folding we cannot say that whether a small integer or a big integer may result.

- type(nil) = {$\overline{\texttt{nil}}$}. “The type of the expression nil, which returns the nil object, is {$\overline{\texttt{nil}}$}.” Even if a language, like C++, does not treat nil (actually NULL) as an object, it may be worth doing so during type inference. The prize is a complimentary “NULL-analysis”: types that include $\overline{\texttt{NULL}}$ identify where NULL pointers may show up during execution.

By definition, if an expression or a slot has type T, it also has type T′ for any $T' \supseteq T$. This permits conservative type inference: the inferred types may overestimate what can actually occur during execution. The universal type U is trivially sound for any slot or expression, but it is not a useful type to infer, since it conveys no information! Indeed, the goal is to infer the most precise types where a more precise type is a smaller set.

In a program with n prototypes, there are 2^n possible concrete types. In contrast, a C++ programmer writing “semi-abstract” type declarations is only granted n possible types (one per class). The precision difference between an exponential and a linear number of types is significant. There are concrete types that the C++ programmer cannot express, yet our type inference algorithm can infer.

2.2 The Basic Type Inference Algorithm

The basic type inference algorithm was presented by Palsberg and Schwartzbach [18] as a constraint-solving problem: derive a set of constraints from the program being analyzed, solve the constraints using a fix-point algorithm, and finally map the solution back onto the program to obtain the desired type information. The algorithm has deficiencies when analyzing polymorphic code, but constitutes the core of the improved algorithms, so we review it here. We take a more operational view, presenting type inference as a combined control- and data-flow analysis over the abstract domain of types. This abstract interpretation [9] perspective allows a direct correspondence between analyzing a program and executing it, making the analysis algorithms easier to understand. Referring to the program being analyzed as the *target program*, there are three steps in the basic algorithm.

Step 1. Allocate type variables. The first step is to associate a *type variable* with every slot and expression in the target program (see Fig. 1). A type variable is simply a variable whose possible values are types (i.e., sets of clone families). Initially all type variables are empty, but the next two steps adds enough clone families to them to make them hold sound types for the slots and expressions they are associated with. Nothing is ever removed from a type variable.

Step 2. Seed type variables. The second step adds a single clone family to certain type variables: the type variables are *seeded.* The goal is to capture the *initial state* of the target program by initializing type variables that correspond to slots or expressions where objects are found initially. For example, the type variable for the slot x←nil becomes {$\overline{\texttt{nil}}$}. Similarly, the type variable for a literal object such as 'bicycle' has $\overline{\texttt{string}}$ added to it. In Fig. 1, a seeded type variable's member is shown as a small dot.

Step 3. Establish constraints and propagate. The last step builds a directed graph whose nodes are the type variables. The edges, which are added one by one, represent *constraints.* A constraint is the type-inference-time equivalent of a run-time data flow.

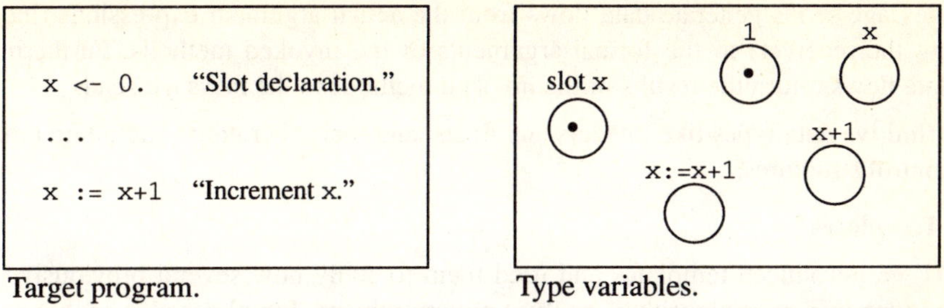

Fig. 1. A type variable is associated with every slot and expression in the target program. A program fragment is shown in the left frame, and the type variables (in no particular order) in the right frame. The type variable for the *slot* x is labelled "slot x" to distinguish it from the *expression* x which reads this slot.

For example, if the target program executes the assignment x:=exp there is a data flow from exp to x. Intuitively, the data flow means that any object that may result from evaluating exp can also be in the x slot. When the algorithm encounters this data flow, an edge is added from exp's type variable to x's type variable, reflecting that type(exp) ⊆ type(x). Fig. 2 depicts this.

Fig. 2. The situation before and after establishing the constraint for x:=exp and propagating.

Whenever an edge is added to the graph, clone families are *propagated* along it. In Fig. 2 all clone families in the exp node are pushed along the arrow to the x node. As more and more constraints are added to the network, the clone families that were originally only in the seeded type variables can flow further and further. The eager propagation ensures that subset relations such as type(exp) ⊆ type(x) always hold: if a clone family is added to type(exp), it is immediately propagated to type(x), reestablishing the subset relation.

Adding constraints makes more propagation necessary. The reverse also holds: when propagation makes the receiver type of a send grow, dynamic dispatch means that the send may invoke new methods, hence more constraints are needed. Thus, Step 3 consists in repeatedly establishing constraints and propagating, until no more can be done.

To ensure soundness, a constraint must be generated for *every* possible data flow in the target program [1]. Different languages have different constructs that produce data flows, but some general examples can be given (more examples are found in [1, 3, 17, 18, 20]):

- Assignments generate data flows from the new value expressions to the assigned variables (Fig. 2).
- Variable reads generate data flows from the accessed variables to the accessing expressions.

- Message sends generate data flows from the actual argument expressions (including the receiver) to the formal arguments of the invoked methods. Furthermore, data flows return the results of the invoked methods to the message sends.
- Primitive data types like integers and floats, and their operations, including built-in control structures.

2.3 Templates

In [1] we introduced templates and used them to study how several previously published type inference algorithms analyze polymorphism. Templates also enable a concise exposition of our new algorithm, so we review them here. Just as methods raise the abstraction level by encapsulating statements, templates raise the abstraction level by encapsulating constraints. Starting with the unstructured constraint graph produced by the basic type inference algorithm, we can carve it into a number of subgraphs, each corresponding to a method in the target program. These subgraphs are templates. More precisely, the *template* for a method M is the subgraph consisting of

- the nodes (type variables) corresponding to expressions, local variables, and formal arguments of M, and
- the edges (constraints) originating from these nodes.

Nodes corresponding to instance variables are not part of any template since instance variables do not belong to any particular method (they still have a type, of course). In the remainder of this paper we work at the template level, to avoid the complexity of dealing with a myriad of individual constraint. For an example of a template, consider the following `max:` method found at the top of the number hierarchy in the Self system (for now it is safe to ignore that the method contains blocks; we discuss them briefly in the appendix):

```
max: a = ( self>a ifTrue: [self] False: [a] ).
```

Fig. 3 shows the template for this method. It is a box with two input type variables at the top, corresponding to the formal arguments `self` and `a`, and a type variable for the result at the bottom. The result type is determined by contributions from two `ifTrue:False:`-templates (a conditional statement in Self is a send of `ifTrue:False:` to `false` or `true`, hence there are connections to templates for the `ifTrue:False:` methods in `false` and `true`, respectively). To simplify the picture, we omitted the constraints for the comparison `self>a` and the constraints propagating its result into the `self` slots of the `ifTrue:False:`-templates. Fig. 3 illustrates how a send, `3 max: 4`, is connected to the `max:`-template. The inference algorithm determines the send's type by propagating the actual argument types through the template(s) of the method(s) that may be invoked. When a send may invoke several methods, its type is the union of the result types of these methods.

2.4 Polymorphism is Analyzed Imprecisely by the Basic Algorithm

We now turn our attention to polymorphic methods. Fig. 4 shows what happens when the target program contains two sends of `max:`, one with integer arguments and the other with float arguments. The basic algorithm infers the type $\{\overline{\texttt{smallInt}}, \overline{\texttt{float}}\}$ for both sends. This is imprecise since invoking `max:` on two integers can "obviously"

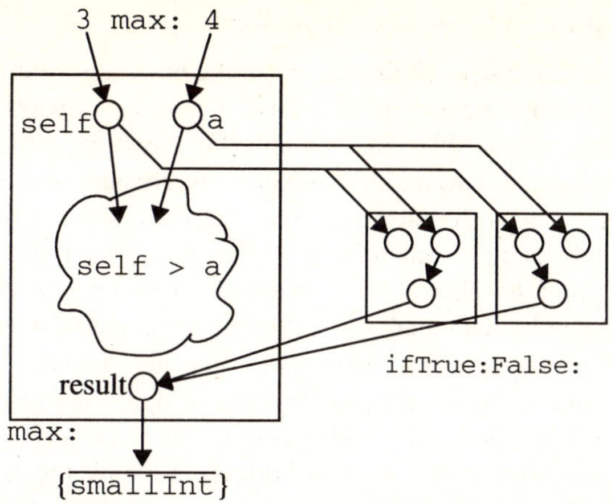

Fig. 3. A template for the max: method and a send connecting to it. The type of the send is determined by propagating the types of actual arguments through the template.

not produce a float or vice versa. The problem is that different types, {smallInt} and {float}, merge to produce the type {smallInt, float} in the input type variables of the max:-template. The merge causes information loss: once merged, the types cannot (easily) be separated and the result is imprecise types for all sends invoking max: with less than the full union type.

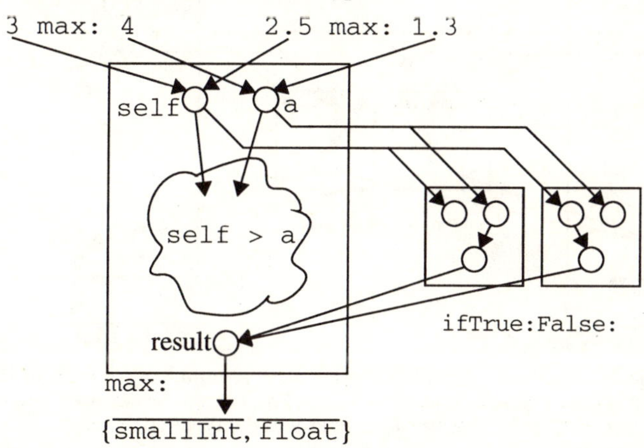

Fig. 4. The basic algorithm infers the imprecise type {smallInt, float} for the above sends of max:, even though one computes the max of two integers and the other the max of two floats.

2.5 Previous Improvements of the Basic Algorithm

The problem with the basic algorithm is that it creates only one max:-template. Its type must then be general (or imprecise) enough to accommodate all uses of max:. An algorithm, like the basic one, that analyzes each method once is called *monovariant*. The improved algorithms are all *polyvariant*: they may analyze methods multiple times by creating more than one template for them.

2.5.1 1-Level and p-Level Expansion Algorithms

Palsberg and Schwartzbach saw the limitations of the basic algorithm and proposed the following polyvariant improvement [17]. *1-level expansion:* always connect different sends in the target program to different templates. For example, if there are two `max:`-sends in the target program, two `max:`-templates are created, one for each send. The intuition is that since two different sends may supply actual arguments of different types, they should not share a template because this causes the types to merge.

The intuition is good, but there are two problems with the 1-level expansion. First, it is inefficient due to redundant analysis. Different sends with the same selector often supply the same argument types, e.g., most sends of + add integers. The 1-level expansion algorithm does not recognize this, and unnecessarily re-analyzes the integer addition method for each such send. (The Self integer addition method is not trivial since it handles type coercions and overflows into bigInts). Second, precision is still inadequate. Fig. 5 shows that the 1-level expansion is just as imprecise as the basic algorithm when applied to the two sends computing maxima of integers and floats. The only difference is that the merging now happens in a pair of `ifTrue:False:`-templates that are shared between two `max:`-templates. These templates are shared because there is only one send of `ifTrue:False:` in the `max:` method.

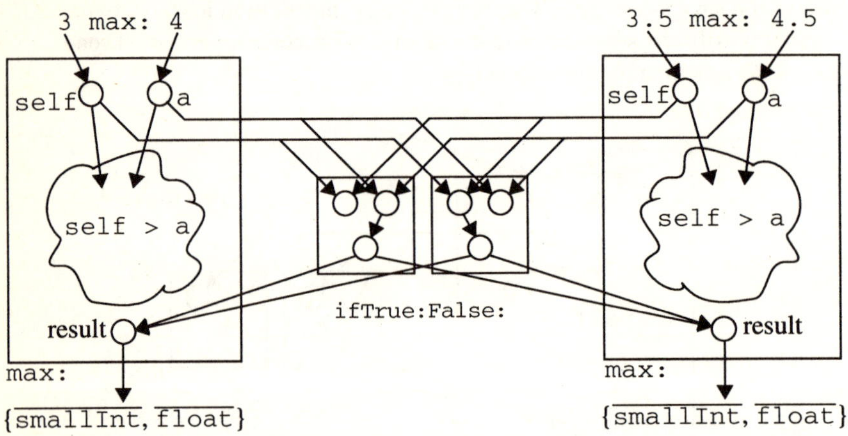

Fig. 5. The 1-level expansion algorithm creates a `max:`-template for each of the two sends, but there is only a single send of `ifTrue:False:` so the two `max:`-templates must share a pair of `ifTrue:False:`-templates and the types still merge.

The obvious way to improve precision is to avoid sharing the `ifTrue:False:`-templates, e.g., by using a *2-level expansion.* While this allows precise type inference for the situation shown in Fig. 5, it is even more inefficient since the second expansion further worsens the redundancy problems. Moreover, many code fragments still cannot be precisely analyzed, e.g., the following method that invokes `max:` twice to compute the max of three numbers, the receiver, x and `y`:

```
max: x Max: y = ( (self max: x) max: y ).
```

This method defeats the 2-level expansion by having a 3-deep polymorphic call chain: `max:Max:`→`max:`→`ifTrue:False:`. In general, a *p-level expansion* algorithm is precise if polymorphic call chains are at most p calls deep, but the worst-case complexity is exponential in p since each expansion incurs a quadratic cost increase [17]. Vitek et al. [25] described this algorithm using the concept of call strings, and Phillips and Shepard [19] applied it to ParcPlace Smalltalk.

2.5.2 The Iterative Algorithm

With the iterative algorithm, Plevyak and Chien [20] broke the unfavorable precision/efficiency trade-off inherent in the expansion algorithms. They simultaneously improved precision and efficiency by allowing a variable amount of expansion in "different parts" of the program. To understand their algorithm, assume we are analyzing these two sends

```
rcvr1 max: arg1.        rcvr2 max: arg2.
```

Consider now this question: *"when is it safe to connect the two sends to a shared template?"* The answer is that the two sends can share a template safely, i.e., without loss of precision, if:

$$\text{type}(\texttt{rcvr}_1) = \text{type}(\texttt{rcvr}_2) \text{ and } \text{type}(\texttt{arg}_1) = \text{type}(\texttt{arg}_2).$$

We call an algorithm which answers the sharing question based upon the above test "ideal." It is precise because it never allows different types to merge, and it is efficient because it avoids redundant analysis by always sharing a template whenever two or more sends invoke a method with the same actual arguments types. Unfortunately, the algorithm is ideal in one more regard: it cannot be implemented. The reason is that the types it compares to decide whether to use a shared template, are the very types being computed. In other words, the ideal algorithm needs to know the types before it can compute them!

Plevyak and Chien found a way out of this dilemma by iterating the type inference. The first iteration is the basic algorithm. In subsequent iterations, the ideal algorithm's sharing test is approximated using the types of the previous iteration. That is, the two sends can share a template in iteration p, if:

$$\text{type}_{p\text{-}1}(\texttt{rcvr}_1) = \text{type}_{p\text{-}1}(\texttt{rcvr}_2) \text{ and } \text{type}_{p\text{-}1}(\texttt{arg}_1) = \text{type}_{p\text{-}1}(\texttt{arg}_2).$$

The iterative algorithm is precise since it can handle arbitrarily deep polymorphic call chains, given enough iterations: after p iterations, the precision is the same as that of the p-level expansion algorithm. The iterative algorithm achieves this precision at a lower expected computational cost because it "selectively" expands the program as is needed to avoid non-equal types merging at calls.

Iteration, while improving precision, also has drawbacks. One is the overhead of iteration, possibly slowing down type inference by a factor roughly equal to the number of iterations required. Implementation complexity may also be an issue: it is non-trivial to map type information across iterations, because the program is expanded differently. In particular, maintaining validity of the previous iteration's type information downstream from a method that is further expanded in the current iteration is a challenge. Finally, it can be hard to know when to stop iterating. In principle, once $p \geq r$, where r is the length of the longest polymorphic call chain, no further precision improvements are possible. In reality, the situation is more complex, due to block specialization and recursion [20] (see also the appendix).

3 The Cartesian Product Algorithm

The previous algorithms aim to obtain precision and efficiency by partitioning sends according to the types of their actual arguments. The iterative algorithm reaches the goal, but incurs the overhead of iteration to harvest timely the type information needed during analysis. The cartesian product algorithm (CPA for short) is fundamentally different. It does not partition sends, but instead turns the analysis of *each* send into a case analysis. Given a send to analyze, CPA computes the cartesian product of the types of the actual arguments. Each tuple in the cartesian product is analyzed as an independent case. This makes exact type information available for each case immediately, thus eliminates the need for iteration. In turn, the type information is used to ensure both precision (by avoiding type merges) and efficiency (by sharing cases to avoid redundant analysis). In the following description of CPA we mainly compare it against the iterative algorithm, since these two are the most powerful algorithms.

The idea behind CPA is best understood by going back to the analogy between program execution and program analysis. During program execution, activation records are always created "monomorphically", simply because each slot contains a single object. Consider for example a polymorphic send that invokes the `max:` method with integer or float receivers. This means that sometimes the send invokes `max:` with an integer receiver, and other times it invokes it with a float receiver. In any particular invocation the receiver is *either* an integer or a float. It cannot be both. We summarize this observation as follows:

There is no such thing as a polymorphic call, only polymorphic call sites.

CPA, unlike the previous algorithms, exploits this observation. CPA creates *monomorphic templates* only. Given a send such as

```
rcvr max: arg.
```

Let R = type(`rcvr`) and A = type(`arg`). Suppose it is (somehow) known that

$R = \{r_1, r_2, ..., r_s\}$ and
$A = \{a_1, a_2, ..., a_t\}$.

In general, of course, these types will not be fully known during type inference; this was the motivation behind the iterative algorithm. In Section 3.1 we explain how it is nevertheless possible to use the types without iterating or even approximating.

To analyze this send, CPA computes the cartesian product of the receiver type and all argument types. In the present case there is only one argument so the cartesian product is a set of pairs. In general it is a set of (k+1)-tuples, where k is the number of arguments.

$$R \times A = \{(r_1,a_1), ..., (r_1,a_t), ..., (r_i,a_j),..., (r_s,a_1), ..., (r_s,a_t)\}.$$

Next, CPA propagates each $(r_i,a_j) \in R \times A$ into a separate `max:`-template. If a `max:`-template already exists for a given (r_i,a_j) pair, it is reused; if no such template exists, a new one is created and made available for this and future (r_i,a_j) pairs in other sends. Finally, the type of the send is obtained as the union of the result types of the templates that the send was connected to. Fig. 6 illustrates the situation with concrete objects for a single send.

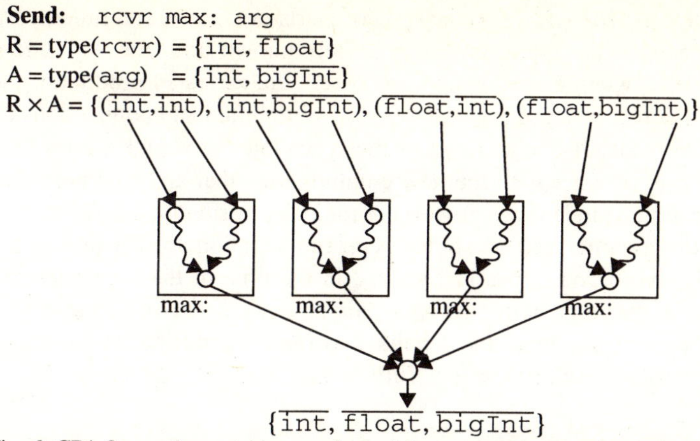

Fig. 6. CPA forms the cartesian product of the receiver type and argument types of the send it is analyzing. Each member of the product is propagated to a template reserved exclusively for that receiver and argument combination. The result type of the send is obtained by collecting the contributions from each template.

In the Self implementation we use a "dictionary" per method to organize the templates. All templates for a method M, no matter which send invoking M caused their creation, are stored in M's dictionary. The dictionaries are keyed by (k+1)-tuples to allow fast retrieval of the template corresponding to a given tuple. Using these structures, the analysis of a send proceeds as follows:

1. Determine the methods M_i ($i = 0, 1, ..., q$) that the send may invoke.
2. Generate the cartesian product (lazily, as described in Section 3.1).
3. For each method M_i and each tuple ($a_0, ..., a_k$) in the cartesian product, look up ($a_0, ..., a_k$) in M's template dictionary. If no matching template is found, create one and add it to the dictionary.
4. Connect the send to the — new or old — template.

To obtain an efficient (and terminating!) algorithm, it is necessary to maintain per-method pools of templates rather than per-send pools, to ensure that different sends whose cartesian products have tuples in common can share templates. It is worth noting that the template dictionaries are not filled up "in advance." Rather, templates are added to them gradually, as new argument combinations (tuples) are encountered during analysis of all the sends in the target program. In fact, it is not possible to know in advance which templates are going to be needed. This only becomes clear gradually, as the analysis is progressing.

3.1 How CPA Can Use Exact Type Information Without Iterating

We have yet to explain how CPA can use the types of arguments and receivers while still in the process of computing them. The iterative algorithm found a way out of this dilemma by iterating and approximating the types with those computed in the previous iteration. CPA avoids the dilemma altogether, using neither approximations nor iteration.

How is this achieved? The key is that, while the iterative algorithm is comparing types to find out whether or not to share templates, CPA computes cartesian products instead. The cartesian product, unlike a type comparison, can be computed correctly, albeit gradually, even if the types are only partially known until the very end of the analysis. Specifically, when a send is first processed, the cartesian product of the *current* members of the receiver and argument types is computed and connections to relevant templates are made. If one or more of the types later grow, CPA goes back and extends the cartesian product with the new combinations that are now possible. This yields a correct solution since types grow monotonically during type inference.

For illustration, assume that we started with the situation shown in Fig. 6, but a new clone family, `rational`, has just arrived in the type of the argument. We first extend the cartesian product with two new pairs: (`int`, `rational`) and (`float`, `rational`). Then we propagate these pairs into (new or old) `max:`-templates and collect the new possible result types. Fig. 7 illustrates all this.

Send: `rcvr max: arg`
R = type(`rcvr`) = {`int`, `float`}
A = type(`arg`) = {`int`, `bigInt`, **`rational`**}
R × A = {(`int`,`int`), (`int`,`bigInt`), (`float`,`int`), (`float`,`bigInt`), **(`int`,`rational`)**, **(`float`,`rational`)**}

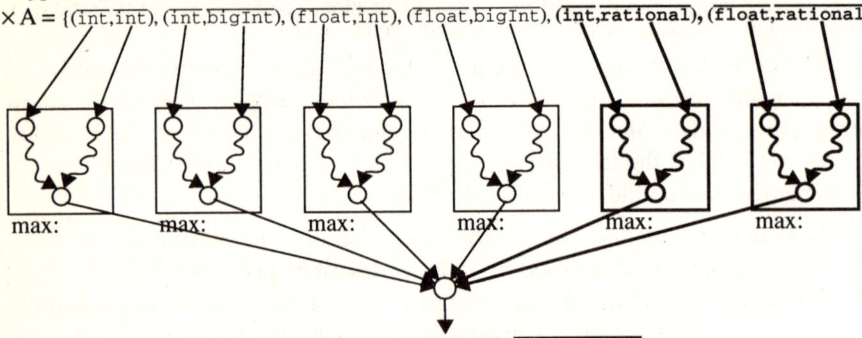

{`int`, `float`, `bigInt`, **`rational`**}

Fig. 7. The cartesian product algorithm tolerates "growing" types in this way: when the type of a receiver or an argument grows, the cartesian product is extended, and the send is connected to additional templates. The new structures are shown in bold above.

Two key properties allow CPA to avoid iteration. First, the cartesian product is a *monotonic* function. If either R or A grows, the cartesian product R × A grows. Second, the cartesian product is applied in a "monotone context": if a cartesian product grows, the correct compensating action is to grow the constraint network. Because CPA manages to preserve monotonicity, it can run in a single pass, yet will on no occasion "regret" a previous action. The iterative algorithm, in contrast, breaks monotonicity because comparing types for equality is not a monotone function. To buy back monotonicity, Plevyak and Chien pays the price of iteration.

Seen in this light, the p-level expansion algorithms form a family of algorithms that apply particularly simple monotonic functions to decide whether or not to share. These functions do not depend on the types being inferred, but merely on the static program text. In [1] such algorithms are called *non-adaptive* because they uniformly apply the same effort throughout the target program rather than focusing on the parts where the most complex polymorphism is found. The iterative algorithm and CPA are *adaptive* because they use type information during inference to concentrate the analysis effort on the demanding parts of the target program.

The hash function algorithm, described in [1, 3], is a hybrid between the 1-level expansion and the cartesian product algorithm. It applies case analysis on receiver types, like CPA, but uses the 1-level expansion for the non-receiver arguments. The hash algorithm is adaptive because it uses receiver types during analysis. Like the two algorithms of which it is a hybrid, it is monotone and can be implemented in one pass.

3.2 Assessing the Cartesian Product Algorithm

CPA is *precise* in the sense that it can analyze arbitrarily deep polymorphic call chains without loss of precision. The reason is that CPA creates monomorphic templates and never allows different tuples from two or more sends to be propagated into the same template. In other words, there is no merging, no matter how deep the call chain is.

CPA is *efficient*, because redundant analysis is avoided. As we have seen before, the key to avoiding redundancy is sharing. Each time an (r_i,a_j) pair can occur in some call of `max:` it is connected to the same shared template. Hence, each combination of a specific receiver and argument is analyzed only once. In contrast, the iterative algorithm may generate templates with overlapping types such as:

Template 1: type(`self`) = {`int`, `float`}
type(`arg`) = {`int`, `bigInt`, `rational`}

Template 2: type(`self`) = {`int`, `float`}
type(`arg`) = {`int`, `bigInt`}

In the above situation, CPA generates more templates than the iterative algorithm (six versus two). This does not necessarily mean that CPA is slower, since the templates it generates have singleton types for the receiver and arguments, hence can be processed faster than templates with larger types.

3.3 Scaling Issues

Both the iterative and cartesian product algorithms may have problems analyzing large programs that are extremely rich in polymorphism. We give two scenarios. The first favors CPA. For simplicity consider a method with one argument (it is straightforward to generalize to an arbitrary number of arguments). Assume that the set of possible receivers and arguments for the method are drawn from these domains:

$P = \{r_1, r_2, ..., r_s\}$ (possible receivers)
$Q = \{a_1, a_2, ..., a_t\}$ (possible arguments)

In the worst case, the iterative algorithm may generate an exponential number of templates, namely one for each subset of P and Q, i.e. 2^{s+t} templates (there are 2^s subsets of P and 2^t subsets of Q). CPA, in contrast, generates at most a polynomial number of templates, namely one for each member P×Q, i.e., s*t templates. So far, though, we have not encountered this worst-case scenario in the programs we have analyzed.

The second scenario favors the iterative algorithm. Assume the target program contains a send whose receiver and 18 arguments (!) have the type {`smallInt`, `bigInt`, `float`}. The cartesian product then has size $3^{19} \approx 10^9$. In this extreme case, even attempting to compute the cartesian product, not to mention creating 10^9 templates, is a bad idea. Again, we have not encountered such extreme polymorphism, but we do apply the following test to determine if we are in danger of starting an unreasonably large computation:

- for each receiver or actual argument type T, test if size(T) ≤ c, where c is some (small) number.

Useful values of c seem to be in the range 3-5, perhaps using different values for receivers and arguments, and possibly letting the value depend on the number of arguments of the send (if there are more arguments, a smaller limit is appropriate). We say that an argument or receiver that fails the test is *megamorphic*. When megamorphic arguments occur, the full cartesian product should no longer be computed. Instead, we create tuples of the form $(x_0, x_1, *, x_3)$ where a star indicates a megamorphic argument. When such a tuple is propagated into a template, the star is expanded to the full megamorphic type.

The contraction of megamorphic arguments is an effective technique to avoid large cartesian products, e.g., the 10^9 cases mentioned above can be collapsed to a single monovariant analysis. The cost, of course, may be loss of precision. To limit the loss, templates should not be shared between sends with and without megamorphic arguments to avoid "polluting" the non-megamorphic cases. The loss can be further limited, e.g., by applying expansions or even iteration to the (few) megamorphic cases.

In practice the exact choice does not seem to matter much. We offer two possible explanations. First, megamorphism is rare. Measuring a number of Self programs we found that 0-4% of the sends have a megamorphic argument if the limit is c = 3. Thus, even if some precision is lost at these sends, the overall consequences are limited. Second, it seems plausible that a programmer who writes a send with two or three kinds of arguments may have distinct cases in mind, but if there are a dozen or more kinds, he is probably exploiting some uniform behavior which in turn limits the loss of precision when the cases are merged during analysis.

3.4 A Case Where the Cartesian Product Algorithm Improves Precision

Even though both the iterative and the cartesian product algorithm avoid losing precision due to merging of types, the property that CPA analyzes each argument combination monomorphically sometimes gives it a precision edge. Consider this method:

```
mod: arg = ( self-(arg*(self div: arg)) ).
```

Assume that `div:` denotes integer division (i.e., a division operator that *fails* if the receiver or argument is not an integer). Consider the analysis of a send, `x mod: y`, in a context where

$$\text{type}(x) = \text{type}(y) = \{\overline{\texttt{smallInt}}, \overline{\texttt{float}}\}.$$

The iterative algorithm will infer that the type of `x mod: y` is $\{\overline{\texttt{smallInt}}, \overline{\texttt{float}}\}$ whereas the cartesian product algorithm will infer the more precise type $\{\overline{\texttt{smallInt}}\}$. Here's how:

- The iterative algorithm analyzes `x mod: y` by connecting it to a `mod:` template in which the type of both `self` and `arg` is $\{\overline{\texttt{smallInt}}, \overline{\texttt{float}}\}$. Then it proceeds to find that the type of `self div: arg` is $\{\overline{\texttt{smallInt}}\}$ (since `div:` fails on floats). So far, the precision is optimal. Next, the iterative algorithm determines the type of arg*(self div: arg). Since arg has type {$\overline{\texttt{smallInt}}$, $\overline{\texttt{float}}$}, the type of the product is {$\overline{\texttt{smallInt}}$, $\overline{\texttt{float}}$}. In turn, the type inferred for self-(arg*(self div: arg)) is {$\overline{\texttt{smallInt}}$, $\overline{\texttt{float}}$}, and finally it is found that the type of x mod: y is {$\overline{\texttt{smallInt}}$, $\overline{\texttt{float}}$}.

- CPA analyzes x mod: y by connecting it to four templates, one for each tuple in the cartesian product of the types of x and y. The template in which both self and arg have type {$\overline{\texttt{smallInt}}$} straightforwardly has result type {$\overline{\texttt{smallInt}}$}. The other three templates have empty result types since in each of them the type of self div: arg is empty (because div: fails on floats and there is no integer "backup"). Hence, CPA combines {$\overline{\texttt{smallInt}}$} and three empty result types, to find that the type of x mod: y is {$\overline{\texttt{smallInt}}$}.

The mod: method was chosen to expose a property of CPA, but similar structures can conceivably be found embedded in more complex situations. It can be argued that enhancements of the iterative algorithm allow such cases to be analyzed precisely. For example, Graver and Johnson use a case analysis within methods to analyze similar structures precisely [10]. We find it preferable, though, to strive for the best precision available using our first tool, the constraints, and consider other enhancements only as they are truly needed.

3.5 Inheritance

To use terminology that most readers are familiar with, we give examples from a class-based language in this section. Inheritance is an important code reuse mechanism in object-oriented programming. Often, inheritance is used in a way that attains substitutability, i.e., ensures that an instance of a subclass can be used wherever an instance of the superclass is expected. Substitutability may also be enforced by the language, although it is not in Self. Even if inheritance is used in this restricted manner, the fact remains that expressions in inherited methods may have different types in the context of a subclass than in the context of a superclass. For instance, a message sent to self may be bound differently when the method is inherited, causing the type to change. Another, and simpler, example is a method that returns self, e.g., a display method implemented for points and inherited by coloured points. The left hand side of Fig. 8 illustrates this situation. Naively, the type inferred for display is {Point, ColourPoint}, because it may be applied to either a point or a coloured point. Propagating this type to a send that invokes display only on coloured points is imprecise: such a send should have the type {ColourPoint}. Compiler writers facing this issue found solutions such as customization [8] where the idea is to recompile a method for each class that inherits it to make the class of self known in the compiled code.

Previous type inference algorithms for object-oriented languages have achieved a similar effect by using a preprocessor to eliminate inheritance [10, 11, 17, 18]. The preprocessor copies methods down into the classes inheriting them. The result of this "expansion" is shown in the right hand side of Fig. 8: there are now two identical methods $\texttt{display}_{\text{Point}}$ and $\texttt{display}_{\text{ColourPoint}}$. The former applies to points only, thus has result type {Point}. The latter applies to coloured points only, and has result type {ColourPoint}. Now, if a send invokes display exclusively on coloured points, its type is {ColourPoint}, since the send is connected to templates for $\texttt{display}_{\text{ColourPoint}}$ only.

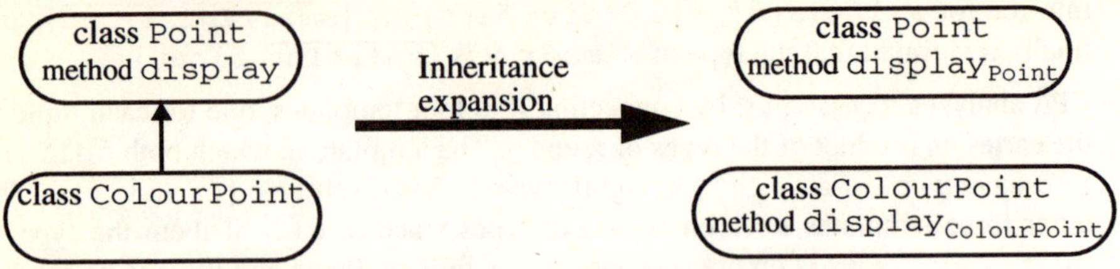

Fig. 8. Most type inference algorithms, but not CPA, have to expand away inheritance to gain precision. The expansion copies inherited methods down into subclasses.

Expanding away inheritance improves precision, because inaccuracies resulting from analyzing a single method in the context of several classes are avoided. The expansion can be expensive, though. In the worst case program size increases quadratically, even for programs using only single inheritance [18]. Care must also be taken to handle overridden methods correctly, including sends to super ("resends"). For Self, there are additional complications: it is non-trivial to eliminate inheritance of state, not to mention dynamic inheritance, by an expansion.

The cartesian product algorithm removes the need for the expansion. It can analyze an unexpanded program with the same precision as an expanded one. The reason is that CPA, unlike other algorithms, always creates templates in which the type of self has exactly one member, i.e., CPA always analyzes a method in the context of one class at a time[2]. Avoiding the inheritance expansion has several advantages:

- *Simplicity.* We reuse an existing mechanism, the cartesian product, instead of applying a special-purpose mechanism to deal with inheritance.
- *Efficiency.* Templates are created only when needed, whereas the static expansion assumes that a method can be invoked on any class inheriting it. (Optimizing the expansion is possible, of course).
- *Generality.* The cartesian product handles inheritance of state, dynamic inheritance, and multiple inheritance. It even supports languages with multiple dispatch (multi-methods) [5, 6], by a straightforward extension to the single-dispatch case: when the cartesian product is generated, each tuple is propagated to a template for the *specific* method that implements the operation for the combination of arguments in the tuple.

3.6 Summary

Table 1 condenses the most important attributes of the algorithms that we have discussed. The hash algorithm [1, 3] is included to show where it fits in, even though we have only touched upon it briefly in this paper. The efficiency column is informal, since it is not based on extensive measurements or theoretical complexity studies of

---

2. The hash function algorithm also has this property [3], but is restricted to singly-dispatched languages.

the algorithms (the latter would require a statistical model of how "typical" programs use polymorphism).

Algorithm	Efficiency	Precision	Adv./contributions	Drawbacks
Basic	Fast	Inadequate	Simple, first	Monovariant (imprecise)
1-level expansion	Slow	Meager	First polyvariant algorithm	Fails on polymorphic call chains of length >1
p-level expansion	Too slow	Good	Parameterized cost/precision trade-off	Gets slow before reaching high precision
Hash	Fast	Good	Good handling of polymorphic receivers	Polymorphic arg's need ad-hoc rules
Iterative	Medium	Better	Better cost/precision trade-off	Iteration overhead, complex
CPA	Fast	Better still	Non-iterative and first to not partition sends	Scaling?

Table 1. Summary of six type inference algorithms.

4 Measurements

We have implemented and tested six type inference algorithms: the basic, the p-level expansion (p = 1, 2, 3, 4), and the cartesian product algorithm, but not the iterative algorithm[3]. The implementation consists of 10,000 lines of Self source code that, in addition to type inference, parses byte codes into expression trees, performs grouping (see appendix), incremental analysis, SSA transformation, and application extraction. We applied the six inference algorithms to four existing programs in the Self system:

- *Factorial:* invocation of the recursive factorial function shown in the introduction.
- *Richards:* an operating system simulator [7].
- *Deltablue:* a multi-way constraint solver [22].
- *Diff:* Mario Wolczko's Self version of the Unix diff command [12].

The programs were analyzed unmodified, with one exception: we had to patch the `_Mirror` primitive to return nothing instead of a mirror (mirrors are a way to write reflective code in Self and reflection is only partially supported by the type inference implementation). Without the patch, both the basic and the 1-level expansion algorithm would get lost in the reflective part of the Self system. The patch was removed when running the other inference algorithms since they are precise enough to avoid falling into the reflective trap[4].

3. We have not implemented the iterative algorithm for Self, hence cannot include it in the following direct comparison. We have refrained from comparing with the numbers published by Plevyak [20] because his system is implemented in a different language than Self (possibly less efficient), and he analyzes different benchmarks, written in a different language.

4. The pure form of the iterative algorithm would also need the patch, since the first iteration is the basic algorithm.

Like most programs, the above four are not self-contained. They reuse and extend existing objects and data structures. For example, the factorial method is only one line of source, but it needs a bigInt implementation which comprises hundreds of lines. To obtain a more useful measure of program size, we applied the extractor described in [4], and measured the size of the resulting self-contained source files. When counting everything, including variable definitions, blank lines, names spaces, etc., Factorial is 1300 lines, Richards 1700 lines, Deltablue 1800 lines, and Diff 5000 lines. Counting method bodies only (i.e., statements and expressions), Factorial is 900 lines, Richards 1100 lines, Deltablue 1200 lines, and Diff 2300 lines.

The extractor is based on type inference and has the property that less precise type information forces it to extract more. We plugged each of the six type inference algorithms into the extractor and measured how many lines and methods were extracted for each test program. The results are shown in Table 2. In general, CPA delivers the smallest extractions, indicating that it is the most precise inference method. On Diff the expansion algorithm improves dramatically when p is increased from 1 to 2, and shows little additional gain past 2. The *increasing* line counts from p=1 to p=2 on Factorial, Richards, and Deltablue are explained by the removal of the reflective patch. The numbers in Table 2 are important beyond indicating type inference precision. A compiler based on type inference compiles fewer methods if it uses CPA than any of the other algorithms (note: the current Self compiler does not use type inference [14]).

	Basic	**1-level**	**2-level**	**3-level**	**4-level**	**CPA**
Factorial	1692 / 678	1667 / 649	2847 / 608	2847 / 608	2847 / 608	1306 / 464
Richards	2117 / 786	2086 / 753	3259 / 698	3259 / 698	3259 / 698	1731 / 560
Deltablue	2199 / 844	2174 / 815	3394 / 784	3392 / 782	3392 / 782	1777 / 600
Diff	74816 / 1582	71598 / 1510	5578 / 1196	5576 / 1194	5547 / 1194	5447 / 1123

Table 2. Number of source lines/methods extracted.

Table 3 compares CPU times of the type inference algorithms, measured on a 50 MHz SparcStation 10. To focus on the type inference algorithms per se, the time spent on grouping objects is omitted. CPA is consistently fastest, although in fairness, it is also the best tuned of the implementations. Remarkably, it is faster than even the basic algorithm analyzing the simpler patched programs. For the expansion algorithms, two opposing trends battle as p increases. On the one hand, precision improves, enabling the analysis to stay clear of "irrelevant" code that is not part of the application. This speeds up type inference. On the other hand, redundancy increases, acting to slow down type inference. Beyond p=2, the effect of the former trend wears off, and the cost of redundancy shows through. Finally note that the basic algorithm's times are lower bounds for the iterative algorithm, since the first iteration is the basic algorithm.

	Basic	**1-level**	**2-level**	**3-level**	**4-level**	**CPA**
Factorial	11	19	17	32	78	9
Richards	21	24	19	37	94	9
Deltablue	22	27	22	43	112	17
Diff	117	250	50	126	377	38

Table 3. Type inference time in seconds (CPU time on a 50 MHz SparcStation 10).

Polyvariance is essential to obtain precision, but too much hurts efficiency. Table 4 contains two numbers for each algorithm/program combination: the average number of times each method was analyzed (the number of templates divided by the number of methods), and the average number of times each expression was analyzed. The second number allows a large method to weigh heavier in the average. The polyvariance degree of CPA is between that of the 2- and 3-level expansion algorithms, yet CPA is faster than these algorithms, because monomorphic templates can be processed faster.

	Basic	1-level	2-level	3-level	4-level	CPA
Factorial	1.0 / 1.0	3.9 / 3.3	6.6 / 4.9	12.1 / 8.7	21.1 / 15.7	6.4 / 5.0
Richards	1.0 / 1.0	4.0 / 3.2	6.5 / 4.7	11.8 / 8.1	20.6 / 14.5	6.2 / 4.7
Deltablue	1.0 / 1.0	4.1 / 3.4	6.6 / 4.8	11.8 / 8.3	20.3 / 14.7	10.8 / 8.3
Diff	1.0 / 1.0	4.8 / 4.0	7.6 / 5.6	14.5 / 10.0	27.3 / 19.1	11.5 / 9.3

Table 4. Number of times each method/expression was analyzed.

Paying the price for a certain amount of polyvariance, it should be used well. Table 5 shows average type sizes over all expressions. The averages are over the polyvariant domains, i.e., if an expression was analyzed twice, it counts twice in the average. CPA achieves the lowest sizes, even compared against the 3- and 4-level expansion algorithms which analyze each expression more times (see Table 4). The expansion algorithms' improvements from p=1 to p=2 are particularly clear in Table 5.

	Basic	1-level	2-level	3-level	4-level	CPA
Factorial	13.41	5.58	1.71	1.67	1.69	1.03
Richards	17.56	8.54	1.85	1.79	1.78	1.04
Deltablue	17.56	8.31	1.92	1.84	1.84	1.11
Diff	37.89	19.0	2.25	2.13	2.13	1.34

Table 5. Average size of types for all expressions.

To conclude the empirical results, it is amusing to see the types inferred by each algorithm for the expression `30 factorial`. As shown in the introduction, the basic algorithm inferred:

{smallInt, bigInt, collector, memory, memoryState, byteVector, mutableString, immutableString, float, link, list, primitiveFailedError, userError, time, false, true, nil, [blk_1], [blk_2], ..., [blk_{13}]}.

The 1-level expansion algorithm did slightly better:

{smallInt, bigInt, collector, memoryState, byteVector, mutableString, immutableString, float, link, list, primitiveFailedError, userError, time, false, true, nil}.

Not surprisingly, the 2-level expansion algorithm was significantly better, although still not perfect:

{smallInt, bigInt, float, primitiveFailedError}.

Both the 3- and 4-level algorithms inferred the same type as the 2-level algorithm. Finally, CPA inferred:

{smallInt, bigInt}.

5 Conclusions

We have presented the cartesian product algorithm. It is based on the key insight that the cartesian product can be used to monotonically and soundly decompose the analysis of a send into a number of monomorphic cases. This decomposition accurately mirrors the situation at program execution time where activation records are monomorphic. It has several advantages:

- *Precision* is sharpened since some methods can be analyzed more precisely in monomorphic contexts. Measurements additionally show that CPA achieves the smallest average size of the inferred types.
- *Efficiency* is improved since monotonicity of the cartesian product allows a 1-pass implementation, yet no redundant analysis is done. Even sends that have only partially overlapping types can share analysis cases. Measurements show that CPA is faster than even the basic algorithm.
- *Generality* is improved. Unlike other algorithms that expand away inheritance, CPA handles it directly, permitting precise analysis of wider range of languages, including ones with inheritance of state, dynamic inheritance, multiple inheritance, and multiple dispatch.
- *Simplicity* is preserved. The core of the algorithm is the familiar cartesian product. Expansions are not required, inheritance elimination is unnecessary, and iteration with mapping of type information across differently expanded versions of the target program is avoided.

CPA addresses parametric polymorphism only. It does nothing to improve the analysis of code with data polymorphism, thus is no better (but also no worse) in this regard than the basic algorithm. What then can be done about data polymorphism? A number of algorithms have been published that target data polymorphism. Analogous to analyzing parametric polymorphism by copying methods, these algorithms copy classes in an attempt to keep different uses of (data) polymorphic instance variables separate. For example, Oxhøj et al. proposed a 1-level class expansion [17], Phillips and Shepard generalized this to p levels [19], and Plevyak and Chien developed an iterative algorithm [20].

While CPA itself does not address data polymorphism, neither does it conflict with the existing algorithms for analyzing data polymorphism. Hence, it is practical to combine CPA with any of these algorithms to obtain a comprehensive type inference system. A particularly interesting question to investigate is how the (iterative, data iterative) combination compares with the (cartesian product, data iterative) combination. The answer is not obvious. The former combination may work well in practice, because the two kinds of iterations can develop the constraint network in parallel. Or the latter combination may excel because CPA's strong handling of parametric polymorphism clears away the brush, giving the data iterative part immediate access to dig out its potatoes.

Acknowledgments. Thanks to Lars Bak, Craig Chambers, Bay-Wei Chang, Ole Lehrmann Madsen, John C. Mitchell, Ivan Moore, David Ungar, Jan Vitek and Mario Wolczko for discussions and comments on earlier drafts of this paper, and to the referees for feedback on the submitted version. The author has been generously supported by The Natural Science Faculty of Aarhus University, The Danish Research Academy, and Sun Microsystems Laboratories. The Self project has been supported by the NSF PYI Grant #CCR-8657631, Sun Microsystems, IBM, Apple Computer, Cray Laboratories, Tandem Computers, NCR, Texas Instruments and DEC.

References

1. Agesen, O., Constraint-Based Type Inference and Parametric Polymorphism. In *SAS'94, First International Static Analysis Symposium,* p. 78-100, Namur, Belgium, Sept. 1994. Springer-Verlag, LNCS 864.
2. Agesen, O., L. Bak, C. Chambers, B.W. Chang, U. Hölzle, J. Maloney, R.B. Smith, D. Ungar, M. Wolczko. *How to use Self 3.0 & The Self 3.0 Programmer's Reference Manual.* 1993. Sun Microsystems Laboratories, 2550 Garcia Avenue, Mountain View, CA 94043, USA. Available by anon. ftp from self.stanford.edu or www: http://self.stanford.edu/.
3. Agesen, O., J. Palsberg, and M.I. Schwartzbach, Type Inference of Self: Analysis of Objects with Dynamic and Multiple Inheritance. In *ECOOP'93, Seventh European Conference on Object-Oriented Programming,* p. 247-267, Kaiserslautern, Germany, July 1993. Springer-Verlag, LNCS 707.
4. Agesen, O. and D. Ungar, Sifting Out the Gold: Delivering Compact Applications from an Exploratory Object-Oriented Programming Environment. In *OOPSLA'94, Object-Oriented Programming Systems, Languages and Applications,* p. 355-370, Portland, Oregon, Oct. 1994.
5. Bobrow, D.G., K. Kahn, G. Kiczales, L. Masinter, M. Stefik, and F. Zdybel, Common-Loops: Merging Lisp and Object-Oriented Programming. In *OOPSLA'86 Object-Oriented Programming Systems, Languages and Applications,* p. 17-29, Portland, Oregon, Sept. 1986.
6. Chambers, C., Object-Oriented Multi-Methods in Cecil. In *ECOOP'92, Sixth European Conference on Object-Oriented Programming,* p. 33-56, June 1992, Utrecht, The Netherlands. Springer-Verlag, LNCS 615.
7. Chambers, C., D. Ungar, Making Pure Object-Oriented Languages Practical. In *OOPSLA'91, Sixth Annual Conference on Object-Oriented Programming Systems, Languages and Applications*, p. 1-15, Phoenix, Arizona, Oct. 1991.
8. Chambers, C., D. Ungar, and E. Lee, An Efficient Implementation of SELF, a Dynamically-Typed Object-Oriented Language Based on Prototypes. *Lisp and Symbolic Computation* 4(3), p. 243-281, Kluwer Academic Publishers, June 1991. (Originally published in Proc. *OOPSLA'89).*
9. Cousot, P. and R. Cousot, Abstract Interpretation: A Unified Lattice Model for Static Analysis of Programs by Construction or Approximation of Fixpoints. In *Conference Record of the Fourth ACM Symposium on Principles of Programming Languages,* p. 238-252, Jan. 1977.
10. Graver, J.O., *Type-Checking and Type-Inference for Object-Oriented Programming Languages*, Ph.D. thesis, University of Illinois at Urbana-Champaign, 1989.
11. Graver, J.O. and R.E. Johnson, A Type System for Smalltalk. In *Conference Record of the Seventeenth Annual ACM Symposium on Principles of Programming Languages*, p. 136-150, San Francisco, California, Jan. 1990.
12. Hunt, J.W. and T.G. Szymanski, A Fast Algorithm for Computing Longest Common Subsequences, *Communications of the ACM*, 20(5), p. 350-353, May 1977.
13. Hölzle, U., Why Static Typing is not Important for Efficiency. In: J. Palsberg & M.I. Schwartzbach (eds.) *Types, Inheritance, and Assignment,* Technical Report, Daimi PB-357, Computer Science Department, Aarhus University, Denmark, June 1991.
14. Hölzle, U. and D. Ungar, Optimizing Dynamically-Dispatched Calls with Run-time Type Feedback. In *PLDI'94, Conference on Programming Language Design and Implementation,* p. 326-336, Orlando, Florida, June 1994.
15. Johnson, R.E., Type-Checking Smalltalk. In *OOPSLA'86 Object-Oriented Programming Systems, Languages and Applications,* p. 315-321, Portland, Oregon, Sept. 1986.

16. Milner, R., A Theory of Type Polymorphism in Programming. *Journal of Computer and System Sciences*, 17, p. 348-375, 1978.
17. Oxhøj, N., J. Palsberg, and M.I. Schwartzbach, Making Type Inference Practical. In *ECOOP'92, Sixth European Conference on Object-Oriented Programming,* p. 329-349, Utrecht, The Netherlands, June 1992, Springer-Verlag, LNCS 615.
18. Palsberg, J. and M.I. Schwartzbach, Object-Oriented Type Inference. In *OOPSLA'91 Object-Oriented Programming Systems, Languages and Applications,* p. 146-161, Phoenix, Arizona, Oct. 1991.
19. Phillips, G. and T. Shepard, *Static Typing Without Explicit Types.* Technical Report, Dept. of Electrical and Computer Engineering, Royal Military College of Canada, Kingston, Ontario, Canada, 1994.
20. Plevyak, J. and A.A. Chien, Precise Concrete Type Inference for Object-Oriented Languages. In *OOPSLA'94, Object-Oriented Programming Systems, Languages and Applications,* p. 324-340, Portland, Oregon, Oct. 1994.
21. Plevyak, J., X. Zhang, and A.A. Chien, Obtaining Sequential Efficiency in Concurrent Object-Oriented Programs. In *Conference Record of the 22nd Symposium on Principles of Programming Languages*, p. 311-321, San Francisco, California, Jan. 1995
22. Sanella, M., J. Maloney, B. Freeman-Benson, A. Borning, Multi-way versus One-way Constraints in User Interfaces: Experience with the DeltaBlue Algorithm. *Software - Practice and Experience,* 23(5), p. 529-566, May 1993.
23. Suzuki, N., Inferring Types in Smalltalk, In *Conference Record of the Eighth Annual ACM Symposium on Principles of Programming Languages,* p. 187-199, Williamsburg, Virginia, Jan. 1981.
24. Ungar, D. and R.B. Smith, SELF: The Power of Simplicity. *Lisp and Symbolic Computing,* 4(3), p. 187-205, Kluwer Academic Publishers, June 1991. (Originally published in Proc. *OOPSLA'87).*
25. Vitek, J., N. Horspool, and J.S. Uhl, Compile-Time Analysis of Object-Oriented Programs. In *Compiler Construction 4th International Conference, CC'92,* p. 236-250, Paderborn, Germany, Oct. 1992, Springer-Verlag LNCS 641.

Appendix

This appendix discusses issues that we have encountered during three years of work on type inference. Tackling them is important to obtain good type inference results, but since they are not central to the understanding of CPA, we only discuss them briefly in this appendix. Most issues are not specific to CPA, nor to Self.

Incrementality. Fast type inference is essential for some applications, e.g., to support browsing during program development. A large speedup can be achieved by reusing templates from one analysis to the next. If a method in the target program is modified, its templates are flushed, but all other templates are kept. Reanalyzing the program is fast because most of the needed templates already exist. Speedups can also be observed *across* programs where shared code often needs to be analyzed only once. Take arithmetic (bigInt's etc.). The first program that uses arithmetic forces analysis of the methods implementing arithmetic. Subsequent programs can be analyzed faster because they can be connected to arithmetic templates that were created during the first analysis. Incremental analysis may be less precise than a full analysis, unless care is taken to avoid that assignments to global state are visible across analyses.

Blocks, closures, and precision. Expressions in blocks may access slots in their lexical environment. To retain overall precision, such accesses must be analyzed precisely. Both blocks in the `max:` method access slots in the lexical environment:

```
max: a = ( self>a ifTrue: [self] False: [a] ).
```

Let $\texttt{a}_{slot}$ denote the slot `a`, and $\texttt{a}_{read}$ the expression which reads the slot `a` in the block `[a]`. Let $type_T$ be the type of a slot or an expression in a template T. Assume we have two `max:`-templates, S and T, for which:

$type_S(\texttt{self}) = type_S(\texttt{a}_{slot}) = \{\overline{\texttt{int}}\}$ and
$type_T(\texttt{self}) = type_T(\texttt{a}_{slot}) = \{\overline{\texttt{float}}\}$.

What should $type(\texttt{a}_{read})$ be? A simple approach is to assume that $\texttt{a}_{read}$ may access $\texttt{a}_{slot}$ in *any* `max:`-template., i.e., $type(\texttt{a}_{read}) = type_S(\texttt{a}_{slot}) \cup type_T(\texttt{a}_{slot}) = \{\overline{\texttt{int}}, \overline{\texttt{float}}\}$. Unfortunately, precise types cannot be inferred under this pessimistic assumption. To do better, analysis must closely parallel execution. Invoking `max:` with an integer argument creates an activation record in which `a` is bound to an integer. When the block `[a]` is evaluated, the result is a closure whose lexical pointer is set to this activation record. Later, when the closure is invoked, the lexical pointer is used to retrieve the value of `a`. To improve type inference precision, this two-phase evaluation of blocks must be simulated. Templates correspond to activation records, so we create type-inference-time closures that have a lexical pointer referring to a template, e.g., (`[a]`, S). When the closure is analyzed, the lexical pointer is used to find, e.g., that $type(\texttt{a}_{\texttt{read}}) = type_S(\texttt{a}_{slot}) = \{\overline{\texttt{int}}\}$. Now it is possible to infer precise types.

The above approach is not specific to Self- or Smalltalk style blocks; e.g., it also applies to Pascal's nested procedures, Scheme's closures and Beta's nested patterns.

Closures and Termination. The precise way to analyze blocks may result in non-termination of type inference, when using an adaptive type inference algorithm such as the iterative algorithm or CPA. The reason is that new templates result in creation of new block closures which in turn may result in creation of new templates. The simplest example is a method which invokes itself with a closure of its own:

```
foo: blk = ( foo: [blk value] ).
```

More complicated cases involve indirect recursion. Plevyak and Chien discuss this in [20]. The general solution is to break the infinite computation by creating a cycle in the constraint graph.

Closures and efficiency. Efficiency of type inference is highly sensitive to the number of closures created. This is due to "self-amplification": more closures result in more templates which in turn result in more closures etc. Consequently, we should create as few closures as possible. However, as outlined above, the simple approach of having only a single closure per block is too imprecise. One way to reduce the number of closures, without impairing precision, is to "fuse" closures when this is safe. Assume we have four templates for `max:`, S and T from above, and U and V with

$type_U(\texttt{self}) = \{\overline{\texttt{int}}\}$, $type_U(\texttt{a}_{slot}) = \{\overline{\texttt{float}}\}$ and
$type_V(\texttt{self}) = \{\overline{\texttt{float}}\}$, $type_V(\texttt{a}_{slot}) = \{\overline{\texttt{int}}\}$.

Even though we have four `max:`-templates, two closures for each of the blocks `[self]` and `[a]` suffice. The reason is that the types in the `[a]` block only depends on the type of $\texttt{a}_{slot}$. This type is the same in S and V, and it is the same in T and U. Creating two closures (`[a]`, {S,V}) and (`[a]`, {T,U}) saves analysis effort because it, in turn, will necessitate fewer `ifTrue:False:`-templates. This optimization complicates matters because closures at analysis time, unlike at execution time, now may have several scopes. For Self, we found the performance gain high enough to be worth the added complexity.

Reaching definitions. Assignments are non-destructive in type inference. They do not erase the old type of a slot they assign to, so clone families keep accumulating in the types for assignable slots. This conservatism is necessary in general, but sometimes we can do better. Four increasingly powerful approaches are: do nothing, eliminate dead initializers, use static single assignment (SSA) form, and propagate definitions through the call graph as it is constructed during type inference. In the Self implementation we have tested the first three approaches, but only for local slots. ("Instance slots" are harder to deal with because they may both be aliased and represent multiple locations). We found that the simple elimination of unused initializers pays off significantly, and that SSA is only slightly better. We suspect that this is because most local slots are initialized to `nil`, but immediately assigned to something more useful; simply getting rid of $\overline{\texttt{nil}}$ from the type of the slot achieves most of what can be obtained.

Coupled arguments. Assume that type(`x`) = {$\overline{\texttt{int}}$, $\overline{\texttt{float}}$} and type(`y`) = {$\overline{\texttt{int}}$, $\overline{\texttt{float}}$}. The send `x+y` connects to four templates, one for each of the four tuples in the cartesian product of the types of `x` and `y`. In contrast, the send `x+x` should only connect to two templates: ($\overline{\texttt{int}}$, $\overline{\texttt{int}}$) and ($\overline{\texttt{float}}$, $\overline{\texttt{float}}$), since if the receiver is an integer, so is the argument (the form of the send enforces that the receiver and argument is the same object). The receiver and argument are *coupled.* Coupling need not involve the exact same object, just objects that are (somehow) bound to be in the same clone family. In general, determining if two arguments are coupled is not computable, but safe approximations are possible. We implemented a simple approximation, but it had only a marginal effect on analysis of typical Self programs, possibly because we need more powerful detection, but more likely just because coupling *is* rare.

Grouping. The Self type inferencer analyzes an image of objects, not programmer-written source code. Consequently, it may encounter many "similar" objects in the image (e.g., 10,000 point objects that are part of a graph on the display). Inferring types for each object individually is computationally infeasible. To overcome this problem, we group objects according to structural similarity before inferring types [4]. Grouping may cost precision, but speeds up inference since all members of a group can be analyzed "in parallel."

PolyTOIL: A Type-Safe Polymorphic Object-Oriented Language*

Extended Abstract

Kim B. Bruce, Angela Schuett**, and Robert van Gent***

Williams College, Williamstown, MA 01267

Abstract. PolyTOIL is a new statically-typed polymorphic object-oriented programming language which is provably type-safe. By separating the definitions of subtyping and inheritance, providing a name for the type of *self*, and carefully defining the type-checking rules, we have obtained a language which is very expressive while supporting modular type-checking of classes. The *matching* relation on types, which is related to F-bounded quantification, is used both in stating type-checking rules and expressing the bounds on type parameters for polymorphism. The design of PolyTOIL is based on a careful formal definition of type-checking rules and semantics. A proof of type safety is obtained with the aid of a subject reduction theorem.

Categories: Type systems, design and semantics of object-oriented languages.

1 Introduction

Because of the complexity of object-oriented languages, it has proven to be very difficult to design type-safe statically-typed object-oriented languages which are also very expressive. At one extreme we have statically-typed languages like C++ [ES90] and Object Pascal [Tes85] which come close to type safety, but whose rigid and inflexible type systems result in the need for type casts in order to express the programmer's desires. At the other extreme are untyped or weakly typed languages like Smalltalk [GR83], which are prone to run-time errors of the form "message not understood." Somewhere between these extremes are languages like Eiffel [Mey92], which provides a conservative link-time "system validity check" to pick up errors missed by the type checker, and Beta [MMMP90], which builds in run-time checks to pick up errors which cannot be detected reliably by the type-checker.

* This research was partially supported by NSF grant CCR-9121778. The full paper is available via anonymous ftp from cs.williams.edu in pub/kim/PolyTOIL.dvi or on the world-wide web through http://cs.williams.edu/~kim.

** Current address: Department of Electrical Engineering and Computer Science, University of California at Berkeley.

*** Current address: Department of Computer Science, Stanford University.

The language PolyTOIL is the culmination of a series of design efforts to build a type-safe language based on progress in the theoretical understanding of object-oriented languages. In [Bru93], we introduced a statically-typed, functional, object-oriented language, TOOPLE. This and subsequent papers [Bru94, BCK94, BCD+93] provided typing rules and both denotational and operational semantics for the language. These papers included proofs of the relative consistency of the operational and denotational semantics, a subject-reduction theorem, the type safety of the type-checking rules, and the decidability of the type-checking problem.

Because most object-oriented programming languages are imperative, it was clearly desirable to extend this work to create an imperative object-oriented language. The language TOIL [BvG93, vG93] was designed to satisfy this goal while retaining the same nice features as TOOPLE. The extension of TOIL to PolyTOIL is obtained by adding an unusual form of bounded polymorphism which provides a very flexible yet safe language for object-oriented programming. In this paper we report on the design, type-checking rules, and semantics of PolyTOIL.

A minimal list of features that should be supported in any object-oriented programming language includes:

- **Objects**, consisting of both state and operations.
- **Classes**, to generate objects (though delegation would be a reasonable alternative).
- **Message sending**, as a way of specifying computation.
- **Instance variables**, representing state.
- **Subclasses**, to support reuse of the instance variables and methods of an existing class in defining a new class.
- **Subtypes**, depending only on object interfaces, to provide a mechanism for programmers to use an object of one type in a context which expects one of a different but related type.
- Keywords, *self* and *super*, representing the receiver of a message and its superclass, respectively.

Other desirable features supporting reuse include:

- **Information hiding**, ensuring that applications do not depend on the implementation details of objects.
- **Parameterized types and (bounded) polymorphic functions**, allowing a programmer to abstract over a type in order to define a related family of types or operations.
- **Modular type-checking**, providing greater support for the reuse of class definitions by allowing subclasses to be type-checked with knowledge only of the type of the superclass, rather than its code. This provides support for separately compiled classes and eliminates the necessity of repeatedly type-checking methods when they are inherited from superclasses.

The language PolyTOIL satisfies all of these requirements and is provably type safe. PolyTOIL also has the following important features.

PolyTOIL treats classes as first-class values, allowing them to be values of variables, to be passed as parameters, and to be returned as values of functions. This simplifies many of the problems with initializing objects and provides greater flexibility in support of such things as parameterized subclasses. We also provide more flexibility in the definition of subclasses by allowing the programmer to change the types of over-ridden methods to be subtypes of the corresponding types in the superclass.

Separating the subclass and subtype hierarchies in PolyTOIL allows greater expressibility while providing type safety. We introduce a new relation on types that we call "matching" which corresponds more closely than subtyping to the subclass hierarchy. This relation, which is weaker than subtyping on object types, is very useful both in expressing the type-checking rules for classes and in determining when messages can be sent to objects. The major difference between our earlier languages, TOIL (for Typed Object-oriented Imperative Language) and PolyTOIL is the support for polymorphic functions. We express constraints on type parameters by requiring that a type match a given object type. As we shall see in the next section, constraining types using matching is much more useful that using the subtype relation.

While we have a number of results on the type system and semantics of PolyTOIL, in this paper we focus on type safety. We include and explain the type-checking rules as well as a natural (operational) semantics. The natural semantics is environment-based and corresponds closely to an interpreter which we have implemented for the language. We prove a subject-reduction theorem, from which follows the type safety of the system. One consequence is that the computation of a well-typed term will never result in sending a message to an object that it will not understand. The proof of subject reduction (which is included in the full paper) is interesting in that it applies to an environment-based natural semantics for a polymorphic language.

In Section 2 of this paper we discuss the design of PolyTOIL. We include an extended example which illustrates the flexibility of the language. In Section 3 we provide the formal syntax and type-checking rules for PolyTOIL. In Section 4 we provide the natural semantics and discuss the subject-reduction and type-safety theorems for PolyTOIL. In Section 5 we compare our development of PolyTOIL with other similar work on statically-typed imperative object-oriented programming languages. In the final section we discuss more recent work and future plans for PolyTOIL.

2 Language Design for Type Safety

We presume that the reader is familiar with the basic notions of object-oriented languages, including object, class, subclass, method, and instance variable. Recall that type σ is a subtype of type τ, written $\sigma <: \tau$, if an element of type σ can be used in any context expecting an element of type τ.

The distinction between subclasses and subtyping is illustrated clearly in [CHC90]. It is possible to have subclasses which do not generate subtypes, and subtypes which do not arise from subclasses. Thus if one is interested in designing a statically typed object-oriented language, type safety will require either restricting subclasses to be those which generate subtypes or separating the subclass and subtype hierarchies. In the interest of maximizing expressibility we have chosen to separate these hierarchies.

Types in programming languages provide interfaces which can be used to determine whether certain operations or constructs are legal. They typically do not include semantic information. Classes in object-oriented languages include the bodies for methods as well as initial values for instance variables. Since this is semantic information, we conclude that it is more appropriate to think of classes as values than as types.

Because classes and objects are used in different ways (classes can be extended or modified to form subclasses or instantiated to create objects, while messages can be sent to objects in order to perform actions), it is important to give classes and objects different types. A class type, written $ClassType(\sigma, \tau)$, includes information on the types of the record of instance variables, σ, and methods, τ, while an object type, *ObjectType* τ, reveals only the types of methods.

Virtually all object-oriented languages include a construct *self* (sometimes named *this* or *Current*) which is used either explicitly or implicitly within a method to refer to the object executing the method. In order to statically type check a method in which *self* occurs, we must be able to determine its type. This is harder than it might appear at first sight.

Let c be a class and *ObjectType* τ be the type of objects generated by c. If *self* occurs in method m in class c, one might expect to assign *self* the type *ObjectType* τ. However the method m might also be inherited in a subclass c' of c. In this new context, *self* represents an object generated from c', which likely has a different type. If we wish to be able to type check the method m only the first time it appears, and not repeatedly type check it every time it is inherited, we must do the type checking under weaker assumptions on the type of *self*.

In order to do this, we must know what changes are allowed in the types of methods in subclasses. As explained in [Bru94], to preserve type safety the body of a method m with type τ_m in a class c may only be overridden in a subclass with a new method as long as the type τ'_m of the replacement method is a subtype of τ_m. This motivates the definition of the *matching* relation, $<\#$, between object types. *ObjectType* τ' $<\#$ *ObjectType* τ if for every method name, m, in τ there is a corresponding method in τ', and the type of m in τ' is a subtype of its type in τ. (An example of two types which match, but are not subtypes is given later in this section. Formal definitions of matching and subtyping are given in the next section.)

In order to accomodate the possible changes to the types of methods in subclasses, we introduce the special type, *MyType*, to represent the external type of *self* (where instance variables are hidden). In order to ensure that methods remain type safe when inherited in subclasses, methods are type checked under the assumption that *MyType* $<\#$ *ObjectType* τ.[4] By type checking under this assumption, we need not worry about the type safety of the method when it is inherited in subclasses.

Most statically-typed object-oriented programming languages (including C++ and Object Pascal) do not include a keyword like *MyType* to express the type of *self*, and instead are forced to assume its type is the same as the objects being defined by the class. In order to preserve type safety, the language designer must then restrict the user from changing the types of methods when they are overridden in a subclass. As a result it becomes impossible to properly redefine methods which take parameters or return a result whose type should correspond to that of the receiver.

Eiffel [Mey92] rejects this rigidity and includes a construct similar to *MyType* (which is written *like Current*). Unfortunately, the adoption of a covariant rule for parameters of methods and the identification of subclasses with subtypes leads to type insecurities [Coo89], which must be compensated for with a link-time "system validity check."

We avoid these problems while preserving much of the expressibility of Eiffel by separating the class and subtype hierarchies, providing more careful type-checking rules, and providing support for bounded polymorphism using matching. The result is a language that is provably safe, while being significantly more flexible than such statically-typed object-oriented languages as C++ and Object Pascal.

Before providing a complete example of a PolyTOIL program to illustrate the language features, we mention a few issues that arise when imperative features are combined with subtyping.

According to the definition of subtyping, it should be possible to assign to a variable an expression whose type is a subtype of that of the variable. That is, if $T <: U$, e_T is an expression of type T, and x_U is a variable of type U, one would like to allow the assignment $x_U := e_T$. As usual, we accomodate this in the run-time system by requiring that all objects be implemented as references. A variable of object type either contains a reference to the instance variables and methods of an object or contains a nil reference, which is denoted by the constant *nil*. *Nil* is considered an element of each object type, including *MyType*.

If x is a variable holding values of type τ, the type checker treats x as having type *ref* τ. Because these reference types are both receivers and producers of values, they have no non-trivial subtypes (see [Rey80]). Similar problems obstruct the use of subtyping with call-by-reference parameters. For instance, a procedure might take a formal parameter of type T and assign it a new object of that type. If an actual parameter, u, of type $U <: T$ is passed in to the procedure, it will

[4] We also introduce a special type *SelfType* to represent the internal type of *self*. In this internal view, *self* has access to its instance variables. A built-in function, *close*, converts *self* from the internal to the external view. The implemented language PolyTOIL hides this distinction by automatically inserting instances of *self* and *close* where needed so that the programmer need not be concerned with this distinction or even know about *SelfType*.

be assigned a value of type T. This would create a hole in the type system which would show up if a message m belonging to U but not T were sent to u after the procedure returns.

To avoid adding special rules, PolyTOIL only supports call-by-constant-value parameters. It is illegal to assign to a formal parameter in a procedure or function. Of course, it is legal to send a message to such a parameter, requesting it to perform an action (which may result in a change to that object's instance variables). As a result, this mechanism, similar to that used in Eiffel, is more flexible than it might first appear.

PolyTOIL supports the definitions of parameterized types (functions from types to types) and polymorphic functions (functions from types to values). In order to provide finer control over the types which may be passed in as parameters, the language allows the programmers to constrain a type parameter to match a given object type.

To illustrate the expressiveness of PolyTOIL, a relatively sophisticated sample PolyTOIL program which defines and uses singly and doubly-linked lists is given in Appendix A. We point out a few interesting features below.

Parameterized types are represented in PolyTOIL as functions from types to types. For instance, *OrdList_type* and *OrdList_class_type* are functions which take a type, U, matching *Node_type*, and return an object and class type, respectively. The language also supports bounded polymorphic functions which return values. *OrdList_class* is a function which takes a type, U, matching *Node_type* and returns a class with type *OrdList_class_type[U]*. Bounded matching can be shown to be equivalent to F-bounded polymorphism [CCH+89], but is expressed in a simpler and more readily understood form.

As illustrated in the definition of *Node_class*, a common way of specifying initial values of instance variables is to write a function which takes the initial values as parameters and returns a class. Other languages (such as C++, Eiffel, and Turbo Pascal's object extensions) often require the introduction of a new language mechanism (*e.g.*, constructors or creation routines) to initialize objects. We accomplish this by the combination of "new" and functions returning classes. This is just one of several ways in which having classes as first-class values is very helpful.

The use of *MyType* permits the implicit recursive definition of object types. For instance, the type *Node_class_type* in the Appendix has an instance variable of type *MyType*, while methods *get_next* and *attach_right* respectively return a value of type *MyType* and take a parameter of type *MyType*. When a message is sent to an object, all occurrences of *MyType* in the method body and its type are replaced by the type of the object. Thus if o is an object of type *Node_type*, the type of *o.get_next* is *func():Node_type*, while the type of *o.attach_right* is *proc(Node_type)*. Because the instance variable *next* in *Node_class_type* has type *MyType*, each object generated from a class with that type also contains a (hidden) instance variable of type *Node_type*.

In the example, *DNode_class*, a class generating doubly-linked nodes, is defined via inheritance from *Node_class*.[5] This is accomplished by adding a new instance variable and methods as well as modifying *attach_right*. All of the instance variables and methods of *Node_class(v)* are inherited by *DNode_class(v)*. Because the types of methods and instance variables are specified using *MyType*, the meaning of the types changes automatically. (This would not happen if the type *Node_type* were written with all occurrences of *MyType* replaced by the name *Node_type*.) Thus, if *node* is of type *Node_type* and *dble_node* is of type *DNode_type*, the value returned from *node.getnext()* will have type *Node_type*, while the value returned from *dble_node.getnext()* will have type *DNode_type*. This makes it possible to polymorphically define homogeneous data structures.

New objects are created by applying *new* to a class. The instance variables of the new object are initialized to the values specified in the class. Classes may be returned from functions in PolyTOIL. *Node_class* is a function which takes a value of type *Num_type* and returns a class, while *OrdList_class* takes a type which matches *Node_class* and returns a class for a linked list composed of that kind of node. *OrdList_class* can be applied to either *Node_type* or *DNode_type* to create a linked list since *DNode_type* <# *Node_type*. In the first case we end up with a singly-linked list, while in the second case we have a doubly-linked list. This is a very powerful and flexible mechanism for creating new objects in a parametric way.

It is worth noting here that one cannot write the program in this way in either C++ or Object Pascal, because the types of the methods and instance variables of *DNode_class* are all different from the corresponding types in the superclass, *Node_class*, because of the use of *MyType*.

We note here that while *DNode_type* <# *Node_type*, it is *not* a subtype. Suppose we write the following procedure:

```
break_it = procedure(sn1, sn2: Node_type)
           begin
              sn1.attach_right(sn2)
           end;
```

Because Eiffel assumes subclasses generate subtypes, it would allow the call of `break_it(dnode,lnode)` for *dnode* of type *DNode_type* and *lnode* of type *Node_type*. If allowed, this call would result in a run-time error when *lnode* is sent the *set_prev* message from within *attach_right*. PolyTOIL would not allow one to deduce that *DNode_type* <: *Node_type*, and hence would not allow the use of actual parameter *dnode* for *sn1*.

As in the definition of *OrdList_class*, it is often more important to know what messages can be safely sent to an object than to know whether or not it is a subtype of some other type. Thus we choose to support a form of bounded polymorphism where the bound is expressed in terms of matching.

A further example of the usefulness of matching is obtained by noting that the sample program can be further parameterized to make it more flexible. Define

[5] Technically, we define a function which returns a subclass of the class returned by evaluating *Node_class(v)*.

```
Comparable = ObjectType {ge:func(MyType):bool;
                         eq:func(MyType):bool}
```

Note that *Num_type* <# *Comparable*, though again it will *not* be a subtype. Now we can parameterize each of *Node_type, Node_class_type, DNode_type, DNode_class_type, OrdList_type*, and *OrdList_class_type* to take a parameter T <# *Comparable* within *TFunc* headers. All occurrences of *Num_type* within the bodies of the associated methods will now be changed to T. The result is a collection of classes which can be used to generate either singly or doubly-linked lists with elements of any type supporting appropriate *ge* and *eq* methods.

3 A Formal Definition of PolyTOIL Syntax

In this section we present the formal definitions of types and terms, and provide type-checking rules for PolyTOIL. The language is presented here with an abstract syntax which differs in inessential ways from that used in the earlier examples.

Definition 1. Let $\mathcal{V}$ be an infinite collection of type variables, $\mathcal{L}$ be an infinite collection of labels, and $\mathcal{C}$ be a collection of type constants which includes at least the type constants *Bool, Num, COMMAND, UNIT*, $\bot$, and $\top$. The simple pre-type expressions of PolyTOIL with respect to $\mathcal{V}$. $\mathcal{L}$, and $\mathcal{C}$ are given by the following context-free grammar. We assume $t \in \mathcal{V}$, $c \in \mathcal{C}$, and $m_i \in \mathcal{L}$ in the following.

$$\begin{aligned}\tau ::= {} & t \mid c \mid \mathit{ref}\ \tau \mid \mathit{func}(\tau_1){:}\ \tau_2 \mid \mathit{func}(\mathit{atype}\ t){:}\ \tau \mid \mathit{func}(t <\!\#\ \tau_1){:}\ \tau_2 \mid \\ & \{m_1{:}\ \tau_1, \ldots, m_n{:}\ \tau_n\} \mid \mathit{ClassType}(\tau_1, \tau_2) \mid \mathit{VisObjType}(\tau_1, \tau_2) \mid \\ & \mathit{ObjectType}\ \tau\end{aligned}$$

The *kinds* of the language are collections of constructors. The simplest kinds are the collection of all types and collections of types which match an object type. The higher-order kinds are collections of functions whose domains are restricted to be one of the simple kinds.

$$K ::= \mathit{TYPE} \mid \mathit{TYPE}^{\#\tau} \mid \mathit{TYPE} \Rightarrow K \mid \mathit{TYPE}^{\#\tau} \Rightarrow K$$

The pre-constructors represent elements of the various kinds. They are types, higher-order functions with types as parameters, or applications of these functions to types.

$$\kappa ::= \tau \mid \mathit{TFunc}[T{:}\ \mathit{atype}]\kappa \mid \mathit{TFunc}[T <\!\#\ \tau]\kappa \mid F[\tau]$$

The type constant *COMMAND* is the type of an imperative command expression. *UNIT* is a type whose only value is written () and is used when typing parameterless functions. The type $\bot$ is a subtype of all object types. It contains the element *nil* which is used in our sample program. The type $\top$ is a supertype of all object types, and (in our current implementation) contains built-in *clone* and *deep_clone* methods which are (implicitly) inherited by all object types. Reference types are the types of variables. The three function types represent the types of normal functions, polymorphic functions, and bounded polymorphic functions.

VisObjType(σ, τ) represents the type of the internal view of objects generated from a class with type *ClassType*(σ, τ). The external view represented by the type *ObjectType* τ does not expose the instance variables. Both σ and τ in these types must be record types.

Because programs in the implemented language are not allowed to use *ref*, record, or *VisObjType* types or the type constants *COMMAND, UNIT*, $\top$, or $\bot$, these types do not complicate the language seen by programmers. However, they are useful in writing the type-checking rules for the language.

The kinds give us a way to classify higher-order functions from types to types. For simplicity, we restrict the domains of these functions to either be *TYPE* or $TYPE^{\#\tau}$ for some type τ. *TYPE* represents the collection of all types, while $TYPE^{\#\tau}$ represents the collection of all (object) types which match τ.

The constructors include all types, functions from types (or bounded collections of types) to constructors, and the application of constructors to types. We omit the axioms and rules for determining which are the legal type and constructor expressions in this conference paper.

The axioms and rules for $<:$, $<\#$, and type-checking are given with respect to a set, C, of simple type constraints, which provide information about type variables. These definitions are mutually recursive.

Definition 2. Relations of the form t: *TYPE*, $t \leq \tau$, and t $<\#$ τ, where t is a type variable and τ is a type expression, are said to be ***simple type constraints***. A ***type constraint system*** is defined as follows:

1. The empty set, ϵ, is a type constraint system.
2. If C is a type constraint system and t is a type variable which does not appear in C, then $C \cup \{t\text{: } TYPE\}$ is a type constraint system.
3. If C is a type constraint system such that $C \vdash \tau\text{: } TYPE$, and t is a type variables which does not appear in C or τ, then $C \cup \{t \leq \tau\}$ is a type constraint system.
4. If C is a type constraint system such that $C \vdash \tau <\# \top$, and t is a type variable which does not appear in C or τ, then $C \cup \{t\ <\#\ \tau\}$ is a type constraint system.

The restriction that $C \vdash \tau <\# \top$ in the last clause ensures that τ will be an object type.

The axioms and rules for $\leq$ and $<\#$ are similar to those for TOOPLE and can be found in Appendix B. Neither class nor reference types have non-trivial subtypes. The subtyping rule for object types is adapted from the rule for determining subtypes of recursive types in [AC93]. It is more difficult to satisfy than the corresponding matching rule for objects. In particular, if an object type has a method with parameter of type *MyType*, then it cannot have any non-trivial subtypes. On the other hand, a type formed by adding new methods will always "match" the original. Note that only object types are related by "matching."

Applications of *TFunc* terms in type expressions are evaluated before type checking by explicitly substituting actual parameters for formal parameters in the bodies. We do not include subtyping rules for higher-order constructors (*e.g.*, $C \vdash F \leq G$ iff $C \cup \{t\colon TYPE\} \vdash F(t) \leq G(t)$). These would not be difficult to include, but are omitted from the language for simplicity. Because we evaluate *TFunc* applications before type checking, they are also less important than they might otherwise be.

In the examples presented earlier, we used a concrete syntax which is understood by our interpreter. Here we use a de-sugared abstract syntax which is closer to the way expressions are held internally. In particular, the key words *var* and *method* separating instance variable and method definitions are dropped in favor of a pair of record expressions, and *val* must be applied to a variable to obtain its value. Procedures are modeled by functions which return the unique value, *command*, of type *COMMAND*. All functions and procedures are written in Curried form.

We distinguish between instance variable access and message sending in the abstract syntax by writing $o \Leftarrow m$ for message sending and $o.v$ for accessing instance variables. In the concrete syntax, an unaccompanied message name, m, or instance variable, v, denoted sending a message to *self* or extracting the instance variable of *self*. However, in the abstract syntax we require that these be written explicitly as $self \Leftarrow m$ or $self.v$.

In this conference paper we will omit the discussion of declarations in PolyTOIL. See the full paper [BSvG94] for details. The syntax of blocks, expressions and commands of the language are given as follows:

Definition 3. The set of pre-terms of PolyTOIL over a set C of constants is given by the following context-free grammar:

$$\begin{array}{l}
Block ::= begin\ S\ return\ E\ end \\
E ::= x \mid c \mid val\ E \mid function(v{:}\,\sigma){:}\,\tau\ Block \mid function(t{:}\,atype){:}\,\tau\ Block \mid \\
\quad function(t <\!\# \sigma){:}\,\tau\ Block \mid E(E') \mid E[\tau] \mid \{m_1 = E_1, \ldots, m_n = E_n\} \mid \\
\quad E.m_i \mid class(E_1, E_2) \mid new\ E \mid E \Leftarrow m_i \mid E.v_i \mid \\
\quad class\ inherit\ E\ modifying\ x_1, \ldots, x_n \\
\qquad\qquad (\{v_{i_1} = E_1, \ldots, v_{i_k} = E_k\}, \{m_{j_1} = E'_1, \ldots, m_{j_l} = E'_l\}) \\
S ::= x := E \mid if\ E\ then\ E_1\ else\ E_2 \mid while\ E\ do\ S \mid S; S'
\end{array}$$

The intended meaning of these terms should be clear from our previous discussion. The type-checking axioms and rules for PolyTOIL are given in terms of a type constraint system, C, as defined earlier, and a *variable type assignment*, E, which assigns types to free variables.

Definition 4. A variable type assignment, E, is a finite set of associations between variables and type expressions of the form $x\colon \tau$, where each x is unique in E. If the relation $x\colon \tau \in E$, then we write $E(x) = \tau$.

The collection of terms of PolyTOIL with respect to C, E is the set of pre-terms which can be assigned types with respect to the type-assignment axioms and rules. The most interesting of these are included in Appendix D.

The type-assignment rules for the commands and non-object-oriented expressions should be relatively clear, while those for the object-oriented expressions may require some extra explanation.

The type-assignment rule, *Class*, involves several interesting features. As suggested earlier, the reserved word *self* may be used inside the methods of a class to refer to the object which is executing the method (though *self* may not be used in the initial values of instance variables). Because instance variables are not visible outside of an object's methods, it is convenient to assign *self* two types, an internal type, *SelfType*, in which the instance variables are visible, and an external type, *MyType*, which hides the instance variables. The reserved word *self* represents an internal view of the object, and has type *SelfType*. The reserved word *close*: *SelfType* → *MyType* is used to convert a term (usually *self*) from the internal type to the external type of the receiver. (Again, this coercion is inserted automatically in the interpreter for the language, so a programmer need not be aware of it.) Since *SelfType* is the internal type of the object, it cannot appear in the type of any instance variable or method of the object.

Recall that the class contains initial values for the instance variables, while the objects contain locations at which those initial values are stored. The function $RecToMem(\{v_1{:}\,\sigma_1; \ldots; v_n{:}\,\sigma_n\}) = \{v_1{:}\, \textit{ref}\ \sigma_1; \ldots; v_n{:}\, \textit{rcf}\ \sigma_n\}$, is used to convert a record type into one in which the type of each field is a reference to the type in the original.

Finally, recall that values of instance variables and method bodies should be type checked so that they are guaranteed to be type correct when inherited in a subclass. Thus we must type check these terms only under relatively weak assumptions on the possible values of *SelfType* and *MyType*.

With this background we can now understand the type-assignment rule, *Class*, as indicating that to type check a class term one must ensure that the records of initial values of instance variables and of methods have the desired types. This type checking is done assuming that $SelfType <: VisObjType(\sigma, \tau)$ and $MyType <\# \; ObjectType\ \tau$, since any subclass of the class being type checked must satisfy these constraints. We also assume that *self* and *close* have the appropriate types in type checking methods. By the subtyping rule for *VisObjType*, which converts types of instance variables using *RecToMem*, the subtype may not change the type of any instance variable, but may only add new ones.

The type-assignment rules for subclasses (classes with *inherit* clauses) are similar to *Class*, but require type checking the new or modified components. It is not necessary to type check inherited methods or instance variables, since they were already type checked under assumptions which are still valid in the subclass. (In fact, even stronger assumptions hold in the subclass.) Unlike C++ or Object Pascal, one may replace a method in a class by one in the subclass whose type is a subtype of the original.

The type-checking rule for message sending is interesting in that it uses the matching relation. A simpler version of the rule given in the appendix would be:

$$Msg' \quad \frac{C, E \vdash o\colon ObjectType\{m_1\colon \tau_1; \ldots; m_n\colon \tau_n\}}{C, E \vdash o \Leftarrow m_i\colon \tau_i[ObjectType\{m_1\colon \tau_1; \ldots; m_n\colon \tau_n\}/MyType]}$$

Unfortunately, this simple rule is not sufficient to handle the case in which a message is sent to *self*. That case would be written as $close(self) \Leftarrow m$, where $close(self)$ has type $MyType <\!\# \; ObjectType\; \tau$. Since we cannot write the type of $close(self)$ in the form $ObjectType\; \tau'$, the simple rule, (*Msg'*), is not applicable, and we must use the more complex rule given in the appendix.

We can get by with a simpler rule for instance variables. Since we assume $SelfType <: VisObjType(\sigma, \tau)$, we can deduce $self\colon VisObjType(\sigma, \tau)$ by subsumption. We do need to remember, however, that the instance variable actually has type $ref\ \sigma_i$, since it is a variable.

4 An Operational Semantics for PolyTOIL

In this section we sketch a natural (operational) semantics for PolyTOIL. This semantics is similar to that given in [BCK94] for TOOPLE. We also state a subject-reduction theorem and show how it can be used to prove that our type-assignment rules are safe.

The natural semantics for PolyTOIL provides a description of the reduction rules for a simple interpreter for the language. An environment keeps track of the current values of identifiers, while the store keeps track of what values are stored in currently active locations in memory. The semantic rules reduce a term, M, with associated environment, ρ, and current store, s, to a pair consisting of an irreducible value, V, and an updated store, s'. We write this as $(M, \rho, s) \downarrow (V, s')$.

There are a number of semantic decisions involving binding time that must be made carefully in order to provide a useful language. For instance, in order for *new* to create new objects each time it is invoked, it is important that locations for instance variables are not allocated when their initial values are declared in a class. Instead, they can only be allocated when a new object is created.

Suppose the initial values of instance variables or method bodies depend on global variables. When should they be evaluated? In TOOPLE, we waited until new objects were created, but, because it was a functional language, it made no real difference. In PolyTOIL, we employ eager evaluation in computing the initial values of instance variables specified in classes, while method bodies (since they are protected by function or procedure abstraction) do not evaluate variables until they are actually invoked by a message.

Another complication is that methods may refer to *self* and *super*. Yet the values of these reserved words are not known at the time a method body is provided in a class definition. Thus the instantiation of the corresponding values must be postponed until the new object is created.

The *irreducible values* in PolyTOIL are elements of base types, locations, functions (represented as *closures*, which are pairs of terms and environments), and records, classes, and object values with irreducible components. To assist in proving the subject-reduction theorem we presume that each location in the store is associated with a fixed type. We write Loc_τ for the collection of locations holding values of type τ, and interpret the type *ref* τ as Loc_τ.[6] *ObjectType* τ will be interpreted as $\bigcup_\sigma Loc_{VisObjType(\sigma,\tau)} \cup \{nil\}$, where σ ranges over record types. (We ignore error terms resulting from sending messages to *nil* in this conference paper.) If we think of terms of the form $obj(a, e)$ as representing objects whose instance variables are visible, objects with hidden instance variables are interpreted as references to those with visible instance variables. (See the full paper for more information on "obj" terms and closures.)

The store is infinitely extensible. The function *GetNewLoc* takes a store, s, a type, τ, and a value V of type τ, and returns an unused location $l \in Loc_\tau$, along with a new store, s'. The new store is the same as s, except that the location l holds the value V. The notation $s[l \mapsto V]$ is used to denote the updated store.

Because PolyTOIL supports the application of polymorphic functions to type expressions, and because some other constructs (such as records and regular function definitions) include type expressions as part of the terms, types will necessarily appear in our reduction rules. However, we also include some other type information in the rules in order to make it simpler to prove soundness via the subject-reduction theorem. Aside from indicating the amount of memory necessary to be allocated for a new variable, this extra typing information is inessential to the evaluation of terms.

Because the language is polymorphic, the types of terms can involve type variables. The environment keeps track of the values of these type variables. Because the result of evaluating a term is a pair of an irreducible value and a state, and because our terms involve type information, we will substitute in the values of type variables from the environment as part of the computation. We use the notation τ_ρ to stand for the result of replacing free variables in a type expression, τ, by the values assigned to them by the environment, ρ.

As stated earlier, the natural semantics rules (a selection of which can be found in Appendix E), reduce a term with associated environment and store to a pair consisting of an irreducible value and an updated store. An environment, ρ, is a (finite) mapping of names to irreducible values, while a store, s, is a (finite) mapping of locations to irreducible values. A state is consistent iff for each type τ and location $l \in Loc_\tau$, $s(l)$ has type τ. Because we wish to maintain a consistent state, allocation of new memory via *GetNewLoc* (*e.g.*, in expressions of the form *new* c) requires the type of memory being allocated and an initial value of that type.

Function expressions reduce to closures. Regular function applications proceed as expected by first reducing the function to a closure and the argument to a value. The body of the function is then reduced using the closure's environment, which is updated to interpret the formal parameter as the actual parameter's value.

---

[6] It would be possible instead to have a single collection of locations and simply keep a "store environment" which keeps track of the intended types of allocated locations, but the approach used here seemed a bit simpler.

Polymorphic functions are applied to type expressions. While there are no reduction rules for type expressions, we must handle properly any type variables contained in the type parameter. As a result, we replace the type variables in the parameter by the values assigned by the current environment. We then update the closure's environment with this modified type expression before evaluating the body of the function.

Class expressions are reduced by evaluating the initialization code for instance variables and method expressions in an environment which does not include interpretations of *self*, *close*, *SelfType*, or *MyType*.

The most complex rule is for *new c*. In *new c*, the expression *c* is first reduced to an irreducible value of the form $class(IV, Methods)$. New locations are allocated for each of the instance variables of the object and the initial values of the instance variables are stored in those locations. Then a new location is allocated to hold the object. The value returned is the new location, into which is stored a term of the form $obj(newIV, newMethods)$. $NewIV$ is defined to be the record of locations of the new instance variables, $newMethods$ is obtained from $Methods$ by replacing all free occurrences of *self* by $obj(newIV, Methods)$, *close* by the appropriate specialized $close_{(\sigma,\tau)}$, and the types *SelfType* and *MyType* by the types $VisObjType(\sigma, \tau)$ and $ObjectType\ \tau$. Notice that we must be careful to allocate memory corresponding to types in which the free type variables have been replaced by the values assigned by the environment. The rule for $close_{(\sigma,\tau)}\ o$ is not shown, but is interpreted similarly.

Since *new c* and $close_{(\sigma,\tau)}\ o$ are the only ways of constructing terms of type $ObjectType\ \tau$, no irreducible values of these types will have free occurrences of *self* or *close*. As a result, the natural semantics of sending a message to an object is trivial. Just look up the value stored in the location corresponding to the object and extract the appropriate method value.

Extracting the value of instance variables from (visible) objects, like sending messages, simply involves extracting the location from the record of instance variables.

Rather than attempting to write one all-encompassing rule for *inherit* terms, we include only one representative case. The semantics of inheritance is the obvious one. The new or modified values are added to or replace the corresponding values in the original class. *Super*, when applied to *self*, returns the record of methods of the superclass.

With some additional definitions and technical results about closures and substitutions, it is possible to state and prove a subject-reduction theorem which ties together the type-checking rules with the natural semantics. The subject-reduction theorem states that if we evaluate a term in a "consistent" environment and state, we obtain a pair consisting of an irreducible term and a consistent state, such that the irreducible term has the same type as the original term. (A careful statement of the theorem can be found in the full paper.) The proof proceeds by induction on the length of a computation. The general approach is similar to that taken in [BCD+93], but with extra complications due to the fact that class definitions do not contain explicit names for *self* and *MyType*. (This explicit annotation of classes was omitted in PolyTOIL because of the rarity of occurrences of nested classes.) The greatest new difficulties to overcome in this imperative language include handling of environments (*e.g.*, in closures) and ensuring that the state is always typed correctly.

By adding semantic rules which generate a value *stuck* when none of the original rules apply, a simple proof by induction using the subject-reduction theorem shows that no computation gets "stuck." That is, all computations either result in an irreducible value of the appropriate type or loop forever. (We note that sending a message to the *nil* object generates an explicit error value rather than generating "stuck." One must clearly be very careful in inserting "error" results versus "stuck". See the full paper for details.) This theorem ensures the type safety of the language.

5 Comparison with Other Work

PolyTOIL is a very expressive, yet type-safe, statically-typed object-oriented programming language. Its type system is more powerful and flexible than other statically-typed languages like C++ and Object Pascal, while avoiding the type-checking problems of Eiffel.

An important difference between PolyTOIL and these other typed object-oriented languages is that the subtype and subclass hierarchies are no longer identified. If they are identified then one is either left with an unsafe language (either by design, or with conventions that require many type casts – essentially by-passing the type system), a language with limited expressibility, or a language which requires extra run-time or link-time checks in order to preserve type safety.

In PolyTOIL the types of instance variables and methods may be given in terms of *MyType*. Thus when a subclass is defined, the types of the instance variables and methods automatically change to reflect that of the new object type.

The combination of the use of *MyType* and bounded polymorphism using matching provides much of the flexibility found in languages using the (unsafe) "covariant" rule for changing types of parameters in subclasses. A "covariant" type system, such as that found in Eiffel, would consider *DNode_type* to be a subtype of *Node_type* in the example in Appendix A. This leads to type errors unless a link-time global analysis of a program is added to identify those places where type-related errors could arise. PolyTOIL does not need this kind of global analysis in order to ensure type safety.

We see PolyTOIL as providing a sound semantic basis for a new generation of object-oriented programming languages which offer both increased expressibility and a safe type system. An example of this impact is the language Strongtalk [BG93], which has adopted essentially the typing rules for TOIL (along with a few extensions) in order to type check a subset of Smalltalk.

The language Theta [DGLM94] was developed independently of this work, but shares many of the features of PolyTOIL. In particular it supports a mechanism for constraining polymorphism which is equivalent to our use of bounded matching. The authors also argue that this mechanism is more useful than bounds on type parameters based on subtyping. Unfortunately, Theta does not appear to include a *MyType* construct, and it appears that inherited methods must be type checked again in the context of the subclass. The paper claims that Theta is type safe but provides no supporting evidence. We expect that the results of this paper can be used to add flexibility to their type system, while providing a proof of its type safety.

The Emerald language [BH91] seems to have been the first to explicitly identify the relation of matching as distinct from subtyping. While Emerald does not contain classes, it supports the use of bounded matching to restrict polymorphic functions.

The theoretical work most similar to that described here is [ESTZ94]. That paper presents an analysis of a statically-typed object-oriented language, LOOP, which is similar to PolyTOIL, although it lacks support for polymorphic functions. Results include proofs of type safety as well as the decidability of type checking.

There are a few important differences between PolyTOIL and LOOP. LOOP allows the use of *self* in the initial values of instance variables (though at the cost of a substantially more complex semantics for object creation), and supports multiple inheritance. Its subtyping rules for object types differ substantially from those for PolyTOIL. It includes folding and unfolding rules for object types (similar to those typically used with recursive types), which allow one to replace *MyType* by the type it represents. On the other hand, LOOP does not include our rule for subtyping object types. As a result, object types which involve *MyType* generally do not have subtypes.

LOOP does not explicitly identify the concept of "matching", though it appears that the concept is implicitly supported in the type-checking rules for methods. The typing rules for subclasses indicate that inherited methods should be type checked in the context of the subclass definition, but this does not seem to be necessary. It would be interesting to design a language which combined the strengths of LOOP and PolyTOIL.

The proof of type safety for LOOP differs from that sketched here in that LOOP is first given a somewhat complicated translation into an imperative language, SOOP, which supports F-bounded polymorphism, but has no object-oriented features. The proof of type-soundness for SOOP can then be lifted to LOOP. The operational semantics of LOOP is given via this translation into SOOP, while we provide a direct natural semantics for PolyTOIL.

Other researchers have performed interesting investigations of imperative object-oriented languages by looking at translations into simpler calculi. Pierce, [Pie93], has extended his encoding of object-oriented languages in higher-order bounded lambda calculi [PT94] to imperative languages. The semantics is somewhat simpler than the semantics of PolyTOIL, requiring one fewer fixed-point operator in creating types of objects. However, there is a corresponding loss of expressibility in that methods like the `attach_right` method of `node_class_type` in Appendix A, which have parameters of type *MyType*, may not be written as methods of the class.

Abadi and Cardelli have written a series of papers [AC94c, AC94b, AC94a] investigating a series of low-level object calculi designed to serve as a foundation for higher-level object-oriented programming languages. Interesting new unpublished results by the same authors show that one of these calculi can be used to model TOOPLE and PolyTOIL. Such a foundational object calculus should make it easier to explore new language features and prove type safety.

6 Further Results and Extensions to PolyTOIL

A proof of the decidability of a type-checking algorithm for TOIL appears in [vG93]. It is very similar to the one described in [BCD+93] for TOOPLE. It is easy to extend this to PolyTOIL because of the simplicity of our subtyping rule for polymorphic types. (It omits the problematic rule for bounded polymorphic types which leads to undecidability.) We have built a prototype interpreter for PolyTOIL which is based on the natural semantics given here.

Though not included here, there is also a denotational semantics for TOIL (which should be easily extensible to PolyTOIL), along with a proof of the soundness of type-checking with respect to the denotational semantics (similar to that in [Bru93] and [Bru94]). See [vG93] for details.

Recent work with Leaf Petersen and Jasper Rosenberg at Williams College involved adding new features to the language, improving the interpreter, and improving the readability of the concrete syntax. New features added include new control constructs, recursive types, arrays and other base types, a short-hand type-inclusion notation (similar to that of Rapide [KLM94]), programmer control over visibility of methods, We also added a new subtyping rule which allows us to deduce more subtype relations. The new rule states that if $\sigma <\# \tau$ and all occurrences of *MyType* in τ are positive then σ is a subtype of τ. We have also written and run a large number of PolyTOIL programs which have led us to these changes and have provided us with greater confidence in the strength and flexibility of the language. A reference and users' manual for PolyTOIL are currently being written.

The type system for PolyTOIL allows the programmer greater flexibility than most statically type languages, while providing assurance that the static type checking rules guarantee type safety. We are somewhat concerned, however, at the added complexity for the programmer in needing to keep track of two related, yet different, orderings on types: subtyping and matching. In writing a number of PolyTOIL programs we were somewhat surprised to find that we relied on matching quite heavily, but rarely used subtyping. Current research is involved in exploring the possibility of designing an object-oriented language which supports matching, but not subtyping, while still providing sufficient expressibility for programmers.

References

[AC93] Roberto Amadio and Luca Cardelli. Subtyping recursive types. *ACM Transactions on Programming Languages and Systems*, 15(4):575–631, 1993.

[AC94a] Martin Abadi and Luca Cardelli. An imperative object calculus. Manuscript, 1994.

[AC94b] Martin Abadi and Luca Cardelli. A theory of primitive objects: second-order systems. In *Proc. ESOP '94*. Springer-Verlag, 1994. to appear.

[AC94c] Martin Abadi and Luca Cardelli. A theory of primitive objects: untyped and first-order systems. In *Proc. Theoretical Aspects of Computer Software*. Springer-Verlag, 1994. to appear.

[BCD+93] K. Bruce, J. Crabtree, A. Dimock, R. Muller, T. Murtagh, and R. van Gent. Safe and decidable type checking in an object-oriented language. In *Proc. ACM Symp. on Object-Oriented Programming: Systems, Languages, and Applications*, pages 29–46, 1993.

[BCK94] K. Bruce, J. Crabtree, and G. Kanapathy. An operational semantics for TOOPLE: A statically-typed object-oriented programming language. In S. Brookes, M. Main, A. Melton, M. Mislove, and D. Schmidt, editors, *Mathematical Foundations of Programming Semantics*, pages 603–626. LNCS 802, Springer-Verlag, 1994.

[BG93] Gilad Bracha and David Griswold. Strongtalk: Typechecking Smalltalk in a production environment. In *Proc. ACM Symp. on Object-Oriented Programming: Systems, Languages, and Applications*, pages 215–230, 1993.

[BH91] A. Black and N. Hutchinson. Typechecking polymorphism in Emerald. Technical Report CRL 91/1 (Revised), DEC Cambridge Research Lab, 1991.

[Bru93] K. Bruce. Safe type checking in a statically typed object-oriented programming language. In *Proc. ACM Symp. on Principles of Programming Languages*, pages 285–298, 1993.

[Bru94] K. Bruce. A paradigmatic object-oriented programming language: design, static typing and semantics. *Journal of Functional Programming*, 4(2):127–206, 1994.

[BSvG94] Kim B. Bruce, Angela Schuett, and Robert van Gent. PolyTOIL: A type-safe polymorphic object-oriented language. Technical report, Williams College, 1994.

[BvG93] Kim B. Bruce and Robert van Gent. TOIL: A new type-safe object-oriented imperative language. Technical report, Williams College, 1993.

[CCH+89] P. Canning, W. Cook, W. Hill, J. Mitchell, and W. Olthoff. F-bounded quantification for object-oriented programming. In *Functional Prog. and Computer Architecture*, pages 273–280, 1989.

[CHC90] William R. Cook, Walter L. Hill, and Peter S. Canning. Inheritance is not subtyping. In *Proc. 17th ACM Symp. on Principles of Programming Languages*, pages 125–135, January 1990.

[Coo89] W.R. Cook. A proposal for making Eiffel type-safe. In *European Conf. on Object-Oriented Programming*, pages 57–72, 1989.

[DGLM94] Mark Day, Robert Gruber, Barbara Liskov, and Andrew C. Meyers. Abstraction mechanisms in Theta. Technical report, MIT Laboratory for Computer Science, 1994.

[ES90] Margaret A. Ellis and Bjarne Stroustrop. *The annotated C^{++} reference manual.* Addison-Wesley, 1990.

[ESTZ94] J. Eifrig, S. Smith, V. Trifonov, and A. Zwarico. Application of OOP type theory: State, decidability, integration. In *Proceedings of OOPSLA '94*, pages 16–30, 1994.

[GR83] A. Goldberg and D. Robson. *Smalltalk-80: The language and its implementation.* Addison Wesley, 1983.

[KLM94] Dinesh Katiyar, David Luckham, and John Mitchell. A type system for prototyping languages. In *21st ACM Symp. Principles of Programming Languages*, pages 138–150, 1994.

[Mey92] B. Meyer. *Eiffel: the language.* Prentice-Hall, 1992.

[MMMP90] O. Madsen, B. Magnusson, and B. Moller-Pedersen. Strong typing of object-oriented languages revisited. In *OOPSLA-ECOOP '90 Proceedings*, pages 140–150. ACM SIGPLAN Notices,25(10), October 1990.

[Pie93] Benjamin C. Pierce. Mutable objects. Technical report, University of Edinburgh, 1993.

[PT94] Benjamin C. Pierce and David N. Turner. Simple type-theoretic foundations for object-oriented programming. *Journal of functional programming*, 4:207–247, 1994. An earlier version appeared in Proc. of POPL '93, pp. 299-312.

[Rey80] J.C. Reynolds. Using category theory to design implicit conversions and generic operators. In N.D. Jones, editor, *Semantics-Directed Compiler Generation*, pages 211–2580. Springer-Verlag Lecture Notes in Computer Science, Vol. 94, 1980.

[Tes85] L. Tesler. Object Pascal report. Technical Report 1, Apple Computer, 1985.

[vG93] Robert van Gent. *TOIL: An imperative type-safe object-oriented language.* Williams College Senior Honors Thesis, 1993.

Appendices

A Sample PolyTOIL Program

```
program linkedlist;
type
   Num_type = ObjectType {ge: func(MyType):bool;
                          eq: func(MyType):bool;
                          get_val: func():num;
                          set_val: proc(num)};
   Num_class_type = ClassType ({val: num},
                               {ge:...; set_val: proc(num)})

   Node_type = ObjectType {get_next: func():MyType;
                           get_val: func():Num_type;
                           set_next: proc(MyType);
                           set_val: proc(Num_type);
                           attach_right: proc(MyType)};
```

```
   Node_class_type = ClassType ({val: Num_type ; next: MyType},
                                {get_next: ...});

   DNode_type = ObjectType {get_next: func():MyType;
                            set_next: proc(MyType);
                            get_val: func():Num_type;
                            set_val: proc(Num_type);
                            get_prev: func():MyType;
                            set_prev: proc(MyType);
                            attach_right: proc(MyType)};
   DNode_class_type = ClassType ({val: Num_type ; next: MyType},
                                 {...});

   OrdList_type = TFunc[U <# Node_type]
                        ObjectType {find: func(Num_type):bool;
                                    add: proc(U)};
   OrdList_class_type = TFunc[U <# Node_type]
                        ClassType ({head: U}, {find:...});

const
   Num_class = class
            var val = 0: num;
            methods
              ge = function(other: MyType): bool
                begin return val >= other.get_val(); end;
              ... : Num_class_type;
   Node_class = function(v: Num_type): Node_class_type
      begin
         return class
            var val = v: Num_type;
                next = nil: MyType;
            methods
               get_next = function(): MyType
                  begin   return next;  end;
               set_next = procedure(nxt: MyType)
                  begin  next := nxt;   end;
               get_val = ...; set_val = ...;
               attach_right = procedure(nxt: MyType)
                  begin  set_next(nxt);  end;  ...
      end;
   DNode_class = function(v: Num_type): DNode_class_type
      begin
         return inherit Node_class(v) modifying attach_right
            var prev = nil: MyType;
            methods
```

```
            get_prev = ...;  set_prev = ...;
            attach_right = procedure(nxt: MyType)
               begin set_next(nxt); nxt.set_prev(self) end;
      end;
   OrdList_class=function(U <# Node_type): OrdList_class_type[U]
      begin
         return class
            var  head = nil: U;
            methods
               find = function(match: Num_type): bool ... end;
               add = procedure(new_node:U)
                  var  prev: U;  current: U;
                  begin
                     if head = nil then
                        head := new_node;
                        new_node.set_next(nil);
                     else if head.get_val().ge(new_node.get_val())
                        then
                           new_node.attach_right(head);
                           head := new_node;
                     else ...
      end;  -- function
var num_obj: Num_type;
    lnode: Node_type;                       -- singly linked node
    dnode: DNode_type;                      -- doubly linked node
    slist: OrdList_type[Node_type];         -- singly linked list
    dlist: OrdList_type[DNode_type];        -- doubly linked list
begin
    num_obj := new (Num_class);
    num_obj.set_val(1);
        -- create singly linked list
    slist := new (OrdList_class(Node_type));
        -- create doubly linked list
    dlist := new (OrdList_class(DNode_type));
    dnode := new (DNode_class(num_obj));
    dlist.add(dnode);
    printBool (dlist.find (num_obj));
end.
```

B Selected Subtyping Rules

We include only the rules for selected type constructors.

$$\textit{Bound--Bound}(\ <:\ )\qquad \frac{C \cup \{u <\!\!\# \gamma\} \vdash \tau[u/t] <: \tau'[u/t']}{C \vdash (\mathit{Func}(t <\!\!\# \gamma)\colon\ \tau) <:\ (\mathit{Func}(t' <\!\!\# \gamma)\colon\ \tau')},$$

where u does not occur in C, τ or τ'.

$$Func(<:) \quad \frac{C \vdash \sigma' <: \sigma, \; C \vdash \tau <: \tau'}{C \vdash Func(\sigma)\colon \tau \; <: \; Func(\sigma')\colon \tau'},$$

$$Rec(<:) \quad \frac{C \vdash \sigma_j <: \tau_j, \text{ for } 1 \le j \le k, \;\; C \vdash \sigma_j\colon TYPE, \text{ for } k \le j \le n}{C \vdash \{m_1\colon \sigma_1; \ldots; m_k\colon \sigma_k; \ldots; m_n\colon \sigma_n\} <: \{m_1\colon \tau_1; \ldots; m_k\colon \tau_k\}},$$

$$VisObj(<:) \quad \frac{C \vdash RecToMem(\sigma) <: RecToMem(\sigma'), \; C \vdash \tau <: \tau'}{C \vdash VisObjType(\sigma, \tau) <: VisObjType(\sigma', \tau')},$$

$$Obj(<:), \quad \frac{C \cup \; \{t\colon TYPE, s <: t\} \vdash \tau[s/Mytype] <: \tau'[t/Mytype]}{C \vdash ObjectType \; \tau <: ObjectType \; \tau'}.$$

where neither s nor t may occur free in C, τ, or τ'.

C Selected Matching Rules

Matching is a preorder on object types with $\top$ as maximum element. The most important structural rule is:

$$ObjectType(<\#) \; \frac{C \cup \{Mytype <\# ObjectType \; \sigma\} \vdash \sigma <: \tau}{C \vdash ObjectType \; \sigma <\# ObjectType \; \tau},$$

D Selected Type-Checking Rules

Type Assignment Rules (Commands):

$$Assn \quad \frac{C, E \vdash X\colon ref \; \tau, \;\; C, E \vdash M\colon \tau}{C, E \vdash X := M\colon \text{COMMAND}}$$

$$Cond \quad \frac{C, E \vdash B\colon Bool, \;\; C, E \vdash S\colon \text{COMMAND}, \;\;\; C, E \vdash T\colon \text{COMMAND}}{C, E \vdash if \; B \; then \; S \; else \; T \; end : \text{COMMAND}}$$

Similar rules exist for *while* loops and sequencing.

Type Assignment Rules (Expressions):

$$Function \quad \frac{C, E \cup \{v\colon \sigma\} \vdash Block\colon \tau}{C, E \vdash function \; (v\colon \sigma) \; Block\colon \; (func \; (\sigma)\colon \tau)}$$

$$BdPolyFunc \quad \frac{C \cup \{t <\# \gamma\}, E \; \vdash Block\colon \tau}{C, E \vdash function \; (t <\# \gamma) \; Block\colon \; (func \; (t <\# \gamma)\colon \tau)}$$

FuncAppl
$$\frac{C, E \vdash f\colon func(\sigma)\colon \tau, \quad C, E \vdash M\colon \sigma}{C, E \vdash f(M)\colon \tau}$$

BoundFuncAppl
$$\frac{C, E \vdash f\colon func(t <\# \gamma)\colon \tau, \quad C \vdash \sigma <\# \gamma}{C, E \vdash f(\sigma)\colon \tau[\sigma/t]}$$

Class
$$\frac{C^{IV}, E \vdash e_1\colon \sigma, \quad C^{METH}, E^{METH} \vdash e_2\colon \tau}{C, E \vdash class(e_1, e_2)\colon ClassType(\sigma, \tau)}$$

where $C^{IV} = C \cup \{MyType <\# ObjectType\ \tau\}$,
$C^{METH} = C^{IV} \cup \{SelfType <:\ VisObjType(\sigma, \tau)\}$,
$E^{METH} = E \cup \{self\colon SelfType, close\colon func(SelfType)\colon MyType\}$
Neither *MyType* nor *SelfType* may occur free in C or E.
τ must be the type of a record of functions.

Object
$$\frac{C, E \vdash c\colon ClassType(\sigma, \tau)}{C, E \vdash new\ c\colon ObjectType\ \tau}$$

Msg
$$\frac{C \vdash \gamma <\# ObjectType\{m\colon \tau\}, C, E \vdash o\colon \gamma}{C, E \vdash o \Leftarrow m\colon \tau[\gamma/MyType]}$$

InstVar
$$\frac{C, E \vdash o\colon VisObjType(\{v_1\colon \sigma_1; \ldots; v_n\colon \sigma_n\}, \tau)}{C, E \vdash o.v_i\colon ref\ \sigma_i}$$

Inherits
$$\frac{\begin{array}{c} C, E \vdash c\colon ClassType(\{v_1\colon \sigma_1; \ldots; v_m\colon \sigma_m\}, \{m_1\colon \tau_1; \ldots; m_n\colon \tau_n\}), \\ C^{IV} \vdash \tau_1' <: \tau_1, \quad C^{IV}, E \vdash a_{m+1}\colon \sigma_{m+1}, \quad C^{IV}, E \vdash a_1'\colon \sigma_1, \\ C^{METH}, E^{METH} \vdash e_{n+1}\colon \tau_{n+1}, \quad C^{METH}, E^{METH} \vdash e_1'\colon \tau_1' \end{array}}{\begin{array}{l} C, E \vdash inherit\ c\ modifying\ v_1, m_1 \\ \qquad (\{v_1 = a_1'\colon \sigma_1, v_{m+1} = a_{m+1}\colon \sigma_{m+1}\}, \\ \qquad \{m_1 = e_1'\colon \tau_1', m_{n+1} = e_{n+1}\colon \tau_{n+1}\})\colon \\ ClassType(\{v_1\colon \sigma_1; \ldots; v_{m+1}\colon \sigma_{m+1}\}, \\ \qquad \{m_1\colon \tau_1'; m_2\colon \tau_2; \ldots; m_{n+1}\colon \tau_{n+1}\}) \end{array}}$$

where $C^{IV} = C \cup \{MyType <\# ObjectType\ \{m_1\colon \tau_1'; \ldots; m_{n+1}\colon \tau_{n+1}\}\}$,
$C^{METH} = C^{IV} \cup \{SelfType <:\ VisObjType(\{v_1\colon \sigma_1; \ldots; v_{m+1}\colon \sigma_{m+1}\}, \{m_1\colon \tau_1'; \ldots; m_{n+1}\colon \tau_{n+1}\})\}$
$E^{METH} = E \cup \{self\colon SelfType, close\colon func(SelfType)\colon MyType, super\colon SelfType \rightarrow \{m_1\colon \tau_1; \ldots; m_n\colon \tau_n\}\}$
Neither *MyType* nor *SelfType* may occur free in C or E.

Subsump
$$\frac{C \vdash \sigma <: \tau, \quad C, E \vdash e\colon \sigma}{C, E \vdash e\colon \tau}$$

Type Assignment Rules (Commands):

Assn $$\frac{C, E \vdash x\colon ref\ \tau, \quad C, E \vdash M\colon \tau}{C, E \vdash x := M\colon \text{COMMAND}}$$

Cond $$\frac{C, E \vdash B\colon Bool, \ C, E \vdash S\colon \text{COMMAND}, \quad C, E \vdash T\colon \text{COMMAND}}{C, E \vdash \text{if } B \text{ then } S \text{ else } T \text{ end}\colon \text{COMMAND}}$$

While $$\frac{C, E \vdash B\colon Bool, \ C, E \vdash S\colon \text{COMMAND}}{C, E \vdash \text{while } B \text{ do } S \text{ end}\colon \text{COMMAND}}$$

StmtList $$\frac{C, E \vdash S\colon \text{COMMAND}, \ C, E \vdash T\colon \text{COMMAND}}{C, E \vdash S;\ T\colon \text{COMMAND}}$$

E The Natural Semantics of PolyTOIL

Expressions:

FuncAppl $$\frac{\begin{array}{c}(M, \rho, s^0) \downarrow (\langle \text{function}(v\colon\sigma)B, \rho_f\rangle, s^1),\\ (N, \rho, s^1) \downarrow (V_1, s^2), \quad (B, \rho_f[v \mapsto V_1], s^2) \downarrow (V, s^3)\end{array}}{(M(N), \rho, s^0) \downarrow (V, s^3)},$$

BdPolyFuncAppl $$\frac{\begin{array}{c}(M, \rho, s^0) \downarrow (\langle \text{function}(t <\!\# \gamma)B, \rho_f\rangle, s^1),\\ (B, \rho_f[t \mapsto \tau_\rho], s^1) \downarrow (V, s^2)\end{array}}{(M[\tau], \rho, s^0) \downarrow (V, s^2)},$$

Class $$\frac{(a, \rho', s) \downarrow (V_a, s'), \quad (e, \rho', s') \downarrow (V_e, s'')}{(\text{class}(a, e), \rho, s) \downarrow (\text{class}(V_a, V_e), s'')},$$

where $\rho' = \rho \backslash \{self, close, SelfType, MyType\}$

New $$\frac{\begin{array}{c}(c, \rho, s) \downarrow (\text{class}(\{iv_1 = V_1\colon \sigma'_1, \ldots, iv_n = V_n\colon \sigma'_n\}, Methods), s^0),\\ (newLoc_i, s^i) = GetNewLoc\ s^{i-1}\ \sigma''_i\ V'_i, \ \text{for } 1 \leq i \leq n,\\ (newLoc_{n+1}, s^{n+1}) = GetNewLoc\ s^n\ VisObjType(\sigma', \tau')\ o'\end{array}}{(\text{new } c, \rho, s) \downarrow (newLoc_{n+1}, s^{n+1})},$$

where $\sigma' = \sigma_{\rho'} = \{iv_1\colon \sigma'_1; \ldots; iv_n\colon \sigma'_n\}$, $\tau' = \tau_{\rho'}$
for $\rho' = \rho \backslash \{self, close, SelfType, MyType\}$,
$\sigma''_i = \sigma'_i[MyType \mapsto ObjectType\ \tau']$
$V'_i = V_i[MyType \mapsto ObjectType\ \tau'])$,
$newIV = \{iv_1 = newLoc_1\colon ref\ \sigma''_1, \ldots, iv_n = newLoc_n\colon ref\ \sigma''_n\}$,
$o' = \text{obj}(newIV, Methods)$,
if $Methods = \{\langle f_1, \rho_1\rangle, \ldots, \langle f_k, \rho_k\rangle\}$

$$\text{then } \mathit{newMethods} = \{\langle f_1, \rho'_1\rangle, \ldots, \langle f_k, \rho'_k\rangle\}$$
$$\text{where for } 1 \le i \le k,$$
$$\rho'_i = \rho_i[\mathit{self} \mapsto o', \mathit{close} \mapsto \mathit{close}_{(\sigma',\tau')},$$
$$\mathit{SelfType} \mapsto \mathit{VisObjType}(\sigma', \tau'), \mathit{MyType} \mapsto \mathit{ObjectType}\ \tau']$$

Message
$$\frac{(o, \rho, s) \downarrow (\mathit{Loc}, s'),\quad s'(\mathit{Loc}) = \mathrm{obj}(V_a, \{m_1 = V_1{:}\, \tau'_1, \ldots, m_n = V_n{:}\, \tau'_n\})}{(o \Leftarrow m_i, \rho, s) \downarrow (V_i, s')},$$

InstVble
$$\frac{(o, \rho, s) \downarrow (\mathrm{obj}(\{iv_1 = V_1{:}\, \sigma'_1, \ldots, iv_n = V_n{:}\, \sigma'_n\}, V_e), s')}{(o.iv_i, \rho, s) \downarrow (V_i, s')},$$

Inherit
$$\frac{\begin{array}{c}(c, \rho, s) \downarrow (\mathrm{class}(V_a, \{m_1 = V_1{:}\, \tau'_1, \ldots, m_{upd} = V_{old}{:}\, \tau'_{old}, \\ \ldots, m_n = V_n{:}\, \tau'_n\}), s'), \\ (u, \rho', s') \downarrow (V_{new}, s'')\end{array}}{\begin{array}{c}(\text{class inherit } c \text{ modifying } m_{upd};\ (\{\}, \{m_{upd} = u{:}\, \tau'_{new}\}), \rho, s) \downarrow \\ (\mathrm{class}(V_a, \{m_1 = V_1{:}\, \tau'_1, \ldots, m_{upd} = V_{new}{:}\, \tau'_{new}, \\ \ldots, m_n = V_n{:}\, \tau'_n\}), s'')\end{array}},$$

where $sup = \langle \text{function}(\mathit{self}{:}\, \mathit{SelfType}).\ \{m_1 = V_1{:}\, \tau'_1, \ldots, m_{upd} = V_{old}{:}\, \tau'_{old}, \ldots, m_n = V_n{:}\, \tau'_n\}, \rho\rangle$

$\rho' = \rho[\mathit{super} \mapsto \mathit{sup}] \setminus \{\mathit{self}, \mathit{close}, \mathit{SelfType}, \mathit{MyType}\}$

$\tau'_i = (\tau_i)_{\rho'}$.

Commands:

Assign
$$\frac{(X, \rho, s) \downarrow (\mathit{Loc}, s'),\quad (M, \rho, s') \downarrow (V, s'')}{(X{:=}\, M, \rho, s) \downarrow (\text{command}, s''[\mathit{Loc} \mapsto V])},$$

Conditional$_{true}$
$$\frac{(B, \rho, s) \downarrow (\text{true}, s'),\quad (M, \rho, s') \downarrow (\text{command}, s'')}{(\text{if } B \text{ then } M \text{ else } N \text{ end}, \rho, s) \downarrow (\text{command}, s'')},$$

Conditional$_{false}$
$$\frac{(B, \rho, s) \downarrow (\text{false}, s'),\quad (N, \rho, s') \downarrow (\text{command}, s'')}{(\text{if } B \text{ then } M \text{ else } N \text{ end}, \rho, s) \downarrow (\text{command}, s'')},$$

while$_{true}$
$$\frac{\begin{array}{c}(B, \rho, s) \downarrow (\text{true}, s'),\quad (S, \rho, s') \downarrow (\text{command}, s''), \\ (\text{while } B \text{ do } S \text{ end}, \rho, s'') \downarrow (\text{command}, s''')\end{array}}{(\text{while } B \text{ do } S \text{ end}, \rho, s) \downarrow (\text{command}, s''')},$$

while$_{false}$
$$\frac{(B, \rho, s) \downarrow (\text{false}, s')}{(\text{while } B \text{ do } S \text{ end}, \rho, s) \downarrow (\text{command}, s')},$$

Sequence
$$\frac{(C_1, \rho, s) \downarrow (\text{command}, s'),\quad (C_2, \rho, s') \downarrow (\text{command}, s'')}{(C_1;\ C_2, \rho, s) \downarrow (\text{command}, s'')}$$

Object Imaging

Satish R. Thatté*

Abstract

As heterogeneous and distributed object systems become more common, interoperability of system components is becoming a pressing issue. One important challenge in making such component-based systems work is support for object transport. Earlier data transport standards such as XDR focused primarily on marshalling RPC parameters and results for transport between different processor architectures. Effective use of the potential benefits of heterogeneous distributed object systems will require object transport at many levels of abstraction and granularity, ranging from small objects exchanged via RPC to large multimedia documents transferred across environments via the world-wide web. To emphasize the transformations involved, we refer to the problem of producing copies of objects across different environments as object imaging. In this paper we propose a very general notion of object imaging in which a flexible knowledge-base in the form of a dual logic of conversion and conformance is used to represent elements of imaging knowledge as composable combinators. This approach has the potential to seamlessly cover the entire range of imaging problems from simple primitive datatypes to complex object structures, and supports a variety of notions about conformance of object and interface types, including the multiple-inheritance single-interface object model of CORBA and the inheritance-averse multiple-interface model of COM.

1 Introduction

One of the benefits expected from object-oriented technology in software construction is the possibility of building open evolving software systems from collections of interoperable components. Potential components include class libraries, single-focus tools of the kind that are expected to be integrated using technologies such as OpenDoc [3] and OLE [4], and system components such as databases and file systems. A fundamental problem in establishing interoperability of components is support for object transport between components residing in different execution environments. The granularity of objects involved in transport may vary greatly. They may be as small as complex numbers or as large as compound documents involved in drag-and-drop operations.

*Department of Mathematics and Computer Science, Clarkson University, Potsdam, NY 13699-5815. E-mail: `satish@sun.mcs.clarkson.edu`.

The considerably simpler related problem of transporting both simple and complex data values has been addressed in the context of RPC mechanisms with marshalling schemes. Marshalling is concerned with issues like byte order, floating point representations, and data layout in arrays and records. This has been tackled traditionally with external data representation standards like XDR [23], which establish a one-to-one correspondence between standard atomic and aggregate types in different execution environments. Such marshalling schemes are clearly not capable of supporting transport of abstract objects, although they are necessary as a lower-level layer on which object transport can be built in a distributed object system. For various reasons, the leading component oriented object models being developed today, CORBA [17] and COM [15], do not treat object transport as a primary operation. Their default assumption is that objects are passed-by-reference, *i.e.*, only references to objects[1] are transported, not objects themselves. We therefore begin with an explanation of the need for transport of abstract objects, and the shortcomings of current approaches to the problem.

Motivations for Object Imaging

When components exchanging objects reside in different processes, there are many situations in which it is desirable or even necessary to make a copy of an object in the receiving environment rather than merely copying a reference. Examples occur at many levels of granularity:

- It is clearly impractical to expect small objects (such as complex numbers) to be used remotely since such objects tend to be numerous and the operations on them tend to be simple. Using such objects remotely would be prohibitively expensive. This problem is most likely to come up in passing parameters anbd results at the RPC level.

- A large object may be transported because accessing it remotely may impose an unacceptable cost in response time. Transport of multi-media document parts by world-wide web browsers is a good example.

- An object may be part of an aggregate such as a compound document on a remote system where the aggregate needs to be made persistent. Since the object may be transient in its original location, it may need to be transported for "embalming" purposes.

- Remote use may be simply impossible due to platform mismatches. For instance, if a user drags an icon for a document residing on a Macintosh and drops it on an icon representing an application on a machine running Windows, the Windows application will not in general be able to use the document remotely—it will need a local copy produced via (probably both hardware and software) format conversions.

[1] In the case of COM, it would be more accurate to say references to interfaces.

Effective interoperability standards must therefore support some notion of object transport. In the presence of heterogeneity, the only practical proposition *in general* is to transport (state) representations only, not code for methods, since code is extremely difficult to migrate even across software platforms, let alone hardware ones. Specifically, we must assume that when transporting an object O of class C_1 from environment E_1 to environment E_2, there is a *corresponding* class C_2 in E_2 which can provide the same functionality if the representation of O is transported to E_2[2]. It is therefore more appropriate to call this process object *imaging* rather than object transport. Object imaging includes and generalizes the current data transport protocols based on representation standards such as XDR. The imaging of abstract types is a more general problem than the transport of data structure representations—the polar and cartesian representations of complex numbers are identical as data structures. The problem considered in this paper is to identify the kinds of knowledge required to support a general notion of object imaging and to find an appropriate knowledge representation scheme.

Shortcomings of Current Approaches

Some of the essential mechanisms for object imaging are offered by several currently available systems. The specification for the common services layer on top of CORBA reflects current practice by offering standard copying [18] and externalization [19] services (the former as one of the life-cycle services)[3]. The copying service is expected to be a restricted version of what is possible with externalization. The externalization service provides a standard way for an object to produce an external representation of its state, using a flat stream format suitable for persistent storage and network transport. The service also provides a way to internalize such a stream in a different environment using an appropriate "object factory" to produce a corresponding object there. It is obviously possible to combine existing data transport protocols with the externalization service to achieve object imaging. The primary model for externalization is the various wire-format standards used in distributed systems for marshalling data structures. The same idea can be extended to larger objects with proposed standards such as the Rich Text Format (RTF) and the Graphical Interchange Format (GIF). The main current alternative to standard formats is custom conversions when the target type is known, as is often the case in drag-and-drop operations, for instance. This approach has been popular in desktop applications such as word processors.

Although both of these approaches are compatible with the externalization model, they have the disadvantage of making very strong assumptions about

[2] The representation could be treated in either a "shallow" or "deep" manner during transport. The treatment of graph structures is also a well-known problem addressed in the OMG services proposals [18, 19].

[3] The uniform data transfer and structured storage services associated with COM implement related functionality. For expository purposes we focus on the CORBA services. The following remarks can be paraphrased for the corresponding COM services as well.

the relationship between the object types involved in imaging. Many people advocate standards in interfaces and formats as a way of achieving interoperability in open object systems. However, the process of arriving at standards is difficult, both because software technology changes rapidly and because software vendors compete on the basis of product differentiation at least as much as on performance. Standard formats are therefore not likely to be available for most objects. On the other hand, custom conversions assume a degree of mutual knowledge that is contrary to the goals of open systems. For instance, pictures are commonly stored in GIF, JPEG and TIFF formats among others. Consider sending a GIF-formatted picture over the web to remote environments where the available viewers in each support only one of the other two formats. Given the lack of a standard format, custom conversions are called for. Knowledge about all these formats must therefore be available inside each source object in order to externalize appropriate representations for all possible target types. This clearly goes against fundamental principles of object design in open systems since this extraneous knowledge makes such objects fragile and subject to continual change due to the introduction of new picture formats, new requirements such as encryption, and so on. Each object ought to know only how to externalize/internalize its own state in a standard way, and knowledge of transformation to other formats can and should be maintained and applied externally. In short, the complexity of imaging in an evolving heterogeneous environment is difficult to handle *entirely* with *closely coupled* approaches based on custom converters or format standards. We need a *loosely coupled* approach based on a uniform knowledge-representation framework which provides an umbrella under which many approaches can coexist and evolve as object types are introduced, converters added, standards established.

Goals for an Imaging Service

The considerations above provide support for our claim that object imaging is a problem that needs to be investigated in its own right, rather than being seen as a simple application of existing or proposed mechanisms in the realm of distributed objects. Among other things, the imaging process needs an open evolving knowledge-base that registers convertibility relationships between atomic and parameterized data and object types and the corresponding conversions. In fact, one may need multiple knowledge-bases of this kind since imaging occurs at many layers in a distributed object system, and each layer potentially has different requirements. For instance, at the networking level, imaging processes are statically determined, and compiled into RPC stubs, whereas at the user-interface level, imaging tends to be triggered dynamically by spontaneous user actions such as following connections in a hypertext web document or drag-and-drop in a compound document based on OpenDoc or OLE. The knowledge-base for RPC level imaging would therefore be used primarily by a compile-time tool such as RPCGEN, and since performance requirements at this level are often stringent, the use of declarative specifications in conjunction with techniques such as deforestation [27] to optimize the conversions to and from wire-formats is important. The knowledge-base for document-level imaging, in contrast, would most likely be a part of an *imaging service* similar to naming, security, and other run-time services.

In this paper we focus on knowledge-representation issues that are independent of the specific requirements of any particular layer. For generality, the knowledge-base needs to incorporate the following principles:

- Knowledge representation based on relationships between atomic and parameterized types.
- Seamless integration of primitive and user-defined types[4].
- Composability of imaging knowledge along two dimensions:
  - Part/whole composition based on the use of parameterized types in the construction of type expressions.
  - Sequential composition based on transitivity, *i.e.*, multi-step imaging.
- Complete automation of the reasoning processes involved in imaging.

Leaving aside network transport, the fundamental process in object imaging is type transformation. Both externalization and internalization can be represented as type transformations. External representation transformations such as GIF-to-JPEG can also be seen as type transformations. Moreover, the notion of type covers both primitive data values and abstract objects. A type-centric knowledge-base therefore facilitates the ability to freely combine imaging knowledge along all of the dimensions mentioned above. Such a knowledge-base will in practice consist of a conversion registry for object types, and will have to deal with many systems issues such as distributed reasoning using knowledge from multiple registries, uniform scripting models for conversion scripts, activation protocols for stand-alone converters, and so forth. These issues are not discussed in this paper. which confines itself to *symbolic* knowledge-representation and reasoning.

Motivation for Conformance Considerations

We propose an approach to knowledge representation based on two main elements: an order-sorted conversion logic and a logic of sort conformance, linked by the sorts and signatures of type constants and constructors. The need for a conversion logic is obvious given that the main computational process to be automated in object imaging is the inference and application of conversions between object types. For instance, the isomorphism (symmetric convertibility relation)

---

[4] Apart from its intuitive appeal, erasing the distinction between primitive and user-defined types is important in practice because user-defined types are often transformed to standard data structures during multistep imaging.

```
class Printable {
  public:
    virtual void print(ostream&) = 0;
};

template<class Key, class Value> class Table
                                   : public Printable {
  public:
    void update(Key,Value);
    Value lookup(Key);
    Table merge(Table&);
    void print(ostream& o=cout) { rep.print(o); }
  private:
   struct Pair : public Printable {
     Key index; Value val;
     void print(ostream& o)
               { o << index; o << val; }
     int operator==(Pair& p) { index == p.index; }
   };
   List<Pair> rep;
};
```

Figure 1: A Template Class: `Table`

$$\texttt{polar(r)} \quad \underset{\texttt{internalize}}{\overset{\texttt{externalize}}{\rightleftarrows}} \quad \texttt{key} \times \texttt{r} \times \texttt{r}$$

might express the externalization process for a general notion of polar complex numbers. The product constructor × is used here to represent `structs`. The type parameter `r` is the real number type (such as `vax_float` or `powerpc_double`) used for representing the real and imaginary parts, and the `key` type is meant to identify the appropriate "object factory" for internalizing the representation. It is best thought of as a type tag. Conversions are essentially rewrite rules. Rewriting logics satisfy the composability requirements mentioned above and are also amenable to automated reasoning. We have used a similar conversion logic in [24] to express type conversions in polymorphic functional languages.

The role and form of the conformance logic are perhaps less obvious. Unlike the primitive universal type constructors such as products and arrays, user-defined parameterized types typically make *assumptions* about the functionality supported by the type parameters they are prepared to accept. The knowledge base for imaging needs to formalize and use these constraints to check that types and conversions are well-formed, and to limit the application of conversions to ensure that functionality constraints on the parameters of type constructors are not violated.

A simple RPC-level example will suffice to illustrate these points. Consider the C++ container class template `Table` given in Figure 1. The type parameters `Key` and `Value` of `Table` are not free. The way they are used in the implementation structure `Pair` implies that the operation `<<` is defined on all objects of types `Key` and `Value`, and `==` is defined on all objects of type `Key`. No mention is made of any inheritance relationship between any specific classes and the type parameters—the constraints require only available functionality.

Now suppose we have a type constructor `list`. We might wish to use the conversion from a list of pairs to a pair of lists by declaring the rule

```
list(a × b)  ⟶  list(a) × list(b)
```

where, unlike C++, we use ordinary parantheses to construct type expressions. The symbol ⟶ denotes one-step convertibility. The actual conversion function can be used as a tag when it is of interest, as in the isomorphism for complex number types above. Assuming that `int` supports both `==` and `<<`, and instances of `list` support `<<`, the type `Table(int,list(int × bool))` is well-formed. Now by the usual laws of rewriting, we should be able to claim

```
Table(int,list(int × bool))  ⟶  Table(int, list(int)×list(bool))
```

However, the C++ `iostream` library does not define `<<` as an operation for arbitrary `structs`, and so, starting with a well-formed type we are in danger of creating an ill-formed type by the application of a perfectly reasonable looking conversion. The point to note is that type conversion does not in general preserve interfaces. Maintaining the integrity of compound types in the conversion process therefore requires consideration of interface types as distinct from object types and specification of conformance relationships between the two.

Designing an Abstract Conformance Framework

One of the difficulties in choosing a symbolic representation for interface types is the variety of specific notions of interface and conformance that must be covered if the choice is to claim generality. For instance, conformance constraints for type parameters in programming languages are based either on subtyping or on functionality. Eiffel [14] uses an object type as an upper bound for each type parameter of a generic type and checks the integrity of compound types at compile-time using (inheritance-based) subtyping. Conformance for the type parameters of templates in C++ [8] is based on available functionality, and is enforced by the linker. In theoretical terms, parametric polymorphism in Eiffel is bounded [6] while in C++ it is F-bounded [5].

Component oriented systems such as OpenDoc [3] and OLE [4] tend to require their components to support *multiple* interfaces. However, as a result of differences in the underlying object models (CORBA and COM respectively), they use radically different notions of conformance. OpenDoc uses objects with single principal interfaces which constitute object types, and a notion of conformance based on interface inheritance, similar to most statically typed languages. Multiple interfaces are merged using multiple inheritance. OLE expects objects to offer multiple independent interfaces. Moreover, COM strongly discourages the use of inheritance in *defining* interfaces (as opposed to implementing them). Conformance of interface types in OLE therefore reduces to identity, except for the root `IUnknown` interface. On the other hand, object type and interface type are potentially distinct concepts in OLE/COM, since access to one interface can be used to gain access to other interfaces on the same object using the `QueryInterface` operation. Both the actual and the expected type of a COM *object* therefore represents multiple interface types.

The use of `QueryInterface` in COM also implies the existence of *conditional* interfaces, since a container might decide at run-time whether or not to offer an interface based on the availability of certain interfaces in its components. Conditional interfaces are also possible in languages like C++ where "functionality marshalling" for type parameters occurs at link-time based on need. The available interface(s) corresponding to a compound object type therefore need not be fixed. Functionality marshalling also brings up the issue of wrapper generation. When a COM object needs to masquerade as a CORBA object, or vice versa, one could wrap the object with an appropriate veneer to make this possible. In general, an object type is capable of supporting many interfaces not intrinsic to it with some adaptation. Such adaptability relations can be thought of as coercions realized by wrappers. In determining conformance of object types when used as parameters, it is important to take coercibility into account, and the conformance logic should be able to invoke wrapper generation automatically as needed.

It is desirable to use a uniform symbolic framework for all these diverse contexts because conversions often cross conformance-domains. For instance, an RPC call from a C++ client may send object parameters to an Eiffel-based server, or a content object may be dragged from an OpenDoc compound document and dropped into an OLE container. We therefore need an interface formalism that is abstract enough to admit a variety of interpretations, and has enough structure to represent the relation of conformance between object and interface types, provide for inheritance of interfaces and adaptability via wrapper generation, and represent the necessary interaction between the conformance logic and the reasoning algorithms for conversion. We believe that the notion of sorts from order-sorted equational logic can be adapted to fit the bill, if we extend the sort structure with appropriate intersection sorts.

In the rest of this paper, we illustrate the range of imaging problems with examples in Section 2, and present a (preliminary) formal approach to a general solution in Section 3. Related work is reviewed briefly in Section 4.

2 Symbolic Knowledge Representation

The examples used in this section to illustrate knowledge representation issues use two kinds of conversion rules. The standard rule is of the form $t \longrightarrow u$, where t and u are type expressions, possibly containing formal parameters in the form of variables. This defines a one-way or irreversible conversion. A good example of such a conversion would be `document` $\longrightarrow$ `postscript` which represents a rendering of a document for printing on a PostScript printer. Reasoning with such rules permits inference of multistep relations of the form $t \overset{*}{\longrightarrow} u$. However, very often conversion relations are reversible. We occasionally refer to such relations as isomorphisms although that is not strictly correct since there is no guarantee that, for instance, converting a Word document to WordPerfect form and then back to Word form will reproduce the original. Such reversible relations are common enough to merit the notation $t \longleftrightarrow u$ for a reversible rule, and $t \overset{*}{\longleftrightarrow} u$ for a multistep reversible conversion. Practically all the examples in this section use reversible conversions.

Primitive Types

We start with simple examples involving primitive types, an extension of the problem tackled by systems such as XDR. For clarity, we leave out the conversion functions in convertibility relations. Inference of conversions is not difficult given that we can find a proof for the simpler convertibility relationship between types.

Suppose we are concerned about interoperation of components that may reside on computers based on either the Vax or the PowerPC architecture. We start by expressing the convertibility of arrays between the two environments. However, instead of using a direct equation, we choose to reflect actual practice by equating each array type to a common data format used in the distributed object infrastructure.

$$\texttt{vax\_array(a)} \longleftrightarrow \texttt{xdr\_array(a)} \qquad \texttt{ppc\_array(a)} \longleftrightarrow \texttt{xdr\_array(a)}$$

This allows easy extension of the equivalence to other architectures. We use the convention that wire format type names are prefixed with `xdr_`. Now given additional isomorphisms for atomic types

$$\begin{array}{ll} \texttt{vax\_float} \longleftrightarrow \texttt{xdr\_float} & \texttt{vax\_int} \longleftrightarrow \texttt{xdr\_int} \\ \texttt{ppc\_float} \longleftrightarrow \texttt{xdr\_float} & \texttt{ppc\_int} \longleftrightarrow \texttt{xdr\_int} \end{array}$$

we can obviously prove equational theorems such as

$$\texttt{vax\_array(vax\_float)} \overset{*}{\longleftrightarrow} \texttt{ppc\_array(ppc\_float)}$$

representing marshalling/unmarshalling processes currently used in RPC systems.

The treatment of record types needs more care. Records can often be conveniently represented using cross products, since field labels are not important for portability when it is appropriate to treat records as multisets (or bags). On the other hand, records sometimes need to be treated more like abstract types as in the XDR system (illustrated in the complex number marshalling example below). In the former case, the type

```
struct { int x;  float y;  int z[10]; }
```

can be represented as $\texttt{int} \times \texttt{float} \times \texttt{<int>}$. The product constructor in this context is naturally associative and commutative—the same symbolic representation can be used for

```
struct { float y; struct c { int x; int z[10]; } w; }
```

Associativity and commutativity are represented by the conversions

$$\texttt{a} \times (\texttt{b} \times \texttt{c}) \longleftrightarrow (\texttt{a} \times \texttt{b}) \times \texttt{c} \qquad \texttt{a} \times \texttt{b} \longleftrightarrow \texttt{b} \times \texttt{a}$$

and the corresponding pairs of maps can be used to adjust address alignment and similar details if necessary.

As an example of an equivalence that is *not* supported by typical RPC-oriented marshalling mechanisms, tables (finite maps from keys to values) can be represented as a pair of sequences or as a sequence of pairs (among other possibilities). The equivalence of the two representations can be expressed as:

$$\texttt{T\_array(a} \times \texttt{b)} \longleftrightarrow \texttt{T\_array(a)} \times \texttt{T\_array(b)}$$

where `T_array` is treated as a template for array types. We can now prove that the representation of a table mapping strings to floats on a Vax can be transformed to the slightly different representation of a similar table on a PowerPC:

$$\begin{aligned} &\texttt{vax\_array(vax\_string)} \times \texttt{vax\_array(vax\_float)} \\ \overset{*}{\longleftrightarrow}\ &\texttt{ppc\_array(ppc\_string} \times \texttt{ppc\_float)} \end{aligned}$$

In fact, since the *order* of fields in a record is unimportant

$$\begin{aligned} &\texttt{vax\_array(vax\_string)} \times \texttt{vax\_array(vax\_float)} \\ \overset{*}{\longleftrightarrow}\ &\texttt{ppc\_array(ppc\_float} \times \texttt{ppc\_string)} \end{aligned}$$

By a simple process of accumulation of obvious knowledge about isomorphism relations, we have reached the point where the equivalence of relatively complex representation types can be inferred, reaching considerably beyond what is possible with traditional marshalling techniques.

Atomic Object Types

Now consider the problem of expressing the standard equivalence between the cartesian and polar representations of complex numbers as part of a framework for interoperation of numerical simulation components. Specifically, we would like to be able to marshall a polar complex number as a parameter in the client and unmarshall it as a cartesian complex number in the server. The two atomic object types are `ppc_polar` and `cray_cartesian`. Given the likely absence of a wire-format standard for complex numbers, the marshalling cannot be done directly unless we tag the data and expect the server to "make it right". We would ideally like to simply express the necessary knowledge symbolically and let a system like RPCGEN use it to insert the appropriate conversions. One approach to this is to expose the representation of each object type in the form of a structure, except in this case the identity of the structure is important in distinguishing between the polar and cartesian forms.

`ppc_polar` $\longleftrightarrow$ `ppc_polar_struct`
`cray_cartesian` $\longleftrightarrow$ `cray_cart_struct`

We follow the convention of using names appended with `_struct` for structure types with significant identities. The computational cost of such exposure can be made negligible, using private inheritance in C++ for instance. The correspondance between the exposed representations represents local conversions:

`ppc_cart_struct` $\longleftrightarrow$ `ppc_polar_struct`
`cray_cart_struct` $\longleftrightarrow$ `cray_polar_struct`

Finally, the marshalling and unmarshalling of the exposed cartesian representations is symbolized by:

`ppc_cart_struct` $\longleftrightarrow$ `xdr_cart_struct`
`cray_cart_struct` $\longleftrightarrow$ `xdr_cart_struct`

which allows us to prove `ppc_polar` $\overset{*}{\longleftrightarrow}$ `cray_cartesian` and automatically generate the corresponding conversions for marshalling and unmarshalling. This example is meant to illustrate an approach to transport of abstract atomic objects. In the case of complex numbers, given the restriction to two representations, a more direct approach may be viable and attractive.

Compound Object Types

We now consider an entirely different kind of example to demostrate the range of applicability of the symbolic notation. The approach used above is clearly applicable to conversion knowledge regarding atomic document types such as `word_win` (Word for Windows) and `wp_mac` (WordPerfect on a Macintosh). With the advent of object linking and embedding technologies such as OpenDoc and OLE, a document can be seen as a container with many different kinds of content elements, such as text, spreadsheets, drawings, pictures, and even sound and video. A traditional application such as Word plays two conceptually separate roles as both a container widget and a text widget. If we separate these roles and use types to represent pure roles, we would have atomic types for content widgets like `word_mac` and `quattro_win` and type constructors for container widgets like `c_wp_mac` (WordPerfect in its container role on a Macintosh). An actual compound document might be of the compound type `c_wp_mac(wp_mac,excel_mac)`, *i.e.*, a WordPerfect container with WordPerfect text and Excel spreadsheet content elements. Traditional custom conversion utilities (usually bundled with applications) could be represented by relations of the form

`wp_mac` $\longleftrightarrow$ `wp_win`   `excel_win` $\longleftrightarrow$ `quattro_win` representing cross-platform and cross-widget conversions, respectively[5]. Similarly, container conversions would yield non-atomic relations such as[6]

```
c_wp_mac(a,b)  ⟷  c_word_mac(a,b)
c_wp_mac(a,b)  ⟷  c_wp_win(a,b)
```

which represents a WordPerfect to Word container conversion on the Macintosh platform, and WordPerfect container conversion from a Macintosh to a Windows format, assuming two distinct kinds of content elements. Now if a user drags a document of type `c_wp_mac(wp_mac,excel_mac)` to the Word icon on a Windows machine where Quattro is the only spreadsheet installed, the drag-and-drop manager can derive and use the isomorphism

```
c_wp_mac(wp_mac,excel_mac)  ⟷  c_word_win(word_win,quattro_win)
```

to infer the necessary (multistep) conversions and apply them transparently without user intervention. Actually, this example cheats a little by ignoring the dependence of compound document containers on standard interfaces they expect content objects to support. The symbolic representation of this dependence is an important topic to which we now turn.

Sorts and Signatures

A full-fledged formalism for interface types is not desirable as part of a reasoning system based on rewriting. As we noted in the introduction, it is sufficient to introduce a notion of *sorts* in the conversion logic. In practical terms, a sort represents an interface type as distinct from an object type—we use the word *type* to refer to an *object* type throughout this section. Formally, a sort has two natural interpretations: an intensional one and an extensional one. The intension of a sort is the set of features supported by any type that possesses the sort. The extension is the set of ground types that possess the sort. Constraining a type *variable* with a sort simply constrains the variable to range over the extension of that sort. Intuitively, a ground type has a sort exactly when it conforms to the interface functionality required by the sort. Each type has at least one sort, and may have more. Multiple interfaces can be directly represented by intersection sorts as we see below. For a CORBA object type τ, the statement that τ possesses a sort s means that the principal interface represented by τ inherits from the interface(s) represented by s. For a COM object type τ, the same statement means that objects of type τ expose the interface(s) corresponding to s.

The conversion logic obviously needs the extensional interpretation of sorts. Introducing sorts there requires adding simple annotations to each variable in a conversion rule. An annotation `a`:$\mathcal{X}$ constrains the type variable `a` to sort $\mathcal{X}$. For instance, suppose we want to represent a direct isomorphism

[5] Of course, the availability of these conversions is often restricted to one-way conversions.
[6] There is a technical problem with the number of parameters for container types. The number obviously varies, but this could be handled, by using schemas of relations.

$$\texttt{polar(r)} \underset{\texttt{polarize}}{\overset{\texttt{cartify}}{\rightleftarrows}} \texttt{cartesian(r)}$$

between complex number types on a given platform, using a type parameter to represent the real and imaginary parts, instead of treating each possible combination of architecture, precision, and complex number form as a distinct type. The type parameter cannot meaningfully range over all types, since a type such as, say, `string`, cannot be used to represent the parts of a complex number—it does not support the operations required of such a part. This constraint can be expressed by restricting the range of the type variable. Suppose we let sort $\mathcal{R}$ represent the functionality of real number operations (or the set of real number types such as `vax_float` and `ppc_double`). We could then have:

$$\texttt{polar(r:}\mathcal{R}\texttt{)} \longleftrightarrow \texttt{cartesian(r:}\mathcal{R}\texttt{)}$$

If we let $\mathcal{T}$ represent the sort with no functionality, *i.e.*, the set of all ground types, then $\mathcal{R}$ is a subsort of $\mathcal{T}$ (denoted by $\mathcal{R} \leq \mathcal{T}$) if we use the natural order based on the subset relationship between sort extensions. The conversion theory we are constructing is therefore not only many-sorted, it is naturally *order sorted*: we have a quasi-ordered set of sorts such as $\mathcal{T}$ and $\mathcal{R}$, (type) variables have sorts representing their range, and (type) constants and constructors have signatures representing their relationships to sorts. For instance, suppose we have a sort of "number-like" types (those which support the four basic arithmetic operators) called $\mathcal{N}$. Any type constructed by the type constructor `polar` clearly belongs to $\mathcal{N}$. The signatures of the constructors $\times$ and `polar` therefore could be given as

$$\texttt{polar} : \mathcal{R} \rightarrow \mathcal{N} \qquad\qquad \times : (\mathcal{T}, \mathcal{T}) \rightarrow \mathcal{T}$$

and we have the sort structure $\mathcal{R} \leq \mathcal{N} \leq \mathcal{T}$. In general, a type constructor has a signature that shows the relationship between the functionality it expects its parameters to support and the functionality supported by the types it constructs. Note that a type constructor need not have a unique signature. For instance, suppose we use $\mathcal{E}$ to represent the sort of types which support an equality operation. It is not hard to see that $\times$ *could also* have the signature $\times : (\mathcal{E}, \mathcal{E}) \rightarrow \mathcal{E}$ since equality on products can be defined pointwise given that it is defined on the two parts in the product. Moreover, if we assume that the functionality associated with $\mathcal{R}$ and $\mathcal{N}$ does not include equality, then we have $\mathcal{E} \leq \mathcal{T}$ but neither $\mathcal{N} \leq \mathcal{E}$, nor $\mathcal{E} \leq \mathcal{N}$, and hence our sort structure is no longer linearly ordered.

In the terminology used in the literature on order-sorted algebra, operators such as $\times$, which possess multiple signatures, are called *polymorphic* operators. Polymorphic type constructors offer flexible *conditional* functionality.

Signatures influence type composition in two ways. They decide if a type expression is well formed, and if it is, which sort(s) the expression may claim. For instance, suppose `float:`$\mathcal{R}$, `float:`$\mathcal{E}$, but `string` does not possess sort $\mathcal{R}$. Then `polar(string)` is ill-formed, but `polar(float)` is well-formed and possesses *two unrelated* sorts: $\mathcal{N}$ and $\mathcal{E}$ (the latter using the additional signature for `polar` given below).

The functionality associated with sorts is naturally additive, in particular because an object may support multiple interfaces. Combining two sorts results in an *intersection* of the sorts (seen as sets of types). We use $\sqcap$ to represent the intersection operator for sorts, in keeping with the lattice-like structure being constructed. If $s = s_1 \sqcap \cdots \sqcap s_k$ is an intersection sort, then τ is an instance of s iff it is an instance of each s_i. Of course, $\sqcap$ is an associative and commutative operation, and $s_1 \sqcap \cdots \sqcap s_k \;\leq\; s_i$ for $1 \leq i \leq k$. This is an intrinsic subsort relation—no wrapper generation is involved.

Intersection means merger through multiple inheritance for CORBA interfaces, which means that the sort hierarchy parallels the interface hierarchy and subsorts are essentially subtypes. In COM, an object type τ conforms to a sort $s = s_1 \sqcap \cdots \sqcap s_k$ only if it exposes interfaces corresponding to each atomic sort s_i. Note that τ may also expose additional interfaces, in which case its *principal* sort would be a subsort of s. Thus, the sort structure constructs a conformance hierarchy for COM where none existed before—*conformance in COM is based on subsort rather than subtype relations*, specifically on subsorts constructed as intersection sorts.

Even in the absence of multiple interfaces, as in the context of functionality requirements for template type parameters in C++, elevating intersection sorts to the status of first-class sorts helps to avoid a confusing proliferation of overlapping sorts. For instance, if we use $\mathcal{P}$ to represent the sort of printable types, then the signature of the `Table` template of Figure 1 can be given as

$$\texttt{Table} : (\mathcal{E} \sqcap \mathcal{P},\ \mathcal{P}) \rightarrow \mathcal{P}$$

instead of having to declare a new sort that combines the functionality of $\mathcal{E}$ and $\mathcal{P}$. Similarly, `polar` may also claim

$$\texttt{polar} : \mathcal{R} \sqcap \mathcal{E} \rightarrow \mathcal{E}$$

Finally, continuing the hypothetical compound documents example from previous sections, suppose the interfaces `Text`, `SpreadSheet` and `Document` define text, spreadsheet and document objects, respectively, and `RenderMac` represents objects that can be rendered and interactively modified on a Macintosh screen. In this case `c_word_mac` might have the signature

$$(\texttt{Text} \sqcap \texttt{RenderMac},\ \texttt{SpreadSheet} \sqcap \texttt{RenderMac}) \rightarrow \texttt{Document}$$

and perhaps a second signature based on the COM persistence framework

$$(\texttt{IPersistFile},\ \texttt{IPersistFile}) \rightarrow \texttt{IPersistFile}$$

meaning that if the text and spreadsheet types given to `c_word_mac` are capable of persistence, so is the resulting document type, otherwise not. In this way the dependencies of available interfaces for a `c_word_mac` object can be specified precisely and independently.

Conformance Checking and Wrapper Generation

Simple conformance checking, where the interface/functionality is intrinsic to the object type, is routine and well understood. More sophisticated structural conformance and interface adaptability relations based on subtyping for recursive types have been considered in the literature [2, 26], but we will not be concerned with them here. Our main concern is with conformance based on user-specified methods for generating auxiliary interfaces on demand. The details of how auxiliary interfaces are realized are highly platform-dependent. For instance, a CORBA object could support a new interface by interposition of an auxiliary object that delegates actual execution to the underlying intrinsic interface. This does not affect the identity of the object since CORBA specifically excludes identity checking on references precisely to support such interposition [9][7]. A COM object can achieve the same effect more directly through aggregation, since the problem of interface conflicts does not arise.

The initial examples in the following illustrate sort and signature declarations using a simple applicative notation for the intensional aspects of sorts, *i.e.*, sort definitions. We choose to make the type of `self` explicit in the signatures of operations. In standard object-oriented typing notations, including CORBA IDL, the signatures of intrinsic operations leave out the type of the recipient object. Technically, this is important in establishing subtype relationships corresponding to inheritance—due to the contravariant subtyping for intrinsic operations, making the type of the recipient explicit as an argument type would invalidate structural subtyping and substitutability, and fail to account for the polymorphic nature of such operations. However, the functionality represented by sorts may, in general, be a mixture of intrinsic and extrinsic operations, *e.g.*, in a system like C++-templates, where expected functionality for type parameters is not tightly organized into named interfaces, but is implied by usage. For instance, the printability constraint on the parameters of class `Table` in the introduction refers to an extrinsic (and overloaded) operation `<<` since the object used to select the appropriate implementation is the *second* parameter. We would also like to leave open the possibility of accounting for constructs that do not follow "standard" object-oriented practice, *e.g.*, multimethods in CLOS. Such explicit "self" parameters are also used in CORBA and COM language bindings.

The following sort declaration defines the functionality of number-like types:

sort $\mathcal{N}$ **contains** T **given**
$\{\ + : T \times T \to T,\ - : T \times T \to T,\ * : T \times T \to T,\ / : T \times T \to T\ \}$

where T plays the role of a prototypical instance of $\mathcal{N}$. The operator signatures in a sort declaration use only the prototypical instance and ground types. Every type constant and constructor has one or more signatures which must be declared and validated. For instance, we can establish the signature `int:`$\mathcal{N}$ using a **signature** declaration:

[7] Of course, the support for CORBA's agnostic approach to object identity is by no means universal in the CORBA community [21].

```
signature int : 𝒩 with
    { + = intAdd, - = intSub, * = intMul, / = intDiv }
```

where we assume for the sake of example that `intAdd`, *etc.*, are the integer arithmetic operations, each of which has the type `int×int→int`. Note that the declaration of the signature is accompanied by actual implementations of the required operations which can be (automatically) checked to ensure the validity of the signature. This can be thought of as instructions for the construction of a function table similar to the standard implementation of an interface in COM[8]. The declarations of equality and printable sorts can be given as:

```
sort ℰ contains T given { == : T × T → bool }
sort 𝒫 contains T given { << : ostream × T  → void }
```

where the operation `<<` exhibits multimethod-like flexibility by using the *second* parameter to select its implementation in order to accommodate standard C++ output syntax. As an example of a nonatomic signature, the signature of the type constructor `Table` from Figure 1 might then be declared as

```
signature Table : (ℰ⊓𝒫, 𝒫) → 𝒫 with
    { str << tab = tab.print(str) }
```

If we want to use the expression `Table(int,string)` as an instance of sort $\mathcal{P}$, we must use `signature` declarations to show that `int` is an instance of both $\mathcal{E}$ and $\mathcal{P}$ (and therefore of sort $\mathcal{E} \sqcap \mathcal{P}$) and `string` is an instance of $\mathcal{P}$ as well. The fact that `<<` for `int` may be defined in the iostream library as intrinsic to class `ostream` while `<<` for `string` may be user-defined and extrinsic to both `ostream` and `string` is not a problem since we make no distinction between the two situations.

The rest of the examples are based on compound document types and are meant to illustrate some situations that would trigger wrapper generation and some of the ways signatures and wrapper generation procedures might be specified in an environment based on well-defined named interfaces. Suppose we use `PO` to represent the basic interface for persistence in CORBA, and `P` to represent a similar interface in COM. We may have the following signatures for two containers:

```
wp_win   : (PO, PO) → PO                word_win  : (P, P) → P
```

We may also have the container conversion rule

```
wp_win(x : PO, y : PO) ⟶ word_win(x : P, y : P)
```

where the notation `x : PO` is used to declare that variable `x` can only be instantiated with type that are instances of sort `PO`. Note that the use of identical variable names on the two sides reflects the correspondence between the parts, even though their expected sorts differ. We may then need to infer

[8] CORBA does not define an implementation standard.

$$\texttt{wp\_win(pict\_win, chart\_win)} \longrightarrow \texttt{word\_win(pict\_win, chart\_win)}$$

if we cause a document of type `wp_win(pict_win, chart_win)` to be opened by a `word_win` server. The right-hand side is well-formed only if wrappers can be applied to the type parameters to change their sort. There are two ways such wrapper generation capabilities can be specified. One is to provide declarations analogous to `signature chart_win : P with ..` which directly specifies how to synthesize the required interface based on the underlying object type. This is possible with CORBA but may be inconvenient with COM because COM objects do not have principal interfaces. For COM, a subsort declaration $\texttt{PO} \leq \texttt{P}$ would be more appropriate. In general, a subsort declaration may assume multiple interfaces. For example, if an interface `EQ` is assumed besides `PO` to construct `P` then the declaration would be $\texttt{PO} \sqcap \texttt{EQ} \leq \texttt{P}$. Of course, such an explicit subsort declaration (as opposed to the implicit subsort relations established by intersection) must be accompanied by code that synthesizes the supersort interface given the subsort interface(s).

We conclude this section with an example where the imaging system is used more like a trading system. Suppose we have a different drag-and-drop gesture that causes a dropping of a document of type `wp_win(pict_win,chart_win)` on a `word_win` server icon to be interpreted as the attempted conversion

$$\texttt{wp\_win(pict\_win, chart\_win)} \overset{*}{\longrightarrow} \texttt{word\_win(x : P, y : P)}$$

where the target type is incompletely specified. The imaging system must then find target object types with the specified sorts (in this case `P`) for the types being "traded in": `pict_win` and `chart_win`. This may involve wrapper generation, actual conversion, or both.

3 Reasoning Algorithms for Imaging

In this section we describe a formal approach to reasoning about imaging. The idea is to formalize the problem space illustrated by the examples of the last section. The ideas presented here should not be viewed as finished theoretical results—they are more properly seen as a first attempt at formalizing the problem and an approach to a solution. Among the shortcomings of the present solution is the fact that we pay no attention to heuristics for optimizing either the efficiency of the algorithm or the efficiency of the derived conversions. A naive reasoning algorithm will in general yield unnecessarily long proofs leading to inefficient conversions that proceed through too many intermediate stages. It would be nice if the reasoning algorithm guaranteed a most efficient proof. This is a difficult problem for which theoretically complete solutions are unlikely in the case of unrestricted conversion theories [7]. However, there may be heuristic approaches that yield good results.

We assume a basic familiarity with the ideas and terminology of term rewriting (see [10] for a survey of rewriting concepts and results). Although the discussion in this section is entirely in terms of order-sorted term algebras and rewriting systems, it is important to keep in mind that terms are object type expressions, and term rewriting corresponds to object conversions.

Delineating the Problem

Conversion rules are rewrite rules and the basic reasoning problem in imaging is a version of the classical word problem in algebra: determining whether two ground terms (in this case type expressions) are equivalent in the conversion theory. Since we allow asymmetrical conversion rules, equivalence must be replaced by reducibility in the corresponding rewriting theory. There are three additional aspects we need to consider:

1. Convertibility proofs must be accompanied by conversion functions/scripts.
2. The algebraic signature being order-sorted, sort checking is necessary and wrapper generation may be needed during rewriting.
3. The conversion target may be incompletely specified, *i.e.*, it may be a term containing variables, as in the "trading service" example above.

As we have noted before, the details of conversion functions and scripts are highly platform and context dependent and the technical problems that will be encountered in synthesizing and using them are likely to be "systems" oriented and cannot be addressed in a general reasoning framework. The mere identification of required conversions given a convertibility proof is a trivial problem rather similar to the problem of constructing a parse tree given a parsing proof. The same comments apply to wrapper generation relative to sort checking. In the formal notation and algorithms developed here, we therefore focus on convertibility proofs and sort checking, and ignore code synthesis. The problem of incompletely specified targets in rewriting, on the other hand, is both very important and amenable to a general solution. It forces us to generalize the problem under consideration to one of *order-sorted matching under reduction.* This specific problem has not been considered in the literature on order-sorted reasoning since it does not occur in the context of standard theorem-proving applications, but the ideas needed to solve it are substantially the same as in the well-understood problem of order-sorted equational unification and matching.

Finally, there is one aspect of practical object systems that is difficult to model formally, though not difficult to deal with in practical reasoning algorithms. Containers in compound document systems are equipped to hold an arbitrary number of parts with possibly different degrees of functionality. The symbol for a container thus has an infinite number of signatures. An infinite algebraic signature is not a problem in itself, but since containers are often involved in transformations, the rule-base also becomes theoretically infinite. In practice this is easy to deal with using rule and signature schemata but such schemata would unnecessarily complicate the formal system so we leave them out and assume that each symbol has a finite number of signatures.

The impact of sorts on the reasoning algorithms goes beyond preserving the well-formedness of type expressions. The fundamental processes in reasoning about imaging is term rewriting, which in turn is based on *matching* of rule-templates with actual expressions. Matching is a special case of unification, and unfortunately, unification in the presence of order-sorted signatures is considerably more problematic than in the unsorted case. To avoid excessive nondeterminism, it would help to ensure that free unification in the algebra of types is *unitary*, *i.e.*, for any set of equations there is a complete set of unifiers with at most one element. Smolka, *et al* [22] show that a finite algebraic signature is unitary if it is regular, coregular and downward complete. Moreover, for unitary algebraic signatures, unification and matching can be implemented in quasi-linear time in a straightforward way [13]. Regularity is simply the property that every expression has a principal (least) sort. This is not a problem since, as we see below, we can transform the signature to ensure a unique signature for each symbol, and therefore a unique sort for each term, at the cost of giving up something we don't have anyhow: sort preservation during conversion. Coregularity is also trivial given this, since it merely requires that there is a least restrictive way to construct a sort using a given function symbol. Downward completeness—the existence of infimums for finite sets of sorts—is more problematic since it requires us to support *arbitrary* sort intersections. In a heterogeneous environment, this might mean, for instance, that objects must be able to support both CORBA and COM interfaces simultaneously, which might not be possible. On the other hand, many practical systems may be homogeneous enough to guarantee downward completeness of the sort structure, allowing for an efficient rewriting procedure.

Notation and Definitions

We work with a finite set of ordered sorts and a finite signature consisting of function symbols with *unique* signatures. There is a denumerable set of variables for use in conversion rules and in the reasoning process. Each variable may possess several sorts, but its sort in each occurrence must be specified. These restrictions are the reverse of the usual ones where function symbols are permitted multiple signatures but variables are restricted to single sorts. In our case, change of signatures for a function symbol (type constant or constructor) must in general trigger wrapper generation to assemble the corresponding functionality, so it is convenient to treat it as a transformation. This amounts to an implicit transformation of the actual algebraic signature. On the other hand, since conversions do not in general preserve interfaces, variables may change sorts as part of a conversion rule. To help keep track of which part in an original compound type corresponds to which part in a transformed one, the identity of the variables must be maintained.

Let $(S, \leq)$ denote a quasi-ordered set of sorts and Σ an algebraic signature of function symbols. Σ consists of a family of subsignatures $\Sigma_{w,s}$. Each $f \in \Sigma_{w,s}$ has the signature $w \rightarrow s$, where w is a possibly empty sequence $s_1 s_2 \cdots s_k$ of sorts. For instance, the signature for `Table` may be $s_1 s_2 \rightarrow s$ where $s_1 = \mathcal{E} \sqcap \mathcal{P}$,

$s_2 = \mathcal{P}$ and $s = \mathcal{P}$. The signature for **int** might be $\Lambda \rightarrow \mathcal{N}$, where Λ is the empty sequence. We also have a denumerable set $\mathcal{V}$ of variables. Each occurrence of a variable must be tagged with a sort $s \in S$, but different occurrences of the same variable may be tagged with different sorts. The set of well-sorted terms over Σ and $\mathcal{V}$ is denoted by $\mathcal{T}_\Sigma(\mathcal{V})$, or just $\mathcal{T}$ when Σ and $\mathcal{V}$ are known from the context. $\mathcal{T}_\Sigma$ denotes the set of ground terms, *i.e.*, terms without variables. Every well-formed term has at least one sort. A term t can be an instance of a sort s in one of four ways:

1. $t \in \Sigma_{\Lambda,s}$, *i.e.*, t is a constant of sort s.
2. $t = x^s$, *i.e.*, t is a variable of sort s.
3. $t = f(t_1, \ldots, t_k)$, $f \in \Sigma_{s_1 \cdots s_k, s}$, and each t_i is an instance of sort s_i.
4. t is an instance of a sort s' and $s' \leq s$.

Substitutions are maps from $\mathcal{V}$ to $\mathcal{T}$ which map a *finite* number of variables (the *domain* of the substitution) to terms other than themselves (the *range* of the substitution). Substitutions are extended to apply to terms in the usual way. The application of a substitution ξ to a term t is denoted by ξt. The composition of two substitutions ξ and ζ is denoted by $\xi\zeta$—$(\xi\zeta)\, t{=}\xi(\zeta t)$. We shall assume that all substitutions are idempotent—a substitution σ is idempotent if and only if $\sigma\sigma = \sigma$. Substitutions must respect sorts, *i.e.*, if $\sigma x^s = t$ for a substitution σ, then t must be an instance of the sort s. A substitution ξ may be restricted to a subset of its domain. We write $\xi|_V$ to denote ξ restricted to V. By definition, $\xi|_V\, x = \xi x$ if $x \in V$, and $\xi|_V\, x = x$ otherwise. A *ground* substitution ξ is said to be *more general* than ξ' modulo R for a set V of variables (written $\xi \leq_R^V \xi'$) if and only if $\forall x \in V.\ \xi x \xrightarrow{*} \xi' x$. The relation $\leq_R^V$ is reflexive and transitive but not necessarily antisymmetric.

The knowledge base, for the purposes of this section, consists of a set R of conversion rules of the form $t \longrightarrow u$, where $t, u \in \mathcal{T}_\Sigma(\mathcal{V})$. R generates the usual rewriting relation $\xrightarrow[R]{*}$, which is just the reflexive, transitive and congruence closure of R. In forming the congruence closure, sorts are assumed to be respected, *i.e.*, well-sortedness takes precedence over congruence.

The general problem we need to solve can be denoted by $t \xrightarrow[R]{?} u$, where $t \in \mathcal{T}_\Sigma$ is a ground term and $u \in \mathcal{T}_\Sigma(\mathcal{V})$ is a linear term (a linear term does not have more than one occurrence of any variable). A solution of such a problem is a ground substitution σ such that $t \xrightarrow[R]{*} \sigma u$. Such a substitution will be called an *R-matcher* for $t \xrightarrow[R]{?} u$. In the process of solving $t \xrightarrow[R]{?} u$, the problem typically gets reduced to a set $\{s_1 \xrightarrow[R]{?} t_1, \ldots, s_k \xrightarrow[R]{?} t_k\}$ of subproblems[9]. It is therefore convenient to consider such a set to be the general form of a reduction problem.

[9] Some of these problems may have terms with variables on both sides. See below.

The notion of an R-matcher extends to the set form naturally—a matcher for a set will solve *all* problems in the set simultaneously. We shall use P to denote such an arbitrary set of reduction problems. Let $M_R(P)$ denote the set of *all* R-matchers of P and $Var(P)$ the set of variables occurring in P. We say that $MM_R(P)$ is a *minimal complete* set of R-matchers for P if and only if

- $MM_R(P) \subseteq M_R(P)$
- $\xi \in M_R(P) \Rightarrow \exists \xi' \in MM_R(P),\ \xi' \leq_R^{Var(P)} \xi$
- $\forall \xi, \xi' \in MM_R(P),\ \xi' \leq_R^{Var(P)} \xi \Rightarrow \xi = \xi'$.

The three conditions can be thought of as *correctness, completeness* and *minimality* conditions respectively. Completeness and minimality also imply that the R-matchers in $MM_R(P)$ are *most general.*

The problem is to find an algorithm that finds a minimal complete set of R-matchers for a general problem P. Such an algorithm can be naturally expressed in the rule-based style of [10]. We give an algorithm in Table 1 that nondeterministically finds most general R-matchers subject to the assumption that the reduction theory is Ω-free, *i.e.*, if $f(t_1, \ldots, t_n) \xrightarrow[R]{*} f(u_1, \ldots, u_n)$ then $t_1 \xrightarrow[R]{*} u_1, \ldots, t_n \xrightarrow[R]{*} u_n$. The function **bridge** used in the algorithm is defined as follows. Given that R consists of the set of rules:

$$
\begin{array}{rcl}
f_1(t_{11}, \ldots, t_{1m_1}) & \longrightarrow & g_1(u_{11}, \ldots, u_{1n_1}) \\
 & \vdots & \\
f_k(t_{k1}, \ldots, t_{km_k}) & \longrightarrow & g_k(u_{k1}, \ldots, u_{kn_k})
\end{array}
$$

we construct the directed graph $\mathcal{G}_R = (\mathcal{N}_R, \mathcal{E}_R)$ with

$$
\mathcal{N}_R = \{f_1, \ldots, f_k, g_1, \ldots, g_k\} \qquad \mathcal{E}_R = \{(f_i, g_i) : 1 \leq i \leq k\}
$$

bridge(f, g, R) succeeds if and only if there is a path from f to g in $\mathcal{G}_R$ and in that case it returns the first rule $s \longrightarrow v$ along the path.

A formal proof of the correctness and completeness of the algorithm is boyond the scope of this paper. The following notes mention some of the ideas on which the algorithm is based, and explain the relationship between the constraints on R assumed above and the algorithm.

The algorithm is in the form of a set of rules for transforming the problem set P. The objective is to reduce P to a so-called *solved form* by repeated application of the rules. A solved form consists of units of the form $t \xrightarrow[R]{?} x^s$ where t is an instance of s. This can be interpreted as a substitution, especially since t is always a ground term and hence the substitution is idempotent.

We assume that P starts out as a set $\{t \xrightarrow[R]{?} u\}$ where t is ground. Although **Conflict** introduces nonstandard problem units $t \xrightarrow[R]{?} u$ where t is not ground,

Delete	$P \cup \{s \xrightarrow[R]{?} s\} \;\Rightarrow P$
Decompose	$P \cup \{f(t_1, \ldots, t_n) \xrightarrow[R]{?} f(u_1, \ldots, u_n)\}$
	$\Rightarrow\; P \cup \{t_1 \xrightarrow[R]{?} u_1, \ldots, t_n \xrightarrow[R]{?} u_n\}$
Conflict	$P \cup \{f(t_1, \ldots, t_n) \xrightarrow[R]{?} g(u_1, \ldots, u_m)\}$
	$\Rightarrow\; P \cup \{f(t_1, \ldots, t_n) \xrightarrow[R]{?} s,\; v \xrightarrow[R]{?} g(u_1, \ldots, u_m)\}$,
	if **bridge** (f, g, R) returns $(s \longrightarrow v) \in R$
	F, otherwise (assuming $f \neq g$)
Instantiate	$P \cup \{f(t_1, \ldots, t_n) \xrightarrow[R]{?} x^s\},\; f \in \Sigma_{w,s'},\; s' \not\leq s$
	$\Rightarrow\; P \cup \{f(t_1, \ldots, t_n) \xrightarrow[R]{?} g(x_1^{s_1}, \ldots, x_k^{s_k}),$
	$g(x_1^{s_1}, \ldots, x_k^{s_k}) \xrightarrow[R]{?} x^s\}$,
	if $g \in \Sigma_{s_1 s_2 \cdots s_k, s''},\; s'' \leq s$ and **bridge** (f, g, R) succeeds
	F, otherwise
Propagate	$P \cup \{f(t_1, \ldots, t_n) \xrightarrow[R]{?} x^s\},\; f \in \Sigma_{w,s'},\; s' \leq s$
	$\Rightarrow\; \{x^s \mapsto f(t_1, \ldots, t_n)\} P \cup \{f(t_1, \ldots, t_n) \xrightarrow[R]{?} x^s\}$,

Table 1: SC–MATCH: Rules for R-matching for Simple Conversion Problems

it is possible to ensure that there is always at least one unit of the standard form in P. The basic strategy is to always attack a standard unit with **Decompose**, **Conflict** or **Instantiate** until only **Propagate** is applicable. Applications of **Propagate** can then be used to reduce another unit to standard form, unless P is already in solved form. Note that the actual convertibility proof consists of all the conversion steps generated by uses of **Conflict**.

4 Related Work

Object imaging is recognized as a fundamental problem in the connectivity of distributed object systems, and the Uniform Data Transfer and Structured Storage services associated with COM as well as the Life-Cycle and Externalization services in the Common Services layer on top of CORBA address the problem to a limited extent. We are not aware of any concrete proposal that goes beyond a simple externalize-transport-internalize model. An interesting overview of the imaging problem is given by Konstantas [11] in the context of a general discussion of interoperability.

The idea of using type isomorphism for representation transformations was used in our earlier work in the context of polymorphic functional languages [24], where the primary reasoning mechanism was equational unification. Although the unification problem for arbitrary equational theories is undecidable, and multiple most general unifiers create semantic problems, we were able to show that for a reasonably broad class of user-defined type equations, implicit conversions among multiple representations can be supported in practice even in the presence of ML-style type *reconstruction* since the corresponding equational theories are unitary [25].

In the broader context of object system interoperability, interface transformations are a related and complementary area of research. Object imaging is limited by the availability of object factories for internalization in the remote environment. Although the required functionality may be supported by the objects produced by the factory the exact interface required may not be supported. In such cases automated interface transforms can be used to produce proxy objects with the right interface. Pintado and Junod [20] discuss a scheme where such proxies are created manually. We were able to show that some recently developed algorithms for subtyping with recursive types [2] can be extended to largely automate the process of interface matching and synthesis of proxy objects [26].

Finally, there has been quite a bit of recent work in extending the very notion of object type to include interaction protocols [1, 12, 16, 28] which is likely to have an impact on object imaging by refining notions of object types and type matching.

5 Conclusions

We have presented an outline of the technical issues involved in an object imaging service, with the main emphasis on knowledge representation ideas. We have made no attempt to give a mapping of our ideas to a specific distributed object technology platform such as CORBA or COM, with detailed specification of service structure and interfaces, and relationship to other services and the basic object model. Such a mapping will result in a conversion registry for object types, and as we mentioned before, will have to deal with many systems issues such as distributed reasoning using knowledge from multiple registries, uniform scripting models for conversion scripts, activation protocols for standalone converters, and so forth. We hope to deal with these problems in another paper.

References

[1] R. Allen and D. Garlan. Beyond definition/use: Architectural interconnection. In *Proceedings of the workshop on interface definition languages*, 1994. Published as School of CS, Carnegie Mellon University technical report, CMU-CS-94-WIDL-1.

[2] Roberto M. Amadio and Luca Cardelli. Subtyping recursive types. In *Proceedings of Eighteenth POPL Symposium*, pages 104–118. ACM Press, January 1991.

[3] Apple Computer, Inc. *OpenDoc Technical Summary*, October 1993. Version 1.0.

[4] Kraig Brockschmidt. *Inside OLE 2.* Microsoft Press, 1994.

[5] Peter Canning, William Cook, Walter Hill, Walter Olthoff, and John C. Mitchell. F-bounded polymorphism for object-oriented programming. In *Proceedings of Fourth International Conference on Functional Programming Languages and Computer Architecture (FPCA'89), London, U.K.* ACM Press, Addison-Wesley, 1989.

[6] Luca Cardelli and Peter Wegner. On understanding types, data abstraction and polymorphism. *Computing Surveys*, 17(4), 1985.

[7] D.E. Cohen, K. Madlener, and F. Otto. Separating the intrinsic complexity and the derivational complexity of the word problem for finitely presented groups. *Mathematical Logic Quarterly*, 39:143–157, 1993.

[8] Margaret A. Ellis and Bjarne Stroustrup. *The annotated C++ reference manual.* Addison-Wesley, 1990.

[9] William Harrison. *The Importance of Using Object References as Identifiers of Objects.* Object Management Group, 1994. OMG Document 94–6–12.

[10] J.-P. Jouannaud and C. Kirchner. Solving equations in abstract algebras: a rule-based survey of unification. In J.-L. Lassez and G. Plotkin, editors, *Computational Logic. Essays in honor of Alan Robinson*, chapter 8, pages 257–321. MIT Press, 1991.

[11] Dimitri Konstantas. Object oriented interoperability. In *Proceedings of the 7th European Conference on Object-Oriented Programming (ECOOP 93)*, pages 80–102. Springer-Verlag, 1993. LNCS 707.

[12] Doug Lea and Jos Marlowe. PSL: protocols and pragmatics for open systems. Manuscript, August 1994.

[13] J. Meseguer, J.A. Goguen, and G. Smolka. Order-sorted unification. *Journal of Symbolic Computation*, 8(4):383–413, 1989.

[14] Bertrand Meyer. *Eiffel the Language.* Prentice Hall, 1992.

[15] Microsoft Corp. and Digital Equipment Corp. *Common Object Model Specification (Introduction), Draft Version 0.2*, October 1994. OMG Document 94.10.9.

[16] Oscar Nierstrasz. Regular types for active objects. In *Proceedings of the Eighth Annual ACM Conference on Object-Oriented Programming Systems, Languages and Applications (OOPSLA 93)*, pages 1–15. ACM Press, 1993. Special Issue of SIGPLAN Notices 28(10).

[17] Object Management Group. *The Common Object Request Broker: Architecture and Specification*, 1993. OMG Document 93–12–43 Revision 1.2.

[18] Object Management Group. *Common Object Services Specification, Volume I*, 1994. OMG Document 94.1.1 (includes specifications for Naming Service, Lifecycle Service, and Event Notification Service).

[19] Object Management Group. *Object Externalization Service*, 1994. Joint Proposal by IBM and Sunsoft, OMG TC Document 94.6.21.

[20] Xavier Pintado and Betty Junod. Gluons: support for software component cooperation. In D. Tsichritzis, editor, *Object Frameworks*. Centre Universitaire d'Informatique, Université de Genève, 1992.

[21] Michael Powell. *Objects, References, Identifiers and Equality White Paper*. Object Management Group, 1993. OMG Document 93–7–5.

[22] G. Smolka, W. Nutt, J.A. Goguen, and J. Meseguer. Order-sorted equational computation. In M. Nivat and H. Aït-Kaci, editors, *Resolution of equations in algebraic structures, Volume 2*. Academic Press, 1989.

[23] Sun Microsystems. *Network Programming Guide*, 1990.

[24] Satish R. Thatté. Coercive type isomorphism. In *Proceedings of the Fifth Conference on Functional Programming Languages and Computer Architecture (FPCA'91)*, pages 29–49. ACM Press, 1991.

[25] Satish R. Thatté. Finite acyclic theories are unitary. *Journal of Symbolic Computation*, 15(2), February 1993.

[26] Satish R. Thatté. Automated synthesis of interface adapters for reusable classes. In *the Proceedings of the 21st Annual ACM Symposium on Principles of Programming Languages (POPL'94)*. ACM Press, 1994.

[27] Philip Wadler. Deforestation: Transforming programs to eliminate trees. In *Proceedings of Second European Symposium on Programming*. Springer-Verlag, 1988. LNCS 300.

[28] Daniel M. Yellin. Interface, protocols, and the semi-automatic construction of software adaptors. In *Proceedings of the Ninth Annual ACM Conference on Object-Oriented Programming Systems, Languages and Applications (OOPSLA 94)*. ACM Press, 1994.

Optimization of Object-Oriented Programs Using Static Class Hierarchy Analysis

Jeffrey Dean, David Grove, and Craig Chambers

Department of Computer Science and Engineering
University of Washington
Seattle, WA 98195-2350 USA
{jdean,grove,chambers}@cs.washington.edu

Abstract. Optimizing compilers for object-oriented languages apply static class analysis and other techniques to try to deduce precise information about the possible classes of the receivers of messages; if successful, dynamically-dispatched messages can be replaced with direct procedure calls and potentially further optimized through inline-expansion. By examining the complete inheritance graph of a program, which we call *class hierarchy analysis*, the compiler can improve the quality of static class information and thereby improve run-time performance. In this paper we present class hierarchy analysis and describe techniques for implementing this analysis effectively in both statically- and dynamically-typed languages and also in the presence of multi-methods. We also discuss how class hierarchy analysis can be supported in an interactive programming environment and, to some extent, in the presence of separate compilation. Finally, we assess the bottom-line performance improvement due to class hierarchy analysis alone and in combination with two other "competing" optimizations, profile-guided receiver class prediction and method specialization.

1 Introduction

Object-oriented languages foster the development of reusable, extensible class libraries and frameworks [Johnson 92]. For example, the InterViews graphics framework [Linton *et al.* 89] defines a collection of interacting base classes. The base classes define a set of messages that are to be defined or overridden in subclasses. Clients of the framework specialize it to their use by providing application-specific subclasses of the framework's base classes with the appropriate operations defined. Other frameworks have a similar structure, exploiting inheritance and dynamic binding of messages to make library code customizable and malleable.

Heavy use of inheritance and dynamically-bound messages is likely to make code more extensible and reusable, but it also imposes a significant performance overhead, compared to an equivalent but non-extensible program written in a non-object-oriented manner. In some domains, such as structured graphics packages, the performance cost of the extra flexibility provided by using a heavily object-oriented style is acceptable. However, in other domains, such as basic data structure libraries, numerical computing packages, rendering libraries, and trace-driven simulation frameworks, the cost of message passing can be too great, forcing the programmer to avoid object-oriented programming in the "hot spots" of their application. For example, hybrid languages like C++ [Stroustrup 91], Modula-3 [Nelson 91, Harbison 92], and CLOS [Bobrow *et al.* 88, Gabriel *et al.* 91] provide non-object-oriented built-in array data structures that are more efficient than would be a typical class-based extensible implementation using dynamically-dispatched fetch and store operations, Sather [Omohundro 94, Szypersky *et al.* 93] allows the programmer to explicitly select where subtype polymorphism is allowed, trading away reusability for performance, and it is common practice in C++ programming to avoid virtual function calls along common execution paths, sometimes leading to contorted, hard-to-understand and hard-to-extend code.

Compilers can reduce the cost of dynamically-dispatched messages in a number of ways. For example, *static class analysis* identifies a superset of the set of possible classes of objects that can be stored in variables and returned from expressions. Sometimes class analysis determines that the receiver of a message can be an instance of only one class, allowing the dynamically-dispatched message to be replaced with a direct procedure call (i.e., *statically-bound*) at compile-time and further optimized using inline expansion if the target procedure is small. If static class analysis determines that the receiver of a message can be one of a small set of classes, the dynamically-dispatched message can be replaced with a "type-case" expression, implemented with a series of run-time class tests, each branching to direct procedure calls implementing that case; executing one or two run-time class tests followed by an inlined version of the called procedure can be faster than performing a general run-time method lookup, particularly if additional optimizations of the called and calling methods can take place after inlining. Several other compiler techniques have been investigated for reducing the cost of message passing:

- *Profile-guided receiver class prediction* can support a type-casing-style optimization where static analysis is unable to determine precise information about the receiver of a message. The profile information representing the expected receiver class distribution of particular messages or call sites can be hard-wired into the compiler [Deutsch & Schiffman 84, Chambers *et al.* 89], gathered and exploited on-line [Hölzle & Ungar 94], and/or gathered off-line and exploited via recompilation [Garrett *et al.* 94, Calder & Grunwald 94].
- *Method specialization* can produce faster specialized versions of a method for particular inheriting subclasses; each specialized version can be optimized for the particular class or classes of the receiver for which the method is being specialized. Specializations for a given source method can be produced obliviously for each inheriting subclass [Kilian 88, Chambers & Ungar 89, Lea 90, Lim & Stolcke 91] or they can be produced selectively for groups of inheriting subclasses guided by execution frequency profiles [Dean *et al.* 95].

Class hierarchy analysis is another idea for speeding messages. When the compiler compiles a method, it knows statically that the receiver of the method is some subclass *S* of the class *C* containing the method. Unfortunately, in the absence of additional information, the compiler cannot optimize messages sent to the method's receiver, because the subclass *S* may override any of C's dynamically-dispatched methods. Class hierarchy analysis resolves this dilemma by supplying the compiler with complete knowledge of the program's class inheritance graph and the set of methods defined on each class. In the presence of this global information about the program being compiled, the compiler can infer statically a specific set of possible classes given that the receiver is a subclass of the class *C*, and messages sent to the method's receiver can be optimized. In particular, if there are no overriding methods in subclasses, a message sent to the method's receiver can be replaced with a direct procedure call and perhaps inlined. This sort of optimization would be especially important in the case of highly-extensible frameworks, where a great deal of flexibility is incorporated in the form of dynamically-dispatched messages within the framework base classes, but where only a limited portion of the potential flexibility is exploited by any particular application. For example, InterViews supports the display and manipulation of arbitrary graphical shapes, but if a particular application only implements a rectangle concrete subclass, then all the dynamically-dispatched calls within the framework for manipulating arbitrary shapes can be replaced with direct calls to the appropriate rectangle methods.

Class hierarchy analysis has long been known informally as a possible optimization among implementors of optimizing compilers for object-oriented languages, but we are unaware of any previous studies of the effectiveness and costs of this technique. Moreover, class hierarchy analysis is just one of a number of candidate optimizations that could be incorporated into an optimizing compiler, and the question remains as to which is the most cost-effective combination to include. In this paper we perform such a study:

- We describe several implementation techniques for efficiently incorporating class hierarchy analysis into a compiler, in particular into an existing static class analysis framework. Our techniques scale to support multi-method-based languages; efficient compile-time method lookup in the presence of multi-methods is substantially harder than for mono-methods.
- We address programming environment concerns of achieving fast turnaround for programming changes and supporting independent development of libraries, which could be adversely affected by a whole-program analysis such as class hierarchy analysis.
- We measure the run-time performance benefit and compile-time cost of class hierarchy analysis on several large programs written in Cecil [Chambers 92, Chambers 93], a pure object-oriented language with multi-methods. Moreover, we also measure the run-time performance benefits and compile-time costs of profile-guided receiver class prediction and method specialization separately and in combination with class hierarchy analysis.

The next section of this paper describes our integration of class hierarchy analysis into static class analysis and addresses programming environment concerns. Section 3 reports on our experimental evaluation of class hierarchy analysis, profile-guided receiver class prediction, and method specialization. Section 4 describes some related work and Section 5 offers some conclusions.

2 Class Hierarchy Analysis

By exploiting information about the structure of the class inheritance graph, including where methods are defined (but not depending on the implementation of any method nor on the instance variables of the classes), the compiler can gain valuable static information about the possible classes of the receiver of each method being compiled. To illustrate, consider the following class hierarchy:

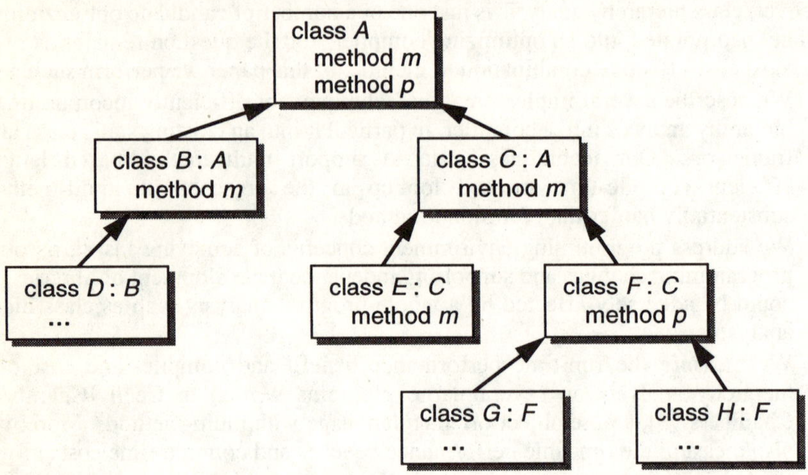

Consider the situation where the method *p* in the class *F* contains a send of the *m* message to self. *m* is declared to be a virtual function (there are several implementations of *m* for subclasses of *A*, and the right implementation should be selected dynamically). As a result, with only static intraprocedural class analysis the *m* message in *F*::*p* must be implemented as a general message send. However, by examining the subclasses of *F* and determining that there are no overriding implementations of *m*, the *m* message can be replaced with a direct procedure call to *C*::*m* and then further optimized with inlining, interprocedural analysis, or the like. This reasoning depends not on knowing the exact class of the receiver, as with most previous techniques, but rather on knowing that no subclasses of *F* override the version of *m* inherited by *F*. Class hierarchy analysis is a direct method for determining this without programmer intervention.

2.1 Alternatives to Class Hierarchy Analysis

Other languages have alternative approaches for achieving a similar effect. In C++ a programmer can declare whether or not a method is virtual (methods default to being non-virtual). When a method is not declared to be virtual, the compiler can infer that no subclass will override the method,[1] thus enabling it to implement invocations of the method as direct procedure calls. However, this approach suffers from three weaknesses relative to class hierarchy analysis:

- The C++ programmer must make explicit decisions of which methods need to be virtual, making the programming process more difficult. When developing a reusable framework, the framework designer must make decisions about which

1. Actually, C++ non-virtual functions can be overridden, but dynamic binding will not be performed: the static type of the receiver determines which version of the non-virtual method to invoke, not the dynamic class.

operations will be overridable by clients of the framework, and which will not. The decisions made by the framework designer may not match the needs of the client program; in particular, a well-written highly-extensible framework will often provide flexibility that goes unused for any particular application, incurring an unnecessary run-time performance cost. In contrast, class hierarchy analysis is automatic and adapts to the particular framework/client combination being optimized.

- The virtual/non-virtual annotations are embedded in the source program. If extensions to the class hierarchy are made that require a non-virtual function to become overloaded and dynamically dispatched, the source program must be modified. This can be particularly difficult in the presence of separately-developed frameworks which clients may not be able to change. Class hierarchy analysis, as an automatic mechanism, requires no source-level modifications.
- A function may need to be virtual, because it has multiple implementations that need to be selected dynamically, but within some particularly subtree of the inheritance graph, there will be only one implementation that applies. In the example above, the *m* method must be declared virtual, since there are several implementations, but there is only one version of *m* that is called from *F* or any of its subclasses. In C++, *m* must be virtual and consequently implemented with a dynamically-bound message, but class hierarchy analysis can identify when a virtual function "reverts" to a non-virtual one with a single implementation for a particular class subtree, enabling better optimization. In particular, it is always the case that a message sent to the receiver of a method defined in a leaf class will have only one target implementation and hence can be implemented as a direct procedure call, regardless of whether or not the target method is declared virtual. For the benchmark programs discussed in Section 3, slightly more than half of the message sends that were statically bound through class hierarchy analysis could not have been made non-virtual in C++ (i.e., had more than a single definition of the routine).

In a similar vein, Trellis [Schaffert *et al.* 85, Schaffert *et al.* 86] allows a class to be declared with the no_subtypes annotation and Dylan [Dyl92] allows a class to be sealed, both of which inform the compiler that no subclasses exist. These annotations allow the compiler to treat the class as a leaf class and compile all messages sent to objects statically known to be of the class as direct procedure calls. Sealing has similar weaknesses relative to class hierarchy analysis as do non-virtual functions in C++: programmers have to predict in advance, in the source code, which classes are to be sealed, and opportunities for static binding will be missed, relative to class hierarchy analysis, when a class has unknown subclasses but none of the subclasses override certain methods.

2.2 Implementation

To make class hierarchy analysis effective, it must be integrated with intraprocedural static class analysis. Static class analysis is a kind of data flow analysis that computes a set of classes for each variable and expression in a method; the compiler uses this information to optimize dynamically-bound messages, type-case statements as in Modula-3 and Trellis, and other run-time type checks. Previous frameworks for static class analysis in dynamically-typed object-oriented languages have defined several representations for sets of classes [Chambers & Ungar 90]:

Representation	Description	Source	Use
Unknown	the set of all classes	method arguments; results of non-inlined message sends; contents of instance variables	
Class(*C*)	the singleton set $\{C\}$	true branch of run-time class tests; literals	supports static binding of sends; eliminating run-time type checks
Union(S_1, ..., S_n)	union of class sets	control flow merges	supports "type-casing" if small union of classes
Difference(S_1, S_2)	difference of two class sets	false branch of run-time class tests	avoids repeated tests

Earlier frameworks focused on the singleton class set as the primary source of optimization: if the receiver of a message is a singleton class set, then the message lookup can be resolved at compile-time and replaced with a direct procedure call to the target method. Unions of class sets were optimized only through a type-casing optimization, if the union combined a small number of classes.

2.2.1 Cone Class Sets

Class hierarchy analysis changes the flavor of static class analysis. The initial class set associated with the receiver of the method being analyzed is the set of classes inheriting from the class containing the method; in the earlier example, the receiver of *F*'s *p* method is associated with the set $\{F, G, H\}$. It would be possible to use the Union set representation to represent the class set of the method receiver, but this could be space-inefficient for the large receiver class sets of methods declared high up in the inheritance hierarchy. Consequently we introduce a new representation for the kind of regular class sets inferred by class hierarchy analysis, the Cone:

Representation	Description	Source	Use
Cone(*C*)	the set of all subclasses of the class *C*, including *C*	class hierarchy analysis of method receiver; static type declarations	supports static binding of sends

Class hierarchy analysis annotates the method's receiver with a cone set representation for the class containing the method. A simple optimization of this representation is to use the

Class(*C*) representation rather than Cone(*C*) if *C* is a leaf class. (This framework for representing static class analysis information is similar to Palsberg and Schwartzbach's static type system [Palsberg & Schwartzbach 94].) Cones tend to be concise summaries of sets of classes: in our implementation, when compiling a 52,000-line benchmark program with 957 classes, the average cone used for optimization purposes contained 12 concrete classes, and some cones included as many as 93 concrete classes.

In a statically-typed language, cones can be used to integrate static type declarations into the static class analysis framework: for a variable declared to be of static type *C*, any static class information inferred for the variable is intersected with Cone(*C*). This integration is crucial to adapting techniques developed for dynamically-typed object-oriented languages to work effectively for statically-typed object-oriented languages. For hybrid languages, built-in non-object-oriented data types like integers and arrays can be considered their own separate classes, as far as static class analysis is concerned; CLOS takes a similar view on integrating the standard Lisp data types with user-defined classes.

2.2.2 Method Applies-To Sets

If only singleton class sets support static binding of messages, then only leaf classes would benefit from class hierarchy analysis. However, this is unnecessarily conservative: even if the receiver of a message has multiple potential classes, if all the classes inherit the same method, then the message send can be statically bound and replaced with a direct procedure call. For instance, in the earlier example, the class set computed for the *m* message sent to the receiver of the *F*::*p* method is {*F*, *G*, *H*}, but all three classes inherit the same implementation of *m*, *C*::*m*. Our measurements indicate that nearly 50% of the messages statically bound using class hierarchy analysis have receiver class sets containing more than a single class. To receive the most benefit from class hierarchy analysis, static binding of messages whose receivers are sets of classes should be supported. One approach would be to iterate through all elements of Union and Cone sets, performing method lookup for each class, and checking that each class inherits the same method; however, this could be slow for large sets (e.g., cones of classes with many subclasses).

We have pursued an alternative approach that compares whole sets of classes at once. We first precompute for each method the set of classes for which that method is the appropriate target; we call this set the *applies-to* set. (In our compiler, we compute the applies-to sets of methods on demand, the first time a message with a particular name and argument count is analyzed, to spread out the cost of this computation.) Then at a message send, we take the class set inferred for the receiver and test whether this set overlaps each potentially-invoked method's applies-to set. If only one method's applies-to set overlaps the receiver's class set, then that is the only method that can be invoked and the message send can be replaced with a direct procedure call to that method. (To avoid repeatedly checking a large number of methods for applicability at every call site in the program, our compiler incorporates a compile-time method lookup cache that memoizes the function mapping receiver class set to set of target methods. In practice, the size of this cache is reasonable: for a 52,000-line program, this cache contained 7,686 entries, and a total of 54,211 queries of the cache were made during compilation.)

The efficiency of this approach to compile-time method lookup depends on the ability to precompute the applies-to sets of each method and the implementation of the set overlaps test for the different representations of sets. To precompute the applies-to sets, we first construct a partial order over the set of methods, where one method M_1 is less than another M_2 in the partial ordering iff M_1 overrides M_2. For the running example, we construct the following partial order:

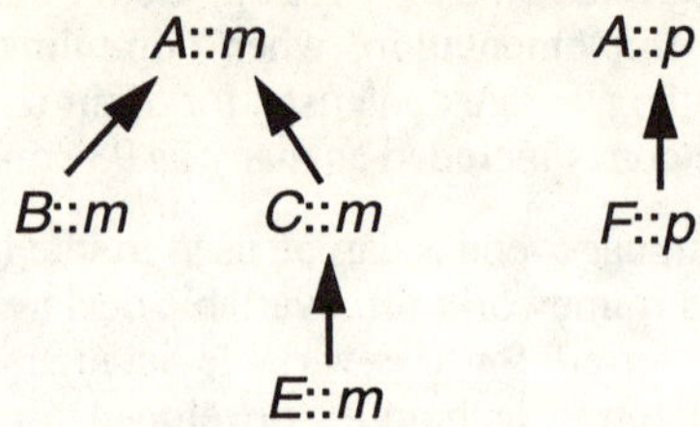

Then for each method defined on class *C*, we initialize its applies-to set to Cone(*C*). Finally, we traverse the partial order top-down. For each method *M*, we visit each of the immediately overriding methods and subtract off their (initial) applies-to sets from *M*'s applies-to set. In general, the resulting applies-to set for a method *C*::*M* is represented as Difference(Cone(*C*), Union(Cone(D_1), ..., Cone(D_n))), where D_1, ..., D_n are the classes containing the directly-overriding methods. If a method has many directly-overriding methods, the representation of the method's applies-to set can become quite large. To avoid this problem, the subtracting can be ignored at any point, it is safe though conservative for applies-to sets to be larger than necessary.

The efficiency of overlaps testing depends on the representation of the two sets being compared. Overlaps testing for two arbitrary Union sets of size *N* is $O(N^2)$,[1] but overlaps testing among Cone and Class representations takes only constant time (assuming that testing whether one class can inherit from another takes only constant time [AK *et al.* 89, Agrawal *et al.* 91, Caseau 93]): for example, Cone(C1) overlaps Class(C2) iff C1 = C2 or C2 inherits from C1. Overlaps testing of arbitrary Difference sets is complex and can be expensive. Since applies-to sets in general are Differences, overlaps testing of a receiver class set against a collection of applies-to Difference sets could be expensive. To represent irregular applies-to sets more efficiently, we convert Difference sets into a flattened BitSet representation. Overlaps testing of two BitSet class sets requires $O(N)$ time, where *N* is the number of classes in the program. In practice, this check is fast: even for a large program with 1,000 classes, if bit sets use 32 bit positions per machine word, only 31 machine word comparisons are required to check whether two bit sets overlap. In our implementation, we precompute the BitSet representation of Cone(*C*) for each class *C*, and we use these bit sets when computing differences of Cones, overlaps of Cones, and membership of a class in a Cone.

When compiling a method and performing intraprocedural static class analysis, the static class information for the method's receiver is initialized to Cone(*C*), where *C* is the class containing the method. It might appear that the applies-to set computed for the method would be more precise initial information. Normally, this would be the case. However, if an overriding method contains a `super` send (or the equivalent) to invoke the overridden method, the overridden method can be called with objects other than those in the method's applies-to set; the applies-to set only applies for normal dynamically-dispatched message sends. If it is known that none of the overriding methods contain `super` sends that would invoke the method, then applies-to would be a more precise and legal initial class set.

1. Since the set of classes is fixed, Union sets whose elements are singleton classes could be stored in a sorted order, reducing the overlaps computation to O(*N*).

2.2.3 Support for Dynamically-Typed Languages

In a dynamically-typed language, there is the possibility that for some receiver classes a message send will result in a run-time message-not-understood error. When attempting to optimize a dynamic dispatch, we need to ensure that we will not replace such a message send with a statically bound call even if there is only one applicable source method. To handle this, we introduce a special "error" method defined on the root class, if there is no default method already defined. Once error methods are introduced, no special efforts need be made to handle the possibility of run-time method lookup errors. For example, if only one (source) method is applicable, but a method lookup error is possible, our framework will consider this case as if two methods (one real and one error) were applicable and hence block static binding to the one real method. Similarly, if a message is ambiguously defined for some class, more than one method will include the class in its applies-to set, again preventing static binding to either method.

Knowledge of the class hierarchy and the location of defined methods can improve the results of receiver class prediction, a common technique used when the available static class information is not precise enough to lead to static binding of a message send. If the compiler can predict the expected class(es) of the message's receiver, either based on the name of the message and a hard-wired table in the compiler (as in Smalltalk-80 and the Self-91 system) or on dynamic profile data (as in the Self-93 system and Cecil), then it can insert run-time class tests for the expected classes. The compiler generates a full message send to handle any unexpected classes that occur at run-time:

Before Class Prediction:	After Class Prediction:

`a := s.area();`	`if (s.class == Rectangle) {`
	  // statically bind to rectangle's area; inline if small
	  `a := s.Rectangle::area();`
	`} else if (s.class == Circle) {`
	  // statically bind to circle's area; inline if small
	  `a := s.Circle::area();`
	`} else {`
	  // a full message send to handle unexpected cases
	  `a := s.area();`
	`}`

In dynamically-typed languages, if the compiler can prove statically that the classes being tested exhaust the set of classes for which the message is correctly defined, then the final "unexpected" case can be replaced with a run-time message lookup error trap. (In statically-typed languages, using class hierarchy information to convert static type declarations into Cone class set representations accomplishes a similar purpose.) Such a lookup error trap might take up less compiled code space than a full message send, but more importantly in some languages it is known not to return to the caller. Thus, the error branch never merges back into the main stream of the program, and the compiler learns that only the predicted class(es) are possible after the message. In the above example, if analysis of the class hierarchy reveals that Rectangle and Circle are the only classes implementing the area message, then the third case can be replaced with an error trap. After the area message, the compiler will know that s is either a Rectangle or a Circle, enabling it to better implement later messages sent to s. (In a statically-typed language, class hierarchy analysis coupled with static type declarations would have shown s to refer to either a Rectangle or a Circle all along.) In the absence of class hierarchy information, the compiler must assume that some other class could implement the area message (or, in a statically-typed language, that some other class could be a subtype of the Shape static type), and consequently include support for the third "unexpected" case. When compiling our 52,000-line benchmark program, elimination of unexpected cases using class hierarchy analysis occurred 3,232 times; 3,004 of these occurrences optimized basic messages such as if and not, which might not be necessary in a less pure language lacking user-defined control structures.

2.2.4 Support for Multi-Methods

The above strategy for static class analysis in the presence of class hierarchy analysis and/or static type declarations works for singly-dispatched languages with one message receiver, but it does not support languages with multi-methods, such as CLOS, Dylan, and Cecil. To support multi-methods, we associate methods not with sets of classes but sets of *k*-tuples of classes, where *k* is the number of dispatched arguments of the method.[1] To represent many common sets of tuples of classes concisely, we use *k*-tuples of class sets: a *k*-tuple $<S_1, ..., S_k>$, where the S_i are class sets, represents the set of tuples of classes that is the cartesian product of the S_i class sets. To represent other irregular sets of tuples of classes, we support a union of class set tuples as a basic representation.

Static class analysis is modified to support multi-methods as follows. For each method, we precompute the method's applies-to *tuple* of class sets; this tuple describes the combinations of classes for which the method should be invoked. For a multi-method specialized on the classes $C_1, ..., C_k$, the method's applies-to tuple is initialized to $<\text{Cone}(C_1), ..., \text{Cone}(C_k)>$. When visiting the directly-overriding methods, the overriding method's applies-to tuple is subtracted from the overridden method's tuple. When determining which methods apply to a given message, the *k*-tuple is formed from the class sets inferred for the *k* dispatched message arguments, and then the applies-to tuples of the candidate methods are checked to see if they overlap the tuple representing the actual arguments to the message.

Efficient multi-method static class analysis relies on efficient overlaps testing and difference operations on tuples. Testing whether one tuple overlaps another is straightforward: each element class set of one tuple must overlap the corresponding class set of the other tuple. Computing the difference of two tuples of class sets efficiently is trickier. The pointwise difference of the element class sets, though concise, would not be a correct implementation. One straightforward and correct representation would be a union of *k* *k*-tuples, where each tuple has one element class set difference taken:

$$<S_1, ..., S_k> - <T_1, ..., T_k> \equiv \bigcup_{i=1..k} <S_1, ..., S_{i-1}, S_i - T_i, S_{i+1}, ..., S_k>$$

If the $S_i - T_i$ element set is empty, then the *i*-th *k*-tuple is dropped from the union: its cartesian-product expansion is the empty set. Also, if two tuples in the union are identical except for one position, they can be merged into a single tuple by taking the union of the element class sets. Both optimizations are important in practice.

1. We assume that the compiler can determine statically which subset of a message's arguments can be examined as part of method lookup. In CLOS, for instance, all methods in a generic function have the same set of dispatched arguments. In Cecil, the compiler examines all methods with the same name and number of arguments and finds all argument positions that any of the methods is specialized upon. It would be possible to consider all arguments as potentially dispatched, but this would be substantially less efficient, both at compile-time and at run-time, particularly if the majority of methods are specialized on a single argument.

For example, consider the following class hierarchy and multi-methods (`x@`*X* is the syntax we use for indicating that the `x` formal argument of a multi-method is specialized for the class *X*):

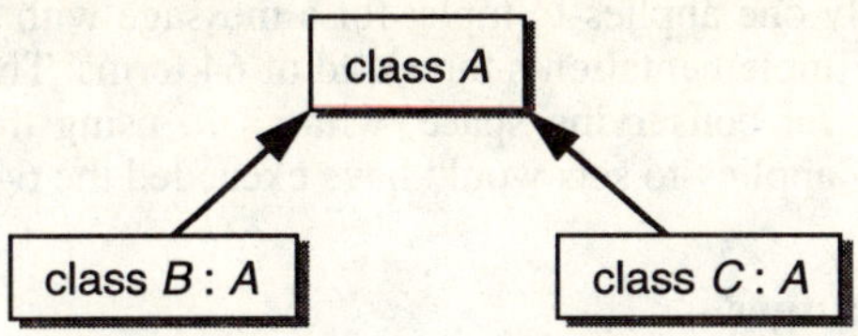


```
m(r@A, s@A, t@A) { ... }

m(r@B, s@C, t@A) { ... }
```

Under both CLOS's and Cecil's method overriding rules, the partial order constructed for these methods is the following:

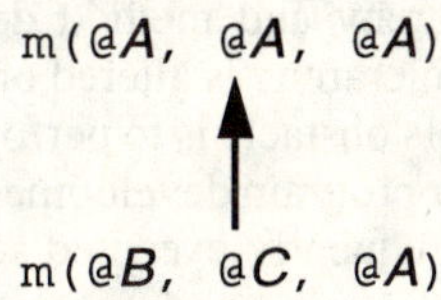

The applies-to tuples constructed for these methods, using the formula above, are:

`m(@A, @A, @A)`: $\langle\{A,C\}, \{A,B,C\}, \{A,B,C\}\rangle \cup \langle\{A,B,C\}, \{A,B\}, \{A,B,C\}\rangle$

`m(@B, @C, @A)`: $\langle\{B\}, \{C\}, \{A,B,C\}\rangle$

(The third tuple of the first method's applies-to union drops out, since one of the tuple's elements is the empty class set.)

Unfortunately, for a series of difference operations, as occurs when computing the applies-to tuple of a method by subtracting off each of the applies-to tuples of the overriding methods, this representation tends to grow in size exponentially with the number of differences taken. For example, if a third method is added to the existing class hierarchy, which overrides the first method:

```
m(r@C, s@B, t@C) { ... }
```

then the applies-to tuple of the first method becomes the following:

`m(@A, @A, @A)`: $\langle\{A\}, \{A,B,C\}, \{A,B,C\}\rangle \cup \langle\{A,C\}, \{A,C\}, \{A,B,C\}\rangle \cup$
$\langle\{A,C\}, \{A,B,C\}, \{A,B\}\rangle \cup \langle\{A,B\}, \{A,B\}, \{A,B,C\}\rangle \cup$
$\langle\{A,B,C\}, \{A\}, \{A,B,C\}\rangle \cup \langle\{A,B,C\}, \{A,B\}, \{A,B\}\rangle$

To curb this exponential growth problem, we have developed (with help from William Pugh) a more efficient way to represent the difference of two overlapping tuples of class sets:

$$\langle S_1, \ldots, S_k\rangle - \langle T_1, \ldots, T_k\rangle \equiv \bigcup_{i=1..k} \langle S_1 \cap T_1, \ldots, S_{i-1} \cap T_{i-1}, S_i - T_i, S_{i+1}, \ldots, S_k\rangle$$

By taking the intersection of the first *i*-1 elements of the *i*th tuple in the union, we avoid duplication among the element tuples of the union. As a result, the element sets of the tuples are smaller and tend to drop out more often for a series of tuple difference operations. For the three multi-method example, the applies-to tuple of the first method is simplified to the following:

`m(@A, @A, @A)`: $\langle\{A\}, \{A,B,C\}, \{A,B,C\}\rangle \cup \langle\{C\}, \{A,C\}, \{A,B,C\}\rangle \cup$
$\langle\{C\}, \{B\}, \{A,B\}\rangle \cup \langle\{B\}, \{A,B\}, \{A,B,C\}\rangle$

As a final guard against exponential growth, we impose a limit on the number of class set terms in the resulting tuple representation, beyond which we stop narrowing (through subtraction) a method's applies-to set. We rarely resort to this final ad hoc measure: when compiling a 52,000-line Cecil program, only one applies-to tuple, for a message with 5 dispatched argument positions, crossed our implementation's threshold of 64 terms. The intersection-based representation is crucial for conserving space: without it, using the simpler representation described first, many applies-to sets would have exceeded the 64-term threshold.

2.3 Incremental Programming Changes

Class hierarchy analysis might seem to be in conflict with incremental compilation: the compiler generates code containing embedded assumptions about the structure of the program's class inheritance hierarchy and method definitions, and these assumptions might change whenever the class hierarchy is altered or a method is added or removed. A simple approach to overcoming this obstacle is to perform class hierarchy analysis and its dependent optimizations only after program development ceases. A final batch optimizing compilation could be applied to frequently-executed software just prior to shipping it to users, as a final performance boost.

Class hierarchy analysis can be applied even during active program development, however, if the compiler maintains enough intermodule dependency information to be able to selectively recompile those parts of a program invalidated after some change to the class hierarchy or the set of methods. In previous work, we have developed a framework for maintaining intermodule dependency information [Chambers *et al.* 95]. This framework is effective at representing the compilation dependencies introduced by class hierarchy analysis.

In the dependency framework, intermodule dependencies are represented by a directed, acyclic graph structure. Nodes in this graph represent information, including pieces of the program's source and information resulting from various interprocedural analyses such as class hierarchy analysis, and an edge from one node to another indicates that the information represented by the target node is derived from or depends on the information represented by the source node. Depending on the number of incoming and outgoing edges, we classify nodes into three categories:

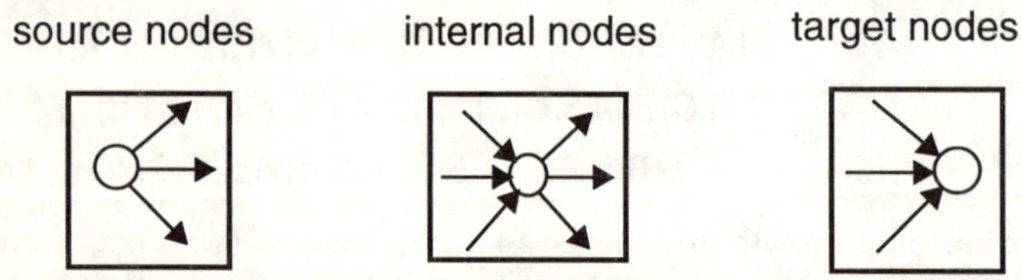

- *Source nodes* have only outgoing dependency edges. They represent information present in the source modules comprising the program, such as the source code of procedures and the class inheritance hierarchy.
- *Target nodes* have only incoming dependency edges. They represent information that is an end product of compilation, such as compiled `.o` files.
- *Internal nodes* have both incoming and outgoing edges. They represent information that is derived from some earlier information and used in the derivation of some later information.

The dependency graph is constructed incrementally during compilation. Whenever a portion of the compilation process uses a piece of information that could change, the compiler adds an edge to the dependency graph from the node representing the information used to the node representing the client of the information. When changes are made to the source program, the compiler computes what source dependency nodes have been affected and propagates invalidations downstream from these nodes. This invalidates all information (including compiled code modules) that depended on the changed source information.

In our compiler, static class analysis queries a compile-time method lookup cache to attempt to determine the outcome of message lookups statically; this cache is indexed with a message name and a tuple of argument class sets and returns the set of methods that might be called by such a message. To compute an entry in the method lookup cache, the compiler tests the applies-to tuples of methods with a matching name, in turn examining the BitSet representation of the set of classes represented by a Cone class set, which was computed from the underlying class inheritance graph. To support selective recompilation of optimized code, dependency graph nodes are introduced to model information derived from the source code:

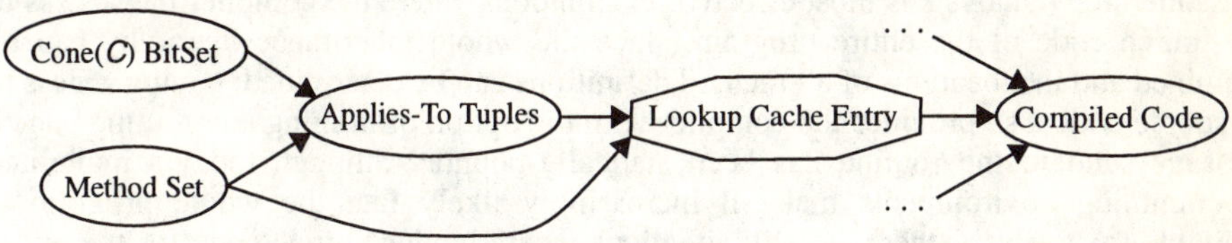

- one kind of dependency node represents the BitSet representation of the set of subclasses of a class (one product of class hierarchy analysis),
- another kind of dependency node represents the set of methods with a particular name (another product of class hierarchy analysis),
- a third kind of dependency node represents the applies-to tuples of the methods, which is derived from the previous two pieces of information, and
- a fourth kind of dependency node guards each entry in the compile-time method lookup cache.

If the set of subclasses of a given class is changed or if the set of methods with a particular name and argument count is changed, the corresponding source dependency nodes are invalidated. This causes all downstream dependency nodes to be invalidated recursively, eventually leading to the appropriate compiled code being invalidated and subsequently recompiled.

To support greater selectivity and avoid unnecessarily invalidating any compiled code, some of the internal nodes in the dependency framework are *filtering nodes*. When invalidated, a filtering node will first check whether the information it represents really has changed; only if the information it represents has changed will a filtering node invalidate its successor dependency nodes. The compile-time method lookup cache entries are guarded by such filtering nodes. If part of the inheritance graph is changed or a new method is added, then downstream method lookup results *may* have changed, but often the source changes do not affect all potentially dependent method lookup cache entries. By rechecking the method lookup when invalidated, and squashing the invalidation if the method lookup outcome was unaffected by a particular source change, many unnecessary recompilations are avoided.

Empirical evaluation using a trace of a month's worth of actual program development indicates that the dependency-graph-based approach reduces the amount of recompilation required during incremental compiles by a factor of seven over a coarser-grained C++-style header file scheme, in the presence of class hierarchy analysis, and by a factor of two over the Self compiler's previous state-of-the-art fine-grained dependency mechanism [Chambers & Ungar 91]. Of course, more recompilation occurs in the presence of class hierarchy analysis than would occur without it, but for these traces the number of files recompiled after a programming change is often no more than the number of files directly modified by the changes. A more important concern with our current implementation is that many filtering nodes may need to be checked after some programming changes, and even if few compiled files are invalidated, a fair amount of compilation time is expended in checking caches. The size of the dependency graph is about half as large as the executable for the program being compiled, which is acceptable in our program development environment; coarser-grained dependency graphs could be devised that save space at the cost of reduced selectivity. Further details are available elsewhere [Chambers *et al.* 95].

2.4 Optimization of Incomplete Programs

Class hierarchy analysis is most effective in situations where the compiler has access to the source code of the entire program, since the whole inheritance hierarchy can be examined and the locations of all method definitions can be determined; having access to all source code also provides the compiler with the option of inlining any routine once a message send to the routine has been statically-bound. Although today's integrated programming environments make it increasingly likely that the whole program is available for analysis, there are still situations where having source code for the entire program is unrealizable. In particular, a library may be developed separately from client applications, and the library developer may not wish to share source code for the library with clients. For example, many commercial C++ class libraries provide only header files and compiled `.o` files and do not provide complete source code for the library.

Fortunately, having full source code access is not a requirement for class hierarchy analysis: as long as the compiler has knowledge of the class hierarchy and where methods are defined in the hierarchy (but not their implementations), class hierarchy analysis can still be applied, and this information usually is available in the header files provided for the library. When compiling the client application, the compiler can perform class hierarchy analysis of the whole application, including the library, and statically bind calls within the client application. If source code for some methods in the library is unavailable, then statically-bound calls to those methods simply won't be able to be inlined. Static binding alone still provides significant performance improvements, particularly on modern RISC processors, where dynamically-dispatched message send implementations stall the hardware pipeline. Furthermore, some optimizing linkers are able to optimize static calls by inlining the target routine's machine code at link time [Fernandez 95], although the resulting code is not as optimized as what could be done in the compiler.

Using class hierarchy analysis when compiling a library in isolation is more difficult, since the client program might create subclasses of library classes that override methods defined in the library. The sealing approach of Dylan and Trellis can provide the compiler with information about what library classes won't be subclassed by client applications, supporting class hierarchy-based optimizations for those classes at the cost of reduced extensibility. Alternatively, the compiler could choose to compile specialized versions of methods applicable only to classes present in the library. For example, in a data structure library, the compiler could compile specialized versions of methods for array, string, hash table, and other frequently-used classes; generic versions of methods would also be compiled to support any subclasses of these library classes defined by client applications. In previous work, we have developed a profile-guided algorithm that examines the potential targets of sends in a routine and derives a set of profitable specializations based on where in the class hierarchy these target routines are defined [Dean *et al.* 95]. This specialization algorithm detects call sites where class hierarchy analysis is insufficient to statically-bind message sends, and produces versions of methods specialized to truncated cones of the class hierarchy. Empirical measurements indicate that this algorithm applied to a complete 52,000-line Cecil program improves performance by 50% or more with only a 5% to 10% compiled code space increase, although we would expect a larger relative space overhead if the algorithm were applied to a library in isolation.

In summary, although class hierarchy analysis is most effective when the whole program is available, it can still be applied in situations where only portions of the program are available. Using the techniques described above, it can be applied to incomplete programs and to libraries independent of client applications, at some cost in missed optimization opportunities and/or increased compiled code space.

3 Empirical Assessment

Class hierarchy analysis, method specialization, and profile-guided receiver class prediction are all techniques for increasing the amount of class information available to the optimizer at compile time. All three represent different, and partially overlapping, approaches to solving the same fundamental problem: enabling the static binding of dynamic dispatches. In this section, we examine the effectiveness of these three approaches in isolation and in combination, focusing on the following questions:

- What is the impact of class hierarchy analysis on program performance?
- How effective is class hierarchy analysis in comparison to specialization? Can additional benefit be gained from combining class hierarchy analysis and specialization?
- How much benefit does class hierarchy analysis confer to a system that already performs profile-guided receiver class prediction?

We examine these issues in the context of the Vortex optimizing compiler for Cecil, a pure object-oriented language with multi-methods. Table 1 describes the five medium-to-large Cecil programs that we used as benchmarks. Appendix A includes the raw performance data.

Table 1: Cecil Benchmarks

Program	Lines[a]	Description
Richards (Rich)	400	Operating systems simulation
Deltablue (Delta)	650	Incremental constraint solver
InstrSched (Instr)	2,400	MIPS global instruction scheduler
Typechecker (Type)	17,000[b]	Cecil static typechecker
Compiler (Comp)	43,800[b]	Vortex optimizing compiler

a. Not including 8,500-line standard library.

b. The typechecker and compiler share approximately 12,000 lines of code.

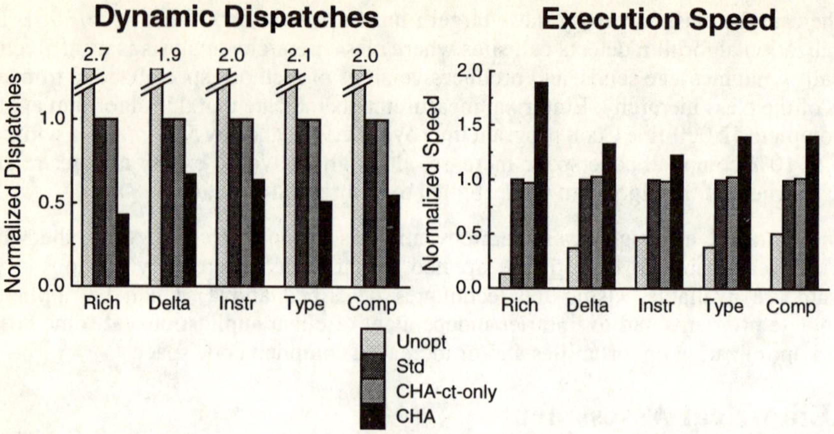

Figure 1: Number of dynamic dispatches and execution speed

3.1 Effectiveness of Class Hierarchy Analysis

Since class hierarchy analysis provides the compiler with additional information about the classes of program variables (in particular the receiver(s) of the message being compiled), we would expect that the compiler would be able to statically bind more dynamic dispatches. Additionally, as discussed in Section 2.2.3, in some situations the compiler can determine when unexpected cases of a message send are guaranteed to fail, thus improving the quality of static analysis downstream of the send.

To measure the impact of class hierarchy analysis, we compiled the benchmark programs using the following set of compiler optimizations:

- ***unopt:*** No optimizations.
- ***std***: Standard static intraprocedural analyses, including iterative intraprocedural class analysis, inlining, hard-wired class prediction for a small set of common messages, closure optimizations, extended splitting [Chambers & Ungar 90] and other standard intraprocedural optimizations such as CSE, constant folding and propagation, and dead code elimination.
- ***cha-ct-only***: Standard (*std*) augmented by a limited usage of class hierarchy analysis. The results of class hierarchy analysis are used only to optimize the uncommon cases after run-time class tests, as described in Section 2.2.3.
- ***cha***: Standard augmented by class hierarchy analysis. Class hierarchy analysis is used to provide class information about the receiver(s) of a method and to determine when messages sends are guaranteed to fail.

Figure 1 shows the dynamic number of dynamic dispatches and the execution speeds of the benchmark programs, normalized to those of *std*. Augmenting standard intraprocedural techniques with class hierarchy analysis resulted in a 23% to 89% improvement in execution speed for these applications. Since the performance difference between *std* and *cha-ct-only* was negligible, we can conclude that almost all of the runtime benefits seen in *cha* are due to additional receiver class information and not from optimizing the unexpected branches of class tests inserted by hard-wired class prediction, therefore we expect the improvements due to class hierarchy analysis to be significant even in object-oriented languages lacking used-defined control structures.

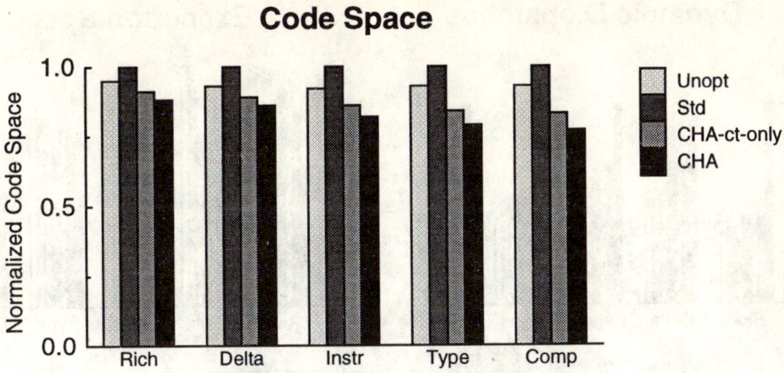

Figure 2: Compiled Code Space

In addition to improving execution speed, class hierarchy analysis reduces compiled code size, as shown in figure 2. Executables compiled with class hierarchy analysis were 12% to 21% smaller than *std* executables. By comparing the relative heights of the bars we can see that most of this reduction in code space was due to the replacement of call sites which are guaranteed to result in a message-not-understood error by a simple call to an error routine. Such call sites mainly occurred in the off branches of class tests inserted by hard-wired class prediction and thus, one would expect that class hierarchy analysis would have a smaller impact on compiled code space in languages without user-defined control structures.

3.2 Class Hierarchy Analysis and Specialization

Method specialization creates multiple copies of a single source method, each one of which is compiled with more precise static class information about the method receiver(s) thus enabling static binding and inlining of messages sent to self. Class hierarchy analysis makes a similar contribution. In some sense, specialization and class hierarchy analysis are competing approaches to gaining the same sort of information. An important question, then, is "what are the relative benefits and costs of the two techniques?" Since a specialized method has exact class information about the receiver(s) of the method, we would expect that specialization would yield better results than class hierarchy analysis, but specialization accrues its benefits at the cost of increased compiled code space. In this section, we examine the impact of class hierarchy analysis and method specialization, both in isolation and in combination, using the following set of compiler optimizations:

- ***std***: Standard static intraprocedural analyses, as described in Section 3.1.
- ***cha***: Standard augmented by class hierarchy analysis.
- ***cust-k***: Standard augmented by the *customization* form of method specialization. Customization is the specialization strategy used in Self, Trellis, and Sather implementations where a specialized version of a method is generated for each inheriting subclass. We extended customization to handle multi-methods by specializing on all combinations of subclasses of the dispatched arguments.[1]

1. We used profile data to determine which of the specializations produced by *cust-k* actually needed to be generated, since it was infeasible to actually compile them all. In effect, this simulates Self-style dynamic compilation.

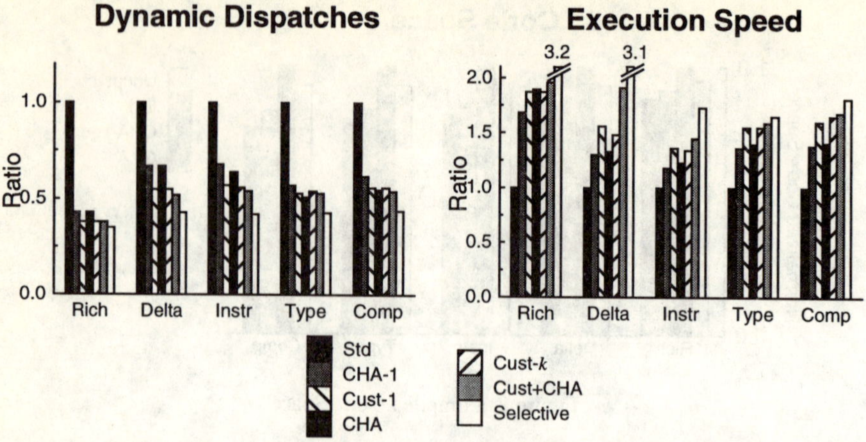

Figure 3: Number of dynamic dispatches and execution speed

- ***cust-1***: Standard augmented by customization on only the first receiver. Customization on only the first receiver is more feasible in practice than customizing on all combinations of receivers in the case of multi-methods.
- ***cha-1***: Standard augmented by class hierarchy analysis for only the first receiver, to compare against *cust-1*.
- ***cust+cha***: Standard augmented with both *cust-k* and class hierarchy analysis.
- ***selective***: Standard augmented with class hierarchy analysis and a selective specialization algorithm that combines a profile-derived weighted call graph and class hierarchy analysis to select candidates for specialization [Dean *et al.* 95].

Figure 3 shows the normalized number of dynamic dispatches and execution speeds for the benchmark programs compiled with these seven configurations. As expected, in most cases customization had a larger impact than class hierarchy analysis, speeding up programs by 48% to 87%. Combining class hierarchy analysis and naive customization (*cust+cha*) yielded only small additional benefits. However, the runtime benefits of customization came at the cost of a large increase in compiled code space and compile time. *Cust-1* executables were 2.5 to 3.5 times larger than *std* executables and *cust-k* executables are too large to actually be built using standard static compilation techniques; even in a system with dynamic compilation, *cust-k* would require compiling roughly 1.5 to 2 times as many methods as *std*. In contrast, *cha* executables were 12% to 21% smaller than *std*. By far, the best results were achieved by *selective,* which increased execution speed by 52% to 210% while increasing compiled code space by only 4% to 10%.

3.3 Class Hierarchy Analysis and Profile-Guided Receiver Class Prediction

Profile-guided receiver class prediction has been shown to substantially improve the performance of applications written in pure object-oriented languages. It is unclear whether or not adding class hierarchy analysis to a system that already performs profile-guided receiver class prediction would result in any significant improvements [Hölzle 94]. To examine this question, we utilized the following compiler configurations:

- ***std***: Standard intraprocedural optimizations as described in Section 3.1.
- ***cha***: Standard augmented by class hierarchy analysis

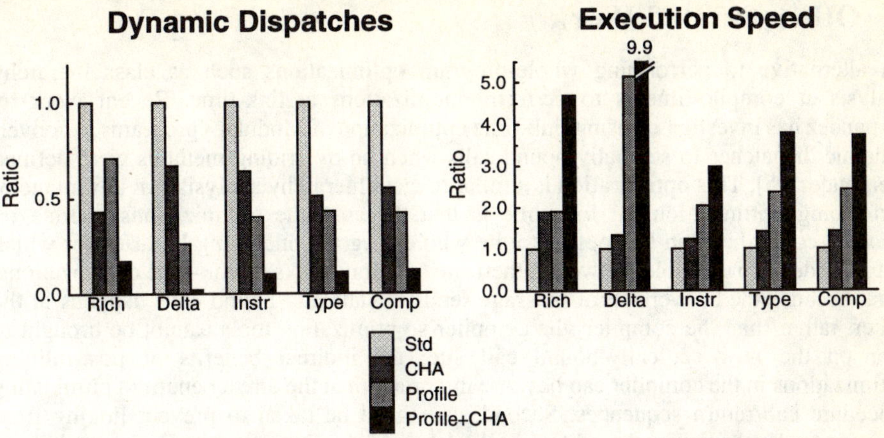

Figure 4: Number of dynamic dispatches and execution speed

- ***profile***: Standard augmented with profile-guided receiver class prediction.
- ***profile+cha***: Standard augmented with profile-guided receiver class prediction and class hierarchy analysis.

Figure 4 shows the normalized number of dynamic dispatches and execution speeds of the applications. These numbers show that profile-guided receiver class prediction is the most effective of the three techniques in isolation, improving application execution speeds by 90% to 410% over s*td*. However, augmenting profile-guided receiver class prediction with class hierarchy analysis (*profile+cha*) yielded surprisingly large additional improvements of 45% to 125% over *profile* alone. Part of this improvement can be explained by a reduction in the number of call sites at which the compiler, due to a lack of sufficient static class information, is forced to fall back on profile information and insert explicit class tests. However, the improvements can not solely be explained by this effect, since combining the two optimizations yields larger benefits than can be explained even by assuming that their benefits in isolation are completely additive. For example, in the Compiler benchmark, *cha* is 41% faster than *std* and *profile* is 142% faster than *std*. Multiplying these two speedups results in a projected speedup of 241% over *std,* which is smaller than the observed speedup of 272%. By examining the number of dynamic dispatches, we can see that it is not the case that *profile+cha* is able to eliminate more dispatches than the sum of *profile* and *cha* (in the Compiler benchmark, *cha* eliminated 45% of the dynamic dispatches present in *std* and *profile* eliminated 58%, but *profile+cha* only eliminated 88%). We believe that the large speedups observed in *profile+cha* are due to the increased effectiveness of other compiler optimizations, such as CSE and register allocation, that was enabled by the simplified control flow graphs produced by this configuration.

In our implementation of profile-guided receiver class prediction, we only insert class tests if the target method is a desirable candidate for inlining; if the target method is not going to be inlined, then we leave the call site unchanged. In the Richards benchmark, several of the frequently-called methods are too large to be inlined, but can be statically-bound by class hierarchy analysis. This explains why *profile* eliminated fewer dynamic dispatches than *cha* for the Richards benchmark.

4 Other Related Work

An alternative to performing whole-program optimizations such as class hierarchy analysis at compile-time is to perform optimizations at link-time. Recent work by Fernandez has investigated using link-time optimization of Modula-3 programs to convert dynamic dispatches to statically bound calls when no overriding methods were defined [Fernandez 95]. This optimization is similar to class hierarchy analysis. An advantage of performing optimizations at link-time is that, because the optimizations operate on machine code, they can be applied to the whole program, including libraries for which source code is unavailable. However, there are two drawbacks of link-time optimizations. First, because the conversion of message sends to statically-bound calls happens in the linker, rather than the compiler, the compiler's optimization tools cannot be brought to bear on the now statically-bound call site; the indirect benefits of post-inlining optimizations in the compiler can be more important than the direct benefit of eliminating procedure call/return sequences. Second, care must be taken to prevent linking from becoming a bottleneck in the edit-compile-debug cycle. For example, Fernandez's link-time optimizer for Modula-3 performs code generation from a machine-independent intermediate representation for the entire program at every link; Fernandez acknowledges that this design penalizes turnaround time for small programming changes. Additional link-time optimizations would only increase this penalty. In contrast, class hierarchy analysis coupled with a selective invalidation mechanism supports incremental recompilation, fast linking, and compile-time optimization of call sites where source code of target methods is available.

Srivastava has developed an algorithm to prune unreachable procedures from C++ programs at link-time [Srivastava 92]. Although the described algorithm is only used to prune code and not to optimize dynamic dispatches, it would be relatively simple to convert some virtual function calls into direct procedure calls using the basic infrastructure used to perform the procedure pruning.

Interprocedural class analysis algorithms are an important area of current research [Palsberg & Schwartzbach 91, Oxhøj *et al.* 92, Agesen *et al.* 93, Plevyak & Chien 94]. By examining the whole program and solving an interprocedural data flow problem to determine the set of classes that might be stored in each program variable, these algorithms can provide more accurate class sets than intraprocedural static class analysis or class hierarchy analysis. However, current interprocedural class analysis algorithms are relatively expensive to run, assume access to the source code of the entire program (including method bodies), and are not incremental in the face of programming changes. Nevertheless, as these algorithms mature, it will be interesting to compare the run-time benefits and compile-time costs of interprocedural class analysis against class hierarchy analysis and the other techniques examined in Section 3. Agesen and Hölzle have compared the effectiveness of profile-guided receiver class prediction alone to interprocedural class analysis alone for a suite of small-to-medium sized Self programs, but they did not report on the effectiveness of combining the two techniques [Agesen & Hölzle 95].

5 Conclusions

Class hierarchy analysis is a promising technique for eliminating dynamically-dispatched message sends automatically. Unlike language-level mechanisms such as non-virtual functions in C++ and sealed classes in Dylan, class hierarchy analysis improves performance while preserving the source-level semantics of message passing and the ability for clients to subclass any class. To integrate class hierarchy analysis effectively into existing static class analysis frameworks, we introduced the cone representation for a class and its subclasses and constructed applies-to sets for each method to support compile-time method lookup in the presence of cones and other unions of classes. Cones also provide a means for static type declarations to be integrated into static class analysis. Class hierarchy analysis imposes some requirements on the underlying programming environment, particularly to support incremental compilation, but these costs appear to be manageable in practice. These techniques have been implemented in the Vortex compiler for Cecil since the Spring of 1994. In this compiler class hierarchy analysis is always performed as a matter of course, and intermodule dependency links support selective recompilation. The Vortex compiler is itself a 52,000-line Cecil program, undergoing rapid continuous development and extension, providing some evidence that class hierarchy analysis is compatible with a program development environment.

Class hierarchy analysis is only one of a number of optimizations proposed for object-oriented languages; others include method specialization and profile-guided receiver class prediction. We implemented and measured these techniques separately and in combination, on a collection of medium-to-large Cecil programs, to try to determine which techniques are most effective and where the techniques could profitably be combined. Of the techniques that we examined, profile-guided class prediction was the most effective in isolation at improving program performance. However, performing class hierarchy analysis in addition to profile-guided class prediction provided substantial performance improvements over profile-guided class prediction alone. Class hierarchy analysis consumed far less compiled code space than customization, but with smaller performance gains; the best results are achieved by a profile-guided selective specialization algorithm integrated with class hierarchy analysis.

There are two interesting future directions for this work. First, it would be very interesting to extend this performance study to include interprocedural static class analysis algorithms as they mature. Second, the effectiveness of these techniques in pure object-oriented languages like Cecil has been demonstrated, but their effectiveness and relative value when applied to hybrid, statically-typed object-oriented languages such as C++ and Modula-3 remains an open question. We are in the process of porting compiler front-ends for C++ and Modula-3 to the Vortex optimizing compiler back-end in order to be able to perform such experiments.

Acknowledgments

We thank William Pugh for his help in devising a more efficient tuple difference implementation. Charles Garrett performed many of the initial studies of profile-guided receiver class prediction. Vitaly Shmatikov, Ben Teitelbaum, Tina Wong, and Matthew Parker have contributed to the Cecil implementation.

This research is supported in part by an NSF Research Initiation Award (contract number CCR-9210990), an NSF Young Investigator Award (contract number CCR-9457767), a grant from the Office of Naval Research (contract number N00014-94-1-1136), and gifts from Sun Microsystems, IBM, and Pure Software. Stephen North and Eleftherios Koutsofios of AT&T Bell Laboratories provided us with `dot`, a program for automatic graph layout.

Other papers on the Cecil programming language and the Vortex optimizing compiler are available via anonymous `ftp` from cs.washington.edu:/pub/chambers and via the World Wide Web URL http://www.cs.washington.edu/research/projects/cecil.

References

[Agesen & Hölzle 95] Ole Agesen and Urs Hölzle. Type Feedback vs. Concrete Type Analysis: A Comparison of Optimization Techniques for Object-Oriented Languages. Technical Report TRCS 95-04, Department of Computer Science, University of California, Santa Barbara, March 1995.

[Agesen *et al.* 93] Ole Agesen, Jens Palsberg, and Michael I. Schwartzback. Type Inference of SELF: Analysis of Objects with Dynamic and Multiple Inheritance. In *Proceedings ECOOP '93*, July 1993.

[Agrawal *et al.* 91] Rakesh Agrawal, Linda G. DeMichiel, and Bruce G. Lindsay. Static Type Checking of Multi-Methods. In *Proceedings OOPSLA '91*, pages 113–128, November 1991. Published as ACM SIGPLAN Notices, volume 26, number 11.

[AK *et al.* 89] Hassan Aït-Kaci, Robert Boyer, Patrick Lincoln, and Roger Nasr. Efficient Implementation of Lattice Operations. *ACM Transactions on Programming Languages and Systems*, 11(1):115–146, January 1989.

[Bobrow *et al.* 88] D. G. Bobrow, L. G. DeMichiel, R. P. Gabriel, S. E. Keene, G. Kiczales, and D. A. Moon. Common Lisp Object System Specification X3J13. *SIGPLAN Notices*, 28(Special Issue), September 1988.

[Calder & Grunwald 94] Brad Calder and Dirk Grunwald. Reducing Indirect Function Call Overhead in C++ Programs. In *Conference Record of POPL '94: 21st ACM SIGPLAN-SIGACT Symposium on Principles of Programming Languages*, pages 397–408, Portland, Oregon, January 1994.

[Caseau 93] Yves Caseau. Efficient Handling of Multiple Inheritance Hierarchies. In *Proceedings OOPSLA'93*, pages 271–287, October 1993. Published as ACM SIGPLAN Notices, volume 28, number 10.

[Chambers & Ungar 89] Craig Chambers and David Ungar. Customization: Optimizing Compiler Technology for Self, A Dynamically-Typed Object-Oriented Programming Language. *SIGPLAN Notices*, 24(7):146–160, July 1989. In *Proceedings of the ACM SIGPLAN '89 Conference on Programming Language Design and Implementation.*

[Chambers & Ungar 90] Craig Chambers and David Ungar. Iterative Type Analysis and Extended Message Splitting: Optimizing Dynamically-Typed Object-Oriented Programs. *SIGPLAN Notices*, 25(6):150–164, June 1990. In *Proceedings of the ACM SIGPLAN '90 Conference on Programming Language Design and Implementation.*

[Chambers & Ungar 91] Craig Chambers and David Ungar. Making Pure Object-Oriented Languages Practical. In *Proceedings OOPSLA '91*, pages 1–15, November 1991. Published as ACM SIGPLAN Notices, volume 26, number 11.

[Chambers 92] Craig Chambers. Object-Oriented Multi-Methods in Cecil. In O. Lehrmann Madsen, editor, *Proceedings ECOOP '92*, LNCS 615, pages 33–56, Utrecht, The Netherlands, July 1992. Springer-Verlag.

[Chambers 93] Craig Chambers. The Cecil Language: Specification and Rationale. Technical Report TR-93-03-05, Department of Computer Science and Engineering. University of Washington, March 1993.

[Chambers *et al.* 89] Craig Chambers, David Ungar, and Elgin Lee. An Efficient Implementation of SELF – a Dynamically-Typed Object-Oriented Language Based on Prototypes. In *Proceedings OOPSLA '89*, pages 49–70, October 1989. Published as ACM SIGPLAN Notices, volume 24, number 10.

[Chambers *et al.* 95] Craig Chambers, Jeffrey Dean, and David Grove. A Framework for Selective Recompilation in the Presence of Complex Intermodule Dependencies. In *17th International Conference on Software Engineering*, Seattle, WA, April 1995.

[Dean *et al.* 95] Jeffrey Dean, Craig Chambers, and David Grove. Selective Specialization for Object-Oriented Languages. *SIGPLAN Notices*, June 1995. In *Proceedings of the ACM SIGPLAN '95 Conference on Programming Language Design and Implementation.*

[Deutsch & Schiffman 84] L. Peter Deutsch and Allan M. Schiffman. Efficient Implementation of the Smalltalk-80 System. In *Conference Record of the Eleventh Annual ACM Symposium on Principles of Programming Languages*, pages 297–302, Salt Lake City, Utah, January 1984.

[Dyl92] Dylan, an Object-Oriented Dynamic Language, April 1992. Apple Computer.

[Fernandez 95] Mary Fernandez. Simple and Effective Link-time Optimization of Modula-3 Programs. *SIGPLAN Notices*, June 1995. In *Proceedings of the ACM SIGPLAN '95 Conference on Programming Language Design and Implementation.*

[Gabriel *et al.* 91] Richard P. Gabriel, Jon L. White, and Daniel G. Bobrow. CLOS: Integrating Object-Oriented and Functional Programming. *Communications of the ACM*, 34(9):28–38, September 1991.

[Garrett *et al.* 94] Charlie Garrett, Jeffrey Dean, David Grove, and Craig Chambers. Measurement and Application of Dynamic Receiver Class Distributions. Technical Report UW-CS 94-03-05, University of Washington, March 1994.

[Harbison 92] Samuel P. Harbison. *Modula-3*. Prentice Hall, Englewood Cliffs, NJ, 1992.

[Hölzle & Ungar 94] Urs Hölzle and David Ungar. Optimizing Dynamically-Dispatched Calls with Run-Time Type Feedback. *SIGPLAN Notices*, 29(6):326–336, June 1994. In *Proceedings of the ACM SIGPLAN '94 Conference on Programming Language Design and Implementation.*

[Hölzle 94] Urs Hölzle. *Adaptive Optimization for Self: Reconciling High Performance with Exploratory Programming*. PhD thesis, Stanford University, August 1994.

[Johnson 92] Ralph Johnson. Documenting Frameworks Using Patterns. In *Proceedings OOPSLA '92*, pages 63–76, October 1992. Published as ACM SIGPLAN Notices, volume 27, number 10.

[Kilian 88] Michael F. Kilian. Why Trellis/Owl Runs Fast. Unpublished manuscript, March 1988.

[Lea 90] Doug Lea. Customization in C++. In *Proceedings of the 1990 Usenix C++ Conference*, San Francisco, CA, April 1990.

[Lim & Stolcke 91] Chu-Cheow Lim and Andreas Stolcke. Sather Language Design and Performance Evaluation. Technical Report TR 91-034, International Computer Science Institute, May 1991.

[Linton *et al.* 89] M. A. Linton, J. M. Vlissides, and P. R. Calder. Composing User Interfaces with InterViews. *IEEE Computer*, 2(2):8–22, February 1989.

[Nelson 91] Greg Nelson. *Systems Programming with Modula-3*. Prentice Hall, Englewood Cliffs, NJ, 1991.

[Omohundro 94] Stephen Omohundro. The Sather 1.0 Specification. Unpublished manuscript from International Computer Science Institute, Berkeley, CA, 1994.

[Oxhøj *et al*. 92] Nicholas Oxhøj, Jens Palsberg, and Michael I. Schwartzbach. Making Type Inference Practical. In O. Lehrmann Madsen, editor, *Proceedings ECOOP '92*, LNCS 615, pages 329–349, Utrecht, The Netherlands, July 1992. Springer-Verlag.

[Palsberg & Schwartzbach 91] Jens Palsberg and Michael I. Schwartzbach. Object-Oriented Type Inference. In *Proceedings OOPSLA '91*, pages 146–161, November 1991. Published as ACM SIGPLAN Notices, volume 26, number 11.

[Palsberg & Schwartzbach 94] Jens Palsberg and Michael I. Schwartzbach. *Object-Oriented Type Systems*. John Wiley & Sons, 1994.

[Plevyak & Chien 94] John Plevyak and Andrew A. Chien. Precise Concrete Type Inference for Object-Oriented Languages. In *Proceedings OOPSLA '94*, pages 324–340, Portland, Oregon, October 1994.

[Schaffert *et al*. 85] Craig Schaffert, Topher Cooper, and Carrie Wilpolt. Trellis Object-Based Environment, Language Reference Manual. Technical Report DEC-TR-372, Digital Equipment Corporation, November 1985.

[Schaffert *et al*. 86] Craig Schaffert, Topher Cooper, Bruce Bullis, Mike Killian, and Carrie Wilpolt. An Introduction to Trellis/Owl. In *Proceedings OOPSLA '86*, pages 9–16, November 1986. Published as ACM SIGPLAN Notices, volume 21, number 11.

[Srivastava 92] Amitabh Srivastava. Unreachable Procedures in Object-Oriented Programming. *ACM Letters on Programming Languages and Systems*, 1(4):355–364, December 1992.

[Stroustrup 91] Bjarne Stroustrup. *The C++ Programming Language (second edition)*. Addision-Wesley, Reading, MA, 1991.

[Szypersky *et al*. 93] Clemens Szypersky, Stephen Omohundro, and Stephan Murerzw. Engineering a Programming Language: The Type and Class System of Sather. Technical Report 93-064, International Computer Science Institute, Berkeley, CA, 1993.

Appendix A Raw Data

Table 2: Execution Times (seconds)

Configuration	Richards	Deltablue	InstSched	Typechecker	Compiler
unopt	13.410	31.830	25.080	294	2314
std	1.780	11.880	11.870	113	1176
cha-ct-only	1.830	11.490	11.960	110	1152
cha	0.940	8.940	9.670	81	834
cust-1	0.950	7.620	8.710	73	735
cha-1	1.060	9.160	10.030	83	852
cust-*k*	0.950	8.050	8.870	73	712
cust-*k*+cha	0.910	6.220	8.160	71	700
selective	0.560	3.810	6.850	68	650
profile	0.930	2.310	5.830	48	484
profile+cha	0.380	1.200	4.000	40	316

Table 3: Dynamically Dispatched Message Sends (x1000)

Configuration	Richards	Deltablue	InstSched	Typechecker	Compiler
unopt	10,006	13,461	7,505	75,053	470,488
std	3,697	6,980	4,676	36,131	231,659
cha-ct-only	3,697	6,980	4,664	36,028	231,529
cha	1,583	4,668	3,004	18,566	128,400
cust-1	1,414	3,874	2,655	19,301	129,729
cha-1	1,583	4,668	3,192	20,632	143,578
cust-*k*	1,414	3,874	2,637	19,341	129,701
cust-*k*+cha	1,414	3,624	2,516	19,156	125,095
selective	1,278	3,021	1,969	15,478	101,929
profile	619	159	1,890	15,426	98,435
profile+cha	545	157	474	3,902	28,640

Objects with Multiple Most Specific Classes*

Elisa Bertino [1] *Giovanna Guerrini* [2]

[1] Dipartimento di Scienze dell'Informazione
Università di Milano - Milano, Italy
bertino@hermes.mc.dsi.unimi.it

[2] Dipartimento di Informatica e Scienze dell'Informazione
Università di Genova - Genova, Italy
guerrini@disi.unige.it

Abstract. In most object-oriented data models objects must belong to a single most specific class. This exclusive link between an instance and a class is often not adequate to model real-world situations. In this paper, we present an approach where objects can belong to several most specific classes. We formally address how the resulting conflicts can be handled, both for structural and behavioral components of objects. In particular, we formalize a notion of context and characterize the state of an object in terms of the set of its most specific classes. Moreover, we discuss two different dispatching approaches, one allowing context-dependent behavior, the other one ensuring behavior identity.

1 Introduction

One of the advantages of object-oriented data models [3] compared to other data models is that they support a direct representation of real-world domains. These models can represent the structure as well as the behavior of real-world entities. Most object-oriented data models are based on the notion of class; objects with the same structure and behavior are grouped into classes, which are in turn organized in inheritance hierarchies. In most models, real-world entities are represented as instances of the most specific class in which they can be classified[3]. Thus, real-world entities are partitioned into a set of disjoint classes.

However, when modeling application domains, objects are often found that naturally belong to several most specific classes. Consider as an example, a class *person*, whose instances can be classified along orthogonal dimensions, such as *students*, *nobles*, *males* and *females* (the corresponding hierarchy is illustrated in Figure 1(a)). According to the intuitive semantics, a person can be both a student, a noble and a female at the same time. Thus, the object representing this person does not have a unique most specific class, rather it has a set of most specific classes.

* Work partially supported by the EEC under ESPRIT Project 6333 IDEA.

[3] An object o can belong to a set of classes S. We call an element of S that has no subclass in S a *most specific* class of object o.

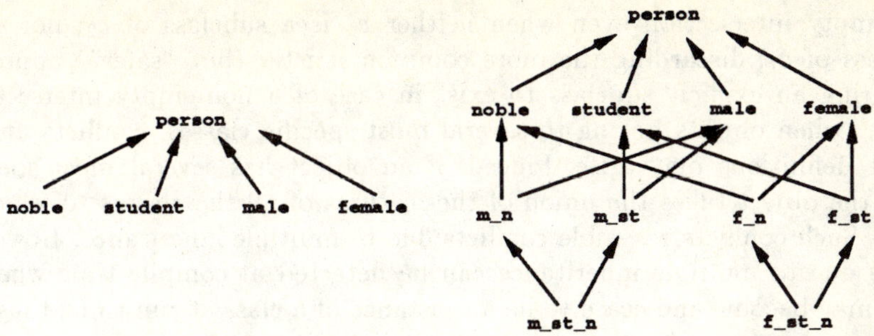

(a) (b)

Fig. 1. (a) Example of class hierarchy, extended in (b) with some meaningful subclasses

Although the above situation can be easily represented in a model with multiple inheritance by defining a subclass (say *noble_student_female*) of all the involved classes, this solution may lead to a lot of artificial subclasses, sometimes referred to as *intersection classes* [15]. Referring to the hierarchy above, the meaningful subclasses of the *person* class are six (see Figure 1(b)). Thus, this approach can lead to a combinatorial explosion of sparsely populated classes, whose sole purpose is to allow an instance to have multiple most specific classes, without adding new state or behavior. Another problem with the multiple inheritance approach is that it only provides a single behavioral context for an object [14]. Indeed name conflicts among features in the superclasses are solved once for ever in the subclass definition (for example by imposing an order on superclasses, or with an explicit qualification mechanism) and the selected feature is the only one always considered whatever the context of the object reference is.

Moreover, there are systems supporting derived (or predicative) classes. That is, classes whose extents are not explicitly manipulated; rather those classes are implicitly populated in that a population predicate is associated with the class specifying sufficient and necessary conditions for an object to belong to the extent of the class. In such models, it is difficult to ensure that an object belong to a unique most specific class, because it depends on the population predicates being disjoint. Referring to the above example, we may consider male, female and student as derived classes, provided that class person has two attributes `sex` and `profession`. In this case classes male, female and student are defined as derived subclasses with population predicates, respectively, `sex =' male'`, `sex =' female'` and `profession =' student'`. In such a situation if a person is inserted in the object database, the insertion may result in an object belonging to several most specific classes and the user may even not realize this fact.

In our model, we take a different approach in that the extents of classes, that are not related via a subclass relationship, are not necessarily disjoint. Thus, in our model, two classes c_1 and c_2, with a common superclass c, may have a non-empty intersection even when neither c_1 is a subclass of c_2, nor c_2 is a subclass of c_1, discarding the more common stricter (but "safer") approach of requiring an explicit subclass to exist in case of a non-empty intersection. However, when objects belong to several most specific classes, conflicts among different definitions may arise. Indeed, if an object has several most specific classes, the object takes the union of the features of all the classes to which it belongs. Such conflicts resemble conflicts due to multiple inheritance. However, conflicts due to multiple inheritance can be detected at compile time whereas objects may become and cease to be an instance of a class at run time, thus the situation is more complicate for multiple class direct membership[4].

In this paper we address the issues arising from multiple direct membership in the context of the Chimera data model [6, 12]. A way of solving conflicts is to impose that each object, though having several most specific classes, has a single *preferred* class. The binding between an object and its preferred class can be either fixed or context-dependent. A fixed binding only depends on the set of most specific classes of the object[5]. By contrast, a context-dependent binding also depends on the expression in which the object reference is contained. In a fixed preferred class approach, the preferred class can be determined by imposing a total ordering on classes, or by allowing each object to specify an ordering on the classes to which it belongs[6], or finally by specifying a reference class for each feature in the instance (with an explicit qualification mechanism). Context-dependent preferred class approach leads to a more more flexible language and models both context-dependent access restrictions and context-specific behavior.

In our approach, the context-dependent preferred class is determined by the static type of the object in the expression containing the object reference. Indeed, each object reference in each Chimera expression is assigned a single static type. We formalize the notion of context of an object reference in terms of static types. Then, we discuss what the state of an object is (in terms of attributes and attribute domains) depending on the set of its most specific classes. We analyze conflicts arising in attribute accesses and method invocations. As far as attribute access is concerned, we can disambiguate each access by taking into account only the context of the object reference. By contrast, when considering method dispatching, if we want to ensure a notion of ***most specific behavior***, the context alone is not enough to properly dispatch the method. Thus, we propose and compare two different dispatching approaches: the first approach ensures context-dependent behavior, the other one ensures behavior identity.

Therefore, the main contributions of this work can be summarized as follows: *i)* formalization of the problem of objects belonging to several most specific

---

[4] An object belonging to a class c is a *direct member* of c if it does not belong to any subclass of c. An object is a *member* of a class c if it is a direct member of c or is a direct member of some subclass of c.

[5] A fixed binding does not mean that the binding is immutable for the object lifetime, since an object may acquire and loose classes dynamically.

[6] A reasonable ordering could be the one determined by the acquisition order of classes, in such a way that the most recently acquired behavior prevails (as in Fibonacci [2]).

classes, which has not been addressed on a formal basis yet; *ii)* proposal and comparison of two different dispatching approaches for messages sent to objects with multiple most specific classes.

The remainder of this paper is organized as follows. In Subsection 1.1 we survey related works. We introduce the relevant characteristics of the Chimera object-oriented data model in Section 2. Section 3 discusses issues related to the inheritance hierarchy. The following sections are specifically devoted to object handling with multiple most specific classes, being Section 4 concerned with structural aspects and Section 5 with behavioral ones (dispatching). Finally, Section 6 concludes the paper.

1.1 Related works

Several papers have addressed the relevance of a more flexible binding between objects and classes, but only few of them elaborate on how to solve name conflicts or how to handle dispatching when objects are members of several most specific classes.

The restriction that an object must be associated with a single most specific type was first pointed out in the framework of the Iris OODBMS [9]. In Iris, arbitrary types can be added to an object. Iris, however, does not support context-dependent behavior since the entire set of types of an object is visible in every context. To avoid conflicts, two different types of an object must not have different methods with the same name.

Stein [16] discusses the motivations for supporting multiple direct membership, but her approach reduces an instance of multiple classes to an instance of a (virtual) subclass-by-multiple-inheritance of its classes. She did not discuss which policy is adopted for conflict resolution. Moreover, no context-dependent behavior can be supported by her approach.

The notions of context-dependent access restriction and context-dependent behavior are by contrast stressed in object data models supporting roles [2, 11, 14]. In these models, two different hierarchies are provided: a class (type) hierarchy and a role hierarchy. These different hierarchies make the model more complex, in that one must choose which features must be modeled as a class and which as a role. Moreover in these approaches, it is not always enforced that (one of) the most specific behavior(s) of the object is exhibited. Among these works, only the work by Albano et Al.[2] deals with the problem of method dispatching for objects with multiple roles. Dispatching is based on the following rules: *i)* the most specific behavior prevails (unless a strict interpretation of messages is explicitly required); *ii)* the most recently acquired behavior prevails. Thus, this approach to dispatching shows some similarities with our preferred class dispatching approach (cf. Section 5.1).

Another approach relaxing the strict object-most specific class link has been proposed by Sciore [15]. In his approach, real-world entities are modeled as object hierarchies where inheritance is determined on a per-object basis, thus merging class-based and prototype-based approaches. When a message is sent to an object, it either directly responds to the message or it delegates the message to its parents. The behavior observed thus depends on the arrangement of the object hierarchy. However, this approach lacks object identity semantics and strong typing.

2 Reference object model

Chimera [6] is a novel database language designed with the aim to integrate active and deductive rules with object-oriented features[7]. Chimera integrates an object-oriented data model, a declarative query language based on deductive rules and an active rule language for reactive processing. The Chimera model is a rather classical object-oriented data model with operations and inheritance; in addition to objects, the model also supports the notion of value classes (extensionally populated) and of views (populated by means of passive rules). The signature of objects describes not only the state (attributes) and the operations for accessing and manipulating object instances, but also integrity constraints and triggers; in addition, class attributes, operations, and constraints collectively apply to classes. The Chimera language integrates object operations (used for manipulating objects), passive rules (used for expressing derived classes and views) and active rules (used for expressing database triggers). In what follows we recall only the aspects of the Chimera formal model relevant for this work. We refer the reader to [12] for a complete definition of the model.

The set of Chimera types $\mathcal{T}$ (that are collection of values) is defined as the union of value types ($\mathcal{VT}$) and object types ($\mathcal{OT}$). Object types are class names and their instances are object identifiers. Value types are defined as follows. They can be either basic domains or structured types built by applying the set, list or record constructors. Named types (possibly constrained) and value classes are also value types.

Definition 1 *[12] The set of Chimera value types $\mathcal{VT}$ is inductively defined as follows*

- *the predefined basic value types (integer, real, bool, character) are value types*
- *if T is a value type or an object type then $list-of(T)$ and $set-of(T)$ are value types*
- *if $T_1,\ldots,T_n$ are value types or object types and $a_1,\ldots,a_n$ are distinct attribute names in $\mathcal{AN}$, then $record-of(a_1 : T_1,\ldots,a_n : T_n)$ is a value type*
- *if T is a value type and Tn is a type name, and Tn is declared as a name for T through a declaration $Tn : T$, then Tn is a (named) value type*
- *if T is a value type, Tn is a type name, and R is a set of rules, and Tn is declared as $Tn : T$ constraint R, then Tn is a (constrained) value type*
- *if T is a value type, Tn is a type name, and S is a set of values, and Tn is declared as $Tn : T$ extent S, then Tn is a value type, which we call value class.* □

[7] A Chimera is a monster of Greek mythology with lion's head, a goat's body and a serpent's tail; each of them represents one of the three components of the language.

We recall from [12] the notion of extension, that is, the set of legal values of each Chimera type. The extension of a type depends on the explicit extent for such types, like value classes and object classes, that have one. To model these extents we introduce a function $\pi = (\pi_V, \pi_O)$, such that π_V assigns a set of values to each value class (*value assignment*), and π_O assigns a set of object identifiers to each object class (*oid assignment*)[8].

Definition 2 *(Type extension) [12]. The extension of the type T under the assignment π (denoted as $[\![T]\!]_\pi$), is defined as follows:*

- $null \in [\![T]\!]_\pi, \forall T \in \mathcal{T}$
- $[\![D_i]\!]_\pi = ED_i$, *for D_i basic domain (ED_i is postulated)*
- *if* $c \in \mathcal{OT}$, $[\![c]\!]_\pi = \pi(c)$
- $[\![set-of(T)]\!]_\pi = 2^{[\![T]\!]_\pi}$, *where 2^S denotes the power set of the set S*
- $[\![list-of(T)]\!]_\pi = \{[v_1, \ldots, v_n] \mid n \geq 0, v_i \in [\![T]\!]_\pi \ \forall i, 1 \leq i \leq n\}$
- $[\![record-of(a_1 : T_1, \ldots, a_n : T_n)]\!]_\pi = \{(a_1 : v_1, \ldots, a_n : v_n) \mid a_i \in \mathcal{AN}, v_i \in [\![T_i]\!]_\pi \ \forall i, 1 \leq i \leq n\}$
- $[\![Tn]\!]_\pi = [\![type(Tn)]\!]_\pi$ *if Tn is an unconstrained named type and type(Tn) is the type denoted by the name*
- $[\![Tn]\!]_\pi = \{v \mid v \in [\![type(Tn)]\!]_\pi$, *v meets constr(Tn)*$\}$ *if Tn is a constrained value type and constr(Tn) denotes its constraint*
- $[\![VC]\!]_\pi = \pi(VC)$ *if VC is a value class.* □

A class[9], in addition to having an extent, is characterized by a structural and a behavioral component. Given a class c, $A(c)$ denotes the set of attributes of that class. Furthermore, $dom(a, c)$, for $a \in A(c)$, denotes the domain of attribute a in class c. Similarly, for the behavioral component of classes, $M(c)$ denotes the set of methods of class c and $sign(m, c)$, for $m \in M(c)$, denotes the signature of method m in class c.

Let $\mathcal{C}$ denote the set of all classes. The user-defined ISA hierarchy is represented through a partial order $\leq_{ISA} \subseteq \mathcal{C} \times \mathcal{C}$ on classes. Moreover, $c <_{ISA} c'$ denotes the relation $c \leq_{ISA} c' \wedge c \neq c'$[10]. In the following, $ISA^*(c) = \{c' \mid c \leq_{ISA} c'\}$ denotes the set of c superclasses, and

$ISA(c) = ISA^*(c) \setminus \bigcup_{c' \text{ such that } c <_{ISA} c'} ISA^*(c')$

denotes the set of direct superclasses of c.

Definition 3 *(Most specific class). Given a set of classes C, ms(C) denotes the set $\{c \mid c \in C \wedge \nexists\, c' \in C$ such that $c' <_{ISA} c\}$. A class c is said a most specific class in C if $c \in ms(C)$.* □

Definition 4 *(Objects). An object is a triple $o = (i, v, CS)$, where*

- *i is the object identifier of o*

---

[8] Thus, if c is a class, $\pi(c)$ is the set of the identifiers of objects members of c.

[9] With the term *class* we refer to object classes, that is classes whose instances are objects, as opposed to value classes, that are collections of values.

[10] In what follows, given an order $\leq$, $<$ denotes the non-reflexive relation obtained from the order $\leq$, that is, $c_1 < c_2$ iff $c_1 \leq c_2$ and $c_1 \neq c_2$.

– *v is a value, called state of o*
– *$CS \subseteq \mathcal{C}$ is the set of most specific classes to which o belongs, that is $CS = ms(\{c \mid c \in \mathcal{C} \wedge i \in [\![c]\!]\})$.* □

Each object is required to be an instance of (at least) a class; therefore, $o \downarrow 3 \neq \emptyset$[11] must hold. Moreover, all the classes in $o \downarrow 3$ are most specific with respect to the others, that is $ms(o \downarrow 3) = o \downarrow 3$.

Starting from the ISA hierarchy on classes and from the inheritance relationships on value types due to constrained value types and value classes, which we suppose expressed by an order $\leq_{ISA_V}$ [12], a subtype relation $\leq_{\mathcal{T}} \subseteq \mathcal{T} \times \mathcal{T}$ is defined as follows.

Definition 5 *(Subtype relation) [12]. Given two types $T_1, T_2 \in \mathcal{T}$, T_2 is a subtype of T_1 (denoted as $T_2 \leq_{\mathcal{T}} T_1$) iff at least one of the following conditions holds:*

– *$T_1 = T_2$ or T_1 and T_2 unconstrained value types with $type(T_1) = type(T_2)$*
– *$T_2 \leq_{ISA_V} T_1$ or $T_2 \leq_{ISA} T_1$*
– *$T_2 = set-of(T_2')$, $T_1 = set-of(T_1')$ and $T_2' \leq_{\mathcal{T}} T_1'$*
– *$T_2 = list-of(T_2')$, $T_1 = list-of(T_1')$ and $T_2' \leq_{\mathcal{T}} T_1'$*
– *$T_1 = record{-}of(a_1 : T_1', \ldots, a_n : T_n')$, $T_2 = record{-}of(a_1 : T_1'', \ldots, a_n : T_n'')$ and for each i, $1 \leq i \leq n$, $T_i' \leq_{\mathcal{T}} T_i''$.* □

$\leq_{\mathcal{T}}$ is a partial order. The notions of *least upper bound* (lub, $\sqcup$) and of *greatest lower bound* (glb, $\sqcap$) with respect to this order have been discussed in [12]. Note that since $(\mathcal{T}, \leq_{\mathcal{T}})$ is a DAG and is not a lattice, *lub*s and *glb*s do not always exist.

2.1 Static and dynamic types

Chimera is a strongly typed database language. When writing a Chimera expression, one must explicitly state the type of each variable used in the expression. This is accomplished in Chimera by using class formulas. Indeed, in Chimera class formulas are used as a typing mechanism. Class formulas are built from class or type names representing unary predicate symbols. Thus, to state in an expression that a variable X is of type T the class formula $T(X)$ is added to the expression. The class formula $T(X)$ has also the effect of stating that $X \in [\![T]\!]$, thus providing a domain for the evaluation of the expression.

The scope of a type assignment for a variable is that of an expression. Each Chimera expression must contain a class formula for each variable. Thus, each variable is associated with a unique type, with respect to which type checking is performed. Declaring a variable X of type T influences type checking in that the only features available for X are those of type T. That is, type checking of the expression, in which X appears, is done regarding X as a term of type T. We say that T is the *static type* of variable X, because it is the type with respect to which the static type checking of the expression containing X is done.

[11] $o \downarrow n$ denotes the n-th component of a tuple o.

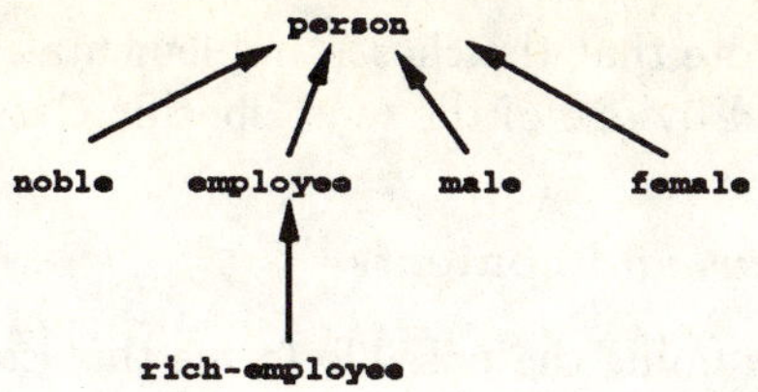

Fig. 2. Class hierarchy of Example 1

At execution time variable X is instantiated with a value of type T. Note that when T is an object type, the variable is instantiated with the identifier of an object member of the class identified by T. This means that the variable may also be instantiated with the identifier of an object which is a direct member of a subclass T' of that class. T' is said to be a *dynamic type* of variable X. However, since we consider objects possibly belonging to several most specific classes, the dynamic type of a variable denoting an object is, in general, not unique. Thus a variable is characterized by a set of dynamic types. The only constraint on those dynamic types is that they must have a common ancestor in the inheritance hierarchy. Moreover, the static type T of the variable denoting the object must be a subtype of this ancestor. Finally at least one dynamic type must be a subtype of the static one. These relationships are stated by the following rule.

Rule 1: Relationship between the static type and the dynamic types of objects

Let $\mathcal{C}$ be a set of classes with the partial order $\leq_{ISA}$. Let $t^s(X)$ be the static type of an object reference X. Let o be an object to which X is instantiated at run-time, and let $o \downarrow 3$ be the set of dynamic types of o. The following relationships hold:

1. $\exists c \in o \downarrow 3$ such that $c \leq_{ISA} t^s(X)$
2. $\exists c \in \mathcal{C}$ such that $\forall c' \in o \downarrow 3 \;\; c' \leq_{ISA} c \wedge t^s(X) \leq_{ISA} c$[12]. □

These relationships between static and dynamic types of an object hold for all kinds of object references, not only for object-denoting variables.

Example 1 Referring to the inheritance hierarchy of Figure 2, consider a variable X declared of type `employee`. At run-time variable X can be instantiated with an object o such that $o \downarrow 3 =$ {`female`, `rich-employee`, `noble`}. The above relationships between $t^s(X) =$ `employee` and $o \downarrow 3$ hold. ◇

The static type of an object is not only exploited to restrict access to a particular context, but may also determine a context-specific behavior. Dynamic types are used for choosing the appropriate method definition to be used on the

[12] Due to the properties of Chimera inheritance hierarchies (cf. Section 3) this is equivalent to the statement that each class in $o \downarrow 3$ and $t^s(X)$ belong to the same strongly connected component $\mathcal{H}_i$ of the inheritance DAG.

object denoted by X. Note that the chosen implementation must always be the implementation provided by one of the most specific classes of the object.

2.2 Object references and contexts

In this subsection we examine the possible forms that can be used in Chimera to denote an object and, for each of them, we show that it is possible in each expression to derive a unique *context* or static type for each expression denoting an object (object reference). The context of an object reference can be derived from the types declared for the variables in the expression and from schema information.

Conceptually, objects are referenced through their identifiers. However, according to the Chimera syntax, object identifiers are regarded as a system feature and they are not accessible by the user. Thus, objects can be denoted by variables, or they can be indirectly denoted by path expressions (containing attribute accesses and method invocations) starting from an object-denoting variable. Thus, an object reference can have one of the following forms:

- an object-typed variable;
- an attribute access $e.a$ where e is an object reference and a is an attribute name;
- a method invocation $e.m(e_1, \ldots, e_n)$ where e is an object reference, m is a method name and $e_1, \ldots, e_n$ are expressions denoting the parameters of the invocation and can be either object references or values.

For the sake of conciseness, we do not address here the detailed forms of values we support in Chimera (basic values, structured values with set, list and record constructors) nor the constructs of record and list field selection. The complete syntax of Chimera expressions is presented in [12].

Since a unique type T is explicitly associated with each variable in each expression (through the class formula mechanism), the static type or context of each variable is known to be T. To deduce the context of object references which are path expressions consisting of attribute accesses and method invocations, we use the following rule. The context derivation rule is expressed through two inference rules[13] to be instantiated letting the metavariable T varying on the set of object types $\mathcal{OT}$ and the metavariable e varying on the set of object references.

Rule 2: Context derivation rule

$$\frac{e : T \quad a \in A(T) \quad dom(a, T) = T'}{e.a : T'} \; T \in \mathcal{OT}$$

$$\frac{e : T \quad m \in M(T) \quad sign(m, T) = T_1 \times \ldots \times T_n \rightarrow T' \quad \forall i, 1 \leq i \leq n, e_i : T_i}{e.m(e_1, \ldots, e_n) : T'} \; T \in \mathcal{OT}$$

□

[13] The meaning of these inference rules is the following: if the conditions in the rule premises (the upper part of the rule) are satisfied, then the rule consequence (the lower part of the rule) can be inferred.

It can be easily shown that, if each value is associated with a unique type, the above rule assigns a unique type to each object reference. Since Chimera typing rules assign a unique type to each value, and since, as deduced above, the context of a variable is uniquely determined, the following result holds.

Proposition 1 *Given an expression, each object reference contained in the expression has a unique context in this expression.*

Example 2 Consider a class c such that $dom(a,c) = c_1$, $dom(b,c) = c_2$ and $sign(m,c) = c_1 \times c_2 \rightarrow c$. The context of the object reference $X.m(X.a, X.b).a$ in an expression containing the class formula $c(X)$ is c_1. ◇

3 Inheritance hierarchies

Chimera supports multiple inheritance. However the constraint is imposed that for multiple inheritance a common ancestor must exist. Therefore a class c can be defined as a subclass of classes c_1 and c_2 only if $ISA^*(c_1) \cap ISA^*(c_2) \neq \emptyset$.

In Chimera inheritance hierarchies are DAGs characterized by a certain number of strongly connected components. Moreover, each strongly connected component of the DAG is characterized by a single node without incoming edges, which we call *root* of the strongly connected component. Indeed, we do not impose the existence of a common root (as an `object` class) of the entire hierarchy, rather the hierarchy is partitioned into multiple strongly connected components, and each component has a single root. Note that an object can belong to several most specific classes only if the classes belong to the same strongly connected component in the DAG, that is, if they have a common ancestor.

The sets of oids in different strongly connected components are therefore disjoint. Consider a set of root classes $c_1, \ldots, c_m$, then Ext_i, for $i = 1, \ldots, m$ denotes the extent of c_i ($[\![c_i]\!]$) which is the extent of the whole strongly connected component rooted at c_i. We may think of the set of all classes $\mathcal{C}$ as partitioned in $\mathcal{H}_1, \ldots, \mathcal{H}_m$, that is, the m distinct hierarchies (corresponding to the m strongly connected components) we have on $\mathcal{C}$.

3.1 A total order on classes

Since an object may have several most specific classes in a hierarchy, a total order $\preceq_i$ of the classes in an inheritance hierarchy $\mathcal{H}_i$ must be provided. Thus it may be useful to choose which is the *preferred* class of an object and therefore to know which methods must be executed for the object. Thus, a total order, denoted as $\sqsubseteq$ and called *ISA-independent order*, is imposed on the classes in the hierarchy. This order may simply be based on the definition order, or it may be specified by the user with **before/after** declarations in class definitions. Alternatively this order may be obtained by considering the definition order as a default, which may be overridden by **before/after** declarations.

Note, however, that the ISA-independent order must be consistent with the ISA order $\leq_{ISA}$. The notion of consistency is formalized as follows.

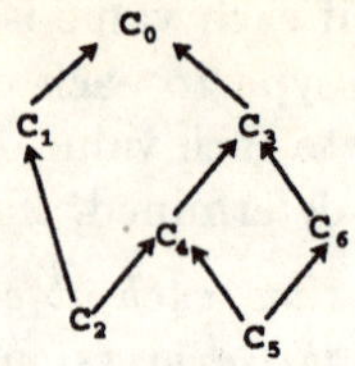

Fig. 3. Inheritance hierarchy $\mathcal{H}_0$ of Example 3

Definition 6 *The total order $\sqsubseteq$ on a set of classes $\mathcal{H}_i$ is said to be consistent with the (partial) ISA order $\leq_{ISA}$ on $\mathcal{H}_i$ if $\forall c_1, c_2 \in \mathcal{H}_i$ such that $c_1 \leq_{ISA} c_2$ does not exist any class $c \in \mathcal{H}_i$ such that the following conditions are satisfied*

- $c_1 \not\leq_{ISA} c$ *and* $c \not\leq_{ISA} c_1$,
- $c_2 \not\leq_{ISA} c$ *and* $c \not\leq_{ISA} c_2$,
- $c_2 \sqsubseteq c \sqsubseteq c_1$. □

We define now a total order on the hierarchy $\mathcal{H}_i$. This total order is obtained by merging the order induced by the ISA relationship with the ISA-independent total order $\sqsubseteq$. The order induced by the ISA relationship dominates the total order, in that for every two classes c_1 and c_2, if $c_1 \leq_{ISA} c_2$ holds, then $c_1 \preceq_i c_2$ holds. There is no need of relating in the order classes from different hierarchies, since they cannot have common instances (the extents of different hierarchies are disjoint).

Definition 7 *Let $\mathcal{H}_i$ be an inheritance hierarchy, $\sqsubseteq$ be an ISA-independent total order on $\mathcal{H}_i$, consistent with the ISA relation $\leq_{ISA}$. A total order on the classes in $\mathcal{H}_i$, denoted as $\preceq_i$, is defined as follows. Let $c_1, c_2 \in \mathcal{H}_i$, then $c_1 \preceq_i c_2$ if*

(i) $c_1 \leq_{ISA} c_2$, *that is, c_1 is a subclass of c_2, or*
(ii) $c_1 \not\leq_{ISA} c_2$, $c_2 \not\leq_{ISA} c_1$, *and* $c_1 \sqsubseteq c_2$ *(that is, neither c_1 is a subclass of c_2 nor vice-versa, but c_1 precedes c_2 in the $\sqsubseteq$ order).* □

Note that in the above definition we have only exploited the order $\sqsubseteq$ to define $\preceq_i$. However, there are different possible options for defining $\preceq_i$ as, for example, getting the ancestors of the two classes at the same level in the DAG and comparing by $\sqsubseteq$ those ancestors or considering the order on levels and comparing by $\sqsubseteq$ only classes at the same level.

Example 3 Consider the inheritance hierarchy of Figure 3. Suppose the ISA-independent order be denoted by the subscripts of class names, that is

$c_0 \sqsubseteq c_1 \sqsubseteq c_2 \sqsubseteq c_3 \sqsubseteq c_4 \sqsubseteq c_5 \sqsubseteq c_6$

whereas the ISA order corresponding to the tree is

$c_2 \leq_{ISA} c_1 \leq_{ISA} c_0$ $\quad$ $c_3 \leq_{ISA} c_0$ $\quad$ $c_2 \leq_{ISA} c_4$

$c_5 \leq_{ISA} c_4 \leq_{ISA} c_3$ $\quad$ $c_5 \leq_{ISA} c_6 \leq_{ISA} c_3$

The ISA-independent order is consistent with the ISA order, and the classes are related in the total order $\preceq_0$ as follows

$c_2 \preceq_0 c_1 \preceq_0 c_5 \preceq_0 c_4 \preceq_0 c_6 \preceq_0 c_3 \preceq_0 c_0$. ◇

Proposition 2 *Let $\mathcal{H}_i$ be an inheritance hierarchy, then the $\preceq_i$ relation defined according to Definition 7 is a total order on $\mathcal{H}_i$. Moreover, this order coincides with $\leq_{ISA}$ when $\leq_{ISA}$ is defined, that is, $\forall c_1, c_2 \in \mathcal{H}_i$ $c_1 \leq_{ISA} c_2 \Rightarrow c_1 \preceq_i c_2$.*

4 Attributes

In this section we consider the structural component of objects. We determine for an object with multiple most specific classes, the state of the object, that is, which are the attributes of the object, and which are the proper domains for these attributes.

Roughly speaking, the state of an object belonging to several most specific classes is the union of the attributes in those classes. However, the sets of attributes in those classes may not be disjoint, that is, *name conflicts* may arise. To handle these situations we introduce the notion of *source* of an attribute. Intuitively, if an attribute belongs to the intersection of the attribute sets of two classes and it has in both classes the same source, that is, it is inherited by a common superclass, then the attribute is semantically unique, and thus the object must have a unique value for this attribute. If, by contrast, the attribute has different sources then the two attributes in the two classes have accidentally the same name, but represent different information, that must be kept in separate ways. Thus, the object may have two different values for the two attributes (a renaming policy is applied).

Example 4 As an example of the first situation, consider the inheritance hierarchy of Figure 1 and suppose that an attribute **`spouse`** is present in class **`person`**. This attribute is inherited by all the subclasses of **`person`**. Consider now an object which is both a noble and a female, then the attribute **`spouse`** belongs to the intersection of the attribute sets of **`noble`** and **`female`**, and it has in both classes the same source (**`person`**), and thus the object has a single attribute **`spouse`** (this corresponds to the intuition that the information carried out by the two attributes in the two different classes is the same).

As an example of the second situation, consider the inheritance hierarchy composed by a class **`person`** and two subclasses **`student`** and **`employee`**. Suppose that in class **`student`** a new attribute **`code`** is defined, representing the number of the student in the university. Suppose moreover, that in class **`employee`** a new attribute **`code`** is defined, representing the number of the employee in the welfare office. Consider now an object which is both an employee and a student, then the attribute **`code`** belongs to the intersection of the attribute sets of **`employee`** and **`student`**, but it has different sources in the two classes: it has source **`employee`** in class **`employee`**, while it has source **`student`** in class **`student`**. Thus the object have two different attributes, say **`student-code`** and **`employee-code`** (this corresponds to the intuition that the information carried out by the two attributes in the two different classes is different). $\diamond$

We now formalize the above notions. We recall that, given a class c, $A(c)$ denotes the set of attributes of that class. Moreover, $A^+(c) = \{a \mid a \in A(c) \wedge \nexists\, c', c <_{ISA} c'$ such that $a \in A(c')\}$ denotes the set of proper (that is, not inherited) attributes of class c.

First, we define the notion of *source* of an attribute. Intuitively, the source of an attribute a in a class c is the most general superclass of c in which the attribute a is defined. Thus, it is the class from which c has inherited attribute a.

However, because of multiple inheritance, there may be two different superclasses of c, not related by the ISA relationship, in which attribute a is defined. In such a situation, we impose that in the definition of class c an explicit specification (through a *qualification mechanism*) is given of the class from which the attribute is inherited. Thus, each class inherits each attribute from one of its superclasses, the most general in the path specified by the qualification mechanism. This unique class is called source of the attribute in the class.

Given the set of classes $\mathcal{C}$, a function $inh^a : \mathcal{C} \rightarrow \mathcal{C}$ is defined for each class c, $c \in \mathcal{C}$, such that $a \in A(c) \setminus A^+(c)$. Given a class c, function inh^a returns the direct superclass of c from which c inherits attribute a. The definition of this function is as follows:

- if a unique class c' exists such that $c' \in ISA(c), a \in A(c')$ then $inh^a(c) = c'$
- otherwise (if more than one class c' exists such that $c' \in ISA(c)$ and $a \in A(c')$) the resolution of name conflicts for multiple inheritance in Chimera requires that in c definition an explicit qualification mechanism is exploited to state from which class attribute a is inherited; if c^q is the qualified class, then $inh^a(c) = c^q$.

We remark that, according to its definition, inh^a is a monotonic (strictly increasing) function, in that $\forall c \in \mathcal{C}$ if $inh^a(c)$ is defined $c <_{ISA} inh^a(c)$ holds.

Let $inh^{a^*} \subseteq \mathcal{C} \times \mathcal{C}$ denote the relation corresponding to the transitive closure of the relation associated with function inh^a[14]. If inh^{a^*} contains two pairs (c, c') and (c, c'') then either $c' <_{ISA} c''$ or $c'' <_{ISA} c'$ holds. Thus, inh^{a^*} contains ascending paths of the inheritance hierarchy. Moreover, given a set of classes C, let $mg(C)$ denote the set $\{c \mid c \in C \wedge \nexists\, c' \in C$ such that $c <_{ISA} c'\}$, that is the set of *most general* classes in C.

Definition 8 *(Source). The source of an attribute $a \in \mathcal{AN}$ in a class $c \in \mathcal{C}$, denoted as $source(a, c)$, is class c if $a \in A^+(c)$. It is a class $c' \in \mathcal{C}$, where $\{c'\} = mg(\{c^* \mid (c, c^*) \in inh^{a^*}\})$, otherwise. The source is undefined if $a \notin A(c)$.* □

Note that for each class $c, c \in \mathcal{C}$, $\{c^* \mid (c, c^*) \in inh^{a^*}\}$ is a totally ordered set with respect to the order $<_{ISA}$. Therefore, if $mg(\{c^* \mid (c, c^*) \in inh^{a^*}\})$ is not empty, it always contains a single element, that is the maximum of the set. As a consequence, the following result holds.

Proposition 3 *Let c be a class, and a be an attribute such that $a \in A(c)$, then $source(a, c)$ is always defined and it is unique.*

We now define which is the set of attributes of an object belonging to two most specific classes.

Definition 9 *Let o be an object such that $o \downarrow 3 = \{c_1, c_2\}$. The set of o attributes is $A(c_1) \uplus A(c_2)$, where the operation $\uplus$ is defined as follows:*

$$\begin{aligned} A(c_1) \uplus A(c_2) = &\{a \mid a \in A(c_1) \cup A(c_2) \wedge a \notin A(c_1) \cap A(c_2)\} \cup \\ &\{a \mid a \in A(c_1) \cap A(c_2) \wedge source(a, c_1) = source(a, c_2)\} \cup \\ &\{c_1\text{-}a \mid a \in A(c_1) \cap A(c_2) \wedge source(a, c_1) \neq source(a, c_2)\} \cup \\ &\{c_2\text{-}a \mid a \in A(c_1) \cap A(c_2) \wedge source(a, c_1) \neq source(a, c_2)\} \end{aligned}$$ □

[14] The relation associated to function inh^a is the set $\{(c, c') \mid c, c' \in \mathcal{C} \wedge inh^a(c) = c'\}$.

Example 5 Consider the inheritance hierarchy composed by class **person** with two subclasses **student** and **employee**. Suppose that

$A(\texttt{person}) = \{\texttt{name}, \texttt{address}, \texttt{spouse}\}$,

$A^+(\texttt{student}) = \{\texttt{code}, \texttt{average\_score}, \texttt{year}\}$,

$A^+(\texttt{employee}) = \{\texttt{code}, \texttt{salary}, \texttt{role}\}$

and therefore

$A(\texttt{student}) = \{\texttt{name}, \texttt{address}, \texttt{spouse}, \texttt{code}, \texttt{average\_score}, \texttt{year}\}$,

$A(\texttt{employee}) = \{\texttt{name}, \texttt{address}, \texttt{spouse}, \texttt{code}, \texttt{salary}, \texttt{role}\}$.

Then,

$A(\texttt{student}) \uplus A(\texttt{employee}) = \{\ \texttt{name},\ \texttt{address},\ \texttt{spouse},\ \texttt{year},\ \texttt{role},\ \texttt{employee} - \texttt{code},\ \texttt{student} - \texttt{code},\ \texttt{average\_score},\ \texttt{salary}\}$. ◇

Operator $\uplus$ is associative. Thus Definition 9 can be easily generalized to arbitrary sets of classes.

We now consider the domain (that is, the set of legal values) for attributes. For the attributes not belonging to the intersection of the attribute sets of the most specific classes of the object, and for the ones that have been renamed because of different sources, the domain is simply the one specified in the class to which the attribute belongs. By contrast, for the attributes in the intersection of the attribute sets of two classes and with the same source, a new domain must be determined. Intuitively, the legal values for an attribute must be legal values for both the attributes in the two classes, that is, they must belong to both the domain.

Definition 10 *Let* $dom(a, c_1) = T_1$ *and* $dom(a, c_2) = T_2$. *Let* o *be an object such that* $o \downarrow 3 = \{c_1, c_2\}$. *Then, value* v *is a legal value for attribute* a *in* o, *if* $v \in [\![T_1]\!] \cap [\![T_2]\!]$. □

Note that the domain of an attribute for an object belonging to several most specific classes cannot be always characterized in terms of an existing type. attribute In particular, if a greatest lower bound of type T_1 and T_2 exists, then the type of the attribute for the object is $T_1 \sqcap T_2$, but a greatest lower bound of two types in the hierarchy does not always exist. Moreover, in Chimera, $[\![T_1 \sqcap T_2]\!] \subseteq [\![T_1]\!] \cap [\![T_2]\!]$ holds for any two types T_1 and T_2, while the converse $[\![T_1]\!] \cap [\![T_2]\!] \subseteq [\![T_1 \sqcap T_2]\!]$ holds only if $T_1 \leq_T T_2$ (or vice-versa). In this case, indeed, $T_1 \sqcap T_2 = T_1$ and $[\![T_1]\!] \cap [\![T_2]\!] = [\![T_1]\!]$ in that $[\![T_1]\!] \subseteq [\![T_2]\!]$. If $T_1 \not\leq_T T_2$ and $T_2 \not\leq_T T_1$, then $T_1 \sqcap T_2$ can be defined only if T_1 and T_2 have a common subclass (by multiple inheritance). However in Chimera if T is a subclass of both T_1 and T_2 ($T_1, T_2 \in ISA(T)$), an object o may exist such that $o \in [\![T_1]\!] \wedge o \in [\![T_2]\!]$ but $o \notin [\![T]\!]$. Indeed, in such a way o can exhibit a context-dependent behavior, while it would not if $o \in [\![T]\!]$.

Example 6 Consider the inheritance hierarchy of Figure 1. Suppose that an attribute **spouse** $\in A(\texttt{person})$ and that $dom(\texttt{spouse}, \texttt{person}) = \texttt{person}$. Then,

spouse $\in A(\texttt{student}), A(\texttt{noble}), A(\texttt{male}), A(\texttt{female})$

and suppose that its domain is refined in the following way:

$dom(\texttt{spouse}, \texttt{student}) = \texttt{person}$

$dom(\texttt{spouse}, \texttt{noble}) = \texttt{noble}$

$dom(\texttt{spouse}, \texttt{male}) = \texttt{female}$
$dom(\texttt{spouse}, \texttt{female}) = \texttt{male}$.

In this case, if an object is a student and a noble, then the domain of the attribute **spouse** for this object can be characterized in terms of an existing type, that is $\texttt{noble} = \texttt{noble} \sqcap \texttt{person} = dom(\texttt{spouse}, \texttt{noble}) \sqcap dom(\texttt{spouse}, \texttt{student})$.

By contrast, if an object is a noble female, since
$dom(\texttt{spouse}, \texttt{noble}) \sqcap dom(\texttt{spouse}, \texttt{female}) = \texttt{noble} \sqcap \texttt{male}$
is not defined, the domain of the attribute **spouse** for this object cannot be characterized in terms of an existing type, but we can only say that the legal values for this attribute are those in $[\![\texttt{noble}]\!] \cap [\![\texttt{male}]\!]$ (that is, to objects belonging to the two most specific classes **noble** and **male**). ◇

Thus, the attributes for which a new domain is determined are the ones which are present in two different classes with a common source. This means that the attribute was defined in a class c (the source) with a domain, say T. Classes c_1 and c_2 have both inherited the attribute, possibly refining its domain into T_1 and T_2, respectively. Due to the refinement condition, both $T_1 \leq_T T$ and $T_2 \leq_T T$ hold. Thus a "compatibility" between types T_1 and T_2 exists, in that they are both subtypes of a common supertype. However, the existence of a common supertype does not ensure neither that $T_1 \sqcap T_2$ is defined nor that a legal value for the attribute exists (that is, $[\![T_1]\!] \cap [\![T_2]\!] \neq \emptyset$). Indeed, referring to the hierarchy of Figure 1, though **male** and **female** have a common supertype (**person**), $\texttt{male} \sqcap \texttt{female}$ is undefined and $[\![\texttt{male}]\!] \cap [\![\texttt{female}]\!] = \emptyset$.

The state of an object (that is, $o \downarrow 2$) is characterized by the set of most specific classes of the object (that is, $o \downarrow 3$) as follows.

Definition 11 *Let o be an object, such that $o \downarrow 2 = (a_1 : v_1, \ldots, a_n : v_n)$. Then:*

- $\biguplus_{c \in o\downarrow 3} A(c) = \{a_1, \ldots, a_n\}$
- $\forall i, 1 \leq i \leq n, v_i \in \bigcap_{c \in o\downarrow 3} [\![dom(a_i, c)]\!]$. □

4.1 Attribute access

We now discuss how an object state can be accessed from outside the object[15]. The attribute renaming, introduced for handling attributes with different sources, is used only for ease of internal representation, but from the outside, both attributes are referred to with the same name. Thus, the problem arises of choosing the correct (that is, the intended) attribute in each expression containing an attribute access.

Referring to Example 5, suppose that we must determine the semantics of the expression `X.code`, where `X` is a variable denoting an object which is both a student and an employee. The choice of accessing an attribute instead of the other one is carried out depending on the *preferred* class of the object, in the context of the specified expression. In our model, to allow different *views* of the object, depending on the context in which it is considered, the preferred class

[15] Note that in Chimera object attributes can be directly accessed, for example in queries.

for the object is determined by the context (static type) of the object reference denoting the object in the considered expression.

Note that the problem of choosing the intended attribute to be accessed arises only for attributes with different sources, because in the case of attributes with common source a single value is stored, and this value is always returned, independently from the class considered for the object.

We now formalize these notions. A function *value* : $\mathcal{O} \times \mathcal{C} \rightarrow \mathcal{V}$ is defined that, given an object o and a class c, if o is a member of c (that is, if $o \downarrow 1 \in [\![c]\!]$), returns the state of object o seen as an instance of class c. This function only returns the fields of the state value proper of the structural component of c. $value(o, c)$ is determined as follows. Let $o \downarrow 2$ be the record value $(a_1 : v_1, \ldots, a_n : v_n)$. Then, for $i = 1 \ldots n$:

- if $a_i \in A(c)$ then $a_i : v_i$ is a field of $value(o, c)$, and
- if $a_i = c\text{-}a'_i$ and $a'_i \in A(c)$, then $a'_i : v_i$ is a field of $value(o, c)$.

Note that, according to its definition, function *value* is well-defined, that is, for each $o \in \mathcal{O}$ and each $c \in \mathcal{C}$ if o is a member of c then $value(o, c)$ is uniquely determined. Indeed, if o is a member of c, o is structurally consistent with respect to the classes to which it belongs, either as direct or indirect member.

Let $t^s(X)$ be the static type of an object reference X. We recall from Section 2 that this type is always unique. Let o be an object to which reference X is instantiated; therefore, $t^s(X)$ is the static type of object o in the current expression. Then, an attribute access $X.a$ is solved by simply returning $value(o, t^s(X)).a$.

Example 7 Consider the inheritance hierarchy of Example 5 and the object

$$o = (i_1, (\texttt{name} : \texttt{'sarah'}, \texttt{address} : \texttt{'genova'}, \texttt{spouse} : i_2,$$
$$\texttt{student-code}{:}643, \texttt{average\_score} : 28, \texttt{year} : 2,$$
$$\texttt{employee-code}{:}14453, \texttt{salary} : 1000, \texttt{role} : \texttt{'secretary'}),$$
$$\{\ \texttt{student, employee}\ \})$$

where i_1 and i_2 are object identifiers. Then,

$$value(o, \texttt{employee}) = (\texttt{name} : \texttt{'sarah'}, \texttt{address} : \texttt{'genova'}, \texttt{spouse} : i_2,$$
$$\texttt{code} : 14453, \texttt{salary} : 1000, \texttt{role} : \texttt{'secretary'}),$$
$$value(o, \texttt{student}) = (\texttt{name} : \texttt{'sarah'}, \texttt{address} : \texttt{'genova'}, \texttt{spouse} : i_2,$$
$$\texttt{code} : 643, \texttt{average\_score} : 28, \texttt{year} : 2),$$
$$value(o, \texttt{person}) = (\texttt{name} : \texttt{'sarah'}, \texttt{address} : \texttt{'genova'}, \texttt{spouse} : i_2).$$

Consider now the attribute access expression $X.$**code**, where X is an object reference which at run-time is instantiated with o:

- if $t^s(X) =$ **person**, an expression containing the attribute access $X.$**code** is not well typed, and causes a type error to occur;
- if $t^s(X) =$ **employee**, the attribute access $X.$**code** is solved as $value(o, \texttt{employee}).\texttt{code}$ and returns the value 14453 (that is, $o \downarrow 2.$**employee-code**);
- if $t^s(X) =$ **student**, the attribute access $X.$**code** is solved as $value(o, \texttt{student}).\texttt{code}$ and returns the value 643 (that is, $o \downarrow 2.$**student-code**).

By contrast, consider the attribute access expression o.**spouse**. If $t^s(X)$ is **person**, **employee** or **student**, the value returned by the expression is i_2, since

$value(o, \texttt{person}).\texttt{spouse} = value(o, \texttt{employee}).\texttt{spouse} =$
$= value(o, \texttt{student}).\texttt{spouse} = i_2$. ◇

Finally, the following result holds, stating that each type correct attribute access $X.a$ is correctly handled by returning $value(o, t^s(X)).a$, in that: *i*) type checking is done with respect to the static type of the object reference X; thus, if $X.a$ is a type correct expression, then for each o member of $t^s(X)$ $value(o, t^s(X)).a$ is defined; *ii*) the value returned by $value(o, t^s(X)).a$ is a legal value for the static type of the expression $X.a$.

Proposition 4 *Let T be the static type of the attribute access $X.a$, and let o be an object to which reference X is instantiated, then $value(o, t^s(X)).a \in [\![T]\!]$.*

Note that the resolution of name conflicts for attributes is fully static, that is, it only makes use of information known at compile time, that is, the database schema and the static types of object references.

5 Methods and dispatching

In this section, we deal with the behavioral component of objects. As an initial remark, note that methods introduce more problems than attributes. An attribute is a stored value for which the only redefinition allowed is a domain refinement but, whatever class the object is seen an instance of, the stored value is the same. By contrast, each class in the hierarchy may define a different implementation for the same method, and for each method invocation on an object, an implementation must be chosen among the most specific ones. Note that different implementations may return different results or may perform different updates on the database state.

According to one of the basic principles of object-orientation, if, due to subtype polymorphism [4], several method implementations are applicable to a method invocation, the implementation specified in the most specific class of the invocation receiver is executed, as it is the one that *most closely matches* the invocation. Thus, the most specialized behavior prevails, according to the classical late binding mechanism. However, in a model where an object is not characterized by a single most specific class, the choice of the method implementation that "most closely matches" the invocation is not obvious.

There are two different approaches to determine the implementation which most closely matches the invocation, among different implementations in different most specific classes of the object. The first approach, which we call *preferred class approach*, is based on the idea that each object has in each context a *preferred* class, among its most specific ones. Thus, each method invocation is dispatched choosing the implementation in the preferred class in the current context. This approach supports a context-dependent behavior, as the same method invocation may be dispatched differently, and thus may return different results and perform different updates, depending on the context where the method is invoked.

The second approach we consider, which we call ***argument specificity approach***, does not determine the preferred class of an object to solve a method invocation, rather it makes use of the other actual arguments in the method call, thus considering the method as a multi-method [1, 7, 10, 13].

In the following subsections we illustrate and compare the two approaches.

5.1 Preferred class

According to this approach, a method invocation is dispatched by taking into account the context-dependent preferred class of the receiver object. As we have seen, in each Chimera expression, each object reference has a single static type. However static typing alone is not enough to assign a preferred class to each object in each expression for method dispatching. Indeed, the static type of the object may not belong to the set of most specific classes of the object. Consider for example an expression where an object reference has the static type `person`. If at run-time the reference denotes an object belonging both to class `noble` and to class `female`, the context of the object reference does not help in choosing the preferred class.

In those cases, we use the total order on classes introduced in Section 3.1. As seen, this order is determined by the definition order of classes, eventually overridden by `before/after` clauses in class definitions. Alternatively, we may consider for each object a total order on its most specific classes, as the one determined by the acquisition order, in such a way that the most recently acquired class precedes the others in the order. We remark that these orders, that may be considered too arbitrary and unpredictable by the user, are taken into account only when the context does not uniquely determine a preferred class for the object. The only alternative in these cases, apart from using these orders, would be to simply not dispatch the message, because it is *ambiguous*.

The preferred class approach is based on both static and dynamic information. The static information consists of the static type of the expression and of the total order on classes. The dynamic information consists of the set of most specific classes of the object; such classes are determined at run-time. The following rule formalizes the preferred class dispatching method. In what follows, $t^s(o)$ denotes the static type of object o, while $o \downarrow 3$ denotes the set of its most specific dynamic types. Moreover in what follows let $\mathcal{H}(o)$ denote the inheritance hierarchy to which object o belongs[16] and let $\preceq_{\mathcal{H}(o)}$ be the total order on the hierarchy to which o belongs, as defined in Section 3.1. Finally, given a set of classes S let $min_{\preceq_{\mathcal{H}(o)}} S$ denote a class which is the minimum among the elements in the set S with respect to the order $\preceq_{\mathcal{H}(o)}$. Since $\preceq_{\mathcal{H}(o)}$ is a total order on $o \downarrow 3$ and thus on $\{c \mid c \in o \downarrow 3 \wedge c \leq_{ISA} t^s(o)\} \subseteq o \downarrow 3$, $min_{\preceq_{\mathcal{H}(o)}} \{c \mid c \in o \downarrow 3 \wedge c \leq_{ISA} t^s(o)\}$ exists and is unique.

---

[16] Note that, since the extents of different hierarchies are disjoint, all the classes in $o \downarrow 3$ belong to the same hierarchy $\mathcal{H}(o)$.

Rule 3: Preferred class dispatching rule

Let $o.m(v_1, \ldots, v_n)$[17] be a method invocation. It is dispatched as follows:

- if $t^s(o) \in o \downarrow 3$, the implementation of m in $t^s(o)$ is selected,
- if $t^s(o) \notin o \downarrow 3$ the implementation of m in $min_{\preceq_{\mathcal{H}(o)}}\{c \mid c \in o \downarrow 3 \wedge c \leq_{ISA} t^s(o)\}$ is selected. □

If we want to privilege the most recently acquired behavior, instead of using the $\preceq_{\mathcal{H}(o)}$ order, we may consider the o acquisition order $\preceq_o$ of the classes in $o \downarrow 3$, where $c \preceq_o c'$ denotes that c has been acquired after c'.

Example 8 Consider the inheritance hierarchy of Figure 1 and let this hierarchy be denoted by $\mathcal{H}_1$. Suppose that for a unary method m, $m \in M(\texttt{noble})$, $m \in M(\texttt{male})$ and $m \in M(\texttt{female})$. Suppose moreover that the classes are related in the ISA-independent order $\sqsubseteq$ as follows

$\texttt{person} \sqsubseteq \texttt{male} \sqsubseteq \texttt{noble} \sqsubseteq \texttt{female}$

and then that the resulting total order $\preceq_1$ is

$\texttt{male} \preceq_1 \texttt{noble} \preceq_1 \texttt{female} \preceq_1 \texttt{person}$.

Consider now the method invocation $o.m(o')$ where $o \downarrow 3 = \{\texttt{noble}, \texttt{female}\}$, so that $\mathcal{H}(o) = \mathcal{H}_1$. Then:

- if $t^s(o) = \texttt{noble}$ the m implementation specified in class `noble` is selected;
- if $t^s(o) = \texttt{female}$ the m implementation specified in class `female` is selected;
- if $t^s(o) = \texttt{person}$ the m implementation specified in class `noble` is selected, since $\texttt{noble} \preceq_{\mathcal{H}(o)} \texttt{female}$. ◇

As illustrated by the previous example, the preferred class dispatching approach models context-dependent behavior. In particular, a given method invocation with a fixed set of parameters may produce different results (both in terms of result values and of database updates), though executed on the same database state, depending on the context of the receiver object reference in the expression containing the invocation.

Under the preferred class approach, any type correct method invocation can be dispatched. To formalize this result the notion of method "dispatchability" must be formalized first. We model dispatching of invocations on method m as a function that, given an object o (and some kind of information used in the dispatching) returns the class in the set of its most specific ones, to which the message $o.m(\_)$ is dispatched. Note that the dispatching function is partial, since if $\nexists\ c \in o \downarrow 3$ such that $m \in M(c)$ then the message cannot be dispatched. Note however that the dispatching function is total on type correct messages. Indeed, if $o.m(\_)$ is type correct, then a class in $o \downarrow 3$ certainly exists such that $m \in M(c)$; such class is either $t^s(o)$ or a subclass of $t^s(o)$.

Let $d^m_{pc} : \mathcal{O} \times \mathcal{T} \rightarrow \mathcal{C}$ denote the function associated with the preferred class dispatching rule, where the first argument is the method receiver and the second one is its context. The following result holds.

[17] We recall that this is the Chimera syntax for method invocation, where o denotes the privileged receiver of the method. Here we consider the actual method invocation, thus $o, v_1, \ldots, v_n$ are the actual values of the formal parameters $e, e_1, \ldots, e_n$ we have considered in Section 2.

Proposition 5 *Let* $o.m(v_1, \ldots, v_n)$ *be a method invocation. The function* d^m_{pc} *is defined for any pair* $(o, t^s(o))$ *such that* $m \in M(t^s(o))$[18].

Finally, note that if the dispatching strategy, based on the preferred class, is used with a contravariant redefinition rule for method arguments, type correctness is ensured.

5.2 Argument specificity

The second approach we consider does not take into account the preferred class of an object, rather it tries to determine the method implementation that most closely matches the invocation by taking into account the types of the actual parameters of the invocation (in addition to the type of the receiver object). This approach is close to multiple dispatching or multi-method approaches where the selection of the method to be executed depends on the types of all the actual arguments of the invocation. In the preferred class approach only the type of the receiver object determines which method is executed and the other arguments only provide values but they play no role in method selection. By contrast, in this approach, the method selection is based on the types of all arguments, the receiver as well as the other ones.

This approach can be regarded as fully dynamic, as opposed to the other, which is only partially dynamic. Indeed, in this approach dispatching is based only on run-time information, that is, the types of the actual parameters of the invocation. Moreover, whereas the previous approach models context-dependent behavior, the argument specificity approach ensures a notion of behavior identity. Indeed, it ensures that a given method invocation, with a fixed set of actual parameters executed on a given database state, returns the same results and produces the same database state, regardless of the expression in which it is contained.

We point out that in Chimera a contravariant redefinition rule is used for method input parameters. As recently discussed by Castagna [5], when using multiple dispatching the input parameter redefinition should be covariant for parameters involved in dispatching, whereas it should be contravariant for other parameters. However, the extension of the Chimera model to allow covariant input parameter refinement is currently under investigation. Note, moreover, that we use multiple dispatching only for choosing an implementation among the ones in sibling classes, and never to choose an implementation among the ones in a path in a given inheritance hierarchy.

In the following we consider multiple dispatching when objects may possibly have multiple most specific classes. Chimera methods, however, are not really multi-methods [10] in that they are associated with classes. Thus, the "privileged receiver", though it is not the only one involved in dispatching, has higher priority with respect to other arguments, in that only implementations in classes that are most specific for the receiver are considered as "candidates" for the dispatching. Thus, the dispatching we propose here is not purely multiple in that

[18] If the method invocation is type correct, then $m \in M(t^s(o))$ holds.

we maintain a form of "privilege" for the receiver of the method: other arguments are taken into account only to choose among sibling implementations, in the different most specific classes of the receiver object.

Let $mst(v) = \{T \mid v \in [\![T]\!] \wedge \nexists\, T' \in T$ such that $T' <_T T, v \in [\![T']\!]\}$ be the set of most specific types of a value. Note that if v is the identifier of an object o then $mst(v) = o \downarrow 3$; otherwise $mst(v)$ is a singleton set containing the (unique) most specific value type of v.

Definition 12 *(Method applicability). A method implementation*
$m : T_1^j \times \ldots \times T_n^j \rightarrow T_r^j$
defined in a class c_j is applicable to a method invocation
$o.m(v_1, \ldots, v_n)$
if $c_j \in o \downarrow 3$ and $\forall i, 1 \leq i \leq n, \exists T_i \in mst(v_i)$ such that $T_i \leq_T T_i^j$. □

Example 9 Consider the class hierarchy of Example 8 where $m \in M(\texttt{noble})$, $m \in M(\texttt{female})$, $m \in M(\texttt{person})$ and consider the following signatures for method m

$sign(m, \texttt{noble}) = \texttt{noble} \rightarrow \texttt{person}$
$sign(m, \texttt{female}) = \texttt{male} \rightarrow \texttt{person}$
$sign(m, \texttt{male}) = \texttt{person} \rightarrow \texttt{person}$.

Consider the method invocation $o.m(o')$

1. if $mst(o) = \{\texttt{noble}, \texttt{female}\}$, $mst(o') = \{\texttt{noble}, \texttt{male}\}$, then both the method in `noble` and the method in `female` are applicable;
2. if, by contrast, $mst(o) = \{\texttt{noble}, \texttt{male}\}$, $mst(o') = \{\texttt{female}\}$, only the method in `male` is applicable. ◇

To define the argument specificity dispatching rule a notion of *method specificity*, that is, an order $\prec$ on methods must be used. This order is exploited in choosing the method to be executed, among the applicable ones. The following rule formalizes the argument specificity dispatching method. For the sake of simplicity, we denote with m^{c_i} (m^{c_j}) method m in class c_i (c_j).

Rule 4: Argument specificity dispatching rule

Let $o.m(v_1, \ldots, v_n)$ be a method invocation, and let $\prec$ be the considered method specificity order. The method invocation is dispatched as follows. Method m in class c is executed if
$m^c = min_\prec\{\, m^{c'} \mid c' \in o \downarrow 3 \wedge m^{c'}$ is applicable $\}$. □

The most specific among the applicable methods is thus executed.

We now discuss how the $\prec$ order can be defined. Consider two method implementations, in class c_i and in class c_j, such that

$sign(m, c_i) = T_1^i \times \ldots \times T_n^i \rightarrow T_r^i$
$sign(m, c_j) = T_1^j \times \ldots \times T_n^j \rightarrow T_r^j$.

A first possibility (which corresponds to the one adopted by Cecil [7] and to the *argument subtype precedence* in [1]) is to define m^{c_i} as more specific than m^{c_j} (denoted as $m^{c_i} \prec_{asp} m^{c_j}$) iff $\forall h, 1 \leq h \leq n, T_h^i \leq_T T_h^j$ and $\exists k, 1 \leq k \leq n, T_k^i <_T T_k^j$. However, if we consider this order on methods there are several ambiguous situations, in which we are not able to dispatch the message.

Example 10 Consider the methods of Example 9, then $m^{\texttt{noble}} \prec_{asp} m^{\texttt{male}}$ and $m^{\texttt{female}} \prec_{asp} m^{\texttt{male}}$ but $m^{\texttt{noble}} \not\prec_{asp} m^{\texttt{female}}$ and $m^{\texttt{female}} \not\prec_{asp} m^{\texttt{noble}}$. Thus, the method invocation in case 1. cannot be dispatched. ◇

Example 11 Let A, B, C be three classes, such that $ISA(A) = C$ and $ISA(B) = C$. Suppose that $m \in M(A)$, $m \in M(B)$ where $sign(m, A) = B \times C \to C$ and $sign(m, B) = C \times A \to C$. The invocation $o.m(o_1, o_2)$ with $o \downarrow 3 = \{A, B\}$, $o_1 \downarrow 3 = \{B\}$, $o_2 \downarrow 3 = \{A\}$ cannot be dispatched, since $m^A \not\prec_{asp} m^B$ and $m^B \not\prec_{asp} m^A$. ◇

The proposed order can then be refined by taking into account an ordering on arguments (for example, a left-to-right ordering). The obtained notion of method specificity, which corresponds to the *argument order precedence* in [1], is defined as follows: m^{c_i} is more specific than m^{c_j} (denoted as $m^{c_i} \prec_{aop} m^{c_j}$) iff $\exists k, 1 \leq k \leq n, T_k^i <_T T_k^j$ and $\forall h, 1 \leq h < k, T_h^i = T_h^j$. However, also considering this order on methods there are still ambiguous situations, in which we are not able to dispatch the message. Referring to Example 9, $m^{\texttt{noble}} \not\prec_{aop} m^{\texttt{female}}$ and $m^{\texttt{female}} \not\prec_{aop} m^{\texttt{noble}}$. Thus, in case 1. of Example 10, the message cannot be dispatched.

Example 12 Consider classes A, B and C such that $ISA(C) = \{A, B\}$ and two classes C_1 and C_2 such that $m \in M(C_1)$, $m \in M(C_2)$ with $sign(m, C_1) = A \to C_1$ and $sign(m, C_2) = B \to C_2$, invocation $o.m(o_1)$, where $o \downarrow 3 = \{C_1, C_2\}$, $o_1 \downarrow 3 = \{C\}$, cannot be dispatched since $m^{C_1} \not\prec_{aop} m^{C_2}$ and $m^{C_2} \not\prec_{aop} m^{C_1}$. ◇

Then, we further refine the proposed order by taking into account an ordering on arguments (for example, a left-to-right ordering) and the total order $\prec_{\mathcal{H}(o)}$ on the classes in the hierarchy to which the method receiver belongs, in addition to the subtype relationship. The resulting notion of method specificity is formalized as follows.

Definition 13 *(Method specificity). Let m^{c_i} denote method m in class c_i and m^{c_j} denote method m in class c_j, with $sign(m, c_i) = T_1^i \times \ldots \times T_n^i \to T_r^i$ and $sign(m, c_j) = T_1^j \times \ldots \times T_n^j \to T_r^j$. m^{c_i} is more specific than m^{c_j} (denoted as $m^{c_i} \prec_t m^{c_j}$) iff $\exists k, 1 \leq k \leq n, T_k^i <_T T_k^j$ or $T_k^i \prec_{\mathcal{H}(o)} T_k^j$ and $\forall h, 1 \leq h < k$, $T_h^i = T_h^j$.* □

Given the method specificity order, the only situations, in which messages cannot be dispatched are when the signatures of the methods in the two classes are the same.

Example 13 Consider the hierarchy of Example 9, with the total order on classes of Example 8. Since $\texttt{male} \prec_{\mathcal{H}(o)} \texttt{noble} \prec_{\mathcal{H}(o)} \texttt{female} \prec_{\mathcal{H}(o)} \texttt{person}$, $m^{\texttt{female}} \prec_t m^{\texttt{noble}}$ holds. Thus, the message in case 1. is dispatched, and the implementation for m defined in class `female` is executed. ◇

We remark that neither by using an *inheritance order precedence* nor a *global type precedence* as in [1] we would be able to dispatch the method invocation of Example 9 in case 1. Moreover, under the argument specificity approach, not all the type correct method invocations can be dispatched. Let $d^m_{as} : \mathcal{O} \times 2^{\mathcal{T}} \times \ldots \times 2^{\mathcal{T}} \rightarrow \mathcal{C}$ be the function associated with the argument specificity dispatching rule, where the first argument is the method receiver and the other ones are the most specific types of the invocation actual arguments. Then, the following result holds.

Proposition 6 *Let $o.m(v_1, \ldots, v_n)$ be a method invocation. Function d^m_{as} is defined on a $n+1$-tuple $(o, mst(v_1), \ldots, mst(v_n))$ if both the following conditions hold:*

- $\exists c \in o \downarrow 3$ *such that* $m \in M(c)$ *and* m^c *is applicable to* $o.m(v_1, \ldots, v_n)$[19]*;*
- $\forall c_i, c_j$, $i \neq j$, *such that both* m^{c_i} *and* m^{c_j} *are applicable to* $o.m(v_1, \ldots, v_n)$ *one of the following conditions holds:*
  - *if* $sign(m, c_i) = T^i_1 \times \ldots \times T^i_n \rightarrow T^i_r$ *and* $sign(m, c_j) = T^j_1 \times \ldots \times T^j_n \rightarrow T^j_r$, $\exists k, 1 \leq k \leq n$, *such that* $T^i_k \neq T^j_k$*;*
  - $\exists c_k$ *such that* m^{c_k} *is applicable to* $o.m(v_1, \ldots, v_n)$ *and* $m^{c_k} \prec_t m^{c_j}$*.*

Finally note that the argument specificity approach ensures the identity of behavior of a method invocation. Indeed, according to Rule 4, a given message $o.m(v_1, \ldots, v_n)$ is dispatched to a class which does not depend on the context $t^s(o)$ of the message receiver in the expression containing the invocation. The argument specificity approach, however, does not ensure type correctness.

6 Conclusions

In this paper we have investigated issues arising from multiple direct membership of objects to classes in the framework of the Chimera object-oriented data model. Both structural and behavioral aspects of objects have been considered. First, the state of an object has been characterized in terms of the set of its most specific classes. A (static) notion of context has been defined and it has been exploited for handling attribute accesses. Then, two different dispatching approaches have been proposed. The two approaches are compared in Table 1. The table summarizes the differences of the two approaches (discussed in detail in Section 5). In the table *applicability* denotes whether the approach is always able to dispatch a message.

	Information exploited	Applicability	Context-dependence	Behavior identity	Static typing
Preferred class	Static and Dynamic	Total	YES	NO	YES
Argument specificity	Dynamic	Partial	NO	YES	NO

Table 1. Comparison between the two proposed dispatching approaches.

Multiple inheritance and multiple class direct membership could seem overlapping design concepts. However, we think that multiple inheritance should

[19] If the method invocation is type correct, then this condition is verified.

be used whenever the obtained class is a semantically meaningful class, with a specific state and behavior (that is, in which new features are added or some features are redefined). By contrast, multiple class direct membership should be used to avoid defining artificial intersection classes and whenever we would like to allow a context dependent behavior.

Currently, only the preferred class approach has been implemented in the Chimera prototype developed at Politecnico di Milano. Indeed, efficient techniques for the argument specificity dispatching approach need to be further investigated. Some efficient techniques for multi-method handling (based on look-up automata) have been proposed [8], that could be extended to our case.

Another possible topic of future work is how to ensure type correctness with the argument specificity dispatching approach. The approach to static type checking for multi-method proposed in [1] could be extended to our case. However, in our approach the confusable methods are much more than in [1] in that an object can have an arbitrary set of types, and the relationship between the static type and the dynamic ones are only those stated by Rule 1.

Finally, we would like to point out that when different implementations for a method are defined in the most specific classes of an object, there are cases in which the most intuitive approach is that of executing both. Consider as an example an *init* method that initializes the class attributes. Problems due to different assignments to the same attribute may however arise. In Chimera, the only way to specify such a behavior is to define a subclass-by-multiple inheritance of the two classes and to redefine the method in the subclass as desired. However, we think that this issue need to be further investigated.

Acknowledgments The ideas presented in this paper have been greatly influenced by discussions with Stefano Ceri and René Bal. We also would like to thank the referees for their comments and suggestions.

References

1. R. Agrawal, L. DeMichiel, and B. Lindsay. Static Type Checking of Multi-Methods. In A. Paepcke, editor, *Proc. Sixth Int'l Conf. on Object-Oriented Programming: Systems, Languages, and Applications*, pages 113–128, 1991.
2. A. Albano, R. Bergamini, G. Ghelli, and R. Orsini. An Object Data Model with Roles. In R. Agrawal, S. Baker, and D. Bell, editors, *Proc. Nineteenth Int'l Conf. on Very Large Data Bases*, pages 39–51, 1993.
3. E. Bertino and L.D. Martino. *Object-Oriented Database Systems - Concepts and Architecture.* Addison-Wesley, 1993.
4. L. Cardelli and P. Wegner. On Understanding Types, Data Abstraction and Polimorphism. *Computing Surveys*, 17:471–522, 1985.
5. G. Castagna. Covariance and Contravariance: Conflict without a Cause. Technical Report LIENS-94-18, Département de Mathématiques et d'Informatique - Ecole Normale Supérieure, Paris, October 1994.
6. S. Ceri and R. Manthey. Chimera: A Model and Language for active DOOD Systems. In *Extending Information System Techology - Second International East-West Database Workshop*, Lecture Notes in Computer Science, pages 9–21, 1994.

7. C. Chambers. Object-Oriented Multi-Methods in Cecil. In O. Lehrmann Madsen, editor, *Proc. Sixth European Conference on Object-Oriented Programming*, Lecture Notes in Computer Science, 615, pages 33–56, 1992.
8. W. Chen, V. Turau, and W. Klas. Efficient Dynamic Look-Up Strategy for Multi-Methods. In M. Tokoro and R. Pareschi, editors, *Proc. Eighth European Conference on Object-Oriented Programming*, Lecture Notes in Computer Science, 821, pages 408–431, 1994.
9. D. H. Fishman et al. Overview of the Iris DBMS. In W. Kim and F. H. Lochovsky, editors, *Object-Oriented Concepts, Databases, and Applications*, pages 219–250. Addison-Wesley, 1989.
10. R. Gabriel, J. White, and D. Bobrow. CLOS: Integrating Object-Oriented and Functional Programming. *Communications of the ACM*, 34(9):28–38, September 1991.
11. G. Gottlob, M. Schrefl, and B. Rock. Extending Object-Oriented Systems with Roles. To appear in *ACM Transactions on Information Systems*, 1994.
12. G. Guerrini, E. Bertino, and R. Bal. A Formal Definition of the Chimera Object-Oriented Data Model. Technical Report IDEA.DE.2P.011.01, ESPRIT Project 6333, May 1994. Submitted for publication.
13. W. Mugridge, J. Hamer, and J. Hosking. Multi-Methods in a Statically Typed Programming Language. In P. America, editor, *Proc. Fifth European Conference on Object-Oriented Programming*, Lecture Notes in Computer Science, 512, pages 307–324, 1991.
14. J. Richardson and P. Schwarz. Aspects: Extending Objects to Support Multiple, Independent Roles. In J. Clifford and R. King, editors, *Proc. of the ACM SIGMOD Int'l Conf. on Management of Data*, pages 298–307, 1991.
15. E. Sciore. Object Specialization. *ACM Transactions on Information Systems*, 7(2):103–122, April 1989.
16. L. A. Stein. A Unified Methodology for Object-Oriented Programming. In M. Lenzerini, D. Nardi, and M. Simi, editors, *Inheritance Hierarchies in Knowledge Representation and Programming Languages*, pages 211–222. John Wiley & Sons, 1991.

A Marriage of Class- and Object-Based Inheritance Without Unwanted Children

Patrick Steyaert Wolfgang De Meuter

Vrije Universiteit Brussel
Programming Technology Lab (PROG)
Pleinlaan 2 - B1050 Brussels - Belgium
email: {prsteyae, wdmeuter}@vnet3.vub.ac.be

Abstract. Class-based languages have often been criticised for their rigidity. Prototype-based languages on the other hand are usually considered too flexible. We claim that this flexibility is inherently correlated to encapsulation problems. We therefore propose a new scale of 'encapsulated' inheritance mechanisms on objects that combine the object model of class-based languages with the inheritance mechanism of prototype-based languages. It is shown that they combine the advantages but shun the disadvantages of both paradigms. A denotational semantics of an exemplar encapsulated inheritance mechanism on objects is given and compared with the standard denotational semantics of class- and object-based inheritance. This comparison confirms our claims.

1 Introduction

In the evolution of object-oriented programming two, largely disjoint, groups of languages have emerged: *class-based languages* and *prototype-based languages*. Both include mature and well established languages: the first group includes languages such as Smalltalk and C++, the second one includes languages like Self.

Languages fitting neatly in this taxonomy are mostly characterised by their use or non-use of classes as a way to express incremental modification. Class-based languages define inheritance on classes while prototype-based languages do this on objects. As argued by Lieberman, this is a reflection of the more philosophical controversy between representing general concepts as abstract sets (or classes) and representing concepts as prototypes (see [10]).

We agree with 'The Treaty of Orlando' [17] that this controversy cannot be decided in one or the other way and that much can be gained from combining the strengths of both viewpoints.

The reaction of *hybrid languages* (such as Hybrid) is to allow both classes and objects to be modified and to offer operators to turn classes into objects (instantiation) and vice versa (promotion) (see [16]). Hybrid languages limit themselves to a straightforward *union* of the distinctive language features of both paradigms thereby combining their advantages but, more importantly, also their disadvantages (figure 1).

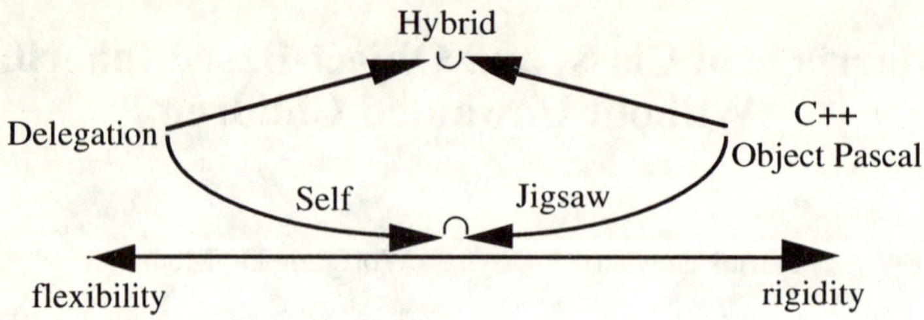

Fig. 1.

More recently, both the prototype- and class-based language research communities have created languages that strive toward an *intersection* of the paradigms (figure 1). Examples of these are attempts to introduce more rigidity into prototype-based languages giving rise to object-based inheritance[1] (see [5, 17]). In the other school, language mechanisms such as mixin-based inheritance and modular inheritance (see [1, 2]) are an improvement for class-based languages as they allow a more flexible creation of class hierarchies. Neither improvement is entirely successful. The latter languages stay in the realm of class-based languages as they still promote a distinction between modifiable templates and non-modifiable objects. On the other hand, there is a general feeling that object-based inheritance is still too flexible. In this paper we will identify the exact reason upon which this feeling is based. We will show that current object-based inheritance languages suffer from an inherent encapsulation problem and that this problem must be solved for them to become viable alternatives to class-based languages.

In order to give sufficient rigour to our arguments we will analyse these problems and propose solutions in a denotational framework. By comparing denotational semantics we will demonstrate that the encapsulation problems are inherently present in object-based inheritance and inherently absent in pure class-based inheritance. The lessons learned in the class-based world will then be used to propose a new family of encapsulated inheritance mechanisms on objects. Finally, we will discuss how these new mechanisms can provide the basis for languages in a successful intersection of classes and prototypes.

2 Terminology and Concepts

In this section we will briefly introduce the basic concepts and semantic domains needed in the remainder of the paper. The object model that is used in the paper is introduced in section 2.1. This is the fairly common treatment of objects modelled as records. Readers unfamiliar with specialisation interfaces should read section 2.2. Section 2.3 introduces the semantic domains for classes and inheritance on classes in the same way as [4]. Section 2.4 introduces our denotational treatment of object-based

---

[1] The behaviour sharing mechanism of prototype-based languages varies from delegation to object-based inheritance. With object-based inheritance parents are determined at object-creation time while delegation usually allows an object to change parents dynamically.

inheritance. It also briefly compares the semantics of class- and object based inheritance.

2.1 Objects and Client Interfaces

In the current state of the art, no general definition of objects is widely accepted. Still a consensus exists that *encapsulation* is one of the distinguishing features of objects (see [12, 13, 15, 18, 20]). An object has an interface which contains the messages it understands and which hides its implementation details. This interface is usually referred to as the object's *client interface*. A record listing all the operations belonging to the client interface of an object thus serves as a natural model for it. Denotationally, objects are therefore modelled as

$$\text{Object} = \text{Ident} \rightarrow \text{Attribute}$$

In this model, message passing is a combination of attribute selection and invocation. Commonly, attributes are methods. Attribute invocation is then a simple procedure invocation thereby passing the actual arguments to the method. In order to respect encapsulation, message passing must be an atomic operation, i.e. selection and invocation must be part of an indivisible whole.

As we will show, existing object-oriented programming languages (OOPLs) not always make it possible to model their 'objects' by the above equation. This is particularly true for prototype-based languages. We will therefore use the term *object* as a general noun to indicate all possible language constructs that can act as receivers of messages. Whenever we want to make a clear distinction we will use the term *encapsulated objects* to indicate 'objects' that can be modelled by the equation and that allow atomic message passing.

2.2 Incremental Modification and Specialisation Interfaces

The power of object-oriented programming lies in its provision for so-called incremental programming techniques. One creates a new program construct R (a 'result') by specifying its differential M (a 'modification') with respect to some existing program construct P (a 'parent') (see [21]).

Inheritance is a specific kind of incremental modification. First of all it is characterised by the fact that modifiers can invoke operations in their parent. Thus the result must be modelled as $R = P + M(P)$. A second characteristic is that modifiers can override operations of the parent with 'late binding of self' which indicates that any self reference made by the parent P will, in the result R, refer to the entire R instead of just P. The semantics of 'late binding of self' will be discussed in section 2.3.

Inheritance requires modifiers to know which parent operations they can invoke and what the effect will be of overriding attributes. This is illustrated in the following example (figure 2). A 'Person' is defined whose client interface contains two operations ('print' and 'getName'). The 'print' operation in 'Person' invokes the 'getName' operation in its implementation. This knowledge is used by the modifying 'Female' to assure that overriding the 'getName' method also has an effect on the result of its (inherited) 'print' method. In general, a parent exposes this kind of knowledge through a second interface, called the *specialisation interface*.

```
Person (name)
        method getName is return name
        method print is self.getName.print

Female Modifies Person
        method getName is return "Ms.".concat(super.getName)

AlternativePerson (name)
        method getName is return name
        method print is name.print
```

Fig. 2.

In this example the specialisation interfaces are implicit: they can only be derived by inspecting the implementations. The issue of specifying specialisation interfaces is outside the scope of this paper (see [8, 9]). This however, does not prevent us to reason about them. Consider figure 2 again. Although specialisation interfaces are left implicit, one can still observe that the 'Female' modification clearly does not fit 'AlternativePerson' with the same result. This is because 'Person' and 'AlternativePerson' have different specialisation interfaces.

Note that the specialisation interface *exposes implementation details* to modifiers. In the above example only a minimal set of implementation details are exported (self and super interactions). Practical programming languages often expose much more to modifiers. For example, most languages also disclose the private variables of a parent through the specialisation interface leading to a form of decapsulated inheritance. Different forms of decapsulation (exposure) of implementation details for modifiers have been discussed in the literature (see [15]).

2.3 Classes

The most popular incremental modification mechanism in OOPLs is inheritance on classes. A class plays at least two different roles: one as a template for the instances that will be created from it, and one as a parent for further refinement by inheritors.

This section explains the denotational counterpart of these roles, which is mainly due to Cook and Palsberg [4].

2.3.1 Classes as Templates

In its most basic form classes are used as templates to create objects with a common behaviour. Denotationally, classes are therefore modelled as *generators of objects* and *instantiation* is an operation that transforms a generator into an object:

Instantiate : Generator → Object

Generator = ... → Object

In this equation the domain '...' from which objects are generated is left open. In OOPLs where objects can refer to themselves, objects are typically modelled as self referential records. This can be abstractly formulated as: self = record (self). Using fixed point analysis, self = record (self) is then rewritten as self =(λs. record(s))self and thus self = Fix(λs. record(s)). Hence, λs. record(s) is a generator function for objects and the exact type of generator functions is given by:

$$\text{Generator}_{\text{Fix}} = \text{Object} \rightarrow \text{Object}$$

Generator functions are used to model classes and instantiation is achieved by taking the fixed point of a generator. The generator domain allows fixing: it is a function of which the argument domain is the same as the result domain.

$$\text{Instantiate} : \text{Generator}_{\text{Fix}} \rightarrow \text{Object} \quad \text{where Instantiate(g)} = \text{Fix(g)}$$

2.3.2 Class-Based Inheritance

As shown by Cook and Palsberg, the model of classes based on generator functions is well suited for extension with inheritance. Generators can be combined with late binding of self to form subclasses. Since subclasses should be potential new parents, inheritance should be an operation converting two generators into a new generator whose self is distributed over all its subparts. This is captured in the following operator

$$\text{Inherit}_{\text{Simple}} : \text{Generator}_{\text{Fix}} \rightarrow \text{Generator}_{\text{Fix}} \rightarrow \text{Generator}_{\text{Fix}}$$

$$\text{Inherit}_{\text{Simple}} = \lambda P.\ \lambda M.\ \left(\lambda \text{self}_{\text{object}}.\ (P\ \text{self}_{\text{object}}) +_r (M\ \text{self}_{\text{object}})\right)$$

where $+_r$ is the right-preferential record combinator.

This model gets slightly more complicated when modifiers are allowed to invoke parent operations (Smalltalk's super-calls). Therefore, modifiers need to be parameterised by a super object. Generators that are parameterised by super objects are called 'wrappers' (see [4]).

$$\text{Wrapper}_{\text{Fix}} = \text{Object} \rightarrow \text{Generator}_{\text{Fix}} = \text{Object} \rightarrow \text{Object} \rightarrow \text{Object}$$

The inheritance operator essentially stays the same. Besides distributing a new 'self' (for late binding) to all subparts, it also provides the modifier M with a reference to the parent.

$$\text{Inherit}_{\text{Cook\&Palsberg}} : \text{Generator}_{\text{Fix}} \rightarrow \text{Wrapper}_{\text{Fix}} \rightarrow \text{Generator}_{\text{Fix}}$$

$$\text{Inherit}_{\text{Cook\&Palsberg}} = \lambda P.\ \lambda M.\ \left(\lambda \text{self}_{\text{object}}\ .\ (P\ \text{self}_{\text{object}}) +_r (M\ (P\ \text{self}_{\text{object}})\ \text{self}_{\text{object}})\right)$$

2.4 Object-Based inheritance

Whereas class-based inheritance involves incremental modification of classes, object-based inheritance does the same on objects. This is illustrated in the following example where objects are modified such that their name is printed with a "Ms." prefix.

```
Rita = Object (name="Rita")
    method getName is return name
    method print is self.getName.print
```

```
Linda = Object (name="Linda")
   method getName is return name
   method print is self.getName.print
method MakeLetterHead ( aPerson )
   return aPerson extended with
      method getName is return "Ms. ".concat super.getName
LetterHeadRita = MakeLetterHead (Rita)
LetterHeadLinda = MakeLetterHead (Linda)
```

Fig. 3.

Object-based inheritance also involves late binding of self but on the level of objects instead of classes. The mechanism of class-based inheritance is therefore entirely shifted to the object level. This requires objects to be modelled by some kind of generators instead of plain records.

Furthermore, as the receiver ('self') can *also* be subject to extension and objects are represented as generators, the interpretation of 'self' should also be a generator. Hence, conventional generators and fixed points will not do the job properly as objects need an *unfixed* rather than a fixed version of themselves for self-reference. The modified generator and wrapper domains are given below.

$$\text{Generator}_{\text{Wrap}} = \text{Generator}_{\text{Wrap}} \rightarrow \text{Object}$$

$$\text{Wrapper}_{\text{Wrap}} = \text{Object} \rightarrow \text{Generator}_{\text{Wrap}}$$

In contrast with the earlier generator domain, the new domain requires self-application instead of taking the fixed point: its argument domain is of the same type as the generator domain itself. We will call this operation 'Wrap'.

$$\text{Wrap} : \text{Generator}_{\text{Wrap}} \rightarrow \text{Object}$$

$$\text{Wrap} = \lambda g\ .\ (g\ g)$$

The quite subtle difference between wrapping and taking a fixed point is illustrated in figure 4.

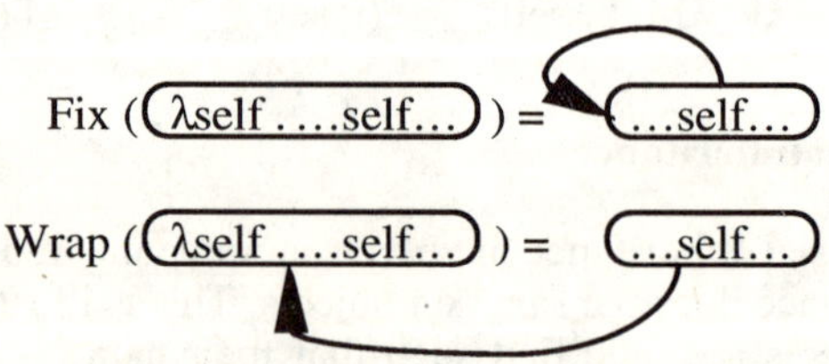

Fig. 4.

Taking the fixed point of a function offers the function an internal version of itself. Wrapping a function on the other hand, gives the function an external version of itself; i.e. it becomes possible for the function to refer to itself as if it were neither wrapped nor fixed.

Three important remarks have to be made here.

First, the previous inheritance *technique* remains applicable but, of course, on the new generator domain.

$$\text{Inherit}_{\text{Objects}} : \text{Generator}_{\text{Wrap}} \rightarrow \text{Wrapper}_{\text{Wrap}} \rightarrow \text{Generator}_{\text{Wrap}}$$

$$\text{Inherit}_{\text{Objects}} = \lambda P.\ \lambda M\ .\ (\lambda \text{self}_{\text{generator}}\ .\ (P\ \text{self}_{\text{generator}}) +_{r} (M\ (P\ \text{self}_{\text{generator}})\ \text{self}_{\text{generator}})\ )$$

From this it can be concluded that *class-based and object-based inheritance share the same inheritance mechanism.* This can be regarded as the semantic counterpart of an insight discovered by Stein who has shown that it is perfectly possible to program 'prototype-style' in a class-based language when classes are treated as objects (see [16]).

Second, the consequence of representing objects as generators is that message passing must always be preceded by wrapping the receiver as the receiver should be provided with a correct self-reference each time a message is sent. This is also the major difference with class-based inheritance. *Class-based and object-based inheritance have a different message passing mechanism and therefore a different object model.*

Finally, it should be noticed that our semantic treatment of object-based inheritance, outlined in this section, can also be used to model class-based inheritance. As argued in [7] this results in a semantics that is less abstract. The same work also gives a more mathematical treatment of the relationship between the fixed-point model and the self-application model, albeit in the context of class-based languages.

3 Object-Based Inheritance Breaches Encapsulation

The main objection against conventional object-based inheritance is that it suffers from an inherent encapsulation problem with respect to specialisation interfaces. This needs some explanation.

In the literature much has been said already about breaching of encapsulation by inheritors. Snyder, for example, discusses how different inheritance strategies allow inheritors to breach the encapsulation of the parent [15]. The most simple form of decapsulation is where an inheritor can directly access the instance variables of its ancestors.

The direct consequence of breaching encapsulation is that a parent of which the encapsulation is violated, *cannot* freely decide to change its implementation: all encapsulation breaching inheritors need to change their implementation with the parent. The solution of Snyder is to introduce encapsulated inheritance: inheriting clients have no direct access to the private attributes of their parent.

This does not prevent all violation of encapsulation however. Late binding of self, which is inherent to inheritance, also involves a form of decapsulation. Take for example a class-based encoding of our person example (figure 2). In this example the female subclass breaks the encapsulation of its person parent class by overriding the getName method, i.e. the person class can not change its implementation without having an effect on the implementation of the female subclass. If, for example, the person class decides to implement its print method in the style of the alternative person class (figure 2) then the female class will need to adapt its implementation also. So, although encapsulation towards inheritors is an important issue, it is clear that inheritors need to breach the encapsulation of their parent class to a certain degree. This is what makes inheritors special. *Not allowing* inheritors to use the specialisation interface of their parent would be a total neglect of the power of inheritance. *Allowing* to use the specialisation interface is a violation of encapsulation.

In class-based languages this is not a serious problem since the inheritance relation is rather static. The set of classes that breach the encapsulation of a parent is limited to a statically known set of inheritors and a clear distinction is made between inheriting and other clients. For object-based inheritance this is not the case.

```
CircleWithExpensiveGoldenWindow is Object
   private variable ExpensiveGoldenWindow
   method DrawInWindow (aWindow)
      ...
   method Draw is
      self.DrawInWindow(ExpensiveGoldenWindow)
WindowThief is Object
   method StealGoldenWindow (aCircle)
      is return (aCircle extended with
         override method DrawInWindow(aWindow)
                 is return aWindow
               ).Draw ; -- this actually does NO drawing

WindowThief.StealGoldenWindow(CircleWithExpensiveGoldenWindow)
```

Fig. 5.

Conventional object-based inheritance allows any object to be extended by any other. Therefore, anyone who can access the client interface of an object can also see its specialisation interface. In other words, with respect to the object involved, no distinction can be made between clients and inheritors. All clients can thus rely on the implementation details exported by the specialisation interface. This can even be stated more strongly. Object-based inheritance makes it impossible for a programmer to specify an *interface* (in the literal sense of the word). A client, dissatisfied with the restrictions a client interface imposes, can always patch up some additional methods in order to enhance its access priorities. This is certainly the case in object-based languages where inheritors have direct access to parent variables. But even in absence of this feature (so called 'encapsulated inheritance' [15]) client interface encapsulation can be breached. This is illustrated in the example in figure 5. By a clever overriding of circle methods, a window thief is constructed that exports the private acquaintance of circle objects to all possible clients.

This breaching of encapsulation towards clients is unacceptable. This is restated in the following design principle:

The Immaculate Client Interface Principle for Objects

An object should not expose any other interface but the client interface to its message passing clients. It must be able to hide its specialisation interface from message passing clients.

Thus, concerning the client/specialisation interfaces a clear distinction must be made between message passing clients and inheriting clients. That object-based inheritance violates this principle is also reflected in its formal semantics. Indeed, in the previous section we showed that object-based inheritance is only possible if objects are modelled as generators instead of encapsulated objects (in order to ensure late binding of self). In such a model, however, any client is allowed to fill in the self parameter of an object at its own will. In other words, the very model of object-based inheritance requires that any client can always pass a new extension as the self parameter of an object. But then a permanent danger exists that a 'dummy'-extension is made with the intention of decapsulating the implementation details of an acquaintance.

Hence, at the semantic level, the encapsulation problems boil down to the fact that languages providing object-based inheritance confuse their objects with explicit language-representations of generators and generator-manipulating operators. Notice that Smalltalk somehow suffers from the same problems. Since everything in Smalltalk is an object (even classes and meta classes), at some point, the implementation of the `subclass:modification` method must take its own generator in order to mix it with the given modifier (read: wrapper). Hence, programming 'prototype-style' in Smalltalk by only making use of classes and omitting instantiation (as was illustrated in [16]) suffers precisely from the same problem. Again this stems from the fact that at some point, deep down in Smalltalk, a generator and a generator manipulating function is used.

Respecting our principle can therefore be expressed in the semantics of OOPLs with the following criterion.

The Object Criterion

An OOPL in which objects can be semantically modelled as encapsulated objects and that has no provisions for explicit generator manipulation is guaranteed to respect the immaculate client interface principle.

Current prototype-based languages do not pass the criterion and certainly do not respect the principle.

As can be deduced from the semantics outlined in section 2.3, the objects of pure class-based languages like Object-Pascal, C++ or Jigsaw (see [1]) can be modelled as encapsulated objects since they are fixed at instantiation time. Furthermore, pure class-based languages allow no explicit generator manipulation as their classes are compile-time structures. Hence, pure class-based languages pass the criterion and seem to be an adequate solution. However, pure class-based languages are a very drastic solution to the problems. They make a clear cut distinction between inheritable classes and non-inheritable objects. Specialisation interfaces are associated only with generators and not with objects. *Objects are not subject to extension* and therefore have no associated specialisation interface.

4 Prototypes With Encapsulated Specialisation Interfaces

Rather than concluding that pure class-based languages are the only solution, we will reconsider the design characteristics of object-based inheritance keeping in mind the need for a clear distinction between inheriting and other clients. A straightforward restriction of the visibility of specialisation interfaces to a limited set of 'inheritor' objects must be approached with caution however. As long as objects can *arbitrarily* subscribe to a specialisation interface, the same set of already discussed problems pops up. Solutions where the object under extension is *not* an active participant in the subscription process are *no* substantial improvements. In the next two sections an inheritance mechanism on objects is proposed that avoids these pitfalls. The result will be an evolutionary step towards an intersection of both paradigms (as indicated in figure 1).

4.1 The General Idea

Respecting the principle does not necessarily preclude inheritance from objects. On the contrary, even within the constraints, a whole scale of inheritance mechanisms remains possible. These mechanisms are characterised by the fact that they encapsulate the specialisation interface. Accordingly, at the semantic level they are characterised by the fact that generators are encapsulated, which is achieved by a hygienic use of wrapped generators to denote objects. Wrapped generators are encapsulated objects and therefore pass the first part of the criterion.

But the semantics of inheritance requires generators. Respecting the second part of the criterion thus implies that inheritance should be an operation of which the mechanics is hidden within the object. Extending an object is then accomplished through its client interface. We call this *encapsulated inheritance on objects*. So, the essence of our solution is that an object itself only provides a client interface but encapsulates a non encapsulated version of itself.

As this might seem a bit fuzzy, let us first give an example.

4.2 An Example Mechanism

The most stable version of encapsulated inheritance on objects that we have at the time of writing is an inheritance mechanism based on *mixin-methods*. Mixin methods were introduced in [19] and [11].

As indicated above, inheritance is an incremental modification mechanism where a modifier M modifies a parent P in order to produce a result R: R = P + M(P). The insight of [6] and [2] is to upgrade these modifiers to explicit language constructs. In language design they are called 'mixins' as they allow a modification to be mixed into a parent. Mixins are an attempt to improve the reusability of code.

The principle of mixin-methods is quite simple. Next to the usual methods, an object can list a number of mixin-methods in its interface. The definition of a mixin-method consists of variable declarations, method declarations and other mixin-methods. Mixin methods can be invoked —like ordinary methods— by sending a message. Upon invocation an extension of the receiving object is returned. This extension contains the declarations that can be found in the definition of the invoked mixin-method. Mixin methods were integrated in our Agora language (see [3]).

The power of this particular form of encapsulated inheritance will now be shown by a kernel version of Agora, called MiniMix. The very simple syntax[1] of MiniMix is given by the following grammar rules[2].

---

[1] See [14] for an excellent introduction to formal syntax and semantics of programming languages.

[2] In the paper only the important aspects of MiniMix will be explained. The interested reader can find a complete formal semantics of MiniMix in the appendix.

$P \rightarrow OE$

A program is an object expression

$OE \rightarrow ME \mid I \mid B \mid$ '**self**' | '**super**' | '**object**' AB

An object expression is (the result of) a message expression, an identifier, a basic object, a pseudo variable or an object created ex-nihilo with an abstraction.

$ME \rightarrow$ '**send**' OE_1 I '(' OE_2 ')'

A message I is sent to an object OE_1 with OE_2 as an actual parameter.

$AB \rightarrow$ '[' AD ']'

$AD \rightarrow$ '**method**' I_1 '(' I_2 ')' OE | '**mixin**' I_1 '(' I_2 ')' AB | AD_1 ';' AD_2

Abstractions are sequences of methods and mixin-methods. They are used to create objects with. Mixins and methods are attribute declarations (AD). They both require a parameter I_2. The result of a method is the evaluation of its body OE while the result of a mixin-method is the object extended with the listed (mixin) methods, i.e. with a given abstraction (AB).

The syntax of the language and its use should be clear by the following MiniMix version of figure 2.

```
object [
    mixin Person (name)
    [ method getName (void) name;
      method print (void)
         send send self getName(void) print(void);
      mixin MakeFemale (void)
       [ method getName (void)
         send "Ms." concat ( send super getName(void))
      ] ];
    mixin AlternativePerson (name)
    [ method getName (void) name;
      method print (void) send name print(void);
      mixin MakeFemale (void)
       [ method getName (void)
         send "Ms." concat( send super getName(void));
        method print (void)
         send send self getName(void) print(void)
      ] ] ]
```

Fig. 6.

Let us now take a look at the semantics in order to explain why mixin-methods do pass the object criterion and therefore follow the immaculate client interface principle.

For the sake of clarity, the semantic domains of MiniMix are summarised below[1].

Object = Ident → Attribute

Attribute = Object → Object

Generator = Generator → Object

Env = Ident → Object

Wrapper = Object → Generator

An object expression is always evaluated using the current unwrapped self ('g' in the equations below), the current environment ('e' in the equations) and the current super object ('p' in the equations). The interpretations of identifiers and pseudo variables then are

$\mathbb{OE}$: **ObjExpr** → Env → Object → Generator → Object

$\mathbb{OE}$ ⟦ **self** ⟧ = λe . λp . λg . (Wrap g)

$\mathbb{OE}$ ⟦**super**⟧ = λe . λp . λg . p

$\mathbb{OE}$ ⟦ I ⟧ = λe . λp . λg . (e I)

The interpretation of self confirms that objects are modelled by encapsulated objects. A self reference is achieved by wrapping the 'current generator'.

The semantics of message passing consists of selecting the appropriate attribute in the interpretation of the receiver and applying this attribute to the semantic object denoting the argument:

$\mathbb{ME}$: **Msg** → Env → Object → Generator → Object

$\mathbb{ME}$ ⟦ **send** OE_1 I (OE_2) ⟧ = λe.λp.λg.(($\mathbb{OE}$⟦ OE_1 ⟧ e p g) I) ($\mathbb{OE}$⟦ OE_2⟧ e p g)

As can be seen in the grammar, an object can be created ex-nihilo by writing an abstraction **object** AB. Therefore, the semantics of ex-nihilo created objects requires understanding the semantics of abstractions. The body of a mixin-method is also an abstraction. Since the body of a mixin-method is a modifier, its denotation is a wrapper and hence abstractions are denoted by wrappers.

$\mathbb{AB}$: **Abstr** → Env → Wrapper

$\mathbb{AB}$ ⟦ **[AD]** ⟧ = λe.($\mathbb{AD}$ ⟦AD⟧ e)

---

[1] We will only consider attributes that are one-argument operations (i.e. Attribute = Object → Object).

An ex-nihilo created (encapsulated!) object is nothing more than a wrapped wrapper with an empty super ($\perp$[1]).

$$\mathbb{OE}\,[\![\, \textbf{object}\ AB \,]\!] = \lambda e\,.\,\lambda p\,.\,\lambda g\,.\,(\mathrm{Wrap}\,(\,\mathbb{AB}\,[\![\, AB \,]\!]\ e\ \perp))$$

An abstraction is a sequence of attribute declarations. As above, all attribute declarations are evaluated making use of the current environment, the current super and the current unwrapped self. This gives us the specification for the semantic function of attribute declarations.

$$\mathbb{AD} : \textbf{AttDec} \rightarrow \mathrm{Env} \rightarrow \mathrm{Object} \rightarrow \mathrm{Generator} \rightarrow \mathrm{Object}$$

A list of attributes is recursively defined by the concatenation of two such other lists. The same therefore goes for its semantics.

$$\mathbb{AD}\,[\![\, AD_1\ ;\ AD_2 \,]\!] = \lambda e.\lambda p.\lambda g.(\mathbb{AD}\,[\![AD_1]\!]\ e\ p\ g) +_r (\mathbb{AD}\,[\![AD_2]\!]\ e\ p\ g)$$

At the lowest level in such a sequence, methods and mixin-methods are declared. This declaration binds a name to a one parameter function containing the effect of invoking the attribute (records are represented as [I→λo.…]).

$$\mathbb{AD}\,[\![\, \textbf{method}\ I_1\ (\,I_2\,)\ OE \,]\!] = \lambda e.\lambda p.\lambda g.\Big[\ I_1 \rightarrow \lambda o.\mathbb{OE}[\![OE\,]\!]\ e[I_2/o]\ p\ g\Big]$$

$$\mathbb{AD}[\![\, \textbf{mixin}\ I_1(\,I_2)\ AB]\!] = \lambda e.\lambda p.\lambda g.\Big[I_1 \rightarrow \lambda o.\Big(\mathrm{Wrap}\Big(\mathrm{Inherit}_{\mathrm{Objects}}\ g\ (\mathbb{AB}[\![AB\,]\!]\ e[I_2/o])\Big)\Big)\Big]$$

In the case of methods the effect is the denotation of the method body expression in the current environment extended with the actual parameter binding. The effect of a mixin invocation is explained by extending the current unwrapped self with the wrapper denoting the mixin-method body $\Big(\mathrm{Wrap}\Big(\mathrm{Inherit}_{\mathrm{Objects}}\ g\ (\mathbb{AB}[\![AB\,]\!]\ e[I_2/o])\Big)\Big)$.

Mixin methods pass the object criterion. By a case analysis of the above semantic clauses, it can be verified that we make a hygienic use of wrapping each time an object is created: ex-nihilo, by invocation of a mixin-method and by returning a self object. Message passing thus involves neither wrapping nor fixing. Furthermore, generators are not expressed as explicit language values.

5 Discussion

5.1 Encapsulated Inheritance on Objects: A Marriage Without Unwanted Children

The most obvious difference between class-based and object-based languages is the difference in inheritance models (i.e. inheritable entities). As is widely known, class-based languages strictly separate their object and inheritance models into objects and classes. Object-based inheritance languages strive towards a unification of these

---

[1] All error handling and undefined values are handled by non-termination as these are not relevant to the paper.

models. The catch however is that *the shift from class-based inheritance to conventional object-based inheritance also involves a dramatical shift in the object model.* The object model employed by conventional object-based inheritance is fundamentally different as it suffers from inherent encapsulation problems.

Under the assumption of the immaculate client interface principle, conventional techniques only made class-based inheritance possible (figure 7 a). The contribution of our work is that we showed that the models *can* be unified without changing the object model. Figure 7 b illustrates the new situation: inheritance on encapsulated objects without the intermediate class construct.

Encapsulated inheritance on objects is a marriage between the object model employed by class-based languages and the inheritance model used in existing object-based inheritance. The semantic counterpart is that it inherits the object domain of the class-based languages of section 2.1 and the generator domain of object-based inheritance given in section 2.3.

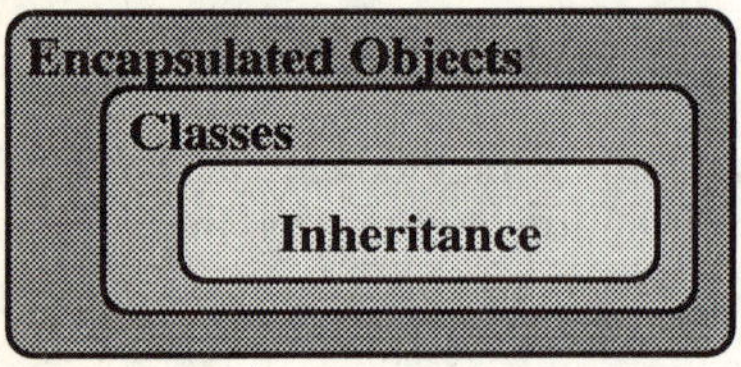

Fig. 7.a.

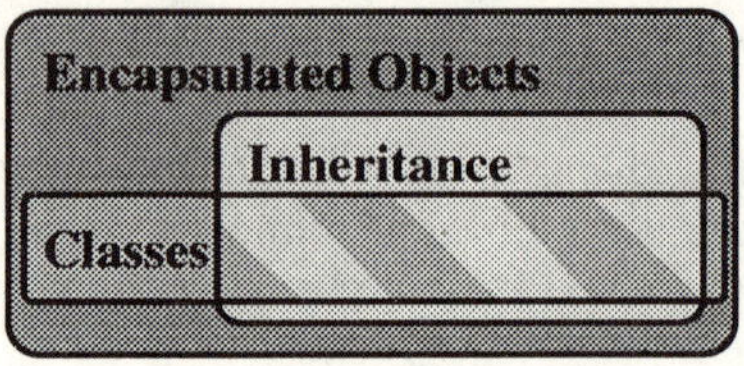

Fig. 7.b.

The above figure also indicates that this allows a possible reconsideration of reintroducing classes in prototype-based languages, for example as a classification mechanism on objects. This problem can now be tackled independently of inheritance.

5.2 Overcoming the Limitations of our Example Mechanism

One of the most fundamental criticisms against mixin-methods is that an object is required to know all its possible extensions in advance.

We claim that this criticism can be refuted by fine tuning the particular way encapsulated generators are brought back into the language development space. Although it requires more research, we already have a few (unstable) versions of Agora in which encapsulated generators can be exposed in a controlled manner.

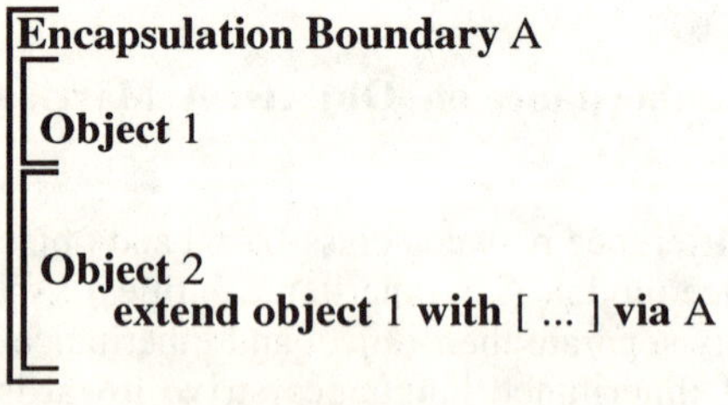

Fig. 8.

Figure 8 shows a very simple example language construct that strives to overcome this criticism. By placing objects together in a module, a controlled exposure of specialisation interfaces is achieved. Objects in the same module can extend each other directly while objects outside the module must go through the client interface. At the semantic level this is achieved by creating a generator environment of all the objects in the module and wrapping this environment - as a background operation - in every object belonging to the module.

A second possible criticism is that the current version of MiniMix (and Agora) allows a mixin-method to see the implementation details of some of its parents, because of the nested scoping of mixin-methods. This is an orthogonal language design decision. Flavours of MiniMix in which the visibility of parent attributes is restricted (as in [15]) can easily be defined within the current framework. For example, a version in which a distinction is made between private variables and protected variables in the style of C++, is perfectly imaginable.

A problem related to this is making specialisation interfaces explicit (see [9]). This is currently under investigation in order to make a statically typed version of MiniMix. Important for the claim made in this paper is that this is, again, orthogonal to the inheritance mechanism underlying MiniMix.

6 Conclusion

We have shown how object-based inheritance suffers from an inherent encapsulation problem concerning specialisation interfaces. We also pointed out that this problem is absent in pure class-based languages where a strict separation between inheritable and non-inheritable entities exists. The source of the problem can be traced back to the semantic level. Although classes and objects can share a common inheritance mechanism, object-based inheritance uses a model of objects that is fundamentally different and does not allow encapsulation.

This enforces us to combine the advantages and omit the shortcomings of both. In a denotational framework, this boils down to actually making a mixture of class-based and object-based inheritance. The result - encapsulated inheritance on objects - combines the clean object model of class-based languages with the more orthogonal inheritance model of object-based inheritance.

Finally, we have proposed an example encapsulated inheritance mechanism under the form of mixin-methods which can be seen as a draft proposal for encapsulated inheritance on objects.

7 Acknowledgements

We owe our gratitude to Theo D'Hondt, Carine Lucas, Serge Demeyer, Wim Codenie, Tom Mens, Marc Van Limberghen, Kim Mens, Niels Boyen and Kris De Volder for reading and giving comments on earlier draft versions of this paper. Furthermore we thank the anonymous referees for their useful comments. We also thank Prof. Theo D'Hondt for promoting our work.

References

[1] G. Bracha. The Programming Language Jigsaw: Mixins, Modularity and Multiple Inheritance. PhD thesis, Department of Computer Science, University of Utah, March 1992.

[2] G. Bracha and W. Cook. Mixin-based Inheritance. In Proceedings of the ACM Joint OOPSLA/ECOOP'90 Conference, ACM Sigplan Notices, 25(10), pp.303-311, ACM Press 1990.

[3] W. Codenie, K. De Hondt, T. D'Hondt, P. Steyaert. Agora: Message Passing as a Foundation for Exploring OO Languages. ACM Sigplan Notices, 29(12), pp. 48-57, ACM Press 1994.

[4] W. Cook and J. Palsberg. A Denotational Semantics of Inheritance and its Correctness. In Proceedings of the OOPSLA'89 Conference, ACM Sigplan Notices Vol. 24(10), pp433-443, ACM Press 1989.

[5] C. Dony, J. Malenfant, P. Cointe. Prototype-Based Languages: From a New Taxonomy to Constructive Proposals and Their Validation. In Proceedings of the OOPSLA'92 Conference, ACM Sigplan Notices Vol. 27(10), pp201-217, ACM Press 1992.

[6] A.V. Hense. Denotational Semantics of an Object-oriented Programming Language with Explicit Wrappers. Formal Aspects of Computing, pp. 3:1-000, 1992.

[7] S.N. Kamin and U.S. Reddy. Two Semantic Models of Object-Oriented Languages. In Theoretical of Object-Oriented Programming, C.A. Gunter and G.C. Mitchell (Eds.), MIT Press, 1994.

[8] G. Kiczales and J. Lamping. Issues in the Design and Documentation of Class Libraries. In Proceedings of the OOPSLA'92 Conference, ACM Sigplan Notices Vol. 27(10), pp435-451, ACM Press 1992.

[9] J. Lamping. Typing the Specialisation Interface. In Proceedings of the OOPSLA'93 Conference, ACM Sigplan Notices Vol. 28(10), pp201-214, ACM Press 1993.

[10] H. Lieberman. Using Prototypical Objects to Implement Shared Behaviour in an Object-Oriented System. In Proceedings of the OOPSLA'86 Conference, ACM Sigplan Notices, 21(11), pp. 214-223, ACM Press, 1986.

[11] C. Lucas, P. Steyaert. Modular Inheritance of Objects Through Mixin-Methods. In Proceedings of JMLC, (Peter Schulthess, ed.), pp. 273-282, Universitätsverlag ulm GmbH, 1994.

[12] T. Mens, K. Mens, P. Steyaert. OPUS, a Formal Approach to Object-Orientation. In Proceedings of FME'94, Formal Methods Europe, pp. 326-345, Lecture Notes in Computer Science 873, M. Naftalin, T. Denvir, M. Bertran (Eds.), Springer-Verlag, 1994.

[13] O. NierStrasz. A Survey of Object-Oriented Concepts. In Object-Oriented Concepts, Databases, and Applications, W. Kim and F.H. Lochovsky (Eds.), pp. 3-21, ACM Press and Addison-Wesley, 1989.

[14] D.A. Schmidt. Denotational Semantics: A Methodology for Language Development. Wm C. Brown Publishers (Dubuque Iowa), 1988.

[15] A. Snyder. Encapsulation and Inheritance in Object-Oriented Programming Languages. In Proceedings of the OOPSLA'86 Conference, ACM Sigplan Notices, 21(11), pp 38-45, ACM Press, 1986.

[16] L.A. Stein. Delegation is Inheritance, In Proceedings of the OOPSLA'87 Conference, ACM Sigplan Notices, 22(12), pp. 138-146, ACM Press, 1987.

[17] L.A. Stein, H. Lieberman, D. Ungar. A Shared View of Sharing: The Treaty of Orlando. In Object-Oriented Concepts, Databases, and Applications, W. Kim and F.H. Lochovsky (Eds.), pp. 31-48, ACM Press 1989.

[18] P. Steyaert. Open Design of Object-Oriented Languages: A Foundation for Specialisable Reflective Language Frameworks. Phd. thesis Vrije Universiteit Brussel, 1994.

[19] P. Steyaert, W. Codenie, T. D'Hondt, K. De Hondt, C. Lucas, M. Van Limberghen. Nested Mixin-Methods in Agora. In Proceedings of ECOOP'93 7th European Conference on Object-Oriented Programming, Lecture Notes in Computer Science 707, O. Nierstrasz (Ed.), pp. 197-219, Springer-Verlag, 1993.

[20] P. Wegner. Dimensions of Object-Based Language Design. In Proceedings of the OOPSLA'87 Conference, ACM Sigplan Notices, 22(12), pp.168-182, ACM Press, 1987.

[21] P. Wegner, S. B. Zdonik. Inheritance as an Incremental Modification Mechanism, or What Like is and Isn't Like. In Proceedings of ECOOP'88 European Conference on Object-Oriented Programming, Lecture Notes in Computer Science 322, S. Gjessing and K. Nygaard (Eds.), pp.55-77, Springer-Verlag 1988.

A Smalltalk-implementation of Agora and a Scheme-implementation of MiniMix are FTP-able from `progftp.vub.ac.be`
See also `progwww.vub.ac.be/prog/proghome.html`

Appendix The Definition of MiniMix

Syntax

I ∈ **Ident** , OE ∈ **ObjExpr**, B ∈ **Basic** , ME ∈ **Msg**, P ∈ **Program**, AB ∈ **Abstr**, AD ∈ **AttDec**

P → OE
OE → ME | I | B | **'self'** | **'super'** | **'object'** AB
ME → **'send'** OE_1 I '(' OE_2 ')'
AB → '[' AD ']'
AD → **'method'** I_1 '(' I_2 ')' OE | **'mixin'** I_1 '(' I_2 ')' AB | AD_1 ';' AD_2

Semantic domains

Object = Ident → Attribute
Attribute = Object → Object
Generator = Generator → Object
Wrapper = Object → Generator
Env = Ident → Object

Semantic Functions

$\mathbb{P}$: **Program**		→ Object
$\mathbb{B}$: **Basic**		→ Object
$\mathbb{OE}$: **ObjExpr**	→ Env → Object → Generator	→ Object
$\mathbb{ME}$: **Msg**	→ Env → Object → Generator	→ Object
$\mathbb{AB}$: **Abstr**	→ Env	→ Wrapper
$\mathbb{AD}$: **AttDec**	→ Env → Object → Generator	→ Object

Semantic clauses

$\mathbb{P}[\![\text{OE}]\!] = \text{Wrap}(\ \mathbb{OE}[\![\text{OE}]\!] \perp \perp)$

$\mathbb{OE}[\![\text{ME}]\!] = \lambda e.\lambda p.\lambda g.\mathbb{ME}[\![\text{ME}]\!]\ e\ p\ g$

$\mathbb{OE}[\![\text{I}]\!] = \lambda e.\lambda p.\lambda g.(e\ I)$

$\mathbb{OE}[\![\text{B}]\!] = \lambda e.\lambda p.\lambda g.\mathbb{B}[\![\text{B}]\!]$

$\mathbb{OE}[\![\textbf{self}]\!] = \lambda e.\lambda p.\lambda g.(\text{Wrap}\ g)$

$\mathbb{OE}[\![\textbf{super}]\!] = \lambda e.\lambda p.\lambda g.p$

$\mathbb{OE}[\![\textbf{object}\ \text{AB}]\!] = \lambda e.\lambda p.\lambda g.(\text{Wrap}\ (\ \mathbb{AB}[\![\text{AB}]\!]\ e \perp \perp))$

$\mathbb{ME}[\![\textbf{send}\ \text{OE}_1\ \text{I}\ (\ \text{OE}_2\ )\ ]\!] = \lambda e.\lambda p.\lambda s.((\mathbb{OE}[\![\text{OE}_1]\!]\ e\ p\ g)\ I\ )\ (\mathbb{OE}[\![\text{OE}_2]\!]\ e\ p\ g)$

$\mathbb{AB}[\![[\ \text{AD}\ ]\ ]\!] = \lambda e.(\mathbb{AD}[\![\text{AD}]\!]\ e)$

$\mathbb{AD}[\![\text{AD}_1\ ;\ \text{AD}_2]\!] = \lambda e.\lambda p.\lambda g.(\mathbb{AD}[\![\text{AD}_1]\!]\ e\ p\ g) +_r (\mathbb{AD}[\![\text{AD}_2]\!]\ e\ p\ g)$

$\mathbb{AD}[\![\textbf{method}\ \text{I}_1\ (\ \text{I}_2\ )\ \text{OE}]\!] = \lambda e.\lambda p.\lambda g.\Big[\ I_1 \to \lambda o.\mathbb{OE}[\![\text{OE}]\!]\ e[I_2/o]\ p\ g \Big]$

$\mathbb{AD}[\![\textbf{mixin}\ \text{I}_1\ (\ \text{I}_2\ )\ \text{AB}]\!]$

$$= \lambda e.\lambda p.\lambda g.\Big[I_1 \to \lambda o.\Big(\text{Wrap}\ \Big(\text{Inherit}_{\text{Objects}}\ g\ \ (\mathbb{AB}[\![\text{AB}]\!]\ e[I_2/o])\Big)\Big)\Big]$$

On Subtyping and Matching

Martín Abadi and Luca Cardelli

Digital Equipment Corporation, Systems Research Center

Abstract. A relation between recursive object types, called *matching*, has been proposed as a generalization of subtyping. Unlike subtyping, matching does not support subsumption, but it does support inheritance of binary methods. We argue that matching is a good idea, but that it should not be regarded as a form of F-bounded subtyping (as was originally intended). We show that a new interpretation of matching as higher-order subtyping has better properties. Matching turns out to be a third-order construction, possibly the only one to have been proposed for general use in programming.

1 Introduction

Subtyping is one of the most basic and best understood concepts in object-oriented programming. The subtyping relation can be defined rather naturally for first-order constructions such as record types, object types, function types, and recursive types [8, 15]. It can be extended to second-order constructions such as quantifiers for polymorphism and for data abstraction [18, 22], and to type operators [20, 34]. In programming, subtyping is the basis for both subsumption and inheritance.

Unfortunately, the subtyping relation does not hold between some recursively defined object types that arise commonly [14, 23]. This failure of subtyping is necessary for soundness. The standard, pragmatic solution is to weaken type definitions so that subtyping is achieved, and to use dynamic type tests to recover lost type information (as for example in Modula-3 [33]). A better solution is to employ Self types (as in [4, 5]), but this helps only for covariant occurrences of recursion variables (e.g., not for binary methods [10]).

Recently, a relation between recursive object types, called *matching*, has been proposed to circumvent this problem [13]. Unlike subtyping, matching does not support subsumption, but it does support inheritance of binary methods and parameterization. The original interpretation of matching was in terms of F-bounded subtyping. We show that a new interpretation of matching as higher-order subtyping has better properties, and produces the expected typing rules.

In the next section we explain the basic issues by means of examples and we hint at a solution based on the informal concept of protocol. In section 3 we introduce the matching relation, which is intended to capture the notion of protocol extension. In section 4 we present type operators, which are a formal counterpart for protocols. In the following two sections, we use type operators to explain matching. In section 5 we discuss a tentative formalization of matching in terms of F-bounded subtyping. In section 6 we present a more satisfactory formalization of matching in terms of higher-order subtyping. In section 7 we apply our techniques to express classes and inheritance.

2 The Power and Limits of Subtyping

In this section we introduce two examples that we use throughout the paper. The first example is that of two types in the subtyping relation. Thanks to subtyping, simple techniques allow us to express classes with inheritance. In the second example, subtyping fails. We describe informally the notion of protocol extension, which is a possible replacement for subtyping.

2.1 Objects Types and Subtyping

We introduce our notation and some basic typing rules in the context of our first example. This example illustrates how subtyping works.

We consider two types Inc and IncDec containing an integer field and some methods:

$$\begin{aligned} \mathrm{Inc} &\triangleq \mu(X)[\mathrm{n}{:}\mathrm{Int},\ \mathrm{inc}^{+}{:}X] \\ \mathrm{IncDec} &\triangleq \mu(Y)[\mathrm{n}{:}\mathrm{Int},\ \mathrm{inc}^{+}{:}Y,\ \mathrm{dec}^{+}{:}Y] \end{aligned}$$

A type of the form $\mu(X)A$ is a recursive type. For now we assume that a recursive type and its unfolding are equivalent, in the sense that we consider $\mu(X)A\{X\} = A\{\mu(X)A\{X\}\}$. We refer to this as the *unfolding property* of recursive types. Thus, we have Inc = [n:Int, inc^{+}:Inc] and IncDec = [n:Int, inc^{+}:IncDec, dec^{+}:IncDec].

A type of the form $[v_i{:}B_i\ ^{i\in I},\ m_j^{+}{:}C_j\ ^{j\in J}]$ is an object type, where the v_i are updatable fields and the m_j are methods; we always indicate a method type by a $^{+}$ sign. For example, the type [n:Int, inc^{+}:Inc] has a field n of type Int and a method inc with result type Inc.

A typical object of type Inc is:

$$\begin{aligned} &p : \mathrm{Inc} \triangleq \\ &\quad [\mathrm{n} = 0, \\ &\quad \ \mathrm{inc} = \varsigma(\mathrm{self}{:}\ \mathrm{Inc})\ \mathrm{self.n} := \mathrm{self.n} + 1] \end{aligned}$$

Here p : Inc means that p has type Inc. The binder ς binds the self variable of the method inc. The code self.n := self.n +1 is the body of the method inc; the method returns the updated self.

The method inc can be understood roughly as the function λ(self: Inc) self.n := self.n +1, of type Inc$\rightarrow$Inc. However, we prefer to avoid the λ notation since the method is never explicitly applied to an argument. Instead, the method is invoked by writing p.inc; when p.inc is executed, p is bound to the self parameter.

Subtyping (<:) is a reflexive and transitive relation on types. For recursive types we have the rule:

$$\mu(X)A\{X\} <: \mu(Y)B\{Y\}$$
$$\text{if } X <: Y \text{ implies } A\{X\} <: B\{Y\}$$

Two recursive types are in the subtyping relation when their bodies are in the subtyping relation under the assumption that the recursion variables are in the subtyping relation [8].

For object types, we have the rule:

$$[v_i{:}B_i\ ^{i\in I}, m_j{}^+{:}C_j\ ^{j\in J}] <: [v_i{:}B_i\ ^{i\in I'}, m_j{}^+{:}C_j'\ ^{j\in J'}]$$
$$\text{if } C_j <: C_j' \text{ for all } j\in J', \text{ with } I'\subseteq I \text{ and } J'\subseteq J$$

A longer object type is a subtype of a shorter one. In addition, the result type of a method may be smaller in a subtype than in a supertype; the type of a field must be the same [2, 5]. The latter condition (the invariance of field types) is necessary for soundness, because fields can be updated.

Object types are often defined recursively; therefore, it is convenient to regard the combination of a recursive type and an object type as a single construction of the form:

$$\mu(X)[v_i{:}B_i\ ^{i\in I}, m_j{}^+{:}C_j\{X\}\ ^{j\in J}]$$

In this view, the recursion variable X is often called "MyType" or "Self": it is the type of the self parameter of methods. Combining the previous rules for subtyping, we obtain the following derived rule for recursive object types:

$$\mu(X)[v_i{:}B_i\ ^{i\in I}, m_j{}^+{:}C_j\{X\}\ ^{j\in J}] <: \mu(Y)[v_i{:}B_i\ ^{i\in I'}, m_j{}^+{:}C_j'\{Y\}\ ^{j\in J'}]$$
$$\text{if } X <: Y \text{ implies } C_j\{X\} <: C_j'\{Y\} \text{ for all } j\in J', \text{ with } I'\subseteq I \text{ and } J'\subseteq J$$

By applying this derived rule to our example, we obtain:

IncDec <: Inc

The subtyping relation between IncDec and Inc allows *subsumption*: we can treat a member of IncDec as a member of Inc. The general rule for subsumption is:

$$\text{if } a : A \text{ and } A <: B \text{ then } a : B$$

2.2 Inheritance

The subtyping relation between IncDec and Inc plays an important role in inheritance. From our perspective, inheritance is obtained by writing sufficiently polymorphic code fragments that can be instantiated and reused for implementing objects of several types. We can express the polymorphism of these fragments with bounded universal quantification. For example, consider a function that increments the field n of its argument and returns the modified argument; this function works for arguments of type Inc, and also for arguments of subtypes of Inc. This is written:

$$\text{pre-inc} : \forall(X<:\text{Inc})X\rightarrow X \ \triangleq$$
$$\lambda(X<:\text{Inc})\ \lambda(\text{self}:X)\ \text{self.n} := \text{self.n}+1$$

To typecheck the body of pre-inc, we use rules implying that if X <: Inc and self:X then self.n:Int and, for b:Int, self.n:=b : X. (See [5] for a discussion of these rules.)

We call a code fragment such as pre-inc a *pre-method*. By polymorphic specialization of pre-inc we can obtain code suitable for implementing the method inc in an object of type Inc or IncDec:

$$\text{pre-inc(Inc)} : \text{Inc}\rightarrow\text{Inc}$$
$$\text{pre-inc(IncDec)} : \text{IncDec}\rightarrow\text{IncDec}$$

Thus, the generic pre-method pre-inc, which was presumably first written for building objects of type Inc, can be reused for building objects of type IncDec, because IncDec <: Inc. The reuse does not require retypechecking the pre-method.

2.3 Classes

Pre-method reuse can be systematized by assembling collections of pre-methods into *classes*. A class for an object type A can be described as a collection of pre-methods and initial field values, plus a way of generating new objects of type A. Such a collection could be taken as primitive; instead, we choose to represent classes as objects [2, 5]. Although it may be mildly confusing at first, this reduction of classes to objects has the advantage of making explicit the typing properties of methods and of object constructors.

In a class for an object type A, the pre-methods are parameterized over all subtypes of A, so that they can be reused (inherited) by any class for any subtype of A. Let A be a type of the form $\mu(X)[v_i{:}B_i{}^{i\in I}, m_j{}^{+}{:}C_j\{X\}{}^{j\in J}]$. As part of a class for A, a pre-method for m_j would have the type $\forall(X<:A)X\rightarrow C_j\{X\}$.

For example, IncClass and IncDecClass are the types of classes for Inc and IncDec, respectively:

$$\begin{aligned}&\text{IncClass} \ \triangleq\\&\quad[\text{new}^{+}{:}\ \text{Inc},\\&\quad\text{n: Int},\\&\quad\text{inc: } \forall(X<:\text{Inc})X\rightarrow X]\end{aligned}$$

IncDecClass $\triangleq$
[new^{+}: IncDec,
n: Int,
inc: $\forall(X<:IncDec)X\to X$,
dec: $\forall(X<:IncDec)X\to X$]

A typical class of type IncClass reads:

incClass : IncClass $\triangleq$
[new = ς(classSelf: IncClass)
[n = classSelf.n,
inc = ς(self:Inc) classSelf.inc(Inc)(self)]
n = 0,
inc = pre-inc]

The code for new is regular: it assembles all the pre-methods and initial field values of the class into a new object. The variable classSelf denotes the incClass object, and classSelf.inc is pre-inc.

Inheritance is obtained by extracting a pre-method from a class and reusing it for constructing another class. For example, the pre-method pre-inc of type $\forall(X<:Inc)X\to X$ in a class for Inc could be extracted and reused as a pre-method of type $\forall(X<:IncDec)X\to X$ in a class for IncDec:

incDecClass : IncDecClass $\triangleq$
[new = ς(classSelf: IncDecClass)[...]
n = 0,
inc = incClass.inc
dec = ...]

This example of inheritance requires the subtyping $\forall(X<:Inc)X\to X <: \forall(X<:IncDec)X\to X$, which follows from the subtyping rules for quantified types and function types:

$\forall(X<:A)B <: \forall(X<:A')B'$	if $A'<:A$ and if $X<:A$ implies $B<:B'$
$A\to B <: A'\to B'$	if $A' <: A$ and $B <: B'$

In summary, inheritance from a class for Inc to a class for IncDec is enabled by the subtyping IncDec <: Inc. Unfortunately, inheritance is possible and desirable even in situations where such subtypings do not exist. As we shall see in the rest of the paper, a more general treatment of inheritance requires a more sophisticated treatment of classes, based on relations between object types other than subtyping.

2.4 Binary Methods

We now consider an example similar to the one of Inc and IncDec, but with binary methods. The first parameter of a binary method is self and the second parameter must have the same type as self. In our example, we consider a recursive object type Max, with a field n and a binary method max. Our intent is that max takes two objects (self and other) and returns the object that has the greatest value for the field n.

$$\text{Max} \triangleq \mu(X)[\text{n:Int}, \text{max}^{+}:X \rightarrow X]$$

We consider also a type MinMax with an additional binary method min:

$$\text{MinMax} \triangleq \mu(Y)[\text{n:Int}, \text{max}^{+}:Y \rightarrow Y, \text{min}^{+}:Y \rightarrow Y]$$

When we attempt to reproduce the development of the previous sections, we immediately run into a difficulty: the subtyping MinMax <: Max does not hold according to the rules we have adopted. Moreover, it would be unsound to ignore this failure, as it is easy to construct examples where allowing MinMax <: Max leads to run-time errors.

Technically, an attempt to prove MinMax <: Max fails at the point where we try to verify that $X \rightarrow X <: Y \rightarrow Y$ under the assumption that $X <: Y$. Since the occurrences of X and Y on the left of $\rightarrow$ are contravariant, we would need $Y <: X$, which is the opposite of the assumption we have available.

We may now observe that the development in section 2.1 relies on the fact that the type for the method inc is covariant with respect to the recursion variable that represents Self. Whenever this covariance condition is violated, as with binary methods, a longer recursive object type is not a subtype of a shorter recursive object type.

The failure of subtyping has dire consequences beyond the loss of subsumption. We can still parameterize over the subtypes of Max, for example writing a pre-method for max:

pre-max : $\forall(X<:\text{Max})X \rightarrow X \rightarrow X \triangleq$
    $\lambda(X<:\text{Max})\ \lambda(\text{self}:X)\ \lambda(\text{other}:X)$
        if self.n>other.n then self else other

However, this parameterization is of no benefit, since the pre-method cannot be specialized at type MinMax. Similarly, we lose inheritability of pre-methods: since $\forall(X<:\text{Max})X \rightarrow X$ is not a subtype of $\forall(X<:\text{MinMax})X \rightarrow X$, the pre-method pre-max cannot be reused in building a class for MinMax.

The lack of inheritance is most disappointing, because the code for pre-max can in fact be given any type of the form:

$$\forall(X<:\mu(Y)[\text{n:Int}, \text{max}^{+}:Y \rightarrow Y, \ldots \textit{(anything)} \ldots])X \rightarrow X \rightarrow X$$

Without inheritance, we may have to rewrite the code for pre-max for many types of this form, retypechecking it in each case. In particular, we may have to write:

$$\text{pre-max}' : \forall(X<:\text{MinMax})X\rightarrow X\rightarrow X \triangleq$$
$$\lambda(X<:\text{MinMax})\ \lambda(\text{self}:X)\ \lambda(\text{other}:X)$$
$$\text{if self.n>other.n then self else other}$$

The body of the pre-method (namely, if self.n>other.n then self else other) does not change. We would be able to reuse pre-max if only we could write down an appropriate polymorphic type for it.

2.5 Protocols

Our difficulties with inheritance can be traced back to the fact that MinMax is not a subtype of Max. Although there is no hope of forcing this subtyping, there is hope of finding some other useful formal relationship between these types. In this section we introduce the notion of *protocol,* in order to capture an intuitive relationship between Max and MinMax. Our discussion is informal, but we will soon see how to formalize the notions described here.

The protocol of an object characterizes its interface, much like the type of the object; the protocol consists of the names of fields and methods of the object, together with their types. The protocol can be derived from the type of the object, and differs from it only by the absence of recursion. Informally, the protocol of a recursive object type $\mu(X)[v_i{:}B_i\ ^{i\in I}, m_j^+{:}C_j\{X\}\ ^{j\in J}]$ is the collection of names and types:

$$v_i{:}B_i\ ^{i\in I}, m_j^+{:}C_j\{\mathbf{Self}\}\ ^{j\in J}$$

For now, we use **Self** as a keyword, without pondering what it means. The protocols of Max and MinMax are:

$$\text{MaxProtocol} \triangleq \text{n:Int}, \text{max}^+{:}\mathbf{Self}\rightarrow\mathbf{Self}$$
$$\text{MinMaxProtocol} \triangleq \text{n:Int}, \text{max}^+{:}\mathbf{Self}\rightarrow\mathbf{Self}, \text{min}^+{:}\mathbf{Self}\rightarrow\mathbf{Self}$$

We introduce also a *protocol-extension* relation, with the following tentative definition:

$$v_i{:}B_i\ ^{i\in I}, m_j^+{:}C_j\{\mathbf{Self}\}\ ^{j\in J}\ \ \textit{extends}\ \ v_i{:}B_i\ ^{i\in I'}, m_j^+{:}C_j'\{\mathbf{Self}\}\ ^{j\in J'}$$
$$\text{if } C_j\{\mathbf{Self}\} <: C_j'\{\mathbf{Self}\} \text{ for all } j\in J', \text{ with } I'\subseteq I \text{ and } J'\subseteq J$$

In this definition, we treat **Self** as a type (and assume, for example, that **Self** <: **Self**). We may now assert that the protocol of MinMax extends the protocol of Max:

$$\text{MinMaxProtocol}\ \ \textit{extends}\ \ \text{MaxProtocol}$$

This is not the same as asserting (incorrectly) that MinMax is a subtype of Max.

When properly formalized, the notion of protocol extension could be used in parameterization, in place of subtyping. For example, when parameterizing over a type X, we would like to be able to express the constraint that the protocol of X extends MaxProtocol, meaning that the protocol of X includes a field n of type Int and a method max of type **Self→Self**. We could then say that, for every such X, the function pre-max has type $X \to X \to X$. We will see how to express this constraint as an appropriate polymorphic type, and will be able to write pre-max so that it is inheritable.

3 Matching

There have been several theoretical and practical approaches that capture concepts similar to that of protocol [14, 17, 21, 24, 25, 27, 28, 29, 30, 32]. Recently, Bruce *et al.* [9, 13] proposed axiomatizing the protocol-extension relation as if it were a relation between recursive object types, called *matching*. In this section we start considering that proposal. We identify some basic properties of matching and then show how we use matching for inheritance of binary methods.

3.1 Basic Properties of Matching

We write $A <\# B$ to mean that A matches B; that is, that the protocol of A extends the protocol of B. We do not yet consider how to prove the assertion $A <\# B$, but we expect to have, for example:

$$\text{IncDec} <\# \text{Inc}$$
$$\text{MinMax} <\# \text{Max}$$

In particular, we may write $X <\# A$, where X is a variable. We may then quantify over all types that match a given one, as follows:

$$\forall(X<\#A)B\{X\}$$

We call $\forall(X<\#A)B$ *match-bounded quantification*, and say that occurrences of X in B are *match-bound*.

Using match-bounded quantification, we can rewrite the polymorphic function pre-inc in terms of matching rather than subtyping:

$$\begin{aligned}&\text{pre-inc} : \forall(X<\#\text{Inc})X\to X \;\triangleq\\ &\quad \lambda(X<\#\text{Inc})\ \lambda(\text{self}{:}X)\ \text{self.n} := \text{self.n}+1\end{aligned}$$

$$\text{pre-inc(IncDec)} : \text{IncDec}\to\text{IncDec}$$

It remains to see why this code fragment typechecks. Some of the necessary properties are:

$$\text{if } X<\#\text{Inc and } x{:}X \text{ then } x.n : \text{Int}$$
$$\text{if } X<\#\text{Inc and } x{:}X \text{ and } b{:}\text{Int then } x.n{:=}b : X$$

Similarly, we can write a polymorphic version of the function pre-max:

$$\begin{array}{l}\text{pre-max} : \forall(X<\#Max)X\rightarrow X\rightarrow X \;\triangleq \\ \quad \lambda(X<\#Max)\ \lambda(self{:}X)\ \lambda(other{:}X) \\ \qquad \text{if } self.n>other.n \text{ then } self \text{ else } other\end{array}$$

$$\text{pre-max}(MinMax) : MinMax\rightarrow MinMax\rightarrow MinMax$$

For typechecking this code fragment, we need:

$$\text{if } X<\#Max \text{ and } x{:}X \text{ then } x.n : Int$$

Thus, the use of match-bounded quantification enables us to express the polymorphism of pre-max. The treatment of pre-max is not substantially different from that of pre-inc: contravariant and covariant occurrences of Self are treated uniformly.

We have not used subsumption in either of these examples. In fact, since we think of matching as protocol extension, we do not expect a subsumption-like property to hold for matching:

$$a : A \quad \text{and} \quad A <\# B \quad \text{need not imply} \quad a : B$$

The properties that we have attributed to matching must hold regardless.

The absence of a subsumption-like property can pose a problem. Knowing that A <# B is not quite as good as knowing that A <: B. For example, imagine that we forget that IncDec <: Inc and attempt to get by with IncDec <# Inc. Then we could not typecheck code such as:

$$\begin{array}{l}inc : Inc\rightarrow Inc \;\triangleq \\ \quad \lambda(x{:}Inc)\ x.n := x.n+1\end{array}$$

$$\lambda(x{:}IncDec)\ inc(x)$$

where we apply a function of type Inc→Inc to an object of type IncDec. We can circumvent this difficulty by turning inc into a polymorphic function of type $\forall(X<\#Inc)X\rightarrow X$:

$$\begin{array}{l}\text{pre-inc} : \forall(X<\#Inc)X\rightarrow X \;\triangleq \\ \quad \lambda(X<\#Inc)\ \lambda(x{:}X)\ x.n := x.n+1\end{array}$$

$$\lambda(x{:}IncDec)\ \text{pre-inc}(IncDec)(x)$$

Thus, at least in this example, we can do without subtyping (and subsumption), provided that we have the foresight of introducing sufficient parameterization. However, this parameterization may be cumbersome.

Despite this example, it is not clear whether matching can completely replace subtyping; we leave this as an open issue. We do not regard matching as a replacement for subtyping, but rather as a complement to subtyping.

3.2 Classes with Matching

We can now revise our treatment of classes from section 2.3, adapting it for matching. A class for an object type A can again be described as a collection of pre-methods and initial field values, plus a way of generating new objects of type A. The pre-methods are now parameterized over all object types matching A, so that they can be inherited by any class for an object type matching A. For example, MaxClass and MinMaxClass are the types for classes for Max and MinMax, respectively:

```
MaxClass ≜
    [new⁺: Max,
     n: Int,
     max: ∀(X<#Max)X→X→X]
MinMaxClass ≜
    [new⁺: MinMax,
     n: Int,
     max: ∀(X<#MinMax)X→X→X,
     min: ∀(X<#MinMax)X→X→X]
```

A typical class of type MaxClass reads:

```
maxClass : MaxClass ≜
    [new = ς(classSelf: MaxClass)
            [n = classSelf.n,
             max = ς(self:Max) classSelf.max(Max)(self)]
     n = 0,
     max = pre-max]
```

The code for new typechecks assuming that Max <# Max, so that classSelf.max(Max)(self) : Max→Max. The pre-method pre-max is as given in section 3.1.

A typical class of type MinMaxClass reads:

```
minMaxClass : MinMaxClass ≜
    [new = ς(classSelf: MinMaxClass)[...]
     n = 0,
     max = maxClass.max,
     min = ...]
```

The implementation of max is taken from maxClass, that is, it is inherited. The inheritance typechecks assuming that ∀(X<#Max)X→X→X <: ∀(X<#MinMax)X→X→X. Thus, we are still using some subtyping and subsumption as a basis for inheritance.

3.3 Discussion

In light of these examples, we may conclude that the idea of a matching relation is attractive:

- The fact that MinMax matches Max is reasonably intuitive, since the textual definition of MinMax does in fact match the textual definition of Max (with Self matching Self, and ignoring the additional components of MinMax). If anything, it is counterintuitive that subtyping should fail.
- Matching handles contravariant occurrences of Self and inheritance of binary methods.
- Matching is meant to be directly axiomatized as a relation between types, so the typing rules of a programming language that includes matching can be explained directly.
- Matching is simple from the programmer's point to of view, in comparison with more elaborate type-theoretic mechanisms that could be used in its place.

By examining examples, we have identified a few necessary properties of matching. However, we still have to settle on the exact typing rules for matching. These rules turn out to be different in proposed languages such as TOOPLE [9] and PolyTOIL [13]. The differences are subtle but fundamental. For example, in PolyTOIL matching is a transitive relation, while in TOOPLE it is not. We may further ask whether matching should be reflexive, or invariant under substitution. These questions, and more, inevitably arise in trying to design a programming language based on a matching relation.

We return to these questions in sections 5 and 6, where we consider two alternative formalizations of matching.

4 Type Operators

As we discussed in section 2, we are looking for formal relationships between the types Max and MinMax. These relationships might suggest a precise definition of matching, clarifying what we mean by the assertion MinMax <# Max; they might also suggest alternatives to matching.

In this section we introduce a theory of type operators that will enable us to express formal relationships between types.

4.1 Type Operators and Recursive Object Types

A type operator is a function from types to types [26]. We use the notations and rules of the lambda calculus for type operators: we write $\lambda(X)B\{X\}$ for the type operator that maps each type X to a corresponding type $B\{X\}$, write $F(A)$ for the application of the type operator F to the type A, and let $(\lambda(X)B\{X\})(A) = B\{A\}$.

We often move back and forth between type operators and their fixpoints. In one direction, we write F* for the fixpoint of the type operator F. In the opposite direction, we have the notation A_{Op}:

$$F^* \quad \text{abbreviates} \quad \mu(X)F(X)$$

$$A_{Op} \quad \text{abbreviates} \quad \lambda(X)D\{X\} \quad \text{whenever } A \equiv \mu(X)D\{X\}$$

When D{X} is an object type $[v_i{:}B_i\ ^{i\in I}, m_j^+{:}C_j\{X\}\ ^{j\in J}]$, the type operator A_{Op} is a formalization of the protocol of A. In this case A_{Op} is $\lambda(X)[v_i{:}B_i\ ^{i\in I}, m_j^+{:}C_j\{X\}\ ^{j\in J}]$; this type operator is analogous to the protocol $v_i{:}B_i\ ^{i\in I}, m_j^+{:}C_j\{\mathbf{Self}\}\ ^{j\in J}$, but differs in being fully formal (e.g., it does not mention the keyword **Self**). In the example of Max and MinMax, we obtain:

$$Max_{Op} \equiv \lambda(X)[n{:}Int, max^+{:}X\rightarrow X]$$
$$MinMax_{Op} \equiv \lambda(Y)[n{:}Int, max^+{:}Y\rightarrow Y, min^+{:}Y\rightarrow Y]$$

The unfolding property of recursive types yields:

$$Max_{Op}{}^* = \mu(X)\, Max_{Op}(X) = \mu(X)\,[n{:}Int, max^+{:}X\rightarrow X] = Max$$
$$Max_{Op}{}^* = Max_{Op}(\mu(X)\, Max_{Op}(X)) = Max_{Op}(Max)$$

Note that A_{Op} is defined in terms of the syntactic form μ(X)D{X} of A. In particular, the unfolding D{A} of A is not necessarily in a form such that $D\{A\}_{Op}$ is defined. Even if $D\{A\}_{Op}$ is defined, it need not equal A_{Op}. For example, consider:

$$D\{X\} \triangleq \mu(Y)\, X\rightarrow Y$$
$$A \triangleq \mu(X)\, D\{X\}$$
$$D\{A\} \equiv \mu(Y)\, A\rightarrow Y \qquad = A$$
$$A_{Op} \equiv \lambda(X)\, D\{X\}$$
$$D\{A\}_{Op} \equiv \lambda(Y)\, A\rightarrow Y \qquad \neq A_{Op}$$

Thus, we may have two types A and B such that A = B but $A_{Op} \neq B_{Op}$. This is a sign of trouble to come.

4.2 F-bounded Subtyping

F-bounded subtyping [14] was invented to support parameterization in the absence of subtyping. In the F-bounded approach, the property $A <: B_{Op}(A)$ is seen as a statement that the protocol of A extends the protocol of B.

We can explain this approach by reference to our examples. One common property of the types Max and MinMax is that they are both pre-fixpoints of Max_{Op}, that is:

$$Max <: Max_{Op}(Max) \qquad (= Max)$$
$$MinMax <: Max_{Op}(MinMax) \qquad (= [n{:}Int, max^+{:}MinMax\rightarrow MinMax])$$

As we said, Max_{Op} is a formalization of the protocol of Max. The property $X <: Max_{Op}(X)$ is seen as asserting that the protocol of X extends the protocol of Max. This view is justified because a recursive object type A such that $A <: [n:Int, max^+:A \to A]$ often has the shape $\mu(Y)[n:Int, max^+:Y \to Y, ...]$.

Since Max and MinMax are both pre-fixpoints of Max_{Op}, it is useful to parameterize over all types X with the property that $X <: Max_{Op}(X)$. Thus, a function of type:

$$\forall(X<:Max_{Op}(X))B\{X\}$$

can be instantiated for the types Max and MinMax, with instances of types B{Max} and B{MinMax}. In particular, this form of parameterization leads to a general typing of pre-max, and permits the inheritance of pre-max:

$$\begin{array}{l} \text{pre-max} : \forall(X<:Max_{Op}(X))X \to X \to X \ \triangleq \\ \quad \lambda(X<:Max_{Op}(X))\ \lambda(self:X)\ \lambda(other:X) \\ \qquad \text{if self.n>other.n then self else other} \end{array}$$

$$\begin{array}{l} \text{pre-max(Max)} : Max \to Max \to Max \\ \text{pre-max(MinMax)} : MinMax \to MinMax \to MinMax \end{array}$$

The code of pre-max is well-typed because $X <: Max_{Op}(X)$ and self:X imply self : $[n:Int, max^+:X \to X]$ by subsumption; similarly, other : $[n:Int, max^+:X \to X]$. The instantiation pre-max(Max) is well-typed because $Max = Max_{Op}(Max)$.

As this example shows, the unfolding property of recursive types is critical. In general, given a function $f : \forall(X<:A\{X\})B\{X\}$, we would expect to be able to write $f(\mu(X)A\{X\})$; but $f(\mu(X)A\{X\})$ is well-typed only if $\mu(X)A\{X\} <: A\{\mu(X)A\{X\}\}$, and this condition holds naturally if $\mu(X)A\{X\} = A\{\mu(X)A\{X\}\}$.

Quantification of the form $\forall(X<:A\{X\})B\{X\}$ is called F-bounded quantification; it is characterized by the constraint $X <: A\{X\}$. This form of quantification is peculiar in that the variable X is bounded by a type where X occurs. We usually encounter F-bounded quantification with A{X} of the form G(X) (for example, $Max_{Op}(X)$).

4.3 Higher-Order Subtyping

A second common property of Max and MinMax can be brought to light by defining a pointwise subtype order on type operators:

$$F \prec: G \qquad \text{if, for all X,} \quad F(X) <: G(X)$$

Just like type operators correspond to protocols, the subtype order on type operators is a direct formalization of the notion of protocol extension.

With this definition, we obtain:

$$\begin{array}{l} Max_{Op} \prec: Max_{Op} \\ MinMax_{Op} \prec: Max_{Op} \end{array}$$

Hence, we may want to parameterize over all type operators X with the property that $X \prec: Max_{Op}$. A polymorphic function of type:

$$\forall(X \prec: Max_{Op})B\{X\}$$

can be instantiated, by application to the type operators Max_{Op} and $MinMax_{Op}$; the corresponding instances have types $B\{Max_{Op}\}$ and $B\{MinMax_{Op}\}$. We need to be careful about how X is used in B{X}, because X is now a type operator. Our general strategy is to take the fixpoint of X whenever required; for example, we can obtain a typing for pre-max, as follows:

$$\begin{aligned}&\text{pre-max} : \forall(X \prec: Max_{Op})X^* \to X^* \to X^* \triangleq \\ &\quad \lambda(X \prec: Max_{Op})\ \lambda(\text{self}:X^*)\ \lambda(\text{other}:X^*) \\ &\qquad \text{if self.n>other.n then self else other}\end{aligned}$$

$$\text{pre-max}(MinMax_{Op}) : MinMax \to MinMax \to MinMax$$

The code of pre-max is well-typed because $X \prec: Max_{Op}$ implies $X^* = X(X^*) <: Max_{Op}(X^*)$ by definition of $\prec:$, and self:X^* implies self : $Max_{Op}(X^*) = [n:Int, max^+:X^* \to X^*]$ by subsumption; similarly, other : $[n:Int, max^+:X^* \to X^*]$.

In this derivation we have used the unfolding property $X^*=X(X^*)$. An alternative, that greatly simplifies the treatment of higher-order theories, is to assume only an explicit isomorphism between each recursive type and its unfolding, with no equality between the types. Two term-level primitives, fold and unfold, realize the isomorphism:

$$\begin{aligned}&\text{fold} : A\{\mu(X)A\{X\}\} \to \mu(X)A\{X\} \\ &\text{unfold} : \mu(X)A\{X\} \to A\{\mu(X)A\{X\}\}\end{aligned}$$

When we abandon the equality $X^*=X(X^*)$, we need to modify the code of pre-max; it suffices to write unfold(self).n and unfold(other).n instead of self.n and other.n.

4.4 Semantic Equivalence

We have encountered types of the forms $\forall(X<:D(X))B\{X\}$ and $\forall(Y \prec: D)B\{Y^*\}$, where D is a type operator and where if X is a type then B{X} is a type. We sketch an informal argument that $\forall(X<:D(X))B\{X\}$ and $\forall(Y \prec: D)B\{Y^*\}$ are semantically equal.

Let us consider a model of types in terms of sets of some sort, such as an ideal model or a per model [6, 7, 11, 16, 19, 31]. In these models, the interpretation of a type is a set, and the interpretation of a type operator is a function on sets. Quantification is interpreted by intersection. Type recursion is interpreted by unique fixpoints of contractive operators.

Let S, F, and G be the interpretations of A, $\lambda(X)B\{X\}$, and D, respectively. Then, $\bigcap_{X \subseteq S} F(X)$ is the interpretation of $\forall(X<:A)B\{X\}$, and fix(F) is the interpretation of $\mu(X)B\{X\}$. Moreover, let $G \preccurlyeq F$ mean that F and G are contractive and that, for all T, $G(T) \subseteq F(T)$ [12]; the interpretation of $\forall(X<:D)B\{X\}$ is $\bigcap_{U\preccurlyeq G} F(U)$. The contractiveness requirement for $G\preccurlyeq F$ is motivated by types of the form $\forall(Y<:D)...Y^*...$: the interpretation of Y^* requires Y to be contractive; additionally we assume that D is syntactically restricted so that its interpretation is a contractive operator. In particular, $\lambda(X)[v_i:B_i\ ^{i\in I}, m_j^+:C_j\{X\}\ ^{j\in J}]$ is a suitable D.

Under these assumptions, we can now prove that $\forall(X<:D(X))B\{X\}$ and $\forall(Y<:D)B\{Y^*\}$ are semantically equal, that is, that $\bigcap_{X\subseteq G(X)} F(X)$ and $\bigcap_{U\preccurlyeq G} F(\text{fix } U)$ are equal sets:

- First, $\bigcap_{U\preccurlyeq G} F(\text{fix } U)$ is included in $\bigcap_{X\subseteq G(X)} F(X)$: If $T\subseteq G(T)$ then there exists H such that $H\preccurlyeq G$ and $(\text{fix } H) = T$. An appropriate choice is $H = \lambda(X)(G(X)\cap T)$. We have that $H\preccurlyeq G$ because $H(X)\subseteq G(X)$ for all X and because contractiveness is preserved by intersection. In addition, $H(T) = G(T)\cap T = T$, since $T\subseteq G(T)$, so T is the fixpoint of H.
- Conversely, $\bigcap_{U\preccurlyeq G} F(\text{fix } U)$ includes $\bigcap_{X\subseteq G(X)} F(X)$: It suffices to notice that if $H\preccurlyeq G$ then $(\text{fix } H) = H(\text{fix } H) \subseteq G(\text{fix } H)$. Therefore, given $H\preccurlyeq G$, there exists $T\subseteq G(T)$ such that $T = (\text{fix } H)$, as needed.

The proof of equality uses a binary intersection operation on types. This operation is available in the models of interest, but is not always available syntactically. Therefore, the equality may not apply to particular syntactic systems.

Despite the equality, the higher-order framework is semantically more expressive than the F-bounded framework. The type $\forall(Y<:D)\forall(Z<:Y)B'\{Y^*,Z^*\}$ is not of the form $\forall(Y<:D)B\{Y^*\}$, because of the plain occurrence of Y in the bound $Z<:Y$. This type has no direct analogue in terms of F-bounded quantification.

4.5 Discussion

F-bounded subtyping and higher-order subtyping are both formal counterparts of protocol extension. These two kinds of subtyping have equal expressive power in many examples; this fact is consistent with the semantic equality established in section 4.4. F-bounded subtyping is appealing because it is a simple extension of second-order subtyping. Higher-order subtyping is appealing because it makes clear that protocols have to do with type operators.

The idea of using higher-order subtyping instead of F-bounded subtyping seems to have occurred to a number of people, including the Abel group at HP (Canning, Cook, Hill, and Olthoff), John Mitchell, and later Luca Cardelli. Although the idea dates back to at least 1989, apparently it was never written down, except in e-mail exchanges. The equality of section 4.4, due to Martín Abadi, appears in a 1990 e-mail exchange.

In the next two sections, we will see how F-bounded subtyping and higher-order subtyping can be used to interpret the matching relation. F-bounded subtyping was the original intended interpretation of matching [9]. Higher-order subtyping is our new interpretation. It is important to ask whether the two interpretations give rise to the same rules. As we will see, they do not. Higher-order subtyping has some definite advantages.

5 Matching as F-bounded Subtyping

Starting in this section, we consider translating a language with a primitive matching relation to a language without it. We refer to the former as the *source* language and to the latter as the *target* language. In this section, the target language is based on F-bounded subtyping.

5.1 The F-bounded Interpretation

The properties of F-bounded subtyping discussed in section 4.2 suggest that we may interpret matching in terms of F-bounded subtyping. To be precise, we would need to write a formal translation. The central idea of the translation is however rather simple; it is expressed by the following two clauses:

$$A <\# B \quad \approx \quad A <: B_{Op}(A)$$
$$\forall(X<\#A)B\{X\} \quad \approx \quad \forall(X<:A_{Op}(X))B\{X\}$$

Since matching is defined on object types of the source language, we must understand the type variable X as ranging only over those types, and not over arbitrary types of the source language. The typing rules of the source language can enforce this constraint, provided there is a separate category of object types, and a way for asserting that a type belongs to this category. An important rule of the source language would say that, under the assumption X <# A, the type variable X is an object type.

This translation is not defined when the right-hand side of <# is a variable, as in the case of cascading quantifiers:

$$\forall(X<\#A)\ \forall(Y<\#X) \ldots \quad \approx \quad ?$$

An expression of the form $\forall(X<:A_{Op}(X))\ \forall(Y<:X_{Op}(Y)) \ldots$ does not make sense as the translation of this type, because X_{Op} is not defined. Hence, we must adopt the restriction that, whenever $\forall(X<\#A)B$ is a type of the source language, the type A must have the form $\mu(X)[v_i{:}B_i{}^{i\in I}, m_j{}^{+}{:}C_j\{X\}{}^{j\in J}]$. Therefore, the type structure supported by this translation is somewhat irregular: type variables are not allowed in places where object types are allowed.

Next we examine other aspects of the F-bounded interpretation, finding several shortcomings.

5.2 Reflexivity and Transitivity

If A is an object type of the source language, then we would expect that A <# A. This reflexivity rule is necessary for justifying the instantiation f(A) of a polymorphic function $f : \forall(X<\#A)B$. According to the F-bounded interpretation, whenever A_{Op} is defined, we obtain:

$$A <\# A \quad \approx \quad A <: A_{Op}(A)$$

because $A = A_{Op}(A)$ by the unfolding property of recursive types. However, if A is a type variable X, then X_{Op} is not defined, so $X <: X_{Op}(X)$ does not make sense. Hence, reflexivity does not hold in general.

Turning now to transitivity, if A, B, and C are object types of the source language, then we would expect that A <# B and B <# C imply A <# C; this would mean:

$$A <: B_{Op}(A) \text{ and } B <: C_{Op}(B) \text{ imply } A <: C_{Op}(A)$$

As in the case of reflexivity, we run into difficulties with type variables. Moreover, we can see that transitivity fails even for closed types, with the following counterexample:

$$A \triangleq \mu(X)[p^+: X \to Int, q: Int]$$
$$B \triangleq \mu(X)[p^+: X \to Int]$$
$$C \triangleq \mu(X)[p^+: B \to Int]$$

We have both A <# B and B <# C, but we do not have A <# C (because $[p^+:A \to Int, q:Int] <: [p^+:B \to Int]$ fails).

We can trace this problem back to the definition of D_{Op}, which depends on the exact syntax of the type D. Because of the syntactic character of that definition, two equal types may behave differently with respect to matching. In our example, we have B = C by the unfolding property of recursive types (which is important for F-bounded quantification, as we discussed in section 4.2). Despite the equality B = C, we have A <# B but not A <# C.

5.3 Matching Self

According to the F-bounded interpretation, two types that look rather different may match. Consider two types A and A′ such that:

$$A \equiv \mu(X)[v_i:B_i{}^{i \in I}, m_j{}^+:C_j\{X\}{}^{j \in J}]$$
$$<\# \mu(X)[v_i:B_i{}^{i \in I}, m_j{}^+:C_j'\{X\}{}^{j \in J'}] \equiv A'$$

This holds when $A <: A'_{Op}(A)$, that is, when $[v_i:B_i{}^{i \in I}, m_j{}^+:C_j\{A\}{}^{j \in J}] <: [v_i:B_i{}^{i \in I}, m_j{}^+:C_j'\{A\}{}^{j \in J'}]$. It suffices that, for every $j \in J'$:

$$C_j\{A\} <: C_j'\{A\}$$

For example, we have:

$$\mu(X)[v:Int, m^+:X] <\# \mu(X)[m^+: [v:Int]]$$

Intuitively, the variable X on the left matches the type [v:Int] on the right. Since

X is the Self variable, we may say that Self matches not only Self but also other types (here [v:Int]). This treatment of Self is both sound and flexible. On the other hand, it can be difficult for a programmer to see whether two types match.

6 Matching as Higher-Order Subtyping

In section 5 we discussed some shortcomings of the F-bounded interpretation. In this section we argue that, in contrast, the interpretation of matching as higher-order subtyping is satisfactory, and specifically that it does not share those shortcomings.

6.1 The Higher-Order Interpretation

The higher-order interpretation relies on two translations of types of the source language. In certain contexts, types in the source language are interpreted as types of the target language, while in other contexts they are interpreted as type operators of the target language.

These two translations, *Type*⟨A⟩ and *Oper*⟨A⟩, can be informally summarized as follows. For object types of the source language, we set:

$$\mathit{Oper}\langle X\rangle \approx \quad \text{(assuming that X is match-bound)}$$
$$X$$

$$\mathit{Oper}\langle \mu(X)[v_i{:}B_i\ ^{i\in I},\ m_j^{+}{:}C_j\{X\}\ ^{j\in J}]\rangle \approx$$
$$\lambda(X)[v_i{:}\mathit{Type}\langle B_i\rangle\ ^{i\in I},\ m_j^{+}{:}\mathit{Type}\langle C_j\{X\}\rangle\ ^{j\in J}]$$

$$\mathit{Type}\langle X\rangle \approx \quad \text{(when X is match-bound)}$$
$$X^*$$

$$\mathit{Type}\langle \mu(X)[v_i{:}B_i\ ^{i\in I},\ m_j^{+}{:}C_j\{X\}\ ^{j\in J}]\rangle \approx$$
$$\mu(X)[v_i{:}\mathit{Type}\langle B_i\rangle\ ^{i\in I},\ m_j^{+}{:}\mathit{Type}\langle C_j\{X\}\rangle\ ^{j\in J}]$$

For other types, we set:

$$\mathit{Type}\langle X\rangle \approx X \quad \text{(when X is not match-bound)}$$
$$\mathit{Type}\langle A\to B\rangle \approx \mathit{Type}\langle A\rangle\to\mathit{Type}\langle B\rangle$$
$$\mathit{Type}\langle \forall(X<\#A)B\rangle \approx \forall(X<:\mathit{Oper}\langle A\rangle)\mathit{Type}\langle B\rangle$$

Here we assume the restriction that, whenever ∀(X<#A)B is a type of the source language, A must be an object type, that is, either a match-bound variable or a type of the form $\mu(X)[v_i{:}B_i\ ^{i\in I},\ m_j^{+}{:}C_j\{X\}\ ^{j\in J}]$. For example, μ(X)[l:∀(Y<#X)B, ...] is not allowed, while ∀(X<#A) [l: ∀(Y<#X)B, ...] is.

When X <# A is the bound of a quantifier, we distinguish the occurrences of X in a type context (as in X→X) from the ones in an operator context (as in ∀(Y<#X)...). The bound is translated as $X <: A_{Op}$; the occurrences of X in a type context are translated as X*, while the occurrences in an operator context are translated simply as X. For instance:

$$Type\langle\forall(X<\#Max)\ \forall(Y<\#X)\ X\rightarrow Y\rangle \approx$$
$$\forall(X<:Max_{Op})\ \forall(Y<:X)\ X^*\rightarrow Y^*$$

This translation is well-defined on type variables, so now there are no problems with cascading quantifiers.

Given these two translations of types, the translation of matching is now:

$$A <\# B \quad \approx \quad Oper\langle A\rangle <: Oper\langle B\rangle \qquad \text{for A,B object types}$$

The higher-order interpretation does not use the unfolding property of recursive types for the *target* language; instead, it uses explicit fold and unfold primitives as explained in section 4.3. On the other hand, the higher-order interpretation is incompatible with the unfolding property of recursive types in the *source* language, because $Oper\langle\mu(X)A\{X\}\rangle$ and $Oper\langle A\{\mu(X)A\{X\}\}\rangle$ are in general different type operators. Technically, the unfolding property of recursive types is not an essential feature and it is the origin of complications; we are fortunate to be able to drop it throughout.

6.2 Reflexivity and Transitivity

Reflexivity is now satisfied by all object types, including variables; for every object type A, we have:

$$A <\# A \quad \approx \quad Oper\langle A\rangle <: Oper\langle A\rangle$$

This follows from the reflexivity of <:, given that $Oper\langle A\rangle$ is a well-defined type operator for every object type A of the source language.

Similarly, transitivity is satisfied by all triples A,B, and C of object types, including variables:

$$A <\# B \ \text{ and } \ B <\# C \ \text{ imply } \ A <\# C \quad \approx$$
$$Oper\langle A\rangle <: Oper\langle B\rangle \ \text{ and } \ Oper\langle B\rangle <: Oper\langle C\rangle$$
$$\text{imply } \ Oper\langle A\rangle <: Oper\langle C\rangle$$

This follows from the transitivity of <:.

6.3 Matching Self

With the higher-order interpretation, the relation:

$$A \equiv \mu(Self)[v_i{:}B_i\ ^{i\in I},\ m_j^+{:}C_j\{Self\}\ ^{j\in J}]$$
$$<\#\ \mu(Self)[v_i{:}B_i\ ^{i\in I},\ m_j^+{:}C_j'\{Self\}\ ^{j\in J'}] \equiv A'$$

holds when the type operators corresponding to A and A′ are in the subtyping relation, that is, when:

$$[v_i{:}Type\langle B_i\rangle^{\,i\in I},\ m_j^{+}{:}Type\langle C_j\{Self\}\rangle^{\,j\in J}]$$
$$<:\ [v_i{:}Type\langle B_i\rangle^{\,i\in I},\ m_j^{+}{:}Type\langle C_j'\{Self\}\rangle^{\,j\in J'}] \qquad \text{for an arbitrary Self}$$

For this, it suffices that, for every j in J':

$$Type\langle C_j\{Self\}\rangle \ <:\ Type\langle C_j'\{Self\}\rangle$$

Since Self is μ-bound, all the occurrences of Self are translated as Self*. Then, an occurrence of Self* on the left can be matched only by a corresponding occurrence of Self* on the right, since Self is arbitrary. In short, *Self matches only itself.* This property makes it easy for programmers to glance at two object types and tell whether they match.

7 Inheritance and Classes via Higher-Order Subtyping

It is possible to make rigorous the translation of section 6, thus proving that matching can be explained in terms of higher-order subtyping. We do not do this here, but instead give further evidence by writing some examples and by showing that the basic properties of matching are supported and that binary methods can be inherited.

In section 3.1, we listed the following expected typings:

if X<#Inc and x:X then x.n : Int
if X<#Inc and x:X and b:Int then x.n:=b : X

The higher-order interpretation induces the following term translations:

if $X \prec: Inc_{Op}$ and x:X* then unfold(x).n : Int
if $X \prec: Inc_{Op}$ and x:X* and b:Int then fold(unfold(x).n:=b) : X*

For the first typing, we have unfold(x):X(X*). Moreover, from $X \prec: Inc_{Op}$ we obtain X(X*) <: Inc_{Op}(X*) = [n:Int, inc:X*]. Therefore, unfold(x):[n:Int, inc:X*], and unfold(x).n:Int.

For the second typing, we have again unfold(x):X(X*) with X(X*) <: [n:Int, inc:X*]. We then use a typing rule for field update in the target language [5]. This rule says that if a:A, c:C, and A <: [v:C,...] then (a.v:=c) : A. In our case, we have unfold(x):X(X*), b:Int, and X(X*) <: [n:Int, inc:X*]. We obtain (unfold(x).n:=b) : X(X*). Finally, by folding, we obtain fold(unfold(x).n:=b) : X*.

Applying our higher-order translation to MaxClass from section 3.2, we obtain:

$$\begin{aligned} &MaxClass \triangleq \\ &\quad [new^{+}{:}\ Max, \\ &\quad n{:}\ Int, \\ &\quad max{:}\ \forall(X \prec: Max_{Op})X^* \to X^* \to X^*] \end{aligned}$$

The corresponding translation at the term level produces:

$$
\begin{array}{l}
\text{maxClass} : \text{MaxClass} \triangleq \\
\quad [\text{new} = \varsigma(\text{classSelf: MaxClass}) \\
\qquad \text{fold}(\\
\qquad\quad [\text{n} = \text{classSelf.n}, \\
\qquad\quad\ \text{max} = \varsigma(\text{self:Max}_{\text{Op}}(\text{Max})) \\
\qquad\qquad\qquad \text{classSelf.max}(\text{Max}_{\text{Op}})(\text{fold}(\text{self}))]), \\
\quad \text{n} = 0, \\
\quad \text{max} = \text{pre-max}]
\end{array}
$$

$$
\begin{array}{l}
\text{pre-max} : \forall(X \mathrel{<\!\!:} \text{Max}_{\text{Op}})X^* \to X^* \to X^* \triangleq \\
\quad \lambda(X \mathrel{<\!\!:} \text{Max}_{\text{Op}})\ \lambda(\text{self}:X^*)\ \lambda(\text{other}:X^*) \\
\qquad \text{if unfold(self).n>unfold(other).n then self else other}
\end{array}
$$

It is easy to check that pre-max is well typed, similarly to the derivation of the first typing above.

The instantiations pre-max(Max_{Op}) and pre-max($\text{MinMax}_{\text{Op}}$) are both legal. Since pre-max has type $\forall(X \mathrel{<\!\!:} \text{Max}_{\text{Op}})X^* \to X^* \to X^*$, this pre-method can be used as a component of a class of type MaxClass. Moreover, a higher-order version of the rule for quantifier subtyping yields:

$$\forall(X \mathrel{<\!\!:} \text{Max}_{\text{Op}})X^* \to X^* \to X^* \quad <: \quad \forall(X \mathrel{<\!\!:} \text{MinMax}_{\text{Op}})X^* \to X^* \to X^*$$

so pre-max has type $\forall(X \mathrel{<\!\!:} \text{MinMax}_{\text{Op}})X^* \to X^* \to X^*$ by subsumption, and hence pre-max can be reused as a component of a class of type MinMaxClass.

8 Conclusions

As we have seen, there are situations in programming where one would like to parameterize over all "extensions" of a recursive object type, rather than over all its subtypes. Both F-bounded subtyping and higher-order subtyping can be used for capturing the notion of extension; however, they are probably too complex for overt use in programming. Using a primitive matching relation is more appropriate. Thus, the concept of matching represents a step forward towards practical and flexible type theories for object-oriented programming.

Still, F-bounded subtyping and higher-order subtyping have an important role to play in explaining the semantics of matching and in justifying its rules. We have presented two interpretations of matching:

$$A \mathrel{<\#} B \quad \approx \quad A <: B_{\text{Op}}(A) \qquad \text{(F-bounded interpretation)}$$

$$A \mathrel{<\#} B \quad \approx \quad A_{\text{Op}} \mathrel{<\!\!:} B_{\text{Op}} \qquad \text{(higher-order interpretation)}$$

As these interpretations show, matching stems from subtyping. The former interpretation motivated the concept of matching, and led to the typing rules of

TOOPLE. The latter interpretation leads to rules that are much closer to the ones of PolyTOIL.

Although both interpretations can be soundly adopted, they require different assumptions and yield different rules. In particular, the higher-order interpretation does not assume the unfolding property of recursive types, which seems necessary for the F-bounded interpretation; this simplification is technically advantageous in a higher-order setting. Additionally, the higher-order interpretation validates reflexivity and transitivity properties for matching; these properties do not hold under the F-bounded interpretation. Thus, we believe that the higher-order interpretation is preferable; it should be a guiding principle for programming languages with matching.

Acknowledgments

We thank Kim Bruce, Benjamin Pierce, and Scott Smith for useful discussions.

References

[1] Abadi, M., **Baby Modula-3 and a theory of objects**. *Journal of Functional Programming* 4(2), 249-283. 1994.

[2] Abadi, M. and L. Cardelli, **A theory of primitive objects: untyped and first-order systems**. *Proc. Theoretical Aspects of Computer Software*. Springer-Verlag. 1994.

[3] Abadi, M. and L. Cardelli, **A semantics of object types**. *Proc. IEEE Symposium on Logic in Computer Science*, 332-341. 1994.

[4] Abadi, M. and L. Cardelli, **A theory of primitive objects: second-order systems.** *Proc. ESOP'94 - European Symposium on Programming*. Springer-Verlag. 1994.

[5] Abadi, M. and L. Cardelli, **An imperative object calculus**. *Proc. FASE'95- Formal Approaches in Software Engineering (to appear)*. Springer-Verlag. 1995.

[6] Abadi, M. and G. Plotkin, **A per model of polymorphism and recursive types.** *Proc. 5th Annual IEEE Symposium on Logic in Computer Science*, 355-365. 1990.

[7] Amadio, R.M., **Recursion over realizability structures**. *Information and Computation* **91**(1), 55-85. 1991.

[8] Amadio, R.M. and L. Cardelli, **Subtyping recursive types**. *ACM Transactions on Programming Languages and Systems* **15**(4), 575-631. 1993.

[9] Bruce, K.B., **A paradigmatic object-oriented programming language: design, static typing and semantics**. *Journal of Functional Programming* 4(2), 127-206. 1994.

[10] Bruce, K.B., L. Cardelli, G. Castagna, The Hopkins Object Group, G.T. Leavens, and B. Pierce, **On binary methods.** (*To appear.*) 1995.

[11] Bruce, K.B. and G. Longo, **A modest model of records, inheritance and bounded quantification**. *Information and Computation* **87**(1/2), 196-240. 1990.

[12] Bruce, K.B. and J.C. Mitchell, **PER models of subtyping, recursive types and higher-order polymorphism**. *Proc. 19nd Annual ACM Symposium on Principles of Programming Languages*, 316-327. 1992.

[13] Bruce, K.B., A. Schuett, and R. van Gent, **PolyTOIL: a type-safe polymorphic object-oriented language.** *Proc. ECOOP'95*. Springer-Verlag. 1995.

[14] Canning, P., W. Cook, W. Hill, W. Olthoff, and J.C. Mitchell, **F-bounded polymorphism for object-oriented programming.** *Proc. ACM Conference on Functional Programming and Computer Architecture*, 273-280. 1989.

[15] Cardelli, L., **A semantics of multiple inheritance.** *Information and Computation* **76**, 138-164. 1988.

[16] Cardelli, L. and G. Longo, **A semantic basis for Quest.** *Journal of Functional Programming* **1**(4), 417-458. 1991.

[17] Cardelli, L. and J.C. Mitchell, **Operations on records.** *Mathematical Structures in Computer Science* **1**(1), 3-48. 1991.

[18] Cardelli, L., J.C. Mitchell, S. Martini, and A. Scedrov, **An extension of system F with subtyping.** *Information and Computation* **109**(1-2), 4-56. 1994.

[19] Cardone, F., **Relational semantics for recursive types and bounded quantification.** *Proc. Automata, Languages and Programming*, 164-178. Lecture Notes in Computer Science 372. Springer-Verlag. 1989.

[20] Compagnoni, A.B., **Higher-order subtyping with intersection types.** *Ph.D. Thesis*, Cip-Data Koninklijke Bibliotheek, Den Haag, Nijmegen. 1995.

[21] Cook, W., W. Hill, and P. Canning, **Inheritance is not subtyping.** *Proc. Seventeenth Annual ACM Symposium on Principles of Programming Languages.* 1990.

[22] Curien, P.-L. and G. Ghelli, **Coherence of subsumption, minimum typing and type-checking in $F_{\leq}$.** *Mathematical Structures in Computer Science* **2**(1), 55-91. 1992.

[23] Danforth, S. and C. Tomlinson, **Type theories and object-oriented programming.** *ACM Computing Surveys* **20**(1), 29-72. 1988.

[24] Day, M., R. Gruber, B. Liskov, and A.C. Myers, **Abstraction mechanisms in Theta.** MIT. 1994.

[25] Eifrig, J., S. Smith, V. Trifonov, and A. Zwarico, **An interpretation of typed OOP in a language with state.** *Proc. OOPSLA'94*, 16-30. 1994.

[26] Girard, J.-Y., **Interprétation fonctionelle et élimination des coupures dans l'arithmétique d'ordre supérieur.** Thèse de doctorat d'état, University of Paris. 1972.

[27] Gunter, C.A. and J.C. Mitchell, ed., **Theoretical Aspects of Object-Oriented Programming.** MIT Press. 1994.

[28] Harper, R. and B. Pierce, **A record calculus based on symmetric concatenation.** *Proc. 18th Annual ACM Symposium on Principles of Programming Languages.* 1991.

[29] Hofmann, M. and B.C. Pierce, **A unifying type-theoretic framework for objects.** *Proc. Symposium on Theoretical Aspects of Computer Science.* 1994.

[30] Katiyar, D., D. Luckham, and J.C. Mitchell, **Polymorphism and subtyping in interfaces.** *ACM SIGPLAN Notices* **29**(8), 22-34. 1994.

[31] MacQueen, D.B., G.D. Plotkin, and R. Sethi, **An ideal model for recursive polymorphic types.** *Information and Control* **71**, 95-130. 1986.

[32] Mitchell, J.C., **Toward a typed foundation for method specialization and inheritance.** *Proc. 17th Annual ACM Symposium on Principles of Programming Languages*, 109-124. 1990.

[33] Nelson, G., ed. **Systems programming with Modula-3.** Prentice Hall. 1991.

[34] Steffen, M. and B.C. Pierce, **Higher-order subtyping.** *Technical Report ECS-LFCS-94-280.* University of Edinburgh. 1994.

Using Metaobject Protocols to Implement Atomic Data Types

R. J. Stroud and Z. Wu

Department of Computing Science, University of Newcastle upon Tyne, UK

Abstract. Many researchers have suggested using atomic data types to implement transactions as a way of achieving atomicity in a modular, encapsulated fashion. However, in practice, implementing user-defined atomic data types is a difficult task. Existing systems fail to make a clean separation between application code and the synchronisation/recovery code needed to guarantee atomicity, and thus make it very hard for programmers to make changes to a system to meet their particular needs. In this paper, we present a metaobject protocol approach to implementing atomic data types. With this approach, application code is implemented at the base level, whilst the synchronisation and recovery code necessary to ensure atomicity is implemented at the meta level in the form of metaobjects. New schemes for ensuring atomicity can be provided for particular applications by introducing new metaobjects into the system without a need to make any changes at the base level. Furthermore, it is possible for an atomic data object to adapt its mechanism for ensuring atomicity dynamically by changing its metaobject at run time.

1 Introduction

Over the past few decades increasing reliance has been placed upon computers to such an extent that many applications are now totally dependent on the correct functioning of their computer systems. A major issue in such applications is preserving the consistency of on-line data in the presence of concurrency and failures. Typically, data consistency is achieved by ensuring that all accesses and updates to shared data objects are made from within atomic activities called transactions. Many researchers have suggested using atomic data types to implement transactions. With this approach, each object that can be accessed concurrently by more than one activity is responsible for ensuring its own atomicity. This use of an object-oriented approach should allow atomicity to be achieved in a modular, encapsulated fashion and enable type-specific object semantics to be exploited to achieve greater concurrency.

In practice, however, implementing user-defined atomic data types is a difficult task. This is because atomic data types define the behaviour of objects in a concurrent and unreliable environment. Thus, in addition to implementing the operations of a normal abstract data type, an atomic data type also needs to implement synchronisation and recovery operations. There are three kinds of approaches to implementing atomic data types: *implicit*, *explicit* and *hybrid*, according to whether the system or the programmer is responsible for implementing the synchronisation and recovery code necessary to ensure atomicity. With an *implicit approach*, the programmer is only responsible for implementing the basic object operations as if for a sequential reliable environment with no concurrency or failure. The system is responsible for implementing the necessary synchronisation and recovery code using knowledge about the object's semantics provided by the programmer. With an *explicit approach*, the programmer is responsible for implementing both the basic object operations and the synchronisation and recovery code. With a *hybrid approach*, the work of implementing the synchronisation and recovery code is shared by the system and the programmer.

The explicit and hybrid approaches fail to achieve a clean separation between application code and the synchronisation/recovery code necessary to ensure atomicity. Their drawbacks are very obvious. Intertwining synchronisation and recovery code with application code makes the implementation of atomic data types very difficult, requiring considerable sophistication on the part of the programmer. Furthermore, it also makes it impossible to change the synchronisation and recovery scheme for an object without re-implementing the object. This prevents changing the mechanism used to ensure atomicity for an existing atomic data object either to support new application requirements or to improve performance. For example, an object that was initially implemented using an optimistic protocol for its synchronisation scheme might need to be re-implemented using a pessimistic protocol later because the conflicts among applications were much higher than anticipated.

An implicit approach does not require the programmer to implement synchronisation and recovery operations. Thus it seems easy to make a clear separation between application code and synchronisation/recovery code. However, in practice, it is not so straightforward. In order to provide type-specific synchronisation and recovery for an object, it is necessary to monitor or control the object's behaviour at run time. The code provided automatically by the system for this purpose must not become intertwined with the application code provided by the programmer. Otherwise, it will be difficult to change the scheme used to ensure atomicity for an atomic data object because different schemes will need different code for monitoring and controlling the object's dynamic behaviour.

In this paper, we present a metaobject protocol approach to implementing atomic data types. With this approach, the application code and the code for ensuring atomicity (i.e. the synchronisation and recovery code) are totally separated from each other. The application code is implemented at the base level, whilst the code for ensuring atomicity is implemented at the meta level in the form of metaobjects. Thus, the behaviour of the system can be modified incrementally using meta level programming. In this way, a new scheme for ensuring atomicity can be supported by introducing new metaobjects into the system without a need to make any change at the base level.

In the next section, the concept of atomic data types is introduced. Section 3 presents our persistent programming language PC++ which supports an implicit approach to defining atomic data types, and analyses the problems with the original implementation of PC++ that led us to consider an alternative implementation based on the use of metaobject protocols. In Section 4, the basic idea of the metaobject protocol approach is described, and the reflective object-oriented programming language used for our experiments is introduced. Section 5 introduces our metaobject protocol for implementing atomic data types and Section 6 demonstrates the flexibility of this protocol by illustrating how it can be used to implement two different synchronisation schemes, one optimistic and one pessimistic. Finally, Section 7 summarises the benefits of a metaobject protocol approach for implementing atomic data types and draws some conclusions.

2 Background and Concepts

Maintaining data consistency in a concurrent and unreliable environment is an important issue for many application systems. To support consistency it is useful to make concurrent activities that access data objects *atomic*. Atomic activities are referred to as *transactions*. Although a transaction usually consists of several operations, the properties of transactions ensure that a transaction is performed atomically. That is, if a transaction commits, it should appear to the outside world as if the entire collection of operations comprising the transaction are performed consecutively, with no intervening operations of other transactions, and without getting part way through and stopping. Transactions simplify the problem of maintaining system consistency by decreasing the number of cases that need to be considered [11].

In order to increase the level of concurrency, many researchers have suggested using the semantics of an application for concurrency control. Semantics-based concurrency control protocols can be broadly classified into two groups depending on whether they are based upon the semantics of transactions or upon the semantics of objects [31]. In the database community, work in this area has largely focused on transactions. Lamport [17] proposed using the semantics of transactions to increase concurrency in database systems. The limitations of the traditional transaction model were demonstrated by Gray [10]. Weikum [34] introduced the multilevel transaction model in which the semantics of operations at different levels are used to increase concurrency.

However, a more object-oriented approach is to use type-specific concurrency control by exploiting the semantics of the data through the definition of abstract data types. A locking protocol based on the notion of commutativity of operations on abstract data types was proposed by Schwarz and Spector [27]. Herlihy, Liskov, and Weihl [14, 33] introduced the concept of atomic data types.

Atomic data types are abstract data types that also have synchronisation and recovery properties. Instances of atomic data types, called atomic objects, are responsible for ensuring their own atomicity. There has been much research into the different issues that arise in implementing atomic data types [4, 6, 27, 32], and a number of systems have been built that support transactions using atomic data types. Examples include Argus [33], Clouds [1], Arjuna [26], TABS [25], and Camelot/Avalon [28]. Although these systems differ in detail, all of them take either an explicit or a hybrid approach to implementing atomic data types. The drawbacks of these approaches were pointed out in the previous section.

A proposal to add user-defined concurrency control to an object-oriented database language was made within the FIDE project [8]. Although the FIDE proposal allows programmers to specify the concurrent behaviour of an atomic data type declaratively and could therefore be used to support an implicit approach. However, it does not deal adequately with recovery. In particular, transactions are required to commit in the same order in which they were initiated, and the problem of cascading aborts is not addressed.

Atkins [2] described an adaptable server for supporting atomic data types that can choose an appropriate concurrency control strategy on the basis of state information, the history of conflicts encountered, or by using preset transaction priorities.

More recently, Guerraoui [12] has proposed using *o-atomicity* to support the composition of atomic data objects, and has outlined an implementation of *o-atomicity* based on an abstract *AtomicObject* class. The idea is that application-specific atomic data types should be derived from a subclass of *AtomicObject* that uses a particular concurrency control protocol to guarantee *o-atomicity.* Optimistic and pessimistic subclasses of *AtomicObject* are presented. Although there are some similarities between this approach and our approach, Guerraoui requires an *access* operation to be invoked internally every time a transaction invokes an operation on an atomic data object whereas we achieve the same effect using meta level programming. Furthermore, Guerraoui uses a hybrid approach to supporting atomic data types whereas we use an implicit approach.

A great deal of work in the field of concurrent object-oriented programming languages has been concerned with the problem of achieving a clean separation between sychronisation code and the code that implements object operations (the so-called "inheritance anomaly" [21, 23, 24, 9, 22]). Our motivation for using a metaobject protocol to support atomic data types is similar except that we are dealing with the issue of transaction concurrency rather than just process concurrency [33].

3 An Implicit Approach for Atomic Data Types

To simplify the task of constructing atomic data types, we have proposed an implicit approach for defining atomic data types and implemented it in a persistent programming language PC++ [36]. In this section, we present a brief description of PC++ and analyse the problems with its implementation that led us to consider using metaobject protocols to implement atomic data types.

3.1 Defining Atomic Data Types

In PC++ a clear separation is made between the *serial specification* of an atomic data type which describes the permissible behaviour of an instance of the type in the absence of concurrency and failures, and the *concurrent specification* which describes how an instance should respond to concurrency and failures. Programmers are required to do very little extra work to make an object type atomic. Except for specifying the concurrent semantics of operations declaratively, an atomic data type is defined just like a normal abstract data type implemented in a sequential, reliable environment. In PC++, a very small language has been developed for users to specify the concurrent semantics of object operations declaratively as an *invalidates* relation. PC++ uses this *invalidates* relation to generate type-specific synchronisation and recovery code automatically.

The *invalidates* relation for a data type describes possible conflicts between operations on instances of the type that would limit concurrency. Given two operations on the same type, p and q, we say that p invalidates q if there is some object d whose value is such that the result of executing q on d might not be the same as the result of executing p and then q on d. By result we mean the result returned by the operation, not the effect the operation has on the object state. However, clearly if p invalidates q for some object d, then p has an effect on the state of d that changes the result of invoking q on d. (Note that it is possible for p to modify the state of d without altering the result of invoking q after p on d and in this case, p would not invalidate q.) Since an *invalidates* relation is only concerned with the names and results of operations and not the effect they have on the object state, it is very easy to check whether a given relation is an *invalidates* relation.

When specifying the *invalidates* relation, each operation is represented by its name and result. The result of an operation is simply characterised as either *failed* or *succeeded* (represented by OK), since usually only this distinction makes a significant difference to *invalidates* relations. The first parameter of an operation can also be taken into account if appropriate. The relationship between two parameters can be classified as: $=$ or $\neq$.

For example, suppose there are two operations: *oper1* and *oper2*. If *oper1* invalidates *oper2* only when their first parameter is the same and both of them succeed, then this conflict can be represented as:

((*oper1, OK*) (*oper2, OK*) =).

In order to define an atomic class in PC++, the programmer need only place a preprocessor directive *atomic* in front of an ordinary C++ class definition, and add an *invalidates* relation part. For example, consider an *Account* class that has an associated set of operations: *credit* money to an account, *debit* money from an account, and *check* the balance of an account. An appropriate *invalidates* relation can be added to a C++ class definition for *Account* to define a PC++ atomic data type as shown in Fig. 1.

In this example, the *invalidates* relation describes four possible conflicts: a successful *credit* invalidates a successful *check*; a successful *debit* invalidates a successful *check*; a successful *debit* invalidates another successful *debit*; and a successful *credit* invalidates a failed *debit*. The interpretation of the *invalidates* relation by the concurrency control mechanism is handled automatically by PC++. Thus, the application code that implements the *Account* class contains no explicit synchronisation code (although it is necessary to indicate whether an operation succeeds or fails by using a special form of *return* statement).

```
atomic class Account
{
private:
        Money    amount;
public:
                 Account();
        Status   credit(Money);
        Status   debit(Money);
        Money    check();
invalidates relation:
        ((credit, OK) (check, OK))
        ((debit, OK) (check, OK))
        ((debit, OK) (debit, OK))
        ((credit, OK) (debit, failed))
};
```

Fig. 1. The class *Account*

3.2 Constructing Transactions

Programmers can construct transactions that access instances of atomic data types using the *Transaction* class provided by the PC++ system. The computation that constitutes the body of the transaction is controlled by an instance of a *Transaction* object associated with the transaction.

The *Transaction* class provides three primitive operations that may be used to declare and control a transaction: *begin_transaction, commit_transaction* and *abort_transaction.* A *begin_transaction* operation starts a transaction which may be terminated by either a *commit_transaction* or an *abort_transaction* operation. A transaction terminated by an *abort_transaction* operation will definitely be aborted, its partial results will be removed. A transaction terminated by a *commit_transaction* operation is not guaranteed to be committed successfully, but programmers will be told whether their attempt to commit the transaction succeeds. The outcome of a *commit_transaction* operation is either a *success,* when the effects of the transaction become permanent, or a *failure*, when the effects of the transaction are removed.

Figure 2 shows a transaction that attempts to transfer some amount of money from one account to another. At first it tries to debit £1000 from account *John*, and if the debit succeeds, it credits £1000 to account *Guang* and commits; otherwise, it aborts.

```
Account      John, Guang;
Transaction  T;

T.begin_transaction();
if (John.debit(1000) == Success)
  {
    Guang.credit(1000);
    T.commit_transaction();
  }
  else
  {
    T.abort_transaction();
  }
```

Fig. 2. A transfer transaction

3.3 PC++ Implementation

From the above description, we can see that it is very simple for programmers to design atomic data types and transactions in PC++. In this subsection, we describe how PC++ provides synchronisation and recovery operations for user-defined atomic data types.

An essential issue for PC++ is how to integrate system-provided synchronisation and recovery code with different kinds of object whilst still allowing type-specific concurrency control. PC++ resolves this issue by using the type inheritance technique of object-oriented programming. The method is quite straightforward. A special type, called *Scheduler*, is provided which implements a specific concurrency control protocol. Atomic data types are translated by the PC++ preprocessor into C++ classes that are derived from this special type and will thereby inherit the underlying concurrency control facility. Furthermore, if the definition of an atomic data type includes type-specific information about the concurrency semantics of its operations, this can be used by the inherited concurrency control mechanism to make synchronisation decisions.

A difficulty particular to an implicit approach is how the system can get the information about the dynamic behaviour of objects necessary to make sychronisation and recovery decisions, because programmers should not be asked to provide it. PC++ overcomes the difficulty via a preprocessor. By preprocessing atomic data type definitions, some code can be added to object operations so that the information necessary for synchronisation and recovery can be collected automatically when object operations are invoked by transactions.

In principle, the type-inheritance technique used by PC++ for providing concurrency control makes it easy to change the synchronisation scheme of an atomic data type. It is only necessary to provide a new type, say *NewScheduler*, that implements the new concurrency control method. Then, user-defined atomic data types that are derived from *NewScheduler* instead of *Scheduler* will automatically use a different mechanism to implement synchronisation and recovery operations.

Unfortunately, the preprocessing approach makes the above flexibility difficult to achieve in practice. Since different concurrency control methods may need to monitor and control the dynamic behaviour of objects in different ways in order to make synchronisation and recovery decisions, implementing a new synchronisation scheme also requires changing the preprocessor so that it generates different code for monitoring and controlling the behaviour of objects. This is not a easy task with a traditional implementation of a preprocessor, especially if the updator is not the original author of the preprocessor. A new approach is required in order to solve this problem.

4 Metaobject Protocols

In order to make PC++ a flexible and extensible system, we re-implemented it using a metaobject protocol approach that opens up the system by using reflection and object-oriented programming techniques. In effect, the metaobject protocol was used as a mechanism for implementing an extensible, flexible, preprocessor. In this section, we introduce the concept of a metaobject protocol and the reflective object-oriented language Open C++ that was used for implementing our metaobject protocols.

4.1 The Basic Idea

Metaobject protocols [16] are interfaces to a system that give users the ability to modify the system's behaviour and implementation incrementally. Reflection and object-oriented programming play a critical role in the metaobject protocol approach. Reflection makes it possible to open up a system's implementation without revealing unnecessary implementation details. Object-oriented programming allows the resulting model of the system's implementation and behaviour to be adjusted locally and incrementally. The crucial difference between an approach based on reflection and an approach based on a preprocessor is *reification*, the process by which a model of the internal workings of the system is presented to the meta level. PC++ required the support of a preprocessor to collect information about the run time behaviour of objects. This information was a reification of the behaviour of the underlying system that was hard-coded into the implementation of the preprocessor. The use of a reflective system allows a more flexible approach to reification.

Reflection [19] is the process by which a system can reason about and act upon itself. In a conventional system, computation is performed on data that represents entities that are external to the computational system. However, a reflective computational system must contain data that represents the structural and computational aspects of the system itself. Moreover, it must be possible to access and manipulate such data from within the system itself, and more importantly, such data must be causally connected to the actual behaviour of the system. Unlike a conventional system, a reflective system allows users to perform computation on the system itself in the same manner as in the application, thus providing users with the ability to adjust the behaviour of the system to suit their particular needs.

In an object-oriented programming environment, reflection can be implemented using metaobjects. Each object is causally connected with a *metaobject* that represents both the structural and computational aspects of the object. Metaobjects can be manipulated in the same manner as "normal" objects. More importantly, changes made to a metaobject will be automatically reflected to the object. Therefore, the computational behaviour of an object can be adjusted to meet a particular requirement without modifying the implementation of the object but rather by changing its metaobject.

Reflection has been used in many application areas: flexible programming [16], concurrent programming [20], distributed systems [5], soft real-time [15], and fault tolerant applications [7]. More generally, [29] argues that reflection can be used as a general approach to addressing non-functional requirements such as fault tolerance and distribution transparency.

4.2 Open C++

For our experiments, we used Open C++ as a reflective programming environment. Open C++ [5] is a C++ preprocessor that provides the programmer with two levels of abstraction: the base level, dedicated to traditional C++ object-oriented programming, and the meta level which allows certain aspects of the C++ programming model to be redefined. For example, method calls to base level objects can be intercepted at the meta level by metaobjects. A base level object that is controlled by a metaobject in this way is called a *reflective object*. In Open C++, metaobjects are just objects whose class is derived from the class *MetaObj*. We will refer to such classes as *metaobject classes*. Open C++ allows the programmer to associate an application class with a metaobject class and arrange for a particular instances of the application class to be reflective, i.e. controlled by a metaobject of the appropriate metaobject class.

In Open C++, a metaobject realises its control on a reflective object by trapping the method calls to the latter. For example, suppose a reflective object *account* is bound to a metaobject *meta_account* as shown in Fig. 3. When a method is called at the base level, the call is trapped and handled at the meta level by a virtual method called *Meta_MethodCall*. This meta method makes it possible to redefine the semantics of a method call for a reflective object. Usually, *Meta_MethodCall* invokes the method at the base level, but it may also perform some extra processing before and/or after the invocation. For example, it can try to set a lock on the object before accessing its state and release the lock afterwards. The definition of *Meta_MethodCall* for *meta_account* is supplied by the class of *meta_account*, i.e. the metaobject class associated with the base level class of *account*.

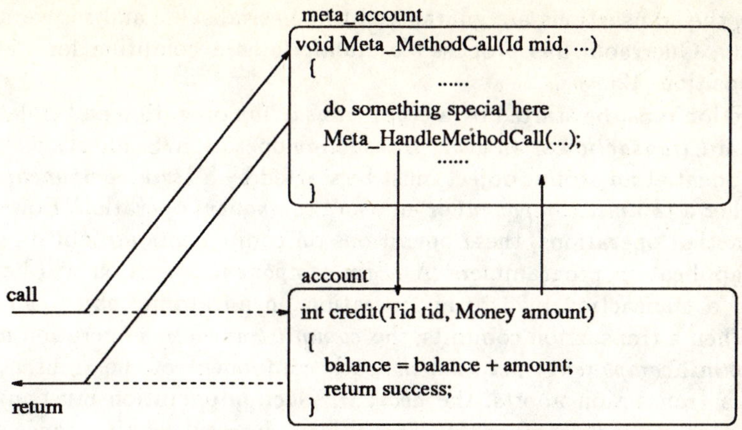

Fig. 3. Invocation trapping in Open C++

5 Using Metaobject Protocols to Implement Atomic Data Types

In this section, we present our metaobject protocol for supporting atomic data types and in the next section we demonstrate the flexibility of our approach with two examples.

5.1 The Computation Model

In our model a system consists of a collection of atomic objects that represent the state of the application, and a collection of transactions that access atomic objects to perform some computations. Atomic objects can only be accessed by operations defined on them and invoked inside a transaction. A transaction usually consists of a series of operations on several atomic objects. The sequence of operations that a transaction invokes on a particular atomic object is referred to as the *transaction component* at that object. An atomic object can deal with invocations from different transactions concurrently. The atomicity of a transaction component at an atomic object is ensured by that atomic object.

There are two kinds of atomicity in a system supporting atomic data objects. The atomicity of transaction components at an atomic object is called *local atomicity* because it deals only with the events involving a particular object. The atomicity of transactions is called *global atomicity* because it deals with events involving all the objects in the system. Generally speaking, the atomicity of a transaction cannot be guaranteed by the atomicity of its components. However, local atomicity is sufficient to ensure global atomicity if certain conditions are satisfied. Weihl [32] has identified three local atomicity properties that result in global atomicity: *static atomicity*, *dynamic atomicity*, and *hybrid atomicity*. If all the atomic objects shared by the transactions in a system provide the same kind of atomicity, the transactions are guaranteed to be serialisable and recoverable. More recently, Guerraoui has proposed *o-atomicity* as a condition for atomic object composition [12].

A transaction must be started by a *begin_transaction* operation and ended by either a *commit_transaction* or an *abort_transaction* operation. Similarly, a transaction component at an atomic object must be started by a *begin_component* and ended by either a *commit_component* or an *abort_component* operation. However, unlike transaction operations, these operations on components are not directly invoked by application programmers. A *begin_component* operation will be executed when a transaction invokes an operation on an atomic object for the first time. When a transaction commits, the *commit_transaction* operation must invoke a *commit_component* operation on each component of the transaction. Similarly, if a transaction aborts, the *abort_transaction* operation must invoke *abort_component* for each component. The object representing the transaction must keep track of which atomic objects are accessed during the transaction so that it can identify the transaction's components.

5.2 Metaobject Protocol Approach

The execution of a transaction component involves two kinds of operations: object operations defined by programmers which we call *functional operations* because they are primarily concerned with the functionality of objects, and local transaction operations provided by the system which we call *non-functional operations* because they do not add new functionality to objects but are used to ensure the correct execution of object operations in an unreliable, concurrent environment. The *begin_component*, *commit_component* and *abort_component* operations that must be provided by every atomic data type are non-functional; the type-specific operations that implement the functionality of an atomic data type are functional although the synchronisation and recovery code associated with the invocation of these operations is non-functional.

The problems with the original implementation of PC++ resulted from mixing up the code implementing functional operations with the code implementing non-functional operations. In order to make a system flexible, we must make a clear separation between the two kinds of code. This can be achieved by taking the metaobject protocol approach introduced in section 4. The use of meta level programming makes it possible to achieve a transparent separation of functional components from non-functional components [29, 30]. Using a metaobject protocol approach, atomic object operations can be implemented by application programmers at the base level as if for a sequential and reliable environment. All of the work required for providing synchronisation and recovery, such as controlling the invocation of object operations, collecting run time object information, validating, committing and aborting transaction components, can be done separately at the meta level.

In Open C++, it is possible to capture the semantics of an atomic data type within our computational model using the *AtomicMetaObj* metaobject class shown in Fig. 4. Metaobject classes that realise particular schemes for ensuring atomicity can be derived from this abstract class.

```
class AtomicMetaObj : public MetaObj
{
public:
                 AtomicMetaObj();
  virtual void   Meta_StartUp();
  virtual void   Meta_MethodCall(Id mid, Id cid, ArgPac& args, ArgPac& rslt);
  virtual int    Meta_BeginComponent(Tid tid);
  virtual int    Meta_CommitComponent(Tid tid);
  virtual int    Meta_AbortComponent(Tid tid);
  virtual void   Meta_NormalOperation(Tid tid, Id mid, id cid, ArgPac& args,
                                                               ArgPac& rslt);
}
```

Fig. 4. A metaobject class for atomic data types

In order to define an atomic data type, the application programmer writes a class definition for the type as if it were implemented in a sequential, reliable environment, and then specifies using an Open C++ directive that the metaobject class of the application class is an appropriate subclass of *AtomicMetaObj*. In other words, atomic data types are implemented by classes whose metaobject class is derived from *AtomicMetaObj*.

When an atomic object is created at run time, Open C++ will automatically create a corresponding metaobject that is an instance of the appropriate subclass of *AtomicMetaObj*. This metaobject will be bound to the application object in such a way that all of the operations that the application invokes on the atomic object are intercepted by the metaobject. The metaobject is responsible for enforcing the particular synchronisation and recovery policies being used to guarantee local atomicity and can control whether the invocation is allowed to proceed at this time or record information about the invocation that will be used for validation later.

The following four operations are provided by the *AtomicMetaObj* class for implementing local atomicity: *Meta_BeginComponent*, *Meta_CommitComponent*, *Meta_AbortComponent*, and *Meta_NormalOperation*.

Open C++ ensures that all the operations invoked on an atomic object are intercepted by the *Meta_MethodCall* operation of the corresponding metaobject. *Meta_MethodCall* will check the category of an intercepted call and then invoke an appropriate operation to deal with the invocation.

The *Meta_MethodCall* operation will invoke the *Meta_BeginComponent* operation when a *begin_component* operation is called on an atomic object. Similarly, the *Meta_CommitComponent* operation is invoked in response to *commit_component* and likewise for *Meta_AbortComponent* and *abort_component*.

When a normal object operation is called on an atomic object from a transaction component, *Meta_MethodCall* will invoke the *Meta_NormalOperation* operation which decides when the invocation is allowed to proceed and records any information necessary for validation at commit time.

In this way, the code for implementing a particular scheme for achieving local atomicity can be clearly separated from the code implementing the functionality of an atomic data type. Therefore, changes to the scheme for achieving atomicity can be made totally transparent to application programmers. Conversely, the code for implementing atomicity is not affected if application programmers make changes to the implementation of the object's operations.

6 Implementing Concurrency Control Methods Using an Atomic Metaobject

In this section, we illustrate the flexibility of our approach and demonstrate the use of the metaobject protocol defined by *AtomicMetaObj* by presenting two different metaobject classes derived from *AtomicMetaObj* that implement an optimistic and a pessimistic concurrency control policy respectively.

6.1 An Optimistic Concurrency Control Metaobject Class

PC++ was developed for a multimedia project called OPERA [18]. Based on our belief that an optimistic concurrency control method is more suitable for real-time multimedia applications than a pessimistic method, PC++ uses an optimistic protocol called the *dual-level validation method* (DLV) [36] as its default concurrency control strategy. In this subsection we describe a metaobject class that uses the DLV method to implement local atomicity for atomic objects. Since we are dealing with local atomicity, we need only consider the effect of a transaction component at a single object.

The Dual-Level Validation Method. We view an atomic object as a two-layered architecture. The higher layer, called the *logical level*, is concerned with the set of abstract operations defined on the object, which are the only means for applications to access the object. The lower layer, called the *physical level*, is concerned with the set of operations provided by the system to manage primitive data objects.

The DLV method is an optimistic protocol. Transactions operate on shadow copies of (components of) objects, relying on commit-time validation to ensure serialisability. The two levels of the DLV method are concerned with the two levels of the object architecture, logical and physical. Logical level validation ensures that a transaction that has used an object and is requesting a commit is serialisable with other transactions. Physical level validation ensures that the logical level object operations are elementary. Logical level validation can be done by making use of the semantics of the object so that greater concurrency can be achieved.

One approach to implementing optimistic concurrency control is to take a *shadow copy* of a whole object at the start of a transaction, or perhaps at the time of the first operation that updates the object. All subsequent invocations are on this copy and are validated against the persistent object when the transaction requests commit [13].

However, our approach is different. Our objects are tree structured with primitive objects as leaves. We assume that objects may be large. Our approach is to take a shadow copy only of the sub-object of the (tree structured) physical object that is required for a given invocation. A copy of a sub-object is taken on the first invocation that updates that part of the object and all subsequent invocations on that sub-object, for read or update, are performed on that shadow.

A transaction, in general, encloses operations on several objects. The sequence of operations that a transaction invokes on a particular object forms the *transaction component* at that object. An execution of a transaction component consists of two, or three phases: a *read phase*, a *validation phase*, and possibly a *write phase*.

During the read phase, an operation invocation is executed immediately. However, if the invocation involves an update, this takes place on a local *shadow copy* of the physical sub-object affected. Each atomic object also maintains a record of which object operations have been invoked by each transaction component, and which physical (sub)objects have been read or written by each transaction component.

The logical validation phase begins when the execution of a transaction component reaches its end. During this phase, an atomic object validates the transaction component to establish whether any of the invocations of the transaction component have been invalidated by the invocations of concurrent transaction components. The information recorded in the previous phase is essential for this validation.

After entering the write phase, a transaction component is validated again by the atomic object to check whether it can be accepted at the physical level. The purpose of this validation is to check whether the values read by the transaction component are still current. If they are, the transaction component is committed by merging its shadow copies into the permanent state. Otherwise the operations of the transaction component are re-executed. Again, the information recorded during the read phase is required for the physical validation and the re-execution.

A more detailed description of the DLV method can be found in [36] and the correctness of the DLV method is proved in [35].

A Metaobject Class for the DLV Method. From the above description of the DLV method, we can see that all the work done at the logical validation phase and the write phase is non-functional. At the read phase, the execution of object operations is functional, but recording information about transaction components is non-functional. We implement the DLV method using a metaobject class called *DlvMetaObj* that is a subclass of *AtomicMetaObj*, as shown in Fig. 5.

```
class DlvMetaObj: public AtomicMetaObj
{
public:
            DlvMetaObj();
    void    Meta_StartUp();
    void    Meta_MethodCall(Id mid, Id cid, ArgPac& args, ArgPac& rslt);
    int     Meta_BeginComponent(Tid tid);
    int     Meta_ValidateComponent(Tid tid, Timestamp tmstp);
    int     Meta_CommitComponent(Tid tid);
    int     Meta_AbortComponent(Tid tid);
    void    Meta_NormalOperation(Tid tid, Id mid, Id cid, ArgPac& args,
                                                          ArgPac& rslt);
protected:
    long    latest_committed;
    struct {
            Tid         tid;
            Timestamp   timestamp;
            Timestamp   last_committed;
            Operation   operations[MaxOpers];
            RWSet       read_set[MaxObjs];
            RWSet       write_set[MaxObjs];
    } history[MaxTrans];
};
```

Fig. 5. The metaobject class for the DLV method

The *latest_committed* variable of a DLV metaobject is used to record the timestamp of the latest committed transaction component at its atomic object. The *history* array is used to record information about each transaction component at that object. The identifier and the timestamp of a transaction component are recorded in *tid* and *timestamp* respectively. The timestamp of the last committed transaction before a transaction component starts is recorded in *last_committed*, whilst the operations performed by each transaction component are recorded in *operations. read_set* and *write_set* are used to record the variables that are read and written by a transaction component respectively.

Whenever a *begin_component* operation is called on an atomic object, the *Meta_MethodCall* operation will invoke the *Meta_BeginComponent* operation. The latter will register the new transaction component with the atomic object, and assign an element of the *history* array as the data buffer to record information related to the transaction component. The behaviour of *begin_component* is shown in Fig. 6.

The *Meta_ValidateComponent* will be invoked by *Meta_MethodCall* when a *commit_component* call is intercepted. It will perform the logical validation by using the information recorded in the *history* array. *Meta_CommitComponent* will be invoked to commit the transaction component if it passes its logical

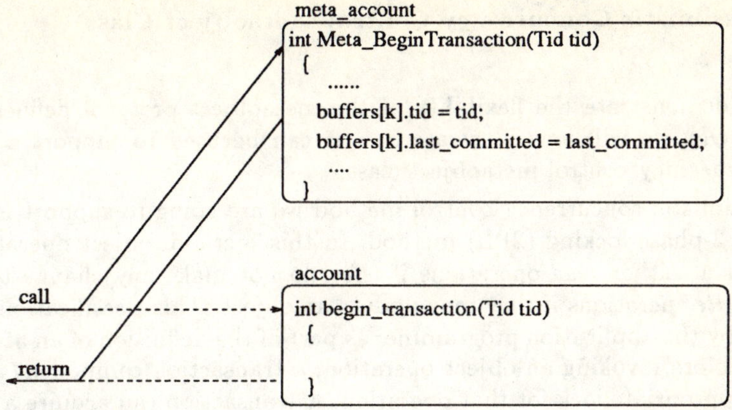

Fig. 6. The behaviour of *begin_component*

validation; otherwise *Meta_AbortComponent* will be invoked to abort it.

When a normal object operation is called on an atomic object from a transaction component, *Meta_MethodCall* will invoke *Meta_NormalOperation*. The *Meta_NormalOperation* operation will first record the method identifier *mId*, the category identifier *cId* and the arguments of the method *args* into the data buffer assigned for the transaction component. It will then invoke the original object operation on the atomic object. After the invocation, it will record the result of the invocation in the data buffer before returning the result to *Meta_MethodCall* which will in turn pass the result to the original caller. The behaviour of a normal object operation is shown in Fig. 7.

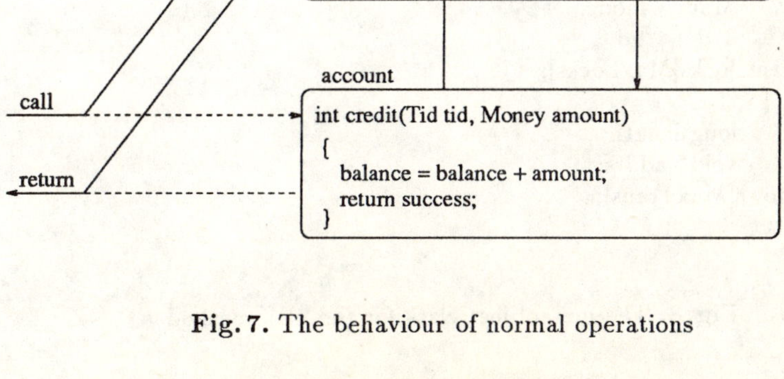

Fig. 7. The behaviour of normal operations

6.2 A Pessimistic Concurrency Control Metaobject Class

In order to demonstrate the flexibility of the metaobject protocol defined by *AtomicMetaObj*, we will now illustrate how it can be used to support a pessimistic concurrency control metaobject class.

The pessimistic concurrency control method we are going to support is the widely used 2-phase-locking (2PL) method. In this method, object operations are classified as either *read* operations if they do not make any change to an object; or *write* operations if they may update an object. This classification will be specified by the application programmer as part of the definition of an atomic data type. Before invoking an object operation, a transaction component must acquire an appropriate lock for that operation. A transaction can acquire a lock on an object only if no concurrent transaction component holds a conflicting lock on the object.

The metaobject class implementing the 2PL method is described in Fig. 8. The *current_locks* field records the current locks set in an object together with their modes and owners. The *shadows* field stores a list of snapshots of the object state.

```
class TplMetaObj: public AtomicMetaObj
{
public:
                TplMetaObj();
    void        Meta_StartUp();
    void        Meta_MethodCall(Id mid, Id cid, ArgPac& args, ArgPac& rslt);
    int         Meta_BeginComponent(Tid tid);
    int         Meta_ValidateComponent(Tid tid, Timestamp tmstp);
    int         Meta_CommitComponent(Tid tid);
    int         Meta_AbortComponent(Tid tid);
    void        Meta_NormalOperation(Tid tid, Id mid, id cid, ArgPac& args,
                                                        ArgPac& rslt);
protected:
    struct {
                Lock   lockid;
                Mode   mode;
                Tid    tid;
    } current_locks[MaxLocks];
    struct {
                long length;
                void* addrs;
    } shadows[MaxTrans];
}
```

Fig. 8. The metaobject class for the 2PL method

Meta_BeginComponent will be invoked when a *begin_component* call is intercepted. It simply makes a snapshot of the object state. *Meta_CommitComponent* will be invoked when a *commit_component* call is intercepted. It needs only to release the locks held by a transaction component. *Meta_AbortComponent* will be invoked when an *abort_component* call is intercepted. It first restores the object to a consistent state by replacing the object state with the snapshot taken for that transaction component, and then releases the lock set by the transaction.

Meta_NormalOperation is invoked when the invocation of an object operation from a transaction component is intercepted. It first tries to acquire an appropriate lock for the transaction component. If successful, it invokes the original object operation, and then returns the result to the caller. This procedure is shown in Fig. 9.

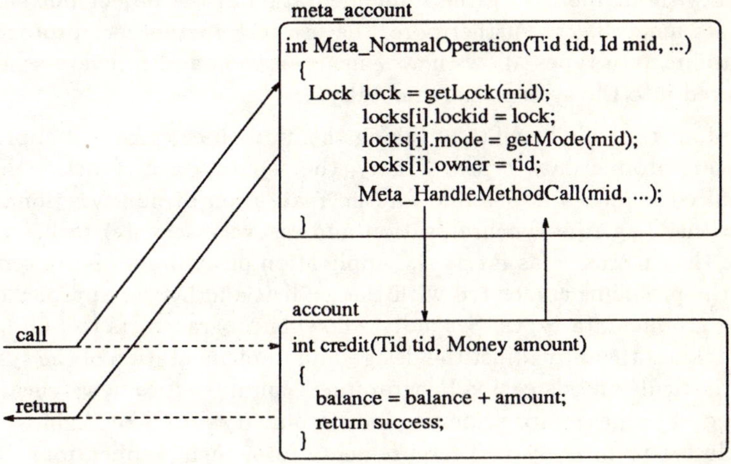

Fig. 9. The behaviour of a normal object operation in 2PL method

These examples have demonstrated that the metaobject protocol defined by *AtomicMetaObj* is flexible enough to support either an optimistic or a pessimistic concurrency control method. Furthermore, because of the separation between the functional and non-functional aspects of the implementation of atomic data types, it is possible for an object to change its synchronisation scheme simply by binding to a different metaobject. This can be done dynamically at run time if the reflective programming environment allows an object to change its metaobject at run time. (The current version of Open C++ does not support this facility.)

7 Summary and Conclusions

Many researchers have suggested using atomic data types to maintain data consistency in a concurrent system. However, existing approaches to implementing atomic data types mix up the code for implementing the functional aspects of an atomic object with the code for implementing the non-functional aspects of an atomic object (e.g. the synchronisation and recovery code used to guarantee atomicity), and this makes it very hard to change the scheme used to implement local atomicity. The metaobject protocol approach presented in this paper solves this problem by using meta level programming to separate the synchronisation and recovery aspects of an atomic data type from its functionality.

With a metaobject protocol approach, non-functional aspects of atomic data types such as synchronisation and recovery are implemented in metaobject classes at the meta level, whilst functional aspects such as object operations are implemented at the base level. This clear separation between the two kinds of code allows either of them to be freely changed without affecting the other. Programmers can change the particular synchronisation and recovery scheme used by an atomic object without modifying the implementation of the object but simply by changing its metaobject. Furthermore, the use of a metaobject protocol to implement atomic data types allows new synchronisation and recovery schemes to be introduced into the system incrementally.

There are four tangible benefits of taking the metaobject protocol approach to implementing atomic data types. Firstly, the separation of functional and non-functional code makes it possible for the realisation of non-functional aspects of atomicity (e.g. the synchronisation and recovery scheme) to be transparent rather than intrusive as far as the application programmer is concerned, thus solving the problems associated with the explicit and hybrid approaches to implementing atomic data types. Secondly, allowing programmers to build new metaobjects enables them to adjust the design and implementation of the system to suit their particular needs easily. Programmers can introduce new synchronisation and recovery schemes for achieving local atomicity simply by defining new metaobject classes to meet special requirements from their applications. Thus the metaobject protocol approach solves the problems associated with the preprocessor approach. Thirdly, permitting each object to have its own metaobject makes it possible for an application to apply different synchronisation and recovery strategies for different objects according to their characteristics. Fourthly, relying on the metaobjects to deal with a wide range of user requirements allows the basic implementation of the system to be simpler and thus easier to analyse with respect to its correctness. Other authors who have experimented with metaobject protocols have reported similar benefits [16, 3, 5, 7, 29].

Although our experiments with using metaobject protocols to implement atomic data types are still at an early stage, and although limitations of the current version of Open C++ prevent us from exploiting important reflective features such as dynamic binding between objects and metaobjects, we have demonstrated the feasibility of our general approach by outlining the implementation of two different schemes for achieving atomicity using metaobject classes derived from an abstract metaobject class defining a protocol for implementing atomic data types. Issues still to be resolved properly before our new implementation can be used as conveniently as the existing PC++ system include the mechanism by which type-specific information about the concurrent semantics of an atomic data type is translated into meta data to be used by the atomic metaobject class to resolve conflicts and ensure serialisability. Since the form that this specification takes may depend on the concurrency control method used, we believe that each metaobject class must be responsible for parsing its own meta data. This is much easier to achieve using an interpreted language such as CLOS than a compiled language such as C++ and it may be necessary to retain some kind of preprocessing mechanism to convert a declarative specification expressed using some form of syntactic sugar by the application programmer into meta data or code to be exploited by the metaobject class. Another topic for future research is the issue of performance although we believe that any inefficiencies inherent in our approach arise from limitations in the implementation of the underlying reflective programming system and that as reflective implementation technologies become better understood, reflection will just come to be viewed as another form of indirection mechanism that is no more expensive to use than inheritance or delegation but can be used to solve a different class of problems.

Acknowledgements

This work has been supported by the University Research Committee of University of Newcastle upon Tyne, and by funding from the ESPRIT Basic Research Action on 'Predictable Dependable Computing Systems' (PDCS-2), grant no. 6232. Thanks must go to members of the OPERA project in Cambridge, especially to Ken Moody and Jean Bacon, and to our colleague at Newcastle, Brian Randell, for many discussions on all aspects of the work. The comments we received from the anonymous referees have also helped us to improve the presentation of this work.

References

1. J. E. Allchin and M. S. McKendry: Synchronization and recovery of actions. In *Proceedings of the 2nd Annual ACM Symposium on Principles of Distributed Computing*, pages 31–44, August 1983.
2. M. S. Atkins and M. Y. Coady. Adaptable concurrency control for atomic data types. *ACM Transactions on Computer Systems*, 10(3):190–225, August 1992.
3. G. Attardi, C. Bonini, and M. R. Boscotrecase. Metalevel programming in CLOS. In *Proceedings of 3rd European Conference on Object-Oriented Programming*, pages 243–256, 1989.
4. B. R. Badrinath and K. Ramamritham. Semantics-based concurrency control: Beyond commutativity. *ACM Transactions on Database Systems*, 17(1):163–199, March 1992.
5. S. Chiba and T. Masuda: Designing an extensible distributed language with meta-level architecture. In *Proceedings of the 7th European Conference on Object-Oriented Programming*, pages 482–501, 1993.
6. P. K. Chrysanthis, S. Raghuram, and K. Ramamritham. Extracting concurrency from objects: A methodology. In *Proceedings of the 17th SIGMOD International Conference on Management of Data*, pages 108–117, 1991.

7. J. Fabre, V. Nicomette, T. Perennou, R. J. Stroud, and Z. Wu. Implementing fault tolerant applications using reflective object-oriented programming. In *Proceedings of the 25th IEEE Symposium on Fault Tolerant Computing Systems*, 1995.
8. N. De Francesco, G. Vaglini, L. V. Mancini, and A. Pereira Paz.: Specification of concurrency control in persistent programming languages. In *Proceedings of the Fifth International Workshop on Persistent Object Systems*, pages 126–143, 1992.
9. S. Frølund. Inheritance of synchronization constraints in concurrent object-oriented programming languages. In *Proceedings of 6th European Conference on Object-Oriented Programming*, pages 185–196, 1992.
10. J. N. Gray: The transaction concept: Virtues and limitations. In *Proceedings of the 7th International Conference on Very Large Data Bases*, pages 144–154, Sept. 1981.
11. J Gray and A. Reuter. *Transaction Processing: Concepts and Techniques*. Morgan Kaufmann Publishers, 1993.
12. R. Guerraoui. Atomic object composition. In *Proceedings of 8th European Conference on Object-Oriented Programming*, pages 118–138, 1994.
13. M. Herlihy: Apologizing versus asking permission: Optimistic concurrency control for abstract data types. *ACM Transactions on Database Systems*, 15(1):96–124, March 1990.
14. M. Herlihy and W. E. Weihl: Hybrid concurrency control for abstract data types. In *Proceedings of the 7th ACM-SIGACT-SIGMOD-SIGART Symposium on Principles of Database Systems*, pages 201–210, March 1988.
15. Y. Honda and M. Tokoro. Soft real-time programming through reflection. Technical Report SCSL-TR-92-016, Sony Computer Science Laboratory, 1992.
16. G. Kiczales, J. des Rivieres, and D. G. Bobrow: *The Art of the Metaobject Protocol*. MIT Press, 1991.
17. L. Lamport: Towards a theory of correctness for multi-user database systems. Technical report, Massachusetts Computer Assoc., 1976.
18. S. L. Lo: *A Modular and Extensible Network Storage Architecture*. PhD thesis, Cambridge University Computer Laboratory, 1994. Technical Report No. 326.
19. P. Maes: Concepts and experiments in computational reflection. In *OOPSLA '87 Proceedings*, pages 147–155, October 1987.
20. S. Matsuoka, T. Watanabe, and A. Yonezawa. Hybrid group reflective architecture for object-oriented concurrent reflective programming. In *Proceedings of the European Conference on Object-Oriented Programming '91*, pages 213–250, July 1991.
21. S. Matsuoka and A. Yonezawa. Analysis of inheritance anomaly in object-oriented concurrent programming languages. In G. Agha, P. Wegner, and A. Yonezawa, editors, *Research Directions in Concurrent Object-Oriented Programming*, pages 107–150. MIT Press, 1993.
22. J. Meseguer. Solving the inheritance anomaly in concurrent object-oriented programming. In *Proceedings of 7th European Conference on Object-Oriented Programming*, pages 220–246, 1993.
23. C. Neusius. Synchronizing actions. In *Proceedings of 5th European Conference on Object-Oriented Programming*, pages 118–132, 1991.
24. S. C. Reghizzi, G. G. de. Paratesi, and S. Genolini. Definition of reusable concurrent software components. In *Proceedings of 5th European Conference on Object-Oriented Programming*, pages 148–166, 1991.
25. A. Z. Spector, J. Butcher, D. S. Daniels, D. J. Duchamp, J. L. Eppinger, C. E. Fineman, A. Heddaya, and P. M. Schwarz: Support for distributed transactions in

the TABS prototype. *IEEE Transactions on Software Engineering*, SE-11(6):520–530, June 1985.

26. S. K. Shrivastava, G. N. Dixon, and G. D. Parrington: An overview of the Arjuna distributed programming system. *IEEE Software*, 8(1):66–73, January 1991.
27. P. M. Schwarz and A. Z. Spector: Synchronizing shared abstract types. *ACM Transactions on Computer Systems*, 2(3):223–250, August 1984.
28. A. Z. Spector, D. Thompson, R. F. Pausch, J. F. Eppinger, D. Duchamp, R. Draves, D. S Daniels, and J. J. Bloch: Camelot: A distributed transaction facility for Mach and the internet—an interim report. Technical Report CMU-CS-87-129, Carnegie Mellon University, 1987.
29. R. J. Stroud: Transparency and reflection in distributed systems. *ACM Operating Systems Review*, 27(2):99–103, April 1993.
30. R. J. Stroud and Z. Wu: Using metaobjects to adapt a persistent object system to meet application needs. In *Proceedings of 6th SIGOPS European Workshop on Matching Operating Systems to Application Needs*, 1994.
31. A. H. Skarra and S. B. Zdonik: Concurrency control and object-oriented databases. In W. Kim and F. H. Lochovsky, editors, *Object-oriented concepts, Databases and Applications*, pages 395–421. ACM Press, 1989.
32. W. E. Weihl: Local atomicity properties: Modular concurrency control for abstract data types. *ACM Transactions on Programming Languages and Systems*, 11(2):249–282, April 1989.
33. W. E. Weihl and B. Liskov: Implementation of resilient, atomic data types. *ACM Transactions on Programming Languages and Systems*, 7(2):244–269, April 1985.
34. G. Weikum: Principles and realization strategies of multilevel transaction management. *ACM Transactions on Database Systems*, 16(1):132–180, March 1991.
35. Z. Wu: *A New Approach to Implementing Atomic Data Types.* PhD thesis, Cambridge University Computer Laboratory, 1994. Technical Report No. 338.
36. Z. Wu, R. J. Stroud, K. Moody, and J. Bacon. The design and implementation of a distributed transaction system based on atomic data types. *Distributed System Engineering*, 1995(2), July 1995.

Meta-level Programming with CodA

Jeff McAffer

Department of Information Science
The University of Tokyo
and
Object Technology International
jeff@acm.org

Abstract. Meta-levels are complex pieces of software with diverse demands in both the computation and interaction domains. Common techniques using just code to express behaviour fail to clearly assign responsibility for a particular behaviour's definition or to provide support for the reuse or integration of existing behaviour descriptions. The techniques of fine-grained decomposition of meta-level behaviour into objects and their subsequent composition into object models provides a framework for creating, reusing and integrating complex object behaviours. Using such a framework, we show that users can develop and integrate quite different object models while retaining a high degree of abstraction and fostering meta-level component reuse.

1 Introduction

Meta-levels are potentially complex pieces of software. They have diverse requirements both for computation and for interaction. Building open meta-level architectures is particularly challenging because of the diversity of behaviours we may wish to describe while maintaining a uniform base-level view of object behaviour.

Many of the current architectures are open but in a restricted sense. They reify various aspects of a particular language or object model and provide infrastructure for change within the scope of that domain. If this is called a 'top-down' approach, we have taken a 'bottom-up' approach. Rather than starting with and then opening a particular object model, we start by describing various notions or views of generic object behaviour and then provide infrastructure for composing these behaviours into specific object models.

This is somewhat related to a basic concept of object-oriented software engineering — decompose a specific problem into generic components and then compose the pieces to solve the problem. From this we get both a solution to our problem and a set of reusable components. In addition, the fine-grained decomposition approach fosters a clear separation between, and definition of, the various components.

Using these techniques at the meta-level, we have developed CodA, a meta-level architecture for describing a wide range of object behaviour models. CodA can be thought of as a generic object engine framework in which users define, on a per-object or even per-use basis, how object's behave computationally. To demonstrate this we present three object models from different computing domains, specifically; concurrency, distribution, and communication.

The abstraction of behaviours into objects encourages reuse and simplifies the combination of object behaviours. While in CodA, object model combination is still a somewhat manual process, we propose that the architecture inherently provides for; the easier identification of points of conflict, isolation of the effects of changing a component, increased reusability of components derived from the combination of object models and easier management of the behaviour space. The addition of some simple annotations for describing component *properties* further enhances these qualities.

The remainder of the paper is organized as follows. The next section details the CodA architecture and in particular, our approach to meta-level factoring. Sections 3, 4 and 5 detail three object models implemented in CodA and section 6 discusses the combination of object models. We relate CodA to other work throughout the paper and summarize these relations in section 7. A further section concludes the paper and points out some directions for future work. Appended to the paper are the standard interface and default implementations for many of the meta-components discussed.

2 The CodA Meta-Architecture

The key concept in the design of the CodA meta-level architecture is the 'decomposition' or 'factoring' of the meta-level into fine-grained objects or *meta-components*. When programming base-level object-oriented systems we typically factor out behaviour, create objects for each factor and then compose these objects into applications. The only difference here is that our 'applications' are *object models* which describe the operation of objects. That is, the meta-level is just an application whose domain happens to be the behaviour[1] of objects.

In factoring the meta-level we developed a relatively generic model of object execution. The meta-level is defined as playing a number of *roles* in the description of base-level object behaviour. Each role is filled by a meta-component and corresponds to some behaviour such as; object execution (both mechanisms and resources), message passing, message to method mapping and object state maintenance. Roles may be filled by many different components and components can sometimes fill several roles. An object's behaviour is changed by explicitly redefining components or by extending the set of roles. Examples in later sections highlight this process.

The CodA meta-level architecture is largely run-time oriented. It does not provide integral support for language constructs like classes which are required for the static description of object behaviour. Rather, these constructs are borrowed from whatever language is used to implement CodA. For example, in the

[1] We use the term *behaviour* to denote *how* an object acts as opposed to *what* it does and so by nature, *behaviour* is a meta-level concept.

Smalltalk implementation, Smalltalk metaclasses are used to define a nice interface for particular object models (i.e., sets of meta-components) which are shared by instances. These interfaces determine which components can be modified and what configurations the meta-level can take. CodA is perhaps 'lower-level' than other systems but this approach allows us to gain a certain measure of language independence while retaining the potential of the architecture.

This is in contrast to the meta-level facilities found in systems like CLOS[7] and ClassTalk[4, 5]. The focus of these systems is different in that they intend to open or extend the functionality of particular language facilities or constructs. As such, they deal with somewhat more static issues and it is natural that their capabilities and constructs be language specific.

CodA differs in two other related ways; granularity and decomposition into objects. A common approach to factoring object execution behaviour (e.g., message sending or method execution) is to create public interface methods on a small number of meta-level objects [8, 6, 7]). That is, object behaviour is decomposed into code at the meta-level. Changes to a behaviour are made by modifying its related interface methods.

Unfortunately, code is inherently more difficult to deal with than objects. Method objects have little support or infrastructure for interaction, change or extension. Without this, describing complex interactions between several behaviours (i.e, groups of interface methods) is confusing. Behaviours are not encapsulated into atomic units and overall responsibility for a behaviour is not clear. Unanticipated behaviours have no clear home for their description and/or state.

Decomposition into objects gives us a higher-level view of behaviour. Objects abstract code, define points of interaction and ease integration. They remove us from the details of implementation code. The boom in micro-kernel operating systems is also witness to these ideas. Rather than creating one large, all encompassing kernel with many functions, we define a small and simple infrastructure and build/use the OS components as needed.

Forming meta-levels by composition has some advantages over techniques such as multiple inheritance (e.g., ClassTalk[4, 5]). The issue here is similar to the "parameterization vs. subclassing" issue — Should we create a generic object which we parameterize by plugging together pieces, or do we create a class hierarchy covering all possible parameter configurations? Unfortunately, the number of possible configurations is a combinatorial function with explosive potential. Just the small number of behaviours we will discuss in this paper translates into hundreds of possible combinations. Apart from the class/metaclass name-space explosion (which can be partially covered up using anonymous metaclasses), we also encounter a method name-space problem where methods from metaclasses which describe different behaviours, collide.

To put this design discussion in more concrete terms, below we give descriptions of the major elements in the CodA object system. In addition to the meta-level infrastructure, there is the set of seven components each of which describes some behaviour in the basic execution model.

2.1 The Meta-level

CodA specifies that every object has a conceptual meta-level. The meta-level is not a single object but rather a *set* of meta-components each of which describes some aspect of base-level object behaviour. The implementation of the meta-level (i.e., these sets of components) is not defined except to say that a particular set, and thus a particular meta-level, can optionally be: *fixed* and allow no changes, *changeable* in that existing components can be replaced or *extensible* by allowing new roles and components to be added to the meta-level.

Meta-level programmers need some way of shifting to the meta-level and of accessing an object's meta-components. This can be done using language constructs as in ABCL/R2's ↑ (up arrow) [8] or by making explicit meta-level objects which are accessed via normal message passing (e.g., CLOS). In CodA we adopt the technique best suited to the base-level language. For example, in the Smalltalk implementation an object's meta-level as a whole is 'represented' by the result of sending meta to some object (e.g., anObject meta). The meta is used for both shifting and accessing. All messages sent to a meta are executed at the meta-level and metas 'broker' (i.e., provide access to) meta-components.

In the implementation, the meta may take many different forms. It may store internally the meta-components it brokers, it may simply fetch them from somewhere or it may create new ones for each request. This is transparent to the user/programmer. When asked, a meta will return the actual component which fills the specified role. Similarly, a meta can be requested to use a particular component for a particular role.

2.2 Meta-level Components

As a basis, CodA defines a default set of seven components which are present at the meta-level of all objects; Send, Accept, Queue, Receive, Protocol, Execution and State. While they do not cover every possible aspect of object behaviour, the set is extensible and the standard seven cover the behaviours essential to common object models. Readers should note that these meta-components are *logically* distinct. In reality, one entity may fill multiple roles. For example, the Queue and Receive components may, in a particular case, be implemented as one physical object. Meta-components can also be shared between objects.

In our discussion below, details such as message selectors are taken from the Smalltalk implementation of CodA. A simplified specification of these meta-component's execution interface is provided in an appendix.

Send. A Send's main role is to manage the potentially complex series of interactions between message sender and receiver ensuring proper transmission and synchronization. This includes protocol negotiation, synchronization and resource management. For example, when sending a synchronous message, the sender's Send must inform the receiver that a completion signal (e.g., reply) is required, how and to where the signal is to be transmitted, and also block the sender until the completion signal is received. The PortedObject model discussed below contains a Send which diverges substantially from the default model.

An object's Send is accessed using anObject meta send{:}. It invokes the message receiver's Accept.

Accept. Accepts define the receiver side of the message passing protocol negotiation and synchronization. They are also responsible for determining if a message is valid and how it should be handled (e.g., queued, processed immediately). Note that *accepting* a message is different from *receiving* a message. Acceptance concerns the interaction between the sender and receiver while receiving is the internal act, by the receiver, of picking the message for processing.

An object's Accept is accessed using anObject meta accept{:}. It is invoked by the message sender's Send and invokes the message receiver's Queue.

Queue. Queuing is the main mechanism of decoupling the execution of message senders and message receivers. Messages which have been accepted but cannot yet be processed must be queued. Once queued, the message's sender can be released to continue executing if the message's protocol allows. There are a great variety of possible queuing policies using a variety of factors to determine in which queue a message should be stored (e.g., by sender or type) and the message's place in that queue (e.g., FIFO, priority).

An object's Queue is accessed using anObject meta queue{:}. It is invoked by the message receiver's Accept and by an object's Receive.

Receive. As noted above, receiving and accepting are different operations. Receiving refers to the actual fetching of the next message for execution. In other words, while Accepts are concerned with how objects synchronize and interact with each other (i.e., inter-object synchronization), Receives deal with intra-object synchronization. When a Receive is asked for the next message to process, it may consider many different physical queues and consult various constraint specifications before determining the next appropriate message. The PortedObject model discussed in section 5 details an example of such a situation.

Note that many architectures implicitly combine the operations of Accept, Queue and Receive into the same object with quite a narrow interface. As such, the implementation or integration of a new scheme for one of these behaviours necessarily impinges on the others. Making them explicit and concrete simplifies the construction of complex behaviours.

An object's Receive is accessed using anObject meta receive{:}. It is invoked by objects when they are looking for the next message to process and invokes the object's Queue.

Protocol. A message, having been received, is translated into a method for execution. This is the primary responsibility of an object's Protocol. The most common mapping is an exact message selector to method name match where methods are examined according to some inheritance scheme. Protocols define both the selection criteria (e.g., exact match) and the search scheme (e.g., single/multiple inheritance). In more complex cases, Protocols may maintain multiple method tables and determine which to use based on some aspect of the base-level or system state.

An object's Protocol is accessed using anObject meta protocol{:}. It is invoked by objects when they need to map a message to a method to execute. That is, typically from an object's Execution.

Execution. For an object to execute methods, it must interact with some system resources (e.g., virtual machines, processes). Executions describe how this interaction occurs. By manipulating its Execution, a programmer can control where and when an object runs as well as its overall importance (e.g., priority) and independence.

Having an explicit execution model also enables methods to be somewhat more abstract and to be executed in different ways depending on the situation. For example, if we are debugging an object, we may wish to execute its methods on a special debugging virtual machine or interpreter whereas normally methods are executed as native machine code. It is the Execution's role is to determine how to execute methods and then execute them.

An object's Execution is accessed using anObject meta execution{:}. Executions are generally invoked by either the Accept or Queue (in the passive case) or by the explicit or implicit invocation of a receive operation (in the active case).

State. Though not directly involved in execution, state is an essential part of an object. The role of a State is to organize and maintain object state. It defines both what slots the object has as well as how the data in those slots is stored. The State *does not* actually hold the data. It simply knows how it can be accessed.

An object's State is accessed using anObject meta state{:}. States are invoked whenever one of the object's slots is accessed.

2.3 Example Meta-level

In Figure 1 we depict the events, meta-components and interactions involved in the sending of a message M from object A to object B (as indicated by the heavy dashed arrow). The shaded areas contain meta-components. Each light arrow is an interaction event (dashed for A's execution thread, solid for B's). The heavy solid arrows indicate the base/meta relationship and go from base-level to meta-level. We have labeled only those meta-components relevant to this particular interaction.

We see that A sends M by interacting with it's Send (1). The Send then transfers M to B's Accept (2) which queues it with the Queue (3). At some point, B will execute a receive operation which invokes the Receive (4) and fetches the next message from the Queue (5). The message is mapped to a method by the Protocol (6) and finally, the message is processed by executing the found method (7). In this way, every aspect of basic execution is reified.

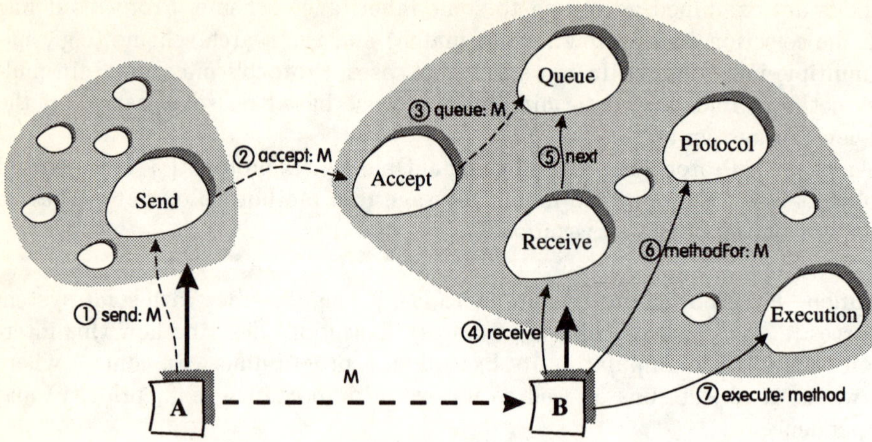

Fig. 1. Sample meta-level configuration and interaction

2.4 Implementation

CodA has been implemented in Smalltalk and much of the remaining discussion draws from that experience. Because CodA deals largely with execution rather than language issues, we have been able to fully integrate it into Smalltalk. For each Smalltalk object we transparently and lazily add the meta-level infrastructure and default meta-components which describe the standard Smalltalk object model. In this implementation, a standard CodA object behaves just like a standard Smalltalk object. Having opened the implementation of a Smalltalk object, we can adjust its behaviour as needed. Objects generally retain their base-level semantics but gain some additional behaviour such as concurrency or distribution.

Using the CodA framework as described above, we have created a library of components with which we have built a number of object models. The following sections describe the design and implementation of three models; ConcurrentObject, DistributedObject and PortedObject as demonstrations of the CodA concepts and design. An appendix contains example implementations of the default behaviours for some meta-components. Our discussion is set in terms of changes to these behaviours.

3 Concurrent Objects

Passive objects are reactive in that they simply respond to external stimulus or input and 'borrow' processing resources from message senders. In the ConcurrentObject model, objects have their own internal *activity* and processing resources (threads). This behaviour is described by a ConcurrentExecution component which fills the Execution role.

A ConcurrentExecution's idling execution behaviour (i.e., what objects do when they are not driven by user code) is similar in intent to that of Actors as seen in [1, 3, 10]. While formal Actors redefine their execution behaviour after every execution, in practice the replacement behaviour is the same; receive and process a message. Our basic activity model is similar; an endless loop, receiving and processing messages. For passive objects, the activity loop is implicit in the runtime system. For ConcurrentObjects, the loop runs explicitly in the threads associated with an object's ConcurrentExecution. The following is an example of such a loop for an object base.

```
| message result |
[true] whileTrue: [
    message := base meta receive receiveFor: base.
    result := self process: message for: base.
    base meta send reply: result to: message for: base]
```

When a message arrives, a passive object's Queue actually calls the object's Execution and directly triggers the processing of the message. That is, there is no queuing, only immediate processing. The Receive is never called explicitly as objects are always implicitly receiving incoming messages. Adding explicit thread(s) and an activity to an object both invokes its Receive and raises the possibility the sender and receiver of a message may be disjoint with respect to execution threads.

In addition to the activity loop, ConcurrentObjects change the Queue to ensure that messages are actually queued rather than passed on to the Execution. StandardQueue (shown below) is an example of such a Queue. It maintains an internal queue structure on which it implements the Queue interface. The actual queuing model used (e.g., FIFO) depends entirely on how we want incoming messages to be ordered (i.e., the object's queuing policy). This is specified by the user in the creation of the StandardQueue.

```
StandardQueue>>nextFor: base
    ^queue next

StandardQueue>>enqueue: message for: base
    queue add: message
```

The ConcurrentObject model does not need to define new message sending mechanisms as the default Send components already include the notions of synchronous, asynchronous and future messages. In the default, passive object case, synchronous sending is the default, future messages represent a promise to compute similar to closures or blocks, and asynchronous messages are mapped to synchronous messages where the result is ignored.

These ideas are included in the default behaviour for two reasons; they are useful in normal object behaviour description and they are relevant to system parallelism, not object concurrency. For example, a distributed system can contain no ConcurrentObjects but still require asynchronous sends.

4 Distributed Objects

The DistributedObject model is a somewhat larger change to object behaviour. In the model, objects live in *spaces*. An object's Execution and State can live in different spaces and can be independently copied, replicated or moved between spaces. Inter-space messaging fits naturally into the normal object model through the use of RemoteReferences or Proxies [14]. The model contains a sophisticated, uniform mechanism for describing how objects are transmitted from space to space (marshaling). The model is equally applicable to passive and active objects and is built largely out of new components/roles (e.g., Marshaling, Replication and Migration) and infrastructure objects (e.g., RemoteReference and Space). Here we present a few of these new structures. More detailed coverage of the DistributedObject model can be found in [9].

Spaces are places in which objects exist (store their state) and execute. A Space is known to every other Space and can be addressed (i.e., sent messages) directly from anywhere in the distributed machine. They manage the mapping between global object ids and local representatives (e.g., RemoteReferences, replica).

A RemoteReference is a local representative or *Proxy*[14] for some remote object. Locally they are just like any other object. They can be stored in instance slots, assigned to variables, passed as arguments, etc. When they are sent a message, the simplest RemoteReference just forwards it to the space containing the real object — the *target*. More sophisticated RemoteReferences process some messages locally while forwarding others to the target.

RemoteReferences are themselves implemented using modified CodA meta-components. According to the CodA execution model, when a message is sent to an object, the sender's Send and the receiver's Accept interact to effect the message transfer. In the DistributedObject case, these meta-components are in different spaces. Local to the sender, the receiver is a RemoteReference and the receiver's Accept is an intelligent RemoteReference to the target's Accept. Rather than performing the normal accept operation, the local Accept *marshals* the message into a stream of bytes and transmits it to the remote space. Once there, it is reconstructed and accepted by the target's Accept. In this way, the DistributedObject model is uniformly applied to all objects in the system, even those at the meta-level.

4.1 Replication

The basic idea of replication is that an object's state can exist in multiple Spaces at the same time. Furthermore, through the use of some distributed consistency schemes, we can maintain the proper semantics of our programs. Schemes for replication range from simple one-off copying (not technically considered replication here) to fully coherent replication. Since this is an entirely new behaviour for objects, it is a new role (Replication) for the meta-level and requires new meta-components for its implementation (The addition of new roles is covered in Section 6). As we will see, the role of the Replication is quite independent of the object's execution and the actual structure of an object's state variables.

To demonstrate replication we develop the partial replication scenario shown in Figure 2. The figure shows two objects, original (in Space 0) and replica (in Space 1). Though not shown, original is actually a 2D N-Body [2] problem solver which calculates the forces exerted by, and movements of, a collection of bodies or *particles* in a 2D plane. N-Body solvers arrange a set of particles in a Quad tree structure according to their physical location and then process each particle individually. Overall, processing consists of a couple tree scans and iterations over the collection of particles.

To distribute this algorithm we divide the particles into subsets which are worked by different solvers, one per Space. The sets however, are not entirely independent since all particles potentially exert forces on all others. As the tree is the central data structure for relating particles to one another, it must be globally known and unique. The solver is a prime candidate for partial replication.

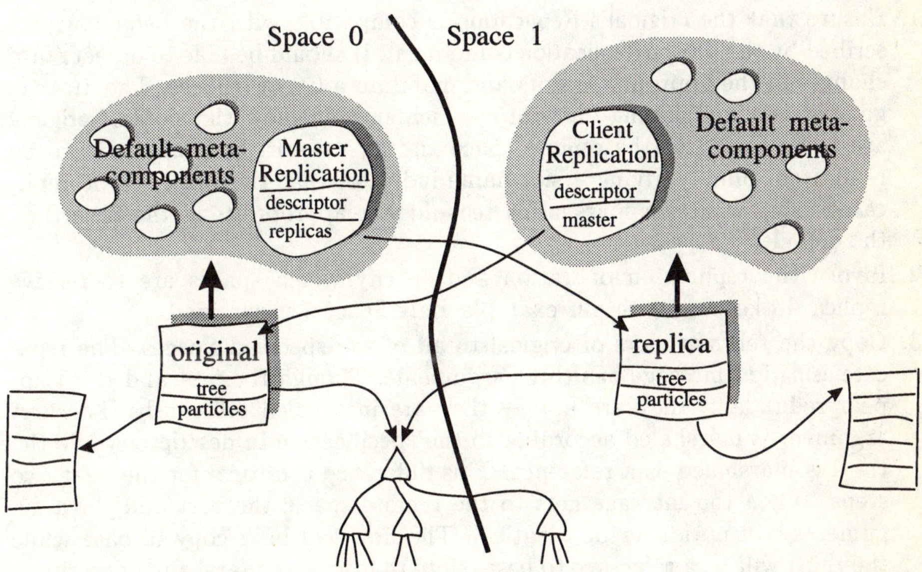

Fig. 2. Distributed object layout

As shown in Figure 2, original, the solver, has two slots; particles and tree. replica is a partial replica of original where the tree slot is consistency managed and the particles slot is not. Every replica in the system shares the same tree but has an independent particle set. The replication of original is done in a series of six steps. Figure 3 shows the required code while the discussion below explains each step.

```
1)  original meta replication asMasterUsing: #('tree') for: original.
2)  original meta replication replicateIn: (Spaces at: 1) for: original

MasterReplication>>replicateIn: space for: base
3)  space replicate: base using: descriptor for: base.
6)  replicas add: space

Space>>replicate: copy using: descriptor for: master
4)  copy meta replication asClientOf: master using: descriptor for: copy.
5)  master become: copy
```

Fig. 3. The making of a replica

1. Ensure that the original's Replication is compatible with the behaviour described by the MasterReplication component. It should be able to detect state changes in the appropriate slots and maintain a list of replicas. The first argument is a marshaling descriptor which specifies how the slots of original are to be copied to the remote space and as a result, how original is to be replicated. Simply giving a slot name indicates that the slot is to be replicated using whatever marshaling technique is appropriate at the time (i.e., the default).
2. Invoke the replication operation and specify which spaces are to receive replica. In keeping with our example, only Space 1 is specified.
3. Copy the relevant slots of original to all of the specified Spaces. The replicate:using:for: message has three arguments. Though the first and third appear redundant, they are not — they are marshaled differently. The first argument is marshaled according to the specification in descriptor while the third is marshaled as a reference. This difference is critical for the next two steps. When the message gets to the remote space, the first and third arguments will no longer be identical. The first will be a copy of base while the third will be a reference to base. Note that though marshaling descriptor specification is a simple addition to the messaging syntax, the details are omitted from this example to improve clarity.
4. Make the remote copy into a replication *client* of original. This is similar to step 1 and executes in the remote Space which will contain replica. copy's meta-level is modified such that all state changes are delegated to master and the Replication knows the identity of its master for future reference.

5. Convert any preexisting remote references to original to be local references to replica. Remote spaces may contain references to master prior to replication. To maintain a consistent view of the world, these remote references should be changed into local references to the newly created replica.
6. Invoke consistency management on the replicated slots of original by adding the Space to the list of consistency controlled replica locations.

In step 1 we hooked the relevant state change operations for original. Note that we do not require a new State component. The existing component's meta-level is manipulated to hook state accesses. This both isolates replication from representation and reduces the possibility of object model conflict. When original's replicated state is changed, its Replication's update:with:for method (shown below) is invoked by the hook. The method simply broadcasts the change in slot to all of original's clients. Typically this would be done by multi-cast messaging for efficiency though here we specify an iterative approach for clarity.

```
MasterReplication>>update: slot with: value for: base
    replicas do: [:space | | rep |
        rep := (base in: space).
        rep meta replication update: slot with: value for: rep]
```

In this example we have shown a relatively lax model of consistency. To implement *strict consistency* requires only the addition of a two phase update protocol between masters and clients and the hooking or delegation of both read and write state accesses on masters and clients rather than just writes. Both of these changes are straightforward and are done using existing meta-level structures and mechanisms.

4.2 Summary

The DistributedObject model, and this example in particular, highlight a central theme to our work — the addition to, or modification of, an object's computational behaviour without changing its base-level code. The result is the ability to use standard class libraries in many different environments. For the N-Body application, the original uniprocessor sequential version required a code change only where a new tree node was created and we wished to explicitly direct its location. Other changes were done to take advantage of the newly introduced concurrency but were not essential.

In terms of distributed object-oriented computation, our model also highlights something which we feel is essential — the ability to talk about distribution on a *per-use* basis rather than just on a per-class or even per-object basis. In the N-Body application (replica creation step 3) we demonstrate the need for use-based marshaling. Also, while our distribution scheme calls for partial replication of the solver objects, someone else's might use a different scheme. Using this architecture, all they need program is the meta-level of individual objects as they are used.

5 Ported Objects

PortedObjects are objects which communicate and behave in a dataflow-like way. They have *ports* or channels over which data flows and when data is available for processing, processing is done. This style of behaviour is interesting in a number of areas. People working in concurrency formalisms like the π-calculus [11] have found channels and ports to be useful in specifying object communication. Most popular data visualization and analysis systems like AVS [16], IRIS/Explorer [15] and parallel system analysis tools like Pablo [13] have dataflow or analysis graph architectures. The model is interesting to us in both regards.

Ported behaviour should be as transparent as possible to the base-level code. For example, in an analysis system we developed, we used a set of generic objects which describe various analysis operations (e.g., filters, collectors, expert systems, DSP processors) and added a set of meta-components which gave these *analysis objects* ported behaviour. The idea was that users (analysts) could then build their own analysis tools by simply connecting existing analysis objects to form the desired analysis graphs.

The addition of porting is done by identifying the parameters and results of each analysis object. Each parameter or result is made into a port on the surface of the object. Users program with PortedObjects by building connections between these ports. 'Programs' are run by feeding data to some of the free parameter ports. Values put in a port are automatically broadcast to all objects connected to that port. When some object in the graph has sufficient input, it processes the data and stores the results in its result ports and so, passes it to the next object. This process continues and data flows through the graph.

5.1 Meta-level Design

The PortedObject meta-level design in CodA is done entirely via modifications to the following five meta-components; Send, Accept, Queue, Receive and Execution.

Send. At the inter-object level, PortedObjects cannot explicitly send messages. They can only store values in their logical output (result) ports. An object cannot tell whether or not storing a result will cause the value to be transmitted to some other object. The meta-level however, can detect the result setting operations and trigger the broadcasting of the new value to all objects connected to the modified port. So, while base-level PortedObjects have no explicit send operations, they implicitly use message sending in their implementation.

A PortedObject's Send behaviour is defined by a generic MultiSend object which provides infrastructure for multi-casting messages to a known set of receivers. For PortedObjects these receivers are represented by ports and connections.

Accept. PortedObjects use MultiAccepts whose behaviour differs from that of normal Accepts only in their support for manipulating ports and connections. This consists mostly of add/remove and connect/disconnect methods in various forms. Also, as messages arrive (via accept:for:), the MultiAccept marks them with the port over which they came and queues them as per normal operation.

Queue. The PortedObject model uses MultiQueues for their Queue component. A MultiQueue supports the sorting of elements into one of many logical queues as defined by some discriminator, in this case, the arrival port. The default Queue interface is augmented with duplicate operations which take an additional parameter, a port identifier.

Receive. A PortedObject's Receive is concerned more with parameter coordination than ports and connections. Some PortedObjects require several inputs to be present before processing can take place. In some cases, processing only makes sense if some set of these parameters are reset from iteration to iteration. In others, a change of one parameter is cause for recalculation. To manage these constraints, PortedObjects use CoordinatedReceives.

When a CoordinatedReceive is asked to receiveFor: by an Execution, it produces the next available message which satisfies the current set of coordination constraints, cSet (see code below). Here cSet represents a very simple system of constraints based on a collection of port identifiers from which it is valid to take a value. As values arrive, their port is removed from cSet. When the set is empty, we know that we have received all the required values and so the object is ready for processing. That is, the receiver is *coordinated*. The initial values for the cSet are derived from information supplied by the programmer as part of the PortedObject definition scheme.

```
CoordinatedReceive>>receiveFor: base
    | message |
    message := base meta queue nextSatisfying: cSet for: base.
    cSet remove: message arrivalPort.
    ^message
```

Execution. Since PortedObjects do not have explicit message passing, we draw a distinction between the implementation receiving and executing a message, and the base-level object itself actually being evaluated. PortedObject evaluation can only happen when the object is coordinated. The messages handled by the Sends and Receives are infrastructure related and serve to transfer data (i.e., parameters and results) and determine coordination.

```
CoordinatedExecution>>process: message for: base
    | method |
    method := base meta protocol methodFor: message for: base.
    self execute: method with: message for: base.
    base meta receive isCoordinated ifTrue: [
        self evaluate: base.
        base meta receive resetCoordinationSet]
```

The main change in a PortedObject's Execution is highlighted by the modified process:for: method shown above. After executing an infrastructure message, the Execution tests for coordination. If the object is coordinated, it is evaluated. After evaluation, the coordination set is reset.

5.2 Compound PortedObjects

In complex PortedObject graphs we would like to be able to think of and manipulate a group of PortedObjects as one. The encapsulation should be completely transparent to objects both inside and outside the group. By taking a generic analysis object and reusing some of the meta-components already described, we can create a *compound* PortedObject as shown in Figure 4.

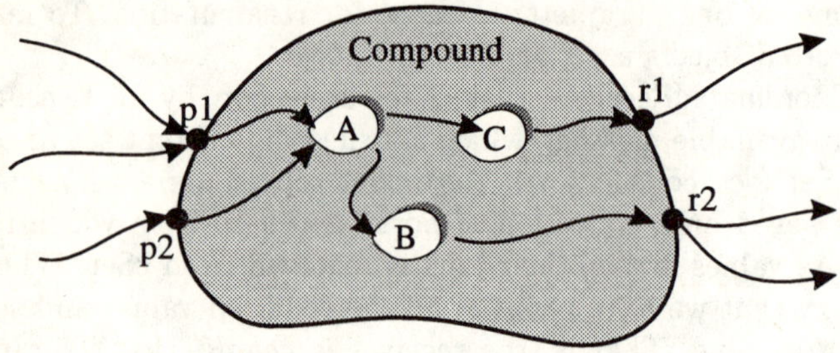

Fig. 4. Compound object example

In the diagram we see three objects (A, B and C) encapsulated in Compound. Compound is itself just a generic analysis object which by default has no ports or particular evaluation behaviour. We have added parameters p1 and p2, and results r1 and r2. The parameters and results are logically linked, as appropriate, to those of the contained objects.

In accordance to the PortedObject model, data values coming to A should come from some PortedObject's Send (e.g., a MultiSend). Compound's Send fits those requirements but it manages the *external* connections for Compound and has no facilities for managing a separate set of *internal* connections. The situation is similar for Compound's result ports and Accept.

An obvious solution is to implement new Send and Accept components which keep two connection lists, one internal and one external. But this would just be duplicating existing behaviour and adding special cases in connection management. An alternative is to use two PortedObjects instead of the single Compound. One would handle the group's parameters and one its results. This however goes against our goal of having the group act as one object.

We take a somewhat novel approach and extend Compound's meta-level to have two new roles, InternalSend and InternalAccept. These roles are actually filled by normal MultiSend and MultiAccept components. Compound's original Accept and Send components remain unchanged and continue to handle all external connections while InternalSend and InternalAccept handle the internal connections. Figure 5 shows the configuration for the parameter side of Compound from Figure 4. Note that p1 and p2 in the two figures are the same.

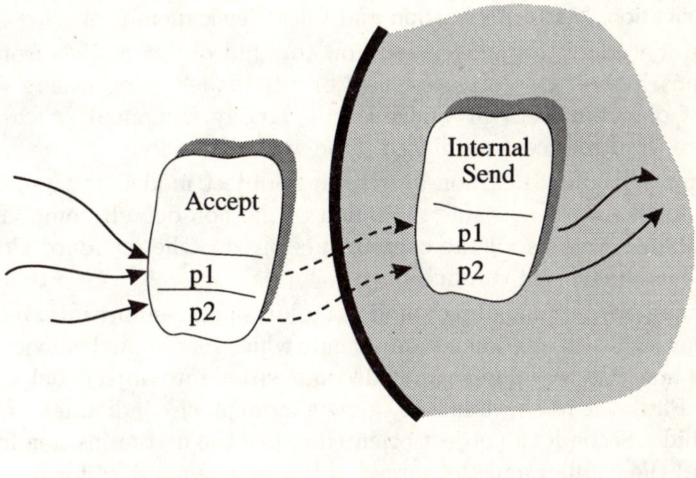

Fig. 5. Compound object parameter handling

Compound's Accept has two ports, p1 and p2, corresponding to its two parameters. Values arriving at those ports are tagged as described above and then passed, at the meta-level, to the corresponding port of Compound's InternalSend. From there they are, as per normal operations, broadcast over the appropriate port's connections to the objects contained in Compound. The structure of the result side is analogous though reversed.

This model is simple and appealing. From a porting and communication viewpoint, all objects have a consistent and uniform model. From a meta-level architecture point of view, it demonstrates how the meta-level is completely extensible and how meta-component defined behaviour is reused. In our original architecture design we never imagined a requirement for having multiple Send or Accept components. In this situation however, it is not only convenient and reusable but is aesthetically pleasing.

6 Putting the Pieces Together

As we have seen, in building object models, we may need to extend the set of roles that the meta-level plays. To do this, we generally create the role and develop at least two components; one which defines some default behaviour and one which defines the new behaviour we specifically want to add to objects. The default component is used when an object's role is accessed but no behaviour (e.g., component) has been explicitly provided. Using this technique, as soon as it is added to the system, all objects have some defined behaviour for the role. Developers are then free to create variations on this default behaviour and substitute them for the default component on individual or groups of objects. For example, the DistributedObject model defines several new roles and we have shown that one of them, Replication, can be filled by three different components; DefaultReplication, MasterReplication and ClientReplication.

Until now we have only discussed how to build object models from scratch. We have not looked at composing new object models from others. The combination of object models in CodA is still largely a manual process but the architecture itself reduces considerably the work to be done.

Combining disjoint (i.e., non-overlapping) object models is straightforward. The new model simply contains the union of the non-default components from the originals. As long as all the components provide the standard CodA interfaces, the new model will run fine.

Combining overlapping object models requires programmer intervention. The general approach is to build new components which merge the behaviour of those being combined. CodA's fine-grained decomposition into objects helps in several ways here. First, the finer granularity gives a more precise indication of where the models collide. Second, the object-orientedness of the decomposition limits both the scope of the conflict and the spread of the change required for its resolution.

Objects also give us an abstraction of behaviour which is easier to use and reuse. Consider two object models X and Y which both redefine the Send component. If we wish to create a model XY (the combination of X and Y) we have to resolve the conflicts between XSend and YSend. If we assume that this resolution creates XYSend, a Send with the properties of both the X and Y models, then the conflict between XSend and YSend has been resolved and need never be resolved again. If the conflict is encountered in the combination of some other models, we can simply reuse XYSend. As we build a library of components, conflict resolution will become more a problem of identifying the existing component with the correct properties than of actually writing code.

The fine-granularity of our design is double edged however. Ad hoc groups of meta-components do not present as nice a package of object behaviour as a single 'meta-object'. Users are faced with a potentially large choice of possible components to fill a particular role. We address this in a number of ways. Relatively simple object models like ConcurrentObjects are represented by methods which configure meta-levels. To use that model, a user just applies the method to the object in question (see the example code below). This simply overwrites any preexisting behaviours.

```
configureAsConcurrentObject: base
    base meta queue: (StandardQueue for: base).
    base meta execution: (ConcurrentExecution for: base)
```

More sophisticated models use base-level language constructs (e.g., classes and metaclasses) as object model representatives. This has the benefit of being integrated with the environment but the drawback of still requiring user-written code.

Using the notion of *properties*, we address both the composition and combination problems. A property is a simple declarative token which points out one way in which a component is different from the default. For example, some of the PortedObject model components are *multi*. Comparing property lists allows us to even more precisely identify conflicts in components. Properties are also used in object model specification. Rather than hardcoding the use of particular components in a model, programmers declaratively specify that, for example, they want a Send with a certain set of properties. Whether a change is required and which actual Send is used is determined dynamically.

Properties, like many categorization systems, suffer from naming problems. Defining and guaranteeing the semantics of a particular property is difficult at best. So, while they do not solve the composition or combination problems, these operations, in a sufficiently rich and consistent component environment, are reduced to property constraint satisfaction.

A completely different approach is component generalization and parameterization. Looking at the models we have defined here, only ConcurrentObjects and PortedObjects overlap in the component domain. Initially we applied the above techniques with success. Then, as we developed other models which also overlapped, we found ourselves generalizing and parameterizing the various components to be more reusable. For example, Executions were changed to take a user supplied code block to define their execution activity. The result was a library of general components which can be setup in many different ways and so can be used in many different situations.

7 Related Work

There are several projects related to our work. We have already mentioned some and relate to a few more below. In general, most previous efforts have either a different focus or different approach with respect to the issues in object behaviour description.

RbCl [6] is similar to CodA in that explicitly supports active objects and factors the meta-level into objects. However, it factors out only a limited set of components and does not provide a framework for their composition and interaction.

The Apertos operating system [17, 18] differs mainly as a result of a different target domain than of the overall architecture. Apertos reifies aspects of object behaviour at the operating system level (e.g., memory management, page faults and device drivers). This level is mostly orthogonal to the current CodA meta-components. It would be interesting to combine the two domains in one framework to get a more complete and far-reaching reification of object behaviour.

Recent work in AL-1/D with distribution control at the meta-level [12] is also similar to ours. They focus on a set of meta-level concepts directly related to distribution requirements. We feel that in fact, in real systems, the issues related to distribution are more far-reaching. They involve heterogeneous state representations and update policies, and demand mechanisms for the control of the intra-object concurrency implicitly introduced by remote referencing. Furthermore, all of this should be possible on a per-use basis. As such, it is appropriate to use a meta-architecture with wider scope. It also appears that the CodA infrastructure and interface is more clearly defined.

Over the years we have been influenced by Actalk [3]. It provides a testbed for describing object behaviours in areas relating primarily to concurrent execution and message passing. Though recent versions are more and more component-based at the meta-level, it is still somewhat monolithic and code-based. Having said that, we are very interested in implementing in CodA, many of the object models available in Actalk.

8 Conclusions and Future Work

By treating the meta-level as "just another application" and applying typical software engineering practices, namely fine-grained decomposition into objects, we have created an extensible, uniform framework for object behaviour description. Object model definition by composition and extension was demonstrated through the development of three object models; ConcurrentObject, DistributedObject and PortedObject. These models show that in CodA, quite diverse object behaviours can be created with relatively minor changes to the meta-level and almost no changes to the base-level.

We have found that the decomposition of behaviour into objects as opposed to code gives meta-level users a higher-level abstraction in which to program. Responsibility for the definition of particular behaviours rests with identifiable, discrete objects rather than being spread through the meta-level code. Individual meta-components have a narrower domain and so are more easily reused. The unruliness of groups of meta-components (as opposed to single 'meta-objects') is addressed via the use of *properties* and the constructs (e.g., classes and metaclasses) available in the implementation environment.

While we have not solved the general object model composition and combination problem, the CodA architecture helps to identify and isolate points of conflict between models. Meta-components provide *firewalls* which limit both the scope of potential conflict and the spread of the changes resulting from its resolution. Components developed to resolve a particular conflict can be reused wherever that conflict occurs so the conflict need only be resolved once. In addition, we propose some simple but potentially useful concepts such as *properties* which ease the burden on meta-level users.

An interesting avenue of future work is to look for techniques which allow the dynamic *compression* and *expansion* of meta-levels. While the separation of meta-level roles into individual objects is logically efficient, it may be less than optimal in implementation. By providing some sort of declarative description of each meta-component's behaviour and expected interactions (e.g., properties), we can automatically combine several components into one. This is analogous to some problems in typing, partial evaluation and code generation. Similarly, by remembering something of their original structure, compressed meta-structures can be expanded into their original form. Using a combination of expansion and compression, monolithic (e.g., compressed) structures can be made open. To change a monolithic meta-level structure, it is first expanded, then changed and finally re-compressed. We believe that this direction holds great promise in the battle to make systems more open and to make open systems more efficient.

9 Acknowledgements

We gratefully thank Jean-Pierre Briot, Pierre Cointe, Nick Edgar and Laurent Thomas for discussions and helpful comments on drafts of this paper.

References

1. G. Agha. *Actors: A Model of Concurrent Computation in Distributed Systems.* Series in Artificial Intelligence. MIT Press, 1986.
2. J. Barnes and P. Hut. A hierarchical $O(N \log N)$ force-calculation algorithm. *Nature*, 324:446–449, 1986.
3. Jean-Pierre Briot. Actalk: A testbed for classifying and designing actor languages in the Smalltalk-80 environment. In S. Cook, editor, *Proceedings ECOOP '89*, pages 109–129, Nottingham, July 1989. Cambridge University Press.
4. Jean-Pierre Briot and Pierre Cointe. Programming with explicit metaclasses in Smalltalk-80. In *Proceedings of OOPSLA '89*, pages 419–431, October 1989.
5. Pierre Cointe. CLOS and Smalltalk: A comparison. In Andreas Pæpcke, editor, *Object-oriented programming: The CLOS perspectives*, pages 215–250. MIT Press, 1993.
6. Yuuji Ichisugi, Satoshi Matsuoka, and Akinori Yonezawa. RbCl: A reflective object-oriented concurrent language without a run-time kernel. In *Proceedings of the International Workshop on Reflection and Meta-level Architecture*, pages 24–35, November 1992. Tokyo, Japan.
7. Gregor Kiczales, Jim des Rivières, and Daniel Bobrow. *The Art of the Metaobject Protocol.* MIT Press, Cambridge, Massachusetts, 1991.
8. Hidehiko Masuhara, Satoshi Matsuoka, Takuo Watanabe, and Akinori Yonezawa. Object-oriented concurrent reflective languages can be implemented efficiently. In *Proceedings OOPSLA '92, ACM SIGPLAN Notices*, pages 127–147, October 1992. Published as Proceedings OOPSLA '92, ACM SIGPLAN Notices, volume 27, number 10.
9. Jeff McAffer. Meta-level architecture support for distributed objects. In preparation.
10. Jeff McAffer and John Duimovich. Actra - An industrial strength concurrent object-oriented programming system. *ACM SIGPLAN OOPS Messenger*, 2(2):82–85, April 1989. Proceedings of the ACM SIGPlan OOPSLA Workshop on Object-Based Concurrent Programming.

11. Robin Milner. The polyadic π-calculus: A tutorial. In *Logic and Algebra of Specification*. Springer Verlag, 1992.
12. Hideaki Okamura and Yutaka Ishikawa. Object location control using meta-level programming. In *Proceedings of the European Conference on Object-Oriented Programming (ECOOP)*, LNCS 821, pages 299–319. Springer Verlag, July 1994.
13. Daniel A. Reed. *An overview of the Pablo performance analysis environment*. Department of Computer Science, University of Illinois, 1992.
14. Marc Shapiro, Yvon Gourhant, Sabine Habert, Laurence Mosseri, Michel Ruffin, and Celine Valot. SOS: An object-oriented operating system – Assesment and perspectives. *Computer Systems*, 2(4):287–337, Fall 1989.
15. Silicon Graphics Inc. *Explorer User's Guide*, 1992.
16. Stardent Computer Inc. *Application Visualization System, User's Guide*, 1989.
17. Yasuhiko Yokote. The Apertos reflective operating system: The concept and its implementation. In *Proceedings OOPSLA '92, ACM SIGPLAN Notices*, pages 414–434, October 1992. Published as Proceedings OOPSLA '92, ACM SIGPLAN Notices, volume 27, number 10.
18. Yasuhiko Yokote, Fumio Teraoka, and Mario Tokoro. A reflective architecture for an object-oriented distributed operating system. In S. Cook, editor, *Proceedings ECOOP '89*, pages 89–106, Nottingham, July 1989. Cambridge University Press.

A Meta-component Specification

The following is a description of the essential meta-components in CodA. Only the protocols needed for actual execution are specified. Others such as those required for configuration are not included as they will vary depending on the capabilities or properties of the component. All specifications are presented in terms of the Smalltalk implementation. The interface also supports a number of convenience methods which combine frequently used operations under one simpler protocol. These are not generally included in the specification. Readers are referred to the body of the paper for explanations of the component's roles.

Note that throughout the interface, the base-object (typically referred to as base) is explicitly specified as an argument. This is done for two main reasons: It allows for meta-components which have a one-to-many relationship with the base-level and it removes the requirement for implicit assumptions regarding the behaviour and arguments associated with an interface. For example, it may not be the case that the *sender* field of a message being sent is actually the object doing the send operation. As a general rule, if a meta-component maintains a one-to-one relationship to the base-level then the base argument is ignored.

A.1 MetaComponent

All meta-components respond to the following messages:

isDefaultBehaviour Answer true if the receiver represents the default behaviour for the role in which it was cast. Answer false if it has been explicitly set by the user.

A.2 Send

Fundamentally there are three different kinds of message sending: synchronous, asynchronous and future. These are realized as different protocols. Variations on the message argument introduce orthogonal concepts such as; express and system messages. Sends also explicitly support the transmission of reply messages as their requirements may be different from that of other message sends.

send: message for: base Send message for base. Defines the default sending behaviour and is typically, though not necessarily, mapped to one of the send operations given below.

send{Async/Sync/Future}: message for: base Send message for base. The sender and receiver are synchronized according to the specified mode (i.e., Async, Sync or Future).

reply: result to: message for: base Reply result to the reply destination listed in message for base. Replies are normal messages but may need to be treated differently to facilitate synchronization and other schemes.

A.3 Accept

accept: message for: base Determine if message can be accepted by base. To accept a message is to promise to consider performing computation based on its contents. It is not an implicit guarantee that the message will be processed but rather that the message has arrived at the destination. The act of accepting a message also involves a preliminary determination of what is to be done with the message. For example, if the message is marked as *express* then it should be considered for immediate execution.

acceptReply: message for: base Replies are normal messages but may need to be treated specially to facilitate synchronization and other schemes.

A.4 Queue

There are a great variety of possible queuing policies and factors in determining in which queue a message should be put and where it should be placed. These policies and factors are generally established via setup parameters on the Queue. The Queue protocol supports methods for enqueuing and dequeuing messages and various forms of message retrieval.

dequeue: message for: base Remove message from the receiver.

enqueue: message for: base Add message to the receiver.

nextFor: base Remove and answer the next available message from the receiver. This defines the default dequeuing behaviour and is typically, though not necessarily, mapped to one of the next operations given below.

blockingNextFor: base Remove and answer the next available message from the receiver. An answer is not given until a message is available.

nonBlockingNextFor: base Remove and answer the next available message or nil if none is available. An answer is always returned immediately.

nextSatisfying: constraints for: base Remove and answer the next available message from the receiver which satisfies the constraints. An answer is not given until such a message is available.

peekFor: base Answer the next available message from the queue or nil if none are available. No messages are removed from the receiver. An answer is always returned immediately.

A.5 Receive

receiveFor: base Answer the next available queued message. This defines the default receiving behaviour and is typically, though not necessarily, mapped to one of the receive operations given below.

nonBlockingReceiveFor: base Answer the next available queued message or nil if none are available. Subsequent calls will not return the same message. An answer is always returned immediately.

blockingReceiveFor: base Answer the next available queued message. Subsequent calls will not return the same message. An answer is not given until a message is available.

A.6 Protocol

methodFor: message for: base Answer the method best suited to processing message. If a method cannot be found then answer some method which will handle the error condition.

A.7 Execution

Executions describe the basic processing activity of an object. How and when they receive, lookup and execute messages. For passive objects this is determined largely by the external thread of control and when other objects send messages to the Execution's base-object(s).

For active objects, the Execution has complete control over these aspects. It must also define what the object does when it is not processing some received message as well as how the object's execution maps onto physical computational resources (e.g., processes and processors). In short, the Execution provides an encapsulation of processing power for the exclusive use of its base-level object(s).

execute: method with: arguments for: base Execute method with arguments on receiver base.

process: message for: base A convenience protocol which combines message to method mapping and method execution. message is processed by first sending methodFor:for: to the relevant Protocol and then execute:with:for: to the receiver.

processImmediately: message for: base Similar to process:for: but the any normal execution currently underway is interrupted with the processing of message.

activityFor: base Answer an evaluable description of base's activity loop.

A.8 State

States describe the physical storage and structure of objects. It is important to note that they do not actually contain the base-level state but simply know how to store and retrieve it. State slots can be named or numbered.

at: id for: base Answer the current value of slot id in base.
at: id put: value for: base Store value in slot id of base.
slotIdsFor: base Answer a list of all the ids for the slots available in base.

B Default Meta-component code

The following are the default implementations for many of the methods mentioned in the body of the paper. They are given as a point of reference so readers can judge the amount of change required to effect the behaviours described.

```
DefaultSend>>send: message for: base
    ^message receiver meta accept
        accept: message for: message receiver

DefaultSend>>reply: result to: message for: base
    | reply |
    reply := message asReply.
    reply arguments: (Array with: result).
    ^reply receiver meta accept
        acceptReply: reply for: reply receiver

DefaultAccept>>accept: message for: base
    ^base meta queue enqueue: message for: base

DefaultAccept>>acceptReply: message for: base
    ^base meta execution processImmediately: message for: base

DefaultQueue>>enqueue: message for: base
    ^base meta execution process: message for: base

DefaultQueue>>nextFor: base
    ^nil

DefaultReceive>>receiveFor: base
    ^base meta queue nextFor: base

DefaultProtocol>>methodFor: message for: base
    ^self lookupTable at: message selector

DefaultExecution>>execute: method with: arguments for: base
    ^method executeFor: base withArguments: arguments
```

```
DefaultExecution>>process: message for: base
    | method |
    method := base meta protocol methodFor: message for: base.
    ^self execute: method with: message args for: base

DefaultExecution>>processImmediately: message for: base
    ^self process: message for: base

DefaultState>>at: id for: base
    ^self slots at: id

DefaultState>>at: id put: value for: base
    ^self slots at: id put: value
```

An Object-Oriented Framework for the Formal Verification of Processors

Laurent Arditi and Hélère Collavizza

Université de Nice – Sophia Antipolis
Laboratoire I3S, CNRS-URA 1376
650, Route des Colles. B.P. 145
06903 Sophia Antipolis Cédex. France
email: arditi@unice.fr, helen@essi.fr

Abstract. We propose an object-oriented approach for the formal verification of processors. This approach has been validated on significant applications. It is based on a class hierarchy that provides the basic components to describe processors at any abstraction level, and to specify verifications to execute.
The originality of our method is to combine an object-oriented model (to ensure *genericity*) and a computer algebra verification system (to ensure *efficiency*). Computer experiments with our framework clearly shown three main advantages: processor descriptions are very easy to write down, the core of the verification system is generic so it may be applied without any modification to different processors, and last, the proof times are very short compared with previous approaches.

1 Introduction

In this section, we first provide general motivations for hardware verification, and then outline our approach in general terms.

1.1 Motivations

In order to produce correct circuits, several verification tools such as correct generators of floor-plans or logic simulators are generally applied during the design process. However, it is widely accepted that the existing CAD tools have two major drawbacks:

- they cannot perform exhaustive proofs: this is due to the combinatorial complexity of the problem,
- they are low-level oriented and therefore they cannot deal with abstract specifications.

For these reasons, attention has been paid these last ten years on general formal verification methods (for a survey and further justifications see [10]). In general, formally verifying a circuit consists in proving that its specification is logically equivalent to its implementation, in the sense of a logical equivalence. More explicitly, the verification process is decomposed in three steps:

- in the first step, a formal model of the specification of the circuit is defined,
- in the second step, a formal model of the implementation of the circuit is defined, and
- in the third step, a proof that for any input and any state variable values, the two models are equal is performed.

This last point amounts to the proof of a universally quantified formula and can be realized using theorem proving techniques such as simplification or inductive reasoning.

1.2 The Problem of Processor Verification

The previous process is crucial when dealing with complex circuits such as processors. The key to the formal verification is the decomposition in successive proofs at successive abstraction levels: a more and more detailed view of the same processor is described [1]. The *specification* of the circuit is then a description of an abstract level (such as the assembly language level), while its *implementation* is a description at a more concrete level (for instance, the microinstruction level or the electronic block model). For each level, one exactly keeps the same description and verification process. The processor is specified as a set of components on which a set of actions is performed.

Let $level_i$ be an abstract specification level, and $level_{i+1}$ a more concrete one. The set of objects at $level_i$ is included in the set of objects at $level_{i+1}$, and an action at $level_i$ is realized at $level_{i+1}$ by composing a set of actions at $level_{i+1}$. So to verify the correctness between two adjacent levels one must show that the following diagram commutes:

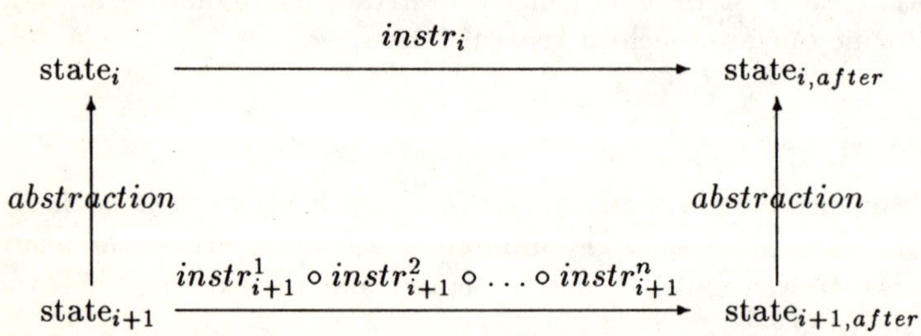

For instance, if $level_i$ is the processor as seen by the assembly programmer, and $level_{i+1}$ is the architecture of the processor, the commutation property of the above diagram means that an assembly instruction is correctly realized by a sequence of microinstructions. Thus, to implement this abstract schema one needs:

- languages to describe states, transitions and abstractions, and
- well-suited proof systems to carry out the transitions and verify the commutation of the diagram.

1.3 Aims of the Paper and Related Works

Several interesting approaches have been proposed to realize formal verification of processors along the lines of the previous general schema, see for instance [7, 11, 18, 21, 22]. However, in our sense, these works display two kinds of shortcomings:

- they are specific to a particular processor. This means that the specification of a new processor must be built from the scratch. As a consequence, they do not provide any user-friendly interface to describe processors and verifications to execute, and
- they are based on very general logical proof tools (such as HOL or Nqthm). However these tools are too complex to support efficiently particular problems.

To overcome the above drawbacks, a new framework for processor verification is presented here. The key idea is to combine a "computer algebra system" and an "object-oriented model" in a single framework. The computer algebra system is used to efficiently simplify expressions. The object-oriented model provides three major advantages:

- the description and verification process is generic, it is the same for all processors and for all specification levels, and
- the object-oriented model is well-suited to the concrete structure of micro processors. As consequence, the specifications are concise and easy to write down, and
- the object classification and the polymorphism of the methods simplify the core of the verification system.

Computer experiments with our framework have shown that not trivial examples can be treated, in a very efficient way (see the comparative Table 2 at the end of the paper), and with a small specification effort.

Layout of the paper: in section 2, we introduce our method on a simple example. In section 3, we present the basis of our verification framework and emphasize the advantages of our object-oriented approach and of the computer algebra system. In section 4 we deal with the implementation of our framework and in section 5 with the results we have obtained so far.

2 Overview of our Method: an Example

Before discussing the technical details of our method, let us introduce it on a simple example.

Assume we are given a simple processor with a memory and one accumulator register and suppose we wish to prove the "addition" instruction in direct memory addressing mode. Let describe this processor at the assembly language level (level_1) and at the microinstruction level (level_2) as follows:

At the assembly language level, the state of the processor consists of the memory "mem", the accumulator register "acc" and the program counter "pc". The addition instruction in direct memory addressing mode involves the two simultaneous transitions:

ADD_{DIR}:	acc := acc + mem [mem [pc](3 to 7)]	acc *is updated*
	pc := pc + 1	pc *is incremented*

"mem[pc]" contains the code of the addition instruction and, "mem[pc](3 to 7)" extracts the 5 highest bits of "mem[pc]" that contain the operand address.

In our object-oriented framework, this will be described as an instance named "proc-$level_1$" of the class `Interpreter` with attributes `state`, `transitions` and `select` (see Sect. 3.1):

- `state` contains the tuple <mem, pc, acc> where each component is built up from an object-oriented library: "mem" is an instance of the `Memory` class while "pc" and "acc" are instances of the `Register` class.
- `transitions` describes the semantics of each instruction. Here, this attribute includes the set of parallel transitions associated with ADD_{DIR} key.
- `select` selects the current instruction that is in memory at address "pc" (here it selects the addition instruction).

At the microinstruction level, a more concrete state is considered. It includes the assembly language level state plus the instruction register "ir", the operand register "rop" and the current microinstruction pointer "mpc". The addition instruction is executed by a sequence of microinstructions M_0, M_1 and M_2, that involves the following transitions:

M_0 :	ir := mem[pc]	ir *receives the instruction code*
	pc := pc + 1	pc *is incremented*
	mpc := 1	M_1 *is the next microinstruction to execute*
M_1 :	rop := ir(3 to 7)	rop *receives the operand address*
	mpc := 2	M_2 *is the next microinstruction to execute*
M_2 :	acc := acc + mem[rop]	acc *is updated*
	mpc := 0	M_0 *is the next microinstruction to execute*

In our framework, the state and transitions at the microinstruction level will be also described as an instance "proc-$level_2$" of class `Interpreter` as follows:

- `state` contains the tuple <mem, pc, acc, ir, rop, mpc>,
- `transitions` includes the definition of the semantics of M_0, M_1, M_2 as described below,

– **select** selects the microinstruction that is in the microprogram memory at address "mpc".

We will see in Sect. 3.1 that the use of same structures for different levels induces more genericity in the proof process.

In order to perform the proof, we must show that the sequence M_0, M_1, M_2 correctly realizes the transitions associated with ADD_{DIR}. The proof is also specified by an instance of the class Proof that has four attributes (see Sect. 3.1):

– **specification** points the object "proc-level$_1$",
– **implementation** points the object "proc-level$_2$",
– **abstraction** defines the state abstraction, that realizes here the hiding of <mem, pc, acc, ir, rop, mpc> into <mem, pc, acc>, and
– **sync** defines the temporal abstraction. Since we assume that the first microinstruction of a microinstruction sequence is always at the address 0 (which is the "fetch" sequence), the predicate **sync** is here "mpc = 0".

To perform this proof, we first take an initial formal value **state** for proc-level$_2$. We then execute the microinstructions selected by **select** of proc-level$_2$ (i.e the microinstruction pointed by "mpc" in the microprogram memory) until **sync** is true. This gives the level$_2$ final state. We also abstract the initial state to obtain the level$_1$ initial state using the **abstraction** attribute. We then execute the instruction selected by **select** of proc-level$_1$ (i.e the instruction pointed by "pc"). This gives the level$_1$ final state. Finally, we verify that level$_1$ final state is an **abstraction** of level$_2$ final state.

In this simple case, the proof does not require any simplification and the state values obtained at the two levels are exactly the same. However, for more complex processors, where addressing mechanisms are much more elaborated, this can involve reducing expressions on bit vectors.

The above specification and proof process will be the same for any processor at any abstraction level.

3 The Framework Basis

In this section, we give further justifications for the object-oriented approach and the use of a computer algebra system.

3.1 Why an Object-Oriented Approach?

The first question that naturally arises is why we choose an object-oriented approach. There are three reasons for that: first, the need for a well-suited model, second, the need for typed processor components and third, the need for genericity. We will illustrate through the next sections of this paper, that the main advantages of object-oriented programming [13, 16] answer to these requirements.

A Well-Suited Model for Processor Description. When teaching computer structure, we usually introduce a processor as a set of components (the data path) that interact according to the signals sent by the sequencer (the control part).

This naturally leads to describe a processor as an object with three attributes:

- `state`: the set of all components visible at the current level,
- `transitions`: a set of state transitions that defines the behaviour of the processor. Each transition is a set of assignments labeled by an instruction key.
- `select`: a function from the processor state that returns the key of the current transition selected by the control part.

The attribute `state` is a set of components that are built out from an object-oriented component library. Thus, its construction takes full benefit of multiple inheritance (see Sect. 4.1).

Processor Components are Strongly Typed Objects. All circuits are built out from the same basic components namely, gates, registers, buses, memories... Each component is characterized by two aspects: its data type and its temporal behaviour and has at least two associated actions: *read* and *write*. Furthermore, some components are specializations of some others. For example, a wire is an instance of a bus (bus of length one), a ROM is an instance of a memory (for which the write action is forbidden). This induces a natural classification of the components that is easily realized with an object-oriented implementation. We will also see that the polymorphism of read and write actions simplifies the core of our verification system.

Specification and Verification Process is Generic. One important point in formally verifying processors, is that the specification and verification process must be reusable for all the processors of a same class. In fact, we need two kinds of genericity:

- *horizontal* genericity: the model should be reusable to specify different processors, and
- *vertical* genericity: at each abstraction level, the same generic model and proof method should be reused.

This leads us to define any processor at any level as an object of the class `Interpreter` that has the three previous attributes `state`, `transitions` and `select`. This ensures the genericity of the description.

In order to ensure the genericity of the proof, a verification between two specification levels is an object of the class `Proof`. This class has two attributes pointing the two interpreters and two others describing the abstraction functions from the implementation to the specification:

- **abstraction**: it defines the state abstraction. It is a function from the implementation to the specification state. It is often a state hiding since the specification state is a subset of the implementation state.
- **sync** defines the temporal abstraction. It is a predicate which value is *true* only when the two levels are synchronized which means that the implementation state corresponds with the start of a transition at the abstract level. This predicate is usually defined as a test on the implementation program counter.

To perform the proof we have to execute a transition at $level_i$ and a sequence of transitions at $level_{i+1}$. The implementation is correct if $level_i$ final state is an abstraction of $level_{i+1}$ final state when **sync** is true.

3.2 Why a Computer Algebra Simplification System?

In order to simplify the expressions involved in state transitions, we use a computer algebra system. This system is less powerful than general provers such as HOL or the Boyer & Moore theorem prover. However, it is enough powerful for processor verification, and furthermore, it is much more efficient and easy to use. It is especially well adapted for this specific problem where expressions to be proved are simple but numerous, and for which efficiency and simplicity must surpass power.

Some other proof systems use rewriting techniques for symbolic expressions (see for example [19, 17]). We choose the computer algebra point of view because it is much more efficient and can easily deal with commutative operators. The simplification of an expression like $(op\ e_1\ \ldots\ e_N)$ is driven by the head operator *op*, so the reduction strategy associated to *op* is used. The underlying algebra includes data types such as naturals, bit vectors, Booleans,...

For example, here are the steps reducing the expression

$$\texttt{bv-nat}(\texttt{bv-concat}(V_1, \texttt{bv-concat}(V_2, V_3)))$$

which is the conversion from bit vectors to naturals of the concatenation of three bit vectors. First, using associativity of concatenation we get

$$\texttt{bv-nat}(\texttt{bv-concat}(V_1, V_2, V_3))$$

By applying a specific reduction rule for conversion we get

$$(\texttt{bv-nat}(V_1) * 2^{\texttt{length}(V_2)} + \texttt{bv-nat}(V_2)) * 2^{\texttt{length}(V_3)} + \texttt{bv-nat}(V_3)$$

Finally by using distributivity of multiplication, we obtain

$$\texttt{bv-nat}(V_1) * 2^{\texttt{length}(V_2)+\texttt{length}(V_3)} + \texttt{bv-nat}(V_2) * 2^{\texttt{length}(V_3)} + \texttt{bv-nat}(V_3)$$

4 The Framework Implementation

Having answered the reasons underlying our system, we are now ready to exhibit its components. They are related to two different aspects: the specification process and the verification process.

The first implementation of our framework (see Fig. 1) is realized using a functional and object-oriented language: STk [8], a Scheme with an object system very close to CLOS [20, 14]. STk is a good compromise in order to combine object paradigms and the ability to carry out formal operations.

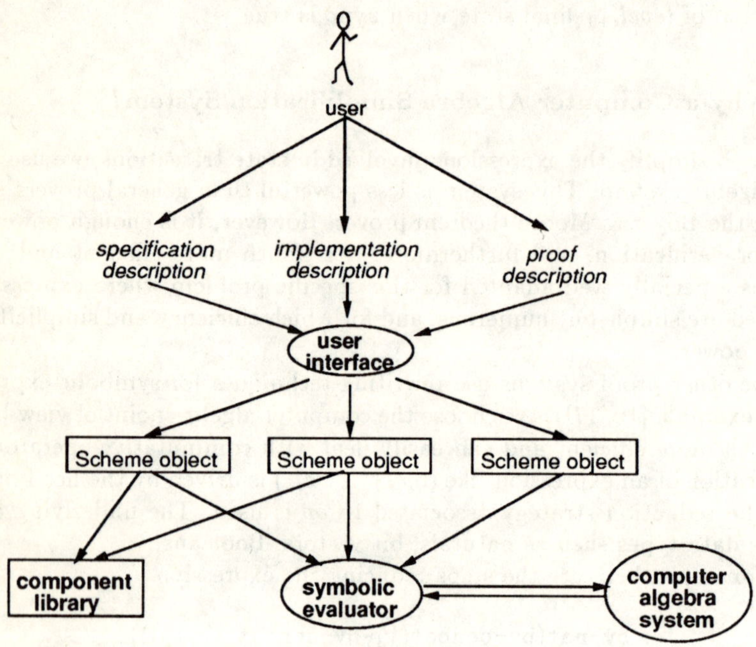

Fig. 1. Overview of the framework

4.1 The Specification Process

We first outline the library from which processor components are built up and then present a specification interface that we have designed in order to facilitate the description process.

A library of components. The attribute `state` of the processor is a set of components built up from a library that consists of a collection of classes describing the variety of structural or behavioural aspects.

Structural Classes: the main data types we use are naturals (**NAT**), bit vectors (**BV**) and arrays of bit vectors (**ARRAY**). Major generic functions are **read** (read contents), **write** (write contents) and **size** (get number of bits). Specific methods are also defined on the different structural classes.

Behavioural Classes: to represent temporal behaviour, we distinguish between what is called in [1] "stored variables" (registers, memories, ...) and "instantaneous variables" (buses or wires). So we have defined the behavioural classes **MEMO** and **NO-MEMO** which are "mixins" [5].

Using multiple inheritance, we get the major component classes to model processors. They have exactly one structural class and one behavioural class as superclasses. Figure 2 shows a simplified class hierarchy.

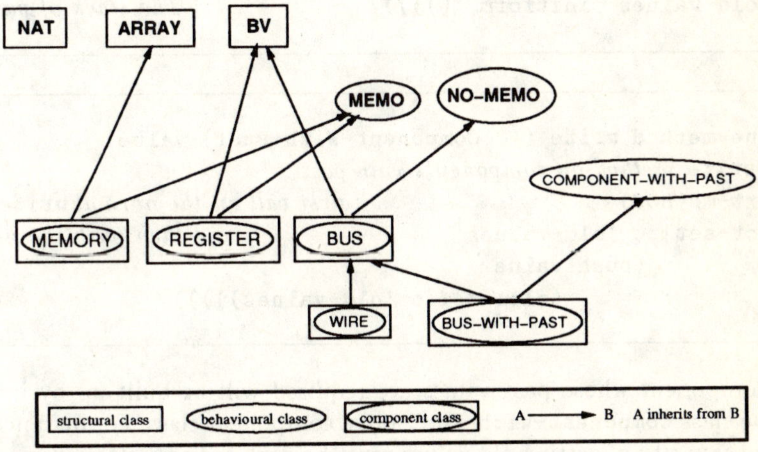

Fig. 2. Hierarchy of component classes

One have to notice that, when building a component class, the behavioural superclass must be more specific than the structural class. In CLOS, this is possible by giving the behavioural class name as the first element of the inheritance list.

Specialized Classes: more specific components such as ROM or stacks, are obtained by specialization of the main classes. Here are examples of class specializations. The first one declares wires as single-bit buses:

```
(define-class Wire (Bus)       ; The wire class inherits from the Bus class.
  ((size :initform 1 :size :getter size))     ; a wire size is always 1.
```

We define below the **Component-With-Past** class. It allows to keep the history of the component values. This is necessary when modeling complex temporal behaviours such as the communication protocol between the processor and the external memory. The **Component-With-Past** class is also a mixin that does not have any parents. Its **write** method calls for **next-method** that writes the bus value and then memorizes the current value in a stack (**old-values** attribute). This does not produce an error because the class is never instantiated alone: it is *one of the superclasses* of a class, the other superclass is a "component class". The **Component-With-Past** class and its **write** method are defined as follows:

```
(define-class Component-With-Past ()
; The Component-With-Past class is a mixin
   ((old-values :initform '())))                    ; The stack of past values
```

```
(define-method write ((c Component-With-Past) value)
; The write method on components with past
  (next-method)                          ; first call on the normal write method
  (slot-set! c 'old-values                       ; and then push the new value
          (push value
                (slot-ref c 'old-values)))))
```

A component whose past values are required will be built up by inheriting from the class **Component-With-Past** and a component class. For instance, buses with the capacity of getting old values must be declared as a class whose parents are **Component-With-Past** and **Bus**:

```
(define-class Bus-With-Past (Component-With-Past Bus)
; The Bus-With-Past class inherits from
; the mixin Component-With-Past and the Bus class.
  ())
```

Interface Facilities. In order to help system designers that are not familiar with Scheme programming, we have designed a textual interface to describe processors in a proof-oriented style. This interface is a simple language to enforce designers to fill all the fields of interpreter and proof objects. Its syntax is coming closer to the standard of Hardware Description Languages: VHDL. Starting from this more readable form, a translator automatically generates the Scheme internal representation (see Fig. 1).

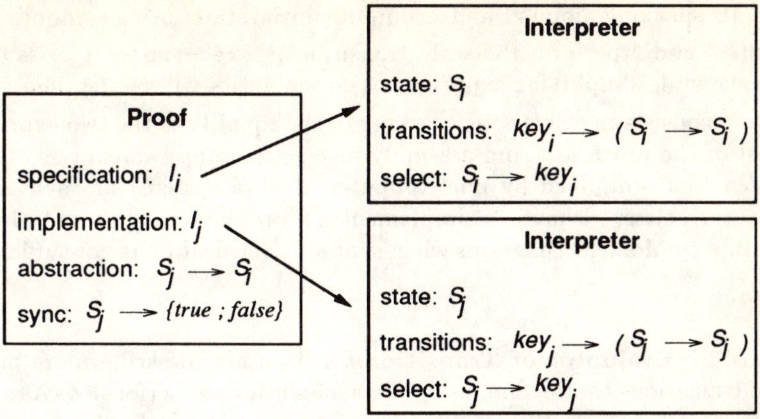

Fig. 3. One proof object and its two interpreters

4.2 The Proof Process

The Verification Steps. Assume we have defined two objects of the class `Interpreter` that specify a processor at levels $level_i$ and $level_j$, and one object of the class `Proof`, that links these two interpreters (Fig. 3). Then, the correctness proof between the two levels is performed according to the following steps:

1. compute an initial state S_j of $level_j$ such that `sync` is true:

$$S_j \texttt{ := init(}state_j\texttt{)}$$

2. take an abstraction S_i of this state:

$$S_i \texttt{ := abstraction(}S_j\texttt{)}$$

3. execute the transition selected by the $level_i$ interpreter to get the $level_i$ final state

$$trans \texttt{ := transitions(select(}S_i\texttt{))}$$
$$S_i \texttt{ := exec-trans(}trans\texttt{, } S_i\texttt{)}$$

4. execute transitions at $level_j$ until both interpreters are synchronized to get the $level_j$ final state:

```
repeat
    trans := transitions(select(Sj))
    Sj := exec-trans(trans, Sj)
until sync(Sj)=true
```

5. verify that $S_i \equiv \texttt{abstraction(}S_j\texttt{)}$

Broadly speaking, points 1 and 2 compute initial states using symbolic values.

Points 3 and 4 perform the state transitions; "`exec-trans`" carries out the transitions while simplifying expressions (its semantics will be detailed next).

Point 5 consists in a syntactic checking of the equality of the two expressions. For most of the processors and assembly instructions the two expressions (that have been first simplified by our computer algebra system) are syntactically equal. Nevertheless, we have also implemented more elaborated proof techniques, such as Binary Moment Diagrams when syntactic verification is not sufficient [2].

A Symbolic Evaluator of Transitions. Let us now describe more precisely how the transitions that define instruction semantics are performed. Assume we are given a transition *dest* := *source*. Then our symbolic evaluator executes this transition as follows:

- call on `read` method to get the value of *source* if it involves processor components,
- call on the simplification system in order to simplify the resulting value if possible,
- call on the `write` method to modify the value of *dest*.

The symbolic evaluator takes convenience of the object-oriented approach. The evaluation process is generic since `read` and `write` are methods associated to all component classes. Of course, it is not the same thing to read a memory or to read a register but these distinct behaviours are discriminated by inheritance.

A short version of the transition execution method is given below:

```
(define-method exec-trans (dest source (i Interpreter))
; This method executes the assignment of dest with the source value
; over components of the interpreter i
  (let ((rs                          ; the real source value is computed as follows:
          (if (component? source i)    ; if it contains a component of i,
              (simplify (read source))               ; read and simplify.
              (simplify source))))                    ; else just simplify
     (write dest rs)))           ; call on the write method on the destination
```

The Verification Kernel. We give here the classes and methods used to implement the proof algorithm. A simplified declaration of the `Interpreter` class is:

```
(define-class Interpreter ()                    ; The Interpreter class:
  ((state :init-keyword :state :getter state)
   (select :init-keyword :select :getter select)
   (transitions :init-keyword :transitions :getter transitions)))
```

Some methods are defined for this class in order to reset, update state...

The Proof class is as follows:

```
(define-class Proof ()                                  ; The Proof class:
  ((s :init-keyword :specification :getter specification)
   (i :init-keyword :implementation :getter implementation)
   (sync :init-keyword :sync :getter sync)
   (abstraction :init-keyword :abstraction :getter abstraction)
   (prove :init-keyword :prove :getter prove)))
```

The `prove` attribute is here to facilitate the proof by cases: it is a set of *all* instructions of the specification interpreter with all their addressing modes.

The method executing the whole proof returns a Boolean showing the correctness. If the proof fails we can get the instruction being proved and the components whose values are wrong.

```
(define-method proof-ok? ((p Proof))
; Returns true if the implementation of p correctly implements its specification
  (mapand (lambda (instr)                        ; All instructions are correct?
            (instr-ok? (specification p) (implementation p)
                       instr (abstraction p) (sync p)))
          (prove p)))
```

The `instr-ok?` method discriminates on multiple arguments. It proves or disproves a single instruction: it returns a Boolean showing the equivalence of the two interpreters `s` and `i`, for instruction `instr`, and using the state and temporal abstractions `abstr` and `sync`.

```
(define-method instr-ok? ((s Interpreter) (i Interpreter)
                          instr abstr sync)
; Returns true if s and i are equivalent when executing the instruction instr
; and using abstraction functions abstr and sync.
  (update-state i (new-state i instr))              ; give i a new state
  (update-state s (abstr i))               ; give s an equivalent new state
  (update-state s (exec (member (select s) (transitions s)) s))
  ; execute the current instruction at the specification level
  (repeat-until
    (update-state i (exec (member (select i) (transitions i)) i))
    ; execute instructions at the implementation level
    (sync i))              ; until the temporal abstraction predicate is true
  (equiv? (abstr i) s))              ; then compare the two final states
```

5 Experimental Results

5.1 Application to Tamarack-3

Tamarack-3 is a benchmark microprocessor described in [9, 12, 19, 22]. Our specification follows the one given in [6] using HOL.

We have specified Tamarack-3 at four levels: the "macro level" which is the assembly level, the "micro level" which is the microinstruction level, the "phase level" which is the decomposition of the "micro level" for each clock phase and the "EBM" which is the structural description of the processor as functional blocks (Fig. 4). We verified the processor in three proof steps between adjacent levels.

At the macro level, components are an accumulator, a register keeping an address to return from subroutines, a program counter, a register latching an external signal of interrupt request, and a register whose value is 1 when an interrupt is being processed. The external memory is also described at this level.

Here is an extract of the specification of Tamarack-3 at the macro level:

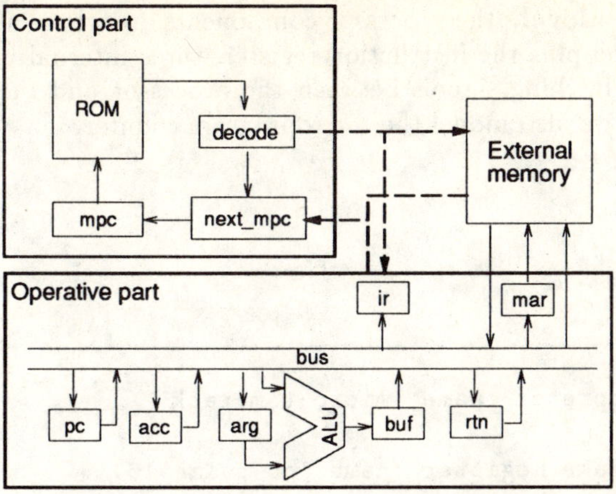

Fig. 4. Structure of the Tamarack-3 microprocessor.

```
(make Interpreter :name 'macro-tamarack
; An instance of the Interpreter class
   :state                          ; The state slot is a list of components
   (list (make Register :name 'pc :size 16)
         ; the program counter is a 16-bit register,
         (make Register :name 'acc :size 16)
         ; as the accumulator
         (make Register :name 'rtn :size 16)
          ; and the return address register,
         (make Memory :name 'mem :size 16)
          ; the external memory is a 16-bit word array,
         (make Register :name 'iack :size 1)
          ; the interrupt acknowledge and
         (make Register :name 'ireq :size 1))
         ; the interrupt request registers are single-bit.
   :select                          ; The select slot is a Lisp expression
   '(if (and ireq (not iack))        ; if an interrupt has to be processed
       ireq-one            ; then return the interrupt pseudo-instruction name
       (decw (fetch mem (address pc))))
                           ; else return the instruction in memory pointed by pc
   :transitions     ; The transitions slot is a list of instruction semantics
   '( (jmp ( (:= pc (fetch mem (address pc))) ))
      ; the jump instruction: assignment to pc
      (adda ( (:= acc (add acc (fetch mem (address pc))))
              (:= pc (inc pc)) ))
      ; the addition instruction: assignment to acc and incrementation of pc
      ...)                                        ; other instructions are here
)
```

At the micro level, the processor components are whose already described at the macro level plus the instruction register, three internal buffer registers, and two registers latching signals between the processor and the external memory. At this level, we also model the microprogram counter.

```
(make Interpreter :name 'micro-tamarack
   :state
   (list (make Register :name 'pc :size 16)
         (make Register :name 'acc :size 16)
         (make Register :name 'rtn :size 16)
         (make Memory :name 'mem :size 16)
         (make Register :name 'iack :size 1)
         (make Register :name 'ireq :size 1)
         (make Register :name 'ir :size 16)      ; the instruction register
         (make Register :name 'arg :size 16)          ; an internal buffer
         (make Register :name 'buf :size 16)               ; another one
         (make Register :name 'mar :size 16)        ; the address register
         (make Register :name 'idle :size 1)      ; for processor/memory
         (make Register :name 'dack :size 1)            ; communication
         (make Register :name 'mpc :size 4))      ; microprogram counter
   :select
   '(case (val4 mpc)                ; the current microinstruction name is
         (0 . u0)           ; u0 when microprogram counter value is 0,
         (1 . u1)           ; u1 when microprogram counter value is 1,
         ... )                                            ; and so on...
   :transitions
   '( (u0                   ; First microinstruction of the fetch sequence:
      ( (:= ir (fetch mem (address pc)))               ; assignment to ir,
        (:= pc (inc pc))                             ; incrementation of pc
        (:= mpc (inc mpc)) ))                                    ; and mpc
     (u1 ( ... ))                 ; specify u1 and other microinstructions
      ...)                                               ; in the same way.
)
```

The proof description between macro and micro levels is:

```
(make Proof :name 'macro-micro-tamarack
    :specification macro-tamarack              ; points the specification
    :implementation micro-tamarack         ; points the implementation
    :abstraction                  ; the state abstraction function is a list where
    ; id is the identity function and nil suppress the corresponding component
    '(id id id id id id nil nil nil nil nil nil nil)
    :sync                       ; the temporal abstraction predicate returns true
    '(= mpc (word4 0))             ; when the microprogram counter value is 0.
)
```

Complete proof. In order to fully prove the Tamarack-3 processor, we have also specified the phase level and the EBM. Our overall goal is to prove that the EBM correctly implements the macro level. In fact we decomposed the proof in three steps: macro versus micro, micro versus phase and phase versus EBM. Transitivity of proofs achieves the complete correctness proof.

5.2 Other Results

We applied our methodology to verify several microprocessors without any change to the `Interpreter` and `Proof` classes, or their methods, nor the proof algorithm of Sect. 4.2. The complexity of these benchmark processors is illustrated in Table 1. The comparative Table 2 shows specification code sizes and proof times for a number of processors already verified with other methods.

Processor	instr.	μinstr.	user registers	word size	addressing modes
AVM-1	30	51	35	32	1
DP-32	20	10	258	32	2
MTI	22	149	38	16	5
Anceau's proc.	8	14	4	16	4
Tamarack-3	8	16	3	16	1

Table 1. Size complexity of processors we specified and proved.

Tamarack-3 and Anceau's processors [1] (pages 181–212) are school processors. Their specifications and proofs do not pose any problem. It is interesting to compare results for Tamarack-3. Stavridou [19] used the OBJ3 theorem prover. It is based on rewriting techniques and one can see that proof time is not acceptable. Furthermore the proof is not automatic. Time proofs in [22] are satisfactory, but to the best of our knowledge, the specifications are given in HOL, which is in our opinion not well-adapted to processor specification.

Processor	#SL	SS (p.)	PT (sec.)	other SS	other PT	ref
AVM-1	4	22	1775	110	58 h	[21]
DP-32	2	9	470			
MTI	2	17	1973			
Anceau's proc.	2	4	183			
Tamarack-3	4	3	197	17	10 days	[19]
				?	360 sec.	[22]

Table 2. Processors we specified and proved. #SL is the number of different specification levels, SS is approximative specification code size in number of pages, PT is proof time in seconds on a SUN IPC workstation. Other SS and other PT are specification sizes and proof times of other works referenced in the "ref" column.

The other processors are rather complex and their proofs emphasize the usefulness of our specification and proof methodology. DP-32 is a processor described in VHDL in [4]. Its verification has raised one error in its implementation. This proof shows that our framework is able to specify, and then to prove, a processor starting from its VHDL description. A VHDL description style provable in our framework has been derived from its verification [3].

AVM-1 [21] has already been verified by Windley using HOL. Our specification is much more concise than his one, and our proof times are also much more satisfactory.

MTI is a processor designed by CNET in France [15]. It has already been studied but never fully proved. Our system discovered several errors in its design.

6 Conclusion

We have presented an object-oriented approach for processor specification and verification. Any processor at any abstraction level is described by an object of the same interpreter class. A proof between two specification levels is an object of the proof class. The main advantages of this approach is that the verification process is reusable. To verify additional processors, we do not need to modify the verification kernel. Furthermore, the specification process is very easy and systematic since it just consists to instantiate predefined classes. The specifications are very concise and the verification times are very satisfactory compared with other methods.

We are now extending our system in two major directions. First, we are developing a graphical interface for processor description. Thanks to the object framework, this will be a very simple task. Second, we will extend the class of processors we are able to prove, to more complex architectures such as DSP or pipelined architectures. We hope that this extension will only consist to an enrichment of the class hierarchy.

Acknowledgments. We are grateful to J.C. Boussard, E. Kounalis and M. Rueher who had the kindness to comment and improve a preliminary version of this paper.

References

1. F. Anceau. *The Architecture of Microprocessors.* Addison-Wesley Publishing Company, 1986.
2. L. Arditi and H. Collavizza. Binary moment diagrams for verifying loops in microprocessor instructions. Technical report, Laboratoire I3S, Université de Nice – Sophia Antipolis, Nov. 1994.
3. L. Arditi and H. Collavizza. Towards verifying VHDL descriptions of processors. Technical report, Laboratoire I3S, Université de Nice – Sophia Antipolis, Jan. 1995.
4. P. J. Ashenden. *The VHDL Cookbook.* Public Domain, Dept. Computer Science, University of Adelaide, South Australia, first edition, July 1990.
5. G. Bracha and W. Cook. Mixin-based inheritance. In *European Conference on Object Oriented Programming / Object-Oriented Programming Systems, Languages and Applications*, October 1990.
6. M. L. Coe and P. J. Windley. Microprocessor verification: A tutorial. Technical Report LAL-92-10, Laboratory for Applied Logic, Brigham Young University, Provo, Utah, 1992.
7. A. Cohn. A proof of correctness of the Viper microprocessor: the first level. In G. Birtwhistle and P. Subrahmanyam, editors, *VLSI Specification, Verification and Synthesis*, pages 27–71, Calgary, Canada, Jan. 1987. Kluwer Acad. Publishers.
8. E. Gallesio. STklos: a Scheme object oriented system dealing with the TK toolkit. In *Xhibition 94*, San Jose, Jul. 1994. ICS.
9. M. Gordon. HOL, a machine oriented formulation of higher order logic. Technical Report 68, University of Cambridge, Computer Laboratory, 1985.
10. A. Gupta. Formal hardware verification methods: a survey. *Formal Methods in System Design*, 1(2/3):151–238, Oct. 1992.
11. W. A. Hunt Jr. Microprocessor design verification. *Journal of Automated Reasoning*, 5(4):429–460, Dec. 1989.
12. J. J. Joyce. Formal verification and implementation of a microprocessor. In G. Birtwhistle and P. Subrahmanyam, editors, *VLSI Specification, Verification and Synthesis*, pages 129–157, Calgary, Canada, Jan. 1987. Kluwer Acad. Publishers.
13. B. Meyer. *Object-Oriented Software Construction.* Prentice Hall International, 1988.
14. A. Paepcke. *Object-oriented programming : the CLOS perspective.* MIT press, 1993.
15. J. Pulou, J. Rainard, and P. Thorel. Microprocesseur à test intégré MTI – description fonctionnelle et architecture. Technical Report NT/CNS/CC/59, CNET, Grenoble, Jan. 1987.
16. J. Rumbaugh, M. Blaha, W. Premerlani, F. Eddy, and W. Lorensen. *Object-oriented Modeling and Design.* Prentice Hall, 1991.
17. R. Sekar and M. Srivas. Equational techniques. In G. Birtwistle and P. Subrahmanyam, editors, *Current Trends in Hardware Verification and Automatic Theorem Proving*, pages 173–217, New-York, 1989. Springer-Verlag.
18. M. Srivas and M. Bickford. Formal verification of a pipelined microprocessor. *IEEE Software*, 7(5):52–64, Sept. 1990.

19. V. Stavridou. *Formal Methods in Circuit Design.* Number 37 in Cambridge Tracts in Theoretical Computer Science. Cambridge University Press, 1993.
20. G. L. Steele Jr. *Common Lisp the Language.* Digital Press, second edition, 1990.
21. P. J. Windley. *The Formal Verification of Generic Interpreters.* PhD thesis, University of California, Division of Computer Science, 1990.
22. Z. Zhu, J. Joyce, and C. Seger. Verification of the Tamarack-3 microprocessor in a hybrid verification environment. In J. J. Joyce and C.-J. H. Seger, editors, *Higher Order Logic Theorem Proving and Its Applications.* 6th *Int. Work. HUG'93,* volume 780 of *LNCS*, pages 253–266, Vancouver, Canada, Aug. 1993. Springer-Verlag.

Incremental Mature Garbage Collection Using the Train Algorithm

Jacob Seligmann Steffen Grarup

Computer Science Department, Aarhus University
Ny Munkegade 116, DK-8000 Århus C, Denmark
E-mail: {jacobse,grarup}@daimi.aau.dk

Abstract

We present an implementation of the *Train Algorithm*, an incremental collection scheme for reclamation of mature garbage in generation-based memory management systems. To the best of our knowledge, this is the first Train Algorithm implementation ever. Using the algorithm, the traditional mark-sweep garbage collector employed by the Mjølner run-time system for the object-oriented BETA programming language was replaced by a non-disruptive one, with only negligible time and storage overheads.

1 Introduction

Many programming languages provide automatic *garbage collection* to reduce the need for memory management related programming. However, traditional garbage collection techniques lead to long and unpredictable delays and are therefore unsatisfactory in a number of settings, such as *interactive* systems, where *non-disruptive* behavior is of paramount importance. *Generation-based* collection techniques alleviate the problem somewhat by concentrating collection efforts on small but hopefully gainful areas of memory, the so-called *young* generations. This reduces the need for collecting the remaining large memory area, the *old*, or *mature*, generation, but in no way obviates it. Traditionally, conventional techniques have been employed for old generation collection, leading to pauses which, although less frequent, are still highly disruptive.

Recently, Hudson & Moss have introduced an exciting new algorithm, the *Train Algorithm*, for performing efficient incremental collection of old generation space [HM92]. Using the algorithm, generational collectors can be extended to provide non-disruptive collection of all generational areas.

In the following, we present the results from a practical implementation of the Train Algorithm [GS93]. Section 2 describes the basic ideas behind the algorithm. Section 3 concerns the practical implementation issues. Section 4 presents the measurement results. Section 5 points out future research directions.

2 The Algorithm

This section deals with the theoretical aspects of the Train Algorithm. For a more detailed presentation of the algorithm including a couple of enlightening examples, see [HM92, GS93].

Section 2.1 outlines the main ideas behind the algorithm and introduces the terminology needed in later sections. (Readers familiar with the algorithm may wish to skip this part.) Section 2.2 identifies and corrects a subtle error in the original algorithm. Section 2.3 addresses the treatment of highly referenced objects.

2.1 The Train Algorithm

2.1.1 The Train Metaphor

The *Train Algorithm* is an incremental garbage collection scheme for achieving non-disruptive reclamation of the oldest generational area, the *mature object space.* The algorithm achieves its incrementality by dividing mature object space into a number of fixed-sized *blocks* and collecting one block at each invocation. The key contribution of the algorithm lies in showing how all garbage (even cyclic structures larger than the size of an individual block) can be recognized and reclaimed while only processing a single block at a time.

To achieve this, the algorithm arranges the blocks into disjoint sets. With a striking metaphor, Hudson & Moss refer to the blocks as *cars*, and to the set of blocks to which a car belongs as its *train.* Mature object space can then be thought of as a giant *railway station* with trains lined up on its tracks, as illustrated in Figure 1.

Just as in real life, cars belong to exactly one train and are ordered within that train. The trains, in turn, are ordered by giving them sequence numbers as they are created. This imposes a global lexicographical ordering on the blocks in mature object space: One block precedes another if it resides in a lower numbered (i.e. older) train; or if both blocks belong to the same train, then if that block has a lower car number (i.e. was added to the train earlier on) than the other. In the example structure shown in Figure 1, Car 1.1 precedes Car 1.2, Car 1.2 precedes Car 1.3, Car 1.3 precedes Car 2.1, and so on.

Intuitively, the Train Algorithm works by constantly clustering sets of related objects. In this way, it eventually collapses any interlinked garbage structure into the same train, no matter how complex. In the following, we shall see how this is achieved.

2.1.2 Car Collection Strategy

Each invocation of the Train Algorithm processes the lowest numbered car of the lowest numbered train in the system. Its space is reclaimed as follows.

First, a check is made to see whether there are any references into the train to which the car being collected belongs. If this is not the case, then the entire train contains only garbage and all its cars are reclaimed immediately. (This

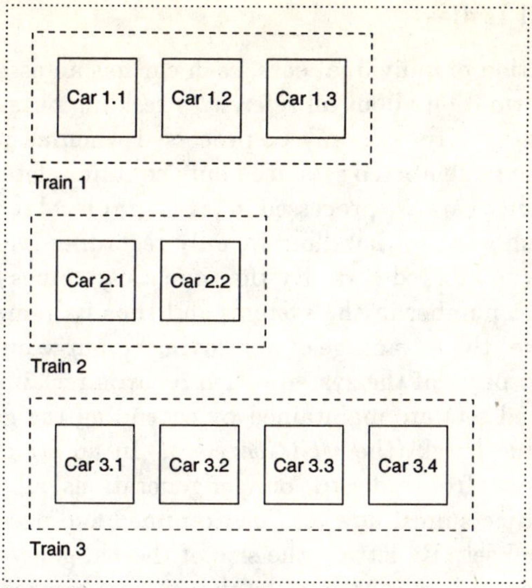

Figure 1: Mature object space structure

is the part of the algorithm which enables large cyclic garbage structures to be recognized and reclaimed, even if they are too big to fit into a single car. Section 2.2 explains why such structures always end up in the same train.)

Otherwise, all objects residing in the car being collected referenced from outside the train are evacuated as follows. Objects referenced from other trains are moved to those trains; objects referenced from outside mature object space are moved to any train except the one being collected. If a receiving train runs full, a new car is simply created and hooked onto its end. Then, in typical copy collector style, evacuated objects are scanned for pointers into the car being collected, moving the objects thus found into the train from which they are now referenced, and so on.

With the transitive closure of all externally referenced objects having been evacuated, the only live objects in the car being processed are those referenced (exclusively) from cars further down the train being collected. Such objects are evacuated to the last car of the train, as are the objects they reference, etc.

At this point, none of the objects remaining in the car being collected are referenced from the outside and are therefore garbage. Thus, the space occupied by the car is reclaimed and the collection is finished.

2.1.3 Tenuring Strategy

The tenuring strategy imposed by the Train Algorithm is simple: Objects promoted from younger generations may be stored in any train except the one currently being collected, or one or more new trains may be created to hold them.

2.1.4 Technical Issues

To facilitate collection of individual cars, each car has an associated *remembered set* containing information about all references residing outside the car pointing into it. Old generation cars will only be processed when all younger generations are collected, so the remembered sets need only contain references from other old generation cars. Since cars are processed in lexicographical order, one can further optimize the remembered set handling by only recording references from higher numbered to lower numbered cars. By the time a car comes up for collection, it will have the lowest number in the system, and thus its remembered set will be complete. This gives the advantage of not having to purge out stale remembered set entries in other parts of the system when a car is reclaimed.

The remembered sets are maintained by extending the generational pointer assignment run-time check (the *write barrier*). In addition to the traditional recording of references from older to younger generations, all pointer assignments between mature objects must now also be examined and possibly recorded in an old car remembered set. By letting the size of the old generation cars be of the form 2^n bytes, allocated on a 2^n byte boundary, one can maintain a *train table* over the train and car number associated with each mature object space block. Given a pointer address, the train table information can be quickly accessed by right-shifting the address n bits and using the result as an index [HMDW91].

2.2 Correctness

Given a garbage structure contained in mature object space, denote the trains holding it the set of *garbage trains*. The structure of this set will not be changed by the mutator because garbage objects are per definition unreachable and therefore immutable. The collector, on the other hand, will cause the set of garbage trains to shrink over time. As each garbage train is processed, the objects residing there are either recognized as garbage and reclaimed or evacuated to higher numbered garbage trains holding references to them. When processing reaches the highest numbered garbage train, the garbage structure will therefore have been collapsed and will be reclaimed.

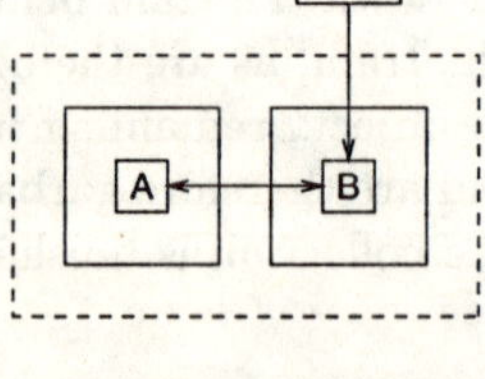

Figure 2: Error situation

This argument, of course, requires that all trains are eventually processed. Unfortunately, the Train Algorithm as presented so far provides no such guarantee. Consider the situation shown in Figure 2. A-B is a live structure, with object B referenced from some root. For the sake of simplicity, objects A and B are assumed to be too big to fit into the same car (more realistically, they could be large interlinked structures). When the car containing A is collected, A is simply moved into a new car at the end of the train. We call such collections *futile* because they neither evacuate, nor reclaim, objects. Now, before the next invocation of the algorithm (in which we would have hoped to evacuate object B), the mutator may change the root reference to point to A instead of B. Thus, at the beginning of the next collection, the overall object structure may be entirely unchanged. If the mutator continues to swap references behind the collector's back, it will force the collector to keep processing the A-B structure, thus never getting around to any of the other trains in the system.

This situation may be prevented as follows. Whenever a futile collection occurs, one of the external references to objects further down the train are recorded. (Such a reference must exist, otherwise the entire train would have been reclaimed.) A reference thus recorded is then used as an additional root for subsequent collections and is not discarded until a non-futile collection occurs. In the example above, this would cause the root reference to be recorded after the first collection, causing object B to be evacuated from the train at the next invocation of the algorithm even though it is no longer directly referenced.

Using this extension, it can be shown that each pass over a train will either reclaim or evacuate at least one object, and the entire Train Algorithm may be proven formally correct [GS93].

2.3 Popular Objects

Since the Train Algorithm processes only a single fixed-size car at a time, there is an upper limit on the number of bytes that are copied at each invocation. However, moving *popular* objects (objects with many pointers to them) could still make the algorithm disruptive. Whenever a popular object is moved, a large remembered set needs to be traversed and all the pointers to the object must be updated. Thus, it is impossible to bound the potential amount of work needed to move even a single object. The classic solution to this problem is to require that all objects be addressed indirectly so that whenever an object is moved, only a single cell needs to be updated. This technique is known to induce significant run-time overheads [Ung86].

As an alternative approach, Hudson & Moss tentatively suggest that cars containing popular objects should not be collected at all. Instead, such cars should be retained, logically (but not physically) moving them to the end of the newest train [HM92, Section 6]. Unfortunately, a closer analysis shows that this approach may leave garbage undetected, so a number of refinements are needed.

First, one cannot simply *retain* popular cars, but must evacuate all non-popular objects from them. Otherwise, garbage contained in or referenced from popular cars will not be detected and reclaimed.

Second, one should not move popular cars to the end of the *newest* train. This would cause large garbage structures scattered across several trains each containing a popular member to survive forever because such structures would never be collapsed. Instead, popular cars should only be moved to the end of the highest numbered train from which they are referenced.

Third, cars containing several unrelated popular objects pose a problem. Such cars will have to be *split* in some way so that each popular object can be moved to the end of the highest numbered train from which it is referenced.

With the popular object treatment outlined above, the Train Algorithm can be shown to correctly identify and reclaim all garbage [GS93]. However, such schemes may be quite costly to implement in practice. Since the remembered sets associated with popular cars may be arbitrarily large, one cannot afford to run through them to find references to non-popular objects, or to find the highest numbered train from which a popular object is referenced. Also, logically split cars are not easily handled in a train table setting. A naive way to overcome these problems would be to associate a remembered set with each object, to always maintain the highest numbered train from which an object is referenced, and to extend the train table with balanced binary search trees for split areas. In practice, more sophisticated solutions are undoubtedly needed to make the popular car approach a viable alternative to pointer indirection.

3 The Implementation

In order to test the Train Algorithm in a realistic setting, we incorporated it into the Mjølner run-time system for the object-oriented BETA programming language [MMN93]. To the best of our knowledge, this is the only implementation of the Train Algorithm to this date.

This section describes the implementation process. Section 3.1 presents the memory layout used in the two systems. Section 3.2 concerns the practical issues that had to be addressed. Section 3.3 discusses the overall implementation efforts.

3.1 Memory Layout

3.1.1 Original Mjølner BETA System

The Mjølner BETA System uses a modern generation-based collector with two generations [KLMM93]. The young generation (the *infant object area*, or *IOA*) consists of two fixed-sized semi-spaces reclaimed using copying collection. The old generation (the *adult object area*, or *AOA*) consists of a series of linked fixed-sized blocks reclaimed using a sophisticated three-phase mark-sweep collection scheme [Bar88]. In addition, large arrays of pointer-less objects are kept in a separate area (the *large value-repetition area*, or *LVRA*) consisting of linked fixed-sized blocks managed using free-lists and periodic compaction.

The advancement age between the two generations is determined adaptively using demographic feedback-mediated tenuring [UJ92]. To record references from old to young objects, a hash table-based remembered set is maintained, using a traditional but quite efficient write barrier to examine pointer assignments at run-time.

3.1.2 New Mjølner BETA System

The Train Algorithm implementation adhered to the general memory layout sketched in Section 2.1, including a train table. We used a car size of 64K bytes.

The global remembered set (recording references from the entire old generation to the young one) was replaced by a remembered set for each car (recording references from that car to the young generation). This approach enabled us to immediately discard the relevant entries when a car was reclaimed, rather than run through a global table to purge out expired references.

3.2 Practical Considerations

There are a number of issues which are left open by the general Train Algorithm description, but which must nevertheless be addressed when implementing it. For instance, one must decide when to create new trains, how often to invoke the algorithm, and whether to treat popular objects specially.

3.2.1 Evacuation Strategy

During a car collection, where should objects referenced from several trains be moved? We chose to evacuate objects to the last car of the train from which they were first seen during the scavenge (or to the last car of the newest train, if referenced from outside mature object space). Moving an object immediately to the highest numbered train referencing it might have given less superfluous copying, but seemed hard to implement efficiently.

Where should objects be moved when they are promoted? As objects were tenured into mature object space, we moved them into the last car of the newest train until the total size of the objects residing there exceeded a certain threshold (the *fill limit*) in which case we chose to create a new train. In this way, we tried to achieve a balance between initially having only a few objects in each train (to avoid accidental object structure infiltration which would require extra passes to disentangle) and putting many objects into each train (to avoid the storage overhead of having many sparsely filled cars in the system). We chose a default fill limit of 90%. The implications of this choice are presented in Section 4.5.

3.2.2 Invocation Frequency

While traditional batch collection algorithms are invoked only when memory runs full, their incremental counterparts must be called often enough to ensure that storage resources are never exhausted. Otherwise, they mutator must be suspended, and the collection becomes disruptive. Similarly, one must choose a collection frequency for the Train Algorithm which on one hand ensures that mature object space does not grow unacceptably full with garbage, but on the other hand does not waste too much time moving live objects around from car to car.

Our approach to finding the right balance was to select a fixed *acceptable garbage percentage* specifying the desired trade-off between speed and storage.

Whenever the amount of garbage detected in mature object space was larger than expected, the collection frequency was automatically increased in order to keep memory consumption down; and whenever the garbage ratio was lower than expected, the collection frequency was decreased to improve the overall performance. In addition, we introduced an upper limit on the number of young generation collections between each old generation collection step. Without such a limit, the algorithm would be called much to seldomly if little or no garbage was detected for a while.

Technically, there were a few obstacles to calculating the garbage ratio. Whereas batch algorithms can compare the size of mature object space before and after a collection, this is not possible in the Train Algorithm setting, where only a small area is collected at each invocation, where some objects may be scanned more frequently than others, and where there are always parts of memory that have not yet been processed. By associating with each train a counter holding the amount of objects tenured directly into it, one can, however, calculate the desired figure. The result is somewhat delayed because it is first obtained when the newest train in the system at counter initialization time is reclaimed, that is, after an entire sweep over mature object space. By initializing a new counter each time the collection of a new train commences, estimates nevertheless become available quite often. This approach turned out to work well in practice [GS93].

3.2.3 Popular Object Treatment

Because of the complications outlined in Section 2.3, we did not implement a full popular object scheme. However, all Mjølner BETA programs contain a special object, the *basic environment object*, which is referenced from a large number of other objects. The basic environment object is always alive by virtue of being one of the garbage collection roots. We therefore isolated it in a specially-marked car for which no remembered set was maintained. Whenever that car came up for collection, we logically moved it to form a new train, rather than physically moving the basic environment object and updating the large number of references to it. The benefits of this approach are demonstrated in Section 4.6.

3.3 Implementation Efforts

Incorporating the Train Algorithm into the Mjølner BETA run-time system meant having to discard practically all the original mature object space reclamation code. However, the rest of the system was left virtually untouched. This was an invaluable asset in debugging and fine-tuning the new system. All in all, the implementation was therefore surprisingly straightforward. The code for the new collector constituted about 2,000 lines of C (including extensive debug consistency checks), or about the same as the original mark-sweep collector.

4 The Results

In this section, we present the main results obtained from our Train Algorithm implementation. For a more detailed account, see [GS93].

Section 4.1 describes the benchmark system. Section 4.2 presents the most important result of our implementation, namely that disruptive old generation collection pauses can be completely removed using the Train Algorithm. Sections 4.3, 4.4, and 4.5 show the reverse side of the coin, namely the time, storage, and copying overheads induced. Section 4.6 concerns the special treatment of popular objects. Section 4.7 looks at the virtual memory behavior of the algorithm.

4.1 Benchmarks

4.1.1 Benchmark Programs

As our main reference point we chose the compilation of the entire Mjølner BETA compiler version 4.4.1 using itself. This program run enjoyed a number of desirable properties. First, it was easily reproducible, thereby ensuring that figures obtained across several runs remained comparable. Second, it ran for a relatively long period of time, so that many objects were promoted during the program execution, and so that quite a few of them died before the compilation was finished. Third, even though the application was not an interactive one, it was still instructive to examine the pause times incurred by the various area collections.

To ensure a wider exposure, we also measured the performance of an interactive run with the Sif hyper-structure editor [MIA90] and a discrete event simulation system modeling a series of orders pipelining through a set of machine queues.

4.1.2 Benchmark System

The tests were carried out using release 2.5.1 of the Sun SPARC variant of the Mjølner BETA System under SunOS 4.1.1. Default system parameters were used for both the original and new implementations, with block sizes of 512K bytes for IOA, AOA, and LVRA (except for the 64K bytes cars in the new implementation) and a 10% tenuring threshold. For the new system a 10% acceptable mature garbage ratio was adaptively aimed for, with an upper limit of ten young generation collections between each Train Algorithm invocation.

Except for the benchmark described in Section 4.7, all measurements were carried out on a 40 MHz Sun SPARC IPX 4/50 workstation equipped with 32M bytes of primary memory. Apart from a few page faults at the beginning of each run, there was practically no virtual memory activity. The times reported in the following are therefore the sum of the user and system CPU times. In practice, this turned out to correspond quite closely to elapsed wall-clock time.

4.2 Collection Pauses

This section presents the old generation collection pauses obtained. Table 1 shows the minimum, median, 90% percentile, maximum, and average amounts of time spent in each Train Algorithm invocation for each of the three benchmark programs. Figure 3 gives a more detailed impression of the pause time distribution for the longest-running benchmark, the compiler compilation.

Application	Compiler		Editor		Simulation	
Method	batch	train	batch	train	batch	train
Pause (min.)	0.27s	0.00s	0.31s	0.00s	0.11s	0.00s
Pause (med.)	1.39s	0.04s	0.49s	0.03s	0.16s	0.01s
Pause (90%)	3.06s	0.06s	0.49s	0.05s	0.17s	0.03s
Pause (max.)	3.21s	0.12s	0.57s	0.08s	0.18s	0.05s
Pause (avg.)	1.71s	0.04s	0.46s	0.03s	0.15s	0.01s

Table 1: Old generation collection pause distribution

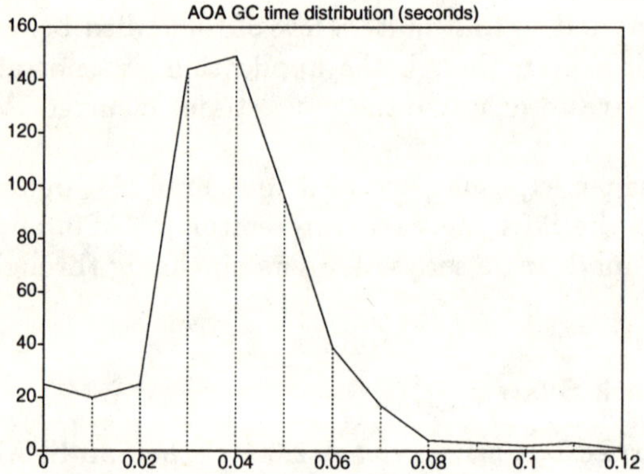

Figure 3: Pause distribution, compiler run

As can be seen, the new collector turned out to be extremely effective. For all three benchmark programs, it replaced a number of highly disruptive old generation collections with a series of non-disruptive ones, each just a few dozen milliseconds long. Thus, the Train Algorithm lived up to its promises of delivering pause times suitable for use in interactive systems.

4.3 Time Overhead

We now take a look at the time overhead incurred by using the Train Algorithm. In addition to the overhead caused in the old generation collector as a direct result of replacing the collection algorithm, we also examine the indirect time overhead caused in the remaining parts of the system (the young generation collector and the mutator) by changing the number of remembered sets, by requiring a more complex write barrier, and so on.

Application	Compiler		Editor		Simulation	
Method	batch	train	batch	train	batch	train
Old collector	17.11s	20.55s	1.37s	1.15s	1.05s	1.86s
Young collector	140.26s	150.14s	8.25s	8.95s	44.26s	32.88s
Mutator	816.09s	808.88s	93.51s	94.02s	183.40s	176.06s

Table 2: Total time distribution

Table 2 shows the total time spent in the various system components. In addition, approximately one second was spent on large object area free-list compaction in the compiler and editor runs. Since the Train Algorithm did not influence large object area management in any significant way, we shall not go further into that issue here.

4.3.1 Old Generation Collector

As could be expected, the price for achieving non-disruptive behavior was a general increase in the total old generation collection time. For the compiler compilation the increase was just above 20%. For the simulation run the increase was more dramatic, nearly 80%. This was mainly because many tenured objects died during the execution, causing the new collector to perform frequent steps (on average once every six young generation collections), thereby scanning nearly twice the amount of mature object space as its batch counterpart. Thus, the time overhead could probably have been replaced by a storage overhead by increasing the acceptable garbage percentage. For the editor session the old generation collection time *fell*. However, the last batch collection occurred just before the end of the run, so estimates obtained over a longer period of time would probably have revealed that the new collector was still somewhat slower.

In any case, the differences in old generation collection times were practically negligible in the overall picture. The extra time spent in the compiler and simulation runs corresponded to merely 0.4% of the total execution time of the programs, and the time (seemingly) saved in the editor session amounted to only 0.2%.

4.3.2 Young Generation Collector

The Train Algorithm approach had its implications on the young generation collector, too. First, the roots for each young object scavenge now had to be found in a number of distinct remembered sets associated with each car, rather than in a single remembered set associated with the entire mature object space.

Second, extra inter-car remembered set insertions had to be performed when objects were promoted.

For the compiler and editor runs, this amounted to an increase of about 0.0025 seconds for each young generation scavenge, or between 7% and 8%. For the simulation run, the result was a *decrease* in young generation collection time of about 25%. In all three cases, we believe that the main reason for the difference was the time spent scanning the remembered sets for roots. In the compiler and editor runs, the accumulated size of the remembered sets associated with the old generation cars far exceeded that of the single remembered set originally employed; in the simulation run, the accumulated size was significantly smaller.

Overall, the differences in young generation collection times corresponded to an increase in execution time of about 1% for the compiler and editor runs, and a decrease of almost 5% for the simulation session.

4.3.3 Mutator

The Train Algorithm approach also affected the mutator performance. On one hand, the run-time pointer assignment checks were slightly costlier, and the new inter-car remembered sets had to be maintained. On the other hand, the large old-to-young generation remembered set was now replaced with one for each car, which typically gave faster insertion times. Also, the train table approach enabled us to handle old and large objects without having to traverse long linked block lists.

For the compiler run, the net result was a 0.9% decrease in mutator time. For the editor session, a 0.5% increase was observed, while the total simulation mutator time decreased by 4%. In the overall picture the differences were, of course, slightly less.

4.3.4 Overall Result

Using the Train Algorithm, the total execution time for the compiler compilation increased by 0.6%, the total execution time for the editor session increased by 1.0%, and the total execution time for the simulation run decreased by 8%.

4.4 Storage Overhead

In addition to the performance overhead, Train Algorithm-based systems affect storage requirements in several ways. First, the inter-car remembered sets take up extra memory. Second, cars are not filled to capacity, but only hold related object structures; also, there is a trade-off between the car collection frequency and the storage required to hold garbage contained in yet unprocessed cars. Third, a train table, if employed, also takes up space.

4.4.1 Inter-Car Remembered Set Overhead

There were an average of 350 entries in each inter-car remembered set for the editor and simulation sessions, and 700 for the compiler run. With the hash table implementation used, this resulted in storage overheads of 6K to 8K bytes per car.

Even though BETA objects are generally highly interlinked because they all contain an environment reference (the *origin*) to their statically enclosing object, this was a surprisingly large figure. However, by fine-tuning the hash function and rehash strategies, we believe that the overhead could be significantly reduced.

4.4.2 Garbage Overhead

To measure the extra storage required to hold unprocessed garbage in the two systems, we performed a series of exhaustive mature object space traversals to determine how many of the objects residing there were actually alive. The result from the compiler run is shown in Figures 4 and 5.

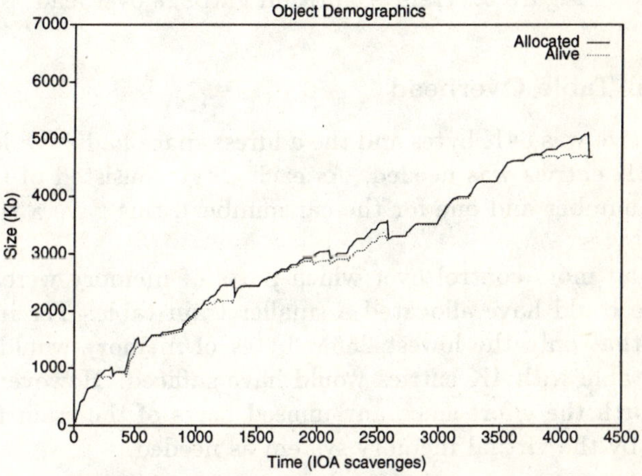

Figure 4: Mark-sweep garbage overhead

In the original system, new mature object space blocks were only allocated if the total old generation capacity was very close to being exhausted after a mark-sweep collection. Therefore, the difference between the two graphs was always less than the size of an old generation block, 512K bytes, as seen in Figure 4. In the Train Algorithm-based system, we chose to aim for a 10% garbage ratio and were quite successful, as seen in Figure 5.

Thus, the storage overhead caused by unprocessed garbage was about 10% for the compiler run. The same behavior was achieved for the editor session, while the old generation storage requirements *fell* a bit for the simulation run, simply because the program needed less old generation space than the size of the single block allocated in the mark-sweep implementation, and because the Train Algorithm collector managed to keep up with the high mortality rate.

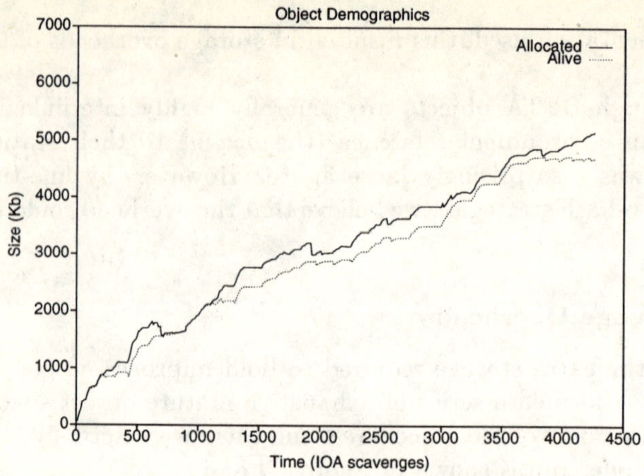

Figure 5: Train Algorithm garbage overhead

4.4.3 Train Table Overhead

Since the car size was 64K bytes and the address space had 2^{32} addresses, a train table with 64K entries was needed. As each entry consisted of two words (one for the train number and one for the car number), this gave a total train table size of 256K bytes.

Had we had more control over which parts of memory were used for heap allocation, we could have allocated a smaller train table. For instance, had it been known that only the lowest 256M bytes of memory would ever be used, a 16K bytes table with 4K entries would have sufficed. However, this may not have been worth the effort since any unused parts of the train table would be swapped out by the virtual memory system as needed.

4.4.4 Overall Result

In total, the old generation storage overhead for the Train Algorithm implementation was between 10% and 20%. In the overall picture, this corresponded to increases in application storage requirements of between 4% and 8%.

4.5 Copying Overhead

Theoretically, the Train Algorithm may require $O(Mn^2)$ invocations to collect a train consisting of n cars, where M is the number of objects containing at least one reference that may fit into a single car [GS93]. In practice this behavior should not be expected because it would require extremely poor locality of reference.

In order to get an impression of the Train Algorithm's practical behavior in this area, we recorded information about the number of cars in each train and the number of collections it took to reclaim one using various fill limits (see

Section 3.2.1). As it turned out, the compiler benchmark gave rise to the most complex object structures. The results of this run are shown in Table 3.

Fill Limit	10%	25%	50%	75%	90%	95%	99%	none
Cars (avg.)	99.8	64.2	57.0	52.7	51.7	51.5	51.4	51.6
Cars (max.)	154	103	94	89	86	86	85	85
Trains (avg.)	59.2	23.8	13.9	9.7	8.3	6.3	3.1	2.9
Trains (max.)	94	36	19	15	13	10	5	3
Length (avg.)	1.7	2.7	4.1	5.4	6.5	8.2	16.8	17.6
Length (max.)	17	22	23	27	32	42	81	79
Passes (avg.)	1.04	1.13	1.10	1.14	1.13	1.15	1.17	1.19
Passes (max.)	2.50	2.00	2.33	2.00	2.00	1.80	1.75	1.65

Table 3: Train structure statistics

The first six rows show the average and maximum number of cars and trains in the system, as well as the train length. The last two rows show the number of passes needed to reclaim each train, expressed as the ratio between the number of invocations performed and the initial length of the train. Thus, a lower ratio signifies less superfluous copying.

As should be expected, lowering the fill limit resulted in more, shorter trains which required fewer passes to be reclaimed. The cost for this behavior was an increase in the number of cars, and thus in the overall storage consumption. However, even in the most storage preserving setting in which new trains were only created when the collection process reached the newest train and needed somewhere else to evacuate objects to, the average amount of redundant copying was less than 20%. Thus, we did not see any signs of worst-case behavior occurring in practice.

4.6 Popular Objects

As described in Section 3.2.3, we chose to create a special car to hold the basic BETA environment object in order to avoid moving it and having to update the multitude of references to it. To investigate the consequences of this approach, we temporarily disabled the special treatment for the compiler run (which had by far the most objects referencing to the basic environment object). The result is shown in Table 4 and Figure 6 (cf. the second column of Table 1, and Figure 3).

As can be seen, the maximum collection time doubled. This was because there were more than 50,000 references to the basic environment object, causing over 200K bytes of pointers scattered throughout mature object space to be updated whenever the car containing it was collected. In addition, the total time spent on old generation collection rose to 26.56 seconds, or nearly 30%. This was because hundreds of inter-car remembered set insertions were now typically required at each collection step as objects referencing the basic environment

Application	Compiler
Method	train
Pause (min.)	0.00s
Pause (med.)	0.04s
Pause (90%)	0.06s
Pause (max.)	0.23s
Pause (avg.)	0.05s

Table 4: No popular treatment, pause table

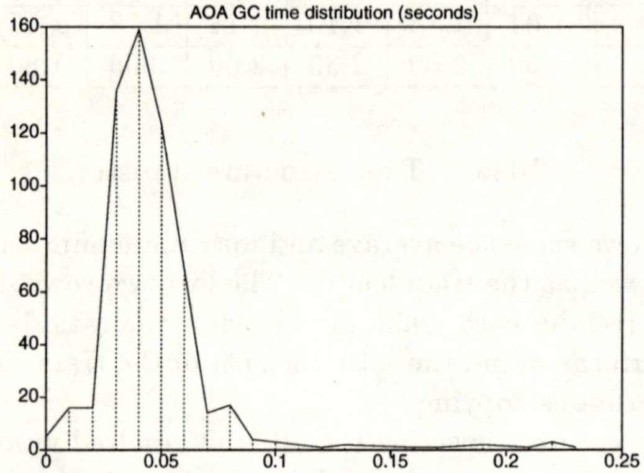

Figure 6: No popular treatment, pause plot

object were evacuated past it.

As can be seen from the figures above, our simple popular object scheme therefore turned out to be highly effective in practice.

4.7 Virtual Memory Behavior

To investigate the virtual memory behavior of the Train Algorithm, we ran the compiler benchmark on a 33 MHz Sun SPARC ELC 4/25 workstation equipped with only 12M bytes of primary memory. Since we only measured user and system time, not elapsed wall-clock time, we were unable to determine the exact amount of time spent on disk swapping. Instead, we monitored the page fault distribution.

The mark-sweep and Train Algorithm collectors scanned roughly the same amount of mature object space during the execution, about 30M bytes. This gave rise to 3,800 page faults in the mark-sweep implementation, and 4,500 in the Train Algorithm implementation. In both cases, this corresponded to around 95% of the total number of page faults. While there were nearly 20% more page faults in the Train Algorithm implementation, they were far better temporally distributed. For instance, the last mark-sweep collection caused over 1,000 pages to be swapped into primary memory, spending 6.4 seconds in the system kernel alone (not counting the disk access). In contrast, the Train Algorithm collector caused an average of less than 10 page faults per collection step. Still, a few collections of cars with large remembered sets caused nearly 100 page faults each, with up to 0.25 seconds spent in the system kernel.

To gain a better impression of the virtual memory behavior of the Train Algorithm, more detailed measurements are required. Nevertheless, our simple experiment seems to indicate that the algorithm is certainly a step in the right direction.

5 Future Work

To understand the full potential of the Train Algorithm, more experiments are needed. For instance, the remembered set implementation seems to play a crucial role. It would be highly instructive to examine the effects of using alternative strategies, such as dirty pages, cards, etc. [HMS92]. Also, further experiments with different car sizes and evacuation strategies would be interesting, as would more work concerning the treatment of popular objects. Finally, the Train Algorithm approach may be applicable in other areas, such as distributed garbage collection or collection of persistent stores.

6 Conclusion

Garbage collection simplifies programming, but has often been considered unfeasible in interactive systems. The most common argument has been that it is impossible to guarantee sufficiently short delays without introducing large overheads. With current hardware and sophisticated reclamation techniques, this is no longer true. Our Train Algorithm implementation shows that collection delays can be brought down to a few milliseconds, with very low maximum delay and a modest increase in storage requirements. Thus, for a large class of interactive applications, there is no need to exclude automatic memory management.

7 Acknowledgments

We wish to thank Ole Lehrmann Madsen and Eric Jul for encouraging us to write this paper. We are also grateful to Søren Brandt, Richard Hudson, Eric Jul, Ole Lehrmann Madsen, Eliot Moss, and Mario Wolczko for reading earlier drafts and providing us with many helpful suggestions.

References

[Bar88] Knut Barra: *Mark/sweep compaction for substantially nested Beta objects*, NCC-Note DTEK/03/88, Norwegian Computing Center, March 1988.

[GS93] Steffen Grarup and Jacob Seligmann: *Incremental Mature Garbage Collection*, M.Sc. thesis, Computer Science Department, Aarhus University, Denmark, August 1993. Also published as Technical Report DAIMI IR-122, Computer Science Department, Aarhus University, Denmark, September 1994. Electronic version available via anonymous ftp from `ftp.daimi.aau.dk` as `pub/thesis/gcthesis.ps.{Z,gz}`.

[HM92] Richard L. Hudson and J. Eliot B. Moss: *Incremental Collection of Mature Objects*, Proceedings of the International Workshop on Memory Management, September 1992, pp. 388–403.

[HMDW91] Richard L. Hudson, J. Eliot B. Moss, Amer Diwan, and Christopher F. Weight: *A Language-Independent Garbage Collector Toolkit*, COINS Technical Report 91-47, University of Massachusetts, Amherst, September 1991.

[HMS92] Anthony L. Hosking, J. Eliot B. Moss, and Darko Stefanović: *A Comparative Performance Evaluation of Write Barrier Implementations*, OOPSLA '92 Proceedings, ACM SIGPLAN Notices, Vol. 27, No. 10, October 1992, pp. 92–109.

[KLMM93] Jørgen L. Knudsen, Mats Löfgren, Ole L. Madsen, and Boris Magnusson (eds.): *Object-Oriented Environments: The Mjølner Approach*, Prentice Hall, 1993.

[MIA90] Mjølner Informatics Report MIA 90-11: *Sif: A Hyper Structure Editor – Tutorial and Reference Manual*, Mjølner Informatics ApS, Science Park Aarhus, 1990.

[MMN93] Ole L. Madsen, Birger Møller-Pedersen, and Kristen Nygaard: *Object-Oriented Programming in the BETA Programming Language*, Addison-Wesley, 1993.

[Ung86] David Ungar: *The Design and Evaluation of a High Performance Smalltalk System*, Ph.D. thesis, University of California, Berkeley, May 1986.

[UJ92] David Ungar and Frank Jackson: *An Adaptive Tenuring Policy for Generation Scavengers*, ACM Transactions on Programming Languages and Systems, Vol. 14, No. 1, January 1992, pp. 1–27.

Message Dispatch on Pipelined Processors

Karel Driesen
Urs Hölzle
Jan Vitek[1]

Abstract. Object-oriented systems must implement message dispatch efficiently in order not to penalize the object-oriented programming style. We characterize the performance of most previously published dispatch techniques for both statically- and dynamically-typed languages with both single and multiple inheritance. Hardware organization (in particular, branch latency and superscalar instruction issue) significantly impacts dispatch performance. For example, inline caching may outperform C++-style "vtables" on deeply pipelined processors even though it executes *more* instructions per dispatch.

We also show that adding support for dynamic typing or multiple inheritance does not significantly impact dispatch speed for most techniques, especially on superscalar machines. Instruction space overhead (calling sequences) can exceed the space cost of data structures (dispatch tables), so that minimal table size may not imply minimal run-time space usage.

Keywords: message dispatch, implementation, performance, computer architecture

1 Introduction

Message dispatch is a central feature of object-oriented languages. Given a receiver object and a selector (i.e., operation name), message dispatch finds the method implementing the operation for the particular receiver object. Since message dispatch is performed at run-time and is a very frequent operation in object-oriented programs, it must be fast. Therefore, the efficient implementation of message dispatch has been the subject of much previous work. Unfortunately, this research has often presented particular dispatch implementations in isolation, without comparing them to other methods. This paper presents several dispatch techniques in a common framework and compares their cost on modern computer architectures. The study includes most previously published dispatch techniques for both statically- and dynamically-typed languages with both single and multiple inheritance.

Any comparative study of dispatch mechanisms must be a compromise between breadth and depth since it is impossible to explore the entire design space in a single paper. While the present study considers several aspects of dispatch mechanisms (such as speed and space efficiency), the main focus is on run-time dispatch performance. But even when considering only run-time dispatch speed, a myriad of issues must be

[1] Author's addresses: Karel Driesen and Urs Hölzle, Department of Computer Science, University of California, Santa Barbara, CA93106, USA; {karel,urs}@cs.ucsb.edu. Jan Vitek, Object Systems Group, Centre Universitaire d'Informatique, Université de Genève, 24 rue Général Dufour, CH-1211 Genève 4, Switzerland; jvitek@cui.unige.ch.

addressed. The remainder of this introduction briefly discusses and justifies the issues we address as well as those we don't.

1.1 Specific measurements vs. analytical models

Previous studies have evaluated the run-time performance of specific dispatch implementations relative to specific systems, languages, and applications; some have not evaluated run-time performance at all. While specific empirical measurements are useful and desirable, they are also limited in scope. Different languages or applications may have different dispatch characteristics, and an implementor who is trying to choose between dispatch techniques may not yet know how the new system relates to the system used for the specific measurements. As discussed below, different processor implementations also change the relative speed of dispatch mechanisms. Any performance comparison using specific measurements will therefore be relative to the particular processors, languages, applications, and run-time systems used.

Therefore, instead of giving concrete measurements, we chose to characterize the performance of each dispatch mechanisms as a function of several configuration parameters that are dependent on the hardware and software environment of the system using the dispatch mechanism. To compare dispatch performance in a new system, an implementor therefore merely needs to measure (or approximate) the values of these performance parameters in that system. By keeping our performance analysis abstract, we hope that this study will be helpful to implementors of a wide range of systems, languages, and applications on a range of hardware platforms.

To help illustrate specific points of trends in the analysis, we also present absolute performance numbers which were obtained by using typical values (taken from previous studies) for the parameters.

1.2 Processor architecture

Dispatch cost is intimately coupled with processor implementation. The same dispatch sequence may have different cost on different processor implementations, even if all of them implement the same architecture (e.g., the SPARC instruction set). In particular, processor pipelining and superscalar execution make it impossible to use the number of instructions in a code sequence as an accurate performance indicator. This paper characterizes the run-time performance of dispatch mechanisms on modern pipelined processors by determining the performance impact of branch latency and superscalar instruction issue. In addition to providing specific numbers for three example architectures, our analysis allows dispatch performance to be computed for a wide range of possible (future) processors. With the rapid change in processor design, it is desirable to characterize performance in a way that makes the dependence on certain processor characteristics explicit, so that performance on a new processor can be estimated accurately as long as the processor's characteristics are known.

1.3 Influence of dynamic typing

In dynamically-typed languages, a program may try to invoke an operation on some object for which the operation is undefined ("message not understood" error).

Therefore, each message dispatch usually needs to include some form of run-time check to guarantee that such errors are properly caught and reported to the user. Most techniques that support static typing can be extended to handle dynamic typing as well. Our study shows the additional dispatch cost of dynamic typing for all dispatch mechanisms that can support it.

1.4 Single versus multiple inheritance

A system using multiple inheritance (MI) introduces an additional difficulty if compiled code uses hard-coded offsets when addressing instance variables. For example, assume that class *C* inherits directly from classes *A* and *B* (Figure 1). In order to reuse compiled code of class *A*, instances of *C* would have to start with the instance variables of *A* (i.e., *A*'s memory layout must be a prefix of *C*'s layout). But the compiled code in class *B* requires a conflicting memory layout (*B*'s instance variables must come first), and so it seems that compiled code cannot be reused if it directly addresses instance variables of an object.

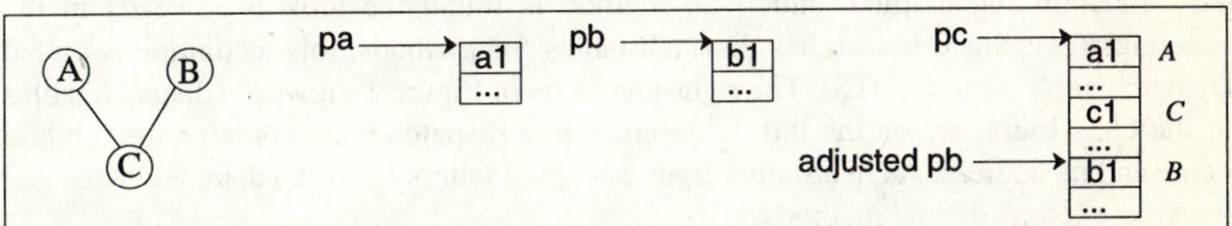

Figure 1. The memory layout of objects of class *A*, *B*, and *C*. Note that the offset of instance variable *b1* is different in instances of *B* versus instances of *C*.

Hard-coded offsets can be retained if the receiver object's address is adjusted just before a *B* method is executed, so that it points to the *B* subobject within *C* [Kro85, ES90].[1] The adjustment can be different for every class that has *B* as a (co-)parent. (If dynamic typing is combined with multiple inheritance it is necessary to keep track of both the unadjusted address and the adjustment.) Strictly speaking, this extra code is not part of method lookup, but if multiple inheritance is allowed, *every* method invocation is preceded by a receiver address adjustment, and thus we chose to include the cost of this adjustment in our study.

1.5 Limitations

This study is limited to single (i.e., receiver-based) dispatch. Since multi-method dispatch techniques (e.g., [KR90, AGS94]) are similar and include single dispatch as an important (very frequent) special case, we hope that the results will nevertheless be useful for implementors or designers of multiple dispatch techniques. Also, we do not consider dynamic inheritance (as used in SELF [CU+91]), i.e., inheritance hierarchies that can change their structure at run-time. Furthermore, we focus on dispatch performance and only briefly discuss other issues such as space overhead and the closed– vs. open–world assumption (see section 6). For space reasons, we consider only the main variant of each technique.

[1] Alternatively, a system could duplicate code (e.g., as in SELF [CUL89]) or access instance variables indirectly (as is done in Eiffel and Sather [MS94]).

A further simplification on the hardware side is that we do not consider every possible processor implementation feature. However, as will be explained in section 5.1, the features we consider represent a very large fraction of past and current processors. Further hardware-related limitations are discussed in section 5.5.

1.6 Overview of the paper

The remainder of this paper is organized as follows. Sections 2 to 4 briefly review the dispatch techniques evaluated. Section 5 presents the results of our performance analysis, and section 6 discusses space costs and other issues.

2 Method lookup techniques

Message lookup is a function of the message name (selector) and the receiver class. If lookup speed was unimportant, lookup could be performed by searching class-specific dispatch tables. When an object receives a message, the object's class is searched for the corresponding method, and if no method is found the lookup proceeds in the superclass(es). Since it searches dispatch tables for methods, this technique is called Dispatch Table Search (DTS). The right-hand side of Figure 2 shows the dispatch tables of the class hierarchy on the left. Each entry in a dispatch table contains the method name and its address. As in all other figures, capital letters (*A*, *B*, *C*) denote classes and lowercase letters denote methods.

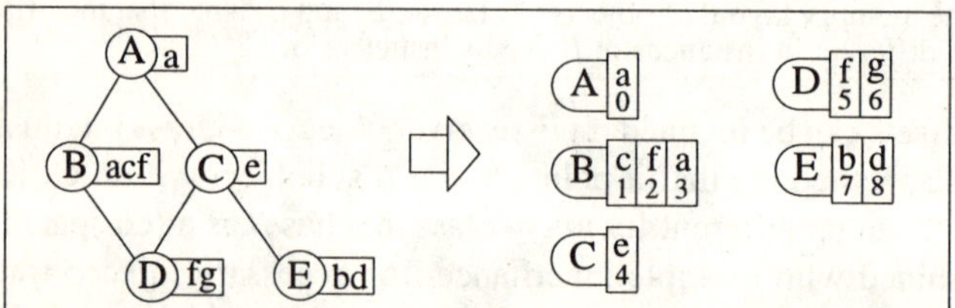

Figure 2. Class hierarchy with corresponding dispatch tables

Since the memory requirements of DTS are minimal (i.e., proportional to the number of methods in the system), DTS is often used as a backup strategy which is invoked when faster methods fail. If desired, DTS can employ hashing to speed up the table search.

All of the techniques discussed in the remainder of this paper improve upon the speed of DTS by precomputing or caching lookup results. The dispatch techniques studied here fall into two categories. *Static techniques* precompute all data structures at compile or link time and do not change those data structures at run-time. Thus, static techniques only use information that can be statically derived from the program's source text. *Dynamic techniques* may precompute some information at compile or link time, but they dynamically update data structures at run-time, i.e., during program execution. Thus, dynamic techniques can exploit run-time information as well as static information. Table 1 lists the techniques we studied.

Each description of a dispatch technique includes pseudo-code illustrating the run-time dispatch. Since our analysis separates out the influence of dynamic typing and multiple

	Acronym	Full Name	Section
static techniques	DTS	Dispatch Table Search (used for illustration only)	2
	STI	Selector Table Indexing (used for illustration only)	4.1
	VTBL	Virtual Function Tables	4.2
	SC	Selector Coloring	4.3
	RD	Row Displacement	4.4
	CT	Compact Tables	4.5
dynam. techn.	LC	Lookup Caching	3.1
	IC	Inline Caching	3.2
	PIC	Polymorphic Inline Caching	3.3

Table 1. Overview of dispatch methods

inheritance/hardwired instance variable offsets, two typographical conventions mark code used to support one of these functions. *Italic code* supports multiple inheritance, and **bold code** supports dynamic typing. Table A-2 in the Appendix contains assembly code sequences.

3 Dynamic techniques

Dynamic techniques speed up message lookup by using various forms of caching at run-time. Therefore, they depend on locality properties of object-oriented programs: caching will speed up programs if the cached information is used often before it is evicted from the cache. This section discusses two kinds of caching: global caching (one large cache per system) and inline caching (one small cache per call site).

3.1 Global lookup caches (LC)

First-generation Smalltalk implementations relied on a global cache to speed up method lookup [GR83, Kra83]. The class of a receiver, combined with the message selector, hashes into an index in a global cache. Each cache entry consists of a class, a selector and a method address. If the current class and selector match the ones found in the entry, the resident method is executed. Otherwise, a dispatch table search finds the correct method, and the new class-selector-method triple replaces the old cache entry (direct-mapped cache). Any hash function can be used; to obtain a lower bound on lookup time, we assume a simple exclusive OR of receiver class and selector.

```
entry = cache[(object->class ^ #selector) & #mask];
if (entry.class == object->class && entry.selector == #selector) {
  adjusted = object + entry.delta;
  entry.func(object, adjusted, arguments); /* cache hit */
} else { /* cache miss: use DTS to find method, and update cache entry e */; }
```

Figure 3. Global lookup cache. Multiple inheritance adds *italicized* code.

To allow hard-coded instance variable offsets in a multiple inheritance context, the receiver is adjusted by #delta.[1] Instance variable accesses in the callee use this adjusted object pointer. Even though LC is considerably faster than dispatch table search (DTS),

[1] To distinguish constants from variables, we precede constants with a hash mark (#) in both C and assembly code.

it still has to compute a hash function for each dispatch. As we shall see, this computation renders LC too slow compared to other techniques. However, LC is a popular fallback method for inline caching.

3.2 Inline caches (IC)

Often, the type of the receiver *at a given call site* rarely varies; if a message is sent to an object of type *X* at a particular call site, it is likely that the next send will also go to an object of type *X*. For example, several studies have shown that the receiver type at a given call site remains constant 95% of the time in Smalltalk code [DS84, Ung87, UP87]. This locality of type usage can be exploited by caching the looked-up method address at the call site. Because the lookup result is cached "in line" at every call site (i.e., no separate lookup cache is accessed in the case of a hit), the technique is called *inline caching* [DS84, UP87].

The previous lookup result is cached by changing the call instruction implementing the send, i.e., by modifying the compiled program on the fly. Initially, the call instruction calls the system's lookup routine. The first time this call is executed, the lookup routine finds the target method. Before branching to the target, the lookup routine changes the call instruction to point to the target method just found (Figure 4). Subsequent executions of the send directly call the target method, completely avoiding any lookup. Of course, the type of the receiver could have changed, and so the prologue of the called method must verify that the receiver's type is correct and call the lookup code if the type test fails.

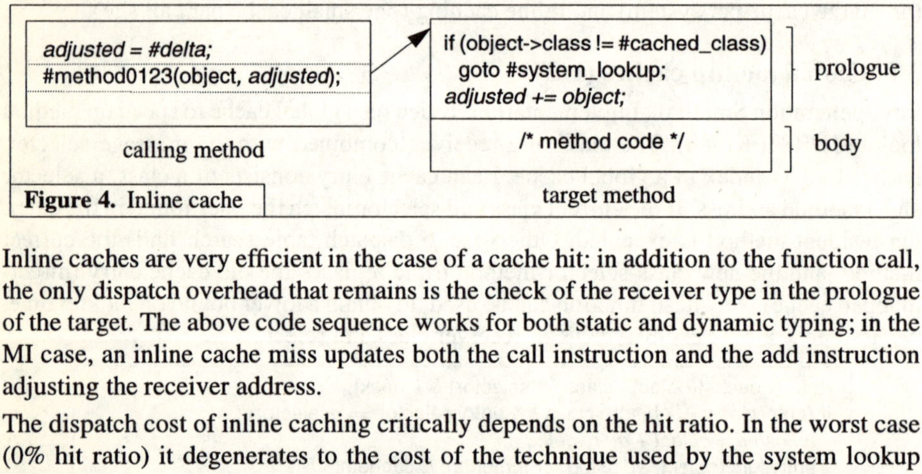

Figure 4. Inline cache

Inline caches are very efficient in the case of a cache hit: in addition to the function call, the only dispatch overhead that remains is the check of the receiver type in the prologue of the target. The above code sequence works for both static and dynamic typing; in the MI case, an inline cache miss updates both the call instruction and the add instruction adjusting the receiver address.

The dispatch cost of inline caching critically depends on the hit ratio. In the worst case (0% hit ratio) it degenerates to the cost of the technique used by the system lookup routine (often, a global lookup cache), plus the extra overhead of the instructions updating the inline cache. Fortunately, hit ratios are usually very good, on the order of 90-99% for typical Smalltalk or SELF code [Ung87, HCU91]. Therefore, many current Smalltalk implementations incorporate inline caches.

3.3 Polymorphic inline caching (PIC)

Inline caches are effective only if the receiver type (and thus the call target) remains relatively constant at a call site. Although inline caching works very well for the majority of sends, it does not speed up a polymorphic call site[1] with several equally likely receiver types because the call target switches back and forth between different methods, thus increasing the inline cache miss ratio. The performance impact of inline cache misses can become severe in highly efficient systems. For example, measurements of the SELF-90 system showed that it spent up to 25% of its time handling inline cache misses [HCU91].

Polymorphic inline caches (PICs) [HCU91] reduce the inline cache miss overhead by caching *several* lookup results for a given polymorphic call site using a dynamically-generated PIC routine. Instead of just switching the inline cache at a miss, the new receiver type is added to the cache by extending the stub routine. For example, after encountering receiver classes A and B, a send of message *m* would look as in Figure 5.

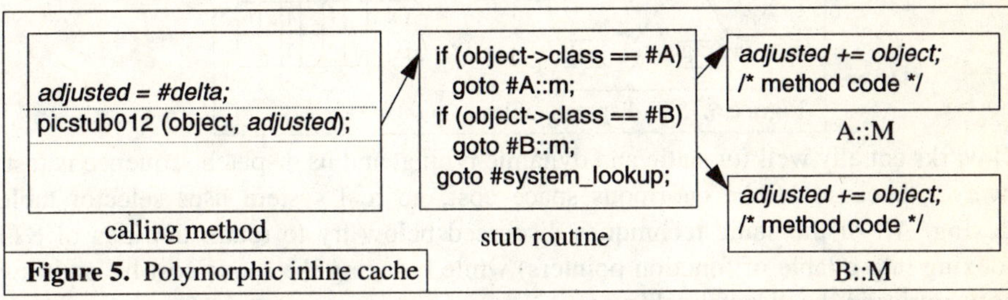

Figure 5. Polymorphic inline cache

A system using PICs treats monomorphic call sites like normal inline caching; only polymorphic call sites are handled differently. Therefore, as long as the PIC's dispatch sequence (a sequence of ifs) is faster than the system lookup routine, PICs will be faster than inline caches. However, if a send is megamorphic (invokes many different methods), it cannot be handled efficiently by PICs. Fortunately, such sends are the exception rather than the rule.

4 Static techniques

Static method lookup techniques precompute their data structures at compile time (or link time) in order to minimize the work done at dispatch time. Typically, the dispatch code retrieves the address of the target function by indexing into a table and performing an indirect jump to that address. Unlike lookup caching (LC), static methods usually don't need to compute a hash function since the table index can be computed at compile time. Also, dispatch time usually is constant[2], i.e., there are no "misses" as in inline caching.

4.1 Selector Table Indexing (STI)

The simplest way of implementing the lookup function is to store it in a two-dimensional table indexed by class and selector codes. Both classes and selectors are

---

[1] We will use the term "polymorphic" for call sites where polymorphism is *actually* used. Consequently, we will use "monomorphic" for call sites which experience only a single receiver type during a program run, even though they might *potentially* be polymorphic.

[2] Here, "constant" means "constant in number of instructions," not "constant in real time" (due to processor cache effects).

represented by unique, consecutive class or selector codes; if a system has *c* classes and *s* selectors, classes are numbered *0..c-1* and selectors are numbered *0..s-1* (Figure 6). Unfortunately, the resulting dispatch table is very large (*O(c*s)*) and very sparse, since most messages are defined for only a few classes. For example, about 95% of the entries would be empty in a table for a Smalltalk image [Dri93b]. With multiple inheritance, every entry consists of a method code address and a delta (the adjustment to the receiver address). To avoid cluttering the graphics, we do not show the latter in any figure.

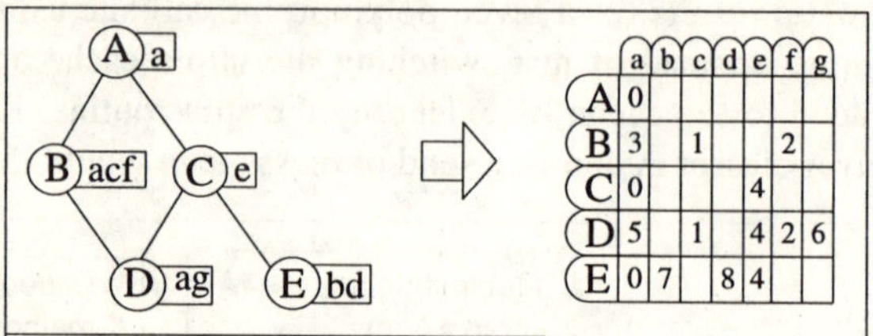

Figure 6. STI dispatch tables

STI works equally well for static and dynamic typing, and its dispatch sequence is fast. However, because of the enormous space cost, no real system uses selector table indexing. All of the static techniques discussed below try to retain the idea of STI (indexing into a table of function pointers) while reducing the space cost by omitting empty entries in the dispatch table.

4.2 Virtual function tables (VTBL)

Virtual function tables were first used in Simula [DM73] and today are the preferred C++ dispatch mechanism [ES90]. Instead of assigning selector codes globally, VTBL assigns codes only within the scope of a class. In the single-inheritance case, selectors are numbered consecutively, starting with the highest selector number used in the superclass. In other words, if a class *C* understands *m* different messages, the class's message selectors are numbered *0..m-1*. Each class receives its own dispatch table (of size *m*), and all subclasses will use the same selector numbers for methods inherited from the superclass. The dispatch process consists of loading the receiver's dispatch table, loading the function address by indexing into the table with the selector number, and jumping to that function.

With multiple inheritance, keeping the selector code correct is more difficult. For the inheritance structure on the left side of Figure 7, functions *c* and *e* will both receive a selector number of 1 since they are the second function defined in their respective class.

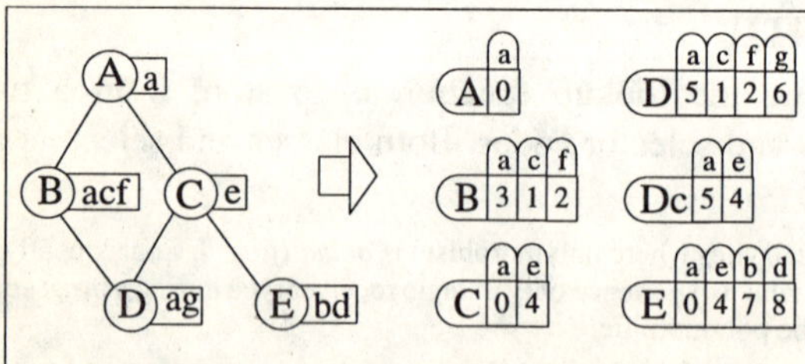


```
object += #tableOffset;
entry = object->table[#selector];
object += entry.delta;
entry.func(object, arguments);
```

Figure 7. VTBL dispatch tables and method call code.

D multiply inherits from both *B* and *C*, creating a conflict for the binding of selector number 1. In C++ [ES90], the conflict is resolved by using multiple virtual tables per class. An object of class *D* has two dispatch tables, *D* and *Dc* (see Figure 7).[1] Message sends will use dispatch table *D* if the receiver object is viewed as a *B* or a *D* and table *Dc* if the receiver is viewed as a *C*. As explained in section 1.4, the dispatch code will also adjust the receiver address before calling a method defined in *C*.

VTBL depends on static typing: without knowing the set of messages sent to an object, the system cannot reuse message numbers in unrelated classes (such as using 0 for the first method defined in a top-level class). Thus, with dynamic typing, VTBL dispatch tables would degenerate to STI tables since any arbitrary message could be sent to an object, forcing selector numbers to be globally unique.

4.3 Selector coloring (SC)

Selector coloring [D+89, AR92] is a compromise between VTBL and STI. SC is similar to STI, but instead of using the selector to index into the table, SC uses the selector's *color*. The color is a number that is unique within every class where the selector is known, and two selectors can share a color if they never co-occur in a class. SC allows more compaction than STI, where selectors never share colors, but less compaction than VTBL, where a selector need not have a single global number (i.e., where the selector *m* can have two different numbers in unrelated classes).

```
entry = object->table[#color];
entry.func(object, entry.delta, #selector, arguments)
```

```
/* method prologue */
if (S != #mySelector) error("Message Not Understood");
adjusted = delta + object;
```

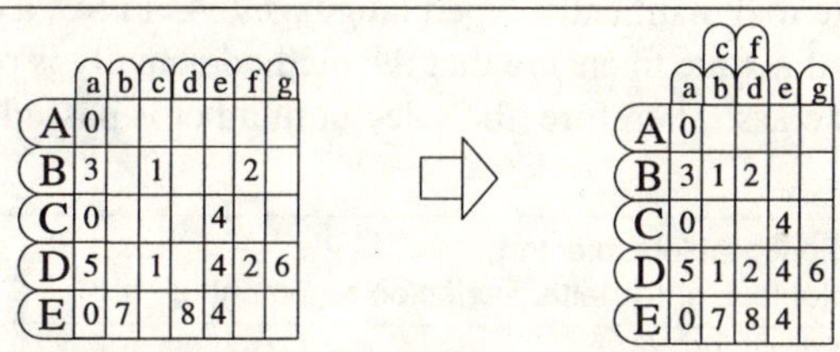

Figure 8. Selector coloring tables, method call code, and method prologue (dynamic typing in **bold**)

Optimally assigning colors to selectors is equivalent to the graph coloring problem[2] which is NP-complete. However, efficient approximation algorithms can often approach or even reach the minimal number of colors (which is at least equal to the maximum number of messages understood by any particular class). The resulting global dispatch table is much smaller than in STI but still relatively sparse. For example, 43% of the entries are empty (i.e., contain "message not understood") for the Smalltalk

[1] Due to limited space, we ignore virtual base classes in this discussion. They introduce an extra overhead of a memory reference and a subtraction [ES90].

[2] The selectors are the nodes of the graph, and two nodes are connected by an arc if the two selectors co-occur in any class.

system [Dri93b]. As shown in Figure 8, coloring allows the sharing of columns of the selector table used in STI.

Compared to VTBL, SC has two potential advantages. First, since selector colors are global, only one dispatch table is needed per class, even in the context of multiple inheritance. Secondly, and for the same reason, SC is applicable to a dynamically-typed environment since any particular selector will have the same table offset (i.e., color) throughout the system and will thus invoke the correct method for any receiver. To guard against incorrect dispatches, the prologue of the target method must verify the message selector, and thus the selector must be passed as an extra argument. Otherwise, an erroneous send (which should result in a "message not understood" error) could invoke a method with a different selector that shares the same color. For example, in Figure 8, message *c* sent to a *E* object would invoke *b* without that check.

4.4 Row displacement (RD)

Row displacement [Dri93a] is another way of compressing STI's dispatch table. It slices the (two-dimensional) STI table into rows and fits the rows into a one-dimensional array so that non-empty entries overlap only with empty ones (Figure 9). Row offsets must be unique (because they are used as class identifiers), so no two rows start at the same index in the master array. The algorithm's goal is to minimize the size of the resulting master array by minimizing the number of empty entries; this problem is similar to parse table minimization for table-driven parsers [DDH84]. [Dri93a] discusses a selector numbering scheme that leaves only 33% of the entries empty for the Smalltalk image. If the table is sliced according to columns (instead of rows), the table can even be filled to 99.7% with an appropriate class numbering scheme [DH95]. Like SC, RD needs only a single table per class even with multiple inheritance, and the technique is applicable to dynamically-typed languages. As in SC, a check is needed in the method prologue, this time to ensure that the method actually is part of the dispatch table of the receiver's class. Therefore, the selector number is passed as an argument to the method.

```
entry = object->table[#selector];
entry.func(object, entry.delta, #selector, arguments);
```

```
/* method prologue */
if (S != #mySelector) error("Message Not Understood");
adjusted = delta + object;
```

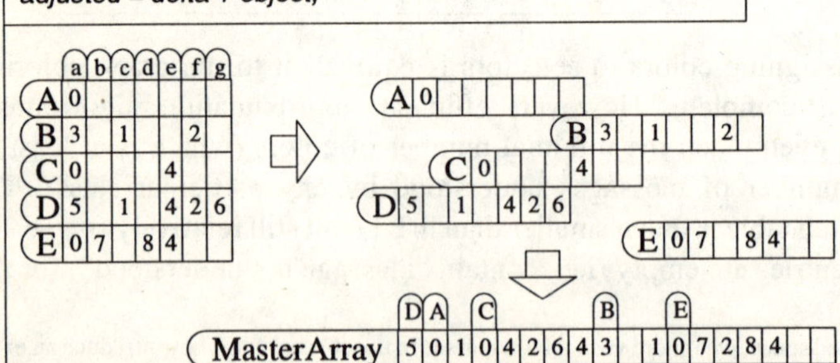

Figure 9. Row displacement tables, method call code, and method prologue

4.5 Compact Selector-Indexed Dispatch Tables (CT)

The third table compaction method [VH94], unlike the two previous methods, generates selector-specific dispatch code sequences. The technique separates selectors into two categories. *Standard selectors* have one main definition and are only overridden in the subclasses (e.g., *a* and *b* in Figure 10). *Conflict selectors* have multiple definitions in unrelated portions of the class hierarchy (e.g., *e* in Figure 10 which is defined in the unrelated classes *C* and *D*). CT uses two dispatch tables, a main table for standard selectors and a conflict table for conflict selectors.

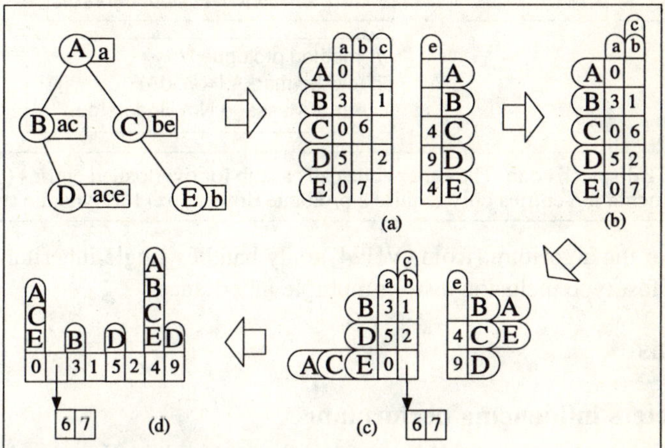

Figure 10. Construction on Compact Tables
(a) main dispatch table and conflict tables for *e*
(b) main dispatch table with *c* and *b* aliased
(c) conflict tables for (*A, B*) and (*C, E*) shared, main dispatch tables for (*A, C, E*) overloaded
(d) dispatch table fitted on a single master array, main dispatch table for (*A, C, E*) trimmed

Standard selectors can be numbered in a simple top-down traversal of the class hierarchy; two selectors can share a number as long as they are defined in different branches of the hierarchy. Such sharing is impossible for conflict selectors, and so the conflict table remains sparse (Figure 10). But the allocation of both tables can be further optimized. First, tables with identical entries (such as the conflict tables for *C* and *E*) can be shared. Second, tables meeting a certain similarity criterion—a parameter to the algorithm—can be *overloaded*; divergent entries refer to a code stub which selects the appropriate method based on the type (similar to PIC). In Figure 10 (a), the entry for selectors *c* and *b* of tables (*A, C, E*) is overloaded. The required level of similarity affects the compression rate (stricter requirements decrease the compression rate) as well as dispatch speed (stricter requirements decrease the number of overloaded entries and thus improve dispatch speed). Finally, dispatch tables are trimmed of empty entries and allocated onto one large master array as shown in Figure 10 (b).

Each class needs at least three fields: class identifier (*cid*), main dispatch table, and conflict table. Because of compression, all methods need a subtype test in the method prologue in dynamically-typed languages. For statically-typed languages, only the code stubs of overloaded entries need such a test. Subtype tests are implemented with a simple series of logical operations (a bit-wise AND and a comparison) [Vit95]. Figure 11 shows the code for a call through a CT dispatch table.

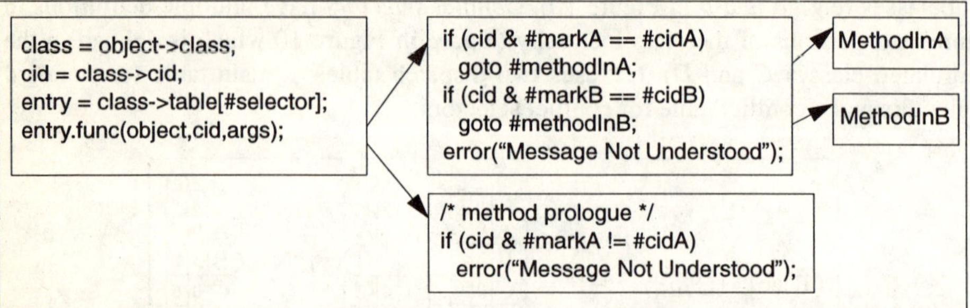

Figure 11. CT dispatch code. The caller code calls a stub for overloaded entries (upper box). Single implementation entries only require a prologue (lower box) for dynamic typing.

This version of the algorithm (from [VH94]) only handles single inheritance, because of the lack of fast type inclusion test for multiple inheritance.[1]

5 Analysis

5.1 Parameters influencing performance

To evaluate the performance of the dispatch mechanisms, we implemented the dispatch instruction sequence of each technique on a simple RISC-like architecture.[2] Table A-2 in the Appendix lists the resulting instruction sequences. Then, we measured the cost of the dispatch sequences for three hypothetical processor implementations. P92 represents a scalar implementation as it was typical of processor designs in 1992. P95 is a superscalar implementation that can execute up to two integer instructions concurrently, representative of current state-of-the art processor designs. Finally, P97 is an estimate of a 1997 superscalar processor with four-instruction issue width and a deeper pipeline. Table 2 lists the detailed processor characteristics relevant to the study.

In essence, these processors are abstractions of current commercial processors that have been reduced to their most important performance features, namely

- *Superscalar architecture*. The processor can execute several instructions in parallel as long as they are independent. Since access paths to the cache are expensive, all but P97 can execute at most one load or store per cycle.
- *Load latency*. Because of pipelining, the result of a load started in cycle i is not available until cycle $i + L$ (i.e., the processor will stall if the result is used before that time).

[1] This problem is tackled in [VH95]. [Vit95] presents a version of the algorithm which improves dispatch speed and shortens the calling sequence. Unfortunately, we have not been able to analyze and measure this new version yet.

[2] Assuming a RISC architecture simplifies the discussion, but our results are not restricted to RISC architectures since pipelined CISC machines have similar performance characteristics. For example, the Intel Pentium processor closely resembles P95.

- *Branch penalty.* The processor predicts the outcome of a conditional branch; if the prediction is correct, the branch incurs no additional cost. However, if the prediction is incorrect, the processor will stall for *B* cycles while fetching and decoding the instructions following the branch [HP90]. We assume that indirect calls or jumps cannot be predicted and always incur the branch penalty.[1]

	P92	P95	P97
max. integer instructions/ cycle	1	2	4
max. loads or stores / cycle	1	1	2
max. control transfers (branch, call) / cycle	1	1	1
load latency (L)[a]	2	2	2
branch prediction	no	yes	yes
branch miss penalty (B)	1[b]	3	6
examples of equivalent commercial CPUs	[M92, Cy90]	[M94, Gw94]	N/A

Table 2. Processor characteristics

[a] To simplify the analysis, we assumed $L > 1$; to the best of our knowledge, this assumption holds for all RISC processors introduced since 1990.
[b] No penalty if the branch's delay slot can be filled. (To improve readability, the instruction sequences in Table A-2 are written without delay slots.) On P95/97, delay slots cannot hide branch latency due to multi-cycle branch penalties and superscalar instruction issue, and thus have no performance benefit.

Virtually all processors announced since 1993 exhibit all three characteristics. We also assumed out-of-order execution for the superscalar machines (P95 and P97). To determine the number of cycles per dispatch, we hand-scheduled the dispatch instruction sequences for optimal performance on each processor. In most cases, a single instruction sequence is optimal for all three processors.

Variable	Typical value	Comments
h_{LC}	98%	lookup cache hit ratio ([CPL83] lists 93% for a very small cache size)
$miss_{LC}$	250[a]	LC miss cost (find method in class dictionaries); conservative estimate based on data in [Ung87]
h_{IC}	95%	inline caching hit ratio; from [Ung87] and [HCU91]
$miss_{IC}$	80[a]+L+LC	IC miss cost; from [HCU91]
m	66%	fraction of calls from monomorphic call sites (PIC) [HCU91, CG94]
k	3.54	dynamic number of type tests per PIC stub (from SELF [Höl94])
p	10%	average branch misprediction rate (estimate from [HP90])
M	1%	fraction of calls from highly polymorphic call sites (> 10 receiver types); conservative estimate (in SELF, $M < 0.1\%$ [Höl94])
$miss_{PIC}$	150[a]+L+LC	PIC miss cost; based on $miss_{IC}$ (overhead for updating the PIC)
s	99.93%	percentage of single (non-overloaded) entries in CT [VH94]
e	2.25	number of tests per overloaded entry in CT

Table 3. Additional parameters influencing performance

[a] Cycles on P92; 20% less on P95 and 33% less on P97.

The performance of some dispatch techniques depends on additional parameters (listed in Table 3). In order to provide some concrete performance numbers in addition to the formulas, we chose typical values for these parameters (most of them based on

[1] But see section 5.5.

previously published performance studies). However, it should be emphasized that these values merely represent one particular data point. Different systems, applications, or languages may well exhibit different parameter values. Thus, the *numbers* below are specific to an example configuration, but the *formulas* in Tables 4 to 6 are general.

5.2 Overview of dispatch costs

Tables 4 to 6 show dispatch costs as a function of processor parameters (L and B) and algorithmic parameters such as miss ratios, etc. Table A-2 in the Appendix lists the exact assembly instruction sequences used, and Table A-3 contains the raw dispatch times in cycles.

	single inheritance		multiple inheritance	
	static typing	dynamic typing	static typing	dynamic typing
LC	h_{LC}*(9+max(7,2L)+(1-h_{LC})*$miss_{LC}$		h_{LC}*(9+max(10,2L))+(1-h_{LC})*$miss_{LC}$	
VTBL	2+2L	N/A	2+2L	N/A
SC	2+2L	4+2L	2+2L	5+2L
RD	3+L + max(L, 3)	7+L+max(3,L)	2+2L+max(3,L)	7+max(5,2L)
CT	s*(2+3L)+(1-s) *(3+3L+7e)	s*(8+3L)+(1-s) *(3+3L+7e)	N/A	N/A
IC	h_{IC} * (2+max(3,L)) + (1-h_{IC}) * $miss_{IC}$		h_{IC} * (3+max(4,L)) + (1-h_{IC}) * $miss_{IC}$	
PIC	m * (2+max(3,L)) + (1-m) * (2+L+2k) + M * $miss_{PIC}$		m * (3+max(4,L)) + (1-m) * (3+L+2k)+ M * $miss_{PIC}$	

Table 4. P92

	single inheritance		multiple inheritance	
	static typing	dynamic typing	static typing	dynamic typing
LC	h_{LC} * (7+2L+B) +(1-h_{LC}) * $miss_{LC}$		h_{LC} * (8+2L+B) + (1-h_{LC}) * $miss_{LC}$	
VTBL	1+2L+B	N/A	see single inher.	N/A
SC	1+2L+B	3+2L+B	see single inher.	see single inher.
RD	1+2L+B	3+2L+B	2+2L+B	5+2L+B
CT	s*(1+3L+B)+(1-s)* (2+3L+B+e(4 +pB))	s*(5+3L+B)+(1-s)* (2+3L+B+e(4 +pB))	N/A	N/A
IC	h_{IC} * (1+L) + (1-h_{IC}) * $miss_{IC}$		h_{IC} * (2+L) + (1-h_{IC}) * $miss_{IC}$	
PIC	m * (1+L)+(1-m)*(2+L+k(1 +pB)) + M * $miss_{PIC}$		m*(2+L)+(1-m)*(2+L+k(1 +pB)) + M * $miss_{PIC}$	

Table 5. P95

Figure 12 illustrates the cycle cost calculation for VTBL. Data dependencies are indicated with arrows, control dependencies with dashed arrows. Instructions handling multiple inheritance are enclosed by dashed circles. The figure shows the order in which instructions are issued into the processor pipeline.[1] An instruction with a dependency on a load instruction executing in cycle i cannot execute before cycle $i + L$ (where L is the load latency). For example, in P92 instruction 2 cannot execute before cycle L

[1] More precisely, the cycle in which the instruction enters the EX stage (this stage calculates the result in arithmetic operations or the effective address in memory operations and branches). For details on pipeline organization, we refer the reader to [HP90].

	single inheritance		multiple inheritance	
	static typing	dynamic typing	static typing	dynamic typing
LC	h_{LC} * (6+2L+B) +(1-h_{LC}) * $miss_{LC}$			
VTBL	1+2L+B	N/A	see single inher.	N/A
SC	1+2L+B	2+2L+B	see single inher.	see single inher.
RD	1+2L+B	3+2L+B	see single inher.	see single inher.
CT	s*(1+3L+B)+(1-s)*(2+3L+B+e(3 +pB))	s*(4+3L+B)+(1-s)*(2+3L+B+e(3 +pB))	N/A	N/A
IC	h_{IC} * (1+L) + (1-h_{IC}) * $miss_{IC}$			
PIC	m * (1+L) + (1-m) * (1+L+k(1 +pB)) + M * $miss_{PIC}$			

Table 6. P97

because it depends on instruction 1 (Figure 12). Similarly, instruction 5 can execute at $L + L$ or $L + 2$ (one cycle after the previous instruction), whichever is later. Since we assume $L > 1$, we retain $2L$. The schedule for P92 also shows that instruction 3 (which is part of the multiple inheritance implementation) is *free*: even if it was eliminated, instruction 5 could still not execute before $2L$ since it has to wait for the result of instruction 2. Similarly, instruction 4 is free because it executes in the delay slot of the call (instruction 5).[1] As a result, VTBL incurs no overhead for multiple inheritance: both versions of the code execute in $2L + 2$ cycles (see Table 4).

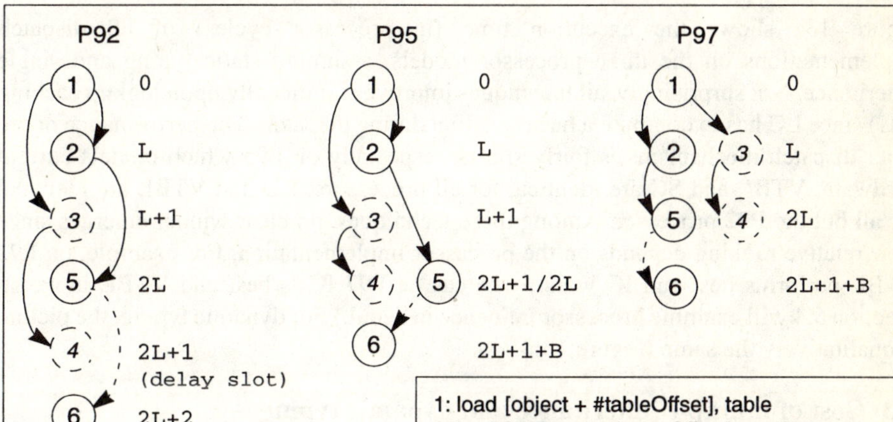

1: load [object + #tableOffset], table
2: load [table + #selectorOffset], method
3: load [table + #deltaOffset], delta
4: add object, delta, object
5: call method
6: <first instruction of target>

Figure 12. VTBL schedules, cycle counts and assembly code. Dependencies are indicated with arrows.

P95 (middle part of Figure 12) can execute two instructions per cycle (but only one of them can be a memory instruction, see Table 2). Unfortunately, this capability doesn't benefit VTBL much since its schedule is dominated by load latencies and the branch latency *B*. Since VTBL uses an indirect call, the processor does not know its target

[1] Recall that P92 machines had a branch latency B = 1, which can be eliminated using explicit branch delay slots; see [HP90] for details. Since we use a fixed branch penalty for P92, B does not appear as a parameter in Table 4.

address until after the branch executes (in cycle *2L*). At that point, it starts fetching new instructions, but it takes *B* cycles until the first new instruction reaches the EX (execute) stage of the pipeline [HP90], resulting in a total execution time of *2L+B+1*. Finally, P97 can execute up to 4 instructions per cycle, but again this capability is largely unused, except that instructions 2 and 3 (two loads) can execute in parallel. However, the final cycle count is unaffected by this change.

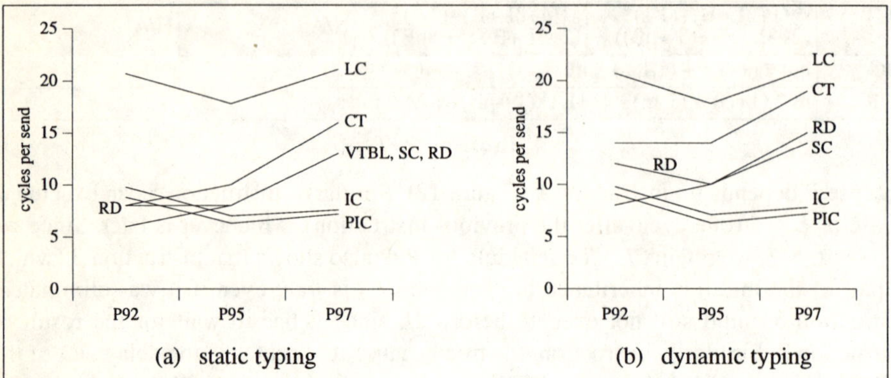

Figure 13. Performance of dispatch mechanisms (single inheritance)

Figure 13a shows the execution time (in processor cycles) of all dispatch implementations on the three processor models, assuming static typing and single inheritance. Not surprisingly, all techniques improve significantly upon lookup caching (LC) since LC has to compute a hash function during dispatch. The performance of the other dispatch mechanisms is fairly similar, especially on P95 which models current hardware. VTBL and SC are identical for all processors; RD and VTBL are identical for all but the P92 processor. Among these techniques, no clear winner emerges since their relative ranking depends on the processor implementation. For example, on P92 VTBL performs best and IC worst, whereas on P97 IC is best and VTBL is worst. (Section 5.4 will examine processor influence in detail.) For dynamic typing, the picture is qualitatively the same (Figure 13b).

5.3 Cost of multiple inheritance and dynamic typing

A closer look at Tables 4 to 6 and Figure 13 shows that supporting dynamic typing is surprisingly cheap for all dispatch methods, especially on superscalar processors like P95 and P97. In several cases (LC, IC, PIC), dynamic typing incurs no overhead at all. For the other techniques, the overhead is still low since the additional instructions can be scheduled to fit in instruction issue slots that would otherwise go unused. Typical overheads are two cycles per dispatch on P95 and one or two cycles on P97. Thus, on superscalar processors dynamic typing does not significantly increase dispatch cost.

The cost of supporting multiple inheritance is even lower. On P97, no technique incurs additional overhead for multiple inheritance, and only LC, RD, and IC incur a one-cycle overhead on P95. (However, recall that we have simplified the discussion of VTBL for

C++ by ignoring virtual base classes. Using virtual base classes can significantly increase dispatch cost in VTBL.)

Since the performance variations between the four scenarios are so small and do not qualitatively change the situation, we will only discuss the case using static typing and single inheritance in the remainder of the paper. The data for the other variations can be obtained from Table A-3 in the Appendix. (Of course, dynamic typing and multiple inheritance can affect other aspects of dispatch implementation; these will be discussed in section 6).

5.4 Influence of processor implementation

According to Figure 13, the cost (in cycles) of many dispatch techniques drops when moving from a scalar processor like P92 to a superscalar implementation like P95. Apparently, all techniques can take advantage of the instruction-level parallelism present in P95. However, when moving to the more aggressively superscalar P97 processor, dispatch cost *rises* for many dispatch techniques instead of falling further as one would expect.[1]

Figure 14a shows that the culprit is the penalty for mispredicted branches. It rises from 3 cycles in P95 to 6 cycles in P97 because the latter processor has a deeper pipeline in order to achieve a higher clock rate and thus better overall performance [HP90]. Except for the inline caching variants (IC and PIC), all techniques have at least one unpredictable branch even in the best case, and thus their cost increases with the cost of a branch misprediction. IC's cost increases only slowly because it has no unpredicted branch in the hit case, so that it suffers from the increased branch miss penalty only in the case of a inline cache miss. PIC's cost also increases slowly since monomorphic calls are handled just as in IC, and even for polymorphic sends its branches remain relatively predictable.

Based on this data, it appears that IC and PIC are attractive dispatch techniques, especially since they handle dynamically-typed languages as efficiently as statically-

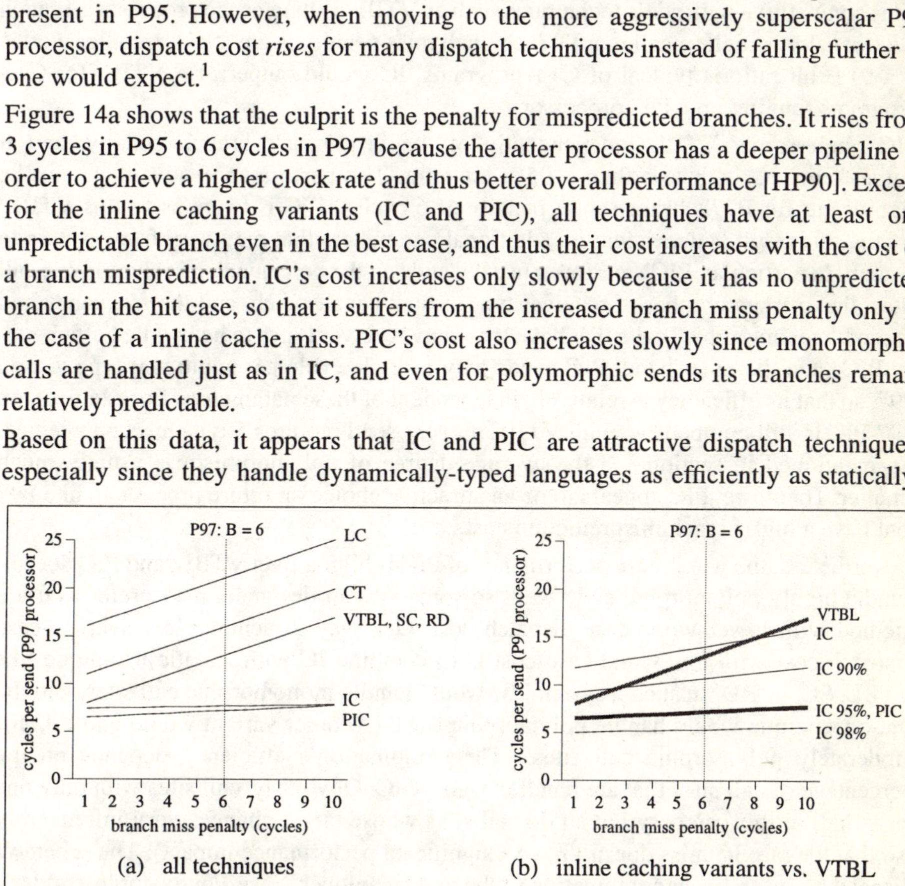

Figure 14. Influence of branch misprediction penalty on dispatch cost in P97

[1] Even though the number of cycles per dispatch increases, dispatch time will decrease since P97 will operate at a higher clock frequency. Thus, while the dispatch cost rises relative to the cost of other operations, its absolute performance still increases.

typed languages. However, one must be careful when generalizing this data since the performance of IC and PIC depends on several parameters. In particular, the dispatch cost of IC and PIC is variable—unlike most of the table-based techniques such as VTBL, the number of instructions per dispatch is not constant. Instead, dispatch cost is a function of program behavior: different programs will see different dispatch costs if their polymorphism characteristics (and thus their inline cache hit ratios) vary. The data presented so far assume a hit ratio of 95% which is typical for Smalltalk programs [Ung87] but may not represent other systems. For example, Calder et al. [CG94] report inline cache hit ratios for C++ programs that vary between 74% and 100%, with an average of 91%. Thus, the performance characteristics of IC and PIC deserve a closer investigation.

Figure 14b compares VTBL with PIC and IC for several inline cache miss ratios. As expected, IC's cost increases with decreasing hit ratio. If the hit ratio is 90% or better, IC is competitive with static techniques such as VTBL as long as the processor's branch miss penalty is high (recall that P97's branch miss penalty is 6 cycles). In other words, if a 91% hit ratio is typical of C++ programs, IC would outperform VTBL for C++ programs running on a P97 processor.

PIC outperforms VTBL independently of the processor's branch penalty, and it outperforms IC with less than a 95% hit ratio. The performance advantage can be significant: for P97's branch miss penalty of 6 cycles, PIC is twice as fast as VTBL. Again, this result is dependent on additional parameters that may vary from system to system. In particular, PIC's performance depends on the percentage of polymorphic call sites, the average number of receiver types tested per dispatch, and the frequency and cost of "megamorphic" calls that have too many receiver types to be handled efficiently by PICs. On the other hand, PIC needs only a single cycle per additional type test on P97, so that its efficiency is relatively independent of these parameters. For example, on P97 PIC is still competitive with VTBL if every send requires 5 type tests on average. As mentioned in section 3.3, the average degree of polymorphism is usually much smaller. Therefore, PIC appears to be an attractive choice on future processors like P97 that have a high branch misprediction cost.

Nevertheless, the worst-case performance of PIC is higher than VTBL, and PIC doesn't handle highly polymorphic code well, so some system designers may prefer to use a method with lower worst-case dispatch cost. One way to achieve low average-case dispatch cost with low worst-case cost is to combine IC with a static technique like VTBL, SC, or RD. In such a system, IC would handle monomorphic call sites, and the static technique would handle polymorphic sites. (Another variant would add PIC for moderately polymorphic call sites.) The combination's efficiency depends on the percentage of call sites that are handled well by IC. Obviously, call sites with only one target fall in this category but so do call sites whose target changes very infrequently (so that the rare IC miss doesn't have a significant performance impact). The scheme's dispatch cost is a linear combination of the two techniques' cost. For example, Calder's data [CG94] suggest that at least 66% of all virtual calls in C++ could be handled without misses by IC, reducing dispatch cost on P97 from 13 cycles for a pure VTBL implementation to $13 * 0.34 + 4 * 0.66 = 5.6$ cycles for VTBL+IC. In reality, the performance gain might be even higher since calls from call sites incurring very few misses could also be handled by IC. Even though this data is by no means conclusive, the potential gain in dispatch performance suggests that implementors should include such hybrid dispatch schemes in their list of dispatch mechanisms to evaluate.

5.5 Limitations

The above analysis leaves a number of issues unexplored. Three issues are particularly important: cache behavior, application code surrounding the dispatch sequence, and hardware prediction of indirect branches.

We do not consider memory hierarchy effects (cache misses); all results assume that memory references will always hit the first level memory cache. If all dispatch techniques have similar locality of reference, this assumption should not distort the results. However, without thorough benchmarking it remains unsubstantiated.

Application instructions surrounding the dispatch sequence (e.g., instructions for parameter passing) can be scheduled to fit in the "holes" of the dispatch code, lowering the overall execution time, and thus effectively lowering dispatch overhead. Therefore, measuring dispatch cost in isolation (as done in this study) may overestimate the true cost of dispatch techniques. Unfortunately, the effect of co-scheduling application code with dispatch code depends on the nature of the application code and thus is hard to determine. Furthermore, the average basic block length (and thus the number of instructions readily available to be scheduled with the call) is quite small, usually between five and six [HP90]. On superscalar processors (especially on P97) most dispatch sequences have plenty of "holes" to accommodate that number of instructions. Thus, we assume that most techniques would benefit from co-scheduled application code to roughly the same extent.

A branch target buffer (BTB) [HP90] allows hardware to predict indirect calls by storing the target address of the previous call, similar to inline caching. This study assumes that processors do not use BTBs; for most current RISC processors, this assumption holds because BTBs are relatively expensive (since they have to store the full target address, not just a few prediction bits) and because indirect calls are very infrequent in procedural programs.[1] However, future processors like P97 might incorporate BTBs since they will have enough transistors available to accommodate a reasonably-sized BTB; some processors (most notably, Intel's Pentium processor and its successor P6) have small BTBs today. Interestingly, BTBs behave like inline caches—they work well for monomorphic call sites but badly for highly polymorphic call sites. For example, the performance of VTBL on such a processor would be similar to the VTBL+IC scheme discussed above. The impact of BTBs on dispatch performance can be estimated by reducing the value of branch penalty B in the formulas of Tables 5 and 6, but the extent of the reduction depends on the BTB miss ratio (i.e., inline cache miss ratio) of the application.

[1] Procedure returns are the exception, but these can be handled more efficiently by a return address prediction buffer [Gw94].

6 Other considerations

Besides the actual speed of message sends, other considerations influence the choice between dispatch techniques. This section discusses the memory costs of dispatch schemes, and how amenable the schemes are to incremental change.

6.1 Memory cost

The space overhead of method dispatch falls into two categories: program code and dispatch data structures. Code overhead consists of the instructions required at call sites and in method prologues; stub routines (PIC & CT) are counted towards the data structure cost. The analysis below ignores per-instance memory costs (such as keeping a type field in each instance), although such costs can possibly dominate all other costs (e.g., if more than one VTBL pointer is needed for a class with a million instances). The space analysis uses the parameters shown in Table 3. Most parameter values are taken

Variable	Value	Comments
m	8,540	total number of methods; from Smalltalk
c	35,042	total number of call sites; from Smalltalk
M	178,264	total number of valid (receiver class, selector) pairs; from Smalltalk
e	4096	entries in LC lookup cache
O_{DTS}	133%	DTS overhead factor = #total entries / #non-empty entries; from Smalltalk
O_{SC}	175%	single inheritance overhead factor for SC; lower bound, from Smalltalk
O_{RD}	101%	single inheritance overhead factor for RD; from [DH95]
O_{CT}	15%	single inheritance compression rate for CT [VH94]
P_{SC}	no data	multiple inheritance overhead factor for SC[a]
P_{RD}	no data	multiple inheritance overhead factor for RD[b]
P_{VTBL}	no data	multiple inheritance overhead factor for CT[c]
k	3.2	average number of cases in a PIC stub; from SELF [Höl94]
f	7.2%	polymorphic call sites, as a fraction of total; from SELF [Höl94]
e	3.49	average number of functions in an overloaded entry (CT)
n	0.07%	overloaded entries, as fraction of total (CT)

Table 7. Parameters used for space cost analysis

[a] As shown in [AR92], the use of multiple inheritance introduces conflicts between selector colors that are hard to deal with and that substantially increase the overhead.
[b] Tables are harder to fit together because multiple inheritance causes more irregular empty regions to appear.
[c] Every time a class inherits from more than one superclass, overridden method entries are stored together with the appropriate delta's. This overhead depends entirely on the way multiple inheritance is used and is not quantifiable without appropriate code metrics.

from the ParcPlace Visualworks 1.0 Smalltalk system and thus model a fairly large application. For the multiple inheritance overhead we do not give typical values because there are none. The few samples in which multiple inheritance is extensively used in [DH95] show that the overhead varies much more than with single inheritance hierarchies (between 215% and 330% for VTBL), and that it is extremely dependent on how frequently MI is used. Therefore we do not give example space data for multiple inheritance. However, it is obvious in [DH95] that $P_{RD} < P_{VTBL} < P_{SC}$ for samples with extensive MI. Table 8 contains formulas for computing the space cost if the overhead is known.

Our analysis assumes that dispatch sequences are compiled in-line; the cost per call site is taken from the code sequences in Table A-2 in the Appendix.[1] Code for secondary techniques (like LC for IC) is not counted since it only appears once and thus should be negligible. Table 8 shows the space cost computation for all techniques. In the formulas, the symbols *D* and *C* refer to data and code cost; D_{LC}, for instance, refers to the data structure cost of LC in *the same column.*

	single inheritance				multiple inheritance			
	static typing		dynamic typing		static typing		dynamic typing	
	code	data	code	data	code	data	code	data
DTS	2c[a]	2m*O_{DTS}	same as SI-ST		same as SI-ST[b]		same as MI-ST	
LC	14c	3e+D_{DTS}	same as SI-ST		17c	4e+D_{DTS}	same as MI-ST	
IC	3c+2m	D_{LC}	same as SI-ST		5c+3m	D_{LC}	same as MI-ST	
PIC	3c+2m	3kfc+D_{LC}	same as SI-ST		5c+3m	4kfc+D_{LC}	same as MI-ST	
VTBL	2c	M	N/A		4c	2M*P_{VTBL}	N/A	
SC	2c	M*O_{SC}	3c+2m	M*O_{SC}	4c+m	2M*P_{SC}	5c+3m	2M*P_{SC}
RD	5c	M*O_{RD}	5c+4m	M*O_{RD}	7c+m	2M*P_{RD}	7c+5m	2M*P_{RD}
CT	4c	M*O_{CT} *(1+en)	4c+7m	M*O_{CT} *(1+en)	N/A			

Table 8. Formulas for approximate space cost (in words)

[a] Two instructions (sethi and setlo) to pass the selector to the lookup routine that actually implements the dispatch table search.

[b] Actually, there is a small overhead involved. Every class needs to store the representational offsets of its ancestors. This is much cheaper than storing an offset for every method understood.

Figure 15 shows the space costs for single inheritance versions of the dispatch techniques, using the classes and methods of the ParcPlace Visualworks 1.0 Smalltalk system as an example. Surprisingly, the code space overhead dominates the overall space cost for six of the eight techniques. Most of that overhead consists of the per-call dispatch code sequence. Much of the literature has been concentrated on the size of dispatch tables, treating call code overhead as equivalent among different techniques ([Ung87] is a notable exception). As demonstrated by the above data, minimizing dispatch tables may not reduce the overall space cost if it lengthens the calling sequence, especially in languages with a high density of message sends, like Smalltalk.[2] Code size can be reduced for most techniques by moving some instructions from the caller to the callee, but only at the expense of a slower dispatch. (LC's code size requirements could be dramatically reduced by doing the lookup out-of-line.)

The size of the immediate field in an instruction significantly impacts the code cost of SC, RD, and CT. This study assumes a 13-bit signed immediate field, limiting the range

[1] We choose not to include the call instruction in each dispatch sequence in the space cost since this instruction is required for direct function calls as well. To include the call instructions, just add c to each entry in Table 8.

[2] Increased code size can also impair execution performance by causing more instruction cache misses.

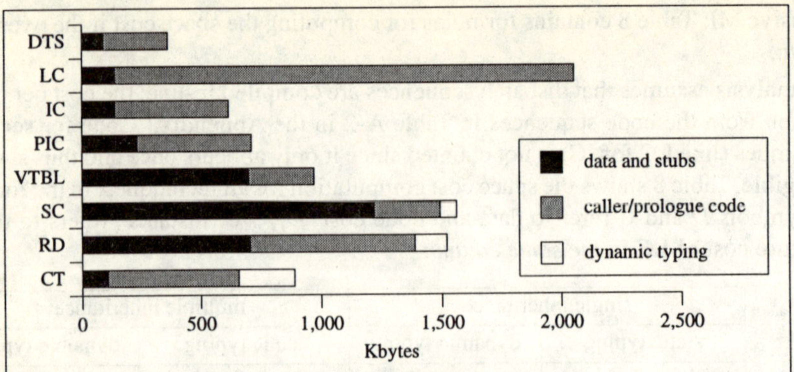

Figure 15. Space overhead for the Smalltalk system

of immediates to -4096..4095.[1] The Smalltalk system measured had 5087 selectors, and thus the selector number fits into an immediate. SC needs only one instruction to load the selector code into a register (see Table A-2), but RD takes two instructions for the same action because the selector offset needs two more bits (both zero) to address a word-aligned method. The same phenomenon increases the method prologue overhead in both RD and CT.[2] In RD, the reduction in data structure size relative to SC is almost offset by a corresponding increase in code size. The data in Figure 15 are thus relative to the processor architecture. For example, for an architecture with larger immediates (or for smaller applications), CT's space advantage over VTBL would double. Of course, the data also depends on application characteristics such as the proportion of call sites versus number of classes, selectors, and methods.

Given these admonitions, IC and PIC apparently combine excellent average speed with low space overhead. The bounded lookup time of SC and RD is paid for with twice as much memory; VTBL is about one third smaller than those two. CT's small data structure size is offset by its code cost.

VTBL, RD, and SC require significantly more data space than DTS because they duplicate information. Each class stores all the messages it *understands*, instead of all the messages it *defines*. For example, in the Smalltalk system a class inherits 20 methods for each one it defines [Dri93b], so the number of entries stored in the class' dispatch table increases by a factor of 20.

Dynamic typing makes a relatively small difference in space cost. Dynamic techniques have no extra overhead because each dispatch already contains a run-time check to test for the cache hit. Static techniques[3] perform the run-time type check in the method prologue, so the overhead grows linearly with the number of defined methods, which is much smaller than the number of call sites.

---

1 The size of immediates varies from architecture to architecture: for example, SPARC has 13 bits, Alpha 8 bits, and MIPS 16 bits.

2 Here the crucial quantity is the number of bits necessary to represent a *cid* (16 bits for the Smalltalk example). For the same reason, CT's dynamic typing cost is higher.

3 Excluding VTBL, which only works for statically-typed languages.

6.2 Other aspects

The choice of a dispatch technique is influenced by considerations other than space cost and execution speed. A detailed discussion of these factors is beyond the scope of this paper, so we will only briefly mention some of them.

- *Responsiveness.* Some static techniques are less suitable for interactive programming environments that demand a high level or responsiveness (i.e., immediate feedback to programming changes). Most static techniques need to recompute some data structures after a programming change. For example, introducing a new method name forces VTBL to rearrange the dispatch table of the affected class and all its subclasses. SC, RD and CT even have to completely recompute their tables from scratch (except in rare cases, e.g., if the new method fits into an empty slot in the dispatch table). For the Smalltalk system, this recomputation can take hours for SC, tens of seconds for RD, and seconds for CT.
- *Support for run-time extensibility.* Many static techniques (e.g., SC, RD, CT) presume knowledge of the entire program, i.e., knowledge of all classes and methods. With dynamic link libraries, the complete set of classes and methods is not known until run time since the classes contained in dynamic libraries are unknown until they are loaded at program start-up time or later during the execution of the program. Thus, these techniques have to recompute the dispatch data structures each time a new library is dynamically loaded.
- *Sharing code pages.* Some operating systems (e.g., Unix) allow processes executing the same program to share the memory pages containing the program's code. With shared code pages, overall memory usage is reduced since only one copy of the program (or shared library) need be in memory even if it is used concurrently by many different users. For code to be shared, most operating systems require the code pages to be read-only, thus disallowing techniques that modify program code on-the-fly (e.g., IC and PIC).

Many of the dispatch techniques discussed here can be modified to address problems such as those outlined above. For example, static techniques can be made more incremental by introducing extra levels of indirection at run-time (e.g., by loading the selector number rather than embedding it in the code as a constant), usually at a loss in dispatch performance. For this study, only the simplest and fastest version of each technique was considered, but any variant can be analyzed using the same evaluation methodology.

7 Related work

Rose [Ros88] analyzes dispatch performance for a number of table-based techniques, assuming a RISC architecture and a scalar processor. The analysis included both dispatch and tag checking code sequences. The study considers some architecture-related performance aspects such as the limited range of immediates in instructions. Other studies have analyzed the performance of one or two dispatch sequences. For example, Ungar [Ung87] analyzes the performance of IC, LC, and no caching on SOAR, a RISC-processor designed to run Smalltalk. Driesen [Dri93b] analyzes algorithmic issues of a number of dispatch techniques for dynamically-typed languages, but without taking processor architecture into account. Hölzle et al. [HCU91] compare IC and PIC for the SELF system running on a scalar SPARC processor. Milton and Schmidt [MS94] compare the performance of VTBL-like techniques for Sather. None of these studies takes superscalar processors into account.

Calder et al. [CG94] discuss branch misprediction penalties for indirect function calls in C++. Their measurements of several C++ programs indicate that inline caching might be effective for many C++ programs (although measurements by Garrett et al. [G+94] are somewhat less optimistic). Calder et al. propose to improve performance with "if-conversion," an inline cache with a statically determined target. For each call site the address of the most frequently called function is determined from execution profiles.

We have considered single dispatch only; multiple dispatch techniques are discussed in [KR90] and [AGS94]. However, singly-dispatched calls are so frequent even in systems offering multiple dispatch that implementations usually special-case these calls. Ingalls [Ing86] shows how to implement multiple dispatch with a sequence of single dispatch, but such implementations may not be optimal [AGS94].

Dispatch overhead can also be reduced by eliminating dispatches (rather than just making them fast). For example, the SELF-93 system inlines 95% of all dispatches [Höl94] with compiler optimizations such as customization [CUL89] and type feedback [HU94]. Similarly, concrete type inference [OPS92, VHU92, APS93, PC94, AH95] or link-time optimizations [App88, Fer95] can determine the concrete receiver types of calls, possibly eliminating dynamic dispatch for many sends.

8 Conclusions

We have evaluated the dispatch cost of a range of dispatch mechanisms, taking into account the performance characteristics of modern pipelined superscalar microprocessors. On such processors, objectively evaluating performance is difficult since the cost of each instruction depends on surrounding instructions and the cost of branches depends on dynamic branch prediction. In particular, some instructions may be "free" because they can be executed in parallel with other instructions, and unpredictable conditional branches as well as indirect branches are expensive (and likely to become more expensive in the future). On superscalar architectures, counting instructions to estimate performance is highly misleading. We have studied dispatch performance on three processor models designed to represent the past (1992), present (1995), and future (1997) state of the art in processor implementation.

We have analyzed the run-time performance of dispatch mechanisms as a function of processor characteristics such as branch latency and superscalar instruction issue, and as a function of system parameters such as the average degree of polymorphism in application code. The resulting formulas allow dispatch performance to be computed for a wide range of possible (future) processors and systems. In addition, we also present formulas for computing the space cost of the various dispatch techniques. Our study has produced several results:

- The relative performance of dispatch mechanisms varies strongly with processor implementation. Whereas some mechanisms become relatively more expensive (in terms of cycles per dispatch) on more aggressively superscalar processors, others become less expensive. No single dispatch mechanism performs best on all three processor models.

- Mechanisms employing indirect branches (i.e., all table-based techniques) may not perform well on current and future hardware since indirect branches incur multi-cycle pipeline stalls, unless a branch target buffer is present. Inline caching variants pipeline very well and do not incur such stalls. On deeply pipelined superscalar processors like the P97, inline caching techniques may substantially outperform even the most efficient table-based techniques.
- Hybrid techniques combining inline caching with a table-based method may offer both excellent average dispatch cost as well as a low worst-case dispatch cost.
- On superscalar processors, the additional cost of supporting dynamic typing or multiple inheritance is small (often zero) because the few additional instructions usually fit into otherwise unused instruction issue slots.
- Instructions (in particular, per-call code) can contribute significantly to the overall space requirements of message dispatch. In our example system, many techniques spend more memory on dispatch code sequences than on dispatch data structures. Thus, minimizing dispatch table size may not always be the most effective way to minimize the overall space cost, and may in some cases even increase the overall space cost.

Even though selecting the best dispatch mechanism for a particular system is still difficult since it involves many factors, the data presented here should allow dispatch speed and space costs to be accurately estimated for a wide range of systems. Therefore, we hope that this study will be helpful to system implementors who need to choose the dispatch mechanism best suited to their needs.

Acknowledgments. The authors would like to thank Lars Bak, Kris De Volder, Brian T. Lewis, Ole-Lehrmann Madsen, Patrick Steyaert, and Mario Wolczko for their comments on earlier versions of this draft.

9 References

[APS93] Ole Agesen, Jens Palsberg, and Michael I. Schwartzbach. Type Inference of SELF: Analysis of Objects with Dynamic and Multiple Inheritance. In *ECOOP '93 Conference Proceedings*, p. 247-267. Kaiserslautern, Germany, July 1993.

[AH95] Ole Agesen and Urs Hölzle. *Type Feedback vs. Concrete Type Inference: A Comparison of Optimization Techniques for Object-Oriented Languages*. Technical Report TRCS 95-04, Department of Computer Science, UCSB, March 1995.

[AGS94] Eric Amiel, Olivier Gruber, and Eric Simon. Optimizing Multi-Method Dispatch Using Compressed Dispatch Tables. In *OOPSLA '94 Conference Proceedings*, pp. 244-258, October 1994. Published as SIGPLAN Notices 29(10), October 1994.

[AR92] P. André and J.-C. Royer. Optimizing Method Search with Lookup Caches and Incremental Coloring. *OOPSLA '92 Conference Proceedings*, Vancouver, Canada, October 1992. Published as SIGPLAN Notices 27(10), October 1992.

[App88] Apple Computer, Inc. *Object Pascal User's Manual*. Cupertino, 1988.

[CG94] Brad Calder and Dirk Grunwald. Reducing Indirect Function Call Overhead in C++ Programs. In *21st Annual ACM Symposium on Principles of Programming Languages*, p. 397-408, January 1994.

[CUL89] Craig Chambers, David Ungar, and Elgin Lee. An Efficient Implementation of SELF, a Dynamically-Typed Object-Oriented Language Based on Prototypes. In *OOPSLA '89 Conference Proceedings*, p. 49-70, New Orleans, LA, October 1989. Published as SIGPLAN Notices 24(10), October 1989.

[CU+91] Craig Chambers, David Ungar, Bay-Wei Chang, and Urs Hölzle. Parents are Shared Parts: Inheritance and Encapsulation in SELF. *Lisp and Symbolic Computation* 4(3), Kluwer Academic Publishers, June 1991.

[CPL83] T. Conroy and E. Pelegri-Llopart. An Assessment of Method-Lookup Caches for Smalltalk-80 Implementations. In [GR83].

[Cy90] Cypress Semiconductors. *CY7C601 SPARC processor*, 1990.

[DDH84] P. Dencker, K. Dürre, and J. Heuft. Optimization of Parser Tables for Portable Compilers. *TOPLAS* 6(4):546-572, 1984.

[DH95] Karel Driesen, Urs Hölzle. Minimizing Row Displacement Dispatch Tables. Technical Report TRCS 95-05, Department of Computer Science, UCSB, March 1995.

[DM73] O.-J. Dahl and B. Myrhaug. *Simula Implementation Guide*. Publication S47, Norwegian Computing Center, Oslo, March 1973.

[DS84] L. Peter Deutsch and Alan Schiffman. Efficient Implementation of the Smalltalk-80 System. *Proceedings of the 11th Symposium on the Principles of Programming Languages*, Salt Lake City, UT, 1984.

[D+89] R. Dixon, T. McKee, P. Schweitzer, and M. Vaughan. A Fast Method Dispatcher for Compiled Languages with Multiple Inheritance. *OOPSLA '89 Conference Proceedings*, pp. 211-214, New Orleans, LA, October 1989. Published as SIGPLAN Notices 24(10), October 1989.

[Dri93a] Karel Driesen. Selector Table Indexing and Sparse Arrays. *OOPSLA '93 Conference Proceedings*, p. 259-270, Washington, D.C., 1993. Published as SIGPLAN Notices 28(10), September 1993.

[Dri93b] Karel Driesen. *Method Lookup Strategies in Dynamically-Typed Object-Oriented Programming Languages*. Master's Thesis, Vrije Universiteit Brussel, 1993.

[Dus89] P. Dussud. TICLOS: An implementation of CLOS for the Explorer Family. *OOPSLA '89 Conference Proceedings*, pp. 215-220, New Orleans, LA, October 1989. Published as SIGPLAN Notices 24(10), October 1989.

[ES90] Margaret A. Ellis and Bjarne Stroustrup. *The Annotated C++ Reference Manual*. Addison-Wesley, Reading, MA, 1990.

[Fer95] Mary F. Fernandez. Simple and effective link-time optimization of Modula-3 programs. To appear in *Proceedings of the SIGPLAN '95 Conference on Programming Language Design and Implementation*, 1995.

[G+94] Charles D. Garrett, Jeffrey Dean, David Grove, and Craig Chambers. *Measurement and Application of Dynamic Receiver Class Distributions*. Technical Report CSE-TR-94-03-05, University of Washington, February 1994.

[GR83] Adele Goldberg and David Robson. *Smalltalk-80: The Language and its Implementation*. Second Edition, Addison-Wesley, Reading, MA, 1985.

[Gw94] Linley Gwennap. Digital leads the pack with 21164. *Microprocessor Report* 8(12), September 12, 1994.

[HP90] John L. Hennessy and David A. Patterson. *Computer Architecture: A Quantitative Approach.* Morgan Kaufmann Publishers Inc. 1990.

[HCU91] Urs Hölzle, Craig Chambers, and David Ungar. Optimizing Dynamically-Typed Object-Oriented Languages with Polymorphic Inline Caches. In *ECOOP '91 Conference Proceedings*, Geneva, 1991. Published as Springer Verlag Lecture Notes in Computer Science 512, Springer Verlag, Berlin, 1991.

[HU94] Urs Hölzle and David Ungar. Optimizing dynamically-dispatched calls with run-time type feedback. In *PLDI '94 Conference Proceedings*, pp. 326-335, Orlando, FL, June 1994. Published as SIGPLAN Notices 29(6), June 1994.

[Höl94] Urs Hölzle. *Adaptive Optimization for Self: Reconciling High Performance with Exploratory Programming.* Ph.D. Thesis, Technical Report STAN-CS-TR-94-1520, Department of Computer Science, Stanford University, 1994.

[Ing86] Daniel H. Ingalls. A simple technique for handling multiple polymorphism. *OOPSLA '86 Conference Proceedings*, p. 347-349, Portland, OR., 1986. Published as SIGPLAN Notices 21(11), November 1986.

[KR90] Gregor Kiczales and Louis Rodriguez. Efficient Method Dispatch in PCL. *Proc. ACM Conference on Lisp and Functional Programming*, 1990. Also in [Pae93].

[Kra83] Glenn Krasner. *Smalltalk-80: Bits of History, Words of Advice.* Addison-Wesley, Reading, MA, 1983.

[Kro85] Stein Krogdahl. Multiple inheritance in Simula-like languages. *BIT* 25, p. 318-326, 1985.

[MS94] S. Milton and Heinz W. Schmidt. *Dynamic Dispatch in Object-Oriented Languages.* Technical Report TR-CS-94-02, The Australian National University, Canberra, January 1994.

[M92] MIPS Inc. *R4000* Technical Brief, 1992.

[M94] MIPS Inc. *R10000* Technical Brief, September 1994.

[OPS92] Nicholas Oxhøy, Jens Palsberg, and Michael I. Schwartzbach. Making Type Inference Practical. In *ECOOP '92 Conference Proceedings*, p. 329-349, Utrecht, The Netherlands, June/July 1992

[Pae93] Andreas Paepcke (ed.). *Object-Oriented Programming: The CLOS Perspective*, MIT Press, 1993.

[PC94] John Plevyak and Andrew A. Chien. Precise concrete type inference for object-oriented languages. In *OOPSLA '94 Conference Proceedings*, pp. 324-340, October 1994. Published as SIGPLAN Notices 29(10), October 1994.

[PW90] William Pugh and Grant Weddell. Two-Directional Record Layout for Multiple Inheritance. In *Proceedings of the SIGPLAN '90 Conference on Programming Language Design and Implementation*, p. 85-91, White Plains, NY, June, 1990. Published as SIGPLAN Notices 25(6), June 1990.

[Ros88] John Rose. Fast Dispatch Mechanisms for Stock Hardware. *OOPSLA'88 Conference Proceedings*, p. 27-35, San Diego, CA, November 1988. Published as SIGPLAN Notices 23(11), November 1988.

[UP83] David Ungar and David Patterson. Berkeley Smalltalk: Who Knows Where the Time Goes? In [GR83].

[Ung87] David Ungar. *The Design and Evaluation of a High-Performance Smalltalk System.* MIT Press, Cambridge, MA, 1987.

[UP87] David Ungar and David Patterson. What Price Smalltalk? In *IEEE Computer* 20(1), January 1987.

[VH94] Jan Vitek and R. N. Horspool. Taming Message Passing: Efficient Method Look-Up for Dynamically-Typed Languages. In *ECOOP '94 Conference Proceedings*, Bologna, Italy, 1994.

[VH95] Jan Vitek and R.N. Horspool, *Fast Constant-Time Type Inclusion Tests*, Unpublished manuscript, 1995.

[Vit95] Jan Vitek. *Compact Dispatch Tables for Dynamically-Typed Object-Oriented Languages.* M.S. Thesis, University of Victoria, B.C., forthcoming.

[VHU92] Jan Vitek, R. N. Horspool, and J. Uhl. Compile-time analysis of object-oriented programs. *Proc. CC'92, 4th International Conference on Compiler Construction*, pp. 236-250, Paderborn, Germany, Springer-Verlag, 1992.

Appendix A. Detailed data

R1	a register (any argument without #)
#immediate	an immediate value (prefix #)
load [R1+#imm], R2	load the word in memory location R1+#imm to register R2
store R1,[R2+#imm]	store the word in register R1 into memory location R2+#imm
setlo #imm, R1	set the least significant part of register R1 to #imm, the rest to 0
sethi #imm, R1	set the most significant part of R1 to #imm[a]
xor R1, R2, R3	bit-wise xor on register R1 and R2[b]. Result is put in R3
and R1, R2, R3	bit-wise and on register R1 and R2. Result is put in R3
add R1, R2, R3	add register R1 to R2 and put result in R3
call R1	jump to address in R1 (can also be immediate), saves return address
comp R1, R2	compare value in register R1 with R2 (R2 can be immediate)
bne #imm	if last compare is not equal, jump to #imm[c]
jump R1	jump to address in R1 (can also be immediate)

Table A-1. Abstract instruction set for Table A-2

[a] sethi always occurs after a setlo in our code. We use the same string to indicate the upper and lower part of #imm, to indicate which instructions depend on the bit length of a particular value.
[b] Operands of arithmetic and logic instructions can be immediates, if the bit length permits.
[c] PC-relative. We do not go into such details, unless they affect code size and/or speed.

SC: Selector Coloring	load [object + #tableOffset], table *store adjusted, [stackptr + #deltaOffset]* load [table + #colorOffset], method *load [table + #deltaOffset], delta* **setlo #selector, selector** call method **comp selector, #methSelector** *add delta, object, adjusted* **bne #messageNotUnderstood**	IC: Inline Caching	load [object + #classOffset], actualClass setlo #class, predictedClass *store adjusted, [stackptr + #deltaOffset]* *add object, #delta, adjusted* call #method[a] comp actualClass, predictedClass bne #inlineCacheMiss
RD: Row Displacement	load [object + #tableOffset], table setlo #selector, selector sethi #selector, selector[b] add table, selector, table load [table], method *store adjusted, [stackptr + #deltaOffset]* *load [table + #deltaOffset], delta* call method **sethi #methSelector, thisSelector** **setlo #methSelector, thisSelector** **comp selector, thisSelector** *add delta, object, adjusted* **bne #messageNotUnderstood**	PIC: Polymorphic Inline Caching	load [object + #classOffset], actualClass comp actualclass, #predictedClass1 *store adjusted, [stackptr + #deltaOffset]* *add object, #delta1, adjusted* call #PIC_nnn[a] bne #2nd jump #method1 2nd: *add object, #delta2, adjusted* comp actualClass, #predictedClass2 bne #3rd jump #method2 3rd: ... last: jump #PICmiss

Table A-2. Instruction sequences

LC: Lookup Caching	load [object + #classOffset], class setlo #cacheAddr, cache sethi #cacheAddr, cache setlo #selectorCode, selector xor class, selector, index and index, #mask, index add cache, index, cache load [cache], cacheClass *store adjusted, [stackptr + #deltaOffset]*[c] load [cache + 4], cacheSelector load [cache + 8], cacheTarget *load [cache + 12], delta* comp class, cacheClass bne #miss comp selector, cacheSelector bne #miss *add delta, object, adjusted* call cacheTarget
VTBL	load [object + #tableOffset], table load [table + #selectorOffset], method *load [table + #deltaOffset], delta* *add object, delta, object* call method (works only for statically-typed languages)
CT: Compact selector-indexed Tables	load [object + #classOffset], class load [class + #tableOffset], table load [class + #cidOffset], cid load [table + #selector], method call method single-implementation (method prologue): **setlo #mask, mask** **sethi #mask, mask** **and mask, cid, cid** **setlo #thisClass, thisClass** **sethi #thisClass, thisClass** **comp thisClass, cid** **bne #messageNotUnderstood** overloaded: setlo #mask1, mask1 sethi #mask1, mask1 and mask1, cid, temp setlo #cid1, cid1 sethi #cid1, cid1 comp cid1, temp bne #2nd jump #method1 2nd: setlo #mask2, mask2 sethi #mask2, mask2 and mask2, cid, temp setlo #cid2, cid2 sethi #cid2, cid2 comp cid2, temp bne #3nd jump #method2 3rd: ... last: jump #messageNotUnderstood

Table A-2. Instruction sequences

[a] The message selector is placed right after this call instruction. This doesn't have any effect on speed, but does increase the code size by one word.

[b] selector offset is unlikely to fit in immediate field of instructions in large applications (see text).

[c] In all code sequences the adjusted receiver address is saved before a call (except in VTBL where it can be reconstructed because every class/superclass combination has its own table with deltas). Actually, this store is only necessary if instance variables can be accessed after the call. Thus, it may be optimized away by the compiler. We do not show the corresponding load, because it is likely to be hidden in the code following the call (on a superscalar processor).

	P92				P95				P97			
	single inh.		multiple inh.		single inh.		multiple inh.		single inh.		multiple inh.	
	static	dyn.	static	dyn.	static	dyn.	static	dyn.	static	dyn.	static	dyn.
LC	20.7		23.6		17.8		18.8		21.1			
VTBL	6.0	N/A	6.0	N/A	8.0	N/A	8.0	N/A	13.0	N/A	13.0	N/A
SC	6.0	8.0	6.0	9.0	8.0	10.0	8.0	10.0	13.0	14.0	13.0	14.0
RD	8.0	12.0	10.0	12.0	8.0	10.0	9.0	12.0	13.0	15.0	13.0	15.0
CT	8.0	14.0	N/A		10.0	14.0	N/A		16.0	19.0	N/A	
IC	9.8		11.9		7.1		8.1		7.8			
PIC	8.8		10.5		6.3				7.2			

Table A-3. Dispatch timings (in cycles)

	single inheritance					
	static typing			dynamic typing		
	code	data	sum	code	data	sum
DTS	274	89	363	same as SI-ST		363
LC	1,916	137	2,053	same as SI-ST		2,053
IC	477	137	614	same as SI-ST		614
PIC	477	231	708	same as SI-ST		708
VTBL	274	696	970	N/A		
SC	274	1,219	1,493	341	1,219	1,560
RD	684	703	1,387	817	703	1,520
CT	548	107	655	782	107	889

Table A-4. Approximate space cost for dispatch in Smalltalk image (in Kbytes)

Do Object-Oriented Languages Need Special Hardware Support?

Urs Hölzle
David Ungar[1]

Abstract. Previous studies have shown that object-oriented programs have different execution characteristics than procedural programs, and that special object-oriented hardware can improve performance. The results of these studies may no longer hold because compiler optimizations can remove a large fraction of the differences. Our measurements show that SELF programs are more similar to C programs than are C++ programs, even though SELF is much more radically object-oriented than C++ and thus should differ much more from C.
Furthermore, the benefit of tagged arithmetic instructions in the SPARC architecture (originally motivated by Smalltalk and Lisp implementations) appears to be small. Also, special hardware could hardly reduce message dispatch overhead since dispatch sequences are already very short. Two generic hardware features, instruction cache size and data cache write policy, have a much greater impact on performance.

1 Introduction

How much can dedicated hardware improve the performance of object-oriented programs? Previous studies have indicated that special hardware can improve performance, and some implementations of object-oriented systems have relied heavily on hardware support. For example, the Xerox Dorado, for a long time the fastest Smalltalk implementation available, contained microcode support for large portions of the Smalltalk virtual machine [Deu83]. Ungar reported that the SOAR system would have been 26% slower without instructions for tagged arithmetic [Ung87]. Williams and Wolczko argued that software-controlled caching improves the performance and locality of object-oriented systems [WW90].

However, none of the systems previously studied employed compiler optimizations specifically aimed at reducing the overhead of message passing. Thus, the results of these studies may overstate the benefits of special hardware features. For this study, we used the SELF-93 implementation [Höl94]. Two factors make it a good vehicle for measuring the execution characteristics of object-oriented programs:

- SELF [US87], like Smalltalk-80 [GR83], is a very pure object-oriented language. All data are objects, and virtually every operation (e.g., instance variable access, integer addition, or control structures like if and while) involves message sends. The pure

[1] Urs Hölzle, Department of Computer Science, University of California, Santa Barbara, CA 93106, USA; urs@cs.ucsb.edu. David Ungar, Sun Microsystems Laboratories, MTV 29-116, Mountain View, CA 94043, USA; ungar@eng.sun.com.

object-oriented language model also inspires a highly object-oriented programming style that makes frequent use of fine-grained abstractions. Thus, if object-oriented programs behaved differently than procedural programs, SELF programs should exhibit these differences in the extreme, much more than programs written in hybrid object-oriented languages like C++. Conversely, if SELF programs behaved just like C programs despite the extreme object-orientedness of the language (because the compiler can reduce the object-oriented source program to C-like object code), then it should also be possible to implement less extreme object-oriented languages in a similar way, so that their programs also behave like C programs.

- The SELF implementation employs several optimizations aimed specifically at reducing the overhead of dynamic dispatch [CUL89, HCU91, CU91, HU94]. With these optimizations, programs run several times faster than comparable Smalltalk programs (since the fastest Smalltalk system uses only a non-optimizing compiler) and about half as fast as optimized C programs (for the benchmarks mentioned in [CU91] and [HU94]). Since the goal of this study was to determine if object-oriented programs still need special hardware support when compiled with state-of-the-art optimization techniques, the SELF-93 implementation was a good match.

We measured the behavior of several large SELF applications with an instruction-level tracing tool. The results of these measurements indicate that even an extremely object-oriented language like SELF can run efficiently on stock hardware (i.e., without special hardware support) since its execution characteristics are surprisingly similar to those of C programs. SELF's instruction mix is similar to that of the SPEC programs, and features like tagged arithmetic instructions or (hypothetical) instructions supporting message lookup all contribute less than 5% to performance. Overall, instruction and data caches can have a much larger impact on performance than the "OO" hardware features.

In the remainder of the paper, we compare SELF's execution characteristics against the C programs of the SPEC benchmark suite and against a suite of C++ programs. Then, we evaluate one feature present in the SPARC architecture (tagged arithmetic instructions) that has previously been shown to improve the performance of (unoptimized) object-oriented programs. We also investigate if hardware-assisted message lookup could improve performance. Finally, we examine the cache behavior of the programs.

2 Methods

The SELF-93 system compiles into native SPARC code, and thus all our data is for the SPARC V8 architecture [SP92]. The measurements were made with a combination of publicly available tools which were adapted for our purposes: the Shade tracing tool [CK93], the Dinero cache simulator [Hill87], and the SPA SPARC simulator [Irl91]. Our simulator models the Cypress CY7C601 chip, a scalar implementation of the SPARC architecture used in the SPARCstation-2 workstation. To reduce the simulation time, execution times were kept relatively short (25M instructions or less, see appendix). However, in a control experiment we ran three of the programs with larger inputs, resulting in execution times around 500M instructions. The resulting data were so similar that we believe the data presented here accurately reflect the behavior of the SELF system.

The SELF programs used for the study consist of large and medium-sized applications (see Table 1). The programs were written by several different programmers and represent a variety of programming styles and problem domains. Thus, we believe that they represent well the spectrum of typical SELF programs. Except for Richards, no program was written specifically as a benchmark, and most programs were in daily use at the time we took the measurements. As typical procedural programs, we chose the integer part of the SPEC89 benchmark suite which is widely used to evaluate the performance of workstations.[1]

	Benchmark	Size[a]	Description
small benchmarks	DeltaBlue	500	two-way constraint solver developed at the University of Washington
	PrimMaker	1,100	program generating "glue" stubs for external primitives callable by SELF
	Richards	400	simple operating system simulator originally written in BCPL by Martin Richards
large benchmarks	CecilComp	11,500	Cecil-to-C compiler compiling the Fibonacci function (the compiler shares about 80% of its code with the interpreter, CecilInt)
	CecilInt	9,000	interpreter for the Cecil language running a short Cecil test program
	Mango	7,000	automatically generated lexer/parser for ANSI C, parsing a 700-line file
	Typeinf	8,600	type inferencer for SELF
	UI1	15,200	prototype user interface using animation techniques[b]
	UI3	4,000	experimental 3D user interface

Table 1. SELF benchmarks

[a] lines of code (excluding blank lines and comments).
[b] time for both UI1 and UI3 excludes the time spent in graphics primitives

To accurately characterize typical SELF and C workloads with our measurements, we use a suite of large and realistic programs. Unfortunately, the flip side of this emphasis on realistic applications is that such applications are available in one language only. Since the development of each of these programs involved a significant programming effort, it would be impractical to translate the programs into other languages. Furthermore, many of the programs (e.g., the user interfaces or the type inferencer) are too tightly coupled with their environment to be translated easily into other languages. Thus, the only two programs that allow direct comparisons between languages are the two smallest programs, Richards and DeltaBlue, which are available in both C++ and

[1] We did not use the floating-point SPEC Fortran benchmarks because we considered them too specific to the scientific computation domain to be usefully compared against other programs.

SELF. But, being relatively small and having few user-defined data structures, these two benchmarks may not by as indicative of real programs as the other applications.

In fact, when comparing programs written in two languages as radically different as SELF and C, to a certain extent one will always compare apples and oranges. Even when comparing the same program written in both languages, the two programs will not perform exactly the same computation. For example, SELF programs include generic arithmetic, overflow checks for integer addition, bounds checks for array accesses, run-time type checking, closures, and garbage collection. Thus, the comparison will never actually compare the same program; at best, the two programs are similar. One could try to maximize the similarity by writing "C-style" programs in SELF or "SELF-style" programs in C, but such contrived programs would no longer be representative of typical programs.

Since the goal of this study was to determine the level of hardware support needed by typical object-oriented programs, and to measure the difference between object-oriented and procedural programs, we felt that choosing large, representative programs from each domain would result in the most predictive results. In other words, realistic characterization of C and SELF workloads was deemed more important than head-to-head comparison of individual programs.

3 Instruction Usage

When designing an architecture, one of the first tasks is to identify frequent operations and then to optimize their performance. Many previous studies have found the execution characteristics of object-oriented languages to be very different from C. For example, Smalltalk studies [Kra83, Ung87] have shown calls to be much more frequent than in other languages. Even for a hybrid language like C++ (which has C at its core and thus shouldn't behave too differently at runtime), significant differences were found. Table 2 shows data from a study by Calder et al. [CGZ94] which measured the

	C++	SPECint92	ratio C++ / SPEC
basic block size	8.0	4.9	1.6
call/return frequency	4.6%	0.7%	6.7
instructions per conditional branch	15.9	6.4	2.5

Table 2. Differences between C++ and C (from [CGZ94])

behavior of several large C++ applications and compared it to that of the SPECint92 suite and other C programs. The study used the GNU C and C++ compilers on the MIPS architecture. Even though C++ is similar in spirit to C, the differences in execution behavior are pronounced: for example, C++ executes almost 7 times more calls and executes less than half as many conditional branches.

Based on these numbers, one would expect a pure object-oriented language like SELF or Smalltalk to be much further away from C, because the language is so radically different from C. (Recall that, for example, even integer addition or if statements involve message sends in SELF.) However, execution behavior is a function not only of the source language characteristics but also of compiler technology, and our data show that the latter can make a big difference. Figure 1 shows the dynamic instruction usage of the four SPECint89 integer benchmarks (written in C) and the nine SELF programs we measured. The data is summarized using box plots[1] (the appendix contains detailed data). The leftmost box in each category represents SELF-only, i.e., the execution of compiled SELF code, excluding any time spent in the runtime system (which is written in C++). The middle box in each category (filled gray) represents complete SELF programs (i.e., all user-mode instructions). We measured both since SELF programs often call routines in the runtime system, for example, to allocate objects or call functions defined in C libraries. Some programs spend one-third of their time in such routines, and separating out SELF-only ensures that our data is not biased by the execution behavior of non-SELF code. On the other hand, showing SELF-only could be misleading as well, since this data may not be representative of the instructions the processor actually executes.

Since there are only four benchmarks in the SPECint89 suite, the individual data points for C are shown directly, and the box plots (dotted) are given for reference only. The SPECint89 data are taken from Cmelik et al [Cme91].

Figure 1 reveals several interesting points:

1. Overall, there are few differences between the SPEC benchmarks and SELF. Often, the differences between the individual SPEC benchmarks are bigger than the difference between SELF and C (in the graph, the SPEC boxes are usually larger than the corresponding SELF boxes).

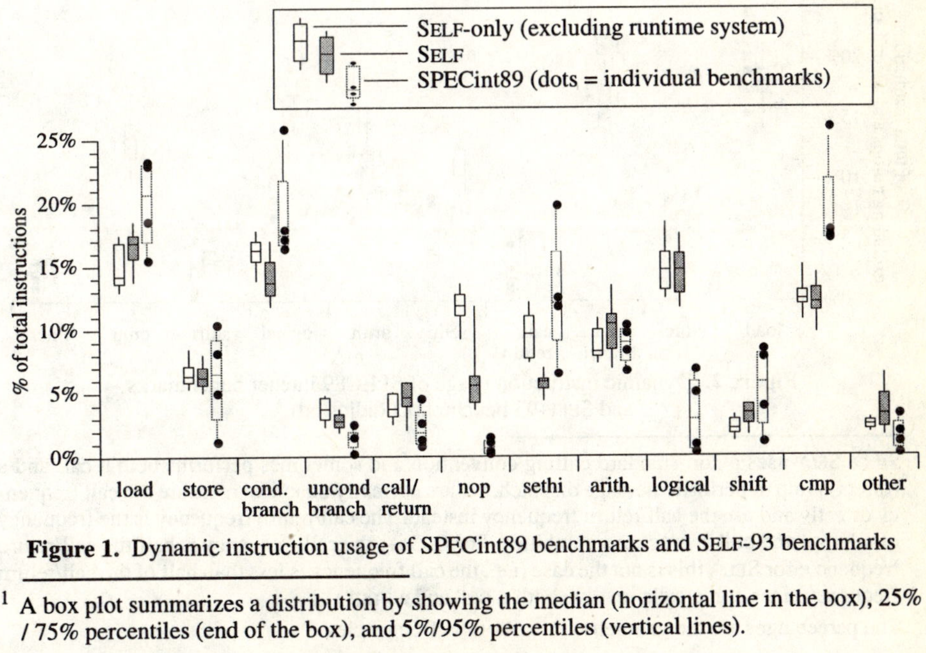

Figure 1. Dynamic instruction usage of SPECint89 benchmarks and SELF-93 benchmarks

---

[1] A box plot summarizes a distribution by showing the median (horizontal line in the box), 25% / 75% percentiles (end of the box), and 5%/95% percentiles (vertical lines).

2. On average, SELF programs execute more no-ops, more unconditional branches, and more logical instructions. However, most these differences can be explained by the simple back end of the current SELF compiler, as explained in more detail below. Thus, they are an artifact of the current compiler back end and are not linked to the object-oriented nature of SELF.

3. SELF's basic block size is very similar to that the SPEC programs, 4.5 vs. 4.4 instructions (geometric means). However, calls and returns[1] are more frequent, occurring every 33 instructions (SELF-only) and 25 instructions (SELF) vs. every 57 instructions in SPEC89. Interestingly, SELF's runtime system (written in C++) has a higher call/return frequency than SELF code.

Before going into a more detailed comparison, we exclude two instruction categories that are distorted by deficiencies in the back end of the SELF-93 compiler. The back end does not fill delay slots (except in fixed code patterns), and thus SELF programs contain many no-ops (6.2% vs. 0.45% for C[2]). Also, it does not optimize branch chains or rearrange code blocks to avoid unconditional branches; thus, the code contains more unconditional branches (2.7% vs. 0.8% in C). Since the presence of these extra instructions distorts the frequencies of other instruction categories, we exclude them in all future graphs in this section.

Figure 2 shows the adjusted execution frequencies. Comparing SELF and SELF-only reveals that the runtime system does not influence the overall behavior much. The only

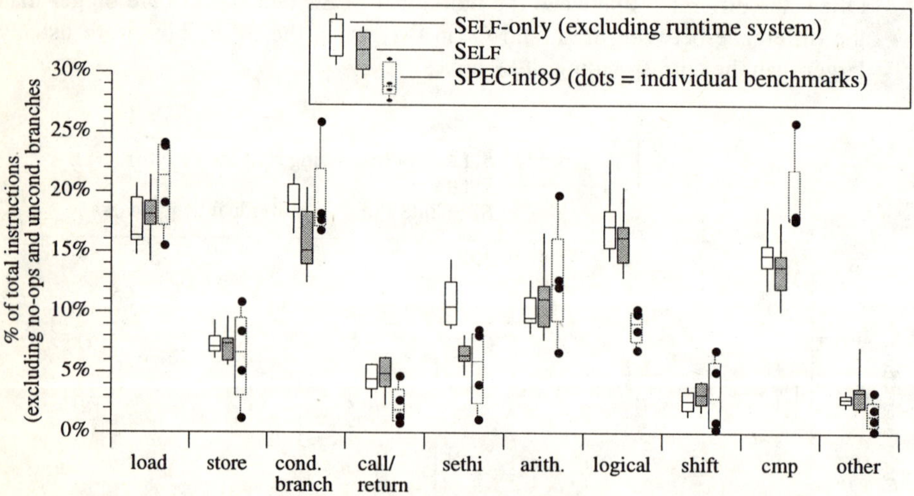

Figure 2. Dynamic instruction usage of SPEC89 integer benchmarks and SELF-93 benchmarks (adjusted)

---

[1] Since SELF uses a non-standard calling convention and sometimes performs both a call and a (direct) jump to perform message dispatch, we are currently unable to measure the call frequency directly and use the call/return frequency instead. The call/return frequency is the frequency of all jmpl and call instructions combined. For C/C++, the call frequency is half the call/return frequency; for SELF, this is not the case (i.e., the call frequency is less than half of the call/return frequency since some calls involve both a call and a jmpl.)

[2] The percentages are the geometric means of the frequencies.

two instruction groups showing a significant difference are conditional branches and sethi instructions. Conditional branches are more frequent in SELF-only than in SELF, but not unusually high compared to the SPEC programs. sethi instructions are used to load 32-bit constants; they are more frequent in compiled SELF code for two reasons. First, the values true, false, and nil are objects in SELF, represented by 32-bit code constants; in contrast, C programs can use the short immediates 0 and 1. Second, object types are represented by the address of the type descriptor, and the implementation of message dispatch compares the receiver's type against the expected type(s) [HCU91]. Since message dispatch is frequent, so are 32-bit constants.

Compared to the SPEC benchmarks, SELF shows few differences. Besides the differences in conditional branches and sethi instructions already mentioned above, only logical instructions and comparisons are markedly different. Logical instructions are more frequent in SELF for two reasons. First, the compiler's back end uses only a simple register allocator, and as a result generates unnecessary register moves. (Move instructions account for roughly half of all logical instructions in SELF.) Second, SELF uses a tagged object representation with the two lower bits as the tag. Dispatch tests involving integers, as well as integer arithmetic operations, test their argument's tag using an and instruction; similarly, the runtime system (e.g., the garbage collector) often extracts an object's tag. Together, these and instructions account for about 25% of the logical instructions.

On average, SELF executes fewer comparisons than the SPEC integer benchmarks. This result surprised us; we expected SELF to execute *more* comparisons since message dispatch involves comparisons and is quite frequent. If SELF used indirect function calls to implement message dispatch, one could explain the lower frequency of conditional branches with the object-oriented programming style which typically replaces if or switch statements with dynamic dispatch; Calder et al. observed this effect when comparing C++ programs to the SPEC C programs [CGZ94]. However, since the SELF implementation uses comparisons (i.e., inline caching [HCU91]) rather than indirect function calls, we cannot explain the difference in this way. It is possible that SELF's optimizer eliminates enough dispatch type tests to lower the overall frequency of comparisons It is also possible that the difference is caused by differences in application characteristics: the frequency of comparisons in the two SELF integer benchmarks (Richards and DeltaBlue) is very close to the frequency of SPEC (Figure 4).

Instruction category	Frequency relative to SPEint89	Reasons for difference
call/return	1.5x higher (SELF-only)	different programming styles; possible compiler deficiencies in SELF-93
logical instructions	1.8x higher (SELF-only)	extra register moves (inferior back end); integer tag tests (and instructions)
sethi (load 32-bit constant)	1.5x higher	true/false/nil are 32-bit constants; message dispatch involves comparisons with 32-bit constants
comparison instructions	1.5x lower	see text

Table 3. Summary of instruction frequency differences between SELF and SPECint89

Table 3 summarizes the main differences in instruction usage. Overall, there are few differences between SELF programs and the SPEC C programs, a surprising result considering how different the two languages are. What is even more surprising is that *SELF-93 is closer to GNU C than is GNU C++*. Figure 3 illustrates this point by

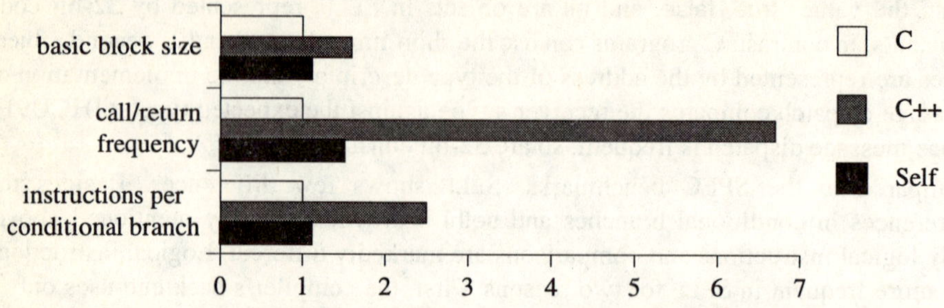

Figure 3. Differences between SELF/C++ and SPEC C programs

summarizing the C++ data from [CGZ94] and our own measurements. In each category, SELF is closer to SPEC than is C++. For example, the basic block size in C++ is 1.6 times higher than SPEC, but in SELF it is only 1.1 times higher than SPEC.

Figure 4 shows the instruction mixes of the two benchmarks available in both C++ and SELF (Richards and DeltaBlue) in comparison to the SPECint median. In general, the data confirm the observations made above: SELF's instruction usage is very similar to SPECint (i.e., C) with the exceptions mentioned in Table 3, and C++ has a much higher call/return frequency (3-4 times higher than SELF) and significantly fewer conditional branches. For virtually all instruction categories, SELF is closer to the SPEC median than is C++.

In summary, our data show that execution behavior is more a function of compiler technology than of the source language characteristics. We believe that much of the

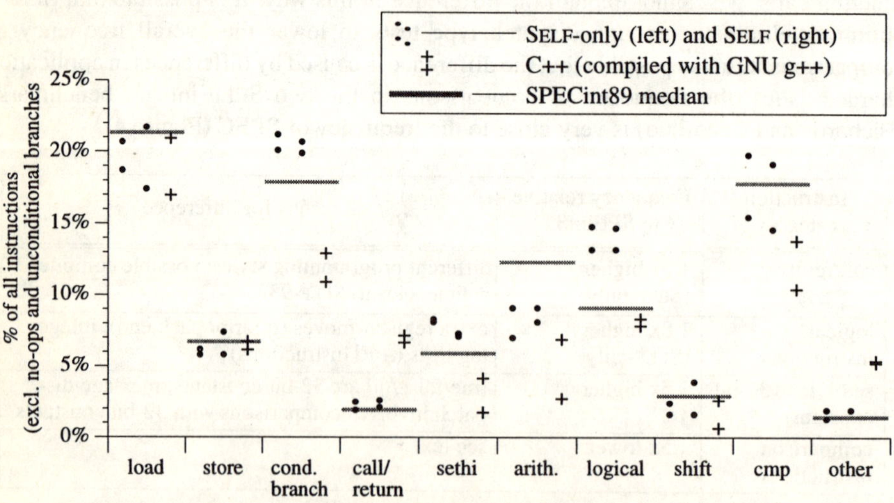

Figure 4. Instruction mix for SELF and C++ on Richards and DeltaBlue

difference between C++ (or other object-oriented languages) and C would disappear if compilers used OO-specific optimizations as well. Of course, until such systems are actually implemented, one cannot be certain that better optimization would indeed bring other object-oriented languages closer to C. However, in light of the data, any claims regarding the necessity of architectural support for an object-oriented language should be regarded with caution unless the system used for the study employs state-of-the-art optimization techniques, or unless such optimizations have been shown to be ineffective for that particular language.

In the next sections, we will examine the performance impact of hardware features that have been found to provide significant speedups when used with non-optimizing compilers. Our goal is to see whether these features still benefit performance in the presence of an optimizing compiler.

4 Hardware Support for Tagged Arithmetic

Tagged integer addition and subtraction instructions are a unique SPARC feature that was motivated by the results of the SOAR project [SUH86]. The special instructions can perform an integer operation, a tag check (assuming a tag in the least significant two bits), and an overflow check in parallel [U+84]. Using a non-optimizing Smalltalk compiler, Ungar reported that SOAR Smalltalk would have been 26% slower without the tagged instructions [Ung87]. Similarly, Lisp machines have included hardware support for tagging [B+87, SH87]. But how useful is hardware support in a system with an optimizing compiler? To answer this question, it is necessary to examine the code generated for integer addition (or subtraction) in SELF-93. Without special hardware, the expression x + y, when specialized for integers, is compiled into the following code:

```
if (x is integer) {             // 3 instructions (test, cond. branch, unfilled delay slot)
  if (y is integer) {           // 2 instructions (fill delay slot with add)
    add(x, y, temp);            // 1 instruction
    if (no overflow) {          // 1 instruction (cond. branch)
      result = temp;            // assign result (instruction in delay slot of branch)
    } else ...                  // handle overflow (code omitted for clarity)
  } else ...                    // handle non-integer y (code omitted for clarity)
} else ...                      // handle non-integer x (code omitted for clarity)
```

The first if implements the dispatch for the "+" message (in a pure object-oriented language, "x + y" means "send the + message to object x, passing object y as a parameter"). The code within the if is the inlined method for integer addition which calls the IntAdd primitive (also inlined) in the standard system. Using the above code sequence, an integer addition takes eight instructions. A better code sequence would fill delay slots, use only one tag test (by first ORing x and y), and eliminate the extra assignment, for a savings of three instructions. The comparison below assumes a six-instruction sequence for integer addition or subtraction.

The ideal code sequence for addition, given the tagged addition instructions available in SPARC, is one instruction:

```
tagged_add_trapIfError(x, y, result);
```

This variant of the tagged add instruction (taddcctv in SPARC syntax) assigns the result register only if both x and y have integer tags and if the addition does not overflow; otherwise, the instruction traps. SELF-93 actually uses a non-trapping variant because the runtime system would need additional mechanisms to handle the traps and recompile the offending compiled code if necessary to avoid taking frequent expensive traps. However, to get an upper bound on the benefits of tagged instructions, we will assume that the ideal system would make maximal use of the tagged arithmetic support and execute all integer additions and subtractions in one cycle.[1]

In addition to integer additions and subtractions, tagged instructions are also useful in integer comparisons (which are similar to subtractions without a check for arithmetic overflow) and other integer tag tests, e.g., tests to verify that the index in an array indexing operation is an integer. For each integer tag test in these operations, we assume an overhead of 2 cycles (test + branch + unfilled delay slot – tagged add). Therefore, the number of cycles saved by tagged arithmetic instructions is 5 * (number_of_adds + number_of_subtracts) + 2 * number_of_other_integer_tag_tests.

program	% integer additions	% integer subtractions	% integer tag tests	estimated benefit of hardware support	benefit with better compiler
CecilComp	0.5%	0.1%	1.8%	6.4%	4.1%
CecilInt	0.1%	0.1%	0.5%	1.7%	1.1%
DeltaBlue	0.6%	0.3%	3.7%	11.9%	7.3%
Mango	0.3%	0.2%	1.4%	5.1%	3.2%
PrimMaker	0.3%	0.1%	1.0%	4.0%	2.6%
Richards	0.4%	0.4%	2.3%	8.3%	5.3%
Typeinf	0.3%	0.2%	1.7%	5.9%	3.7%
UI1	0.6%	0.1%	2.4%	8.1%	5.1%
UI3	0.6%	0.3%	1.9%	8.2%	5.4%
Median	0.4%	0.2%	1.8%	6.4%	4.1%

Table 4. Frequency of integer operations and estimated benefit of tagged instructions

Table 4 shows the frequencies of integer operations in a system making maximum use of tagged instructions. The data include only additions/subtractions executed on behalf of source-level integer addition operations; other additions (e.g., address arithmetic) are excluded since they operate on untagged values. Integer arithmetic instructions are used rarely and represent only about 0.6% of all instructions; other integer tag tests are more frequent, with a median of 1.8%. Without hardware support for tagged integers, SELF would be 6% slower than a system making maximal use of tagged instructions.

[1] Replacing the whole integer addition sequence with a trapping tagged add requires the same optimization as folding the two tag tests into one does (using an or): the compiler has to recognize that there are no instructions between the dispatch test (first integer tag test) and the addition (with the argument tag test). The fact that there are no instructions between the two tests is a result of the current definition of the SELF method for smallInteger addition. Since the definition can be changed by the user, the compiler cannot hardwire the code sequence. A peephole optimizer would suffice, but the current compiler does not perform peephole optimization. Since we assume a one-instruction sequence for the system using tagged instructions, we also assume folded tag tests (6 instructions) for the system without tagged instructions.

However, the true savings are likely to be smaller since we made several simplifying assumptions that all tend to inflate the estimated benefits of tagged arithmetic instructions:

- We assumed that the compiler back end does not eliminate some unnecessary instructions. A better compiler would save one instruction (the extra assignment) per addition and one instruction for each tag test (by filling the delay slot), reducing the performance of tagged instructions from 6.4% to 4.1% (last row of Table 4).
- Counting instructions rather than cycles overestimates the savings because the code sequences are free of memory accesses and could probably execute at close to 1.0 CPI (cycles per instruction), whereas the overall CPI on a SPARCstation-2 is closer to 2 for the benchmark programs. Thus, the sequences replacing tagged instructions consume about 6% of all instructions but only about 3% of all cycles. The exact extent of this overestimation is of course machine-dependent, but we believe the non-tagged instructions could execute with a below-average CPI even on superscalar architectures with high branch penalties because the branches are extremely predictable (the integer type test will almost always succeed, and overflows are rare). Furthermore, existing superscalar SPARC implementations cannot execute the tagged instructions in parallel with other instructions [Sun90] (probably because of the potential trap), and so one tagged instruction consumes as much time as several other instructions (up to three for SuperSPARC [Sun90]).
- We assumed that the compiler has no type information on the arguments of integer additions or subtractions, and thus has to explicitly test both tags for all integer operations. This overestimates the cost of explicit tag checking since one argument may be a constant (e.g., when incrementing a loop index by 1) or otherwise known.

For these reasons, we consider 6% to be a generous upper bound of the benefits of tagged instruction support for the programs in our benchmark suite. For the SPARCstation-2, a more accurate upper bound is probably 2-3% of execution time. Thus, the instructions for tagged addition and subtraction do not improve SELF's performance much. Of course, programs with a higher frequency of integer arithmetic (such as the Stanford integer benchmarks) could benefit more from tagged arithmetic instructions. However, this class of programs is also more amenable to optimizations that eliminate type checks [CU91].

This result stands in marked contrast to Ungar's measurements showing that SOAR would have been 26% slower without instructions for tagged arithmetic [Ung87]. Why the big difference? By analyzing Ungar's data, we could find several reasons for the higher estimate:

- Ungar's data includes speedups from several tagged instructions (such as "load" and "load class") that are not needed in SELF. For example, the "load class" instruction is handled equally fast with a normal load instruction [Höl94]. Including only the tagged arithmetic instructions, Ungar's estimate would be 12%.
- The SOAR code sequences for integer arithmetic without tagged instructions are slowed down because SOAR does not have a "branch on overflow" instruction. With such an instruction, the code sequences would be shorter, reducing the estimated slowdown to 8%.

- Integer arithmetic is more frequent in SOAR than in SELF. In Ungar's benchmarks, arithmetic instructions represent 2.26% of all instructions vs. 0.64% in SELF. We do not know whether this difference is a result of compiler differences or of differences in the benchmarks.

Together, these factors explain the difference between our estimates and the SOAR estimates.

5 Hardware Support for Message Lookup

Object-oriented languages replace traditional direct procedure calls with dynamically-dispatched "indirect" calls, where the target address of the call depends on the type of the receiver (and, in some languages, possibly on one or more arguments). Finding ("looking up") the correct target address was a bottleneck in early Smalltalk implementations [Kra83]. Since message dispatch is extremely frequent in pure object-oriented languages (recall that virtually every operation involves message sends), hardware support could possibly speed up execution.

To test this hypothesis, we measured the time spent in message dispatch (including all integer tag tests). Although the SELF compiler inlines many message sends, it still incurs some dispatch overhead even for inlined message sends to ensure that the correct inlined code sequence is executed. Thus, we include all such type tests in our overhead, as well as the time spent dispatching non-inlined message sends.[1] Message dispatch in SELF is implemented with polymorphic inline caching [HCU91], so that most sends incur only a small overhead (a load and a compare-and-branch sequence) in addition to the cost of a direct call.

Figure 5 shows that most programs spend less than 15% of their time in message dispatching, with the exception of the two smallest programs (Richards and DeltaBlue) whose overhead lies around 25%. At first sight, the relatively high overhead seems to indicate a possible opportunity for hardware support. However, the main reason for the overhead is the extreme frequency of dynamic dispatch. The median time per test is 8

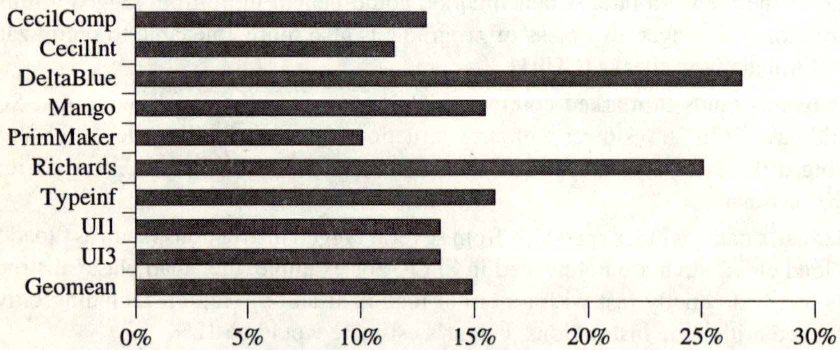

Figure 5. Total time spent in message dispatch

[1] The measurements include everything needed to resolve the target of a message send, but not the actual call/return overhead. All times include cache overhead, assuming the unified 64K direct-mapped cache of the SPARCstation-2.

cycles [Höl94]; for Richards and DeltaBlue, the time per test is even lower (4.5 and 3.4 cycles per test, respectively) since these programs send many messages to integers, so that integer tag tests dominate the dispatch overhead. Dispatch tests are very simple, consisting of two operations (loading the receiver's type and comparing it against a 32-bit constant) that require three to five instructions on a RISC processor. Being so simple, dispatch tests cannot easily be improved with special hardware: the dispatch overhead consists of very many very simple and short tests, and thus there are no expensive computations that could be sped up with special-purpose hardware. The most promising way to reduce the overhead further probably is via compiler optimizations; the current compiler already eliminates more than 75% of all dispatch tests, i.e., less than one in four source-level message sends actually involves runtime dispatch overhead.

6 Instruction Cache Behavior

After examining the performance impact of architectural features targeted specifically at object-oriented languages, we will briefly discuss generic hardware features that influence performance. In particular, the size of the instruction cache has a large impact on SELF's performance. Figure 6 shows the instruction cache miss ratios for a range of direct-mapped caches; all caches use a 32-byte line size. Most of the SELF programs we measured are fairly large, consisting of several hundred Kbytes of code (see Table A-1 in the appendix). For comparison, Figure 6 also includes gcc, the largest SPEC benchmark (about 900 Kbytes). Compared to gcc, the miss ratios of the SELF programs are significantly higher; for most cache sizes, the median miss ratio is 2-3 times higher than gcc's miss ratio.

For caches up to 32K, the misses are dominated by capacity misses; a 4-way associative cache would reduce misses by a factor of 1.4 (see Table A-3 in the appendix). For larger caches, that factor increases, peaking at 4.5 for a 256K cache, indicating that conflict misses play a bigger role in larger caches. However, conflict misses cannot explain the higher cache misses: even with a four-way associative cache, the median miss ratio is twice as high as gcc's (data not shown). Apparently, the temporal locality of SELF programs is significantly worse than that of gcc. One reason might be that object-

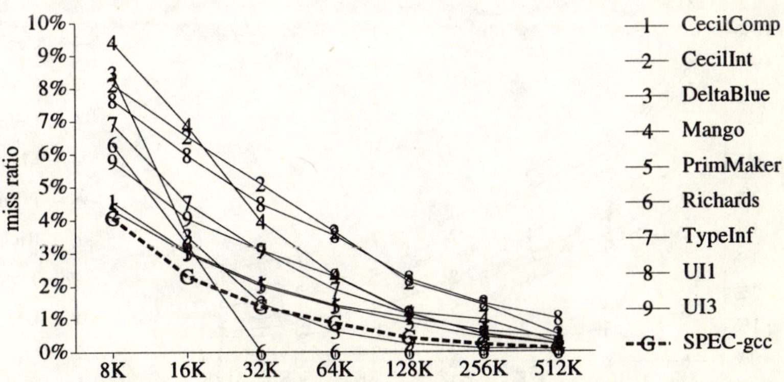

Figure 6. Instruction cache miss ratios of SELF programs (direct-mapped cache, 32-byte lines)

oriented programs have more distributed control and lack the tight loops that would enable good cache behavior even for large programs, or that gcc has an unusually good cache behavior for a program of its size. A more detailed study is beyond the scope of this paper but appears a promising area for future work.

The high instruction cache misses have a substantial performance impact. With a 64K direct-mapped instruction cache with a 26-cycle miss penalty (the miss penalty of a SPARCstation-2), SELF runs 32% slower than it would with an infinitely large cache. Thus, the size of the instruction cache can have a larger influence on performance than all the object-oriented hardware features previously discussed.

7 Data Cache Behavior

Figure 7 shows the data cache read miss ratios for direct-mapped caches with 32-byte lines, write-allocate, and subblock placement. The write-allocate policy has been shown to be beneficial for programs with intensive heap allocation; we will discuss it in more detail below. We assume that there is no cost associated with write misses, i.e., that write buffers can absorb almost all writes (see [DTM94, Rei93, Rei94] for justifications of this assumption).

Even though many SELF programs allocate objects at a rate of about 1 Mbyte/s, the data cache performance is good. For example, the median miss ratio with a 64K cache is 2.4%, which would lead to an overhead of 6% on a SPARCstation-2-like memory system (cache miss time = 26 cycles). Even with an 8K data cache, the median overhead would still be less than 17%. This data is consistent with that of Diwan et al [DTM94] who have measured allocation-intensive ML programs and found very low data cache overheads for the same cache organization (write-allocate, subblock placement). Similar results have also been reported by Reinhold for Scheme programs [Rei93], by Jouppi for the SPEC benchmark suite [Jou93], and by Koopman et al for combinator graph reduction [KLS92]. Such low data cache overheads leave little room for improvement through special cache features (e.g., [PS89, WW90]).

Diwan et al [DTM94] also observed that the data cache overhead of ML programs increased substantially with a write-noallocate policy, i.e., with a cache that does *not*

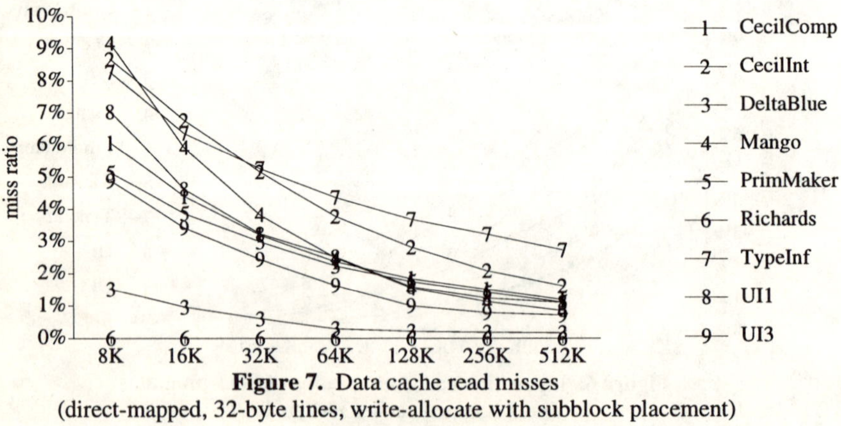

Figure 7. Data cache read misses
(direct-mapped, 32-byte lines, write-allocate with subblock placement)

allocate a cache line on a write miss. This is also true for SELF (see Figure 8). For a 32K cache, write-noallocate increases cache overhead by a median factor of 1.4, and this factor increases with larger caches up to a factor of 1.8 for a 512K cache.

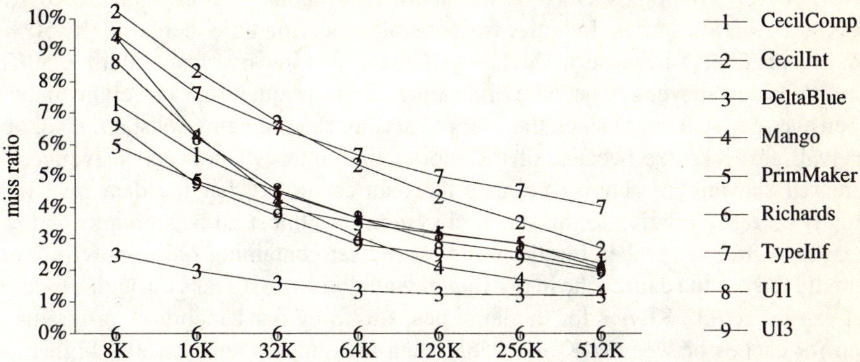

Figure 8. Data read misses (direct-mapped, 32-byte lines, write-noallocate)

For write misses, the impact of the write policy is much higher: while write miss ratios are between 2% and 9% for all programs for write-allocate caches between 8K and 512K, the write miss ratios become truly staggering with write-noallocate caches. Miss ratios range from 20% to over 70% (!) for virtually all cache sizes and show very little improvement with larger caches (see Figure 9). Although we assume that there is no cost associated with write misses, it is still interesting that miss ratios are so high. The main reason is that objects are allocated consecutively in an allocation area. Between two garbage collections, the allocation pointer sweeps through the entire allocation space (400 Kbytes in SELF). Since the fields of newly allocated objects are initialized before they are read, each initializing store will cause a cache miss in a system without write-allocate.

Wilson et al. [WLM92] argue that this allocation behavior will result in especially high cache overheads for direct-mapped caches since the allocation pointer will sweep through the entire cache and evict every single cache line. Therefore, they argue that caches should be associative, and that the size of creation space should be smaller than

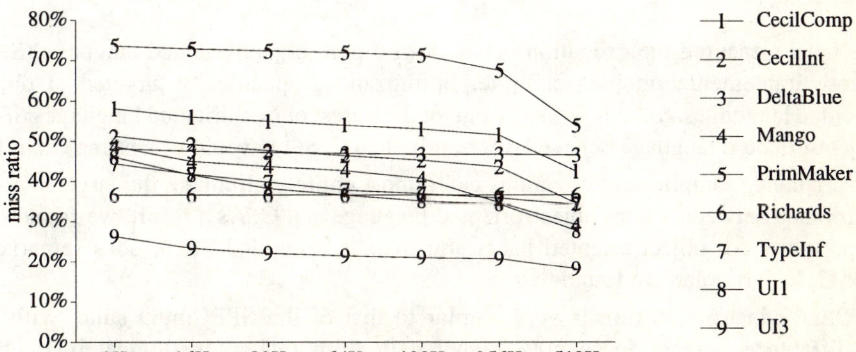

Figure 9. Write miss ratio (direct-mapped, 32-byte lines, write-noallocate)

the cache size. Our data does not support this argument—we cannot detect a significant improvement when going from a 256K cache to a 512K cache, as predicted by Wilson et al. (the allocation area is 400Kbytes).

To test Wilson's hypothesis further, we measured versions of SELF using 50Kbyte and 200Kbyte creation spaces. In both cases, overall execution time increased (by 50% and 10%, respectively) because of higher garbage collection overhead. With a 50Kbyte creation space, scavenges become eight times more frequent but not eight times less expensive (per scavenge) since the root processing time remains constant; also, object survival rates increase because of the shorter time intervals between scavenges. The increased scavenging activity pollutes the data cache, so that the data read misses actually *increase* relative to the standard system for almost all benchmarks and cache sizes. In particular, processing the remembered set containing old-to-new references virtually flushes the data cache in our implementation since it scans through a byte array that can exceed 32 Kbytes for the large heaps used by our benchmark programs. But even for caches between 64K and 256K, data read misses are 50-100% higher when using a 200Kbyte allocation area. Thus, sizing the allocation area to fit into the cache may not yield the best performance even for quite large data caches.

8 Future Work

The results presented here could be extended in several ways. In addition to comparing single-instruction frequencies, comparing the relative frequencies of instruction groups (i.e., instruction pairs or triples) might reveal additional differences or similarities between implementations. Further work is needed to explore the impact of superscalar and out-of-order instruction issue. Of particular interest is the predictability of branches since it has a large impact on superscalar efficiency.

Further research is also needed to determine the cause of the higher instruction cache miss ratios observed in section 6. Since the performance impact of these misses is relatively high, software optimizations to reduce them may be worth investigating. Finally, even though cache-level data locality is good, page-level locality may be poor [WWT87] and thus needs to be studied.

9 Conclusions

We have measured the execution behavior of a pure object-oriented language (SELF) whose implementation uses compiler optimizations specifically targeted at object-oriented languages. SELF is arguably one of the purest object-oriented languages; if any object-oriented language behaved differently than C, SELF would be a prime candidate.

Surprisingly, compiler optimizations can almost entirely eliminate the large semantic difference between a pure object-oriented language and C. As a result, we found little opportunity for object-oriented hardware; overall, compiled SELF looks remarkably like C. In particular, we found that

- SELF's instruction mix is very similar to that of the SPECint89 suite, with few differences except for a 50% higher call/return rate, more logical instructions (partially caused by a simple compiler back end), and fewer comparisons. The basic block size is virtually identical to SPEC.

- In several respects, SELF programs are much more similar to C than are C++ programs compiled without OO-specific optimizations. For example, C++ programs have a much higher call/return frequency and significantly fewer conditional branches. The fact that compiled SELF is more similar to compiled C despite its pure language model is a strong indication that compiler optimizations influence run-time behavior more than language features.
- Even when using optimistic assumptions, SPARC's instructions for tagged arithmetic improve performance by at most 6%; more realistically, the improvement is 2-3%.
- Despite the extreme frequency of dynamic dispatch, hardware support for message lookup is not likely to help, because the dispatch overhead consists of very short code sequences that extra hardware could hardly optimize.
- The data cache behavior of the test programs is good even with small caches, and thus there is little need for special object-oriented caches. Write-allocate caches with subblock placement reduce read miss ratios by up to a factor of two, and write miss ratios by a factor of ten. These findings are consistent with other work for non-object oriented languages [KLS92, Jou93, Rei93, DTM94].
- Instruction cache size significantly impacts performance. For example, doubling the instruction cache from 32K to 64K improves performance by 15% on a SPARCstation-2. This improvement is higher than that of any OO-specific architectural feature we considered.

Our results contradict (and, we believe, supercede) those of earlier studies. While the execution behavior of object-oriented systems *without* optimizing compilers may differ markedly from C programs, it appears that OO-specific optimizations can eliminate most of these differences even for a radically pure object-oriented language like SELF. In light of our data, architectural support for most object-oriented languages appears unnecessary since the semantic gap between language and hardware is better closed by state-of-the-art optimization techniques.

Acknowledgments: We would like to thank everybody who commented on earlier drafts: Bob Cmelik, Karel Driesen, Bill Joy, David Keppel, Randy Smith, and Mario Wolczko.

References

[B+87] C. Baker et al. The Symbolics Ivory processor: a 40 bit tagged architecture Lisp microprocessor. *Proceedings of the 1987 IEEE International Conference on Computer Design*, p. 512-15, Rye Brook, NY, October 1987.

[CGZ94] Brad Calder, Dirk Grunwald, and Benjamin Zorn. *Quantifying Behavioral Differences Between C and C++ Programs.* Technical Report CU-CS-698-94, University of Colorado, Boulder, January 1994.

[CUL89] Craig Chambers, David Ungar, and Elgin Lee. An Efficient Implementation of SELF, a Dynamically-Typed Object-Oriented Language Based on Prototypes. In *OOPSLA '89 Conference Proceedings*, p. 49-70, New Orleans, LA, October 1989. Published as *SIGPLAN Notices 24(10)*, October 1989. Also published in *Lisp and Symbolic Computation 4(3)*, Kluwer Academic Publishers, June 1991.

[CU91] Craig Chambers and David Ungar. Making Pure Object-Oriented Languages Practical. *OOPSLA '91 Conference Proceedings*, Phoenix, AZ, October 1991.

[Cme91] Robert F. Cmelik, Shing I. Kong, David R. Ditzel, and Edmund J. Kelly. An Analysis of MIPS and SPARC Instruction Set Utilization on the SPEC Benchmarks. *ASPLOS IV*, Santa Clara, CA, April 1991.

[CK93] Robert F. Cmelik and David Keppel. *Shade: A Fast Instruction-Set Simulator for Execution Profiling.* Sun Microsystems Laboratories, Technical Report SMLI TR-93-12, 1993. Also published as Technical Report CSE-TR 93-06-06, University of Washington, 1993.

[Deu83] L. Peter Deutsch. *The Dorado Smalltalk-80 Implementation: Hardware Architecture's Impact on Software Architecture.* In [Kra83].

[DTM94] Amer Diwan, David Tarditi, and Eliot Moss. Memory Subsystem Performance of Programs with Intensive Heap Allocation. In *21st Annual ACM Symposium on Principles of Programming Languages*, p. 1-14, January 1994.

[GR83] Adele Goldberg and David Robson. *Smalltalk-80: The Language and its Implementation.* Second Edition, Addison-Wesley, Reading, MA, 1985

[HCU91] Urs Hölzle, Craig Chambers, and David Ungar. Optimizing Dynamically-Typed Object-Oriented Languages with Polymorphic Inline Caches. In *ECOOP '91 Conference Proceedings*, Geneva, 1991. Published as *Springer Verlag Lecture Notes in Computer Science 512*, Springer Verlag, Berlin, 1991.

[HU94] Urs Hölzle and David Ungar. Optimizing dynamically-dispatched calls with run-time type feedback. In *PLDI '94 Conference Proceedings*, pp. 326-335, Orlando, FL, June 1994. Published as *SIGPLAN Notices 29(6)*, June 1994.

[Höl94] Urs Hölzle. *Adaptive Optimization for Self: Reconciling High Performance with Exploratory Programming.* Ph.D. Thesis, Technical Report STAN-CS-TR-94-1520, Department of Computer Science, Stanford University, 1994.

[Hill87] Mark D. Hill. *Aspects of Cache Memory and Instruction Buffer Performance.* Technical Report UCB/CSD 87/381, Computer Science Division, University of California, Berkeley, November 1987.

[Irl91] Gordon Irlam. *SPA—SPARC analyzer tool set.* Available via ftp from cs.adelaide.edu.au, 1991.

[Jou93] Norm Jouppi. Cache Write Policies and Performance. In *ISCA'20 Conference Proceedings*, pp. 191-201, San Diego, CA, 1993. Published as *Computer Architecture News 21(2)*, May 1993.

[Kra83] Glenn Krasner, ed., *Smalltalk-80: Bits of History and Words of Advice.* Addison-Wesley, Reading, MA, 1983.

[KLS92] Philip Koopman, Peter Lee, and Daniel Siewiorek. Cache behavior of combinator graph reduction. *TOPLAS 14(2)*: 265-297, 1992.

[Pat85] David A. Patterson. Reduced Instruction Set Computers. *Communications of the ACM 28 (1)*: 8-21, January 1985.

[PS89] Chih-Jui Peng and Gurindar Sohi. *Cache memory design considerations to support languages with dynamic heap allocation.* Technical Report 860, University of Wisconsin, July 1989.

[PH93] D. N. Pnevmatikatos and M. D. Hill. Cache Performance of the Integer SPEC Benchmarks on a RISC. *Computer Architecture News 18 (2)*: 53-68.

[Rei93] Mark Reinhold. *Cache Performance of Garbage-Collected Programming Languages.* Ph.D. Thesis, Technical Report MIT/LCS/TR-581, Massachusetts Institute of Technology, September 1993.

[Rei94] Mark Reinhold. Cache Performance of Garbage-Collected Programs. In *PLDI '94 Conference Proceedings*, pp. 206-217, Orlando, FL, June 1994. Published as *SIGPLAN Notices 29(6)*, June 1994.

[SUH86] A. Dain Samples, David Ungar, and Paul Hilfinger. SOAR: Smalltalk Without Bytecodes. *OOPSLA '86 Conference Proceedings*, pp. 107-118, Portland, OR, September 1986. Published as *SIGPLAN Notices 21(11)*, November 1986.

[SP92] SPARC International. *The SPARC Architecture Manual (Version 8).* Prentice Hall, NJ, 1992.

[SH87] Peter Steenkiste and John Hennessy. Tags and type checking in LISP: Hardware and Software Approaches. In *ASPLOS II Conference Proceedings*, October 1987.

[Sun90] Sun Microsystems. *The Viking Microprocessor (T.I. TMS S390Z50) User Documentation.* Part No. 800-4510-02, November 1990.

[U+84] David Ungar, Ricki Blau, Peter Foley, A. Dain Samples, and David Patterson. Architecture of SOAR: Smalltalk on a RISC. *11th Annual Symposium on Computer Architecture*, Ann Arbor, Michigan, June 1984.

[Ung87] David Ungar. *The Design and Evaluation of a High-Performance Smalltalk System.* MIT Press, Cambridge, MA, 1987.

[US87] David Ungar and Randall B. Smith. SELF: The Power of Simplicity. In *OOPSLA '87 Conference Proceedings*, p. 227-241, Orlando, FL, October 1987. Published as *SIGPLAN Notices 22(12)*, December 1987. Also published in *Lisp and Symbolic Computation 4(3)*, Kluwer Academic Publishers, June 1991.

[WWT87] Ifor Williams, Mario Wolczko, and Trevor Hopkins. Dynamic Grouping in an Object-Oriented Virtual Memory Hierarchy. In *ECOOP '87 Conference Proceedings*, Special Issue of BIGRE, pp. 87-96, Paris, France, June 1987.

[WW90] Ifor Williams and Mario Wolczko. An Object-Based Memory Architecture. In *Proc. 4th Intl. Workshop on Persistent Object Systems*, Martha's Vineyard, MA, September 1990.

[WLM92] Paul R. Wilson, Michael S. Lam, and Thomas G. Moher. Caching Considerations for Generational Garbage Collection. In *Lisp and Functional Programming '92 Proceedings*, p. 32-42, San Francisco, CA, June 1992.

Appendix A. Detailed data

	Benchmark	static code size (bytes)[a]	dynamic code size (bytes)[b]	Kbytes allocated	dynamic data size (bytes)[c]
small prog.	DeltaBlue	39,960	31,020	332	336,444
	PrimMaker	161,640	128,292	2,435	877,512
	Richards	11,132	10,492	1	1,588
large programs	CecilComp	922,452	547,684	1,283	1,023,996
	CecilInt	268,896	183,280	1,261	773,616
	Mango	239,020	223,056	1,078	958,488
	Typeinf	322,500	128,292	680	1,594,536
	UI1	954,812	625,808	542	746,784
	UI3	164,640	97,192	485	726,728

Table A-1: Benchmark data and instruction size

[a] excluding code in the runtime system
[b] unique instructions referenced (including runtime system)
[c] unique memory locations referenced by load and store instructions (including references by runtime system)

	taddcc	tsubcc	other tag tests	total instructions[a]
CecilComp	90,978	18,921	339,713	19,063,103
CecilInt	14,329	7,314	69,507	14,420,873
DeltaBlue	30,725	16,517	194,005	5,236,611
Mango	82,388	44,062	407,302	28,537,483
PrimMaker	85,040	16,539	261,769	25,742,677
Richards	69,767	61,853	397,965	17,500,114
Typeinf	45,956	22,182	218,912	13,259,725
UI1	54,687	9,225	222,917	9,397,411
UI3	64,637	27,176	195,422	10,324,703

Table A-2: Frequency of integer arithmetic and integer tag tests

[a] assuming optimal use of tagged instructions

cache size	1-way / 4-way misses
8K	1.3
16K	1.35
32K	1.46
64K	1.76
128K	2.27
256K	4.47
512K	3.44

Table A-3: Median increase in miss ratio of direct-mapped vs. 4-way associative cache

Programming as an Experience: The Inspiration for Self

Randall B. Smith and David Ungar

Sun Microsystems Laboratories
2550 Casey, Ave. MS MTV29-116
Mountain View, CA 94043, USA

randall.smith@sun.com david.ungar@sun.com

Abstract. The Self system attempts to integrate intellectual and non-intellectual aspects of programming to create an overall experience. The language semantics, user interface, and implementation each help create this integrated experience. The language semantics embed the programmer in a uniform world of simple objects that can be modified without appealing to definitions of abstractions. In a similar way, the graphical interface puts the user into a uniform world of tangible objects that can be directly manipulated and changed without switching modes. The implementation strives to support the world-of-objects illusion by minimizing perceptible pauses and by providing true source-level semantics without sacrificing performance. As a side benefit, it encourages factoring. Although we see areas that fall short of the vision, on the whole, the language, interface, and implementation conspire so that the Self programmer lives and acts in a consistent and malleable world of objects.

1 Introduction

During the last decade, over a dozen papers published about Self have described the semantics, the implementation, and the user interface. But they have not completely articulated an important part of the work: our shared vision of what programming should be. This vision focuses on the overall experience of working with a programming system, and is perhaps as much a feeling thing as it is an intellectual thing. This paper gives us a chance to talk about this underlying inspiration, to review the project, and to make a few self-reflective comments about what we might have done differently. Although the authors have the luxury of commenting from an overview perspective, the reader should keep in mind that the this work is the result of efforts by the many individuals who have worked in the Self project over the years.

1.1 Motivation

Programmers are human beings, embedded in a world of sensory experience, acting and responding to more than just rational thought. Of course to be effective, programmers need logical language semantics, but they also need things like confidence, comfort, and satisfaction — aspects of experience which are beyond the domain of pure logic. These concerns have traditionally been addressed separately by putting the logic in the language and providing for the rest of experience with the programming environment. The Self system attempts to integrate the intellectual and experiential sides of programming.

In our vision, the Self programmer lives and acts in a consistent and malleable world, from the concrete motor-sensory, to the abstract, intellectual levels. At the lowest, motor-sensory level of experience, objects provide the foundation for natural interaction. Consequently, every visual element in Self, from the largest window to the smallest triangle is a directly manipulable object. At the higher, semantic levels of the language, there are many possible computational models: in order to harmonize with the sensory level, Self models computation exclusively in terms of objects. Thus, every piece of Self data, from the largest file to the smallest number is a directly manipulable object. And, in order to ensure that these objects could be directly experienced and manipulated, we devised a model based on "prototypes." Just as a button can be added to any graphical object, so can a method be added to any individual object in the language, without needing to refer to a class. This prototype model and the use of objects for everything requires a radically new kind of implementation. In Self, implementation, interface, and language were designed to work together to create a unified programming experience.

In the following sections we in turn review the language semantics, the user interface, and the implementation. In each section we will try to point out where we think we succeeded and where we think we failed in being true to the vision.

2 Language Semantics

Self was initially designed by the authors at Xerox PARC [US87]. We employed a minimalist strategy, striving to distill an essence of object and message. Self has evolved over the years in design and implementation at Stanford University and most recently at Sun Microsystems Laboratories. A user interface and programming environment built in Self are part of the system: Self today is a fairly large system, and includes a complete programming environment and user interface framework.

A computation in Self consists solely of objects which in turn consist of slots. A slot has a name and a value. Slot names are always strings, but slot values can be any Self object. A slot can be marked with an asterisk to show that it designates a *parent.* Figure 1 illustrates a Self object representing a two-dimensional point with **x** and **y** slots, a parent slot called **myParent**, and two special assignment slots, **x:** and **y:**, that are used to assign to the **x** and **y** slots. The object's parent has a single slot called **print** (containing a method object).

When sending a message, if no slot name matches within the receiving object, its parent's slots are searched, and then slots in the parent's parent, and so on. Thus our point object can respond to the messages **x**, **y**, **x:**, **y:**, and **myParent**, plus the message **print**, because it *inherits* the **print** slot from its parent. In Self, any object can potentially be a

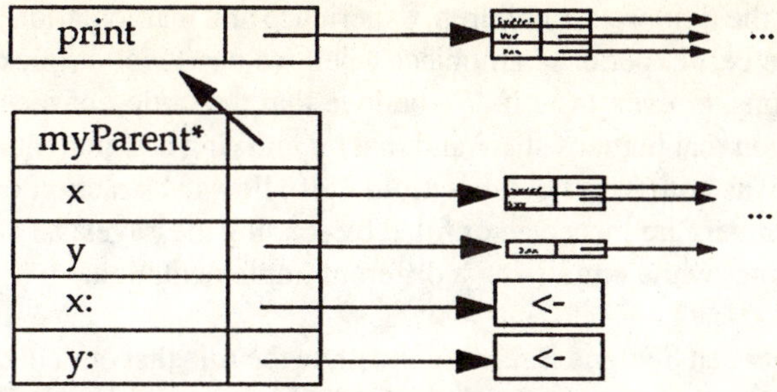

Figure 1. A Self point has **x** and **y** slots, with **x:** and **y:** slots containing the assignment primitive for changing **x** and **y**. The slot **myParent** carries a "parent" denotation (shown as an asterisk). Parent slots are an inheritance link, indicating how message lookup continues beyond the object's slots. For example, this point object will respond to a print message, because it inherits a print slot from the parent.

parent for any number of children, or it can be a child of any object. This uniform ability of any object to participate in any role of inheritance contributes to the consistency and malleability of Self and, we hope, contributes to the programmer's comfort, confidence, and satisfaction.

In addition to slots, a Self object can include code. Such objects are called *methods*; since they do what methods in other languages do. For example, the object in the **print** slot above includes code and thus serves as a method. However in Self, any object can be regarded as a method; a "data" object contains code that merely returns itself. This viewpoint serves to unify computation with data access: when an object is found in a slot as a result of a message send it is *run*; data returns itself, while a method invokes its code. Thus when the **print** message is sent to our point object, the code in the print slot's method will run immediately. This unification reinforces the interpretation that the experience of the client matters, not the inner details of the object used. For example, some soda machines dispense pre-mixed soda, while others dynamically mix syrup and carbonated water on demand. The user does not care to become involved in the distinction, what matters is only the end product, be it soda or the result of a computation.

Of course Self is not the only language that unifies access and computation. For example Beta [MMN93] does too. From a traditional computer science viewpoint, this unification serves to provide data abstraction; it is impossible to tell, even from within an abstraction, whether some value is stored or computed. However when designing Self we also sought to unify assignment and computation; this unification is slightly more unusual. Assignment in Self is performed with assignment slots, such as **x:** and **y:**, which contain a special method (symbolized by the arrow), that takes an argument (in addition to the receiver) and stuffs it in either the **x** or **y** slot. This desire for access/assignment symmetry can be interpreted as arising from the sensory-motor level of experience. From the time we are children, experience and manipulation are inextricably intertwined; we best experience an object when we can touch it, pick it up, turn it over, push its buttons, or even taste it. We believe that the notion of a container is a fundamental intuition that humans share and that by unifying assignment and computation in the same way as access and computation, Self allows abstraction over containerhood; since all containers are inspected or filled by sending messages; any object may pretend to be a container while employing a different implementation.

A contrast between Self and Beta may illustrate the role that our concern for a particular kind of programming experience played in the language design. In Beta, data takes two forms: values and references. Beta unifies accessing values with computation and also unifies assignment of values with computation, but uses a different syntax for accessing or changing references. For example, a data attribute containing a reference to a point would be accessed by saying pt[]-> but a method in the receiver returning a reference to a point would be run by pt->. Giving the programmer two forms of data can be seen as giving the programmer more tools with which to work. More tools can of course be a good thing, but since in our opinion, the value/reference distinction does not really exist at the sensory-motor level of experience, we chose a slightly less elaborate scheme with a single kind of data structuring mechanism. We also believe there are advantages to uniformity in and of itself.

The design of slots in Self has proven to be challenging because of the unified access to state and behavior. In Self the same message can be sent to either read a data slot or run a method in the slot. Where should the distinction be maintained? We have taken the position that method objects are fundamentally different, in that they run non-trivial code whereas data objects just return themselves. Still, this behavior of method objects means that they cannot be directly manipulated because they would run. So we have had to invent primitive objects called *mirrors* as a way of indirectly mentioning methods. Mirrors can be better justified as encapsulators of reflective operations and as relieving each object of the burden of inheriting such behavior. But mirrors can hamper uniformity; it is sometimes unclear whether a method should take a mirror as argument or the object itself. Another approach to unifying invocation and access would be to add a bit to a slot that would record whether or not the slot was a method or data slot. This approach has its own problems: what would it mean to put 17 into a method slot? In our opinion, this issue is not fully resolved.

The treatment of assignment slots in Self is also a bit troublesome. A Self assignment slot is a slot containing a special primitive (the same one for all assignment slots), which uses the *name of the slot* (very odd) to find a corresponding data slot *in the same object* (also odd). This treatment leads to all sorts of special rules, for instance it is illegal to have an object contain an assignment slot without a corresponding data slot, so the code that removes slots is riddled with extra checks. Also, this treatment fails to capture the intuitive notion of a container. Other prototype-based languages address this issue by having a slot-pair be an entity in the language and casting an assignable slot as such a slot pair. Another alternative might be to make the assignment object have a slot identifying its target, so that in principle any slot could assign to any other.

Messages can have extra arguments in addition to the receiver. For example, **3 + 4** sends the message **+** to the object **3**, with **4** as argument. In contrast to many other object-oriented languages numbers are objects in Self, just as in Smalltalk. Because languages like Smalltalk or Self do arithmetic by sending messages, programmers are free to add new numeric data types to the language, and the new types can inherit and reuse all the existing numeric code. Adding complex numbers or matrices to the system is straightforward: after defining a + slot for matrices, the user could have the matrix freely inherit from some slot with code that sends +. Code that sends + would then work for matrices as well as for integers. Self's juxtaposition of a simple and uniform language (objects for numbers and messages for arithmetic in this case) with a sophisticated implementation permits the programmer to inhabit a more consistent and malleable computational universe.

There is more to be said about the language: new Self objects are made simply by copying—there are no special class objects for instantiation (see the later section entitled Prototypes and Classes). The current implementation allows multiple inheritance, which requires a strategy for dealing with multiple parents. It has block closure objects, and threads. (A few constructs that would be somewhat obscure in a language like Self, such as methods contained in the local slots of methods, are not yet supported by the implementation.)

2.1 Discussion

Our desire to provide a certain kind of programming experience has colored Self's stance on some traditional issues:

Type Declarations. In order to understand the design of the Self language it helps to examine the assumptions that underlie language design. In the beginning, there were FORTRAN, ALGOL and Lisp. In all three of these languages the programmer only has to say what is necessary to execute programs. Since Lisp was interpreted, no type information was supplied at all. Since ALGOL and FORTRAN were compiled, it was necessary for programmers to specify primitive type information, such as whether a variable contained an integer or a float, in order for the compiler to generate the correct instructions. As compiled languages evolved, it was discovered that by adding more static declarations, the compiler could sometimes create more efficient code. For example, in PL/I procedures had to be explicitly declared to be recursive, so that the compiler could use a faster procedure prologue for the non-recursive ones.

Programmers noticed that this static declarative information could be of great value in making a program more understandable. Until then, the main benefit of declarations had been to the compiler, but with Simula[1] and PASCAL a movement was born; using declarations both to benefit human readers and compilers.

In our opinion, this trend has been a mixed blessing, especially where object-oriented languages are concerned. The problem is that the information a human needs to understand a program, or to reason about its correctness, is not necessarily the same information that a compiler needs to make a program run efficiently. But most languages with declarations confuse these two issues, either limiting the efficiency gained from declarations, or, more frequently hindering code reuse to such an extent that algorithms get duplicated and type systems subverted.

Self therefore distinguishes between concrete and abstract types. Concrete types (embodied by *maps*) are completely hidden from the Self programmer. Maps are only visible to the implementation, where they are used as an efficiency mechanism. Abstract types on the other hand are notions that the programmer might think about. Self has no particular type manifestation in the language: declarative information is left to the environment. For example, one language level notion of abstract type, the *clone family*, is used in the work of Agesen et. al. [APS93] in their Self type inference work. There is no clone family object in the Self language, but such objects can be created and used by the programming environment. In order to structure complexity and provide the freest environment possible, we have layered the design so that the Self language proper includes only information needed to execute the program, leaving declarative information to the environment. This design keeps the language small, simplifies the pedagogy, and allows users to potentially extend the intensional domain of discourse.

Minimalism. Why have we tried to keep the Self language minimal? It is always tempting to add a new feature that handles some example better. Although the feature had made it possible to directly handle some examples, the burden it imposed in all reasoning about programs was just too much. We abandoned it for Self 3.0. Although adding features seems good, every new concept burdens every programmer who comes into contact with the language.

We have learned the hard way that smaller is better and that examples can be deceptive. Early in the evolution of Self we made three mistakes: prioritized multiple inheritance, the sender-path tie-breaker rule, and method-holder-based privacy semantics.[2] Each was motivated by a compelling example [CUCH91]. We prioritized multiple parent slots in order to support a mix-in style of programming. The sender-path tie-breaker rule allows two disjoint objects to be used as parents, for example a rectangle parent and a tree node parent for a VLSI cell object. The method-holder-based privacy semantics allowed objects with the same parents to be part of the same encapsulation domain, thereby supporting binary operations in a way that Smalltalk cannot [CUCH91].

---

[1] Simula^{TM} is a trademark of a.s. Simula

[2] In all fairness, the first author was across the Atlantic at the time and had nothing to do with it. On the other hand, if he had not wandered off maybe these mistakes could have been avoided.

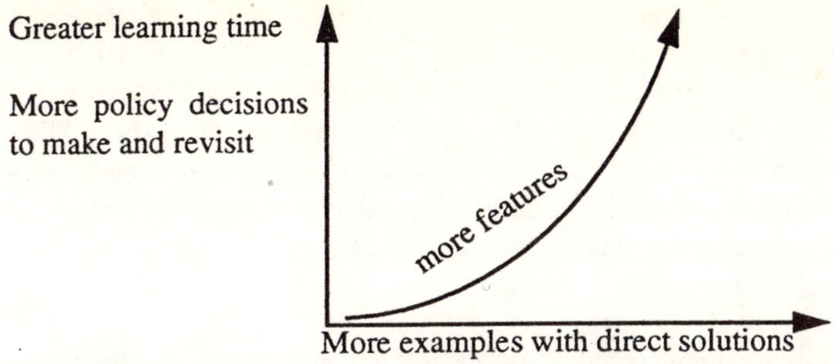

Figure 2. As more features are embedded in the language, the programmer gets to do more things immediately. But complexity grows with each feature: how the fundamental language elements interact with each other must be defined, so complexity growth can be combinatorial. Such complexity makes the basic language harder to learn, and can make it harder to use by forcing the programmer to make a choice among implementation options, a choice which may have to be revisited later.

But each feature also caused us no end of confusion. The prioritization of multiple parents implied that Self's "resend" (call-next-method) lookup had to be prepared to back-up down parent links in order to follow lower-priority paths. The resultant semantics took five pages to write down, but we persevered. After a year's experience with the features, we found that each of the members of the Self group had wasted no small amount of time chasing "compiler bugs" that were merely unforeseen consequences of these features. It became clear that the language had strayed from its original path.

We now believe that when features, rules, or elaborations are motivated by particular examples, it is a good bet that their addition will be a mistake. The second author once coined the term "architect's trap" for something similar in the field of computer architecture; this phenomenon might be called "the language designer's trap."

If examples cannot be trusted, what do we think should motivate the language designer? Consistency and malleability. When there is only one way of doing things, it is easier to modify and reuse code. When code is reused, programs are easier to change and most importantly, shrink. When a program shrinks its construction and maintenance requires fewer people which allows for more opportunities for reuse to be found. Consistency leads to reuse, reuse leads to conciseness, conciseness leads to understanding. That is why we feel that it is hard to justify any type system that impedes reusability; the resultant duplication leads to a bigger program that is then harder to understand and to get right. Such type systems can be self-defeating.[1]

[1] However, by emphasizing the ability to express intuitive relationships, such as covariant specialization, over the ability to do all checking statically, it is possible to do a better job. See [MMM90].

Prototypes and Classes. There are now several fairly mature object-oriented languages based on prototypes. (For overviews see [Blas94], [DMC92], and [SLS94].) These languages differ somewhat in their treatment of semantic issues like privacy, copying, and the role of inheritance. (One notable system, Kevo [Tai93a], [Tai92], [Tai93] does not have delegation or inheritance at all.) All these languages have a model in which an object is in a important sense self-contained. Prototypes are often presented as an alternative to class-based language designs, so the subject of prototypes vs. classes can serve as point of (usually good natured) debate.

However, depending on how one defines "class," one may or may not think that classes are already present in a prototype based system. Some (e.g. [Blas94]) see a Self prototype as playing the role of class, since it determines the structure of its copies. Others note that much of the current Self system is organized in a particular way, using what we call "traits" objects in many places to provide common state and behavior for sharing among children. Such sharing is reminiscent of that provided by a class. However, classes normally also provide the description of an instance's implementation, and a "new" method for instantiation, neither of which are found in a traits object.

In a class-based system, any change (such as a new instance variable) to a class will affect new instances of a subclass. In Self, a change to a prototype (such as a new slot) will not affect anything other than the prototype itself (and its subsequent direct copies).[1] So we have implemented a "copy-down" mechanism in the environment to share implementation information. It allows the programmer to add and remove slots to an entire hierarchy of prototypes in a single operation. Functionality that is provided at the language level in class-based systems has risen to the programming environment level in Self. In general, the simple object model in Self means that some functionality omitted from the language may go back into the environment. Because the environment is built out of Self objects, the copy-down policy can be changed by the programmer. But such flexibility comes with a price. Now, there are two interfaces for adding slots to objects, the simple language level and the copying-down Self-object level. This loss of uniformity could be a source of confusion when writing a program that needs to add slots to objects. Only time will tell if the flexibility is worth the complication.

A brief examination of the emulation of classes in Self will serve to illuminate both the nature of a prototype-based object model and the trade-off between implementing concepts in the language versus in the environment. In order to make a Self shared parent look more like a class, one could create a "new" method in the shared parent. This method could make a copy of some internal reference to a prototype, and so would appear to be an instantiation device. Figure 3 suggests how one might start to make a Smalltalk class out of Self objects. Mario Wolczko has built a more complete implementation of this, and has shown [Wol95] that it works quite well: he can read in Smalltalk source code and execute it as a Self program. There are certain restrictions on the Smalltalk

---

[1] Self prototypes are not really special objects, they are distinguished only by the fact that, by convention, they are copied. Any copy of the prototype would serve as a prototype equally well. Some other prototype-based systems take a different approach.

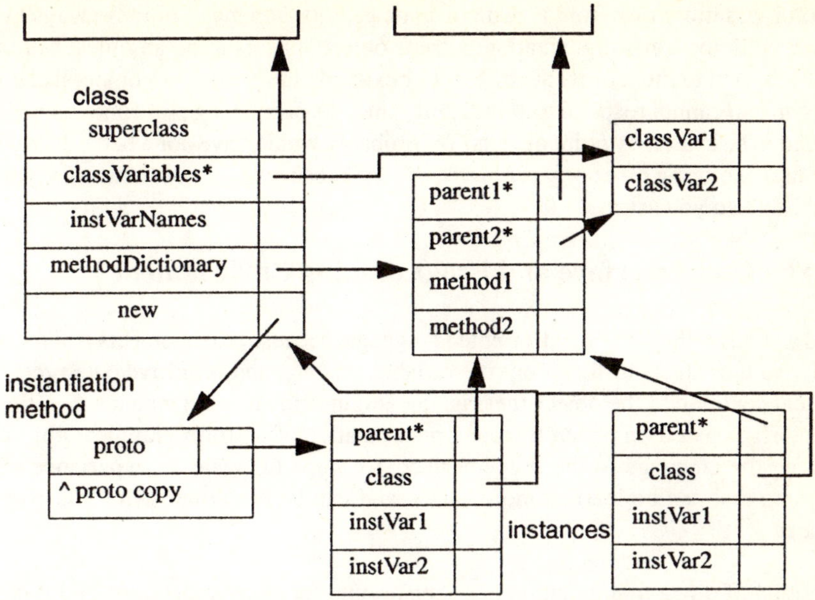

Figure 3. This figure suggests how Self objects might be composed to form Smalltalk-like class structures as demonstrated more completely by Wolczko [Wol95]]. He shows that, with some caveats, Smalltalk code can be read into a Self system, parsed into Self objects, then executed with significant performance benefits, thanks to the Self's dynamically optimizing virtual machine.

source, but thanks to Self's implementation technology, once the code adaptively optimizes, the Self version of Smalltalk code will generally run faster than the Smalltalk version.

Do prototype-based systems like Self have classes? The answer would seem to be that if your definition of class is not satisfied by the existing language elements, you can probably build something quite easily that would make you happy. (It would be difficult to do this kind of trick in a prototype-based language that did not have an inheritance mechanism.) Of course, almost any language can emulate any other, but in this case the classes are built directly out of the prototype-based objects so directly that the classes constructed out of Self objects run faster that those built-in to Smalltalk. General meta-object issues in prototype-based languages are tackled by the Moostrap system [Mul95].

The use of traits might be seen as a carryover from the Self group's Smalltalk experience. Interestingly, it is likely that our old habits might not have done Self justice (as observed in [DMC92].) There are many other ways to organize Self objects other than by prototypes inheriting from a chain of traits parents, and many of these ways avoid a problem with the traits organization: a traits object appears to be an object but in fact cannot respond to most of its messages. For example the point traits object lacks x and y slots and so cannot respond to printString, since its printString slot contains a method intended to be shared by point objects. We probably would have done better to put more effort into exploring other organizations. When investigating a new language, your old habits can lead you astray.

3 The User Interface and Programming Environment

Self is an unusually pure object-oriented language, because it uses objects and messages to achieve the effects of flow control, variable scoping, and primitive data types. This maniacal devotion to the object-message paradigm is intended to match a devotion to a user interface based on concrete, direct manipulation of uniform graphical objects. By matching the language to the user interface, we hope to create an experience of programming that can be learned more easily, and can be performed with less cognitive overhead.

The notion of direct manipulation has been around for many years now, and it is interesting to note that some of the earlier prototype-based systems were visual programming environments [BD81], [Smi87]. The current Self user interface [SMU95], [MS95] enhances the sense of direct manipulation by employing two principles we call *structural reification*, and *live editing*. We will define these principles, and show with an example how the interface brings the feeling of direct object experience to the task of creating objects and assembling applications.

3.1 Structural reification

The fundamental kind of display object in Self is called a "morph," a term borrowed from Greek meaning essentially "thing." Self provides a hierarchy of morphs. The root of the hierarchy is embodied in the prototypical morph, which appears as a kind of golden colored rectangle. Other object systems might choose to make the root of the graphical hierarchy an abstract class with no instances. But prototype systems usually provide generic examples of abstractions. This is an important part of the structural reification principle: there are no invisible display objects. Any descendant of the root morph (or any other morph for that matter) is guaranteed to be a fully functional graphical entity. It will inherit methods for displaying and responding to input events that enable it to be directly manipulated.

In keeping with the principle of structural reification, any morph can have "submorphs" attached to it. A submorphs acts as though it is glued to the surface of its hosting morph. Composite graphical structure typical of direct manipulation interfaces arises through the morph-submorph hierarchy. Again, many systems provide compositing with special "group" objects which are normally invisible. But because we want things to feel very solid and direct, we chose to follow a simple metaphor of sticking morphs together as though glued to each other.

A final part of structural reification arises from the approach to submorph layout. Graphical user interfaces often require that subparts be lined up in a column or row. Self's graphical elements are organized in space by "layout" objects that force their submorphs to line up as rows or columns. John Maloney [MS95] has shown how to create efficient "row and column morphs" as children of the generic morph. These objects are first class, tangible elements in the interface. They embody their layout policy as visible parts of the submorph hierarchy, so the user need only be able to access the submorphs in a structure in order to inspect or change the layout in some way. A possible price of this uniformity is paid by a user who does not wish to see the layout mechanism, but is confronted with it anyway.

An example in section 3.3 will illustrate how structural reification assures that any morph can be seen and can be grabbed, moved and inspected, and assures that graphical composition and layout constraints are physically present in the interface. Structural reification is an important part of making programming feel more tangible and direct.

3.2 Live Editing

Live editing simply means that at any time, an object can be directly changed by the user. Any interactive system that allows arbitrary runtime changes to its objects has a degree of support for live editing. But we believe Self provides an unusually direct interface to such live changes. The key to live editing is provided by Self's "meta menu," a menu that can pop up when the user holds the third mouse button while pointing to a morph. The meta menu contains items such as "resize," dismiss," and "change color" which allow the user to edit the object directly. There are also menu elements that enable the user to "embed" the morph into the submorph structure of a morph behind it, and menu elements that give access to the submorph hierarchy at any point on the screen.

The "outliner" menu item creates a language-level view of the morph under the mouse[1]. This view shows all of the slots in an object, and provides a full set of editing functionality. With an outliner you can add or remove slots, rename them, or edit their contents. Code for a method in a slot can be textually edited: outliners are important tools for programmers. Access to the outliner through the meta menu makes it possible to investigate the language-level object behind any graphical object on the screen.

The outliner supports the live editing principle by letting the user manipulate and edit slots, even while an object is "in use." The example below illustrates how a slot can be "carried" from one object to another, interactively modifying their language level structure.

---

[1] Lars Bak designed the outliner framework for Self.

Popping up the meta menu is the prototypical morph's response to the third mouse button click. All morphs inherit this behavior, even elements of the interface like outliners and pop-up menus themselves. But wait! Pop-up menus are impossible to click on: you find them under your mouse only when a mouse button is already down. To release the button in preparation for the third button click causes the pop-up to frustratingly disappear. Consequently, we provide a "pin down" button, which, when selected, causes the menu to become a normal, more permanent display object. The mechanism is not new, but providing it in Self enables the menu to be interactively pulled apart or otherwise modified by the user or programmer.

Live editing is partly a result of having an interactive system, but is enhanced by features in the user interface. This principle reinforces the feel that the programmer is working directly with concrete objects. The following example will clarify how this principle and the structural reification principle help give the programmer a feeling of a working in a uniform world of accessible, tangible objects.

3.3 Example of Direct Application Construction

Suppose the programmer (or motivated user) wishes to expand an ideal gas simulation, extending the functionality and adding user interface controls. The simulation starts simply as a box containing "atoms" which are bouncing around inside. Using the third mouse button, the user can invoke the meta menu, and select "outliner" to get the Self-level representation of the object (Figure 4). The outliner enables arbitrary language-level changes to the ideal gas simulation.

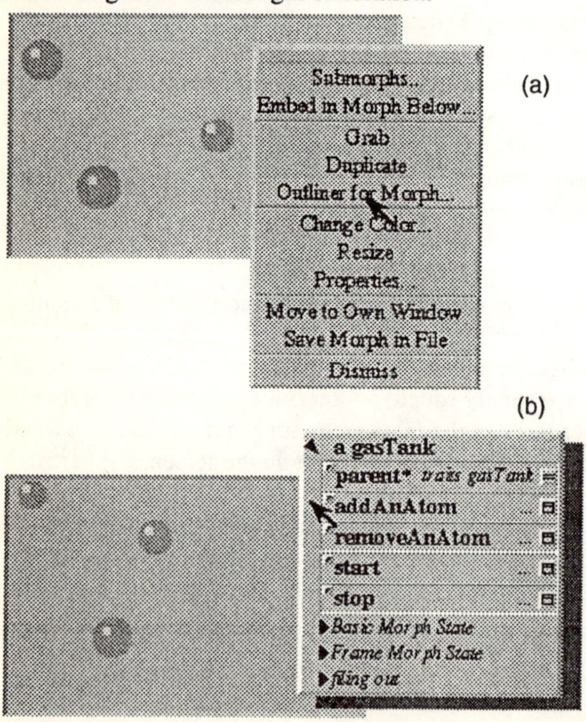

Figure 4. In a Self window, the user pops up the meta menu on the ideal gas simulation (a). Selecting "outliner" gives the Self-level representation to the user, which can be carried and placed as needed (b). (The italic items at the bottom of the outliner represent slot categories that may be expanded to view the slots. Unlike slots, categories have no language level semantics and are essentially a user interface convenience.)

(a)

(b)

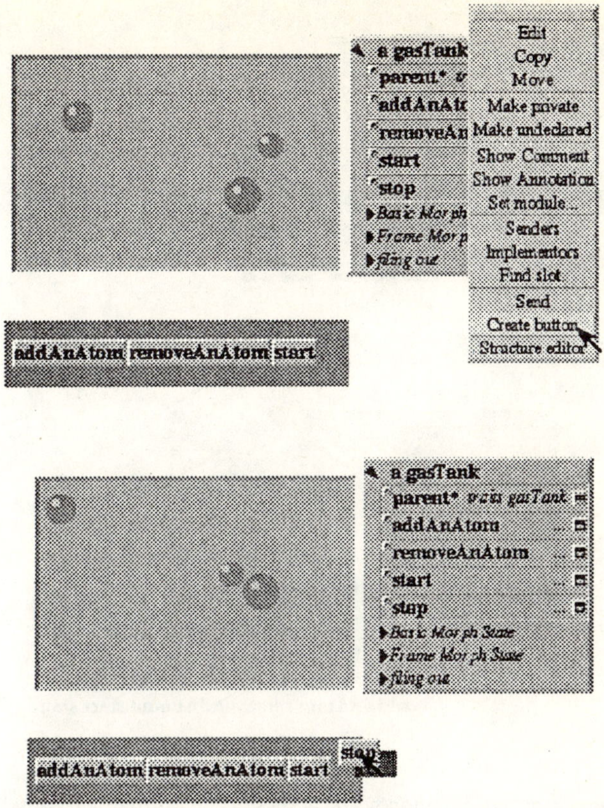

Figure 5. The middle mouse button pop up menu on the "stop" slot (a) enables the user to create a button for immediate use in the user interface (b). This button will be embedded in a row morph, so that it lines up horizontally.

With the outliner, the user can start to create some controls right away. In the outliner, there are slots labeled "start" and "stop." These slots can be converted into user interface buttons by selecting from the middle-mouse-button pop-up menu on the slot (Figure 5). Pressing these buttons starts and stops the bouncing atoms in the simulation. This is an example of live editing at work: in just a few gestures, the programmer has gone through the outliner to create interface elements while the simulation continues to run.

The programmer may wish to create several such buttons, and arrange them in a row. The programmer selects "row morph" from a palette: when the buttons are embedded into the row, they immediately snap into position. Once the row of buttons is created, the programmer wishes to align the row below the gas tank. Again, the programmer can create a column frame: when the gas tank and the button row are embedded into the column frame, they line up one below the next (Figure 6)

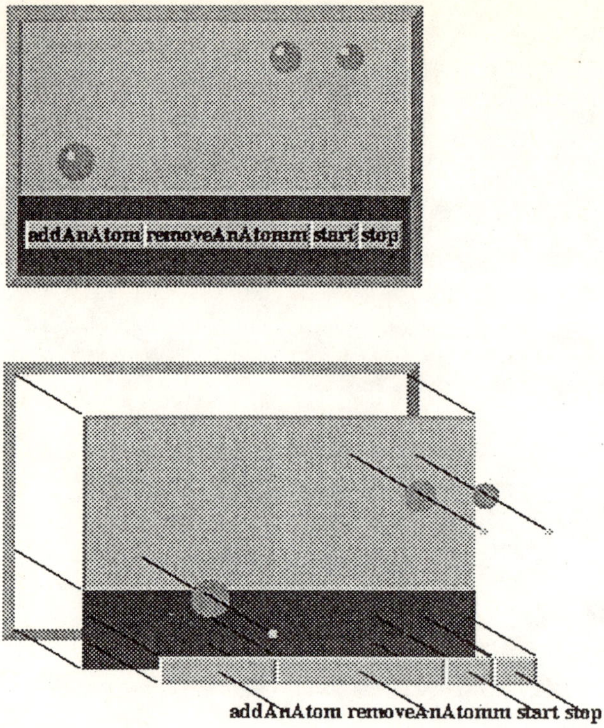

Figure 6. Composite graphical effects are achieved by embedding: any kind of morph can be embedded in any other kind of morph. The ideal gas simulation at left is a compound morph whose embedding relationships are shown at right.

Figure 6 also illustrates how composite graphical effects are achieved through the morph-submorph hierarchy. The interface employs morphs down to quite a low level. The labels on buttons, for example, are themselves first class morphs.

The uniformity of having "morphs all the way down" further reinforces the feel of working with concrete objects. For example, the user may wish to replace the textual label with an icon. The user can begin this task by pointing to the label and invoking the meta menu. There is a menu item labeled "submorphs" which allows the user to select which morph in the collection under the mouse he wishes to denote (see Figure 7). The user can remove the label directly from the button's surface. In a similar way, the user can select one of the atoms in the gas tank and duplicate it. The new atom will serve as the icon replacing the textual label. Structural reification is at play here, making display objects accessible for direct and immediate modification.

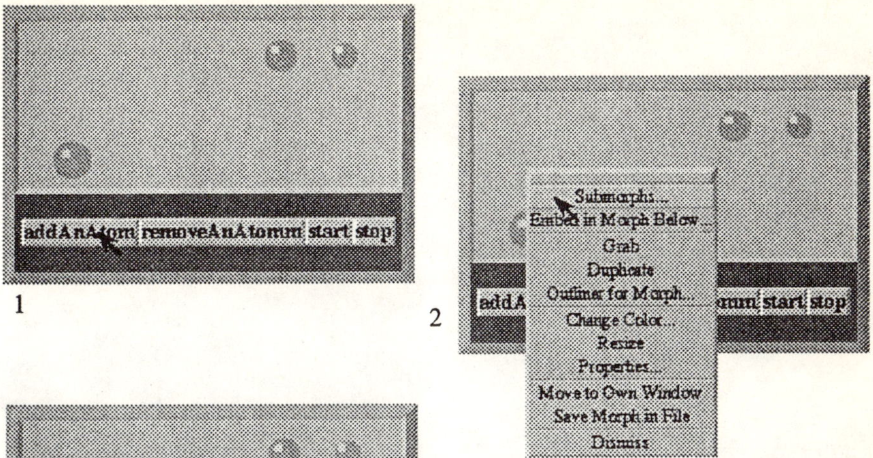

1

2

3

4

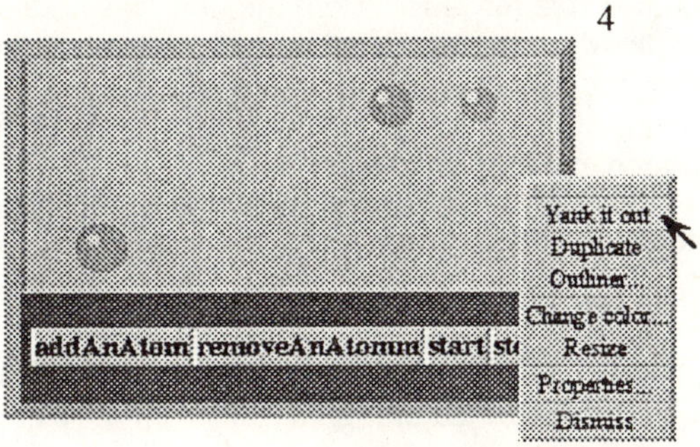

5

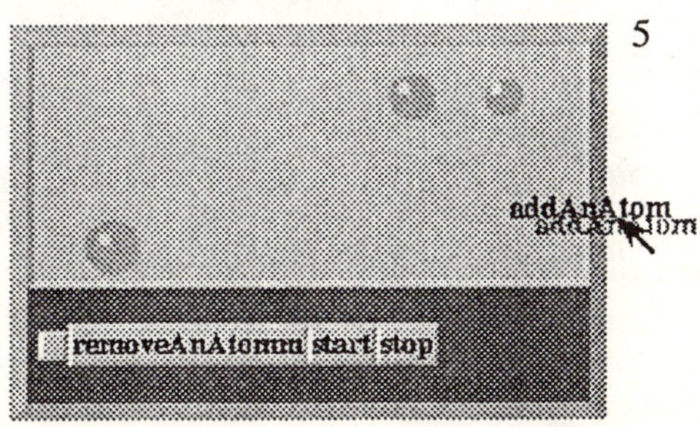

Figure 7. The user wishes to remove the label from the surface of a button. In this series of operations, the user starts by pointing to the label, selects "submorphs" from the meta menu, and selects the label from the resulting menu list. A menu of options is presented, from which the user selects "yank it out". The button, which wraps tightly around its submorphs, shrinks down to a minimum size when it has no submorphs.

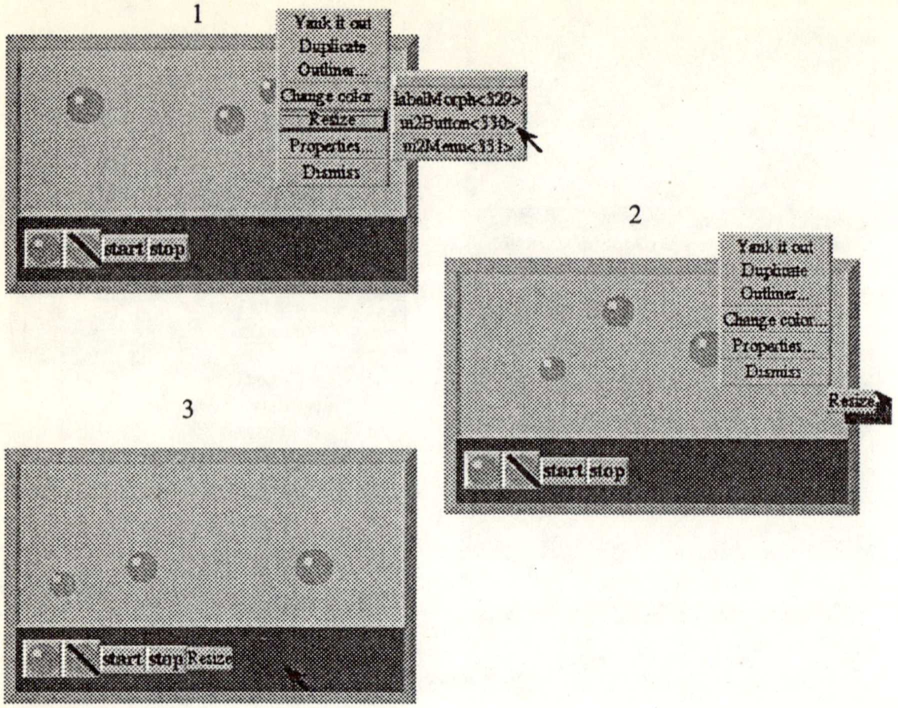

Figure 8. The environment itself is available for reuse. Here the user has created the menu of operations for the gas tank, which is now a submorph of the surrounding frame. He has "pinned down" this menu, by pressing the button at the top of the menu. He can then take the menu apart into constituent buttons: here the is gets the resize button which is then incorporated into the simulation.

As mentioned above, all the elements of the interface such as pop-up menus and dialogue boxes are available for reuse. As an example, the programmer may want the gas tank in the simulation to be "resizable" by the simulation user. The programmer can create a resize button for the gas tank simply by "pinning down" the meta menu and removing the resize button from the menu, as illustrated in Figure 8. This button can then be embedded into the row of controls along with the other buttons.

Figure 9 illustrates how the programmer can modify the behavior of an individual atom to reveal its energy based upon color. A morph has a slot called "rawColor" that normally contains a "paint" object: in this example the programmer replaces that object with a method, so that the paint will be computed based upon energy level. When the change is accepted, the modified slot immediately takes effect. In Figure 10, the programmer is shown copying the slot into the atom's parent object, so that it can be widely shared with other atoms. Of all atoms have a rawColor slot that overrides this slot in the parent. The programmer might at this point remove the rawColor slot from the prototypical atom, so that all new atoms will have this energy-based color.

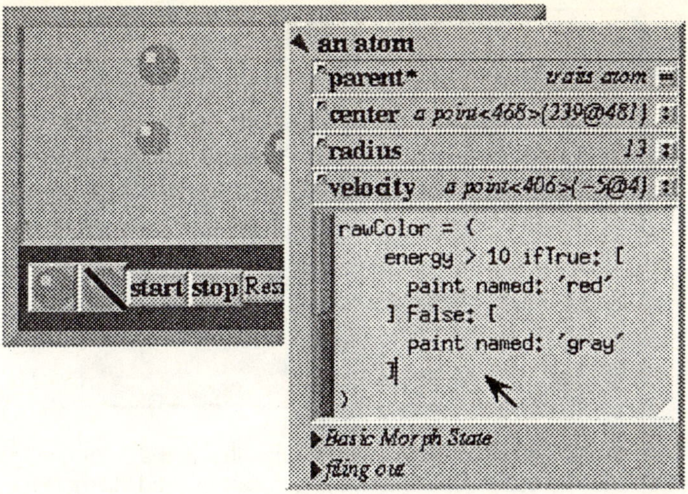

Figure 9. The user has selected one atom on which to experiment. The user changes the "rawColor" slot from a computed to a stored value by editing directly in the atom's outliner.

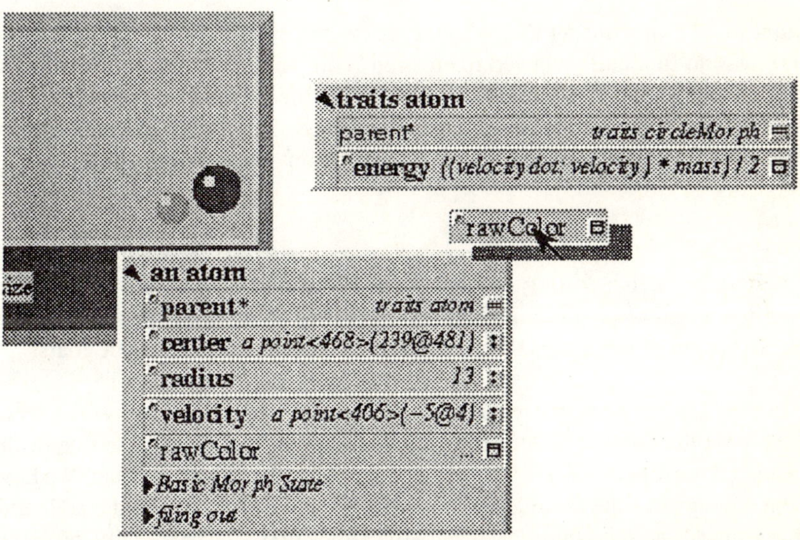

Figure 10. The user copies the modified rawColor slot as a first step in getting the computed method of coloring more widely shared. Because slots can be moved about readily, restructuring changes are relatively light weight, enhancing the sense of flexibility.

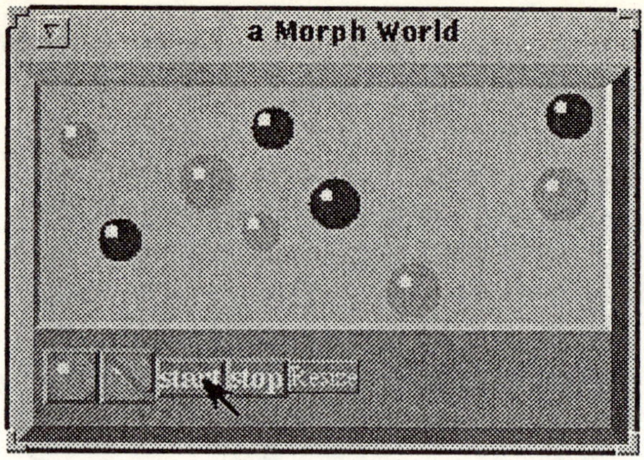

Figure 11. The completed application. The user has invoked a color changing tool that unifies colors across most submorphs, and has invoked the meta menu item "move to own window."

Figure 11 shows the completed application. All the atoms now reveal their energy as they move, and controls for running the simulation appear in a row across the bottom of the object. The programmer has invoked a meta-menu item "move to own window" that wraps the application in its own window-system frame.

It is important to note that during this whole process, the simulation could be left running — there was no fundamental need to enter an "edit" mode, or even stop the atoms from bouncing around. The live editing principle makes the system feel responsive, and is reminiscent of the physical world's concrete presence. Structural reification means that the parts of the interface are visible and accessible for direct modification.

3.4 Issues

While the principles of live editing and structural reification help create the sense of working within a world of tangible malleable objects, we could imagine going further. Here we discuss some of the things that interfere with full realization of our goals.

Multiple views: The very existence of the outliner as a separate view weakens the sense of directness that we are after. After all, when I want to add a slot to one of the simulated atoms, I must work on a different display object, the atom's outliner. We have never had the courage or time to go after some of the wild ideas that would enable unification of any morph with its outliner. Ironically, Self's first interface, Seity, probably did better on this issue [Cha95], [CUS95].

Self's programming environment enforces the constraint that there only be one outliner on the screen at a time for a given object. If the user asks to see some object when its outliner is already on the screen, the outliner will do an animated slide over to the mouse cursor. This constraint encourages identification between the object and its outliner in the programmer's mind. But as we mention above, particularly for morph objects, the identification does not always hold.

Because there is a difference between outliners and the objects they represent, there is a fundamental dichotomy in the system that interferes with the direct object experience goal. Is the programmer to believe that the outliner for some list object really is the list? If so, does the list have a graphical appearance as an intrinsic part of itself? Does the list have an intrinsic display location and a color? We have chosen the easy answer, "no." The object that represents the list to the programmer is not the same as the actual Self list object. Once we take this easy road, it is fundamentally impossible to always maintain the impression that the objects on the screen actually are the Self objects. Unfortunately, it is often clear that outliners are just display stand-ins for the real, invisible Self object, buried somewhere in the computer.

Text and object: There is a fundamental clash between the use of text and the use of direct manipulation. A word inherently denotes something, an object does not necessarily denote anything. That is, when you see the word "cow," an image comes to mind. It is in fact difficult to avoid the image, that is the way words are supposed to work. They stand for things. However, when you manipulate a pencil, what comes to mind? It depends much more on who you are, what the context is, and so on. In other words, a pencil does not by itself denote anything. Consequently, textual notation and object manipulation are fundamentally from two different worlds. The pencil and the word denoting pencil are different entities.

Text is used quite a bit in Self, and its denotational character weakens the sense of direct encounter with objects. For example, many tools in the user interface employ a "printString" to denote an object. The programmer working with one of these tools might encounter the text "list (3, 7, 9)." The programmer might know that this denotes an object which could be viewed "directly" with an outliner. But why bother? The textual string often says all he needs to know. The programmer moves on, satisfied perhaps, yet not particularly feeling like he has encountered the list itself. The mind set in a denotational world is different than that in a direct object world, and use of text creates a different kind of experience.

Issues of use and mention in direct manipulation interfaces are discussed further in [SUC92].

3.5 Summary

The Self user interface helps the programmer feel that he or she is directly experiencing tangible objects. Two design principles help achieve this feeling. First, *structural reification,* assures that the graphical relationships at play in a particular arrangement of submorphs is manifest directly in display objects on the screen. Second, *live editing* means that there is no need for a course grained "edit mode;" rather, objects are always available for immediate and direct editing. The use of textual names for objects, and the distinction between an object and its representation are two problems that weaken the experience of directly working with objects. But on balance, we feel that the Self user interface successfully presents the illusion of being a world of readily modified, physically present objects.

4 Implementing Self

The implementation of a language is usually approached from a mathematical, or mechanistic viewpoint: what is desired is the creation of a program that interprets programs in another language (be the created program a compiler or interpreter). On the other hand, we have taken the view that the goal of the implementation is to fool the user into believing in the reality of the language. Even though Self objects have no physical existence, and there is no machine capable of executing Self methods, the implementation must strive to convince the user otherwise. That is why, despite all the tricks, the programmer can always debug at the source level, seeing all variables and single stepping, and can always change any method, even inlined ones, with no interference from the implementation.

4.1 Transparent Efficiency

The implementation techniques for Self have been presented previously so we will only summarize the briefly here. (See [Hol94], [HU94a], [HCU92], [HCU91], [Cha92], [CU91], [CU90], [CUL89], and [USCH92] for more details.)

Self presented large efficiency challenge because its pure semantics implied that every access, assignment, arithmetic operation and control structure had to be performed by sending a message. Worse yet, the Self user interface's uncompromising stance on structural reification placed further demands on efficiency: everything on the screen down to the smallest triangle is implemented by its own separate object, each with its own redraw and active layout behavior. At the same time, in order to produce the experience of concrete objects, the system had to be as responsive as an interpreter. Self's implementors were confronted with a fundamental problem: to be responsive, the compiler could not afford to spend time on the elaborate optimizations needed for the language, no matter how effective they might be. Caught between Scylla and Charybdis, Self needed something completely different. Instead of relying on a single compiler for both speed and cleverness, Self adopted a hybrid system of two compilers: one fast, the other clever. Instead of always optimizing everything, type feedback permits the system to adaptively optimize code without introducing long pauses.

Figure 12 shows an overview of the compilation process of the system. The first time that a method is invoked, the virtual machine uses dynamic compilation to create an "instrumented" version of the method that counts its invocations and the types of the receivers at each call site. When the invocation counter crosses some threshold, the opti-

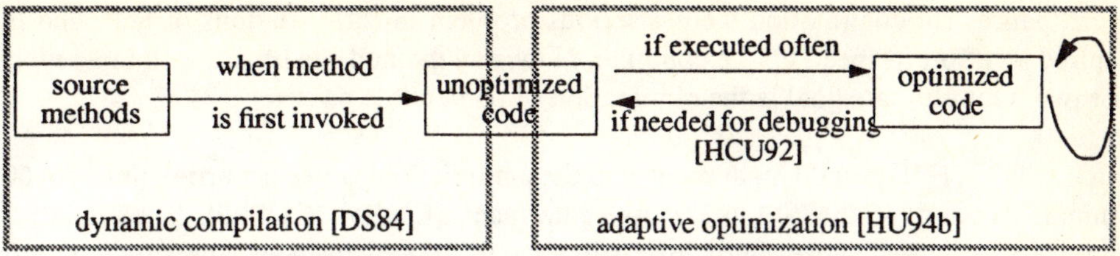

Figure 12. Compilation in the Self system (from [HU94b]).

mizing compiler is automatically invoked and is guided by the counters at the call sites. In this way, Self feeds type information back to the compiler to adaptively optimize code.

Some language implementations force the programmer to choose between interpretation and compilation, or between different modes of compilation. Placing this burden of choice upon the programmer's shoulders can only weaken his confidence in the reality of Self, and force him to consider the difference between the program as written and what really runs. Although Self employs two compilers and a myriad of optimizations, the programmer never chooses nor even knows which have been employed on his code.

Results on two medium-size cross-language benchmarks (Richards and DeltaBlue) suggest that Self runs 2 to 3 times faster than ParcPlace Smalltalk-80[1], 2.6 times faster than Sun CommonLisp 4.0™ using full optimization, and only 2.3 times slower than optimized C++ [HU94a]. Of course, these Smalltalk and Lisp implementations may not include aggressively-optimized compilers, but the C++ language has semantics that make many more concessions to efficiency over purity, simplicity, and safety.

Most implementations strive for efficiency and employ optimizations that show through to the programmer. Tail recursion elimination, for example, optimizes methods that iterate by calling themselves at their ends, but makes it impossible to show a meaningful stack trace. This destruction of information would show through to the user, who might need to see the missing stack frames in order to debug her program. So, Self does not optimize tail-recursion. Instead, endless loops are built in as a primitive operation. There are other optimizations left undone in Self, see [Hol94] for a list.

4.2 Responsiveness

Many systems impose long or unpredictable pauses upon their users. But, a pause in the middle of a user task such as the addition of a slot to an object could ruin the experience of a consistent world. Such pauses, by their very existence, alert users that some mischief is afoot. If the program (be it Self or any other language) were the reality, there would be no pauses upon changing it. Since we believe that such pauses can destroy the fragile illusion of reality, we have striven to reduce them in the Self implementation. In

[1] Smalltalk-80™ is a trademark of ParcPlace Systems.

fact, pauses for compilation were a serious problem in early versions of Self, and inspired an effort to speed up the compiler. Now, any method can be changed in a second or two. Our ultimate goal is the elimination of perceptible pauses.

In [HU94b], Hölzle and Ungar measured the compilation pauses occurring during a 50-minute session of the SELF 3.0 user interface[1] [Cha95] [CUS95]. Their analysis grouped individual pauses into clusters that would be perceived as pauses by the users. The results indicated that there were few intrusive clustered pauses; on a current-generation workstation, only 13 pauses would exceed 0.4 seconds, and on a next-generation machine, none would exceed 0.3 seconds (see Figure 13).

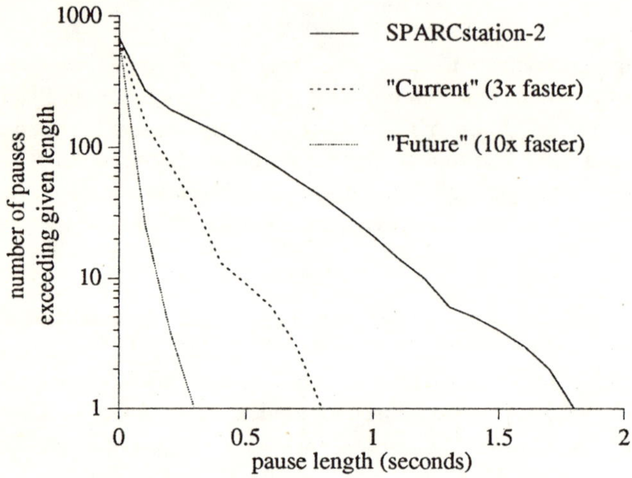

Figure 13. Compilation pauses (from [HU94b]).

Clustering pauses made an order-of-magnitude difference, and reporting individual pauses would have resulted in a distorted, overly optimistic characterization. The idea of pause clustering is one example of how our vision of providing a particular kind of experience to the programmer affects the standards that must be used to evaluate the system.

4.3 Malleability

By now, it should be clear to the reader that our philosophy of implementation as deception places additional burdens on the implementation, such as avoiding inconsistent behavior or unexplainable pauses. What may come as a surprise, though is that a requirement for malleability arises as a logical consequence of this unusual philosophy. For example, in both Smalltalk and Self, the if-then-else control structure is realized by sending a message “ifTrue:IfFalse:” to a boolean object (two arguments are included, a block to execute for true, and another for false). Each boolean simply implements this

[1] The Self 4.0 user interface described in section 3 places more demands on the implementation and its pause behavior is not as good as these measurements suggest.

message with a message that executes the appropriate block; true's ifTrue:IfFalse: method runs the true block and false's runs the false block. If Self or Smalltalk objects are real, if they directly and faithfully execute, if the user is in control, then the user should be able to change these methods and observe the results. But in Smalltalk, extra performance is obtained by short-circuiting this method in the implementation [GR83] and though he may change the method, the programmer cannot alter its behavior. This failure of malleability cannot help but raise disturbing questions and insecurities for the programmer. That is why Self does not short-circuit this or other such methods, even though providing such malleability without an efficiency loss extracts its cost from the implementation.[1]

4.4 Encouraging Factoring and Extensible Control

Our non-traditional approach has led to techniques that provide a very traditional benefit: factoring is free. Suppose two methods in the same object contain several lines in common. By moving the common lines into a new method and sharing the method in both callers, the programmer can centralize them and make the program easier to change. Most implementations of object-oriented programming languages would slow down the program with an additional procedure call, providing a strong disincentive to the programmer for factoring small operations. In C++, for example the programmer must either ask explicitly for inlining (and give up virtual semantics) or pay the price of a many-statement overhead. Since Self relies on automatic inlining, no such price is paid. Consequently Self programmers feel much freer to factor programs, and the system is written in an unusually well-factored style. For example, a do-while loop is implemented with many levels of message passing before bottoming out in primitives. We believe that the performance characteristics of Self's implementation techniques encourage programmers to write programs that are easier to maintain.

In addition to free factoring, the Self implementation makes user-defined control structures as efficient as the built-in ones. Unlike for Smalltalk, there is no disincentive for the programmer to use a block; the implementation in most cases can inline it away. Since we believe that control abstraction is necessary for real data abstraction, making control abstraction free can help encourage programmers to write better programs. We strongly believe that in all languages with user-extensible control, such as Smalltalk and Beta, much benefit could be realized from adopting implementation techniques that put the user-defined control structures on the same footing as the system-defined ones.

4.5 Open Issues

Although the current Self system is in daily use by a number of people, several concerns remain about its implementation.

Overcustomization. The Self compiler creates another copy of a method for each kind of object that inherits it. Sometimes, the method is so trivial that the copies waste code space and compiler time for no good reason.

---

[1] In fact, at first the second author thought the cost would be too great. But Craig Chambers' compiler convinced him otherwise.

Memory Footprint. Because enough information is preserved to maintain source-level semantics, Self takes more space than other systems. Self 4.0 barely fits in a SPARCstation[1] with 32 Mb of real memory. Although we believe that programming time is more precious than memory cost, this resource requirement puts Self out of reach of many current users.

Real-Time Operation. Although much progress has been made in the elimination of perceptible pauses, the system still feels like it "warms up" when running the Self 4.0 environment. Hard real-time operation is not possible with today's system.

User Control. Within the Self group, a debate rages over how much control a user should have over the optimization process. On one hand, users want to be able to tell the system how much, where, and when to optimize. On the other hand, the effort to add this ability might be better spent doing a better job automatically, and giving users this control could distract them from their own tasks and destroy the fragile illusion of Self's reality. So far, we have kept the control over optimization entirely within the virtual machine, as an experiment in the philosophy of implementation as deception.

4.6 Summary

Confidence, comfort, satisfaction—what do these desires imply for implementation techniques? They rarely show up as topics in compiler papers, yet we believe that these goals have exerted a profound influence over Self's implementors.

5 Conclusions

The Self language semantics, implementation, and user interface have been guided by the goal of generating a particular kind of experience for the user of the system. Programmers directly work in a uniform world of malleable objects in a very immediate and direct fashion. Self moves towards giving objects a kind of tangible reality.

The language helps give rise to this experience by its use of prototypes, which provide a copy-and-directly-modify mechanism for changes. Self's treatment of slots with its symmetry for assignment and access reflect the deep connection between perception and manipulation at the sensory-motor level, while also enabling objects to reimplement state as behavior and reflecting an intuition about how objects are behaviorally perceived in the real world.

Self's design departs significantly from other object-oriented languages by separating information needed to run the program from information about the programmer's intentions. It distinguishes abstract types, used for the programmers understanding and reasoning about correctness, from concrete types, used to run and optimize the program. The former is left to the environment, the latter is left to the implementation. In our

[1] SPARCstation™ is a trademark of SPARC International, licensed exclusively to Sun Microsystems Inc.

opinion, this approach avoids a number of undesirable consequences that often follow from attempts to integrate these two forms of information.

Finally, in designing Self, we have learned one lesson by making mistakes: examples can persuade the designer to include additional features which later turn out to produce incomprehensible behavior in unforeseen circumstances. This might be called "the language designer's trap." Minimalism, simplicity and consistency are better guides. They benefit every programmer, not just the ones who need advanced features. We suspect that many of today's object-oriented languages could profit by dropping features.

The Self user interface and programming environment provides a direct object experience for creating objects and assembling applications by adhering to two principals: *Structure reification* makes the graphical containment structure and layout rules themselves appear as graphical objects and assures that any graphical object can be manipulated, displayed, connected to other objects, or customized. *Live editing* ensures that any object may be changed at any time without halting activities. A simple gesture takes the user from any graphical object to its programming-language-level counterpart, just as real-world objects can be taken apart. Consequently, programmers need not pore through long object libraries to find out where to start, but can simply find some graphical widget in the environment, like a button in a menu, that is similar to what they want, and proceed to dissect, inspect, modify and reassemble it. At no time must they retreat from a concrete object to some definition of an abstraction.

Two problems in the user interface interfere with achieving our goal. The existence of multiple views for a graphical object and its Self-level outliner dilutes the experience and these views should be merged. The duality between text and object goes deeper and does not readily present a solution.

The consistency and purity of the Self language together with the ubiquitous use of objects and live layout in the interface place enormous demands on the Self implementation, but more interestingly, the desire to create a particular kind of programming experience imposes its own unique requirements on the implementation. Thus, the implementation foregoes optimizations that cannot be hidden such as tail-recursion elimination. It also supports full source-level debugging, single stepping, and allows the programmer to change any method, even basic ones such as addition and if-then-else, at any time. Since a long pause for compilation would alert the programmer to the existence of a lower level of reality, the implementation works hard to avoid such pauses. We view the implementation not as an interpreter of programs, but rather as a creator of the illusion that the Self objects are real.

Along the way Self's implementation techniques of adaptive recompilation and type-feedback achieve some traditionally-important but rarely achieved goals as well: the elimination of run-time penalty for factoring and for user-defined control structures. A programmer may chop up a method as finely as desired without slowing it down, and may introduce new abstractions that combine control and data without paying a run-time price. These characteristics encourage the create of programmers that are smaller and more malleable.

When all is said and done though, this paper can only suggest, tease, or maybe hint at what it is like to create with Self. In order to most fully appreciate the experience of interacting with a lively, responsive world of objects, effortlessly diving in to change them and create more, freely mixing data and programs, and only getting coffee when you are tired instead of when you change your program, you will have to obtain the Self 4.0 public release and try it out for yourself. May your journey be fruitful.

6 Acknowledgments

The past and present members of the Self group, highly talented individuals each, have made this body of work possible. The authors consider themselves fortunate to have known and worked with them. Sun Microsystems Laboratories has hosted the project for the past four years, for which we are deeply grateful. Special thanks to Mario Wolczko and Ole Lehrmann Madsen for comments on the draft.

7 References

[APS93] Ole Agesen, Jens Palsberg, and Michael I. Schwartzbach. *Type Inference of Self: analysis of Objects with Dynamic and Multiple Inheritance,* in Proc. ECOOP '93, pp. 247-267. Kaiserslautem, Germany, July 1993.

[Blas94] G. Blaschek. **Object-Oriented Programming with Prototypes,** Springer-Verlag, New York, Berlin 1994.

[BD81] A. Borning and R. Duisberg, *Constraint-Based Tools for Building User Interfaces,* ACM Transactions on Graphics 5(4) pp. 345-374 (October 1981).

[CUL89] Craig Chambers, David Ungar, and Elgin Lee. *An Efficient Implementation of Self, a Dynamically-Typed Object-Oriented Language Based on Prototypes.* In OOPSLA '89 Conference Proceedings, pp. 49-70, New Orleans, LA, 1989. Published as SIGPLAN Notices 24(10), October, 1989.

[CU90] Craig Chambers and David Ungar. *Iterative Type Analysis and Extended Message Splitting: Optimizing Dynamically-Typed Object-Oriented Programs.* In Proceedings of the SIGPLAN '90 Conference on Programming Language Design and Implementation, White Plains, NY, June, 1990. Published as SIGPLAN Notices 25(6), June, 1990.

[CU91] Craig Chambers and David Ungar. *Making Pure Object-Oriented Languages Practical.* In OOPSLA '91 Conference Proceedings, pp. 1-15, Phoenix, AZ, October, 1991.

[CUCH91] Craig Chambers, David Ungar, Bay-Wei Chang, and Urs Hölzle, *Parents are Shared Parts of Objects: Inheritance and Encapsulation in Self.* Journal of Lisp and Symbolic Computation, 4(3), Kluwer Academic Publishers, June, 1991.

[Cha92] Craig Chambers. **The Design and Implementation of the Self Compiler, an Optimizing Compiler for Object-Oriented Programming Languages.** Ph.D. Thesis, Computer Science Department, Stanford University, April, 1992.

[CUS95] Bay-Wei Chang, David Ungar, and Randall B. Smith, *Getting Close to Objects,* in Burnett, M., Goldberg, A., and Lewis, T., editors, **Visual Object-Oriented Programming, Concepts and Environments,** pp. 185-198, Manning Publications, Greenwich, CT, 1995.

[Cha95] Bay-Wei Chang, Seity: **Object-Focused Interaction in the Self User Interface,** Ph.D. dissertation, in preparation, Stanford University, 1995.

[DS84] L. Peter Deutsch and Allan M. Schiffman. *Efficient Implementation of the Smalltalk-80 System.* In Proceedings of the 11th Annual ACM Symposium on the Principles of Programming Languages, pp. 297-302, Salt Lake City, UT, 1984.

[DMC92] C. Dony, J. Malenfant, and P. Cointe, *Prototype-Based Languages: From a New Taxonomy to Constructive Proposals and their Validation,* in Proc. OOPSLA '92, pp. 201-217.

[GR83] Adele Goldberg and David Robson, **Smalltalk-80: The Language and Its Implementation.** Addison-Wesley, Reading, MA, 1983.

[HCU91] Urs Hölzle, Craig Chambers, and David Ungar. *Optimizing Dynamically-Typed Object-Oriented Programs using Polymorphic Inline Caches.* In ECOOP' 91 Conference Proceedings, pp. 21-38, Geneva, Switzerland, July, 1991.

[HCU92] Urs Hölzle, Craig Chambers, and David Ungar. *Debugging Optimized Code with Dynamic Deoptimization,* in Proc. ACM SIGPLAN '92 Conferences on Programming Language Design and Implementation, pp. 32-43, San Francisco, CA (June 1992).

[Hol94] Urs Hölzle. **Adaptive Optimization for Self: Reconciling High Performance with Exploratory Programming.** Ph.D. Thesis, Stanford University, Computer Science Department, 1994.

[HU94a] Urs Hölzle and David Ungar. *Optimizing Dynamically-Dispatched Calls with Run-Time Type Feedback.* In Proceedings of the SIGPLAN 94 Conference on Programming Language Design and Implementation, Orlando, FL, June, 1994.

[HU94b] Urs Hölzle and David Ungar. *A Third Generation Self Implementation: Reconciling Responsiveness with Performance.* In OOPSLA'94 Conference Proceedings, pp. 229-243, Portland, OR, October, 1994. Published as SIGPLAN Notices 29(10), October, 1994.

[MMM90] Ole Lehrmann Madsen, Boris Magnusson, and Birger Møller-Pedersen, *Strong Typing of Object-Oriented Languages Revisited.* In ECOOP/OOPSLA'90 Conference Proceedings, pp. 140-149, Ottawa, Canada, October, 1990.

[MMN93] Ole Lehrmann Madsen, Birger Møller-Pedersen, Kristen Nygaard, **Object-Oriented Programming in the Beta Programming Language,** Addison-Wesley Publishing Co., Wokingham, England, 1993.

[Mul95] Phillipe Mulet, **Réflexion & Langages á Prototypes,** Ph.D. Thesis in preparation, Ecole des Mines de Nantes, France, 1995.

[MS95] John Maloney, and Randall B. Smith, *Directness and Liveness in the Morphic User Interface Construction Environment*. In preparation.

[Smi87] Randall B. Smith. *Experiences with the Alternate Reality Kit, an Example of the Tension Between Literalism and Magic,* in Proc. CHI + GI Conference, pp 61-67, Toronto, (April 1987).

[SUC92] Randall B. Smith, David Ungar, and Bay-Wei Chang. *The Use Mention Perspective on Programming for the Interface,* In Brad A. Myers, **Languages for Developing User Interfaces,** Jones and Bartlett, Boston, MA, 1992. pp 79-89.

[SLS94] R. B. Smith, M. Lentczner, W. Smith, A. Taivalsaari, and D. Ungar, *Prototype-Based Languages: Object Lessons from Class-Free Programming (Panel),* in Proc. OOPSLA '94, pp. 102-112 (October 1994). Also see the panel summary of the same title, in Addendum to the Proceedings of OOPSLA '94, pp. 48-53.

[SMU95] Randall B. Smith, John Maloney, and David Ungar, *The Self-4.0 User Interface: Manifesting the System-wide Vision of Concreteness, Uniformity, and Flexibility.* To appear in Proc. OOPSLA '95.

[Tai92] Antero Taivalsaari, **Kevo - a prototype-based object-oriented language based on concatenation and module operations.** University of Victoria Technical Report DCS-197-1R, Victoria, B.C., Canada, June 1992

[Tai93] Antero Taivalsaari, **A critical view of inheritance and reusability in object-oriented programming.** Ph.D. dissertation, Jyvaskyla Studies in Computer Science, Economics and Statistics 23, University of Jyvaskyla, Finland, December 1993, 276 pages (ISBN 951-34-0161-8).

[Tai93a] Antero Taivalsaari, *Concatenation-based object-oriented programming in Kevo.* Actes de la 2eme Conference sur la Representations Par Objets RPO'93 (La Grande Motte, France, June 17-18, 1993), Published by EC2, France, June 1993, pp.117-130

[US87] David Ungar and Randall B. Smith, *Self: The Power of Simplicity,* Proceedings of the 1987 ACM Conference on Object Oriented Programming Systems, Languages, and Applications (OOPSLA), Orlando, FL, October, 1987, pp. 227–242. A revised version appeared in the Journal of Lisp and Symbolic Computation, 4(3), Kluwer Academic Publishers, June, 1991.

[USCH92] David Ungar, Randall B. Smith, Craig Chambers, and Urs Hölzle. *Object, Message, and Performance: How They Coexist in Self.* Computer, 25(10), pp. 53-64. (October 1992).

[Wol95] Mario Wolczko, *Implementing a Class-based Language using Prototypes,* In preparation.

Time and Asynchrony in Interactions among Distributed Real-Time Objects*

Ichiro Satoh** and Mario Tokoro***

Department of Computer Science, Keio University
3-14-1, Hiyoshi, Kohoku-ku, Yokohama, 223, Japan

Abstract. This paper presents a framework for specifying and verifying distributed real-time object-oriented systems. An earlier paper [18] introduced a process calculus for describing distributed objects using local clocks. It was based on synchronous communication and thus could not sufficiently model asynchronous communication in distributed systems. In this paper we propose a new process calculus with the ability to express asynchronous message passing, communication delay, and delayed processing. It can describe temporal and behavioral properties of distributed real-time objects. Based on the new calculus, we develop a verification method by means of algebraic order relations. The relations are speed-sensitive and can decide whether two distributed real-time objects are behaviorally equivalent and whether one of them can perform its behaviors faster than the other. They offer a suitable method for proving the correctness and reusability of real-time objects in asynchronous communication settings. Some examples are shown to demonstrate the calculus and the relations.

1 Introduction

The notion of concurrent object-oriented computation [22] provides a powerful method for designing and developing distributed systems. This is because objects are logically self-contained active entities interacting with one another through message passing while in distributed systems, processors cooperate by sending messages over communication networks. However, these networks have communication delays because of geographic distance, communication bandwidth, and communication protocol overhead. The delay is often non-deterministic and seriously affects the timing of message arrival. Also, for efficiency reasons, communication among remote processors is asynchronous instead of synchronous, although asynchronous communication has its own unpleasant non-deterministic aspects. This is because in synchronous communication the sender must be

---

* Part of this work was done while the first author was visiting Rank Xerox Research Centre, Grenoble Laboratory, France.

** Email: *satoh@mt.cs.keio.ac.jp*, Partially supported by JSPS Fellowships for Japanese Junior Scientists.

*** Email: *mario@mt.cs.keio.ac.jp*, Also with Sony Computer Science Laboratory Inc. 3-14-13 Higashi-Gotanda, Shinagawa-ku, Tokyo, 141, Japan.

blocked for at least the round-trip time of the message, including communication delay.

Therefore, delay and asynchrony in communication create serious difficulties in the design and development of distributed systems, even if these systems are based on the object-orientation concept. To construct correct programs for distributed real-time systems, we need to analyze the influences of delay and asynchrony on the behavioral and temporal properties of the systems. In earlier papers [17, 18] the authors introduced timed extended process calculi, called *RtCCS* and *DtCCS*, for real-time concurrent and distributed object-oriented computing. Unfortunately, these calculi were based on synchronous communication and thus could not provide any general framework for asynchronous interactions among distributed objects.

In this paper we address this problem and propose a new framework of specification and verification for distributed real-time object-oriented systems with these features. The framework consists of two parts: a description language and a verification method for distributed real-time object-oriented systems. The language is formulated as a process calculus [2, 11, 12], because the powerful expressive capability of process calculi allows many features of concurrent objects to be modeled naturally [10, 16]. For example, objects can be viewed as processes; interactions among objects can be seen as communications; and encapsulation can be modeled by the restriction of visible communications. However, ordinary process calculi are based on synchronous communication and lack the notion of time. Therefore, in this paper we develop a new timed extended calculus, called *TACS* (*Timed calculus for Asynchronously Communicating Systems*), with the ability to express communication delay, asynchronous message passing, and delayed processing. It allows us to describe the temporal and behavioral properties of remotely located real-time objects and their asynchronous interactions with communication delay.

Our verification method is formulated on the basis of algebraic relations over objects described in the language. In asynchronous communication settings, a sender object needs only to deliver messages given in its behavioral specification to its receiver objects at *earlier* times than those specified in its temporal specification. It is very convenient to provide a verification method which decides whether or not two objects can send and receive the same messages and whether or not one of them (e.g., an implementation of an object) can perform faster than the another (e.g., the specification of the object). Also, we have many occasions to replace a slower object in a system with a faster object. In such a reconstruction, we need to guarantee that the slower object can really be replaced by the faster object without altering the behavioral properties or lowering the performance characteristics of the whole system. Therefore, we define algebraic order relations which distinguish between behaviorally equivalent objects performing at different speeds. The relations allow us not only to compare two distributed real-time objects with respect to their performances but also to prove that faster objects can behaviorally replace slower objects in a system and that, when the faster objects are embedded, the new system can really perform faster than the old one.

Organization of this paper: In the next section we briefly present our basic ideas concerning the process calculus and then define its syntax and semantics. In Section 3 we define two timed pre-bisimulations that can relate two processes according to their speeds. In Section 4 we briefly survey some related work, and in the final section we make some concluding remarks.

2 Language

The language called *TACS* is formulated as a process calculus [2, 11, 12]. It has the ability to express most features of distributed real-time object-oriented computing: communication delay, asynchronous message passing, delayed processing, and encapsulation. Its syntax and semantics are essentially similar to those of CCS [11], except for the extensions discussed below.[4]

Basic Framework

Before formally defining *TACS*, we summarize its basic ideas.

Non-blocking Message Sending
In distributed systems, communication between remotely located objects is often realized by means of one-way asynchronous message passing. However, most process calculi are essentially based on synchronous communication, and thus we need to introduce the ability to express a *non-blocking message send.*[5] We approach expressing an asynchronous message by creating a process that does not do anything except received by an input port for the message. This is similar to several existing methods [3, 10].

The Passage of Time and Delayed Processing
We assume that time is discrete and that the passage of time in every processor elapses at the same rate.[6] The passage of one time unit is represented as a transition that proceeds synchronously in all objects, written as transition $\leadsto$. Also, most distributed real-time systems have some behaviors that depend on the passage of time. We introduce an operation that explicitly suspends its execution for a specified period, written as $\langle t\rangle$. For example, $\langle t\rangle.S$ is idle for t time units and then behaves as S.

[4] In this paper, for focusing temporal aspects in distributed real-time systems, we avoid introducing the expressive capability of a distributed system where topological connections between objects can change dynamically. However, our calculus can easily model such a system by incorporating it into the port-passing mechanism developed in [12].

[5] In our framework, we assume that the order of message arrival is indeterminate.

[6] By using the method developed in [18], we can easily introduce the ability to express multiple and inaccurate clocks.

Location-dependent Communication Delay
Communication delay is defined as the difference between the time at which an object is ready to send a message and the time at which the message reaches its destination object. The length of communication delay is often dependent on the distance between the locations of the sender and receiver objects. Therefore, we introduce the concept of object (or process) location as developed in [5] and then represent communication delay as a pair consisting of the sender location and the receiver location.[7] Each object has a location name and can receive only the messages that arrive at its location. For example, we write object S at location ℓ sending message a to an object at location ℓ' as $\ell'\uparrow a.S:\ell$.

Syntax

We first define several conventions of notation.

Definition 2.1

- Let $\mathcal{M}$ be an infinite multi-set of message names, ranged over by a,b,....
- Let $\mathcal{L}oc$ be an infinite set of location names, ranged over by ℓ,ℓ_1,ℓ_2,....
- Let $\mathcal{T}$ be the infinite set of the non-negative natural numbers.
- Let $\mathcal{D} \subseteq \mathcal{L}oc \times \mathcal{L}oc \to 2^{\mathcal{T}}$ be a set of multivalued functions, called communication delay functions, ranged over by *delay*,.... □

In our framework, we describe distributed real-time objects by means of the expressions defined below. In order to clarify our exposition, we divide the expressions into two groups: expressions for describing local objects and expressions for describing interactions among remote objects.

Definition 2.2 The set $\mathcal{S}$ of local object expressions, ranged over by $S, S_1, S_2, \ldots$ is the smallest set containing the following expressions:

$$\begin{array}{lll} S ::= & \ell\uparrow a.S & (\textit{Asynchronous Message Send}) \\ \mid & \sum_{i\in I} \downarrow a_i.S_i & (\textit{Selective Message Receive}) \\ \mid & \langle t\rangle\,.\,S & (\textit{Delayed Processing}) \\ \mid & S\,|\,S & (\textit{Parallel Execution}) \\ \mid & S\setminus N & (\textit{Message Encapsulation}) \\ \mid & A \stackrel{\text{def}}{=} S & (\textit{Recursive Definition}) \end{array}$$

The set $\mathcal{P}$ of remote object expressions, ranged over by $P, P_1, P_2, \ldots$ is the smallest set containing the following expressions:

$$\begin{array}{lll} P ::= & S:\ell & (\textit{Located Object}) \\ \mid & P\,|\,P & (\textit{Parallel Execution}) \\ \mid & P\setminus N & (\textit{Message Encapsulation}) \end{array}$$

[7] The concept is used in this paper only for expressing communication dependent on locations; we do not intend to investigate the concept itself.

where N is a subset of $\mathcal{M}$, I is a finite index set $\{1, 2, \ldots, n\}$, t is an element of $\mathcal{T}$, and A is a constant object expression. We assume that in $A \stackrel{\text{def}}{=} S$ if S contains A, A occurs only within subexpressions in S of the form $\sum_{i \in I} \downarrow a_i.S'_i$ or $\langle t \rangle . S'$ $(t > 0)$ in S. We write $\mathbf{0}$ for an empty summation (i.e., $\sum_{i \in \emptyset} \downarrow a_i.S_i$). We also assume that a_i is not an empty name in $\sum_{i \in I} \downarrow a_i.S'_i$ (where $I \neq \emptyset$). We often use the more readable notation $\downarrow a_1.S_1 + \cdots + \downarrow a_n.S_n$ instead of $\sum_{i \in \{1,\ldots,n\}} \downarrow a_i.S_i$ and write $A{:}\ell \stackrel{\text{def}}{=} S{:}\ell$ if $A \stackrel{\text{def}}{=} S$. □

The intuitive meaning of constructors in $\mathcal{S}$ (and $\mathcal{P}$) is as follows:

- $\mathbf{0}$ represents a terminated or deadlocked object.
- $\ell' \uparrow a.S$: sends message a to an object at location ℓ', and continues to execute S without blocking.
- $\sum_{i \in I} \downarrow a_i.S_i$ behaves as S_i if it receives message a_i.
- $\langle t \rangle.S$ is idle for t time units and then behaves like S.
- $S_1 \mid S_2$ allows S_1 and S_2 to execute in parallel.
- $S \setminus N$ encapsulates all messages in set N.
- $A \stackrel{\text{def}}{=} S$ says that A is defined as S. S is allowed to include A.
- $S{:}\ell$ is an object located at ℓ.

We define a function for extracting the name of an object location from P expressions.

Definition 2.3 The function $|\cdot|_{Loc} : \mathcal{P} \to 2^{\mathcal{L}oc}$, which presents the location names of objects, is defined as follows:

$$|S{:}\ell|_{Loc} = \{\ell\}, \quad |P_1|P_2|_{Loc} = |P_2|_{Loc} \cup |P_2|_{Loc}, \quad |P \setminus N|_{Loc} = |P|_{Loc} \ \square$$

Semantics

The operational semantics of *TACS* is given by two kinds of state transition relations: $\rightarrow \subseteq \mathcal{P} \times \mathcal{P}$ (called *behavioral transition*) and $\rightsquigarrow \subseteq \mathcal{P} \times \mathcal{P}$ (called *temporal transition*). Throughout this paper we will use a structural equivalence relation ($\equiv$) over expressions. This is the method followed by Milner in [13] to deal with the π-calculus. The use of the structural equivalence relation allows us to concentrate on the investigation of inequalities between objects as shown in the following section.

Definition 2.4 $\equiv$ is the least syntactic equivalence defined by the following equations:

$$P_1 \mid P_2 \equiv P_2 \mid P_1 \qquad P_1 \mid (P_2 \mid P_3) \equiv (P_1 \mid P_2) \mid P_3 \qquad P \mid \mathbf{0}{:}\ell \equiv P$$
$$(S_1 \mid S_2) : \ell \equiv S_1 : \ell \mid S_2 : \ell \qquad \mathbf{0}{:}\ell \setminus N \equiv \mathbf{0}{:}\ell \qquad S \setminus N{:}\ell \equiv S : \ell \setminus N$$
$$P \setminus N_1 \setminus N_2 \equiv P \setminus N_2 \setminus N_1 \qquad (P \mid \ell' \uparrow a.\mathbf{0}{:}\ell) \setminus N \equiv P \setminus N \mid \ell' \uparrow a.\mathbf{0}{:}\ell \ \text{ where } a \notin N$$
$$\langle 0 \rangle.S{:}\ell \equiv S{:}\ell$$

We now present the operational semantics of our language.

Definition 2.5 *Behavioral transition* $\rightarrow \subseteq \mathcal{P} \times \mathcal{P}$ (written $P \rightarrow P'$) is the least binary relation given by the following axioms and rules.

$$\ell' \uparrow a\,.\,S\!:\!\ell \;\rightarrow\; S\!:\!\ell \mid \langle t\rangle\,.\,\epsilon\!\uparrow\! a.\mathbf{0}\!:\!\ell' \quad (\, t \in \mathit{delay}(\ell,\ell') \text{ and } \ell' \text{ is not } \epsilon)$$

$$\textstyle\sum_{i\in I} \downarrow\! a_i.S_i\!:\!\ell \mid \epsilon\!\uparrow\! a_i.\mathbf{0}\!:\!\ell \;\rightarrow\; S_i\!:\!\ell \mid \mathbf{0}\!:\!\ell$$

$$\frac{P_1 \rightarrow P_1{}'}{P_1 \mid P_2 \rightarrow P_1{}' \mid P_2} \qquad \frac{P \rightarrow P'}{P \setminus N \rightarrow P' \setminus N}$$

$$\frac{S\!:\!\ell \rightarrow S'\!:\!\ell}{A\!:\!\ell \rightarrow S'\!:\!\ell}\;(A \stackrel{\text{def}}{=} S) \qquad \frac{P_1 \equiv P_1{}',\quad P_1 \rightarrow P_2,\quad P_2 \equiv P_2{}'}{P_1{}' \rightarrow P_2{}'}$$

where $\mathit{delay} \in \mathcal{D}$. ϵ is an empty location name. We often write $(\equiv)^* \rightarrow (\equiv)^*$ as $\rightarrow$ when there is not ambiguity. □

Definition 2.6 *Temporal transition* $\leadsto \subseteq \mathcal{P} \times \mathcal{P}$ (written $P \leadsto P'$) is the least binary relation defined by the following axioms and rules.

$$\langle t\rangle\,.\,S\!:\!\ell \leadsto \langle t-1\rangle\,.\,S\!:\!\ell \quad (t > 0) \qquad \epsilon\!\uparrow\! a\,.\,\mathbf{0}\!:\!\ell \leadsto \epsilon\!\uparrow\! a\,.\,\mathbf{0}\!:\!\ell$$

$$\textstyle\sum_{i\in I} \downarrow\! a_i\,.\,S_i\!:\!\ell \leadsto \sum_{i\in I} \downarrow\! a_i\,.\,S_i\!:\!\ell$$

$$\frac{P_1 \leadsto P_1{}',\quad P_2 \leadsto P_2{}',\quad P_1 \mid P_2 \not\rightarrow}{P_1 \mid P_2 \leadsto P_1{}' \mid P_2{}'} \qquad \frac{P \leadsto P'}{P \setminus N \leadsto P' \setminus N}$$

$$\frac{S\!:\!\ell \leadsto S'\!:\!\ell}{A\!:\!\ell \leadsto S'\!:\!\ell}\;(A \stackrel{\text{def}}{=} S) \qquad \frac{P_1 \equiv P_1{}',\quad P_1 \leadsto P_2,\quad P_2 \equiv P_2{}'}{P_1{}' \leadsto P_2{}'}$$

where we often write $(\equiv)^* \leadsto (\equiv)^*$ as $\leadsto$ when there is not ambiguity. □

Remarks on the above transition rules:

- The first axiom of Definition 2.5 shows that a non-blocking message send, $\ell' \uparrow a.S\!:\!\ell$, is translated into two parallel processes: $S\!:\!\ell$ and $\langle t\rangle.\epsilon\!\uparrow\! a.\mathbf{0}\!:\!\ell'$. The former corresponds to the subsequent computation. Note that it can continue to execute without any blocking. The latter corresponds to the asynchronous message. Before it can be received by an object at location ℓ', it is suspended for communication delay time from ℓ to ℓ', written as $\mathit{delay}(\ell,\ell')$. If communication delay is indeterminate, the suspension time is given as a time value of all the possible communication delays non-deterministically.
- The second axiom of Definition 2.5 defines the semantics of message reception. A message can be consumed only by a receiver having a corresponding input port at the same location as the message's destination location.

- Our semantics forces message sending and receiving to be performed as soon as they are executable, without unnecessary delay. This preemptiveness allows us to estimate the necessary execution time of interactions among distributed objects exactly and express several important timed operations, including timeout handling.[8]

In the following section we introduce two order relations with the notion of remote observation, using conceptual observers residing at specified locations. The observers make comparisons between two remote objects (or object groups) by sending arbitrary messages to the objects and receiving messages from them. The observers can know only the length of the passage of time and the messages which arrive at their own locations. They cannot observe any encapsulated computation nor any message passing at locations other than their own ones. The formal representation of the notion is given as labels for behavioral transitions like the weak transitions presented in [11].[9] We define the labeled transitions as follows:

Definition 2.7 Let a range over $\mathcal{M}$, t range over $\mathcal{T}$, and ℓ, ℓ' range over $\mathcal{L}$. The labeled translations are denoted as follows:

- $P \stackrel{\langle t\rangle\uparrow a}{\twoheadrightarrow}_\ell P'$ is defined as $P \rightarrow^* \langle t\rangle\epsilon\uparrow a.\mathbf{0}\!:\!\ell \mid P'$
- $P \stackrel{\langle t\rangle\ell'\downarrow a}{\twoheadrightarrow}_\ell P'$ is defined as $\langle t\rangle\ell'\uparrow a.\mathbf{0}\!:\!\ell \mid P \rightarrow^* P'$
- $P \rightsquigarrow\!\!\!\rightarrow^t P'$ is defined as $P \underbrace{\rightarrow^* \rightsquigarrow \rightarrow^* \quad \cdots \quad \rightarrow^* \rightsquigarrow \rightarrow^*}_{t \text{ times}} P'$

where $P \rightarrow^* P'$ is given as $P \rightarrow \cdots \rightarrow P'$. We often abbreviate $P \stackrel{\langle 0\rangle\uparrow a}{\twoheadrightarrow}_\ell P'$ to $P \stackrel{\uparrow a}{\twoheadrightarrow}_\ell P'$. □

The above labeled transitions have the following intuitive meaning: $P \stackrel{\langle t\rangle\uparrow a}{\twoheadrightarrow}_\ell P'$ means that P behaves as P' and an observer located at ℓ receives message a from P after t time units; $P \stackrel{\langle t\rangle\ell'\downarrow a}{\twoheadrightarrow}_\ell P'$ means that P behaves as P' and an observer located at ℓ sends message a to an object at location ℓ' after t time units. Object P may receive the message if it is located at ℓ'; $P \rightsquigarrow\!\!\!\rightarrow^t P'$ means that P becomes P' after t time units and arbitrary times of internal computations.

The following example illustrates how to describe distributed real-time objects in *TACS*.

Example 2.8 We describe a simple communication protocol for a communication network with transmission delay and failure. The protocol consists of a sender object at location ℓ_S and a receiver object at location ℓ_R. The sender sends a message to the receiver ($\ell_R \uparrow \mathit{send}$) and waits for an acknowledgment

[8] We leave details of a non-preemptive version of this calculus to another paper [20].

[9] We can formalize the relations without using labels for transitions. However, the use of labeled transitions allows us to present and prove some properties of the relations more simply.

($\downarrow ack$). If it does not receive the acknowledgment within eight time units, it retransmits the message. The receiver receives the message ($\downarrow send$) and then returns an acknowledgment ($\ell_S \uparrow ack$). These objects are described as follows:

$$\begin{aligned}
\mathit{Sender}:\ell_S &\stackrel{\text{def}}{=} (\ell_R \uparrow send \,.\, (\downarrow ack.\mathbf{0} + \downarrow timeout \,.\, \mathit{Sender}) \mid \\
&\qquad\qquad \langle 8\rangle \,.\, \ell_S \uparrow timeout \,.\, \mathbf{0}) \setminus \{timeout\} : \ell_S \\
\mathit{Receiver}:\ell_R &\stackrel{\text{def}}{=} \downarrow send \,.\, \ell_S \uparrow ack \,.\, \mathbf{0} : \ell_R
\end{aligned}$$

We assume that communication from ℓ_S to ℓ_R takes 3 ± 1 time units and may occasionally fail, and that communication from ℓ_R to ℓ_S takes 2 ± 1 time units and may occasionally fail.

$$\begin{aligned}
delay(\ell_S, \ell_R) &= \{2, 3, 4\} \cup \{\infty\} \\
delay(\ell_R, \ell_S) &= \{1, 2, 3\} \cup \{\infty\} \\
delay(\ell_S, \ell_S) &= \{0\}
\end{aligned}$$

where ∞ corresponds to a communication failure. By expanding ($\mathit{Sender} : \ell_S$ $\mid$ $\mathit{Receiver} : \ell_R$) $\setminus \{send, ack\}$ in the above transition, we can strictly analyze both the behavioral properties and the temporal properties of the entire system, including the influence of non-determinacy on communication delay.

Due to lack of space, we demonstrate an interaction between the two objects below, when we assume that $delay(\ell_S, \ell_R)$ is three time units and $delay(\ell_R, \ell_S)$ is two time units.

$$\begin{aligned}
&(\mathit{Sender}:\ell_S \mid \mathit{Receiver}:\ell_R) \setminus \{send, ack\} \\
&\to (\langle 3\rangle \,.\, \epsilon \uparrow send \,.\, \mathbf{0}:\ell_R \mid ((\downarrow ack \,.\, \mathbf{0} + \downarrow timeout \,.\, \mathit{Sender}):\ell_S \mid \\
&\qquad \langle 8\rangle \,.\, \ell_S \uparrow timeout \,.\, \mathbf{0}:\ell_S) \setminus \{timeout\} \mid \downarrow send \,.\, \ell_S \uparrow ack \,.\, \mathbf{0}:\ell_R) \setminus \{send, ack\} \\
&\rightsquigarrow^3 (\epsilon \uparrow send \,.\, \mathbf{0}:\ell_R \mid ((\downarrow ack \,.\, \mathbf{0} + \downarrow timeout \,.\, \mathit{Sender}):\ell_S \mid \\
&\qquad \langle 5\rangle \,.\, \ell_S \uparrow timeout \,.\, \mathbf{0}:\ell_S) \setminus \{timeout\} \mid \downarrow send \,.\, \ell_S \uparrow ack \,.\, \mathbf{0}:\ell_R) \setminus \{send, ack\} \\
&\to (((\downarrow ack \,.\, \mathbf{0} + \downarrow timeout \,.\, \mathit{Sender}):\ell_S \mid \\
&\qquad \langle 5\rangle \,.\, \ell_S \uparrow timeout \,.\, \mathbf{0}:\ell_S) \setminus \{timeout\} \mid \ell_S \uparrow ack \,.\, \mathbf{0}:\ell_R) \setminus \{send, ack\} \\
&\to (((\downarrow ack \,.\, \mathbf{0} + \downarrow timeout \,.\, \mathit{Sender}):\ell_S \mid \\
&\qquad \langle 5\rangle \,.\, \ell_S \uparrow timeout \,.\, \mathbf{0}:\ell_S) \setminus \{timeout\} \mid \langle 2\rangle \,.\, \epsilon \uparrow ack \,.\, \mathbf{0}:\ell_S \mid \mathbf{0}:\ell_R) \setminus \{send, ack\} \\
&\rightsquigarrow^2 (((\downarrow ack \,.\, \mathbf{0} + \downarrow timeout \,.\, \mathit{Sender}):\ell_S \mid \\
&\qquad \langle 3\rangle \,.\, \ell_S \uparrow timeout \,.\, \mathbf{0}:\ell_S) \setminus \{timeout\} \mid \epsilon \uparrow ack \,.\, \mathbf{0}:\ell_S) \setminus \{send, ack\} \\
&\to (\mathbf{0}:\ell_S \mid \mathbf{0}:\ell_R) \qquad\qquad \textit{(successful)}
\end{aligned}$$

3 Verification for Distributed Real-Time Objects

This section presents two algebraic order relations on distributed real-time objects with respect to speed. In the last few years, many timed equivalence relations for synchronously communicating processes (or objects) have already been explored in timed extended process calculi (for example see [14, 15, 17]). These relations equate two processes only when their temporal and behavioral properties completely match. The temporal strictness of these relations is appropriate in verifying synchronously communicating real-time objects. This is because in synchronous communication settings every sender object must synchronize with its receiver. Therefore, even if a sender object can send a message earlier than its temporal specification, the object may not send it then if its receiver object is not fast enough.

On the other hand, in asynchronous communication settings, sender objects do not have to synchronize with their receiver objects and thus may send messages as soon as they are able to. Therefore, in these settings real-time objects do not need to completely match their own temporal specification, and need only to deliver messages to their receiver objects at times earlier than those given in their specifications. This reveals that in the verification of asynchronously communicating real-time objects, "speed-sensitive" order relations are more suitable and practical than the above timed equivalences. In this section, we investigate algebraic order relations that decide whether two real-time objects are behaviorally equivalent and whether one of them can perform *faster* than the other.

Relating Objects with Respect to Speed

Before defining the relations, we first illustrate the basic idea behind them. Suppose two simple objects: $A_1 \stackrel{\text{def}}{=} \langle 1 \rangle . \ell {\uparrow} a.S : \ell_A$ and $A_2 \stackrel{\text{def}}{=} \langle 3 \rangle . \ell {\uparrow} a.S : \ell_A$, where ℓ is a conceptual observer's location. A_1 can send message a to the observer after one time unit, and A_2 can send the same message after three time units. That is, A_1 can send the message sooner than A_2. Therefore, we would consider object A_1 to be *faster* than object A_2. Now we define such a speed-sensitive order relation based on the notion of the observation bisimulation [11].

Definition 3.1 A binary relation $\mathcal{R} \subseteq (\mathcal{P} \times \mathcal{P}) \times \mathcal{T} \times 2^{\mathcal{L}oc}$ is a *t-speed pre-bisimulation* on L if $(P_1, P_2) \in \mathcal{R}_t^L$ ($t \in \mathcal{T}$ and $L \subseteq \mathcal{L}oc$) implies, for all $a, b \in \mathcal{M} \cup \{\epsilon\}$, $\ell, \ell' \in L$, and $d \in \mathcal{T}$;

$$\text{(i) } \forall \ell_1, \forall m_1, \forall P_1' : \ P_1 \stackrel{\langle d \rangle \ell_1 \downarrow a}{\twoheadrightarrow}_{\ell} \rightsquigarrow\!\!\rightarrow^{m_1} \stackrel{\uparrow b}{\twoheadrightarrow}_{\ell'} P_1' \ \textit{then}$$
$$\exists \ell_2, \exists m_2, \exists P_2' : \ P_2 \stackrel{\langle d \rangle \ell_2 \downarrow a}{\twoheadrightarrow}_{\ell} \rightsquigarrow\!\!\rightarrow^{m_2} \stackrel{\uparrow b}{\twoheadrightarrow}_{\ell'} P_2' \ \textit{and} \ (P_1', P_2') \in \mathcal{R}_{t-m_1+m_2}^L$$
$$\text{(ii) } \forall \ell_2, \forall m_2, \forall P_2' : \ P_2 \stackrel{\langle d \rangle \ell_2 \downarrow a}{\twoheadrightarrow}_{\ell} \rightsquigarrow\!\!\rightarrow^{m_2} \stackrel{\uparrow b}{\twoheadrightarrow}_{\ell'} P_2' \ \textit{then}$$
$$\exists \ell_1, \exists m_1, \exists P_1' : \ P_1 \stackrel{\langle d \rangle \ell_1 \downarrow a}{\twoheadrightarrow}_{\ell} \rightsquigarrow\!\!\rightarrow^{m_1} \stackrel{\uparrow b}{\twoheadrightarrow}_{\ell'} P_1' \ \textit{and} \ (P_1', P_2') \in \mathcal{R}_{t-m_1+m_2}^L$$

where $\ell_1 \in |P_1|_{Loc}$, $\ell_2 \in |P_2|_{Loc}$. We let $P_1 \preceq_t^L P_2$ if there exists a t-speed pre-bisimulation on L such that $(P_1, P_2) \in \mathcal{R}_t^L$. We call $\preceq_t^L$ *t-speed order* on L. We shall often abbreviate $\preceq_0^L$ as $\preceq^L$. □

In the above definition, $\mathcal{R}_t^L$ is a family of relations indexed by a non-negative time value t. Intuitively, t is the relative difference between the time of P_1 and that of

P_2; that is, it means that P_1 precedes P_2 by t time units.[10] $\preceq_t^L$ starts with a pre-bisimulation indexed by t (i.e., $\mathcal{R}_t^L$) and can change t as the bisimulation proceeds only if $t \geq 0$. L corresponds to the set of the locations of conceptual observers. The bisimulation makes two objects interact with the observers (i.e., arbitrary objects) at L and relates them according to the temporal and behavioral results of the interactions. P_1 (or P_2) may be an object or a group of objects at the same or different locations.

We here state the informal meaning of $P_1 \preceq_t^L P_2$. We first assume that conceptual observers are at locations in L and that P_1 precedes P_2 by t time units. An observer at location ℓ ($\ell \in L$) sends a message to P_1 after d time units (written as $P_1 \overset{\langle d \rangle \ell_1 \downarrow a}{\twoheadrightarrow}_\ell$ in (i)). It also sends the same message to P_2 after d time units (written as $P_2 \overset{\langle d \rangle \ell_2 \downarrow a}{\twoheadrightarrow}_\ell$ in (ii)). An observer at location ℓ' ($\ell' \in L$) then receives return messages from P_1 and P_2 after m_1 time units and m_2 time units, respectively (written as $\rightsquigarrow^{m_1} \overset{\uparrow b}{\twoheadrightarrow}_{\ell'} P_1'$ and $\rightsquigarrow^{m_2} \overset{\uparrow b}{\twoheadrightarrow}_{\ell'} P_2'$). If the arrival time of the return message from P_1 is earlier than that from P_2,[11] and if P_1' and P_2' can be successfully observed in $(P_1', P_2') \in \mathcal{R}_{t-m_1+m_2}^L$ in the same way, the observers judge that P_1 and P_2 are behaviorally equivalent and that P_1 can perform its behaviors *faster* than P_2.

We show several basic properties of the order relation below.

Proposition 3.2 Let $P, P_1, P_2, P_3 \in \mathcal{P}$ $t, t_1, t_2 \in \mathcal{T}$, and $L \subseteq \mathcal{L}oc$ then,

(1) $P \preceq_t^L P$

(2) *If* $P_1 \preceq_{t_1}^L P_2$ *and* $P_2 \preceq_{t_2}^L P_3$ *then* $P_1 \preceq_{t_1+t_2}^L P_3$

where for all $\ell \in L$ and $\dot{\ell} \in |P|_{Loc}$, $delay(\ell, \dot{\ell})$ and $delay(\dot{\ell}, \ell')$ are constant. □

From these results, we see that $P \preceq^L P$ and that if $P_1 \preceq^L P_2$ and $P_2 \preceq^L P_3$ then $P_1 \preceq^L P_3$. Hence, $\preceq^L$ is a preorder relation.

Proposition 3.3 Let $P_1, P_2 \in \mathcal{P}$, $L \subseteq \mathcal{L}oc$, and $t, t_1, t_2 \in \mathcal{T}$ then,

(1) *If* $P_1 \preceq_t^L P_2$ *and* $t \leq t'$ *then* $P_1 \preceq_{t'}^L P_2$

(2) *If* $P_1 \preceq_t^L P_2$ *and* $L' \subseteq L$ *then* $P_1 \preceq_t^{L'} P_2$ □

This proposition is significant in revealing the meanings of the indexes of $\preceq_t^L$. (1) means that P_1 performs at most t time units faster than P_2 and thus P_1 can still perform at most t' time units faster than P_2 if $t \leq t'$. (2) means that L in $\preceq_t^L$ corresponds to all the locations at which the observers can send and receive messages, and two objects ordered by an observer can be still ordered by another observer having a more limited scope $L' \subseteq L$.

[10] This means that the performance of P_1 is at most t time units faster than that of P_2.

[11] Note that P_2 already precedes P_1 by t time units. Thus, the relative difference between the arrival time of the message from P_2 and that from P_1 is $t - m_1 + m_2$ time units.

Proposition 3.4 Let $S_1{:}\ell, S_2{:}\ell, P_1, P_2 \in \mathcal{P}$, $L \subseteq \mathcal{L}oc$, and $t, d \in \mathcal{T}$ then,

(1) *If* $S_1{:}\ell \ \preceq_t^L\ S_2{:}\ell$ *then* $\downarrow a.S_1{:}\ell \ \preceq_t^L\ \downarrow a.S_2{:}\ell$

(2) *If* $S_1{:}\ell \ \preceq_t^L\ S_2{:}\ell$ *then* $\ell'\!\uparrow a.S_1{:}\ell \ \preceq_t^L\ \ell'\!\uparrow a.S_2{:}\ell$

(3) *If* $P_1 \ \preceq_t^L\ P_2$ *then* $P_1 \setminus N \ \preceq_t^L\ P_2 \setminus N$ □

When for all $\ell' \in L$, $t, d \in \mathcal{T}$, $delay(\ell, \ell') = delay(\ell', \ell) = 0$, from $S_1{:}\ell \ \preceq_t^L\ S_2{:}\ell$, $\langle d\rangle.S_1{:}\ell \ \preceq_t^L\ \langle d\rangle.S_2{:}\ell$ is derived.

Remark We defined a speed order relation where the index t may not be zero in order to investigate its basic properties. However, we will usually use $\preceq_0^L$ in verifying systems.

Example 3.5 We present some examples to demonstrate how $\preceq^L$ works. To simplify, we assume that communication delay can be ignored.

(1) $\langle 1\rangle.\ell\!\uparrow a.\langle 3\rangle.\ell\!\uparrow b.\mathbf{0}{:}\ell' \ \preceq^L\ \langle 2\rangle.\ell\!\uparrow a.\langle 2\rangle.\ell\!\uparrow b.\mathbf{0}{:}\ell'$ *where* $\ell \in L$

We verify this relation. We assume the following relation

$$\mathcal{R}_0^L = (\,\langle 1\rangle.\ell\!\uparrow a.\langle 3\rangle.\ell\!\uparrow b.\mathbf{0}{:}\ell', \langle 2\rangle.\ell\!\uparrow a.\langle 2\rangle.\ell\!\uparrow b.\mathbf{0}{:}\ell'\,).$$

We first prove that the relation satisfies (i) in Definition 3.1. If $\langle 1\rangle.\ell\!\uparrow a.\langle 3\rangle\, \ell\!\uparrow b.\mathbf{0}{:}\ell' \rightsquigarrow\!\!\!\rightarrow^1 \xrightarrow{\uparrow a}\!\!\!\rightarrow_\ell \langle 3\rangle\, \ell\!\uparrow b.\mathbf{0}{:}\ell'$ then

$$\langle 2\rangle.\ell\!\uparrow a.\langle 2\rangle.\ell\!\uparrow b.\mathbf{0}{:}\ell' \rightsquigarrow\!\!\!\rightarrow^2 \xrightarrow{\uparrow a}\!\!\!\rightarrow_\ell \langle 2\rangle.\ell\!\uparrow b.\mathbf{0}{:}\ell' \text{ and } (\langle 3\rangle.\ell\!\uparrow b.\mathbf{0}{:}\ell', \langle 2\rangle.\ell\!\uparrow b.\mathbf{0}{:}\ell') \in \mathcal{R}_{0-1+2}^L.$$

Moreover, $\langle 3\rangle.\ell\!\uparrow b.\mathbf{0}{:}\ell' \rightsquigarrow\!\!\!\rightarrow^3 \xrightarrow{\uparrow b}\!\!\!\rightarrow_\ell \mathbf{0}{:}\ell'$ then

$$\langle 2\rangle.\ell\!\uparrow b.\mathbf{0}{:}\ell' \rightsquigarrow\!\!\!\rightarrow^2 \xrightarrow{\uparrow b}\!\!\!\rightarrow_\ell \mathbf{0}{:}\ell' \text{ and } (\mathbf{0}{:}\ell', \mathbf{0}{:}\ell') \in \mathcal{R}_{1-3+2}^L.$$

We can verify that $\mathcal{R}_0^L$ satisfies (ii) in Definition 3.1 in the same way.

(2) $\langle 1\rangle.\downarrow a.\langle 3\rangle.\ell\!\uparrow b.\mathbf{0}{:}\ell' \ \not\preceq^L\ \langle 2\rangle.\downarrow a.\langle 2\rangle.\ell\!\uparrow b.\mathbf{0}{:}\ell'$ *where* $\ell \in L$

It is enough to consider a counterexample. Suppose $\langle 1\rangle.\downarrow a.\langle 3\rangle.\ell\uparrow b.\mathbf{0} : \ell' \xrightarrow{\langle 3\rangle\ell'\downarrow a}\!\!\!\rightarrow_\ell \rightsquigarrow\!\!\!\rightarrow^3 \langle 3\rangle.\ell\!\uparrow b.\mathbf{0}:\ell'$, while $\langle 2\rangle.\downarrow a.\langle 2\rangle.\ell\!\uparrow b.\mathbf{0}:\ell' \xrightarrow{\langle 3\rangle\ell'\downarrow a}\!\!\!\rightarrow_\ell \rightsquigarrow\!\!\!\rightarrow^3 \langle 2\rangle.\ell\!\uparrow b.\mathbf{0}{:}\ell'$. Clearly, $(\langle 3\rangle.\ell\!\uparrow b.\mathbf{0}{:}\ell', \langle 2\rangle.\ell\!\uparrow b.\mathbf{0}{:}\ell')$ is not a speed pre-bisimulation.

(3) Next, assume these objects are allocated on different processors. For all $\ell \in L$, the communication delay from ℓ_1 to ℓ is three time units and that from ℓ_2 to ℓ is one time units: $delay(\ell_1, \ell) = \{3\}$ and $delay(\ell_2, \ell) = \{1\}$. we have:

$$\langle 2\rangle.\ell\!\uparrow a.\langle 2\rangle.\ell\!\uparrow b.\mathbf{0}{:}\ell_2 \ \preceq^L\ \langle 1\rangle.\ell\!\uparrow a.\langle 3\rangle.\ell\!\uparrow b.\mathbf{0}{:}\ell_1$$

Cooperationability for Distributed Real-Time Objects

It is very convenient to develop a pre-congruence with respect to speeds in order to guarantee substitutability between two ordered objects. However, there is a problem in defining such a pre-congruence with temporal inequality. Suppose four objects: $A_1:\ell_A \stackrel{\text{def}}{=} \langle 1\rangle.\ell_B{\uparrow}a.\mathbf{0}:\ell_A$, $A_2:\ell_A \stackrel{\text{def}}{=} \langle 4\rangle.\ell_B{\uparrow}a.\mathbf{0}:\ell_A$, $B_1:\ell_B \stackrel{\text{def}}{=} ((\downarrow a.B'+\downarrow b.B'')\,|\,\langle 2\rangle.\ell_B{\uparrow}b.\mathbf{0})\setminus\{b\}:\ell_B$, and $B_2:\ell_B \stackrel{\text{def}}{=} \langle 1\rangle.((\downarrow a.B'+\downarrow b.B'')\,|\,\langle 2\rangle.\ell_B{\uparrow}b.\mathbf{0})\setminus\{b\}:\ell_B$, where $delay(\ell_A,\ell_B)=0$. Clearly $A_1 \preceq^L A_2$ and $B_1 \preceq^L B_2$ hold, but $A_1|B_1 \preceq^L A_2|B_2$ does not hold. This fact reveals that a slower object cannot always be replaced by a faster object in a parallel composition with other objects. This anomaly is traced to contexts that restrict the capability to execute a particular computation due to the passage of time, for example *timeout* handling in B_1 and B_2. In order to define a rational pre-congruence with respect to speed, we here define another order relation which is a little more strict than the $\preceq^L_t$ relation, and a restricted expression of $\mathcal{P}$.

Definition 3.6 A binary relation $\mathcal{R} \subseteq (\mathcal{P}\times\mathcal{P})\times\mathcal{T}\times 2^{\mathcal{L}oc}$ is a *t-timed pre-bisimulation* on L if $(P_1,P_2)\in\mathcal{R}^t_L$ ($t\in\mathcal{T}$ and $L\subseteq\mathcal{L}oc$) implies, for all $a,b\in\mathcal{M}$, $\ell,\ell',\in L$, $\dot{\ell}\in|P_1|_{Loc}\cup|P_2|_{Loc}$, and $d_1,d_2\in\mathcal{T}$ such that $d_1\le d_2+t$;

(i) $\forall m_1,\forall P_1':\ P_1 \stackrel{\langle d_1\rangle\dot{\ell}\downarrow a}{\twoheadrightarrow}_{\ell} \rightsquigarrow\!\!\twoheadrightarrow^{m_1} P_1'$ *then*
$\quad\forall m_2,\exists P_2':\ P_2 \stackrel{\langle d_2\rangle\dot{\ell}\downarrow a}{\twoheadrightarrow}_{\ell} \rightsquigarrow\!\!\twoheadrightarrow^{m_2} P_2'$ *and* $(P_1',P_2')\in\mathcal{R}^L_{t-m_1+m_2}$

(ii) $\forall m_2,\forall P_2':\ P_2 \stackrel{\langle d_2\rangle\dot{\ell}\downarrow a}{\twoheadrightarrow}_{\ell} \rightsquigarrow\!\!\twoheadrightarrow^{m_2} P_2'$ *then*
$\quad\forall m_1,\exists P_1':\ P_1 \stackrel{\langle d_1\rangle\dot{\ell}\downarrow a}{\twoheadrightarrow}_{\ell} \rightsquigarrow\!\!\twoheadrightarrow^{m_1} P_1'$ *and* $(P_1',P_2')\in\mathcal{R}^L_{t-m_1+m_2}$

(iii) $\forall m_1,\forall P_1':\ P_1 \rightsquigarrow\!\!\twoheadrightarrow^{m_1} \stackrel{\uparrow b}{\twoheadrightarrow}_{\ell'} P_1'$ *then*
$\quad\exists m_2,\exists P_2':\ P_2 \rightsquigarrow\!\!\twoheadrightarrow^{m_2} \stackrel{\uparrow b}{\twoheadrightarrow}_{\ell'} P_2'$ *and* $(P_1',P_2')\in\mathcal{R}^L_{t-m_1+m_2}$

(iv) $\forall m_2,\forall P_2':\ P_2 \rightsquigarrow\!\!\twoheadrightarrow^{m_2} \stackrel{\uparrow b}{\twoheadrightarrow}_{\ell'} P_2'$ *then*
$\quad\exists m_1,\exists P_1':\ P_1 \rightsquigarrow\!\!\twoheadrightarrow^{m_1} \stackrel{\uparrow b}{\twoheadrightarrow}_{\ell'} P_1'$ *and* $(P_1',P_2')\in\mathcal{R}^L_{t-m_1+m_2}$

For $P_1,P_2\in\mathcal{P}$, we let $P_1 \trianglelefteq^L_t P_2$ if there exists a t-timed pre-bisimulation on L such that $(P_1,P_2)\in\mathcal{R}^L_t$. We call $\trianglelefteq^L_t$ *t-timed order* on L. We shall often abbreviate $\trianglelefteq^L_0$ as $\trianglelefteq^L$. □

This relation is basically similar to $\preceq^L_t$ except that the observers of $\trianglelefteq^L_t$ are slightly stricter. That is, whereas the observer of $\preceq^L_t$ sends a message to the concerned objects after the same number of time units, the observer of $\trianglelefteq^L_t$ sends a message to the slower object after arbitrarily more time units than the number of time units after which it sends the message to the faster object. To allow easier discussion hereafter, we define the following restricted expression.

Definition 3.7 Let $P\in\mathcal{P}$ and $L\subseteq\mathcal{L}oc$, if $P \trianglelefteq^L_0 P$, we call P a *non-timeout* expression on L. □

From Definition 3.6, we directly know that for all $P_1,P_2,P_3\in\mathcal{P}$, If $P_1 \trianglelefteq^L_{t_1} P_2$ and $P_2 \trianglelefteq^L_{t_2} P_3$ then $P_1 \trianglelefteq^L_{t_1+t_2} P_3$. Hence, $\trianglelefteq^L_0$ is a preorder relation on non-timeout expressions.

Proposition 3.8 Let $P_1,P_2\in\mathcal{P}$, $L\subseteq\mathcal{L}oc$, and $t\in\mathcal{T}$ then,

(1) *If* $P_1 \trianglelefteq_t^L P_2$ *then* $P_1 \preceq_t^L P_2$

(2) *If* $P_1 \trianglelefteq_t^L P_2$ *and* $L' \subseteq L$ *then* $P_1 \trianglelefteq_t^{L'} P_2$ □

The first above result shows that $\preceq_t^L$ at least includes $\trianglelefteq_t^L$.

Proposition 3.9 Let $P_1, P_2 \in \mathcal{P}$, $delay_1, delay_2 \in \mathcal{D}$ such that for all $\ell \in L$, $\ell_2 \in |P_2|_{Loc}$: $delay_1(\ell, \ell_2) \leq delay_2(\ell, \ell_2)$ and $delay_1(\ell_2, \ell) \leq delay_2(\ell_2, \ell)$,

If $P_1 \trianglelefteq_t^L P_2$ *assuming* $delay_1$ *then* $P_1 \trianglelefteq_t^L P_2$ *assuming* $delay_2$ □

This proposition shows that a slower object is still slower even from an observer residing at a further location. However, we cannot assume the similar proposition about the first expression. That is, for all $delay_1, delay_2 \in \mathcal{D}$ such that $\forall \ell \in L, \ell_1 \in |P_1|_{Loc}$: $delay_1(\ell, \ell_1) \geq delay_2(\ell, \ell_1)$ and $delay_1(\ell_1, \ell) \geq delay_2(\ell_1, \ell)$ then, from $P_1 \trianglelefteq_t^L P_2$ assuming $delay_1$, $P_1 \trianglelefteq_t^L P_2$ assuming $delay_2$ is not usually derived. This is because the observer of $\trianglelefteq_t^L$ cannot notice any difference between its ordered objects before the observer receives their first messages.

Proposition 3.10 Let $S_1 : \ell, S_2 : \ell, P_1, P_2 \in \mathcal{P}$, $L \subseteq \mathcal{L}oc$, and $t \in \mathcal{T}$ then,

(1) *If* $S_1 : \ell \trianglelefteq_0^L S_2 : \ell$ *then* $\downarrow a.S_1 : \ell \trianglelefteq_0^L \downarrow a.S_2 : \ell$

(2) *If* $S_1 : \ell \trianglelefteq_t^L S_2 : \ell$ *then* $\ell' \uparrow a.S_1 : \ell \trianglelefteq_t^L \ell' \uparrow a.S_2 : \ell$

(3) *If* $P_1 \trianglelefteq_t^L P_2$ *then* $P_1 \setminus N \trianglelefteq_t^L P_2 \setminus N$ □

When for all $\ell' \in L$, $delay(\ell, \ell') = delay(\ell', \ell) = 0$, if $S_1 : \ell \trianglelefteq_t^L S_2 : \ell$ and $t_1 \leq t_2$ then $\langle t_1 \rangle.S_1 : \ell \trianglelefteq_t^L \langle t_2 \rangle.S_2 : \ell$. We next show a significant fact for proving substitutability between two behaviorally equivalent objects with different speeds.

Proposition 3.11 Let $P_1, P_2, Q_1, Q_2 \in \mathcal{P}$ be non-timeout expressions on L such that $|P_1|_{Loc}, |P_2|_{Loc}, |Q_1|_{Loc}, |Q_2|_{Loc} \subseteq L$ then, when $P_1|Q_1$ and $P_2|Q_2$ are non-timeout expressions on L,

If $P_1 \trianglelefteq_t^L P_2$ *and* $Q_1 \trianglelefteq_t^L Q_2$ *then* $P_1 | Q_1 \trianglelefteq_t^L P_2 | Q_2$ □

We directly know that if $P_1 \trianglelefteq^L P_2$ then $P_1|Q \trianglelefteq^L P_2|Q$. Intuitively, the result shows the following theoretically and practically significant facts:

- If two objects are behaviorally equivalent and one of them can perform faster than the other, the faster object can be behaviorally substituted for the slower one in a parallel composition.
- A parallel composition between the faster objects can really perform faster than one between the slower ones. That is, a system embedded with the faster objects can really perform faster than one embedded with the slower ones.

Remark The expressive power of non-timeout expressions is weaker than that of $\mathcal{P}$ because any expressions which contain the anomalous contexts mentioned above are no longer definable; for example, $((\downarrow a.A_1 + \downarrow b.A_2) \,|\, \langle 2 \rangle.\ell\uparrow b.\mathbf{0}) \setminus \{b\} : \ell$ and $(\langle 2 \rangle.\downarrow a.\mathbf{0} \,|\, \langle 4 \rangle.\downarrow a.\mathbf{0}) : \ell$. However, we insist that this is not an unreasonable restriction because we never lose the expressive capability for time-dependent operations which make some other event executable due to the passage of time. This restriction never affects any required expressiveness of the language in describing real-time systems which contain no timeout handling, including hard real-time systems.[12]

Example of Verification

For the remainder of this section we will present an example of the verification of distributed real-time objects to demonstrate how the order relations work.

Example 3.12 We consider two printing service systems in a distributed system. The first system consists of two remotely located objects: a printer object ($Printer_1$) at location ℓ_P and a console object ($Console_1$) at location ℓ_C. We denote the location of their environment as ℓ.

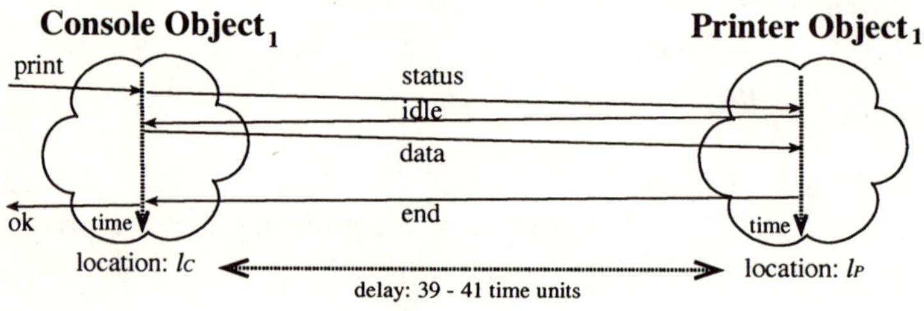

Fig. 1. The first printing service system

- Upon reception of a message ($\downarrow print$) from the environment, the console object queries the status of the printer object ($\ell_P\uparrow status$). If it receives a permission message to send data ($\downarrow idle$), it sends data to the printer ($\ell_P\uparrow data$) after an internal execution for 5 time units and waits for a completion notice of the print ($\downarrow end$). After receiving the notice, it sends a message to the environment ($\ell\uparrow ok$).

[12] On the contrary, every expression in $\mathcal{P}$ can satisfy all the propositions presented in this section, if we alter the fourth rule of Definition 2.6 into "$P_1 \leadsto P_1'$ and $P_2 \leadsto P_2'$ imply $P_1|P_2 \leadsto P_1'|P_2'$". However, this alternation allows an executable communication to be suspended for arbitrary periods of time. We leave further details of this alternative semantics to another paper [20].

- The printer object waits for a query message ($\downarrow status$) and then returns its status ($\ell_C \uparrow idle$) after 5 time units and waits for data transmission ($\downarrow data$). It returns a print completion notice ($\ell_C \uparrow end$) after an internal execution of 60 time units.

The two objects are described as follows:

$$Console_1 : \ell_C \stackrel{\text{def}}{=} \downarrow print . \ell_P \uparrow status . \downarrow idle . \langle 5 \rangle . \ell_P \uparrow data . \downarrow end . \ell \uparrow ok . \mathbf{0} : \ell_C$$

$$Printer_1 : \ell_P \stackrel{\text{def}}{=} \downarrow status . \langle 5 \rangle . \ell_C \uparrow idle . \downarrow data . \langle 60 \rangle . \ell_C \uparrow end . Printer_1 : \ell_P$$

The first system is described as a parallel composition of the objects as follows:

$$(Printer_1 : \ell_P \mid Console_1 : \ell_C) \setminus N_1 \quad \text{where } N_1 \stackrel{\text{def}}{=} \{status, idle, data, end\}$$

Next, we consider the second printing system. It consists of three remotely located objects: a printer object ($Printer_2$) at location ℓ_P, an agent object ($Agent$) at location ℓ_A, and a console object ($Console_2$) at location ℓ_C. The agent object interacts with the printer object and the console object. The printer object is identical to that in the first system except for its message destinations.

- Upon reception of a message ($\downarrow print$), the console object sends a printing request to the agent object ($\ell_A \uparrow req$) and then waits for a notice of printing start ($\downarrow started$). After receiving the notice, it sends a message to the environment ($\ell \uparrow ok$).
- The agent object receives a printing request message ($\downarrow req$). After an internal execution of 20 time units, it queries the printer about its status ($\ell_P \uparrow status$). If the agent object receives the status ($\downarrow idle$), it sends data to the printer ($\ell_P \uparrow data$) after an internal execution of 20 time units, and then sends a message to the console ($\ell_C \uparrow started$). After that, it waits for next print request ($\downarrow req$) while waiting for a print completion notice ($\downarrow end$) from the printer object.

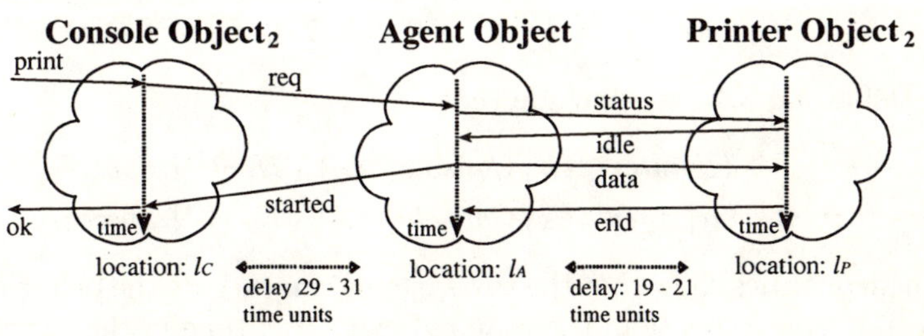

Fig. 2. The second printing service system

These objects are described as follows:

$$Console_2 : \ell_C \stackrel{\text{def}}{=} \downarrow print \,.\, \ell_A \uparrow req \,.\, \downarrow started \,.\, \ell \uparrow ok \,.\, \mathbf{0} : \ell_C$$

$$Agent : \ell_A \stackrel{\text{def}}{=} \downarrow req \,.\, \langle 20 \rangle \,.\, \ell_P \uparrow status \,.\, \downarrow idle \,.\, \langle 20 \rangle \,.\, (\ell_P \uparrow data \,.\, \ell_C \uparrow started \,.\, \downarrow end \,.\, \mathbf{0} \mid Agent) : \ell_A$$

$$Printer_2 : \ell_P \stackrel{\text{def}}{=} \downarrow status \,.\, \langle 5 \rangle \,.\, \ell_A \uparrow idle \,.\, \downarrow data \,.\, \langle 60 \rangle \,.\, \ell_A \uparrow end \,.\, Printer_2 : \ell_P$$

The whole second system is described as a parallel composition of the three objects as follows:

$$(Printer_2 : \ell_P \mid Agent : \ell_A \mid Console_2 : \ell_C) \setminus N_2 \quad \text{where } N_2 \stackrel{\text{def}}{=} \{req, status, idle, started, data, end\}$$

We here compare the performances of these systems. We first assume that the communication delay between ℓ_C and ℓ_P is 40 ± 1 time units, that between ℓ_A and ℓ_P is 20 ± 1 time units, and that between ℓ_C and ℓ_A is 30 ± 1 time units.

$$\begin{aligned} delay(\ell_C, \ell_P) &= delay(\ell_P, \ell_C) = \{39, 40, 41\} \\ delay(\ell_C, \ell_A) &= delay(\ell_A, \ell_C) = \{29, 30, 31\} \\ delay(\ell_A, \ell_P) &= delay(\ell_P, \ell_A) = \{19, 20, 21\} \end{aligned}$$

We also assume that other communication channels among these locations do not exist. Using the timed order relation, the two systems are related as follows:

$$\begin{aligned} &(Printer_1 : \ell_P \mid Console_1 : \ell_C) \setminus N_1 \\ &\quad \trianglelefteq^L (Printer_2 : \ell_P \mid Agent : \ell_A \mid Console_2 : \ell_C) \setminus N_2 \\ &\qquad \text{where } L \subseteq \mathcal{L}oc \text{ such that } \ell, \ell_A, \ell_C, \ell_P \in L \end{aligned}$$

The above result shows that the two systems are behaviorally equivalent but that the first system can perform faster than the second one.

Also, by using the speed order relation, we can verify that the systems satisfy their specification. For example, let $Spec : \ell_C$ be the specification of the printing systems:

$$Spec : \ell_C \stackrel{\text{def}}{=} \downarrow req \,.\, \langle 300 \rangle \,.\, \ell \uparrow ok \,.\, \mathbf{0} : \ell_C$$

By using Definition 3.1, we conclude that:

$$\begin{aligned} (Printer_1 : \ell_P \mid Console_1 : \ell_C) \setminus N_1 &\preceq^{\{\ell\}} Spec : \ell_C \\ (Printer_2 : \ell_P \mid Agent : \ell_A \mid Console_2 : \ell_C) \setminus N_2 &\preceq^{\{\ell\}} Spec : \ell_C \end{aligned}$$

The above inequalities show that the two systems can execute the behaviors given in the specification faster than the required execution time in the specification.

Next we will consider a reconstruction (or an improvement) of the second system. Suppose another agent object (a new implementation) described as the following $Agent' \ell_A$:

$$Agent' : \ell_A \stackrel{\text{def}}{=} \downarrow req \,.\, \langle 5 \rangle \,.\, \ell_P \uparrow status \,.\, \downarrow idle \,.\, \langle 5 \rangle \,.\, (\ell_P \uparrow data \,.\, \ell_C \uparrow started \,.\, \downarrow end \,.\, \mathbf{0} \mid Agent') : \ell_A$$

When we apply the two agent expressions to Definition 3.6, we know the following result:

$$\mathit{Agent}' : \ell_A \trianglelefteq^L \mathit{Agent} : \ell_A$$

The above inequality tells that *Agent* and *Agent′* are behaviorally equivalent and *Agent′* can perform faster than *Agent*. In order to improve the performance of the whole second system, we replace *Agent* by *Agent′* in the system. We will need to verify that the new second system really performs faster than the old one and does not change any behavioral properties. From the inequality and Proposition 3.11, we can directly know the following desired fact:

$$(\mathit{Printer}_2 : \ell_P \mid \mathit{Agent}' : \ell_A \mid \mathit{Console}_2 : \ell_C) \backslash N_2 \\ \trianglelefteq^L (\mathit{Printer}_2 : \ell_P \mid \mathit{Agent} : \ell_A \mid \mathit{Console}_2 : \ell_C) \backslash N_2$$

This demonstrates that *Agent′* can be behaviorally substituted for *Agent* in the second system and that the new second system can perform faster than the old one.[13] Moreover, by using the timed order relation we can compare the new system and the first system.

$$(\mathit{Printer}_2 : \ell_P \mid \mathit{Agent}' : \ell_A \mid \mathit{Console}_2 : \ell_C) \setminus N_2 \\ \trianglelefteq^L (\mathit{Printer}_1 : \ell_P \mid \mathit{Console}_1 : \ell_C) \setminus N_1$$

This holds for $\preceq^L$ as well as $\trianglelefteq^L$.

4 Related Work

A number of frameworks for specifying and verifying distributed real-time systems have already been proposed based on temporal logic, automata, and process calculi. However, although there is a close relationship between delay and asynchrony in communication, general theories for modeling both delay and asynchrony seem to have been neglected in favor of ad hoc methods. On the other hand, several formal models for concurrent object-oriented computation have already been devised. Among these, process calculus [2, 6, 11, 12] is a well-studied theory that can naturally model concurrent objects as communicating processes. In this section we compare our work with some existing process calculi for modeling asynchronous communication and real-time.

Recently, several researchers have explored process calculi-related frameworks for asynchronous communication (with or without object orientation settings). Most of these frameworks introduced auxiliary mechanisms: buffering, for example see [3, 7]. However, these extensions are not always suitable for dealing with computational aspects of process calculi. On the other hand, Honda and Tokoro in [10], and Agha et al. in [1] proposed process calculi based on the notion of actor-like objects with asynchronous communication [9]. In particular, the

[13] Note that all the expressions in this example are non-timeout.

calculus in [10] which expresses asynchronous messages as newly created output processes, is very similar to ours. It also provides an equivalence theory for asynchronous communicating objects. However, its purpose is to construct a purely theoretical foundation for asynchronous communication with port passing, and it does not provide any support for the notion of time.

There have been many timed extensions of process calculi for synchronous communication, for example [8, 15, 17]. There is a notable work by Moller and Tofts in [14], in which the authors studied a preorder relation over timed processes with respect to speed based on the bisimulation concept [11] like ours. However, their order relation is seriously dependent on synchronous communication and thus cannot deal with asynchronous communication. Also their calculus, unlike ours, allows an executable communication to be suspended for arbitrary periods of time. As a result, the calculus cannot exactly analyze the execution time of systems, and their relation shows only that one process may *possibly* execute faster than another. Such a speed sensitive order relation does not seem to have been explored within process calculi in asynchronous communicating settings.

Baeten and Bergstra in [3] proposed a process calculus with the ability to express asynchronous communication channels with latency and failure, based on a timed extended calculus of ACP [2]. Their calculus introduces asynchronous messages through the creation of processes corresponding to the messages and like ours, describes communication delay as a suspension of the created process for the length of the delay time. However, it does not have any speed-sensitive order relation for asynchronously communicating processes.

5 Conclusion

In this paper we proposed a framework for specifying and verifying for distributed real-time object-oriented systems and studied its basic properties. The framework is formulated on the basis of a new timed extended process calculus. The calculus is unique among existing process calculi in expressing both delay and asynchrony in communication. It provides a powerful method for describing temporal and behavioral properties of remotely located real-time objects and their asynchronous interactions with communication delay. We also presented two speed-sensitive order relations. The relations are defined based on the bisimulation concept and can decide whether two real-time objects are behaviorally equivalent and whether one of them can perform its behaviors faster than the other. One of the relations allows us to guarantee that faster objects can be behaviorally substituted for slower ones in a system and that the system embedded with the faster objects can perform even faster than the system embedded with the slower objects. Since in asynchronous communication settings it often is necessary only to verify that real-time objects can perform faster than required by their specification, these relations offer a theoretical and practical foundation for proving the correctness and reusability of asynchronously interacting real-time objects.

Finally, we would like to point out some further issues. Our framework is not sensitive to the order of message arrival; but in several distributed systems, arriving messages are often queued in FIFO order. We therefore are very interested in developing a process calculus that takes the arrival order of messages into account. In this paper we inherently assume the existence of a global clock, but in distributed systems each processor often follows its own local clock. We have already developed a method for describing multiple local clocks in [18]. We plan to introduce the method into the framework presented in this paper. We developed some techniques to define semantics for object-oriented real-time languages with synchronous communication primitives based on a timed extended process calculus in [19]. We believe that the calculus presented here allows us to define semantics of object-oriented real-time languages with various asynchronous communication mechanisms.

Acknowledgments We are grateful to J. Sifakis (VERIMAG) for discussions on the topics treated here. We would like to thank to R. Pareschi, J.-M. Andreoli, K. Beesley (Rank Xerox Research Centre), and V. Vasconcelos (Universidade Nova de Lisboa) for giving significant comments on earlier versions of this paper, and anonymous referees for providing many constructive and valuable suggestions.

References

1. Agha, G., Mason, I., Smith, S., and Talcott, C., *Towards a Theory of Actor Computations*, Proceedings of CONCUR'92, LNCS 630, p565-578, August, 1992.
2. Baeten, J. C. M., and Bergstra, J. A., *Process Algebra*, Cambridge University Press, 1990.
3. Baeten, J. C. M., and Bergstra, J. A., *Asynchronous Communication in Real Space Process Algebra*, Proceedings of Formal Techniques in Real-Time and Fault-Tolerant System, LNCS 591, p473-491, May, 1991.
4. Bergstra, J. A., and Klop, J. W., *Process Algebra with Asynchronous Communication Mechanisms*, Seminar on Concurrency, LNCS 197, p76-95, 1985.
5. Boudol, G., Castellani, I., Hennessy, M., and Kiehn, A., *A Theory of Processes with Localities*, Proceedings of CONCUR'92, LNCS 630, p108-122, August, 1992.
6. Brinksma, E., *A tutorial on LOTOS*, Proceedings, IFIP Workshop on Protocol Specification, Testing and Verification, p73-84, North-Holland, 1986.
7. de Boer, F.S., Klop, J.W., and Palamidessi, *Asynchronous Communication in Process Algebra*, Proceedings of LICS'92, p137-147, June, 1992.
8. Hennessy, M., *On Timed Process Algebra: a Tutorial*, Technical Report 2/93, University of Sussex, 1993
9. Hewitt, C., *Viewing Control Structures as Pattern of Passing Messages*, Journal of Artificial Intelligence, Vol. 8, No.3, 1977.
10. Honda, K., and Tokoro, M., *An Object Calculus for Asynchronous Communication*, Proceedings of ECOOP'91, LNCS 512, p133-147, June, 1991.
11. Milner, R., *Communication and Concurrency*, Prentice Hall, 1989.
12. Milner, R., Parrow. J., Walker, D., *A Calculus of Mobile Processes*, Information and Computation, Vol.100, p1-77, 1992.
13. Milner, R., *Functions as Processes*, Mathematical Structures in Computer Science, Vol.2, No.2, p119-141, 1992.

14. Moller, F., and Tofts, C., *Relating Processes with Respect to Speed*, Proceedings of CONCUR'91, LNCS 527, p424-438, August, 1991.
15. Nicollin. X., and Sifakis, J., *An Overview and Synthesis on Timed Process Algebras*, Proceedings of Computer Aided Verification, LNCS 575, p376-398, June, 1991.
16. Nierstrasz, O. M., and Papathomas, M., *Viewing Objects as Patterns of Communicating Agents*, Proceedings of ECOOP/OOPSLA'90, October, p38-43, 1990.
17. Satoh, I., and Tokoro, M., *A Formalism for Real-Time Concurrent Object-Oriented Computing*, Proceedings of OOPSLA'92, p315-326, October, 1992.
18. Satoh, I., and Tokoro, M., *A Timed Calculus for Distributed Objects with Clocks*, Proceedings of ECOOP'93, LNCS 707, p326-345, July, 1993.
19. Satoh, I., and Tokoro, M., *Semantics for a Real-Time Object-Oriented Programming Language*, Proceedings of IEEE International Conference on Computer Languages, p159-170, May, 1994.
20. Satoh, I., and Tokoro, M., *A Formalism for Remotely Interacting Processes*, Proceedings of Workshop on Theory and Practice of Parallel Programming, November, 1994. Also a revised version will appear in LNCS, 1995.
21. Tokoro, M., and Satoh, I., *Asynchrony and Real-Time in Distributed Systems*, Proceedings of Parallel Symbolic Computing: Languages, Systems, and Application, LNCS 748. p318-330, 1993.
22. Yonezawa, A., and Tokoro, M., editors, *Object-Oriented Concurrent Programming*, MIT Press, 1987.

Object Protocols as Functional Parsers

Gert Florijn

Utrecht University, Department of Computer Science
P.o. Box 80.089, 3508 TB Utrecht, the Netherlands
E-mail: *florijn@cs.ruu.nl*

Abstract. A service definition is an abstract specification of the behavior of a software component. It provides the interface between the users of an object and its (hidden) implementation. A protocol can be a part of a service definition. It captures the conditions under which interface operations can be invoked. This is of use for the designers of clients, but also for implementers of the service, at least if the protocol mechanism provides automatic (static or dynamic) acceptability checking of invocations or messages. Existing protocol formalisms are mostly based on finite state machines that describe legal orderings of messages. This is too limited, however, to model more complex services or to handle conditions that go beyond the ordering (such as access-control or time-dependencies) without referring to a service implementation.

In this paper we explore a grammar-based approach to protocol definition, i.e. we define protocols as non-deterministic grammars extended with provisions for parallellism. The resulting protocols not only define legal message sequences but can also impose context-sensitive constraints on properties of messages, like its sender or a time stamp. Protocotols are truly abstract, i.e. independent of the implementation of a service. Since we want to investigate the kinds of constructs needed in specifying protocols we do not introduce a new notation, but instead express protocols as parsers written in a lazy functional language using a technique called combinator parsing. Besides giving a complete picture of the semantics of the constructs this also allows us to show how dynamic protocol checking can be provided. The approach is illustrated through several examples and its potential and limitations are discussed.

Keywords: service definitions, interface definitions, protocols, functional programming.

1 Introduction and background

Encapsulation is one of the cornerstones of object-oriented development. The separation between the interface of externally visible operations of an object and its hidden implementation provides a firewall that limits the effects of changes to a system. As long as the interface of an object stays the same, its internal operation can be adapted without affecting the rest of the system.

The specification of an object-interface – a *service definition* – thus is an important element of an object-oriented design. It defines the operations that are part of the interface and specifies their behaviour. This involves two viewpoints: 1) the conditions under which the operations can be used and 2) the conditions that the implementation of the operations should meet.

A service definition therefore is a contract that enables clients and implementors to cooperate [Meyer88]. It should be sufficiently detailed to allow (designers of) clients to know how a particular component providing the service should be used. Similarly, it should provide an implementor of the service with enough information to choose a suitable implementation. To give the implementer enough freedom it is important that a service definition is abstract, and does not reflect any particular implementation.

In most programming languages, interfaces are defined in terms of signatures of operations. This is insufficient for both viewpoints. Service implementors need to know more about the required behaviour, while clients need to know more about when and how operations can be invoked. This can involve constraints on data that cannot be captured in the typing-system, but also legal orderings of operations, e.g. a file that must be opened before it can be read or written. In concurrent object-oriented languages these conditions are perhaps even more important since they define the synchronization constraints under which messages by senders are accepted by receivers.

Lacking suitable specification constructs, these conditions are mostly captured in comments or in a separate design document written in another language. In most cases these design documents are not part of the implementation of a system, even if a formal specification language is used. The conditions specified in the design have to be coded in the service implementation to make sure that they are checked in an actual system. This situation has obvious drawbacks. We end up with two versions of a service definition that have to be maintained separately. Since there are no direct benefits for a service implementor in maintaining the specification, doing so can become tedious and lead to inconsistencies between code and specification, even in a development environment where formal specifications and implementations are dealt with in an integrated fashion [Perry89, Weide91]. The end-result is that the implementation is the only definition we can trust.

Some programming languages have introduced specific mechanisms to encode the conditions. In Eiffel [Meyer88] for example, we can use assertions: pre- and postconditions that are associated with the (interface) methods of a class. Pre-conditions encode the client perspective and post-conditions encode the behaviour side. Since assertions are represented as boolean expressions in the Eiffel language and thus are executable, there is a direct benefit for clients and implementors because there is no need to add or maintain extra code to check assertions. If a client does not meet a pre-condition, the assertion and thus the invocation will fail. Likewise, failure to meet a post-condition will create an exception that a client may or may not want to handle. However, there is a potential problem with this approach. Since the assertions are part of a class definition which combines both interface definition and implementation (at least if it is not a deferred class), it is all too easy to let assertions refer to implementation aspects. If developers do not use the mechanism properly it is easy to break the encapsulation barrier and thus make service definitions less abstract than they should be.

Experience with mechanisms to define synchronization constraints in concurrent object-oriented languages points out that a separation of these conditions from the implementation would help to prevent the so-called inheritance anomalies [Matsuoka93, Meseguer93]. These can occur when behaviour added to a sub-class can affect the synchronization constraints defined in the super-class.

1.1 Protocols

Ideally, therefore, a service definition is a distinct part of a software component, possibly written in language different from the implementation language. It should be defined independently from any implementation, but still be of use for an actual implementation to prevent the problems of double maintenance.

As far as the client perspective is concerned, *protocols* can meet this goal. A protocol defines the conditions under which a particular interface operation can be performed. Typically this is done by specifying legal sequences of invocations of these operations in terms of a (finite) state machine. The transitions of the state machine are (invocations of) interface operations, while the states represent abstract states of the particular service (not to be confused with the implementation state associated with objects). Consequently, a protocol is defined independently of any particular implementation.

Protocols can be of use in the implementation of a service, at least if the protocol mechanism is linked to the implementation. One way in which this can be done is by dynamic checking. During execution of a program, the state machine for the protocol can act as a recognizer that checks whether incoming messages (invocations) are acceptable or not. By bouncing messages that are refused in the protocol, the service implementor does not have to take the cases excluded by the protocol into account. Protocol mechanisms like this have been introduced in several (concurrent) object-oriented languages, like Procol [Bos89, Laffra92] and Sina [Aksit92].

Nierstrasz [Nierstrasz93] discusses *static* checking of protocol compatibility. He defines the notions of a regular process, a, possibly non-determinstic, finite state machine whose transitions are invocations of interface operations, and of a regular type, a specification of a regular process. Based on this, he defines a subtyping relationship on regular types which allows us to determine statically whether one protocol can replace another, e.g. in the case of inheritance. Similarly, the notion of request satisfiability is derived, which defines whether a client protocol (the behaviour that a client expects of a service) is compatable with the protocol offered by a service.

Protocols defined by finite state machines are not sufficient to handle all situations. Nierstrasz gives the example of a protocol for a stack, where a "pop" operation is only acceptable if the stack is not empty. To model this protocol as a deterministic state machine – i.e. a machine where there is at most one transition labelled with a particular operation from each state – we need an infinite amount of states, where each state corresponds to a stack with a particular number of elements. Since this makes it hard to reason about satisfiability, Nierstrasz proposes to model this by a non-deterministic finite state machine, where a hidden (implementation) decision determines whether a pop leads to the empty or the full state (see figure 1).

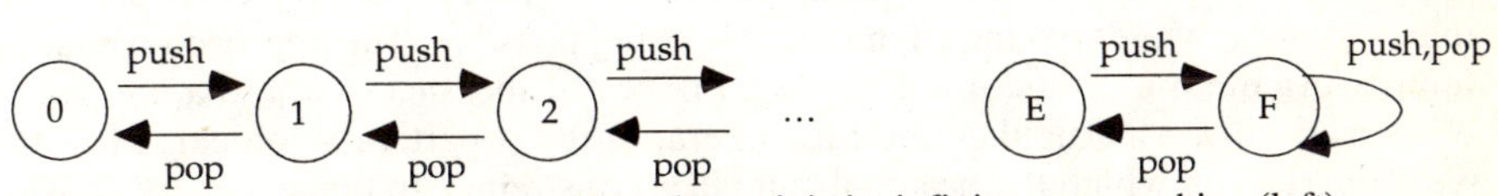

Figure 1: The stack protocol as a deterministic, infinite state machine (left) and as a non-deterministic, finite state machine (right).

In the protocol mechanism offered by Procol, some of this non-determinism can be captured by adding guards to protocol expressions. The guard is a boolean expression that determines which transitions are enabled. Itcan refer to instance variables in the object. In this case we could add a guard referring to an instance variable holding the number of elements currently on the stack, leading to (where + separates alternatives):

```
Obj  STACK(int len)            -- len is max length
 Declare  int n;               -- n is current position

 Protocol (n<len-1): ANY->push + (n>0): ANY->pop
 ...
Endobj STACK;
```

However, this implies a violation of the encapsulation principle – the protocol is not defined in abstract terms but refers to elements of the service implementation (the instance variable n). Clearly, a more abstract way to handle this is necessary, e.g. by letting the guards invoke an interface method of the object such as `isfull` or `isempty`.

A shortcoming of protocols defining only legal sequences is that there other issues involved in deciding whether an incoming message is admissable or not. One aspect is *access-control*: acceptance of an invocation can depend on the identity (or class or another property) of the sender. This is needed for example when update operations performed on the contents of a file object can only be performed by the object that has performed the open operation in an earlier stage. Procol allows access constraints on the class and even the identity of the sender. For example, the keyword ANY in the example above can be replaced by a class name. However, to model the file-protocol it again relies on the implementation. The implementation of the open operation has to record the sender in an instance variable, that can be used to guard subsequent operations.

The access constraints on the file update operations are a particular example of the more general notion of context dependency. Whether or not a particular message is acceptable can depend on properties of earlier messages. In the file-protocol there is a dependency on the sender of an earlier open message. There can also be dependencies on data: arguments passed in a particular invocation may affect legal arguments of future operations. Other aspects like time could play a role, e.g. when other messages should arrive within a certain time-frame after other messages or when there should be a certain delay between invocations.

1.2 About this paper

The aim of this paper is to explore a richer protocol mechanism that can express complex object protocols in an abstract way, i.e. independently of a particular implementation, while making (dynamic) checking possible. The approach we take is grammar-oriented: a protocol defines legal traces of messages, where a message is the invocation of a particular interface operation by a particular object. Messages have properties on which the protocol can place constraints. In this paper we consider the sender, the argument data and time.

Since we want to experiment with the constructs that are needed to model protocols, we do not introduce a new notation. Instead we encode them as non-deterministic, functional parsers written in Gofer, a lazy functional language with strong typing. More specifically, we use a technique called combinator parsing [Hutton92], and express the parsers as monads [Wadler90, Wadler92]. While making the examples somewhat less "easy" to consume, the advantage of using Gofer is that it is easy to define new constructs (e.g. through higher order functions), while at the same time retaining executability. All the examples given are stylized versions of "working" protocols that can be run in Gofer[1].

As indicated before, our goal is that protocols can be specified independently from any service implementation. Therefore we do not introduce a particular (object-oriented) programming language. The basic idea is that once a message is accepted by the protocol, the corresponding operation will be performed on the object on which the protocol parser is active. As a consequence, we assume that normal type checking (checking whether actual and formal arguments and result type are compatible) is done by the underlying language.

The paper is organized as follows. In chapter 2 we introduce to the notation and technology used to express parsers, i.e. we briefly discuss parsing with combinators, monads and Gofer. Chapter 3 shows how parsers can be used for defining protocols by defining parsers of messages. Chapters 4 and 5 provide several examples of protocols, while at the same time extending the expressive power of the parsers with parallellism and shared state. Then, in chapter 6 we discuss incremental checking of protocols by defining an implementation of parsers that will react to individual incoming messages. Finally, in chapter 7, we evaluate the work and discuss some possible extensions and problems.

2 Parsing with Combinators

Parsing in functional languages is very simple. A parser is modeled as function that takes a sequence of input items, tries to match some items from it, and returns a result e.g. a (partial) parse tree. Basic parsers match invididual input items. They are glued together into larger parsers by higher-order functions or combinators [Hutton92] to handle constructs like sequencing or alternatives. Parsers can be non-deterministic: one input-sequence can be parsed in different ways. To model this, the "list of successes" approach is used. Parsers return the results of all possible parses on a given input.

In Gofer, we can define a parser as a function of the following parametrized type:

```
type Parser is a  =  is -> [( a, is )]
```

A parser is function (denoted by the arrow) that takes a state of type `is` (typically, a list of tokens) and produces a list of tuples. Each tuple represents a succesful parse, that is, a result value of type `a` together with the adapted state (typically the remainder of the input that was not parsed).

Parsers are constructed by combining elementary parsers. Two of the basic parsers are: `fail` which always fails, and `okay` which succeeds with a given value as its result:

---

[1]The programs can be obtained via World-Wide Web at URL:
http:://www.cs.ruu.nl/~florijn/reseach/ariadne.html

```
fail    :: Parser is a          okay        :: a -> Parser is
fail xs  = []                   okay v xs    = [ (v,xs) ]
```

Note that the first line in these definitions gives the type of the function. Another basic parser is `item`. It succeeds with the next item of the input, and fails when no input is left.

```
item ::  Parser [a] a
item [] = fail []
item (i:is) = okay i is
```

Note that we assume here that the input is modelled as a list of items of type `a`; `(a:b)` denotes a list whose head element is `a` and whose tail is the list denoted by `b`.

2.1 Combinators

Elementary parsers are combined using combinators. The first one discussed here is `into` which performs a parser on the input and – if it was succesful – performs a second parser on the remaining input. The second parser gets the result of the first parser as an argument. `into` returns the result of the second parser. The second combinator is `orelse`. It applies both parsers on the current input and returns the combined results.

```
infixr 6 `into`
infixr 4 `orelse`

into   :: Parser i a -> (a -> Parser i b) -> Parser i b
(p `into` q) xs = [(r,zs) | (v,ys) <-p xs, (r,zs) <- q v ys]

orelse :: Parser i a -> Parser i a -> Parser i a
(p1 `orelse` p2) xs  =  p1 xs ++ p2 xs
```

`into` and `orelse` are defined as infix operators, where `into` binds more strongly. As follows from the definition, `orelse` concatenates (the ++ operator) the results of attempting both alternatives, implying that a parser returns a list of sucesses. The definition of `into` uses list-comprehension: `[r|v<- e1, r<- e2 v, p r]` denotes the list of `r`'s obtained by iterating v over the values returned by `e1`, binding `r` to the result of applying `v` to `e2` and checking whether `p v` is true.

The fact that parsers are functions means that we can combine them easily and write higher order functions. Take for example the function `oneof` which succeeds when one parser of a list of parsers suceeds and which returns the result of that match. We must insert the `orelse` operator between all the parsers:

```
oneof   :: [Parser a b]  -> Parser a b
oneof l = foldr1 orelse l
```

For a real application a few other definitions are useful. The first is `sat`. It succeeds when the next input item satisfies a given predicate, and returns the input item if successful. Using `sat` it is easy to define `lit`, which matches a literal item in the input

```
sat  ::  (a -> Bool) -> Parser [a] a
sat p = [ (r,xs') | (r, xs') <- item xs, p r]

lit :: Eq i => [i] -> Parser [i] i
lit x = sat (==x)
```

Now we can define a parser that matches nested parenthesized expressions from a string of characters and returns the nesting-depth (an integer):

```
nest :: Parser [Char] Int
nest = (lit '(' `into` (\_ -> nest `into` (\d ->
                         lit ')' `into` (\_ -> okay (d + 1)))))
        `orelse` okay 0  -- empty alternative
```

Here we use the lambda abstraction (`\args -> expr`) to turn parsers in a form suited for use with `into`. The underscore character is used if we are not interested in naming the argument. Note that this definition requires (Parser i) to be a monad (see below). Finally, to actually run a parser on some input, we define:

```
parse :: Parser i a -> i -> [(a,i)]
parse p xs = [(x,s) | (x,s) <- p xs]
```

Applying "`parse nest "(())"`" will produce a list of two results: one with depth 2 that consumed all input, and one with depth 0 that consumed no input.

2.2 Parsers as monads

Given our definitions we can define parsers as monads [Wadler90, Wadler92]. Conceptually, monads allow us to make a distinction between a value and the computation that produces that value. Specifically, a monad `m a` denotes a computation of type `m` which, when evaluated, will produce a value of type `a`. To define a type as (various kinds of) monads we have to give definitions for certain functions. Using the monad constructor classes [Jones93] defined in Gofer, this results in the following definitions (the comments indicate the type of the function in terms of a monad `m`):

```
instance Monad   (Parser i) where
         result = okay   -- result :: a -> m a
         bind   = into   -- bind   :: m a -> (a -> m b) -> m b
```

The main advantage of defining parsers as monads is that we can now glue together parsers using "`bind`" and "`result`". If we change the implementation of parsers, the definitions of our parsers can remain unchanged, as long as the new implementation can again be mapped to a monad, that is, as long as we can define new implementations for `bind` and `result`. By adding a few more definitions, for a zero element and for the concatenation:

```
instance Monad0    (Parser i) where
         zero   = fail   -- zero :: m a

instance MonadPlus (Parser i) where
         (++)   = orelse-- (++) :: m a -> m a -> m a
```

we can even use monad-comprehensions to define our parsers. Monad comprehensions are similar to list-comprehensions (in fact, the list is a monad). To illustrate this, we give two definitions of `seq` which performs two parsers in sequence and returns the combined results in a tuple:

```
seq :: Monad m => m a -> m b -> m (a,b)
p1 `seq` p2 = p1 `bind` (\a -> p2 `bind` \b -> result (a,b))
p1 `seq` p2 = [ (a,b) | a <- p1, b <- p2]
```

The second form is internally transformed to something similar to the first form. Note that this version of `seq` works for any datatype that is a monad. We illustrate the use monad comprehensions further by defining a few other combinators. The first is `serie` which matches a list of parsers in sequence and returns the combined results as a list. The second one is `option`, which implements the optional construct. If the argument parser succeeds, its result is returned (in a list), otherwise the empty list is returned. In fact, these functions also operate on any monad of the given class. Finally, we define `many` and `many1` that succeed when the argument parsers matches zero or more (one or more for `many1`) times:

```
serie :: Monad m => [m a] -> m [a]
serie [] = result []
serie (p:ps)  = [ a:as | a <- p, as <- serie ps ]

option :: MonadPlus m => m a -> m [a]
option p    =   [ [x] | x <- p] ++ result []

many, many1  :: MonadPlus m => m a -> m [a]
many  p = [ (f:r) | f <- p, r <- many p] ++ [[]]
many1 p = [ (f:r) | f <- p, r <- many p]
```

3 Protocols as message parsers

A protocol is a specification of the conditions under which messages are acceptable to an object that implements a service. By modelling protocols as functional parsers that match incoming messages, we can specify the protocol independently of a particular implementation. In this section we illustrate the general idea by defining a suitable representation for messages, and by discussing a simple example.

3.1 The general idea

Conceptually, the protocol parsers are used as a per-object arbiter function operating on incoming messages. There will be a running instance of a protocol parser for each object that should meet the protocol. If an incoming message is accepted by the protocol, it will lead to a method invocation. If the message is rejected, we assume that the sender is informed of this, e.g. by an exception. Objects could run concurrently, e.g. with synchronization between sender and receiver on the acceptance of a message by the protocol (as in Procol). In this case we expect that multiple incoming messages are queued for handling by the protocol.

As mentioned before, we do not consider any concrete (object-oriented) programming language for which the protocol mechanism is used. As a consequence we do not consider the type-checking of invocations of interface methods. The main reason for this is that we want to focus on the constructs needed to define protocols. Adding type-checking would muddle the definitions and make the discussion too language-specific. So, although type checking could be introduced in the protocol (constraints on arguments for example are possible, see the next chapter) we assume that it is handled by the programming language implementation itself (e.g. in the compiler). In particular, we assume that type-checking is performed before a message is passed to the protocol for deciding whether it is acceptable.

As far as the implementation of protocol parsers is concerned, we assume for the time being that the complete input, i.e. all the messages that are sent to an object, is available in a list. The implementation of incremental checking that is necessary for pratical applications is discussed in chapter 6.

3.2 Message representation

Protocols are parsers of messages. Any constraint defined in the protocol must thus be defined in term of information associated with incoming messages. So, if we want to impose constraints on the sender of a message, the sender should be part message structure that is offered to the protocol. In this paper we consider three of such properties, i.e. the data that makes up the arguments, the identity of the sender object and a timestamp denoting the moment the message was sent. Additional properties that could be of interest would be the location from which a message is sent (in a distributed system) or the class of the object that sent the message (as used in Procol).

In Gofer terminology this means that a message is a tuple consisting of an operation name or selector, arguments (data), the sender and a timestamp. As far as data values are concerned, we take a simple approach (see the discussion about type-checking above). We consider elementary values of type Text and Number and composite values of type Set and Record, a mapping from names to values. We can express this through the following types:

```
type Selector    = String
type Sender      = String
type Timestamp   = String
type Message     = (Selector, Value, Sender, Timestamp)

type Label = String
type Assoc = (Label, Value)
type Env   = [Assoc]

data Value = Text String
           | Number Int
           | Set [Value]
           | Rec [Assoc]
           | None          -- No value

assoc x ((y,v):as) | x == y = v
                   | otherwise = assoc x as
```

In addition to this, we define a number of functions that extract certain elements out of `message` tuples or `value` tuples:

```
timestamp (_,_,_,x) = x        tv (Text i) = i
sender (_,_,x,_)    = x        nv (Number i) = i
value (_,x,_,_,)    = x        sv (Set i) = i
selector (x,_,_,_)  = x
```

For the implementation of the examples it is also necessary to make the `message` and `value` types instances of classes `Eq` and `Ord`, so that they can be compared and ordered. These definitions have been omitted here, but involve defining two comparison functions on each type.

3.3 A simple example: the file-protocol

If we assume that the input is a (complete) list of `message` tuples we now can actually define and run protocols. We can use `sat` to match specific messages, since it applies a predicate on the next input item. For convenience we define a parser `lmsg` which matches any message with a particular selector. Recall that the message is a 4-tuple as defined above.

```
lmsg :: Parser [Message] Message
lmsg l = sat (\(s,v,o,t) -> s == l)
```

Using combinators defined earlier we can write a simple protocol parser for a file object (henceforth the type definitions for the parsers have been omitted for brevity):

```
file = many session

session = [ (o,rw,c) | o <- lmsg "open", rw <- readwrite,
                       c <- lmsg "close" ]

readwrite = many ( oneof [lmsg "read", lmsg "write"] )
```

The parser `session` matches one valid walk-through of the protocol and returns the messages that were parsed in a 3-tuple. The combinator `many` is used to match zero or more or occurences of read or write operations and to get the "infinite" loop providing multiple sessions on the same file.

4 Examples of protocol parsers

In this section we illustrate the expressive power of parsers by discussing several examples. In the course of this discussion we also introduce some new combinators. We begin with variations of stack protocols that show how context-dependency and access-control can be provided. Then, we show how dynamic instantiation of parsers can be used to model a fairly complex voting protocol. We conclude this section with some discussion.

4.1 Simple stacks

In the introduction we discussed the protocol for stacks. Using the existing combinators, we can define a simple stack protocol in a straightforward fashion:

```
stack     = many push
push      = [ f | f <- lmsg "push", r <- full]
full      = [ r | f <- many push,   r <- lmsg "pop" ]
```

The basic parser is `stack` that represents the empty stack. The parser `full` is invoked whenever an item is pushed onto the stack. Each invocation of `full` thus corresponds to a stack with a particular number of items on it. `Full` can handle arbitrarily many extra "pushes" (which lead to recursive invocations) but it will complete by matching the "pop" of the item that was pushed onto the stack just before this particular invocation. Compared to the state-machine solutions in the introduction, this solution thus creates a (possibly infinite) list of states. Since the return values of parsers are not really relevant in this case, the `push` parser returns the "push" message while the `full` parser returns the "pop" message.

Obviously, real-life stacks are not infinite in size, but have an – implementation determined – maximum size. To incorporate this into our definitions is – conceptually – simple. We can let the protocol query the underlying component for its maximum number of elements, count the number of states generated so far and use this in checking the acceptability of an incoming "push" message. The examples below illustrate the general mechanisms to do this.

4.2 Context sensitivity

Now suppose that we want to adapt the definition of stacks such that the items pushed on it are non-negative numbers in non-descending order, i.e. the number on stack position *i* should be greater or equal to the number that is below it. We now would like the protocol to reflect this constraint, so that messages that want to push a wrong value are rejected.

Basically what we do here is introduce context sensitivity. A message is only accepted if its properties conform to properties of other messages that were parsed earlier. Modelling this particular case is relatively easy by adding parameters to our parsers and by passing the data values of messages around:

```
stack2   = many (push2 0)
push2 n = [ f | f <- sat (\(l,v,u,t) ->
                                l == "push" && n <= nv v),
                r <- full2 (nv (value f))]
full2 n = [ r | f <- many (push2 n), r <- lmsg "pop" ]
```

The parser that handles "push" is given the number that is currently on the top of the stack as an argument (or zero if the stack is empty). A push message now has to have a number value that is larger than or equal to this value. This is coded in an application of `sat`. The new "top" number is passed on to `full` and the process continues.

4.3 Access control

A perhaps more appealing application of context-sensitivity occurs when we use protocols to encode access-control: constraints on who can send a message to this particular object. The stack protocol serves again as the vehicle for the example: we want to enforce that items that are pushed on a stack are removed by other objects than the ones that pushed them on the stack. So the sender of a message that pushed item *i* on the stack should be different from the sender of the corresponding pop. Again we use parameters to pass this context information around:

```
stack3   = many (push3 "arbitrary object-id")
push3 n = [ f | f <- lmsg "push",   r <- full3 (sender f)]
full3 n = [ r | f <- many (push3 n),
                r <- sat (\(l,v,u,t) -> l == "pop" && u /= n)]
```

The `sat` application in `full3` only succeeds if the sender is not equal to the sender that pushed the item and that was passed as an argument to `full3`.

Obviously, a similar approach could be used to add access control to the file protocol that was introduced earlier. Since we only consider the sending object as part of the message we cannot express constraints on the class of the sender (e.g. all the push messages should come from objects of class X). Of course, this could be repaired easily by adding the class information to the message.

4.4 The voting protocol

As a final example in this section we discuss a fairly complex protocol that can handle a voting session on a particular topic. The definition given here is an adapted version of an example introduced in [Florijn94].

The idea is that a software component performs the bookkeeping surrounding a vote on a particular topic. The vote is broken down into three "phases". In the preparation phase the initiator of the vote defines the topic, the choices that voters can make, the participants that can cast a vote, the time at which voting can start and the deadline before which votes should be cast. In phase two, the actual votes are cast. It is a bounded period of time (from start to deadline). Of course, each participant can only vote once, and can only chose one of the given options. Voting may or may not be compulsory. In the final phase, the results of the vote can be inspected by the participants and by the initiator. We assume that intermediate results cannot be inspected.

The top level parser of this protocol is straightforward. It decomposes into parsers for the three phases. Likewise, the parser for the preparation phase matches the messages that define the various initial settings.

```
voting  = [ (p,v,i) | p <- prepare, v <- votes p,
                      i <- inspect p ]

prepare = [ (tv (value t)),ps,cs,tv (value s),tv (value d)) |
                  t  <- lmsg "topic", ps <- voters,
                  cs <- choices, s  <- lmsg "starttime",
                  d  <- lmsg "deadline" ]

voters  = [ Set (map value x) | x <- many1 (lmsg "voter") ]
choices = [ Set (map value x) | x <- many1 (lmsg "choice") ]
```

Note that we represent senders and timestamps (the starting time and the deadline) as strings. Also we assume that the topic and the choices that can be made are represented as strings. Furthermore, this definition is not complete. It lacks a check for the fact that voters and choices do not contain duplicates and there is no access control check for the fact that all these messages are sent by one particular sender, the initiator object. Adding these constraints is easy, so we will not do it here.

Once the preparation phase is completed, we enter the voting-phase. Basically this involves the reception of "vote" messages from all voters identified earlier (assuming that voting is compulsory). One constraint on these votes is that they must occur within the time-frame identified. This is a variation on the constraints defined above. The other constraints to check are that each voter votes precisely once, and that each vote makes a choice from the set of choices identified earlier. We model this by "generating" suitable combinations of parsers using the sets of voters and choices defined during preparation.

The elementary parser is `vote` which succeeds when a particular choice c is made by a particular voter object p within the time-frame between b and e:

```
vote p c b e = sat (\(l,v,u,t) ->
         l == "vote" && p == u && v == c && b <= t && t <= e)
```

Given a particular voter p, the set of choices cs, the start time b and the deadline e, we can define a parser that accepts one of all possible choices as follows (and returns the message that was parsed succesfully):

```
pvote p cs b e = oneof [ vote p c b e | c <- sv cs]
```

Note that the list comprehension here generates a list of parsers, handled by `oneof`. Similarly, we can generate a series of parsers for the set of participants and thus define the version of the parser for `votes` that returns the set of choices made from the vote messages.

```
votes (t,ps,cs,b,e) = [ Set (map value x) |
            x <- serie [ pvote (tv p) cs b e | p <- sv ps]]
```

The problem with this definition is that we use the `serie` combinator. The votes by the participants now are expected to arrive in a particular order. Of course, this is undesired: we want to accept all possible permutations of votes [Cameron94]. We need a new combinator `unordered` that will match a list of parsers occurring in arbitrary order. Defining `unordered` is conceptually simple. We generate all possible permutations of the list of parsers, put each permutation in a `serie`, and combine the set of permutations as alternatives using `orelse`, relying on lazy evaluation to optimize the actual generation and evaluation of alternatives:

```
unordered ps = oneof (map serie (perms ps))
              where gaps [] = []
                    gaps (x:xs) = xs:(map (x:) (gaps xs))
                    perms [] = [[]]
                    perms l = [ x:p | (x,r) <- zip l (gaps l),
                                      p <- perms r]
```

Note that there is one flaw in this solution: the order of the results is not fixed but depends on the alternative actually found. To correct this, we must add functions to re-order each alternative once it has been matched. We will not discuss this further here. Applying `unordered` in our example completes the definition of `votes`:

```
votes (t,ps,cs,b,e) = [ Set (map value x) |
       x <- unordered [ pvote (tv p) cs b e | p <- sv ps]]
```

The restriction on compulsory voting can be removed easily by using `option`:

```
votes2 (t,ps,cs,b,e) = [ Set (map value (concat x)) |
         x <- unordered [ option (pvote (tv p) cs b e) |
                                   p <- sv ps]]
```

The final part of this protocol is the parser for `inspect`. It is straightforward, omitting the check on the senders and on the time stamp that would be similar to examples provided earlier:

```
inspect p  = many (lmsg "inspect")
```

4.5 Discussion

At this point it is worthwile to reflect on the work so far. A crucial element is that protocols are defined indepently of any implementation. This means that most of the problems surrounding the inheritance anomaly can be avoided [Matsuoka93,

Meseguer93]. For example, creating a sub-class of stacks with a method pop2 that pops the two top elements of a stack implies the definition of the new method and the definition a new protocol for this sub-class, but does not affect any *existing* definitions in the super-class. A similar approach applies when adding a sub-class with a method ppop which can not be invoked directly after a preceding push operation.

Another observation to be made is that the variations on stacks discussed above only differ in the protocol, and not in the visible interface methods or their semantics. This holds an interesting promise for creating different classes by vaiation in the protocol, and not in the actual service implementation.

5 Parallellism and shared state

The previous section has illustrated some of the expressive power of functional parsers. We have modelled non-trivial protocols that involve context-sensitivity and dynamic instantiation to express constraints on data, time and senders. In this section we discuss an extension to our formalism, i.e. the ability to express parallellism in the protocol. This is needed among others for modelling objects that support multiple roles. Based on this we also introduce shared state among parallel parsers.

5.1 The need for parallellism

The parser for voting assumes that inspection of the results is only done after all the votes have been cast, or more precisely, after the deadline for voting has passed. Suppose however that we want to allow such inspection to occur in parallel with the casting of votes. How can we model this?

At first it would seem that the `unordered` combinator could be of use here. Using the existing definitions of `votes` and `inspect`, the top-level procedure for `voting` would become:

```
voting = [ (p,v, i)| p <- prepare,
                       [v,i] <- unordered [votes p, inspect p]]
```

Unfortunately, this does not work. `Unordered` matches any permutation of its argument parsers, but does not provide interleaving of the parsers invoked by them, which is what we need. We want to allow the messages accepted by `inspect` and all the parser it invokes to occur arbitrarily interleaved with the "vote" messages accepted by `votes` and its descendants.

What is needed therefore is a combinator `par` that takes two parsers, matches arbitrary interleavings of the items matched by the two parsers and returns the results in an orderly fashion. The type signature of this combinator is:

```
par :: Parser i a -> Parser i b -> Parser i (a,b)
```

Using this combinator, the definition of voting with parallel inspection now becomes:

```
voting = [ (p,v,i) | p <- prepare,
                       (v,i) <- votes p `par` inspect p ]
```

The implementation of this combinator requires a revision of the implementation of the parsers. Roughly speaking it means that parsers internally do not return values directly, but *continuations* whose execution is interleaved in all possible ways using the definition of the merge-operator from process algebra [Baeten90]. The details of this are beyond the scope of this paper, but are described fully in [Florijn94]. There we also define a constructor `atomic`, that prevents interleaving of its argument parser and turns it into an atomic action again.

The voting protocol is not the only case in which parallellism is needed. In [Florijn94] for example we discuss an electronic-mail protocol in which messages can be added to arbitrarily nested discussion threads. Here we give two other examples: a file-protocol with a single writer and multiple readers, and a shared drawing object with coordination control.

5.2 Parallel file access

First consider the file-protocol defined earlier. It models exclusive access to a file object for the client that has opened it. In practice, we may want a more elaborate definition, where multiple clients can have a file opened for read-access, but only one client at a time can have a file opened for write-access. The visible behaviour of such an object can be seen as the parallel composition of two protocols: one that handles writers and one for readers. So:

```
file = reading `par` writing
```

The protocol that controls the writers is simple:

```
writing = many writer

writer = [ o | o  <- lmsg "openw",
               rw <- many (oneof [read (sender o),
                                  write (sender o)]),
               c  <- close (sender o)]

read n  = sat (\(l,v,u,t) -> l == "read" && u == n)
write n = sat (\(l,v,u,t) -> l == "write" && u == n)
close n = sat (\(l,v,u,t) -> l == "close" && u == n)
```

To model multiple readers, we need the parallel composition again. After an open for read has occurred, a parallel parser is "forked" to handle other opens for read:

```
reading = [ o | o <- lmsg "openr",
                _ <- reader (sender o) `par` reading]

reader n = [ (r,c) | r <- many (read n), c <- close n ]
```

5.3 A shared drawing object

As another example, consider a shared drawing object. It provides operations to access and manipulate the drawing, e.g. to add graphical objects to the drawing or to remove them. Multiple client objects have read access but only one client has write access (the owner). Write permission is not handled by the clients themselves, but by a separate "moderator" object. It can transfer ownership from one client to another dynamically.

The shared drawing object performs two roles: on the one hand it offers the operations to access and update the drawing to the client objects, while on the other hand it offers operations to change ownership to the moderator object. Using parallel composition we get the following definition for the top-level:

```
drawing = [(i,w,m) | i <- init,
                       (w,m) <- work (snd i) `par` mod (fst i)]
```

In the initialization we identify the moderator and the initial owner and return them for use by other parsers:

```
init = [ (txtval m, txtval o) | m <- lmsg "moderator",
                                o <- lmsg "owner" ]
```

The work involves many read or update operations, while the moderate part involves changes of ownership.

```
work o = many (oneof [ readop, changeop o])

changeop o = sat (\(l,v,u,t) -> l == "change" && u == o)

mod m = many (sat (\(l,v,u,t) -> l == "transfer" && u == m)
```

The flaw in this protocol is obvious immediately. We want the constraint in the `work` parser to be affected by a change in owner that is handled by the moderator parser. While parameter passing can be used to pass the initial owner, it is insufficient for communication between two parallel parsers. What is needed in this case is some kind of state (e.g. an environment: a mapping from names to values) that is shared between these two parallel parsers.

Implementing the shared state means that we have to generalize the "input state" handled by parsers. Instead of assuming a list of items, it now becomes a more complex entity consisting of the items and an environment. This composite state object is then passed from one parser to another. Again, the implementation of this is beyond the scope of this paper, but defined in [Florijn94]. Here we focus on how the mechanisms provided there are used to model this particular case.

The shared state is a modelled as an environment, a mapping from labels (strings) to values (of type Value). It is manipulated through two functions that are modelled as parsers. The first, `eadd`, adds a label, value tuple to the environment. The second, `elup`, searches the environment for a given label and returns the corresponding value. Using these two parsers, we can re-model the protocol for the shared drawing object as follows:

```
drawing = [ (i,w,m) | i <- ini,(w,m) <- work `par` moderate]

ini     = [ m | m <- lmsg "moderator", o <- lmsg "owner",
                _ <- eadd ("moderator", value m),
                _ <- eadd ("owner", value o)]

work     = many (oneof [ readop, changeop])
readop   = lmsg "read"
changeop = atomic ([c | o <- elup "owner",
                        c <- sat (\(l,v,u,t) ->
                                l == "change" && u == tv o)])

moderate = many transfer
transfer = atomic  ([c | m <- elup "moderator",
                         c <- sat (\(l,v,u,t) ->
                                 l == "transfer" && u == tv m),
                         o <- eadd ("owner", value c)])
```

Note that we use atomic here to guarantee that accessing and updating the environment is an atomic action whose constituents cannot be interleaved with other actions.

5.4 Discussion

One of the main advantages of the parallel combinator is to combine different sub-protocols into one. This could prove useful, for example, in the case of multiple inheritance. Suppose we want to combine the stack service defined earlier with a locking behaviour where a locked stack can not accept any messages besides an unlock message [Matsuoka93]. The locking behaviour can be described – essentially – by the following protocol:

```
locking = many dolock
dolock  = lmsg "lock" `seq` lmsg "unlock"
```

Of course, more elaborate checks could be added, e.g. to ensure that the unlock is performed by the same sender as the lock message.

Combining the locking service with the stack service on the protocol level now is simple (assuming that `stack` refers to the protocol of the stack service):

```
lockedstack = stack `par` atomic (locking)
```

Note that the `atomic` combinator is needed here to ensure that no intermediate stack operations are performed during locking.

There are two points worth mentioning here. First, the locking behaviour is pure coordination, so, no actual class definition for locking is necessary; adding in the protocol definition suffices. Obviously, this also holds for some of the examples above. The moderated drawing protocol, for example, includes messages used purely for coordination; they do not have to correpond to interface methods of the underlying object. Second, combining protocols is not always this easy, especially if more elaborate synchronization is needed between the protocols that are combined. While the shared state between parallel protocols offers the basic mechanisms to handle this, more study is needed as to how easy combinations can be made.

Finally, the examples given in this section (and also in [Florijn94]) suggest that our protocol formalism could be used to describe cooordination among multiple objects, e.g. clients, a server and work-allocators or moderators. In fact, this is one of the main motives of our research; we want to define and implement a flexible coordination system for hybrid processes in which human activities are combined with automated steps.

6 Incremental protocol checking

In the previous sections we have seen how message-parsers can be used to model even complex object protocols in a fairly straightforward and elegant way. The parsers are executable: when run with a list of input messages a message parser will return a list of successful parses, each of which consists of the result produced and the remainder of the input that was not handled. The non-determinism in the grammar is thus handled by attempting all possible parses. However, if we want to consider parsers as an implementation tool, this is not acceptable. We need a situation where for each incoming message it is immediately clear whether or not it is acceptable. In other words, we want to make our parsers deterministic and incremental.

In this section we show that this can be done. We give a simple implementation that doesn't cause changes to any of the protocols defined earlier. That is, while the implementation of parsers is changed, the way in which they are used and combined remains unaffected because we use monads. The key to the solution is that if there is no input available, a parser should return a continuation, a construct that can be evaluated whenever new input becomes available and that continues the parsing process. These continuations are collected and handled by a special driver function that handles the incoming input. Note that we apply incremental checking here to parsers without parallellism, but a similar approach also works for parsers with parallellism.

6.1 Parsers with continuations

We adapt the basic type of parsers given earlier to accommodate continuations. The new definition is:

```
type Parser s a = s -> [ PStat a s ]

data PStat  a s  = Done s a
                 | Maybe s (Parser s a)
```

A parser thus not directly returns a result, but a value of type `PStat`. Such a value is either a final result (constructor `Done`) or a continuation (constructor `Maybe`). A result is a combination of the value and the resulting (input) state. The continuation is a combination of the input state and a parser that still has to be performed. Such a value is only returned if we reach the (temporary) end of the input stream. Whenever new input becomes available, the continuation can be reinvoked.

A few of our basic parsers (introduced in section 2) have to be adapted to accommodate the new definitions. Since their type signatures remain the same these have been omitted. Also we introduce a new parser maybe:

```
okay v  s = [Done s v]
fail s = []

(p1 `into` p2) xs = [ bi |
                 pi <- p1 xs,
                 bi <- case pi of
                       Maybe i' p' -> maybe (p' `into` p2) i'
                       Done  i' a  -> (p2 a) i' ]

(p1 `orelse` p2) xs = p1 xs ++ p2 xs

maybe :: Parser s a -> Parser s a
maybe p s = [Maybe s p]
```

The essential part is the definition of `into` since `into` is used to compose parsers out of smaller ones. It shows how the result of applying the first parser affects further handling. A `Maybe` result means that the whole `into` construct is not completed, but should be retried at a later point. A `Done` result means that the result of `into` is the same as the result of applying the second parser on the adapted input. This can again be a `Done` or a `Maybe`.

Given these function definitions we can define our new parsers as monads. In fact we can use the same definitions as used before. Since all the protocol parsers defined in the previous sections are monad expressions, this means that these definitions still work, but now with a different implementation.

6.2 Input representation

Maybe values are created when the input stream is temporarily empty, i.e. when no messages are currently available. To abstract from a particular representation of the input state we define a new constructor class for it. A constructor class defines a class of types by defining a number of functions that should be implemented on types that are instances of the class (as with the monad definitions before). In this particular case we introduce functions that check whether the input is currently empty, that deliver the next element (and the adapted state) and that add items to the input. Also, we introduce the list as an instance of this class.

```
class ParsingState s where
        next ::  s a -> (a,s a)
        unput :: a -> s a -> s a
        isempty :: s a -> Bool

instance ParsingState [] where
        next (i:is) = (i,is)
        unput a xs = append xs a where
                 append (x:xs) i = append xs i
                 append [] i = [i]
        isempty [] = True
        isempty x = False
```

Using these definitions we can give a new implementation of item, the basic parser that returns the next item in the input or that returns a continuation if the input is temporarily empty. Of course, now the input is a type in the ParsingState class:

```
item ::   ParsingState t => Parser (t a) a
item s = let (x,y) = next s
          in  if (isempty s)
             then maybe item s
             else okay x y
```

6.3 Incremental checking

The final part in providing incremental checking is the implementation of a driver routine that handles incoming messages and the set of continuations and determines whether the next message is acceptable or not. The basic strategy is to derive a first set of continuations based on the empty input. Then, an incoming message is added to the input states of all continuations and these continuations are evaluated. If this does not result in any new continuations, the parser may have completed successfully or not. In the first case, the original parser could be restarted. In the second case, the message is refused and the previous set of continuations is used for the next message.

In the implementation below we represent the decisions as text strings that are returned. Also we assume that the whole list of incoming messages is available to the driver routine which handles them one at a time. In this way we could check for an "end of input" condition indicating that no further messages will arrive (these checks have been omitted here, so we assume an infinite list of input items). It is trivial to adapt this function to handle real input, e.g. typed by a user or coming from a file. We would then have to add a conversion from text strings to the message tuple. This is not relevant for the point we try to make, so it is omitted here.

```
iparse p s input = doiparse (parseconts (parse p s)) input
  where doincrparse ps inp =
        let -- ps is the current set of continuations
            -- h is the input item handled next
            -- t is the remainder of the input
            -- res is the set of results from applying the
            --      continuations in ps to this input item

            (h:t) = inp
            res = concat (map spa ps)
                  where spa (p',s') = parse p' (unput h s')
        in
         if (null (parseconts res))   -- no continuations?
         then if (null (parseresults res)) -- no termination?
              then "Msg refuse" ++  (doiparse ps t)
              else "Terminated; should restart protocol"
         else "Msg accept" ++ (doiparse (parseconts res) t)
```

The definition is straightforward. It relies on a few auxiliary functions that actually run a parser on an input state or that select particular types of responses (results or continuations) which have consumed all the input. We give the definitions here for sake of completeness:

```
parse p xs = [ pi | pi <- p xs]

parseresults ps = concat (map x ps)
                  where x (Done s r)     | isempty s = [(r,s)]
                                         | otherwise = []
                        x _ = []

parseconts ps = concat (map x ps)
                  where x (Maybe s p)    | isempty s = [(p,s)]
                                         | otherwise = []
                        x _ = []
```

7 Conclusions

This paper has explored techniques for modelling complex service protocols independently from any particular service implementation. A protocol provides clients of a software component with information as to when and how particular interface operations can be perfomed. On the other hand, a protocol can be of use for a service implementer, if checking of protocol conformance is automated.

We propose a grammar-oriented approach, where protocols are separate entities in a service definition, and are defined as grammars. Dynamic checking of protocols is then possible by generating suitable recognizers for the grammar. To explore the constructs that are needed we have defined protocols as (functional) parsers that impose constraints on (sequences of) incoming messages. The available constructs make it easy to model context-sensitivity and to constrain properties of messages, like the sender or a time-stamp. The non-determinism provided by parsers has been extended with parallellism and shared state. As demonstrated in section 6, incremental checking of protocols can be provided, making the technique, at least in principle, suitable for dynamic checking in actual systems.

The examples we have given show that fairly complex protocols can be modelled in an elegant and straightforward way. The advantages of treating protocols as independent, but executable, specifications have also become obvious. By changing the protocol we can change the visual behaviour of a class (or even an individual object) without any changes to the implementation. In fact, the behaviour of a component that is purely dedicated to coordination (such as the ownership of a shared drawing, or the locking behaviour) does not require a service implementation, but can be handled directly and exclusively with protocols. Similarly, combinations of protocols (using the `par` combinator), occuring e.g. in multiple inheritance, can be modelled. So, in this way, some of the inheritance anomalies can be avoided. Going even further – and in fact one of the main motives behind our research – the approach allows us to coordinate the behaviour of multiple objects.

While modelling protocols in this fashion is attractive, there are still several open ends to be explored and problems to be dealt with. First, while Gofer provides an excellent framework to experiment with these ideas, it is nothing more than that. Ultimately we want a high-level language or notation for describing protocols. This paper suggests some of the constructs that would have to be included, like context-sensitivity and dependencies among parallel parsers that communicate via the shared environment. Besides adding syntactic sugar, defining a protocol language also implies finding a balance between expressiveness and efficiency. The availability of non-determinism combined with the parallel combinator makes the current protocol formalism powerful, but dynamic checking – at least in our naive implementation – too expensive for practical applications where decisions on message acceptation have to be made within a couple of milliseconds. We are currently looking at more efficient implementation schemes, but it is possible that restrictions to the formalism, e.g. by enforcing that the set of message-selectors accepted by two parallel parsers must be disjunct, are needed to make a highly efficient implementation possible. In a similar vein, the desire to provide static checking could lead to further restrictions regarding the expressive power.

Since the protocol is fully independent from the implementation, protocol state changes are only caused by messages. State changes caused by the implementation should thus be modelled as messages sent to the object itself. One example would be a file object that should be closed automatically if the client hasn't accessed it within a given time frame. The object should send the close message to itself at the appropriate time. It remains to be seen, however, to what extent this separation of concerns can be maintained. Can all preconditions be expressed in the protocol, or should the implementation of an operation be allowed to refuse a message that is accepted by the protocol? Implementing this would be trivial: we can include the result of handling an accepted message in the decision whether or not a state-change in the incremental checking algorithm.

One obvious way to extend the scope of our formalism is to include more message properties. In addition to the class of the senders we could include for example the location (i.e. machine) of the sender, to enforce a particular communication strategy in a distributed system. In a similar fashion it might be reasonable to make certain properties of the current object (like the identity or the location) available to model constraints.

For a more direct integration with object-oriented languages we need a more explicit notion of protocol inheritance. The idea would be that a sub-protocol could give new definitions of certain parse functions, add additional messages that can be accepted or impose additional constraints. Another interesting extension would be to introduce reflection and to make the protocol (and its current state) available for querying by clients. Similar to the `respondsTo:` method in Smalltalk, a client could ask the protocol of an object whether a particular message currently is acceptable or not. Obivously, there is a strong relationship between protocols for dynamic checking and reflective object-oriented systems. Our protocol can be seen as a function based on the reification of the message delivery primitive. By the same token, a protocol could be extended with provisions to handle certain meta-messages itself like finding out who performed the last message send, or how many messages haven been handled by the object.

Acknowledgements

The work described here is a part of the Ariadne project where we investigate computer support for hybrid office processes, which are complex information-processing activities involving contributions by people and tools. Doaitse Swierstra initiated this project and suggested the use of functional parsers to model processes. Jeroen Fokker provided an introduction to combinator parsing. Erik Meijer pointed the way in the introduction of the parallel combinator and the use of monads. Many thanks go to the anonymous referees for pointing me to the existing work in this field.

References

[Aksit92] M. Aksit, L. Bergmans and S. Vural, "An Object-Oriented Language-Database Integration Model: The Composition-Filters Approach", in *Proceedings ECOOP'92*, Utrecht, the Netherlands, Springer Lecture Notes in Computer Science vol. 615, O. Lehrmann Madsen (Ed), 1992.

[Baeten90] J. Baeten (Ed.), *Applications of Process Algebra*, vol. 17, Cambridge Tracts in Theorethical Computer Science. Cambridge University Press, 1990.

[Bos89] J. van den Bos and C. Laffra, "PROCOL A Parallel Object Language with Protocols," in *Proceedings of the 1989 OOPSLA Conference,* New Orleans, Louisiana, September 1989.

[Cameron94] Robert D. Cameron, "Extending Context Free Grammars with Permutation Phrases," *ACM Letters on Programming Languages and Systems*, vol. 2, no. 1-4, March-December 1994.

[Florijn94] Gert Florijn, "Modelling Office Processes with Functional Parsers", Technical Report, Utrecht University, November 1994.

[Hutton92] Graham Hutton, "Higher-Order Functions for Parsing," *Journal of Functional Programming*, vol. 2, no. 3, July 1992.

[Jones93] Mark Jones, "A System of Constructor Classes: Overloading and Implicit Higher-Order Polymorfism," in *Proceedings FPCA'93,* 1993.

[Laffra92] C. Laffra, "PROCOL: a Concurrent Object Language with Protocols, Delegation, Persistence and Constraints," Ph.D. thesis, Erasmus Universiteit, Rotterdam, the Netherlands, May 1992.

[Matsuoka93] S. Matsuoka and A. Yonezawa, Highly Efficient and Encapsulated Re-use of Synchronization Code in Concurrent Object-Oriented Languages, in *Proceedings of the 1993 OOPSLA Conference,* Andreas Paepcke (Ed.), Washington D.C., USA, 1993.

[Meyer88] B. Meyer, *Object-Oriented Software Construction.* Prentice Hall, 1988.

[Meseguer93] J. Meseguer, "Solving the Inheritance Anomaly in Concurrent Object-Oriented Programming", in *Proceedings of ECOOP'93*, Springer Verlag, Lecture Notes in Computer Science, 1993.

[Nierstrasz93] Oscar Nierstrasz, "Regular Types for Active Objects," in *Proceedings of the 1993 OOPSLA Conference,* Andreas Paepcke (Ed.), Washington D.C., USA, 1993.

[Perry89] D.E. Perry, "The Inscape Environment," in *Proceedings 11th International Conference on Software Engineering,* Pittsburgh, Pennsylvania, May 1989, pp. 2–12.

[Wadler90] P. Wadler, "Comprehending Monads," in *ACM Conference on LISP and Functional Programming,* Nice, France, June 1990.

[Wadler92] P. Wadler, "The Essence of Functional Programming," in *19th Annual Symposium on Principles of Programming Languages,* Santa Fe, New Mexico, January 1992.

[Weide91] B.H. Weide, W.F. Ogden, and S.H. Zweben, "Reusable Software Components," in *Advances in Computers*, M.C. Yovits, Ed. Academic Press, 1991.

Interface-Based Protocol Specification of Open Systems using PSL

Doug Lea[1] and Jos Marlowe[2]

[1] SUNY at Oswego / NY CASE Center
[2] Sun Microsystems Laboratories

Abstract. PSL is a framework for describing dynamic and architectural properties of open systems of components. PSL extends established interface-based tactics for describing the functional properties of open systems to the realm of protocol description. PSL specifications consist of logical and temporal rules relating *situations*, each of which describes potential states with respect to the *roles* of components, role attributes, and the issuance and reception of events. A specialized form, PSL/IDL supports protocol description in CORBA systems.

1 Open Systems

Open systems have been defined[28, 1, 65] as encapsulated, reactive, and spatially and temporally extensible systems: They are composed of possibly many *encapsulated* components, each of which is normally described as an *object*. Each component supports one or more public *interfaces*. The inner workings of each component are separately specified via a normally inaccessible *implementation* description (often a *class*). Open systems are *reactive* in that they do not just perform a single one-time service; most functionality is provided "on-demand", in reaction to a potentially endless series of requests. Open systems are *spatially extensible* when components need not bear fixed connectivity relations among each other. They may interact via message passing mechanisms ranging from local procedure calls to multi-threaded invocations to asynchronous remote communication. And open systems are *temporally extensible* to the extent to which their components and functionality may be altered across a system's lifetime, typically by adding new components and new component types (perhaps even while the system is running) and/or updating components to support additional functionality.

For example, an open system supporting financial trading might include a set of components that "publish" streams of stock quotes, those that gather quotes to update models of individual companies, those serving as traders issuing buys and sells of financial instruments, and so on. Such a system possesses each of the above features: It relies on interfaces (e.g., `QuotePublisher`) with multiple implementations. It contains reactive components handling a constant influx of messages. It is intrinsically distributed in order to deal with world-wide markets. And it may evolve in several ways across time; for example to accommodate a new company listed on an exchange, or to replace components computing taxes with interoperable versions reflecting tax law changes.

2 Interfaces

Interface declarations provide a basis for specifying capabilities in open systems at varying levels of precision and formality. An interface describes only those services that other components may depend on, in terms of a set of constraints (e.g., a collection of required operation signatures[8]) on a family of components, not necessarily a complete or closed (nonextensible) description of any given component. Any implementation(s) that provide requisite functionality may be used. Subtyping regimes allow one interface to be described as an extension, refinement, or specialization of one or more superinterfaces. Conversely one interface may abstract a subset of the functionality described in one or more subinterfaces. Typically, base interfaces describe only those operations that are involved in a set of related interactions, and "fatter" interfaces are derived via multiple inheritance[52]. At an extreme, an interface might include only a single service operation. Interface subtyping allows systems to include multiple interoperable implementations of common services, and sets of component types that specialize on common core features.

Systems constructed according to the OMG CORBA [51] model are among the best examples of interface-based development. In CORBA, component interfaces are described in CORBA IDL, an interface description language indicating only the functional properties of provided services in terms of operation signatures. Implementations are often process-level components distributed across machines, communicating via message passing mechanisms mediated by an object request broker (ORB) that directs requests to their destinations.

Roles. While not always phrased as such, interface-based specification intrinsically relies upon the distinction between *roles*[66, 59, 6, 18] and the components that implement those roles. This notion follows ordinary usage distinguishing between a role in a particular play performance (e.g., *Hamlet*) and the actor or actors playing the role (e.g., *Richard Burton* or *Lawrence Olivier*). While the term "role" is sometimes applied to a description of a role rather than its instantiation, we reserve the term "interface" for descriptions, and just "role", or for emphasis, "role instance" for instantiations. A role may be thought of as a typed, abstract *access channel*[63, 4] providing a *subjective view*[62, 25] of one or more interaction participants[33], where each view is described by an interface.

Interface specifications deal only with roles, not *implementation objects*. In fact, implementations need not be conceptualized as objects in the usual narrow sense of the term. They may also consist of finer-grained instantiations (activations) of single procedures, or coarser-grained process-level components. Role-based development methods enforce an opaque layering of roles on top of implementation-level objects, in just the same sense that common object-oriented methods in turn enforce an opaque layering of objects on top of machine-level memory cells, CPUs, etc.

In classic modular development methods, there is typically exactly one implementation type per interface type and vice versa. In most object-oriented languages, there may be multiple implementation subclasses per interface. But in general, interface-based specification admits a *many-to-many* relationship between roles and objects: One implementation object may support several otherwise unrelated interfaces concurrently, or different interfaces across time. Conversely, one role may be implemented by several otherwise unrelated objects connected to the same channel. Each may implement a subset of operations, or redundantly implement all of them. CORBA systems support such mappings by reifying some aspects of roles as "interface objects" that relay messages to implementations (see Section 11).

For example, an `OfficeManager` role might be implemented using a `Person` object, or a `Robot` object, or a set of job-sharing `Persons`, or even a mechanism causing a new `SpecialtyWorker` object to be constructed to handle each incoming service request. A `Person` object might additionally play the roles (hence "export" the interfaces) of `Parent`, `Driver`, `Customer`, etc. perhaps all at the same time. Multiple roles, each seen from a different client, may be associated with the same `Person` implementations; for example (using boxes for roles and ellipses for objects):

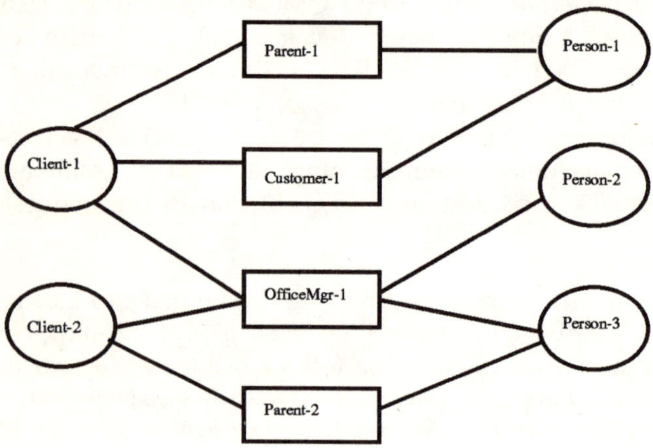

3 Extending Interface Specification

Common interface-based specification techniques are limited in their ability to deal with dynamics, architecture, and quality of service. An interface alone defines only "syntactic" conformance: Implementations must respond to the listed operations. An interface adorned with descriptions of the nature of operation arguments and results defines per-operation functional conformance. But even this does not always provide sufficient information for designers and implementors to ensure that components in open systems behave as desired. A new interface-compatible component may not actually interoperate with an existing one if it fails to send the same kinds of messages to other components in the course of providing services. Such concerns often overwhelm those surrounding service functionality[21, 20, 27].

The remainder of this paper describes PSL, a framework for specifying the dynamic and architectural properties of open systems. An associated technical report [39] contains additional syntactic details, examples, and elaborations omitted from this paper because of space limitations.

PSL adds four kinds of specification constructs to interfaces: Abstract *attributes* are descriptions of properties that may vary across time. These include the special properties `in` and `out` describing the reception and issuance of messages. *Situations* are contexts in which attributes assume particular values. *Protocols* describe required temporal relationships among the instances ("realizations") of situations. *Constraints* describe invariant relationships among the values of attributes.

PSL differs from most other approaches to specification (see Section 12) by mirroring the intrinsic *incompleteness* of open systems. PSL specifications document sets of properties and constraints without claiming that these fully describe a system, or ruling out the existence of unmentioned components, situations, or events. Thus, PSL lacks some familiar constructs found in "closed-world" formalisms. In particular: (1) PSL does *not* support the use of *frame axioms* asserting that properties that are not otherwise mentioned in one situation are not changed from those in predecessors. (2) PSL does *not* contain *step operators* asserting that given states occur at the "next time step" after others; thus that there are no intervening situations. (*Step* is also implicit in the description of transitions in most state models.) (3) PSL does *not* support *leaf interfaces* asserting that interfaces have no possible extensions; thus that instances do not support additional operations. (4) PSL does *not* contain any notion of a *leaf state* asserting that a situation has no possible subsituations; thus that no further state decomposition or unmentioned events exist. These omissions make way for the kinds of refinement and extensibility necessary in the development of open systems.

Types and Interfaces in PSL. As a basis for specification, PSL relies on any framework for declaring interfaces, operations, and pure value types such as integers, records, etc. Rather than establishing a novel syntax, we illustrate using PSL/IDL, a concrete syntax for PSL with CORBA IDL value and interface types and C++-style expressions. All PSL/IDL constructs appear as annotations within `protocol module` declarations. Protocol modules have the syntactic properties of IDL `modules` but contain only type declarations, attribute function declarations, and/or `rules` declarations that consist of an optionally named parameterized scope containing one or more rules. Because textual representations of even simple protocol rules stretch the limits of readability and writability, we simultaneously define PSL/IDL-G, a semigraphical form corresponding in simple ways to the textual version.

PSL/IDL uses C++ expression syntax over CORBA IDL value types. Predicates are `boolean` expressions. For convenience, we add the logical *implies* operator ("-->") and its left-sided version, *is implied by* ("<--") to the list of boolean operators. Within expressions, commas may be used as low-precedence *and* separators. To make them more useful in specifications, PSL/IDL predefines common pure value functions (`head`, `tail`, `empty`, `contains`, `prepend`, `append`, `concat`, `equal`, `remove`) on IDL `sequence` and `string` types.

Handles. A role may have finite temporal existence. However, the lifetime of a role need not be coextensive with that of any given implementation object. Instead, lifetime properties are described with respect to the *liveness* of *handles* used to access instances. In PSL, each distinct instance of a role is ascribed a unique handle. Handle types are abstractions of names[47], references[51], ports[63], and static labels used to identify role instances and message destinations. Handle types may include values that do not provide access to implementations (as in the case of "null" and "dangling" references), in which case we say that the handle is not `live`. The relation "==" among handle values denotes only ("shallow") value equality, not necessarily identity or equality of implementation-level components. PSL/IDL handle values are expressed using the syntax of IDL `objrefs`. These serve as both references to instances of IDL `interfaces` (*not* necessarily their implementations) and destinations of CORBA messages. However, as discussed in [39], PSL handle values need not bear a one-to-one relation with CORBA `objref` implementations.

4 Attributes

An attribute (also known as a *state function*[38, 33]) is an abstract property ascribed to zero or more role instances, and possibly assuming different values across time. In PSL, attributes are abstract functions of handle and/or other value type arguments. The relationship between abstract attributes and their implementations (if any) is outside the scope of PSL proper. For example, the attribute `isOpen` is a hypothetical function that might actually be computed or approximated as a side-effect-free procedure, a function whose value is deduced by an analytic tool, and/or a "derived" function that is symbolically definable or otherwise constrained in terms of other attributes. The use of an attribute in PSL does not commit implementations to "know" its values in any computational sense, and even if implemented, does not mandate that the value be computed by any component it describes.

In PSL/IDL, attributes are declared as auxiliary functions within the scope of a `protocol module` using normal IDL/C++ function syntax, and where all function arguments are explicit. (The IDL keyword `attribute` is not used in PSL to avoid conflict with its IDL usage in implicitly declaring "get" and "put" *operations*.) For example:

```
protocol module fm { boolean isOpen(File f); /*...*/ };
```

Event Predicates. A PSL *event predicate* is a special kind of attribute representing the issuance or reception of any kind of explicit communication among participants, including operation requests, operation replies, asynchronous messages, and exceptions. For each kind of message M possible in a system, we assume the existence of a corresponding record type $MessageType_M$ that minimally includes fields describing the message "selector" (e.g., operation name) and arguments (if any). All messages are assumed to be *handle-directed.* A handle describing the intended receiver role is a required part of any communication. Similarly, messages corresponding to a procedural operation that returns a reply (or perhaps just a "`void`" completion indication) include a handle describing the "return address" of the caller. We also assume an abstract function `reply[`*msg*`]` that represents a reply message (not its issuance) of the appropriate type for a given procedural request *msg*, and a function `throw[`*msg*`]` that represents an exception reply message for a request.

Messages themselves are not used directly in PSL. Instead, PSL contains two families of special attribute functions, `in` and `out`. The construct `in(`*m*`) by(`*p*`)`, where *m* is of some type $MessageType_M$ and *p* is a handle value, denotes a context in which a particular message instance *m* has been received by participant *p*, and `out(`*m*`) by(`*p*`)` denotes a context in which *m* has been issued by *p*. The `by(`*p*`)` suffixes are optional and seldom needed. When otherwise unconstrained, omission reflects lack of concern about which participant issues or receives a message.

PSL event predicates are otherwise treated as attribute functions that happen to have predefined characteristics. Event predicates are monotonic attributes, behaving as persistent "latches". Once `out(`*m*`) by(`*p*`)` is true for a particular *m* and *p*, it is true forever more; similarly for `in(`*m*`) by(`*p*`)`. This reflects the fact that events never "unhappen". Once a predicate describing the occurrence of an event becomes true, it never becomes false. Situations and rules may thus be phrased in terms of events that have occurred at any time [44].

PSL/IDL event predicates use IDL messages as arguments to `in` and `out`. PSL/IDL message types are abstractions of the `CORBA Request` type [51], with a shorthand handle-based message syntax delimited by angle-brackets:

m = < *dest->op(args)* >

Here, *m* is an instance of an implicitly "pattern-matched" message type corresponding to the form of the message expression; *dest* is a handle indicating the destination role instance of the message; *op* is an operation name literal; and *args* are arguments, each of some value type as defined in a corresponding interface. Messages need not be named, and values are referenced directly rather than through the implicit fields of *m*. As a notational convenience, a `reply` or `throw` without a bracketed message argument refers to the most closely associated message whenever this is unambiguous. Examples:

```
in( <aFile->write(c)> )              // write req received by aFile
out( reply[<aFile->read()>](c) ) // c sent as reply to read
out( throw(exc) ) by(aFile)         // exc thrown by aFile
```

5 Situations

The concept of a situation extends the common notion of abstract object state[43, 7]. Situations describe *partial* views of possible system-wide states, factored with respect to possibly several roles. In PSL, situations are represented by parameterized declarative expressions describing "interesting" commonalities of transient *possible worlds* in terms of relevant attribute and event predicate values. In PSL/IDL, a situation is represented as a parameterized predicate. We provide a full notation in [39], but use here an abbreviated form in which situations are defined within `rules` declarations as boolean C++ expressions within braces. (PSL/IDL-G notation is the same except that situations are demarcated by solid rounded boxes inside a dashed `rules` box.) Expressions may reference attributes and event predicates, named arguments and in-line local declarations. For example, the following situation describes the state of a `File` being open:

```
rules f1(File f) { { isOpen(f) } };
```

Realizations. In the same sense that a class is instantiated by an object, and an interface is instantiated by a role, a situation is said to be instantiated by a *realization*. And just as interfaces describe the properties of an unbounded family of potential implementations, situations describe the properties of an unbounded family of potential realizations. However, realizations are not *explicitly* instantiated by programmers. They just unfold over the course of system execution. For example, the realizations of the above `isOpen` situation include all "snapshots" of a system in which such a `File` is open. The manner in which such realizations are observed or inferred in executing systems is outside the scope of PSL proper (see Section 11).

A realization is thus a partial description of an arbitrarily brief instance, an *actual world* in which the predicate describing a situation holds. Realizations represent individual observations, mappings, or inferences about concrete system behavior, characterized by expressions describing attribute and event predicate values. A realization is said to *match* one or more situations if all features required in the situation(s) are present. The matching relation, $s \propto S$ for realization s and situation S, holds if the situation predicate for S can be made true using the values in s (see [39]). Two or more realizations may all match the same situation but in different ways because they differently instantiate free parameters listed in the situation.

6 Protocol Rules

PSL temporal operators describe conditions under which realizations occur. They are defined in terms of an underlying temporal dependency relation $a \preceq b$ among two *realizations* a and b. If $a \preceq b$, then a happens no later than b (see Section 11). But since it would not be very productive to describe protocols via orderings among individual occurrences, PSL protocol rules are instead described at the level of situations (classes of realizations). Each of the following operators relates the occurrences of realizations of a predecessor situation A and successor situation B:

*A*s lead to *B*s: $A \blacktriangleright B \stackrel{\text{def}}{=} \forall a : a \propto A \Rightarrow \exists b : b \propto B \wedge a \preceq b$

*A*s enable *B*s: $A \blacksquare B \stackrel{\text{def}}{=} \forall b : b \propto B \Rightarrow \exists a : a \propto A \wedge a \preceq b$

*A*s pair with *B*s: $A \blacklozenge B \stackrel{\text{def}}{=} (A \blacktriangleright B) \wedge (A \blacksquare B)$

Rules are collections of situations linked by temporal operators. In PSL/IDL-G, rules are expressed via lines connecting situations through corresponding symbols drawn on the outside of the predecessor situation to the same symbol drawn on the inside of the successor situation. In PSL/IDL, these operators are designated as `lead`, `enable` and `pair` respectively. In PSL/IDL (but not necessarily in PSL/IDL-G), the "earlier" situation is always to the left of the "later" one. PSL/IDL situations are implicitly parameterized by the arguments listed in their `rules`, as well as all declarations in their predecessor situation(s).

Leading. The "forward reasoning" operator $A \blacktriangleright B$ is akin to a state transition, applying to cases in which *A*s always precede *B*s. However, unlike a state transition, $A \blacktriangleright B$ does not indicate that instances of *B* form the "next" situations after those of *A*. Instead, an instance occurs at some unspecified time after an instance of *A* occurs, in a manner that neither requires nor precludes concurrency with respect to any other non-conflicting rules. Also, unlike state transitions, the orderings are not explicitly "triggered" by events. Instead predicates on events are listed as aspects of the situations themselves. For example, a protocol rule for a relay operation that sends `m2` whenever `m1` is received takes the form (in PSL/IDL and PSL/IDL-G respectively):

```
{in(m1)} lead {out(m2)}
```

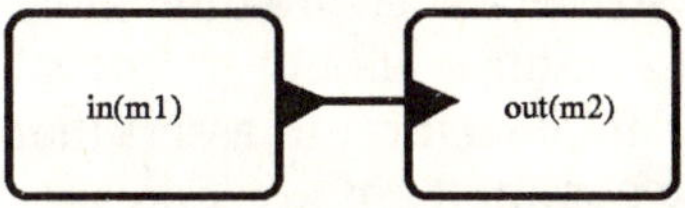

This rule does not in any way imply that `Relay` operations must be single-threaded. Because there are no constraints indicating otherwise, two or more different "threads" of this rule may be active concurrently, each triggered by a realization corresponding to a different instance of an `m1` message. On the other hand, this specification does not preclude implementation via a single-threaded relay object either.

Enabling. The "backward reasoning" operator $A \blacksquare B$ is used for relations in which *A enables B*, applying to cases in which *B*s are always preceded by *A*s. (Or are "caused" by *A*s, under some interpretations of this overloaded term.) For example, a desirable rule in most systems is the *no spurious replies* rule; for any procedural message `req`:

```
{in(req)} enable {out(reply[req]())}
```

This rule says that replies are sent only if messages are received. It does not say that requests always lead to replies, only that replies are never sent unless preceded by requests. In PSL/IDL, this rule is considered to be predefined for all procedural requests, since it is enforced by CORBA.

Separate rules may link multiple right-hand-sides to the same left-hand-side to describe multiple possible effects. For example, we could add another rule stating that `req` may lead to an exception, and link it to the first rule, reflecting the fact that rules are combined conjunctively (i.e., implicitly $\wedge$'ed):

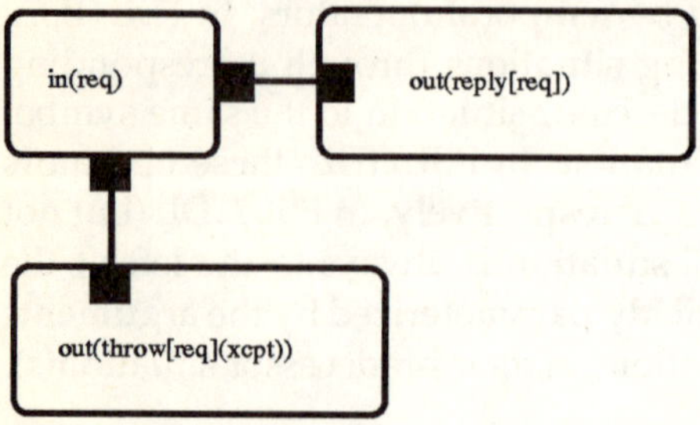

Pairing. The $A \leftrightarrow B$ operator is used for if-and-only-if relations, in which both every A is followed by a B, and every B is preceded by an A; thus As and Bs occur only in pairs. For example, another desirable global rule is the *one-to-one delivery rule*, for any `m`:

```
{out(m)} pair {in(m)}
```

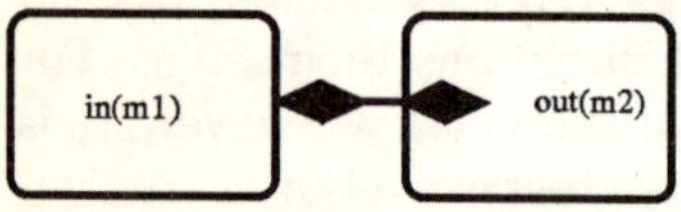

This says that all and only those messages that have been issued are ultimately received. The ◆ relation may be used to provide guarantees about procedural operations. For example, we could strengthen the above ■ form to assert that a reply to `req` must be issued, thus precluding the possibility of exceptions or other non-procedural behavior:

```
{in(req)} pair {out(reply[req]())}
```

Sequences. A single rule may include chains of situations connected by temporal operators to describe sequencing. We express sequences of, for example, the leads-to operator as $A \blacktriangleright B \blacktriangleright C$. This indicates $(A \blacktriangleright B) \wedge (B \blacktriangleright C)$ while also extending scoping so that expressions in C may reference terms in A. For example, a special protocol in which a relay outputs `m3` after receiving message `m1` followed by `m2` could include a rule of the form:

```
{in(m1)} lead {in(m2)} lead {out(m3)}
```

If we did not care about the ordering of `m1` and `m2`, we would have written this using simple conjunction of event predicates:

```
{in(m1), in(m2)} lead {out(m3)}
```

On the other hand, if we wanted to claim that this `m1-m2` ordering were the only one possible, we would add the rule:

```
{in(m1)} enable {in(m2)}
```

7 Constraints

Some conditions must *always* hold, across all possible contexts. PSL constraint rules limit the set of possible system states to those in which listed expressions hold. For a trivial example, if we declared attribute `notOpen(File f)`, we would want to claim that its value is always equal to `!isOpen(f)`. The PSL notation for static constraints is based on the "□"*necessity* operator of temporal and modal logic[19,64]. The expression □*p* indicates that *p* invariantly holds for all time, over all possible worlds. In PSL/IDL `rules` declarations, brace-demarcated expressions describing necessary restrictions among attribute values are prefaced by `inv`. For example:

```
rules f1(File f) { inv {notOpen(f) == !isOpen(f)} };
```

Constraints may be used to describe system-wide messaging policies. For example, CORBA (like most systems) enforces the policy that either a normal reply or an exceptional reply can be issued for procedural request `req`, but at most one of these. Using the PSL construct `unique(`*expr*`)`, which is false if there is more than one match to *expr*, these constraints may be expressed as:

```
inv { out(reply[req]()) -->   !out(throw[req](x)) }
inv { out(throw[req](x)) -->  !out(reply[req]()) }
inv { unique(reply[req]()) }
inv { unique(throw[req](x)) }
```

Relating Attributes to Events. Once a predicate describing the occurrence of an individual event becomes true, it never becomes false. Thus, event predicates "latch" from left to right in PSL linked situations. For any event predicate *e*, if *e* holds in *A*, then it also holds in all successors of *A*. For example, the following two rules for simple relays are equivalent:

```
{in(m1)} lead {out(m2)}
{in(m1)} lead {in(m1), out(m2)}
```

This "latching" property of event predicates does *not* necessarily hold for arbitrary attributes. For example, if there were an unconstrained attribute `ok(Relay r)`, and we required that `ok(r)` persist as true across these two situations, we would have to write:

```
{in(m1), ok(r)} lead {out(m2), ok(r)}
```

Such unconstrained attributes are notoriously troublesome in practice [43, 11, 17]. When attributes are not tied to events, there are no global rules stating how values change as a function of events. Any required variation or invariance in the values of unconstrained attributes across time must be explicitly tracked in individual protocol rules. Constraint rules may be used to avoid such problems, by linking the values of arbitrary attributes to the occurrence particular events. For example, supposing that our unrealistically simple `File` may be opened and closed only once, we might supply constraints indicating how attribute `isOpen` varies with `open` and `close` events:

```
rules fl(File f) {
 inv { isOpen(f) -->   out(reply[<f->open()>]()) }
 inv { out(reply[<f->close()>]()) -->  !isOpen(f) }
};
```

Here, the first constraint says that if a file is open, then it must have at some time replied to an open request (but not necessarily vice versa). The second says that if the file has ever replied to a close request, then it must not be open. These might be buttressed with a description of a FileFactory operation that guarantees that isOpen is true upon reply of its result. On the other hand, if a File could be implemented by a special kind of object that is initially open upon construction without requiring an explicit open operation, then the first constraint would have to be weakened or eliminated.

To further illustrate, consider an Account interface, along with a protocol module declaring abstract bal and serialNo, along with simple postcondition style rules stating that mkAcc initializes them, getBalance returns bal, setBalance changes bal, and getSerialNo reports serialNo. A set of inv rules adds further constraints:

```
interface Account {
 void  setBalance(in float b);
 float getBalance();
 long  getSerialNo();
};

interface AccountFactory {
 Account mkAcc(in long s, in float b);
};

protocol module accountm {
 float bal(Account a);
 long  serialNo(Account a);
 rules (Account a, AccountFactory f, long s, float b) {
  {in(<f->mkAcc(s, b)>)}  pair
   {out(reply(a)), live(a), bal(a) == b, serialNo(a) == s}
  {in(<a->getBalance()>)}  pair {out(reply(bal(a))}
  {in(<a->setBalance(b)>)} pair {out(reply()), bal(a) == b}
  {in(<a->getSerialNo()>)} pair {out(reply(serialNo(a)))}

  inv {(bal(a) == b) -->
       out(reply[<f->mkAcc(x,b)>](a)) ||
       out(reply[<a->setBalance(b)>]()) }
  inv {(serialNo(a) == s) -->
      out(reply[<f->mkAcc(s,b)>](a)) }
  inv {unique(out(reply[<f->mkAcc(s,b)>](a)) }
  inv {unique(in(s = <a->setBalance(b)>), !out(reply[s]())) }
 };
};
```

The four invariants establish the following constraints:

1. The `setBalance` and `mkAcc` operations are the *only* ones that affect the value of attribute `bal`. Without such a constraint, there is no requirement that this reasonable and often implicitly assumed encapsulation property holds. This is expressed by relating `bal` to values associated with replies from either of the two operations.
2. The `serialNo` is always the one established by the factory operation. Note that because roles need not bear a one-to-one relation to implementation objects, it is not possible in PSL to ascribe such "initial" properties to roles that hold across all instantiations. Instead, factory[53] operations are used to establish instances for which particular properties hold.
3. Initialization occurs at most once per account.
4. The processing of `setBalance` requests is not subject to arbitrary interleavings (i.e., that they proceed serially), thus precluding multithreaded implementations. The restriction that no two `setBalance` operations operate concurrently can be expressed by saying that any message that has been received but not replied to is `unique`.

8 Subsituations

Like interfaces, states and classes, situations may be specialized into *subsituations*. Subsituation relations are analogs of the subtype relations underlying interface inheritance. Mechanics follow those for ordinary sets defined via predicates. For example, situation Q: {`in(readrequest) && isOpen(f)`} is a subsituation of P: {`in(readrequest)`} in which case we say that $Q \subseteq P$.

If $Q \subseteq P$, then fewer possible realizations match Q than P. Every situation is a subsituation of the empty situation {} (or equivalently {*true*}), which is matched by all realizations. The situation {*false*} (matched by no realizations) is a subsituation of all others. We say that expression *expr holds* in situation S if $S \subseteq \{ expr \}$. Conversely, we define set-like union and intersection operators in terms of the corresponding boolean relations on their component expressions [17, 62]. In PSL/IDL $A \cap B$ is expressed as $\{expr_A\}$ `&&` $\{expr_B\}$, and $A \cup B$ as $\{expr_A\}$ `||` $\{expr_B\}$.

The simplest and most common means of constructing a subsituation is to "strengthen" an expression by *and*'ing an independent predicate p, since $A \cap \{p\} \subseteq A$. Strengthening may also occur by replacing a predicate with one that implies it. For example, a situation including `out(`m`)` might be strengthened by replacing it with the more committal `out(`m`)by(`p`)`.

Partitions. PSL does not use any special notation to *declare* that one situation is a subsituation of another except in the special case of disjoint union where $S = S_1 \oplus S_2 \oplus \ldots \oplus S_n$. This represents a set of subsituations that are constrained to completely partition a situation-space S. Partitioned subsituations must be exhaustive and mutually exclusive. Partitioning is thus one way to express the notion that one situation "disables" another[67].

In PSL/IDL, partitions are enclosed in `case`. Successive cases are interpreted in the same way as `case`, `cond`, and `if ...elsif` statements in most languages, implicitly negating the expressions in all previous `cases`. The special trailing situation `default` matches only if all previous cases fail, thus acting as a generalized `else`.

Conditional protocol rules can be expressed using partitions. Ordering operators "distribute" through situation partitionings to describe conditional paths. Since ordering operators have lower precedence than the `&&` operator combining situations, expressions common to all partitions can be described in a situation linked by `&&` to the `cases`. For example, to indicate that a `TRUE` reply is enabled if some function `ok` holds, and conversely for `FALSE`:

```
{ out(req) } pair
{ in(req) } && {
 case { ok(req) } enable { out(reply(TRUE)) }
 case { default } enable { out(reply(FALSE)) } }
```

In PSL/IDL-G, partitioning is indicated via nested StateCharts [24]. Each enclosed box represents a partition. The special trailing "else" box contains only the expression `default`. Expressions common to all partitioned subsituations may be listed outside of the nested boxes. The accompanying fragment of a PSL/IDL-G protocol for a simple `File` illustrates some of the interplay between conditionals and temporal operators.

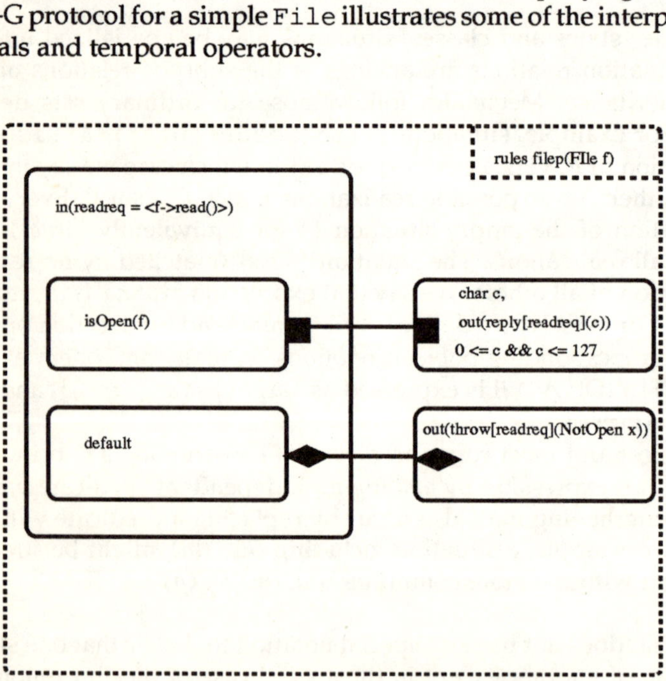

In this example, the use of ■ linking the "normal" `read` reply indicates that a situation in which a reply is generated occurs only when a file is open and receives a read request, but may not occur at all so far as can be determined from the perspective of the roles parameterized within the current `rules` declaration. For example, there may be "downstream" errors stemming from internal invocations that are not visible at this scope or level of specification. However, if a reply occurs, the return value `c` is subject to the listed constraints that amount to a guarantee that the return value is a 7-bit character value.

In contrast, the "exceptional" reply situation is linked via $\blacklozenge$, indicating that (only) when a read request is received by a file that is not open, an exception reply to the request is always generated. This does *not* indicate that this is the only context in which the `NotOpen` exception is thrown. It says instead that this is the only context in which it is thrown *as a reply to* `read`. If for some reason we had wanted to make the weaker claim that `NotOpen` is possible but not guaranteed, we would have used $\blacksquare$. Had we wanted to make the differently weaker claim that `NotOpen` is always issued not only here, but perhaps also in some other context (i.e., even if the file is open) we would have used $\blacktriangleright$.

9 Refinement

Protocol refinement is the act of introducing new rules that apply in more specific situations than do general rules, without invalidating these more general rules. Refinement is thus an additive process, where rules accumulate, each adding specificity in a narrower context. The opposite of refinement is generalization, in which a weaker set of rules is introduced in a broader context. In PSL, refinements are normally localized to new interfaces bearing subinterface relations to the originals. Specialized protocol declarations may be attached to (parameterized by) instances of subinterfaces. Similarly, generalizations may be attached to superinterfaces.

PSL/IDL-annotated interfaces are always refinements of those described in IDL only. When two kinds of PSL/IDL interfaces differ in protocol but not operation signatures (for example, when protocols differ across "local" versus "remote" versions of components), it may be necessary in practice to construct "dummy" IDL interface types just to give the two types different names [5].

Of course, not all reasonable modifications are valid refinements. For example, instances of a protocol description could differ in that one corrects an error, or removes unwanted behavior, or describes a subtly different protocol, or imposes additional constraints due to changed or overlooked requirements. Valid refinements are generally limited to the following techniques, that may also be applied in reverse in the course of generalization. These techniques reflect properties of PSL that hold for all situations A, B, C containing predicates meaningful in their scopes:

$A \blacktriangleright \{\, true \,\}$	$A \blacksquare \{\, false \,\}$
$\{\, false \,\} \blacktriangleright A$	$\{\, true \,\} \blacksquare A$
$A \blacktriangleright B, B \blacktriangleright C \vdash A \blacktriangleright C$	$A \blacksquare B, B \blacksquare C \vdash A \blacksquare C$
$A \blacktriangleright B, B \blacklozenge C \vdash A \blacktriangleright C$	$A \blacksquare B, B \blacklozenge C \vdash A \blacksquare C$
$A \blacklozenge B, B \blacktriangleright C \vdash A \blacktriangleright C$	$A \blacklozenge B, B \blacksquare C \vdash A \blacksquare C$

$A \blacktriangleright B \cap C \vdash A \blacktriangleright B$	$A \blacksquare B \cup C \vdash A \blacksquare B$
$B \cup C \blacktriangleright A \vdash B \blacktriangleright A$	$B \cap C \blacksquare A \vdash B \blacksquare A$
$B \blacktriangleright A, C \subseteq B \vdash C \blacktriangleright A$	$C \blacksquare A, C \subseteq B \vdash B \blacksquare A$
$A \blacktriangleright C, C \subseteq B \vdash A \blacktriangleright B$	$A \blacksquare B, C \subseteq B \vdash A \blacksquare C$

Adding Rules. New rules relating new situations, as well as new constraints, may be added so long as they do not conflict with existing ones. For example, if `ReadWriteFile` is defined as a subinterface of `ReadFile`, new rules applicable to `write` operations may be defined in `rules` for `ReadWriteFile`. The `rules` for `ReadFile` would also still hold for all `ReadWriteFile` instances.

Splicing Situations. A new situation S may be spliced among existing ordered situations A and B, so long as the original relation between A and B is maintained. Thus, $A \blacktriangleright B$ may be extended to $A \blacktriangleright S \blacktriangleright B$, or to $A \blacktriangleright B \blacktriangleright S$, or to the separate $(A \blacktriangleright S) \wedge (A \blacktriangleright B)$, and so on. Splicing allows arbitrarily complex subprotocols to be inserted between existing end-points. For example, an original version of a rule for a procedural operation might list only the request and reply. A refinement may then specify internal structure such as an interaction with a helper:

```
{in(req)} enable
   {out(reply[req]())}

{in(req)} pair {out(h = <helper->help()>)} enable
   {in(reply[h]())} pair {out(reply[req]())}
```

Note that even though the ■ was juggled around, the original sense of the relation is maintained. If necessary, this may be checked formally. For example here, the refined rule is of the form $(A \blacktriangleleft\!\blacktriangleright B) \wedge (B \blacksquare C) \wedge (C \blacktriangleleft\!\blacktriangleright D)$. From the first two clauses we see that $A \blacksquare C$. Then applying the last clause, we obtain $A \blacksquare D$, as required by the original rule.

Subdividing Situations. A situation may be split into subsituations, so long as all ordering relations are maintained across all paths along all subsituations. For example, an initial rule for a boolean operation might only list that a reply occurs, while a refinement splits apart the conditions under which it replies true versus false:

```
{in(req)} enable {out(reply(b))}

{in(req)} && {
  case {badstuff()} enable  {out(reply(FALSE))}
  case {default}    enable  {out(reply(TRUE))} }
```

Strengthening Relations. The relation $A \blacktriangleright B$ or $A \blacksquare B$ may be strengthened to $A \blacktriangleleft\!\blacktriangleright B$ when this does not conflict with other existing rules. For example, a preliminary version of a rule may use ■ to indicate that a particular exception may result from a certain request in a certain condition. Assuming that no other existing rules indicate otherwise, a refinement may instead use ◆ to make the stronger claim that this exception is *always* generated under this condition. Similarly, we could strengthen the previous example to use the ◆ operator instead of ■ if we were sure that the listed situations represented the only ways in which the TRUE and FALSE replies could occur.

Weakening and Strengthening Situations. If relation $A \blacktriangleright B$ holds in an original specification, a refinement may add a new rule $A' \blacktriangleright B'$, where $A \subseteq A'$ and $B' \subseteq B$. The reverse relation holds for ■. These are situational analogs of type conformance and substitutability[58], ensuring that rules applying in the original versions continue to hold even when refined. For example, consider an $A \blacktriangleright B$ rule for a Relay r with attribute broken:

```
{in(m1), !broken(r)} lead {out(m2)}
```

In a refined version $A' \blacktriangleright B'$, we could have a weaker left-hand-side ($A \subseteq A'$) and a stronger right-hand-side ($B' \subseteq B$), leading to a stronger rule that subsumes the original version:

```
{in(m1)} lead {out(m2) by(r)}
```

The opposite maneuver would be either superfluous or an error: If the second rule had been the original specification, then it would have already covered the first rule. And if we had wanted to *restrict* the second rule to the first, the relation would not be a refinement; we would create an unrelated (on this dimension) protocol and/or interface.

10 Describing Interactions

Consider a set of transaction components in which Coordinators help arrange the actions of Transactors, with IDL interfaces:

```
typedef long TID;

interface Transactor {
 boolean join(in TID tid);
 boolean commit(in TID tid)
 void    abort(in TID tid)
};

interface Coordinator : Transactor {
 TID     begin();
 boolean add(in TID tid,in Transactor p) raises (TransError);
};
```

The overall design is that Coordinators create (via begin) transaction identifiers (TIDs) that are used to index transactions. Each transaction consists of a group of Transactor members, added via the add operation. As indicated by the use of interface inheritance, members may be other Coordinators. Each Transactor may be asked to join a transaction, and to commit or abort it. The application operations that each component performs within transactions (perhaps bank account updates) are not described in this set of interfaces.

To capture some of this in PSL/IDL, we declare a protocol module, starting off with a declaration of attribute members to represent the handles of all members of a given transaction. There may be several sets of members maintained by each Coordinator, each referenced via its transaction identifier (tid). The associated constraint precludes the existence of any additional operations or rules that cause p to become a member unless they somehow invoke add. We also declare auxiliary function validtid and corresponding constraint to show how the notion of a valid transaction id is related to event predicates. A transaction identifier tid is valid if it was created as the result of a begin operation, but becomes invalid when the subject of any abort or commit request:

```
sequence<Transactor> members(Coordinator c, TID tid);
boolean validtid(Coordinator c,TID tid);

rules(Coordinator c, Transactor p, TID t){
 inv { contains(members(c,t), p) -->
       out(reply[<c->add(p,t)>](TRUE)) }
 inv { validtid(c, tid) -->  out(reply[<c->begin()>](tid)) }
 inv { in(<c->abort(tid)>) -->  !validtid(c, tid) }
 inv { in(<c->commit(tid)>) --> !validtid(c, tid) }
};
```

Two sample protocol rules are also shown in the accompanying PSL/IDL-G declaration. The first rule says that on receiving a begin request, the Coordinator replies with a tid value that has never been used before. This statement, along with the above constraints on validtid amount to a promise that each tid value returned by begin is unique and valid for the length of the transaction.

The main "thread" in the second rule says that upon receiving an add request for a Transactor p with a valid tid, a coordinator invokes p's join operation. If it then receives a TRUE reply, p is then a member of members and the operation completes successfully. The other cases are "error paths"; one causing an exception, and the other a simple FALSE reply. Additional situations and relations would surely be included in a more realistic specification. For example, it may describe cases dealing with the possibility that !live(p) (i.e., if p were not a live handle), the use of timeouts, and so on.

We may also rework a more specialized version of the add rule by parameterizing over both the Coordinator and the Transactor roles. The accompanying partial PSL/IDL-G declaration of rules addp(Coordinator

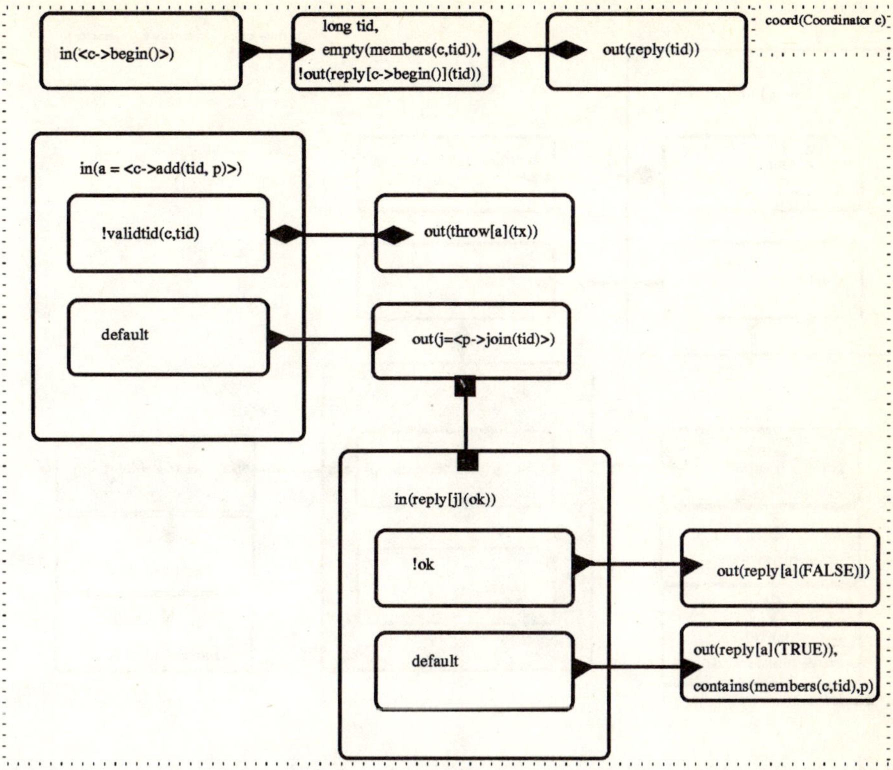

c, Transactor p) assumes for simplicity that p replies FALSE to join only if it is already a member of the transaction. For emphasis, situations describing the view of the Transactor are shaded. One sense in which this protocol is more committal is that rather than relying on a *one-to-one delivery rule* to match the p->join request with its reception (and similarly for the join reply), this version directly connects the associated situations for these particular communication partners. Such rules may be seen as the specification analog of multimethods[17].

Along a different dimension, we could have presented a less committal version by omitting various situations if we happened not to care about them for the sake of this protocol declaration, and then perhaps inserted them later as refinements. For example, the join reply and its acceptance might have been elided without changing the ordering requirements of the remaining situations.

11 Foundations

PSL constructs are based on structures describing possible worlds, as found in model theory and temporal and modal logic[31, 19, 64]. These serve as the basis for several frameworks for specifying possibly distributed systems

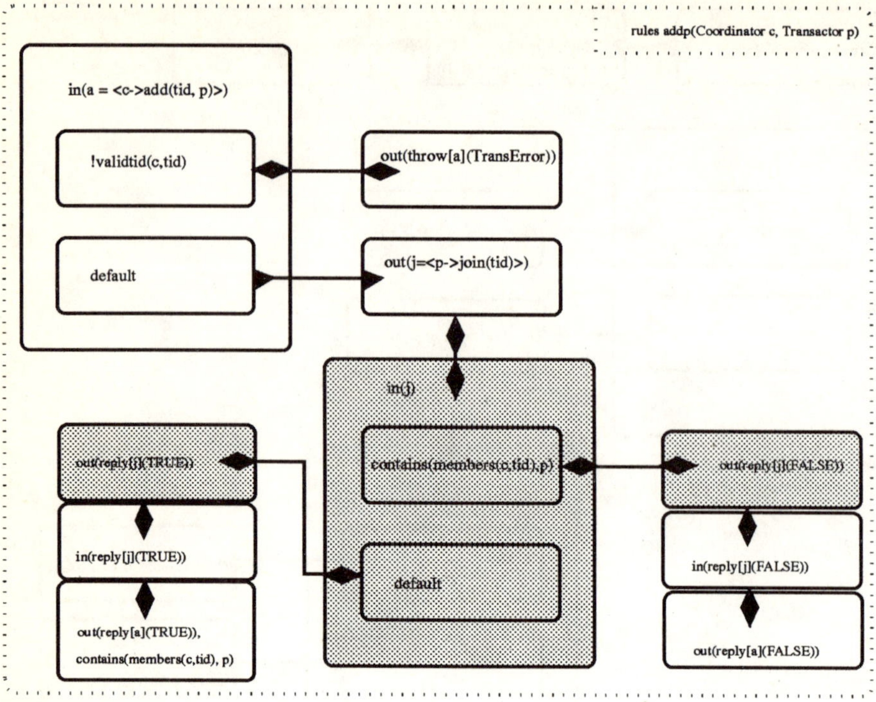

[38, 42, 14, 34, 6], as well as related applied temporal reasoning systems in AI and object-oriented logic programming [43, 3, 15].

Possible world structures are of the form **<W, V, R>**. **W** is a set of worlds. **V** is a set of value expressions over some basis, with an associated function $\phi(p, w)$, which is true if expression p holds in world w. **R** represents any number of defined relations among the worlds in **W**. Chief among them is the relation generated by constraints. PSL □ rules define the set of all worlds that are possible, and a corresponding relation containing every pair of possible worlds.

PSL situations define a another family of "static" equivalence relations $\mathbf{R}_\sigma$. Situation S describes that set of worlds for which its defining predicate P_S holds given the values in the world (i.e., $\{w \mid \phi(P_S,w)\}$). In PSL this is expressed in terms of the matching relation, $\propto$, between values holding in worlds and situation predicates. The corresponding relation $\mathbf{R}_S$ contains all pairs of worlds that are members of this set.

The relation $\mathbf{R}_\preceq$ serves as the basis for PSL ordering operators. This relation is simplest to describe formally when expressions are restricted to event predicates on fixed messages[23, 67, 57]. In this case, expressions in **V** are just characteristic predicates of sets of event occurrences, and $\phi(e,w)$ is true if w contains the events of e. For example, suppose a satisfies e_a = `out(m1)` for some message `m1`, and b satisfies e_b = `out(m1) && in(m1)`. The relation $a \preceq b$ states that $e_b \Rightarrow e_a$. The `out(m1)` event has not "gone away" in B. In fact, if $a \preceq b$, `out(m1)` holds no later than the realization in which `in(m1)` holds as well. Thus, when restricted to events, the relation $\mathbf{R}_{\preceq}$ contains all *(a,b)* such that the set of events described by e_a must be be a subset of that described by e_b. When expressions are liberalized to allow reference to arbitrary attributes, the $\preceq$ relation is no longer definable in this semi-automatic manner, since it is not necessarily the case that $e_b \Rightarrow e_a$. Constraint rules must be supplied to describe how arbitrary attributes vary with respect to events.

Application of these constructs to particular systems relies on *mappings* from PSL to concrete implementation code and/or observations. These include (1) mappings between roles and implementation objects; (2) mappings between event predicates and concrete communication occurrences; (3) mappings between expressions defining situations and realizations observed or inferred in concrete code and/or its execution; and in some cases (4) mappings of the initial conditions of the system of interest. These generate an operational semantics that in turn allows construction of corresponding design methods and tools; for example simulation, prototyping, verification, visualization, testing, and monitoring. This also allows PSL to be used as a scripting language in which prococol specifications are directly compiled into default implementations.

While the use of PSL in some systems would require development of auxiliary configuration languages and tools to establish mappings, the particular features of PSL/IDL along with those of CORBA permit simpler tactics: PSL/IDL uses the same value type system as CORBA IDL. OMG standards in turn already map IDL value types to those of various implementation languages [54]. PSL/IDL message types map directly to those used in CORBA. Observations of messages may be used to establish instantiation of corresponding event predicates. Also CORBA Object Request Brokers (ORBs) and repositories maintain information relating values that are used as message destinations and the locations of concrete implementation components. These may be relied on to maintain implicit mappings between interface instance handles and implementation objects. And the initial conditions of most CORBA applications amount only to the initialization of a small number of components, avoiding the need for extensive description of static configuration properties.

CORBA also supports development of the instrumentation needed for dynamic execution tools. Event monitoring may be accomplished through interpositioning; the placement of intercepts between communicating components to tap communication traffic[68]. However, even if attention is restricted to event predicates, mapping communications to event predicates, and in turn realizations of particular situations, and in turn rule instantiations is not a trivial matter in a distributed open system (see [39]). However, provided that such observational apparatus is available, one could create, for example, a monitoring tool reporting whether realizations matching listed situations occurred and whether the corresponding ordering rules were observed.

12 Related Work

Protocol specification, architectural description, and approaches to dynamics in general have a long history. While all such approaches may be related at some level, they differ significantly in their theoretical bases, definitional primitives, and range of usability. The ways in which PSL constructs support interface-based specification of open systems distinguish it from other frameworks:

Preconditions and Postconditions [29] and specification systems based upon them [35], employ the construct $\{A\}\ s\ \{B\}$, asserting that program fragment s brings a program from a state obeying A to one obeying B. The PSL constructs $A \blacktriangleright B$ and $A \blacksquare B$ have similar usages, but split the different senses of this relation when applied to ordered events. PSL may be used to express the kinds of assertions typically associated with operation postconditions, but applies them to arbitrary "evaluation points" rather than necessarily only upon issuance of a reply. PSL does not include any language-specific operational semantics, and omits reference to s. PSL also differs in its scoping and parameterization of predicates.

Abstract Data Types (ADTs) [40, 61] describe functional properties of "black box" components via preconditions, postconditions, and invariants, without describing the nature of their dynamic dependencies or interactions. PSL attributes and constraints share a similar basis, but are used primarily to describe interaction constraints.

Architecture Description Languages (ADLs), module interconnection languages, and related approaches [41, 4] usually extend an ADT-style basis to describe static configuration and communication properties of sets of components. This focus on statics varies in degree across languages. PSL may be construed as variant ADL best suited for systems with few fixed configuration properties beyond those of their general purpose communication substrates; for example, ORB-mediated communication in CORBA systems.

Object-Oriented Analysis notations [60, 33, 17] describe classes of objects in terms of attributes, relations, states, operations, and messaging, at varying degrees of formality. PSL generalizes, extends and reworks the dynamic aspects of such concepts to apply to interfaces of components in open systems, in a manner compatible with other role-based frameworks [6, 59, 66, 25]. Unlike some other approaches [2, 68] that add protocol specifications to object-oriented interfaces, PSL does not assume any particular model or mechanism relating these interfaces and roles to classes and objects.

Linguistic Approaches to Pragmatics [50] address the context-specific dynamics of communication (speech acts) among participants, while semantics abstracts over situations to address context-independent meanings. This distinction provides a useful conceptual basis for approaching these qualitatively different aspects of interaction, and serves as a guide to the kinds of phenomena that PSL is intended to capture.

Process Calculi [46] and specification languages based upon them model systems as collections of abstract processes communicating via messages, where each process and communication act obeys a particular abstract computation model. In contrast, PSL specifications are non-constructive. They do not rely on a particular computational model beyond that implied by minimal assumptions about message passing in open systems. PSL specifications contain sets of constraints on behavior that may be implemented by any kind of component meeting the constraints.

History-based Frameworks [44, 49, 32, 13, 22] specify actions that occur under given patterns of event histories. These patterns are most often described in terms of regular expressions or variants thereof. Because PSL deals with roles in potentially distributed systems, events as seen by a given instance are not necessarily totally orderable. They can be ordered only by $\preceq$, not the strict $\prec$ relation that may be seen by any particular implementation *object*. Thus PSL history patterns cannot be described as languages or regular expressions[56]. They are instead indicated by linked situations. Also, an event occurrence is construed in PSL as just one kind of attribute (although one with a special interpretation) ascribable to a role. Other kinds of attributes can be defined as well. For example, one set of instances of a `File` interface may be "born" in an `isOpen` state, while others are not.

Event-based Frameworks [37, 56, 9] are typically based on orderings defined over raw events. The PSL $\preceq$ relation serving as the basis for protocol operators is defined in a fashion similar to such orderings, but ranges over abstract instances of situations described via event predicates and other arbitrary attributes, not instances of events themselves. When restricted to event predicates, these are related in a simple way under the intended mapping to raw events: If the instances of two events are ordered, then so are the corresponding instances of event predicates. PSL operators, situations, and partitionings are more closely related to corresponding constructs in *event structures* and its variants[67, 23, 57], as adapted for use in interface-based specification.

The most important differences between PSL and other approaches reflect instrinsic properties of open systems development. But they also weaken analytic properties. Closed-world models are uniformly more powerful than PSL in addressing questions about liveness, deadlock, interference, and aliasing [48, 30], which often have no definitive answers in open systems. Closed-world models may still have a place in open system development, but only when applied to descriptions of classes and objects. Object implementation code does what it does, and nothing more. While interface-level open system development cannot exploit this fact, it is sometimes profitable (but see [36]) to rely on fixed known implementation properties when constructing individual components.

Acknowledgments. This work was supported in part by a Sun Microsystems Labs collaborative research grant to the first author. Thanks to the Sun PrimaVera and Vantage groups, and to Alistair Cockburn, Dennis de Champeaux, Desmond D'Souza, Peter O'Hearn, Alan Pope, Doug Schmidt, Bob Sproull, and Carolyn Talcott for helpful discussions and comments.

References

1. Agha, G., *ACTORS: A Model of Concurrent Computation in Distributed Systems,* MIT Press, 1986.
2. Aksit, M., L. Bergmans, & S. Vural, "An Object-Oriented Language - Database Integration Model: The Composition-Filters Approach", *Proceedings, ECOOP '92,* LNCS 615, Springer-Verlag, 1992.
3. Alexiev, V., *Mutable Object State for Object-Oriented Logic Programming: A Survey,* Technical Report TR 93-15, Department of Computing Science, University of Alberta, 1993.
4. Allen, R., & D. Garlan, "Formal Connectors", Technical Report CMU-CS-94-115, Carnegie Mellon University, 1994.
5. America, P., "A Parallel Object-Oriented Language with Inheritance and Subtyping", *Proceedings, OOPSLA '90,* ACM, 1990.
6. Arapis, C., *Dynamic Evolution of Object Behavior and Object Cooperation,* Thesis, University of Geneva, 1992.
7. Barwise, J., "Constraints, Channels, and the Flow of Information", in j. Peters (ed.) *Situation Theory and its Applications, Volume 3,* CSLI Lecture Notes, Stanford University, 1993.
8. Baumgartner, G., & V. Russo, "Signatures: A C++ Extension for Type Abstraction and Subtype Polymorphism", *Software---Practice and Experience,* 1994.
9. Birman, K., & R. Van Renesse, *Reliable Distributed Computing with the Isis Toolkit,* IEEE Computer Society Press, 1994.
10. Booch, G., *Object-Oriented Analysis and Design,* Benjamin Cummings, 1993.
11. Borgida, A., J. Mylopoulos, & R. Reiter, "...And nothing else changes: The frame problem in procedure specifications". *Proceedings Fifteenth International Conference on Software Engineering,* IEEE, 1993.
12. Buhr, R. & R. Casselman, "Architecture with Pictures", *Proceedings, OOPSLA '92,* ACM, 1992.
13. Campbell, R. H., & A. N. Habermann, "The Specification of Process Synchronization by Path Expressions". *Lecture Notes in Computer Science 16,* Springer-Verlag, 1974.
14. Chandy, K. & J. Misra, *Parallel Program Design: A Foundation,* Addison-Wesley, 1988.
15. Davison, A., "A Survey of Logic Programming Based Object-Oriented Languages", in G. Agha, P. Wegner, & A. Yonezawa (eds.) *Research Directions in Concurrent Object-Oriented Programming,* MIT Press, 1993.
16. de Champeaux, D., Verification of Some Parallel Algorithms, *Proceedings, 7th Annual Pacific Northwest Software Quality Conference,* Portland, OR, 1989.
17. de Champeaux, D., D. Lea., & P. Faure, *Object-Oriented System Development,* Addison-Wesley, 1993.
18. D'Souza, D., & A. Wills, *Catalysis -- Practical and Rigorous Object Development,* Techincal Report, ICON Computing, 1995.
19. Emerson, E., "Temporal and modal logic". J. van Leeuwen (ed.), *Handbook of Theoretical Computer Science, Volume B,* MIT press, 1990.
20. Gamma, E., R. Helm, R. Johnson, & J. Vlissides. *Design Patterns,* Addison-Wesley, 1994.
21. Garlan, D., & M. Shaw, "An Introduction to Software Architecture". In V. Ambriola and G. Tortora (eds.) *Advances in Software and Knowledge Engineering,* vol II, World Scientific Publishing, 1993.
22. Gatziu, S., & K. Dittrich, "Events in an Active Object-Oriented Database System", *Proceedings, 1st International Workshop on Rules in Database Systems,* 1993.

23. Gupta, V., "Concurrent Kripke Structures", *Proceedings of the North American Process Algebra Workshop* Cornell CS-TR-93-1369, 1993.
24. Harel, D., "StateCharts: A Visual Formalism for Complex Systems", *Science of Computer Programming*, 8, 1987.
25. Harrison, W., & H. Ossher, "Subject-Oriented Programming", *Proceedings, OOPSLA '93*, ACM, 1993.
26. Harrison, W., *The Importance of Using Object References as Identifiers of Objects*, Document 94.6.12, Object Management Group, 1994.
27. Helm, R., I. Holland, & D. Gangopadhyay, "Contracts: Specifying Behavioral Compositions in Object-Oriented Systems", *Proceedings, OOPSLA '90*, ACM, 1990.
28. Hewitt, C., P. Bishop, & R. Steiger, "A Universal Modular ACTOR Formalism for AI", *Third International Joint Conference on Artificial Intelligence*, Stanford University, August 1973.
29. Hoare, C.A.R., "An Axiomatic Basis for Computer Programming", *Communications of the ACM*, 12, 1969.
30. Hogg, J., D. Lea, R. Holt, A. Wills, & D. de Champeaux, "The Geneva Convention on the Treatment of Object Aliasing", *OOPS Messenger*, April 1992.
31. Hughes, G.E., & Cresswell, M.J. *An Introduction to Modal Logic*, Methuen, 1971.
32. Jagadish, H., & O. Shmueli, "Composite Events in a Distributed Object-Oriented Database" *Distributed Object Management*, Morgan Kaufmann, 1994.
33. Jarvinen, H., R. Kurki-Suonio, M. Sakkinnen, & K. Systa, "Object-Oriented Specification of Reactive Systems". *Proceedings, International Conference on Software Engineering*, IEEE, 1990.
34. Jarvinen, H. *The Design of a Specification Language for Reactive Systems*, Technical Report 95, Tampere University of Technology, 1992.
35. Jones, C., *Systematic Software Development Using VDM*, Prentice Hall, 1986.
36. Kiczales, G. *Open Implementations*, Forthcoming book.
37. Lamport, L., "Time, Clocks, and the Ordering of Events in Distributed Systems", *Communications of the ACM*, 21(7), 1978.
38. Lamport, L., *The Temporal Logic of Actions* SRC Research Report 79, Digital Equipment Corp, 1991.
39. Lea, D., & J. Marlowe, *PSL: Protocols and Pragmatics for Open Systems*, Technical Report, Sun Microsystems Laboratories, 1994.
40. Liskov, B., & J. Guttag, *Abstraction and Specification in Program Development*, MIT Press, 1986.
41. Luckham, D., L. Augustin, J. Kenney, J. Vera, D. Bryan, & W. Mann, "Specification and Analysis of a System Architecture Using Rapide", *IEEE Transactions on Software Engineering*, 1994.
42. Manna, Z., & A. Pneulli, *The Temporal Logic of Reactive and Concurrent Systems*, Springer-Verlag, 1991.
43. McCarthy, J. & P.J. Hayes, "Some Philosophical Problems from the Standpoint of Artificial Intelligence", in D. Michie and B. Meltzer (eds.), *Machine Intelligence 4*, Edinburgh University Press, 1969.
44. McCarthy, J. *Elephant 2000: A Programming Language Based on Speech Acts*, Unpublished Manuscript, Stanford University, 1994.
45. Meseguer, J., "A Logical Theory of Concurrent Objects and its Realization in the Maude Language", in G. Agha, P. Wegner, & A. Yonezawa (eds.) *Research Directions in Concurrent Object-Oriented Programming*, MIT Press, 1993.
46. Milner, R., *Communication and Concurrency*, Prentice Hall International, 1989.

47. Milner, R., J. Parrow, & D. Walker, "A Calculus of Mobile Processes", *Information and Computation*, vol 10, pp1-77, 1992.
48. Mullender, S. (ed.) *Distributed Systems*, 2nd ed., Addison-Wesley, 1993.
49. Nierstrasz, O. "Regular Types for Active Objects", *Proceedings, OOPSLA '93*, ACM, 1993.
50. Newmeyer, F. *Linguistics: The Cambridge Survey*, Cambridge University Press, 1988.
51. OMG, *Common Object Request Broker Architecture and Specification*, Document 91.12.1, Object Management Group, 1991.
52. OMG, *Response to the Object Management Group Object Services Task Force Request for Information*, Document 91.11.6. Object Management Group, 1992.
53. OMG, *Common Object Services Specification*, Document 94.1.1, Object Management Group, 1994.
54. OMG, *IDL C++ Language Mapping Specification*, Document 94.8.2, Object Management Group, 1994.
55. Powell, M., *Objects, References, Identifiers and Equality*, Document 93.7.5, Object Management Group, 1993.
56. Pratt, V.R., "Modeling Concurrency with Partial Orders", *International Journal of Parallel Programming*, 15 (1), 1986.
57. Pratt, V.R., *Chu Spaces: Complementarity and Uncertainty in Rational Mechanics*. Technical Report, Stanford University, 1994.
58. Raj, R., E. Tempero, H. Levy, A. Black, N. Hutchinson, & E. Jul, "Emerald: A General Purpose Programming Language", *Software---Practice and Experience*, 1991.
59. Reenskaug, T. *The Object Industry: The Large Scale Provision of Customized Software*, Addison-Wesley, forthcoming.
60. Rumbaugh, J., M. Blaha, W. Premerlani, F. Eddy, & W. Lorensen, *Object-Oriented Modeling and Design*, Prentice Hall, 1991.
61. Sankar, S. & R. Hayes "ADL: An Interface Definition Language for Specifying and Testing Software", in *Proceedings of the Workshop on Interface Definition Languages*, ACM SIGPLAN Notices, 1994.
62. Scholl, M., C. Laasch, & M. Tresch, "Updatable Views in Object Oriented Databases", in C. Delobel, M. Kifer & Y. Masunaga (eds.) *Deductive and Object-Oriented Databases*, Springer-Verlag, 1991.
63. Strom, R., D. Bacon, A. Goldberg, A. Lowry, D. Yellin, & S. Yemeni, *Hermes: A Language for Distributed Computing*, Prentice Hall, 1991.
64. von Benthem, J. *The Logic of Time*, Kluwer, 1991.
65. Wegner, P., "Tradeoffs between Reasoning and Modeling", in G. Agha, P. Wegner, & A. Yonezawa (eds.) *Research Directions in Concurrent Object-Oriented Programming*, MIT Press, 1993.
66. Wieringa, R., & W. de Jonge, "The Identification of Objects and Roles", Technical Report TR-267, Faculty of Mathematics and Computer Science, Vrije Universiteit, 1993.
67. Winskel, G., "An Introduction to Event Structures", *REX'88: Linear Time, Branching Time and Partial Order in Logics and Models for Concurrency* Lecture notes in Computer Science 354, Springer-Verlag, 1988.
68. Yellin, D., & R. Strom. "Interfaces, Protocols, and the Semi-Automatic Construction of Software Adaptors", *Proceedings, OOPSLA '94*, ACM, 1994.

Experience Using Design Patterns to Evolve Communication Software Across Diverse OS Platforms

Doug Schmidt[1] and Paul Stephenson[2]

[1] Department of Computer Science, Washington University, St. Louis, MO, USA
[2] Ericsson Inc., Cypress, CA, USA

Abstract. Design patterns help to improve communication software quality since they address a fundamental challenge in large-scale software development: *communication of architectural knowledge among developers*. This paper makes several contributions to the study and practice of design patterns. It presents a case study that illustrates how design patterns helped to reduce development effort and project risk when evolving an object-oriented telecommunication software framework across UNIX and Windows NT OS platforms. Second, the paper discusses the techniques, benefits, and limitations of applying a design pattern-based reuse strategy to commercial telecommunication software systems.

1 Introduction

Developing communication software that is reusable across OS platforms is hard. Constraints imposed by the underlying OS platforms often make it impractical to reuse existing algorithms, detailed designs, interfaces, or implementations directly. This paper describes how we evolved an object-oriented framework from several UNIX platforms to the Windows NT Win32 platform. Fundamental differences in the I/O mechanisms available on Windows NT and UNIX platforms precluded the direct black-box reuse of framework components. We were, however, able to achieve significant reuse of the *design patterns* underlying the framework.

Design patterns capture the static and dynamic structures of solutions that occur repeatedly when producing applications in a particular context [1, 2, 3]. Systematically incorporating design patterns into the software development process helps improve software quality since patterns address a fundamental challenge in large-scale software development: *communication of architectural knowledge among developers*. In this paper, we describe our experience with a design pattern-based reuse strategy. We have successfully used this strategy at Ericsson to develop a family of object-oriented telecommunication system software based on the ADAPTIVE Service eXecutive (`ASX`) framework [4].

The `ASX` framework is an integrated collection of components that collaborate to produce a reusable infrastructure for developing communication software. The framework automates common activities (such as event demultiplexing, event handler dispatching, connection establishment, routing, configuration of application services, and concurrency control) performed by communication software. At Ericsson, we have used the `ASX` framework to enhance the flexibility and reuse of network management software, which monitors and manages telecommunication switches across multiple hardware and software platforms.

During the past year, we ported the ASX framework from several UNIX platforms to the Windows NT platform. These OS platforms possess significantly different mechanisms for event demultiplexing and I/O. To meet our performance and functionality requirements, it was not possible to reuse several key components in the ASX framework directly across the OS platforms. It was possible, however, to reuse the underlying design patterns embodied by the ASX framework, which reduced project risk significantly and simplified our re-development effort.

The remainder of the paper is organized as follows: Section 2 presents an overview of the design patterns that are the focus of this paper; Section 3 examines the issues that arose as we ported the components in the Reactor framework from several UNIX platforms to the Windows NT platform; Section 4 summarizes the experience we gained, both pro and con, while deploying a design pattern-based system development methodology in a production software environment; and Section 5 presents concluding remarks.

2 Overview of Design Patterns

A design pattern represents a recurring solution to a design problem within a particular domain (such as business data processing, telecommunications, graphical user interfaces, databases, and distributed communication software) [1]. Design patterns facilitate architectural level reuse by providing "blueprints" or guidelines for defining, composing, and reasoning about the key components in a software system. In general, a large amount of experience reuse is possible at the architectural level. However, reusing design patterns does not necessarily result in direct reuse of algorithms, detailed designs, interfaces, or implementations.

This paper focuses on two specific design patterns (the Reactor [5] and Acceptor patterns) that are implemented by the ASX framework. The ASX components, and the Reactor and Acceptor design patterns embodied by these components, are currently used in a number of production systems. These systems include the Bellcore and Siemens Q.port ATM signaling software product, the system control segment for the Motorola Iridium global personal communications system [6], a family of system/network management applications for Ericsson telecommunication switches [7], and a Global Limiting System developed by Credit Suisse that manages credit risk and market risk.

The design patterns described in the following section provided a concise set of architectural blueprints that guided our porting effort from UNIX to Windows NT. By using the patterns, we did not have to rediscover the key collaborations between architectural components. Instead, our development task focused on determining a suitable mapping of the components in the pattern onto the mechanisms provided on the OS platforms. Finding an appropriate mapping was non-trivial, as we describe below. Nevertheless, our knowledge of the design patterns significantly reduced redevelopment effort and minimized the level of risk in our projects.

2.1 The Reactor Pattern

The Reactor is an object behavioral pattern that decouples event demultiplexing and event handler dispatching from the services performed in response to events. This separation of concerns factors out the demultiplexing and dispatching mechanisms (which are independent of an application and thus reusable) from the event handler processing policies (which are specific to an application). The Reactor pattern appears in many single-threaded event-driven frameworks (such as the Motif, Interviews [8], System V STREAMS [9], the ASX OO communication framework [4], and implementations of DCE [10] and CORBA [11]).

The Reactor pattern solves a key problem for single-threaded communication software: *how to efficiently demultiplex multiple types of events from multiple sources of events within a single thread of control.* This strategy provides coarse-grained concurrency control that serializes application event handling within a process at the event demultiplexing level. A consequence of using the Reactor pattern is that the need for more complicated threading, synchronization, or locking within an application is often eliminated.

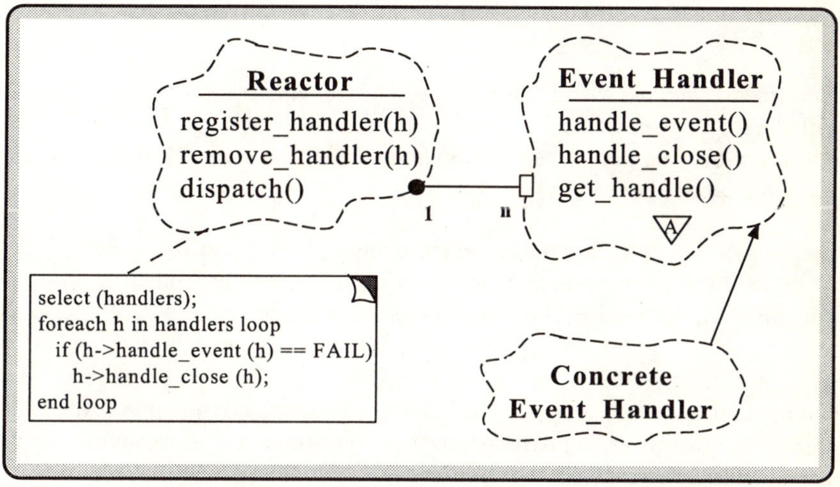

Fig. 1. The Structure and Participants in the Reactor Pattern

Figure 1 illustrates the structure and participants in the Reactor pattern. The `Reactor` defines an interface for registering, removing, and dispatching `Event Handler` objects. An implementation of this interface provides a set of application-independent mechanisms. These mechanisms perform event demultiplexing and dispatching of application-specific event handlers in response to events. The `Event Handler` specifies an abstract interface used by the `Reactor` to dispatch callback methods defined by objects that register to handle input, output, signal, and timeout events of interest. The `Concrete Event Handler` selectively implements callback method(s) to process events in an application-specific manner. The `Timer Queue` supports the dispatching of `Event Handlers` based on time.

Figure 2 illustrates the collaborations between participants in the Reactor pattern. These collaborations are divided into two modes:

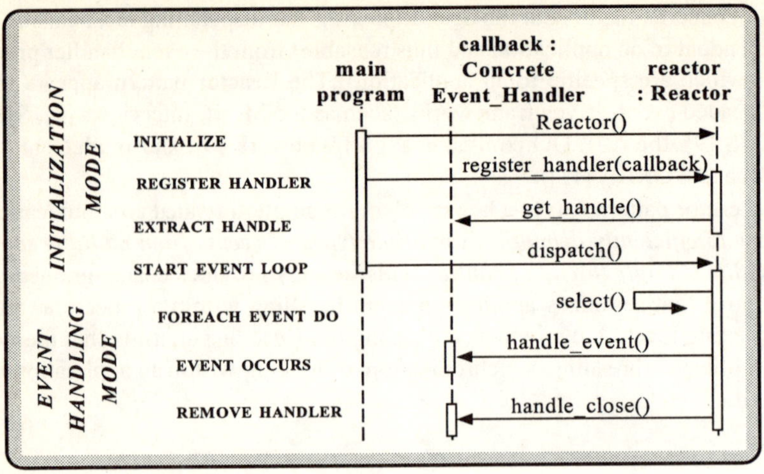

Fig. 2. Object Interaction Diagram for the Reactor Pattern

1. *Initialization mode* – where `Concrete Event Handler` objects are registered with the `Reactor`;
2. *Event handling mode* – where methods on the objects are called back to handle particular types of events.

An alternative way to implement event demultiplexing and dispatching is to use multi-tasking. In this approach, an application spawns a separate thread or process that monitors an event source. Every thread or process blocks until it receives an event notification. At this point, the appropriate event handler code is executed. Certain types of applications (such as file transfer, remote login, or teleconferencing) benefit from multi-tasking. For these applications, multi-threading or multi-processing helps to reduce development effort, improves application robustness, and transparently leverages off of available multi-processor capabilities.

Using multi-threading to implement event demultiplexing has several drawbacks, however. It may require the use of complex concurrency control schemes; it may lead to poor performance on uni-processors [4]; and it is not available on many OS platforms. In these cases, the Reactor pattern may be used in lieu of, or in conjunction with, OS multi-threading or multi-processing mechanisms.

2.2 The Acceptor Pattern

The Acceptor is an object creational pattern that decouples passive connection establishment from the service performed once the connection is established. This separation of concerns enables the application-specific portion of a service to vary independently of the mechanism used to establish the connection. The Acceptor pattern appears in network "superservers" (such as `inetd` [12] and `listen` [13]). These superservers utilize a master Acceptor process that listens for connections on a set of

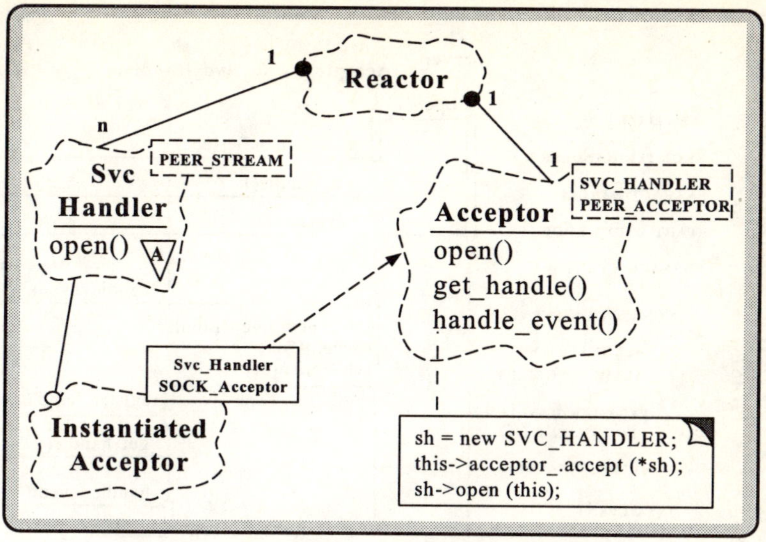

Fig. 3. Structure and Participants in the Acceptor Pattern

communication ports. Each port is associated with a communication-related service (such as the standard Internet services `ftp`, `telnet`, `daytime`, and `echo`). When a service request arrives on a monitored port, the acceptor process accepts the request and dispatches an appropriate pre-registered handler to perform the service.

The Acceptor pattern solves several problems encountered when writing communication software (particularly servers) using interfaces like sockets [12] and TLI [13]:

1. How to avoid writing the same connection establishment code over and over again for each server;
2. How to make the connection establishment code portable across platforms that may contain sockets but not TLI, or vice versa;
3. How to ensure that a passive-mode descriptor is not accidentally used to read or write data.

Figure 3 illustrates the structure and participants in the Acceptor pattern. This pattern leverages off the Reactor pattern's `Reactor` to passively establish multiple connections within a single thread of control. The `Svc Handler` specifies an abstract interface for defining a service; it inherits from `Event Handler` (not shown in this figure). `Svc Handler` is parameterized by a `PEER STREAM` endpoint. The `Acceptor` connects this endpoint to its peer when a connection is successfully established. The `Acceptor` implements the strategy for establishing connections with peers. It is parameterized by a particular type of `SVC HANDLER` (which performs a service in conjunction with a connected peer) and a `PEER ACCEPTOR` (which is the underlying IPC mechanism used to passively establish the connection). Parameterized types are used to enhance portability since the Acceptor pattern's connection establishment strategy is independent of the type of service and the type of IPC mechanism. The programmer supplies arguments for these types to produce an `Instantiated Acceptor`.

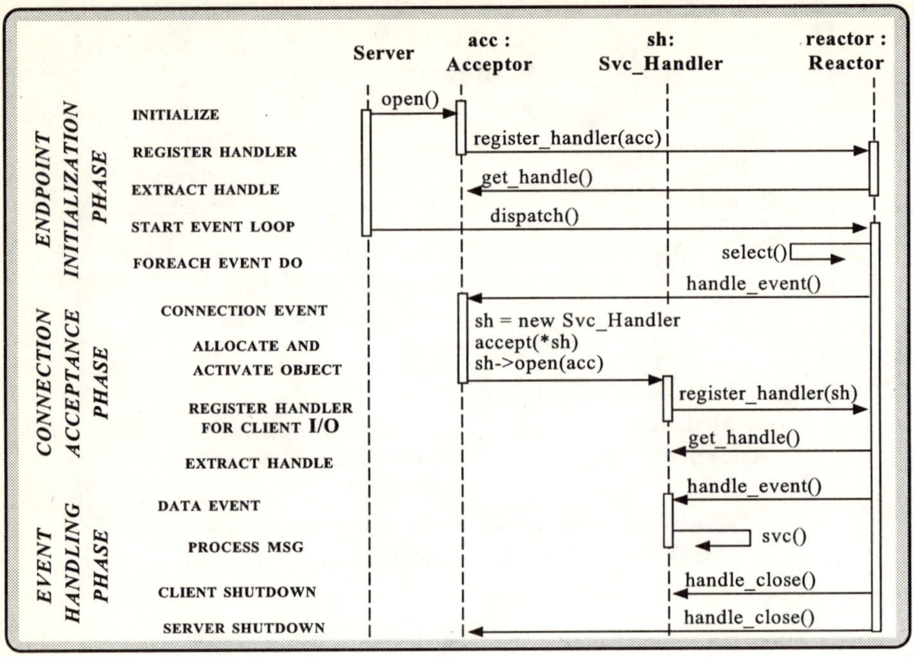

Fig. 4. Object Interaction Diagram for the Acceptor Pattern

Figure 4 illustrates the collaboration among participants in the Acceptor pattern. These collaborations are divided into three phases:

1. *Endpoint initialization phase* – which creates a passive-mode endpoint and listens for connections from clients;
2. *Connection acceptance phase* – which creates a new `Svc Handler` object, accepts the connection into it, and then activates the `Svc Handler`
3. *Event handling phase* – which may employ the Reactor pattern discuss in Section 2.1 to process incoming events.

3 Evolving Design Patterns Across OS Platforms

3.1 Motivation

Our experience at Ericsson demonstrated that explicitly incorporating design patterns into the software development process is beneficial. Design patterns focus attention on the stable aspects of a system's software architecture. In addition, patterns emphasize the strategic collaborations between key participants in the architecture without overwhelming developers with excessive details. Abstracting away from low-level implementation details is essential for system software since OS platform constraints often preclude direct reuse of system components.

We observed that without concrete exemplars, however, developers at Ericsson found it hard to understand and apply a particular pattern to components they were building. To address this concern, this section provides a technically rich, motivating, and detailed (yet comprehensible) roadmap that we used at Ericsson to successfully shepard other developers into the realm of patterns. In this section, we discuss how the Reactor and Acceptor design patterns were implemented and evolved on BSD and System V UNIX platforms, as well as on Windows NT.

The discussion below outlines the relevant functional differences between the various OS platforms and describes how these differences affected the implementation of the design patterns. To focus the discussion, C++ is used as the implementation language. However, the principles and concepts underlying the Reactor and Acceptor patterns are independent of the programming language, the OS platform, and any particular implementation. Readers who are not interested in the lower-level details of implementing design patterns may skip ahead to Section 4. In this section we summarize the lessons we learned from using design patterns on several projects at Ericsson.

3.2 The Impact of Platform Demultiplexing and I/O Semantics

The implementation of the Reactor pattern was affected significantly by the semantics of the event demultiplexing and I/O mechanisms in the underlying OS. There are two types of demultiplexing and I/O semantics: *reactive* and *proactive*. Reactive semantics allow an application to inform the OS which I/O handles to notify it about when an I/O-related operation (such as a read, write, and connection request/accept) may be performed without blocking. Subsequently, when the OS detects that the desired operation may be performed without blocking on any of the indicated handles, it informs the application that the handle(s) are ready. The application then "reacts" by processing the handle(s) accordingly (such as reading or writing data, accepting connections, etc.). Reactive demultiplexing and I/O semantics are provided on standard BSD and System V UNIX systems [12].

In contrast, proactive semantics allow an application to proactively initiate I/O-related operations (such as a read, write, or connection request/accept) or general-purpose event-signaling operations (such as a semaphore lock being acquired or a thread terminating). The invoked operation proceeds asynchronously and does not block the caller. When an operation completes, it signals the application. At this point, the application runs a completion routine that determines the exit status of the operation and potentially starts up another asynchronous operation. Proactive demultiplexing and I/O semantics are provided on Windows NT [14] and VMS.

For performance reasons, we were not able to completely encapsulate the variation in behavior between the UNIX and Windows NT demultiplexing and I/O semantics. Thus, we could not directly reuse existing C++ code, algorithms, or detailed designs. However, it was possible to capture and reuse the concepts that underlay the Reactor and Acceptor design patterns.

3.3 UNIX Evolution of the Patterns

Implementing the Reactor Pattern on UNIX The standard demultiplexing mechanisms on UNIX operating systems provide reactive I/O semantics. For instance, the UNIX `select` and `poll` event demultiplexing system calls inform an application which subset of handles within a set of I/O handles may send/receive messages or request/accept connections without blocking. Implementing the Reactor pattern using UNIX reactive I/O is straightforward. After `select` or `poll` indicate which I/O handles have become ready, the `Reactor` object reacts by invoking the appropriate `Event Handler` callback methods (*i.e.*, `handle_event` or `handle_close`).

One advantage of the UNIX reactive I/O scheme is that it decouples (1) event detection and notification from (2) the operation performed in response to the triggered event. This allows an application to optimize its response to an event by using context information available when the event occurs. For example, when `select` indicates a "read" event is pending, a network server might check to see how many bytes are in a socket receive queue. It might use this information to optimize the buffer size it allocates before making a `recv` system call. A disadvantage of UNIX reactive I/O is that operations may not be invoked asynchronously with other operations. Therefore, computation and communication may not occur in parallel unless separate threads or processes are used.

The original implementation of the Reactor pattern provided by the ASX framework was derived from the `Dispatcher` class category available in the InterViews object-oriented GUI framework [8]. The `Dispatcher` is an object-oriented interface to the UNIX `select` system call. InterViews uses the `Dispatcher` to define an application's main event loop and to manage connections to one or more physical window displays. The `Reactor` framework's first modification to the `Dispatcher` framework added support for signal-based event dispatching. The `Reactor`'s signal-based dispatching mechanism was modeled closely on the `Dispatcher`'s existing timer-based and I/O handle-based event demultiplexing and event handler dispatching mechanisms.[3]

The next modification to the `Reactor` occurred when porting it from SunOS 4.x (which is based primarily on BSD 4.3 UNIX) to SunOS 5.x (which is based primarily on System V release 4 (SVR4) UNIX). SVR4 provides another event demultiplexing system call named `poll`. `Poll` is similar to `select`, though it uses a different interface and provides a broader, more flexible model for event demultiplexing that supports SVR4 features such as STREAM pipe band-data [12].

The SunOS 5.x port of the `Reactor` was enhanced to support either `select` or `poll` as the underlying event demultiplexer. Although portions of the `Reactor`'s internal implementation changed, its external interface remained the same for both the `select`-based and the `poll`-based versions. This common interface improves networking application portability across BSD and SVR4 UNIX platforms.

A portion of the public interface for the BSD and SVR4 UNIX implementation of the Reactor pattern is shown below:

```
// Bit-wise "or" to check for multiple activities per-handle.
enum Reactor_Mask {
```

[3] The `Reactor`'s interfaces for signals and timer-based event handling are not shown in this paper due to space limitations.

```
  READ_MASK = 01, WRITE_MASK = 02, EXCEPT_MASK = 04
};

class Reactor
{
public:
  // Register Event_Handler according to the Reactor_Mask(s)
  // (i.e., "reading," "writing," and/or "exceptions").
  virtual int register_handler (Event_Handler *, Reactor_Mask);

  // Remove handler associated with the Reactor_Mask(s).
  virtual int remove_handler (Event_Handler *, Reactor_Mask);

  // Block process until I/O events occur or a timer
  // expires, then dispatch Event_Handler(s).
  virtual int dispatch (void);

// ...
};
```

Likewise, the `Event Handler` interface for UNIX is defined as follows:

```
typedef int HANDLE; // I/O handle.

class Event_Handler
{
protected:
  // Returns the I/O handle associated with the
  // derived object (must be supplied by a subclass).
  virtual HANDLE get_handle (void) const;

  // Called when an event occurs on the HANDLE.
  virtual int handle_event (HANDLE, Reactor_Mask);

  // Called when object is removed from the Reactor.
  virtual int handle_close (HANDLE, Reactor_Mask);

// ...
};
```

The next major modification to the `Reactor` extended it for use with multi-threaded applications on SunOS 5.x using Solaris threads [15]. Adding multi-threading support required changes to the internals of both the `select`-based and `poll`-based versions of the `Reactor`. These changes involved a SunOS 5.x mutual exclusion mechanism known as a "mutex." A mutex serializes the execution of multiple threads by defining a critical section where only one thread executes the code at a time [15]. Critical sections of the `Reactor`'s code that concurrently access shared resources (such as the `Reactor`'s internal dispatch table containing `Event Handler` objects) are protected by a mutex.

The standard SunOS 5.x synchronization type (`mutex_t`) provides support for *non-recursive* mutexes. The SunOS 5.x non-recursive mutex provides a simple and efficient form of mutual exclusion based on adaptive spin-locks. However, non-recursive mutexes possess the restriction that the thread currently owning a mutex may not reacquire the mutex without releasing it first. Otherwise, deadlock will occur immediately.

While developing the multi-threaded `Reactor`, it quickly became obvious that SunOS 5.x mutex variables were inadequate to support the synchronization semantics required by the Reactor. In particular, the Reactor's dispatch interface performs callbacks to methods of pre-registered, application-specific event handler objects as follows:

```
void Reactor::dispatch (void)
{
  for (;;) {
    // Block until events occur.
    this->wait_for_events (this->handler_set);
    // Obtain the mutex.
    this->lock->acquire ();

    // Dispatch all the callback methods
    // on handlers who contain active events.

    foreach handler : h in this->handler_set
      if (h->handle_event (handler, mask) == FAIL)
        // Cleanup on failure.
        h->handle_close (handler);

    // Release the mutex.
    this->lock->release ();
  }
}
```

Callback methods (such as handle_event and handle_close) defined by Event Handler subclass objects may subsequently re-enter the Reactor object by calling its register_handler and remove_handler methods as follows:

```
// Global per-process instance of the Reactor.
extern Reactor reactor;

// Application-specific method called back by the Reactor.

int Acceptor::handle_event (HANDLE handle,
                            Reactor_Mask)
{
  Concrete_Event_Handler *new_handler =
    new Concrete_Event_Handler;

  *new_handler = this->accept (handle);

  // Re-enter the Reactor object.
  reactor.register_handler (new_handler, READ_MASK);
  // ...
}
```

In the code fragment shown above, non-recursive mutexes will result in deadlock since (1) the mutex within the Reactor's dispatch method is locked throughout the callback and (2) the Reactor's register_handler method tries to acquire the same mutex.

One solution to this problem involved recoding the Reactor to release its mutex lock before invoking callbacks to application-specific Event Handler methods. However, this solution was tedious and error-prone. It also increased synchronization overhead by repeatedly releasing and reacquiring mutex locks. A more elegant and efficient solution used *recursive* mutexes to prevent deadlock and to avoid modifying the `Reactor`'s concurrency control scheme. A recursive mutex allows calls to its `acquire` method to be nested as long as the thread that owns the lock is the one attempting to re-acquire it.

The current implementation of the UNIX-based Reactor pattern is about 2,400 lines of C++ code (not including comments or extraneous whitespace). This implementation is portable between both BSD and System V UNIX variants.

Implementing the Acceptor Pattern on UNIX To illustrate the Reactor and Acceptor patterns, consider the event-driven server for a distributed logging service shown in Figure 5. Client applications use this service to log information (such as error notifications, debugging traces, and status updates) in a distributed environment. In this service, logging records are sent to a central logging server. The logging server outputs the logging records to a console, a printer, a file, or a network management database, etc.

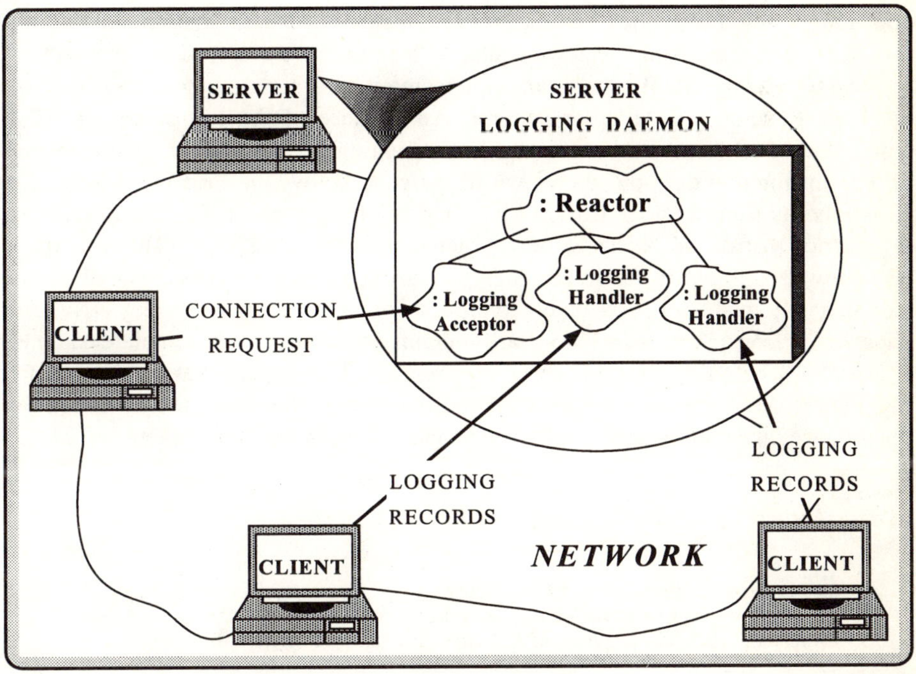

Fig. 5. The Distributed Logging Service

In the architecture of the distributed logging service, the logging server shown in Figure 5 handles logging records and connection requests sent by clients. These records and requests may arrive concurrently on multiple I/O handles. An I/O handle identifies a resource control block managed by the operating system.[4]

The logging server listens on one I/O handle for connection requests to arrive from new clients. In addition, a separate I/O handle is associated with each connected client. Input from multiple clients may arrive concurrently. Therefore, a single-threaded server must not block indefinitely reading from any individual I/O handle. A blocking `read` on one handle may significantly delay the response time for clients associated on other handles.

A highly modular and extensible way to design the server logging daemon is to combine the Reactor and Acceptor patterns. Together, these patterns decouple (1) the application-independent mechanisms that demultiplex and dispatch pre-registered `Event Handler` objects from (2) the application-specific connection establishment and logging record transfer functionality performed by methods in these objects.

Within the server logging daemon, two subclasses of the `Event Handler` base class (`Logging Handler` and `Logging Acceptor`) perform the actions required to process the different types of events arriving on different I/O handles. The `Logging Handler` event handler is responsible for receiving and processing logging records transmitted from a client. Likewise, the `Logging Acceptor` event handler is a factory that is responsible for accepting a new connection request from a client, dynamically allocating a new `Logging Handler` event handler to handle logging records from this client, and registering the new handler with an instance of a `Reactor` object.

The following code illustrates an implementation the server logging daemon based upon the Reactor and Acceptor patterns. An instance of the `Logging Handler` template class performs I/O between the server logging daemon and a particular instance of a client logging daemon. As shown in the code below, the `Logging Handler` class inherits from `Event Handler`. Inheriting from `Event Handler` enables a `Logging Handler` object to be registered with the `Reactor`. This inheritance also allows a `Logging Handler` object's `handle_event` method to be dispatched automatically by a `Reactor` object to process logging records when they arrive from clients. The `Logging Handler` class contains an instance of the template parameter `PEER IO`. The `PEER IO` class provides reliable TCP capabilities used to transfer logging records between an application and the server. The use of templates removes the reliance on a particular IPC interface (such as BSD sockets or System V TLI).

```
template <class PEER_STREAM>
class Logging_Handler : public Event_Handler
{
public:
  // Callback method that handles the reception of logging
  // transmissions from remote clients.  Two recv()'s are
  // used to maintain framing across a TCP bytestream.

  virtual int handle_event (HANDLE, Reactor_Mask) {
    long len;
    // Determine logging record length.
    long n = this->peer_stream_.recv (&len, sizeof len);
```

[4] Different operating systems use different terms for I/O handles. For example, UNIX programmers typically refer to these as *file descriptors*, whereas Windows programmers typically refer to them as *I/O HANDLEs*. In both cases, the underlying concepts are the same.

```
    if (n <= 0) return n;
    else {
      Log_Record log_record;

      // Convert from network to host byte-order.
      len = ntohl (len);
      // Read remaining data in record.
      this->peer_stream_.recv (&log_record, len);

      // Format and print the logging record.
      log_record.decode_and_print ();
      return 0;
    }
  }

  // Retrieve the I/O handle (called by Reactor when
  // Logging_Handler object is registered).

  virtual HANDLE get_handle (void) const {
    return this->peer_stream_.get_handle ();
  }


  // Close down the I/O handle and delete the object
  // when a client closes the connection.

  virtual int handle_close (HANDLE, Reactor_Mask) {
    delete this;
    return 0;
  }

private:
  // Private ensures dynamic allocation.
  ~Logging_Handler (void) { this->peer_stream_.close (); }

   // C++ wrapper for data transfer.
   PEER_STREAM peer_stream_;
};
```

The Logging Acceptor template class is shown in the C++ code below. It is a generic factory that performs the steps necessary to (1) accept connection requests from client logging daemons and (2) create SVC HANDLER objects that are used to perform an actual application-specific service on behalf of clients. Note that the Logging Acceptor object and the SVC HANDLER objects it creates run within the same thread of control. Logging record processing is driven reactively by method callbacks triggered by the Reactor.

The Logging Acceptor subclass inherits from the Event Handler class. Inheriting from the Event Handler class enables an Logging Acceptor object to be registered with the Reactor. The Reactor subsequently dispatches the Logging Acceptor object's handle_event method. This method then invokes accept of the SOCK Acceptor, which accepts a new client connection. The Logging Acceptor class also contains an instance of the template parameter PEER Acceptor. The PEER Acceptor class is a factory that listens for connection requests on a well-known communication port and accepts connections when they arrive on that port from clients.

```
// Global per-process instance of the Reactor.
extern Reactor reactor;

// Handles connection requests
// from a remote client.

template <class SVC_HANDLER,
          class PEER_ACCEPTOR,
          class PEER_ADDR>
class Logging_Acceptor : public Event_Handler
{
public:

  // Initialize the Logging_Acceptor endpoint.

  Logging_Acceptor (PEER_ADDR &a): peer_acceptor_ (a) {}

  // Callback method that accepts a new connection, creates
  // a new SVC_HANDLER object to perform I/O with the client
  // connection, and registers the object with the Reactor.

  virtual int handle_event (HANDLE, Reactor_Mask) {
    SVC_HANDLER *handler = new SVC_HANDLER;

    this->peer_acceptor_.accept (*handler);
    reactor.register_handler (handler, READ_MASK);
    return 0;
  }

  // Retrieve the I/O handle (called by Reactor
  // when an Logging_Acceptor object is registered).

  virtual HANDLE get_handle (void) const {
    return this->peer_acceptor_.get_handle ();
  }

  // Close down the I/O handle when the
  // Logging_Acceptor is shut down.

  virtual int handle_close (HANDLE, Reactor_Mask) {
    return this->peer_acceptor_.close ();
  }
private:
  // Factory that accepts client connections.
  PEER_ACCEPTOR peer_acceptor_;
};
```

The C++ code shown below illustrates the main entry point into the server logging daemon. This code creates a `Reactor` object and an `Logging Acceptor` object and registers the `Logging Acceptor` with the `Reactor`. Note that the `Logging Acceptor` template is instantiated with the `LOGGING HANDLER` class, which performs the distributed logging service on behalf of clients. Next, the main program calls `dispatch` and enters the `Reactor`'s event-loop. The `dispatch` method continuously handles connection requests and logging records that arrive from clients.

The interaction diagram shown in Figure 6 illustrates the collaboration between the

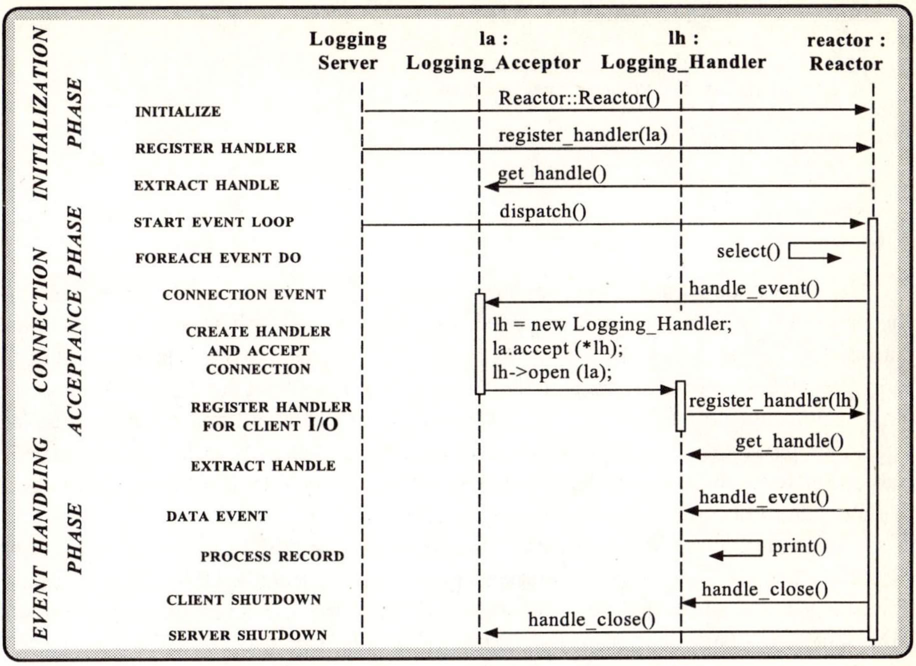

Fig. 6. Server Logging Daemon Interaction Diagram

various objects in the server logging daemon at run-time. Note that once the `Reactor` object is initialized, it becomes the primary focus of the control flow within the server logging daemon. All subsequent activity is triggered by callback methods on the event handlers controlled by the `Reactor`.

```
// Global per-process instance of the Reactor.
Reactor reactor;

// Server port number.
const unsigned int PORT = 10000;

// Instantiate the Logging_Handler template.
typedef Logging_Handler <SOCK_Stream> LOGGING_HANDLER;

// Instantiate the Logging_Acceptor template.
typedef Logging_Acceptor<LOGGING_HANDLER,
                         SOCK_Acceptor,
                         INET_Addr> LOGGING_ACCEPTOR;
int
main (void)
{
  // Logging server address and port number.
  INET_Addr addr (PORT);

  // Initialize logging server endpoint.
  LOGGING_ACCEPTOR acceptor (addr);
```

```
  reactor.register_handler (&acceptor, READ_MASK);

  // Main event loop that handles client logging
  // records and connection requests.

  reactor.dispatch ();

  /* NOTREACHED */
  return 0;
}
```

The C++ code example shown above uses templates to decouple the reliance on the particular type of IPC interface used for connection establishment and communication. The `SOCK Stream`, `SOCK Acceptor` and `INET Addr` classes used in the template instantiations are part of the `SOCK SAP` C++ wrapper library [16]. `SOCK SAP` encapsulates the `SOCK STREAM` semantics of the socket transport layer interface within a type-secure, object-oriented interface. `SOCK STREAM` sockets support the reliable transfer of bytestream data between two processes, which may run on the same or on different host machines in a network [12].

By using templates, it is straightforward to instantiate a different IPC interface (such as the `TLI SAP` C++ wrappers that encapsulate the System V UNIX TLI interface). Templates trade additional compile-time and link-time overhead for improved run-time efficiency. Note that a similar degree of decoupling also could be achieved via inheritance and dynamic binding by using the Abstract Factory or Factory Method patterns described in [1].

3.4 Evolving the Design Patterns to Windows NT

This section describes the Windows NT implementation of the Reactor and Acceptor design patterns performed at Ericsson in Cypress, California. Initially, we attempted to evolve the existing `Reactor` implementation from UNIX to Windows NT using the `select` function from the Windows Sockets (WinSock) library.[5] This approach failed because the WinSock version of `select` does not interoperate with standard Win32[6] I/O HANDLEs. Our applications required the use of Win32 I/O HANDLEs to support network protocols (such as Microsoft's NetBIOS Extended User Interface (NetBEUI)) that are not supported by WinSock version 1.1. Next, we tried to reimplement the `Reactor` interface using the Win32 API system call `WaitForMultipleObjects`. The goal was to maintain the original UNIX interface, but transparently supply a different implementation.

Transparent reimplementation failed to work due to fundamental differences in the proactive vs. reactive I/O semantics on Windows NT and UNIX outlined in Section 3. We initially considered circumventing these differences by asynchronously initiating a 0-sized `ReadFile` request on an overlapped I/O HANDLE. Overlapped I/O is an Win32 mechanism that supports asynchronous input and output. An overlapped event

[5] WinSock is a Windows-oriented transport layer programming interface based on the BSD socket paradigm.

[6] Win32 is the 32-bit Windows subsystem of the Windows NT operating system.

signals an application when data arrives, allowing `ReadFile` to receive the data synchronously. Unfortunately, this solution doubles the number of system calls for every input operation, creating unacceptable performance overhead. In addition, this approach does not adequately emulate the reactive output semantics provided by the UNIX event demultiplexing and I/O mechanisms.

It soon became clear that directly reusing class method interfaces, attributes, detailed designs, or algorithms was not feasible under the circumstances. Instead, we needed to elevate the level of abstraction for reuse to the level of design patterns. Regardless of the underlying OS event demultiplexing I/O semantics, the Reactor and Acceptor patterns are applicable for event-driven applications that must provide different types services that are triggered simultaneously by different types of events. Therefore, although OS platform differences precluded direct reuse of implementations or interfaces, the design knowledge we had invested in learning and documenting the Reactor and Acceptor patterns *was* reusable.

The remainder of this section describes the modifications we made to the implementations of the Reactor and Acceptor design patterns in order to port them to Windows NT.

Implementing the Reactor Pattern on Windows NT Windows NT provides proactive I/O semantics that are typically used in the following manner. First, an application creates a HANDLE that corresponds to an I/O channel for the type of networking mechanism being used (such as named pipes or sockets). The overlapped I/O attribute is specified to the HANDLE creation system call (WinSock sockets are created for overlapped I/O by default). Next, an application creates a HANDLE to a Win32 event object and uses this event object HANDLE to initialize an overlapped I/O structure. The HANDLE to the I/O channel and the overlapped I/O structure are then passed to the `WriteFile` or `ReadFile` system calls to initiate a send or receive operation, respectively. The initiated operation proceeds asynchronously and does not block the caller. When the operation completes, the event object specified inside the overlapped I/O structure is set to the "signaled" state. Subsequently, Win32 demultiplexing system calls (such as `WaitForSingleObject` or `WaitForMultipleObjects`) may be used to detect the signaled state of the Win32 event object. These calls indicate when an outstanding asynchronous operation has completed.

The Win32 `WaitForMultipleObjects` system call is functionally similar to the UNIX `select` and `poll` system calls. It blocks on an array of HANDLEs waiting for one or more of them to signal. Unlike the two UNIX system calls (which wait only for I/O handles), `WaitForMultipleObjects` is a general purpose routine that may be used to wait for any type of Win32 object (such as a thread, process, synchronization object, I/O handle, named pipe, socket, or timer). It may be programmed to return to its caller either when any one of the HANDLEs becomes signaled or when all of the HANDLEs become signaled. `WaitForMultipleObjects` returns the index location in the HANDLE array of the lowest signaled HANDLE.

Windows NT proactive I/O has both advantages and disadvantages. One advantage over UNIX is that Windows NT `WaitForMultipleObjects` provides the flexibility to synchronize on a wide range Win32 objects. Another advantage is that overlapped

I/O may improve performance by allowing I/O operations to execute asynchronously with respect to other computation performed by applications or the OS. In contrast, the reactive I/O semantics offered by UNIX do not support asynchronous I/O directly (threads may be used instead).

On the other hand, designing and implementing the Reactor pattern using proactive I/O on Windows NT turned out to be more difficult than using reactive I/O on UNIX. Several characteristics of `WaitForMultipleObjects` significantly complicated the implementation of the Windows NT version of the Reactor pattern.

First, applications that must synchronize simultaneous send and receive operations on the same I/O channel are more complicated to program on Windows NT. For example, to distinguish the completion of a `WriteFile` operation from a `ReadFile` operation, separate overlapped I/O structures and Win32 event objects must be allocated for input and output. Furthermore, two elements in the `WaitForMultipleObjects` HANDLE array (which is currently limited to a rather small maximum of 64 HANDLEs) are consumed by the separate event object HANDLEs dedicated to the sender and the receiver.

Second, Each Win32 `WaitForMultipleObjects` call only returns notification on a single HANDLE. Therefore, to achieve the same behavior as the UNIX `select` and `poll` system calls (which return a set of activated I/O handles), multiple `WaitForMultipleObjects` must be performed. In addition, the semantics of `WaitForMultipleObjects` do not result in a fair distribution of notifications. In particular, the lowest signaled HANDLE in the array is always returned, regardless of how long other HANDLEs further back in the array may have been pending.

The implementation techniques required to deal with these characteristics of Windows NT were rather complicated. Therefore, we modified the NT Reactor by creating a `Handler Repository` class that shields the `Reactor` from this complexity. This class stores `Event Handler` objects that registered with a `Reactor`. This container class implements standard operations for inserting, deleting, suspending, and resuming `Event Handlers`. Each `Reactor` object contains a `Handler Repository` object in its private data portion. A `Handler Repository` maintains the array of HANDLEs passed to `WaitForMultipleObjects` and it also provides methods for inserting, retrieving, and "re-prioritizing" the HANDLE array. Re-prioritization alleviates the inherent unfairness in the way that the Windows NT `WaitForMultipleObjects` system call notifies applications when HANDLEs become signaled.

The `Handler Repository`'s re-prioritization method is invoked by specifying the index of the HANDLE which has signaled and been dispatched by the `Reactor`. The method's algorithm moves the signaled HANDLE toward the end of the HANDLE array. This allows signaled HANDLEs that are further back in the array to be returned by subsequent calls to `WaitForMultipleObjects`. Over time, HANDLEs that signal frequently migrate to the end of the HANDLE array. Likewise, HANDLES that signal infrequently migrate to the front of the HANDLE array. This algorithm ensures a reasonably fair distribution of HANDLE dispatching.

The implementation techniques described in the previous paragraph did not affect the external interface of the `Reactor`. Unfortunately, certain aspects of Windows NT proactive I/O semantics, coupled with the desire to fully utilize the flexibility of

`WaitForMultipleObjects`, forced visible changes to the `Reactor`'s external interface. In particular, Windows NT overlapped I/O operations must be initiated *immediately*. Therefore, it was necessary for the Windows NT `Event Handler` interface to distinguish between I/O HANDLEs and synchronization object HANDLES, as well as to supply additional information (such as message buffers and event HANDLEs) to the `Reactor`. In contrast, the UNIX version of the `Reactor` does not require this information immediately. Therefore, it may wait until it is *possible* to perform an operation, at which point additional information may be available to help optimize program behavior.

The following modifications to the `Reactor` were required to support Windows NT I/O semantics. The `Reactor Mask` enumeration was modified to include a new `SYNC MASK` value to allow the registration of an `Event Handler` that is dispatched when a general Win32 synchronization object signals. The `send` method was added to the `Reactor` class to proactively initiate output operations on behalf of an `Event Handler`.

```
// Bit-wise "or" to check for multiple activities per-handle.
enum Reactor_Mask {
  READ_MASK = 01, WRITE_MASK = 02, SYNC_MASK = 04
};

class Reactor
{
public:
  // Same as UNIX Reactor...

  // Initiate an asynchronous send operation.
  virtual int send (Event_Handler *, const Message_Block *);

// ...
};
```

Likewise, the `Event Handler` interface for Windows NT was also modified as follows:

```
class Event_Handler
{
protected:
  // Returns the Win32 I/O HANDLE associated with the
  // derived object (must be supplied by a subclass).
  virtual HANDLE get_handle (void) const;

  // Allocates a message for the Reactor.
  virtual Message_Block *get_message (void);

  // Called when event occurs.
  virtual int handle_event (Message_Block *, Reactor_Mask);

  // Called when object is removed from Reactor.
  virtual int handle_close (Message_Block *, Reactor_Mask);

// Same as UNIX Event_Handler...
};
```

When a derived `Event Handler` is registered for input with the `Reactor` an overlapped input operation is immediately initiated on its behalf. This requires the `Reactor` to request the derived `Event Handler` for an I/O mechanism HANDLE, destination buffer, and a Win32 event object HANDLE for synchronization. A derived `Event Handler` returns the I/O mechanism HANDLE via its `get_handle` method and returns the destination buffer location and length information via the `Message Block` abstraction described in [4].

The current implementation of the Windows NT-based Reactor pattern is about 2,600 lines C++ code (not including comments or extraneous whitespace). This code is approximately 200 lines longer than the UNIX version. The additional code primarily ensures the fairness of `WaitForMultipleObjects` event demultiplexing, as discussed above. Although Windows NT event demultiplexing is more complex than UNIX, the behavior of Win32 mutex objects eliminated the need for the separate `Mutex` interface with recursive-mutex semantics discussed in Section 3.3. Under Win32, a thread will not be blocked if it attempts acquire a mutex specifying the HANDLE to a mutex that it already owns. However, to release its ownership, the thread must release a Win32 mutex once for each time that the mutex was acquired.

Implementing the Acceptor Pattern on Windows NT The following example C++ code illustrates an implementation of the Acceptor pattern based on the Windows NT version of the Reactor pattern.

```
template <class PEER_STREAM>
class Logging_Handler : public Event_Handler
{
public:
  // Callback method that handles the reception of logging
  // transmissions from remote clients.  The Message_Block
  // object stores a message received from a client.

  virtual int handle_event (Message_Block *msg, Reactor_Mask) {
    Log_Record *log_record = (Log_Record *) msg->get_rd_ptr ();

    // Format and print logging record.
    log_record.format_and_print ();
    delete msg;
    return 0;
  }

  // Retrieve the I/O HANDLE (called by Reactor when a
  // Logging_Handler object is registered).

  virtual HANDLE get_handle (void) const {
    return this->peer_stream_.get_handle ();
  }

  // Return a dynamically allocated buffer to store
  // an incoming logging message.

  virtual Message_Block *get_message (void) {
    return new Message_Block (sizeof (Log_Record));
  }
```

```
  // Close down I/O handle and delete object when a
  // client closes connection.
  virtual int handle_close (Message_Block *msg, Reactor_Mask) {
    delete msg;
    delete this;
    return 0;
  }

private:
  // Private ensures dynamic allocation.
  ~Logging_Handler (void) { this->peer_stream_.close (); }

  // C++ wrapper for data transfer.
  PEER_STREAM peer_stream_;
}
```

The `Logging Acceptor` class is essentially the same as the one illustrated earlier. Likewise, the interaction diagram that describes the collaboration between objects in the server logging daemon is similar to the one shown in Figure 6. In addition, the application is the same server logging daemon presented above. The primary difference is that Win32 `Named Pipe` C++ wrappers are used instead of the `SOCK SAP` socket C++ wrappers in the main program as shown below:

```
// Global per-process instance of the Reactor.
Reactor reactor;

// Server endpoint.
const char ENDPOINT[] = "logger";

// Instantiate the Logging_Handler template.
typedef Logging_Handler <NPipe_IO> LOGGING_HANDLER;

// Instantiate the Logging_Acceptor template.
typedef Logging_Acceptor<LOGGING_HANDLER,
                         NPipe_Acceptor,
                         Local_Pipe_Name> LOGGING_ACCEPTOR;

int
main (void)
{
  // Logging server address.
  Local_Pipe_Name addr (ENDPOINT);

  // Initialize logging server endpoint.
  LOGGING_ACCEPTOR acceptor (addr);

  reactor.register_handler (&acceptor, SYNC_MASK);

  // Arm the proactive I/O handler.
  acceptor.initiate ();

  // Main event loop that handles client
  // logging records and connection requests.
  reactor.dispatch ();
  /* NOTREACHED */
  return 0;
}
```

The Named Pipe Acceptor object (`Acceptor`) is registered with the Reactor to handle asynchronous connection establishment. Due to the semantics of Windows NT proactive I/O, the `Acceptor` object must explicitly initiate the acceptance of a Named Pipe connection via an `initiate` method. Each time a connection acceptance is completed, the Reactor dispatches the `handle_event` method of the Named Pipe version of the Acceptor pattern to create a new `Svc Handler` that will receive logging records from the client. The `Reactor` will also initiate the next connection acceptance sequence asynchronously.

4 Lessons Learned

Our group at Ericsson has been developing object-oriented frameworks based on design patterns for the past two years [7]. During this time, we have learned many lessons, both positive and negative, about using design patterns as the basis for our system design, implementation, and documentation. This section discusses the lessons we have learned and outlines workarounds for problems we encountered when using design patterns in a production environment.

4.1 Pros and Cons of Design Patterns

Many of our experiences with patterns at Ericsson are similar to those observed on other projects using design patterns, such as the Motorola Iridium project [6]. Recognizing these common themes across different companies increase our confidence that our experiences with patterns generalize to other large-scale software projects. Note that many pros and cons of using design patterns are duals of each other, representing "two sides of the same coin."

• *Patterns are underspecified:* since they generally do not overconstrain implementations. This is beneficial since patterns permit flexible solutions that are customizable to account for application requirements and constraints imposed by the OS platform and network infrastructure.

On the other hand, developers and managers must recognize that learning a collection of patterns is no substitute for design and implementation skills. In fact, patterns often lead team members to think they know more about the solution to a problem than they actually do. For example, recognizing the structure and participants in a pattern (such as the Reactor or Acceptor patterns) is only the first step. As we describe in Section 3, a major development effort may be required to fully realize the patterns correctly, efficiently, and portably.

• *Patterns enable widespread reuse of software architecture:* even if reuse of algorithms, implementations, interfaces, or detailed designs is not feasible. Recognizing the benefit of architectural reuse (which is inherently indirect), compared with more direct forms of reuse, was crucial in the design evolution we presented in Section 3. Our task became much simpler after we recognized how to leverage off our prior development effort and reduce risk by reusing the Reactor and Acceptor patterns across UNIX and Windows NT.

It is important, however, to manage the expectations of developers and managers, who may have misconceptions about the fundamental contribution of design patterns to a project. In particular, at this point in time, patterns do not lead to automated code reuse. Neither do they guarantee flexible and efficient design and implementation. As always, there is no substitute for creativity and diligence on the part of developers.

• *Patterns capture knowledge that is implicitly understood:* once developers are exposed to, and properly motivated by, the concepts of design patterns, we found that they are eager to adopt the nomenclature and methodology. This stems from the fact taht patterns codify knowledge that is already understood intuitively. Therefore, once basic concepts, notations, and pattern template formats are mastered, it is straightforward to document and reason about many portions of a system's architecture and design using patterns.

A drawback to the intuitive nature of patterns is a phenomenon we termed *pattern overload.* In this situation, so many aspects of the project are expressed as patterns that the concept becomes diluted. This situation occurs when existing development practices are relabled as patterns without significantly improving them. Likewise, developers may spend their time recasting mundane concepts (such as binary search or building a linked list) into pattern form. Although this is intellectually satisfying, it may become counter productive if it does not lead to software quality improvements.

• *Patterns help improve communication within and across software development teams:* developers share a common vocabulary and a common conceptual gestalt. By learning the key recurring patterns in their application domain, developers at Ericsson elevated the level of discourse they communicated with their colleagues. For example, once our team understood the Reactor and Acceptor patterns, they used them in other projects that were suited to these architectures.

The focus on design patterns has also helped us to move away from "programming language-centric" views of the object paradigm. This has been beneficial at Ericsson since it enabled experienced developers from different language communities (such as Lisp, Smalltalk, C++, C, and Erlang) to share design expertise of mutual interest.

As usual, however, restraint and a good sense of aesthetics is required to resist the temptation of elevating complex concepts and principles to the level of hyperbole. We noticed a tendency for some developers to adopt a tunnel vision where they would try to apply patterns that were inappropriate simply because they were familiar with the patterns. For example, the Reactor pattern may be an inefficient event demultiplexing model for a multi-processor platform since it serializes application concurrency at a fairly coarse-grained level.

• *Patterns promote a structured means of documenting software architectures:* this documentation may be written at a high-level of abstraction. Abstraction is beneficial since it captures the essential architectural interactions while suppressing unnecessary details.

One of our concerns with conventional pattern catalogs [1, 2], however, is that they are too abstract. We found that in many cases that overly abstract pattern descriptions made it difficult for developers to understand and apply a particular pattern to systems they were building.

4.2 Solutions and Workarounds

Based on our experiences, we recommend the following solutions and workarounds to the various traps and pitfalls with patterns discussed above.

• *Expectation management:* many of the problems with patterns we discussed above are related to managing the expectations of development team members. As usual, patterns are no silver bullet that will magically absolve developers from having to wrestle with tough design and implementation issues. At Ericsson, we have worked hard to motivate the genuine benefits from patterns, without hyping them beyond their actual contribution.

• *Wide-spectrum pattern exemplars:* based on our experience using design patterns as a documentation tool, we believe that pattern catalogs should include more than just object model diagrams and structured prose. Hyper-text browsers, such as Mosaic and Windows Help Files, are particularly useful for creating compound documents that possess multiple levels of abstraction. Moreover, in our experience, it was particularly important to illustrate multiple implementations of a pattern. This helps to avoid tunnel vision and over-constrained solutions based upon a limited pattern vocabulary. The extended discussion in Section 3 is one example of a wide-spectrum exemplar using this approach. This example contains in-depth coverage of tradeoffs encountered in actual use.

• *Integrate patterns with object-oriented frameworks:* Ideally, examples in pattern catalogs [2, 1] should reference (or better yet, contain hyper-text links to) source code that comprises an actual object-oriented framework. We have begun building such an environment at Ericsson, in order to disseminate our patterns and frameworks to a wider audience. In addition to linking on-line documentation and source code, we have had good success with periodic design reviews where developers throughout the organization present useful patterns they have been working on. This is another technique for avoiding tunnel vision and enhancing the pattern vocabulary within and across development teams.

5 Concluding Remarks

Design patterns facilitate the reuse of abstract architectures that are decoupled from concrete realizations of these architectures. This decoupling is particularly useful when developing communication software components and frameworks that are reusable across OS platforms. This paper describes two design patterns, Reactor and Acceptor, that are commonly used to build communication software. Using the design pattern techniques described in this paper, we successfully reused major portions of our telecommunication system software development effort and experience across diverse UNIX and Windows NT OS platforms.

Our experiences with patterns reinforce the fact that the transition from object-oriented analysis to object-oriented design and implementation is challenging. Often, the constraints of the underlying OS and hardware platform influence design and implementation details significantly. This is particularly problematic for communication software, which is frequently targeted for OS platforms that contain non-portable features. In such circumstances, reuse of design patterns may be the only viable means to leverage previous development expertise.

The UNIX version of the `ASX` framework components described in this paper are freely available via anonymous ftp from the Internet host `ics.uci.edu` (128.195.1.1) in the files `gnu/C++_wrappers.tar.Z` and `gnu/C++_wrappers_doc.tar.Z`. This distribution contains complete source code, documentation, and example test drivers for the C++ components developed as part of the ADAPTIVE project [4] at the University of California, Irvine and Washington University.

References

1. E. Gamma, R. Helm, R. Johnson, and J. Vlissides, *Design Patterns: Elements of Reusable Object-Oriented Software*. Reading, MA: Addison-Wesley, 1994.
2. F. Buschmann, R. Meunier, H. Rohnert, and M. Stal, *Pattern-Oriented Software Architecture - A Pattern System*. Wileys and Sons, 1995.
3. J. O. Coplien and D. C. Schmidt, eds., *Pattern Languages of Program Design*. Reading, MA: Addison-Wesley, 1995.
4. D. C. Schmidt, "ASX: an Object-Oriented Framework for Developing Distributed Applications," in *Proceedings of the* 6th *USENIX C++ Technical Conference*, (Cambridge, Massachusetts), USENIX Association, April 1994.
5. D. C. Schmidt, "Reactor: An Object Behavioral Pattern for Concurrent Event Demultiplexing and Event Handler Dispatching," in *Pattern Languages of Program Design* (J. O. Coplien and D. C. Schmidt, eds.), Reading, MA: Addison-Wesley, 1995.
6. D. C. Schmidt, "Experience with a System of Reusable Design Patterns for Motorola Iridium Communication Software," in *Submitted to OOPSLA '95*, (Austin, Texas), ACM, October 1995.
7. D. C. Schmidt and T. Suda, "An Object-Oriented Framework for Dynamically Configuring Extensible Distributed Communication Systems," *IEE/BCS Distributed Systems Engineering Journal (Special Issue on Configurable Distributed Systems)*, vol. 2, pp. 280–293, December 1994.
8. M. A. Linton, J. Vlissides, and P. Calder, "Composing User Interfaces with InterViews," *IEEE Computer*, vol. 22, pp. 8–22, February 1989.
9. D. Ritchie, "A Stream Input–Output System," *AT&T Bell Labs Technical Journal*, vol. 63, pp. 311–324, Oct. 1984.
10. J. Dilley, "OODCE: A C++ Framework for the OSF Distributed Computing Environment," in *Proceedings of the Winter Usenix Conference*, USENIX Association, January 1994.
11. C. Horn, "The Orbix Architecture," tech. rep., IONA Technologies, August 1993.
12. W. R. Stevens, *UNIX Network Programming*. Englewood Cliffs, NJ: Prentice Hall, 1990.
13. S. Rago, *UNIX System V Network Programming*. Reading, MA: Addison-Wesley, 1993.
14. H. Custer, *Inside Windows NT*. Redmond, Washington: Microsoft Press, 1993.
15. J. Eykholt, S. Kleiman, S. Barton, R. Faulkner, A. Shivalingiah, M. Smith, D. Stein, J. Voll, M. Weeks, and D. Williams, "Beyond Multiprocessing... Multithreading the SunOS Kernel," in *Proceedings of the Summer USENIX Conference*, (San Antonio, Texas), June 1992.
16. D. C. Schmidt and T. Harrison, "Object-Oriented Components for High-speed Network Programming," in *Submitted to the Conference on Object-Oriented Technologies*, (Monterey, CA), USENIX, June 1995.

Sharing Properties in a Uniform Object Space

Heiko Kießling and Uwe Krüger

University of Karlsruhe, Department of Informatics,
Operating Systems Research Group
Am Fasanengarten 5, D-76128 Karlsruhe, Germany

Abstract. We consider a system with a uniform object space. In a uniform object space, objects are the primary structural elements of the system. Such a system requires a different way of looking at the problem of sharing properties among objects. We describe the requirements on a suitable model of sharing and linguistic elements in the form of *views* and *patterns* to meet these requirements. With this model, we show that delegation both on the level of objects and as inheritance on the level of classes should only serve as a basis for implementing some of the linguistic elements of the model but not as such an element by itself. The model described in this paper finds itself in the language ARISTARCH/L which supports the object-based operating system ARISTARCH/OS that is under development in SAMOS, a project undertaken by the Operating Systems Research Group at the University of Karlsruhe.

1 Introduction

We consider a system with a uniform object space. The properties of an object in this object space reveal themselves in its *behaviour* observed by other objects. Abstractly speaking, an object shows a changing of behaviour over time. This changing of behaviour is determined by the (abstract) *state* of the object. Enduring structure of behaviour might be called the *behaviour pattern* of the object. In most object-based systems the behaviour pattern of an object is described by its operations. The execution of an operation depends upon the values of local variables. Effectively, these values are interpreted by the operations to represent the abstract state of the object.

In a uniform object space, objects are the primary structural elements of the system. In consequence the notion of an application is only latent as a set of cooperating objects rather than to manifest itself as structural elements of the system, that is a process created out of an object-based program. The elements describing the application, such as classes, do not come to life by calling a program but rather are represented as objects as well. From the uniformity of the object space directly follows the longevity of objects, in the sense that objects may survive the applications that created them. This is because an object may survive the execution of the operation that created it and the execution of an application is only latent as executing an operation of another object. Longevity thus lends itself to preserving existing information even in the face of adaptations by preserving pointers to adapted objects.

2 Requirements

A system with a uniform object space requires a different way of looking at the problem of sharing common behaviour among objects. Based on the preliminary considerations given in the introduction, we shall now put forward the requirements to be met by a suitable model by way of examples.

2.1 Direct Description of Objects

One of these requirements is the ability to directly describe objects instead of classes, as in general is necessary if a class has only one instance. Typical examples are value objects representing numbers, characters or truth values. Classes with only one instance are also common, whenever modules would be chosen in imperative languages. Szyperski [26], for instance, complains about the lack of support of the notion of module by many object-based languages. As examples for its usefulness he gives modules with global constants or mathematical libraries. But since in the kind of system considered here the notions of program and linking are pushed to the background as a consequence of applications being only latent as sets of objects, a module needs a runtime identity. One may now consider the main difference between modules and objects the fact that modules unlike objects lack such a runtime identity. Therefore the requirement of modules turns out to be the requirement of directly describing single objects without classes.

2.2 Direct Description of Aspects of Objects

Objects are often looked at under different aspects by different kinds of applications of the system. For instance, an object representing a person may be regarded as representing a taxpayer by the tax office but an employee by his or her employers. Under different aspects, the same object may show different behaviour.

In most object-based systems, objects owned by different applications work in separate environments. Different aspects of an object modelling the same entity are then represented by different objects in these separate environments. For example, in such a system an application in the tax office would model each person as an object merely representing the taxpayer aspect whereas an application in a company would only allow for the employee aspect. Nevertheless, often cooperation is necessary among different applications. For instance, though taxpayer and employee are represented by different objects, if the income, as an attribute of the employee, changes, the rate of taxation, an attribute of the taxpayer, should change as well. In general, it is necessary for different objects in separate environments to share common state. Most often, this is done by means of shared files, data bases and comparable mechanisms. The uniformity of the object space, however, allows different applications to work at least partially on the same set of objects. The same object now models both the taxpayer and the employee aspect.

Therefore, a dedicated linguistic element to describe aspects seems appropriate. Such an element should allow to describe different aspects separately to the greatest possible extent, but nonetheless in a single object, and to select the aspect of interest at a given time.

2.3 Categorization of Objects

To describe common behaviour of objects, it is necessary to divide them into different *categories* determining this common behaviour. The process of doing so is called *categorization*. It happens for the first time when an object is brought into the system, and in particular when it is created. A category may be defined by the concrete behaviour of its objects, or alternatively based on an abstract notion that separates it from other categories. The former kind of category is called *concrete*, whereas the latter is said to be *abstract*. While a concrete category statically determines behaviour, the behaviour specified by an abstract category may change over time according to the requirements on its objects. The differences between these two kinds of categorization shall now be elucidated by an example.

- By *concrete categorization* an object is assigned to a concrete category based on its behaviour to be modelled. We shall illustrate this by the example of two elephants introduced first by Lieberman [11], Clyde and Fred. Initially, the only elephant in a zoo is Clyde. In a visitor information system Clyde is represented by an object. When the zoo gets Fred, we recognize the similarities between the two of them, therefore putting Fred into the same concrete category as Clyde, which is given by the behaviour shown by the Clyde object at the time of creation of the object representing Fred. Creating an object by concrete categorization therefore means to copy the concrete behaviour of one or several other objects. Now, if Clyde changes his behaviour, for example by losing one of his legs due to an accident, this change should not be passed on to Fred. Because of the accident the object representing Clyde implicitly is assigned to another concrete category, that is it is *recategorized*. Concretely categorizing an object has a *momentary* nature since its membership of a concrete category changes whenever its behaviour changes.
- *Abstract categorization* is the result of an achievement of abstraction by the inventor of the abstract category, thus distinguishing it from other abstract categories. An abstract category therefore is independent of the concrete behaviour of its objects at any time. While a concrete category is determined by the modelled behaviour of its members, an abstract category determines part of the behaviour of its members.
  For example, in a zoo elephants are just one species among others. Therefore, elephants may form an abstract category. Common behaviour among all elephants are their habits. If there is scientific evidence for recently unknown habits, this part of behaviour is changed for all elephants at the same time, whereas their membership of the abstract category of elephants is preserved. Abstractly categorizing an object has a *permanent* nature since membership

is not affected by behaviour changes, but behaviour rather changes for all members at the same time.
Additionally, abstract categorization, in contrast to concrete categorization, in general is not related to the entire behaviour of its members. Parts of the behaviour may not be determined by the abstract category, or only determined in form of a behaviour pattern. For example, every elephant may possess a trunk, but the length of this trunk may be different for each specimen. The length of the trunk is not relevant to the category of elephants, whereas the property to possess one is essential. Altogether, we distinguish three different levels of abstract categorization, which we now shall explain in more conventional terms.

- *Categorization of Behaviour* strongly relates to class variables, as a part of state common to all instances of the class. As operations together with variables determine behaviour, this is synonymous with describing behaviour essential to the abstract category modelled by the class.
- *Categorization of Behaviour Pattern* in general is given by having the same operations for all instances of a class operating on local variables of each instance.
- *No Categorization* to our knowledge is not supported by existing class-based systems. For example, assume now that one of the elephants in the zoo is capable of walking upright. This may or may not be the first step of evolution towards upright walking elephants but, for the moment being, she is really unique. She remains in the same category as her fellows but she still shows a behaviour that distinguishes her from all the others. We may conclude that an important requirement on an object model for a system with a uniform object space is the extensibility of abstractly categorized objects.

In Sect. 1 we have argued that longevity is a natural property of objects in a uniform object space. The different forms of categorization together with longevity lend themselves to preserving existing information in the face of adaptations by systematically adapting single or entire sets of objects while preserving pointers.

Abstract categorization of behaviour may lead to different categories which determine different behaviour nevertheless based on a *common* behaviour pattern. Therefore, an important requirement on languages in a uniform object space is to enable programmers to categorize abstract categories by this common behaviour pattern. We shall elucidate this by the example of a class of character strings. To permit the efficient representation and comparison of strings, often a table is used which holds the different character sequences that occur in strings. Strings themselves merely possess indices into this table, strings containing the same sequence possessing the same index. The table may be thought of as a part of the state of each string that is common to all strings. It finds its natural place in the class of strings which therefore are categorized by using a certain table besides by possessing a common behaviour pattern. If it is not necessary to pass a string out of a certain context, for instance an application, it seems reasonable to use a separate table in this context to achieve higher efficiency. This may be seen even more clearly if we assume a multiple user object space. Such an object space enables several users represented by proxy objects to cooperate with each other via commonly known objects. In this case it may not be just inefficient but plainly wrong to assign to all users the same string class, and thus the same string table, for depending on the functionality supported by strings a user may find out which character sequences are defined by others. This again necessitates multiple string classes for which access may be restricted separately. Put in conventional terms, the requirement is to enable programmers to describe classes with different states but instances which share the same component structure.

Some of the requirements described above seem to be met by delegation both on the level of objects and as inheritance on the level of classes. Lieberman argues for delegation as a means of abstract categorization while object-oriented languages to this end use classes and inheritance. In the following sections we will present a model for describing common behaviour of objects that we believe meets the requirements given above very well. With it we will show that delegation both on the level of objects and as inheritance on the level of classes should only serve as a basis for implementing some of the linguistic elements of the model but not as such an element by itself. The implementation of these elements apart from its relationship to delegation is out of the scope of this paper.

In the following section we will first clarify our terminology. In Sect. 4, we will then present our approach to the description of different aspects of objects. After that, we will deal with the problem of categorization in Sect. 5. Both sections close with a critique of the notion of delegation. In the closing section we will compare our model to related work. The model described here finds itself in the language ARISTARCH/L which supports the object-based operating system ARISTARCH/OS that is under development in SAMOS, a project undertaken by the Operating Systems Research Group at the University of Karlsruhe. Therefore examples are shown in this language but are also explained in the text.

3 Objects

In this section we clarify terminology in a concise way. In the following, we will have to strongly distinguish between the *definition* and the *implementation* of the components of an object. For now it is sufficient to assume *attributes* and *commands* as components. An attribute consists of two commands, one for reading it and one for writing it. These are the terms used when talking about the definition of an object. The implementation of the object describes how attributes and commands are realized. Every command is implemented by a *method*. Accordingly, every attribute is implemented by two methods, one for reading and one for writing, or by a *variable* which implicitly defines these two methods. This allows customizations of attribute implementations similar to, for instance, those in TRELLIS/OWL designed by Schaffert and Cooper [22]. In ARISTARCH/L, definition and implementation of an object are described by means of an *object expression* which may be understood as evaluating to a constant reference to the object. To this end, each object expression has an **IMPLEMENTATION** section which describes both the definition and the implementation of the object and is divided into an **ATTRIBUTES** part and a **COMMANDS** part. Object expressions meet the requirement for direct description of objects stated in Sect. 2.1.

4 Views

4.1 Introduction

Objects are looked at from different aspects by different kinds of applications of the system. For instance, an object representing a person may be regarded as representing a taxpayer by the tax office but representing an employee by his or her employer. To this end, in ARISTARCH/L each object may possess one or more *views*. A view describes an aspect of an object by declaring a logically closed subset of its components, the *interface* of this view. These interfaces are included in the **INTERFACES** section of the object. Besides representing different aspects of an object interfaces of views also serve information hiding.

An object is always considered under one of its views. To achieve this, each reference to an object not only determines its identity but also the view it is currently used under. It is possible, starting from a reference, to get a reference to the same object under another view.

Example 4.1 describes three different aspects of a person in the left code fragment. A general view **Person** is restricted to basic information such as the name (lines 3 to 9). The view **Employee** additionally consists of the personnel number and income (lines 11 to 19), while the view **Taxpayer** (lines 21 to 29) includes the rate of taxation and the tax number[1]. If an object expression describes several different views the **AS** clause may be used to determine the initial view to use the object under (line 31). An application in a tax office may look at the person from its most pleasant aspect that is, a taxpayer, by switching to the appropriate view with the operation **VIEW person AS Taxpayer** (line 12 of the right fragment). The reference obtained by this operation allows access via the interface of the view **Taxpayer** and thus to the attribute **taxrate**. Please note that, as description of an aspect of an object, each view is given exactly once.

Each component may have different *versions of implementation* to cater to the object's different aspects. Hence each attribute and each command may be implemented by several different variables and methods. For example, assume a command **State** giving information about a person. This information for a **Taxpayer** is something different from what it is for an **Employee**. Therefore, a programmer will create at least two versions of the method implementing the command **State**.

4.2 Selecting Versions of Implementation

To execute the correct version of implementation corresponding to a certain view each view possesses a *mapping* which assigns a version to every component. Each

[1] *Derivation* of views allows for such constellations but is deferred to Sect. 4.4.

```
OBJECT
  INTERFACES
    VIEW Person
      ATTRIBUTES
        IMMUTABLE name: tString
      COMMANDS
        State ();
        Action ()
    END VIEW Person;

    VIEW Employee
      ATTRIBUTES
        IMMUTABLE name: tString;
        personnelNumber: INTEGER;
        income: INTEGER
      COMMANDS
        State ();
        Action ()
    END VIEW Employee;

    VIEW Taxpayer
      ATTRIBUTES
        IMMUTABLE name: tString;
        taxNumber: INTEGER;
        IMMUTABLE taxrate: INTEGER
      COMMANDS
        State ();
        Action ()
    END VIEW Taxpayer;
  ...
END OBJECT AS Person -> person
```

```
OBJECT
  ...
  IMPLEMENTATION
    COMMANDS
      TaxReturn (person: tPerson)
        BY METHOD
          DECLARE
            ATTRIBUTES
              t: tTaxpayer BY VARIABLE;
            ...
          DO
            VIEW person AS Taxpayer -> t;
            ... t.taxrate ...
      END TaxReturn;
  ...
END OBJECT -> taxoffice
```

Ex. 4.1. Aspects of a `person`

version must be used in the mapping of at least one view. Since different views may use the same version it is not sensible to describe mappings by syntactically nesting versions into views. Instead, different versions of a component get identifiers which the mapping may refer to. These identifiers are only unambiguous in connection with the identifier of the component. The reason for this is the basic notion of *identifiers as specifications* of components in ARISTARCH/L. The type system of ARISTARCH/L is also based on this notion, and in this respect is comparable to that of EMERALD [3], but out of the scope of this paper.

While in Ex. 4.1 views were merely used to describe different subsets of the components of `person`, Ex. 4.2 employs the command `State` to show the use of different versions specific to views. In the `IMPLEMENTATION` section three versions of the method for `State` are defined (lines 21 to 29), printing the information appropriate to the aspects represented by different views. In the `MAPPINGS` section (lines 4 to 13), the versions are assigned to the views `Person`, `Employee`, and `Taxpayer`, respectively. Components like `State` are marked with the keyword `ASSERTED` (lines 16, 17, 20, and 31). This mark must be carried by all components given in the interface of any view of an object. It has the advantage of hidden components to be immediately recognizable in their implementation.

```
OBJECT
  ...
  IMPLEMENTATION
    MAPPINGS
      VIEW Person ...
        State BY BasicVersion; ...
      END VIEW Person;
      VIEW Employee ...
        State BY EmployeeVersion; ...
      END VIEW Employee;
      VIEW Taxpayer ...
        State BY TaxpayerVersion; ...
      END VIEW Taxpayer
    ATTRIBUTES
      ASSERTED name: tString BY VARIABLE;
      ASSERTED personnelNumber: INTEGER BY VARIABLE;
      ...
    COMMANDS
      ASSERTED State () BY
        VERSION BasicVersion BY METHOD
          Output Personal Data
        END VERSION BasicVersion,
        VERSION EmployeeVersion BY METHOD
          Output Personal and Employee Data
        END VERSION EmployeeVersion,
        VERSION TaxpayerVersion BY METHOD
          Output Personal and Taxpayer Data
        END VERSION TaxpayerVersion
      END State;
      ASSERTED Action () BY METHOD
        ... State (); ...
      END Action;
      ...
END OBJECT AS Person -> person
```

Ex. 4.2. Views and Versions

An object, that is its implementation, may use all of its own components. It does not use them under a specific view, however. Therefore, a generalized way to select versions of implementation for components is needed. For instance, assume that the command `State` giving information about a person now is to be used also for the purpose of debugging other parts of the implementation. To this end, it is called in the methods of the other commands of the object `person`. The problem, however, is to select the right version of the method for `State`. In the given case, it suffices to create several different versions of each method corresponding to the views provided by the object which differ merely in which output command they call. This approach is costly to program, but insufficient as well if the commands to be debugged sometimes are also called directly by the object. In general, if a command was issued by another object under a certain view the versions of implementation for all components used directly or indirectly by the method of this command should also be determined by the view. For this reason, the mapping of a view always has to assign a version to all components of the object, not just to those given in its interface. If for a component there is only one version, it need not be explicitly handled in the mapping section of a view, however.

In Ex. 4.2, the command `Action` is accessible via all views (lines 8, 18, and 28 of the left code fragment of Ex. 4.1) but there is only one method version (lines 31 to 33), this being the reason why there is no entry for `Action` into the `MAPPINGS` section. The method of `Action` calls `State` to print debugging information (line 32). The version for `State` is selected by the view `Action` was called under. So, if `Action` was called under the view `Employee`, the version `EmployeeVersion` of `State` is called. On the other hand, if `Action` was called under the view `Taxpayer`, the version `TaxpayerVersion` of `State` is called.

4.3 Cooperation among Aspects

Despite having several different aspects, an object still possesses a single identity. Different versions for components operate on the same state, at least in part. For instance, a user who thinks of a person as a taxpayer should be able to recognize the adjusted rate of taxation caused by the income being increased by the person's employer. To achieve this, we could describe a version of the write method of `income` that adjusts the rate of taxation as well. The disadvantage of this approach is that if the view `Taxpayer` had been added at some time later we would have had to adapt existing method code requiring understanding it.

It is desirable, therefore, to separate the statements necessary for adjustment of the rate of taxation from those for changing `income`. Generally speaking, it may be necessary in the mapping of a view to assign to a component not just the version of implementation corresponding to the aspect represented by the view, but versions for cooperating aspects as well. With this aim, ARISTARCH/L enables programmers to assign several different versions of implementation to a component in a mapping which are executed in an undetermined order with the same arguments. This is called *combination of versions*. It is possible now to separate the statements necessary for `Taxpayer` from those necessary for `Employee` while at the same time by combination of both versions the rate of taxation gets adjusted whenever an increase of income occurs.

The attribute `income` therefore has two different versions, as shown in Ex. 4.3 (lines 17 to 24). The basic version implements `income` by using a variable which may be changed under the view `Employee`, for instance by the employer. The aspect represented by the view `Taxpayer` cooperates with `Employee` since the rate of taxation depends on the income of the employee. To this end, a method version for writing `income` is defined for `Taxpayer`. By assigning both versions to `income` in the mappings of all views (lines 6, 9, and 12), it is guaranteed that the rate of taxation is adjusted even if the object itself increases income in order to fulfill another task. Nonetheless, as before, other objects may change `income` only via `Employee`. The example also shows how attributes and commands interact. The implementation of `income` by a variable for the aspect represented by `Employee` implicitly defines both method versions for reading and writing, where reading delivers the value most recently written. This makes it possible to cater

```
1  OBJECT
     ...
     IMPLEMENTATION
       MAPPINGS
5        VIEW Person
           income BY BasicVersion, TaxpayerVersion; ...
         END VIEW Person;
         VIEW Employee
           income BY BasicVersion, TaxpayerVersion; ...
10       END VIEW Employee;
         VIEW Taxpayer
           income BY BasicVersion, TaxpayerVersion; ...
         END VIEW Taxpayer

15     ATTRIBUTES
         ...
         ASSERTED income: INTEGER BY
           VERSION BasicVersion BY VARIABLE END VERSION BasicVersion,
           VERSION TaxpayerVersion BY
20           PUT METHOD
               Adjust Rate of Taxation -> taxrate
             END PUT
           END VERSION TaxpayerVersion
         END income;
25       ASSERTED taxrate: INTEGER BY VARIABLE

       COMMANDS
         ...
29 END OBJECT AS Person -> person
```

Ex. 4.3. Cooperation among Aspects

to the aspect of `Taxpayer` by writing a `PUT METHOD` that intercepts any increase of `income` (lines 20 to 22).

One might believe that the undetermined order of execution poses a serious problem. For example, consider a command which changes an employee's benefits, payment policy, and the like at the same time. Each of these modifications necessitates an adjustment of the rate of taxation which may be done by intercepting the command. Unfortunately, the adjustment must be done *after* the changes, a requirement that apparently is in conflict with the undetermined order of execution. The problem disappears by defining versions not intercepting the command itself but rather those commands it calls to do the changes. This is always possible because the methods for both reading and writing an attribute may be customized.

4.4 Derivation of Views

Often an aspect of an object includes another one, that is it constitutes a specialization of another aspect. For instance, we would like to consider an employee a kind of person. To allow the description and exploitation of such relationships, a view may be *derived* from other views. In the course of this, in addition to the components listed in the derived view itself, in general all components from the interfaces of these basic views are inherited by the derived view, with the exception of those given in its `OMITTING` clause.

Dealing with mappings is more demanding than uniting the interfaces. To the fore comes again the idea of identifiers as specifications of components. The versions of implementation for a component given by the mappings of the basic views, the *basic versions*, are combined. This is reasonable because, in a way, the aspects represented by the basic views cooperate with each other in the aspect represented by the derived view. If the mapping of the derived view gives still other versions for a component, they are regarded as *extensions* of the basic versions specific to the corresponding aspect.

This necessitates a linguistic element to describe a version as an extension of its basic versions[2]. It is sufficient to present such an element for methods since attributes are considered pairs of commands and thus are implemented by pairs of methods. The linguistic element sees a method version merely as a sequence of statements. The extended version is produced by combining the sequences of the basic versions with the sequences of the extending versions. The side effect of the extended version on the state of the object therefore consists of the contributions of both the basic and the extending versions. To control the order of these contributions, it is necessary to specify the point at which to execute the statements of the basic versions with regard to those of the extending versions. On the other hand, the linguistic element has to guarantee that basic versions are executed exactly once, for all paths of the method independent of object state and command arguments. In ARISTARCH/L we achieve this by syntactically grouping two sequences of statements around the point of execution of the basic versions, marked by the keyword `BASE METHOD`. All paths through the first sequence thus converge in this point, diverging again in the second sequence. To indicate the point is mandatory, as the programmer of a version does not know *a priori* if it will serve as an extension later. Regarding the extension of variables, we recall that a variable implicitly defines method versions for reading and writing. We establish that the version for reading ignores the results of the basic versions and returns its own value, whereas the version for writing calls the basic versions and then changes its own value.

Example 4.4 makes use of the fact that both `Employee` and `Taxpayer` are specializations of `Person`. Thus, for instance, `Employee` is derived from `Person` and inherits its general interface (line 11). At the same time the mapping is inherited, with the consequence of the version for the `State` command given by `Employee` implicitly being an extension of the version given by `Person`. While the basic version takes care of printing personal data such as the name, the version for `Employee` confines itself to information such as the personnel number. The body of the extension consists of two sequences of statements surrounding the execution of the basic version, `BASE METHOD`, the first one being empty for this example (lines 47 to 48). Accordingly, the method first prints the personal data and then the employee data. The same holds for the view `Taxpayer`.

[2] In ARISTARCH/L, it is possible to directly describe a version as an extension of other versions without the aid of view derivation but this feature is not described in this paper.

```
OBJECT
  INTERFACES
    VIEW Person
      ATTRIBUTES
        IMMUTABLE name: tString
      COMMANDS
        State ();
        Action ()
    END VIEW Person;

    VIEW Employee DERIVED FROM Person
      ATTRIBUTES
        personnelNumber: INTEGER;
        income: INTEGER
    END VIEW Employee;

    VIEW Taxpayer DERIVED FROM Person
      ATTRIBUTES
        taxNumber: INTEGER;
        IMMUTABLE taxrate: INTEGER
    END VIEW Taxpayer;

    VIEW TaxpayingEmployee DERIVED FROM Employee, Taxpayer
    END VIEW TaxpayingEmployee

  IMPLEMENTATION
    MAPPINGS
      VIEW Person
        income BY BasicVersion, TaxpayerVersion;
        State BY BasicVersion; ...
      END VIEW Person;
      VIEW Employee
        State BY EmployeeVersion; ...
      END VIEW Employee;
      VIEW Taxpayer
        State BY TaxpayerVersion; ...
      END VIEW Taxpayer

    ATTRIBUTES ...
    COMMANDS
      ASSERTED State () BY
        VERSION BasicVersion BY METHOD
          BASE METHOD
          DO Output Personal Data
        END VERSION BasicVersion,
        VERSION EmployeeVersion BY METHOD
          BASE METHOD
          DO Output Employee Data
        END VERSION EmployeeVersion,
        VERSION TaxpayerVersion BY METHOD
          BASE METHOD
          DO Output Taxpayer Data
        END VERSION TaxpayerVersion
      END State;
      ...
END OBJECT AS Person -> person
```

Ex. 4.4. Derivation of Views

So the same basic version of `State` may yield different methods by the use of different extensions without replicating code. The other way around, it is also possible to use the same extension with different basic versions. This may be accomplished by assigning this extension to the corresponding component in different views which are derived from yet other views that employ those different basic versions, respectively.

Please note that it suffices to assign the versions of implementation to the attribute `income` in the mapping of `Person` since it is inherited by the derived views. It is also easy to define a view `TaxpayingEmployee` which combines both `Employee` and `Taxpayer` (lines 23 to 24). The implementations for the components of this view are given by combining and extending the versions of all basic views. This especially is true for the implementation of `State` which now consists of all versions including the basic version, and thus now prints *all* information available for a person.

4.5 Views and Delegation

Delegation is regarded as a means for dealing with very different problems. This polyvalence is the main point of our criticism. Some of these problems are mirrored in the requirements given above, and we shall now consider them in turn in the context of our model.

One of those problems is to describe objects with different aspects. Delegation may be used to represent these aspects by different objects. They operate on a common state, at least in part, by using common prototypes, and actually describe a *single* object. Consistently, Dony, Malenfant, and Cointe [6] call such an object a *split object*. The objects representing different aspects may be compared to views in ARISTARCH/L. Delegation takes on the task of mappings. For instance, `Taxpayer` and `Employee` are given by two objects delegating to a third object which represents the view `Person`. Together they form the split object `person`. All three objects possess their own method versions for `State`. Using the *extended self* (Lieberman [11]) the version corresponding to the current aspect is called independent of the site of the call in one of these objects. For example, the version of `Taxpayer` is used even if `State` was called by `Person` if `Taxpayer` indirectly caused the call by delegating an instruction by another object to `Person`. If several views assign the same version of implementation to a component this may be modelled by an object which holds this common version and is delegated to by the objects representing those views. A serious disadvantage of delegation when used for describing different aspects of an object is that it does not support the notion of split objects as logical entities. It also contradicts the notion of prototypes because not different objects with common behaviour are described but aspects of a single split object. In our model, a reference always denotes the whole object while still indicating the aspect currently used via this reference.

Another disadvantage is that delegation also permits the dynamic extension of split objects with other aspects whereas dynamic changeability of an object in general is completely orthogonal to supporting different aspects of objects. It therefore should be realized by a linguistic element that is orthogonal to views. Thus delegation in the case of split objects basically meets two different demands. This gives further evidence for the correctness of our opinion that delegation should only serve as a basis for implementing some of the elements of a linguistic model but not as such an element by itself. Supporting objects with different aspects on the one hand and dynamic changeability of objects on the other hand are separate problems and therefore should be dealt with by separate concepts. Szyperski [26] puts it the way that

> "It is a good rule of thumb to keep the number of concepts in a language small. However, it is always possible to reduce everything to (almost) a single concept. For example, in some functional languages everything is expressed using the single concept of higher-order functions. This tends to make programs hard to grasp. Keeping orthogonality and completeness in mind, it is often preferable to provide *separate concepts for separate problems*. This leads to more natural ways of expressing solutions in a given language."

The *single concept* in languages based on delegation is the delegating object.

5 Categorization of Objects

The linguistic elements introduced hitherto support the description of objects one by one. According to the requirements given above an object-based language should permit both concrete and abstract categorization of objects.

In ARISTARCH/L, concrete categorization of an object is handled by *cloning*. For the following the idea of identifiers as specifications of components comes to the fore again. The clone inherits the views of the cloned prototypes, a view of the clone with a given identifier being implicitly derived from all views with the same identifier of these prototypes. With the components of its prototypes, it also inherits the current states. After cloning has taken place both objects are independent of each other.

In class-based languages abstract categorization of objects is dealt with by each object being an *instance* of a *class*. In ARISTARCH/L, objects may have any number of *instance patterns*, or *patterns* for short, which may be instantiated to objects.

5.1 Patterns

Patterns describe sets of objects of the same kind. To this end, they may possess the same elements as do object expressions, that is components and their versions of implementation as well as various views. An object with several different patterns may now be used to create different kinds of objects according to these patterns. Objects with patterns may be actually regarded as classes with several kinds of instances. Although classes are objects there is no infinite meta regress since objects may as well be described directly by using object expressions.

```
1  OBJECT
     INTERFACES
       VIEW
         PATTERNS
5          PersonPattern INTERFACES
             ...
           END PersonPattern
       END VIEW

10   IMPLEMENTATION
       PATTERNS
         ASSERTED PersonPattern IMPLEMENTATION
           ...
         END PersonPattern
15 END OBJECT -> personclass
```

Ex. 5.1. Description of Patterns

```
NEW PersonPattern OF personclass AS Employee -> employee
```

Ex. 5.2. Creation of Instances

The object `person` described in the previous examples becomes a pattern in Ex. 5.1. The `INTERFACES` section of `person` reappears in the `PATTERNS` section of the `INTERFACES` section of the newly created object `personclass` (lines 5 to 7). This is because the definition of a pattern is required in the interface of a view of a class as to instantiate it under this view. The same holds for the `IMPLEMENTATION` section (lines 12 to 14). A pattern may also possess, as other components may, different versions which are used by different views of the class. This may be used to support several versions tuned to different marginal conditions. For example, we may have two different versions of lists which are optimized for fast random access to elements or for fast insertion of elements, respectively.

An arbitrary number of instances of `PersonPattern` may be created now by using the `NEW` expression. If a pattern describes several different views the `AS` clause may be used to determine an initial view. This is shown in Ex. 5.2.

Besides using a `NEW` expression, an instance of a class may be created by using a pattern when describing an object by an object expression. This allows for abstractly categorized objects with additional behaviour not determined by the category. The procedure is the same as for deriving patterns.

5.2 Derivation of Patterns

To describe common properties of patterns, a pattern may be *derived* from other patterns in much the same way views may. In the course of this, in addition to the views listed in the derived pattern itself, in general all views from the basic patterns are inherited by the derived pattern, with the exception of those given in its `OMITTING` clause. As with cloning, a view of the derived pattern with a given identifier is always implicitly derived from all views with the same identifier of the basic patterns. Therefore, the derivation of patterns is reduced to the derivation of views. Any other views have to be explicitly derived, directly or indirectly, from at least one view of each basic pattern in order to guarantee that a version of implementation is assigned to each inherited component.

The rules given in Sect. 4, for implicitly assigning versions of implementation to components, together with the rule of the above paragraph, regarding views with matching identifiers, allow describing with a minor amount of work constellations in which each pattern has only one anonymous view and for each component there is only one version of implementation. In this case, the rules cause explicit mappings to be superfluous and the views of derived patterns to be implicitly derived from those of their basic patterns. Such constellations are typical of conventional object-oriented languages such as C++. The additional amount of work to be done in ARISTARCH/L to describe them is thus very low.

Different versions of a pattern in connection with derivation yield a controlled form of *or-inheritance* (LaLonde, Thomas, and Pugh [10]). Additionally, similar to attributes and commands, these versions may be extended by the same version used in derived views, respectively. Extension of versions for patterns is reduced to the extension of the components of the pattern according to the mappings of the views. It is not to be mixed up with the derivation of patterns.

The hierarchy of views in Ex. 4.4 may now be used as a starting point for a hierarchy of patterns, as is shown in Ex. 5.3. The different versions of implementation for the components are then distributed among the corresponding patterns so that we may do without explicitly defining them in one pattern. The resulting class possesses several different patterns which can be instantiated separately if they are all listed in the interface of at least one view. `TaxpayingEmployeePattern` describes the complete object `person` also known from the previous examples whereas the other patterns are restricted.

The example also shows the command `Check` in `PersonPattern` (line 23) which is not marked with the keyword `ASSERTED`. A pattern only guarantees the existence of `ASSERTED` components so that the identifier `Check` may not be used in derived patterns such as `TaxpayingEmployeePattern`. But in agreement with the general idea of identifiers as specifications, if a derived pattern defines a version of implementation for `Check` it is considered an extension of the version of `PersonPattern`. Nonetheless, the basic version is hidden from the derived pattern as the latter does not explicitly refer to its identifier and the extension remains correct even if the basic version disappears. In our example, the version of `EmployeePattern` for `Check` implicitly extends the basic version defined in `PersonPattern` (line 27).

5.3 Instances and Class Components

Components of a class at the same time are considered common to all instances of that class. This especially means that an instance may implicitly access the state of its class. In ARISTARCH/L, this essentially works by thinking of patterns

```
OBJECT
  INTERFACES
    VIEW
      PATTERNS
        PersonPattern INTERFACES
          VIEW Person ...
        END PersonPattern;
        EmployeePattern DERIVED FROM PersonPattern INTERFACES
          VIEW Employee DERIVED FROM Person ...
        END EmployeePattern;
        TaxpayerPattern DERIVED FROM PersonPattern INTERFACES
          VIEW Taxpayer DERIVED FROM Person ...
        END TaxpayerPattern;
        TaxpayingEmployeePattern DERIVED FROM EmployeePattern, TaxpayerPattern
        END TaxpayingEmployeePattern
    END VIEW

  IMPLEMENTATION
      PATTERNS
        ASSERTED PersonPattern IMPLEMENTATION ...
            ASSERTED State () BY METHOD ... Basic Version;
            ASSERTED Action () BY METHOD ... ;
            Check () BY METHOD ... Basic Version
        END PersonPattern;
        ASSERTED EmployeePattern IMPLEMENTATION ...
            ASSERTED State () BY METHOD ... Employee Version;
            Check () BY METHOD ... Employee Version
        END EmployeePattern;
        ASSERTED TaxpayerPattern IMPLEMENTATION ...
            ASSERTED State () BY METHOD ... Taxpayer Version;
            Check () BY METHOD ... Taxpayer Version
        END TaxpayerPattern
END OBJECT -> personclass
```

Ex. 5.3. Derivation of Patterns

as being derived from the class. The difference to derivation from another pattern is twofold. First, components of a class exist only once. Second, neither are views of the class inherited by the pattern nor are interfaces of class views inherited by derived views of the pattern. This has the same effect as listing the class views and the components in interfaces in the `OMITTING` clauses of the pattern and the derived views of the pattern, respectively. Therefore, the version of implementation for a class component used by an instance is determined by the current view of the instance. For this reason, each view of a pattern has to be derived, directly or indirectly, from at least one view of the class.

5.4 Nested Patterns

ARISTARCH/L supports classes of instances which are classes themselves, by the means of *nested* patterns. Nested patterns may be derived from other patterns nested inside the same pattern. But they are also inherited by derived patterns like other components. This enables the programmer to derive nested

```
OBJECT
  INTERFACES
    VIEW
      PATTERNS
        StringClassPattern INTERFACES
          VIEW
            PATTERNS
              StringPattern ...
          END VIEW
        END StringClassPattern
    END VIEW

  IMPLEMENTATION
    PATTERNS
      ASSERTED StringClassPattern IMPLEMENTATION
        ATTRIBUTES
          ASSERTED Sequences: tTable
        PATTERNS
          ASSERTED StringPattern ...
      END StringClassPattern
END OBJECT
```

Ex. 5.4. Independent String Classes by Means of Nested Patterns

patterns from patterns nested in a basic pattern as well. It is therefore possible to abstractly categorize classes and thus hierarchies of patterns.

By the means of nested patterns we are now able to solve the problem of describing multiple classes of character strings with different tables of character sequences, as stated in Sect. 2.3. A string class contains the table of different sequences as part of the state common to all strings. In Ex. 5.4, these classes are again abstractly categorized by an object with a corresponding pattern. By instantiating the pattern of this object we get string classes with independent tables of sequences which in turn may be used to create strings implicitly accessing the same table.

Another example shall merely be outlined in the following since it is too complex to be explained in detail here. Access objects for a file may be regarded as instances of this file which are able to implicitly access its content. They permit stateful access of the file, for example, depending on the context of use of the file, to the current record by retaining a record index. Opening such a file then means to create an access object from a pattern contained in the file. There may be very different kinds of files in a file system, for instance sequential files, indexed-sequential files, and direct files. Indexed-sequential files may be thought of as specializations of sequential files, and thus the corresponding pattern may be derived from that for sequential files. All patterns together may be derived from a generic file pattern which, among other components, contains a universal pattern for access objects which is inherited by the other kinds of files. All files on a file system are considered instances of the file system which implicitly have access to its management information. What we have now is an object representing a file system which contains a set of patterns describing various sorts of files which in turn contain patterns describing access objects. Since in general a computer system has several storage devices containing different file systems it is reasonable to finally describe a class of file systems. In this manner, the result is an object with nested patterns of *the first, second, and third order*.

This example clearly explains the way nested patterns extend the expressiveness of previous, object-oriented languages. Each call of a program written in such a language actually creates anew the classes contained in the program with a fresh state. Such programs may be thought of as classes of the second order, that is as objects with patterns which themselves contain other patterns. Unlike nested patterns, however, the conventional model allows neither the derivation of classes of the second order nor describing classes of higher orders.

5.5 Patterns and Delegation

Lieberman [11] proposes delegation as a means for the abstract categorization of objects. Since delegation always refers to another concrete object, *a priori* the entire behaviour of an object is determined by the abstract category. Most of the time this is not what is needed, so the behaviour of the object not part of the abstract category has to be explicitly cancelled or redefined. For example, Dony, Malenfant, and Cointe [6] correctly point out that, corresponding to a behaviour pattern, in most cases, abstract categorization relates only to the component structure of objects whereas their states shall remain independent. Therefore, when using delegation the object has to implement by itself all components carrying state information. The advantage of having a template is thus lost. In the prototype-based language SELF (Ungar and Smith [27]) *trait objects* are used to describe commands common to a set of objects. An object with attributes carrying state delegates its commands to such a trait object. Other objects are created by *cloning* this object, thus using it as a template. Because of this, they possess their own state but delegate to the same trait object. This way of using delegation is a contradiction to the notion of prototypes as concrete objects that also serve as templates because trait objects are stateless and abstract. They just serve as repositories for common commands and therefore may also be treated as optimizations not visible to the user. An additional disadvantage of delegation is the lack of support for concrete categorization.

Delegation may be used as well if access to a common state is the decisive factor for categorization of a group of objects. Lieberman for example describes a set of pens with the same vertical but different horizontal positions. To achieve this, each pen with one exception possesses a variable for the horizontal position only and delegates to the single pen with both coordinates. For instance, we might think of an electrocardiograph here, in which the vertical position common to all pens is given by the position of a carriage relative to a strip of paper. As the actual reason for the common state, an object such as this carriage always exists. It is this carriage that really possesses the part of the state common to all pens. Consequently, in our opinion the implicit access to the common part of the state should not be done by means of delegation, as its carrier may not be considered a prototype of the delegating objects. In our model, the carrier rather is the class of the objects, as classes may also be abstractly categorized. In this example, the carriage would serve as the class of those pens mounted on it. Nested patterns permit to describe a class of carriages, and thus a class of electrocardiographs.

We would like to emphasize that delegation is neither supported by our model in the form of inheritance between classes (Stein [24]). This is an immediate consequence of our criticism of delegation on the level of objects and the notion of classes as objects with patterns. In contrast to conventional object-oriented languages a class, in our terminology an object with a pattern, may not be derived from another class. Nevertheless, categorization of classes is straightforward. If we want to describe a class whose instances are specializations of the instances of another class this corresponds to the conventional notion of a subclass and a superclass. According to the difference between concrete and abstract categorization, our model, besides a tight connection, permits to describe independence between these two classes. In the first case, superclass and subclass are instances of an object with two corresponding patterns, the second derived from the first, respectively. Both patterns contain patterns themselves, the pattern in the second one derived from the pattern in the first one. As a result, if the pattern nested in the first one is modified the pattern contained in the second one changes as well. Nevertheless, in contrast to previous models, the states of these two classes are independent of each other. The second case is given if a programmer wants to reuse a hierarchy of patterns but is neither interested in later changes nor wants to have his or her own modifications taken over into the existing hierarchy. He or she will then provide for this by cloning the superclass and changing the clone to become the subclass.

6 Related Work

6.1 Views

Hailpern and Nguyen [7] propose a model in which the method to be executed not only depends on the target object but also on its client. Consequently, the model really supports views with different versions of implementation for components. The notion of views as such is not present, however. In addition, the model does not relate to the current view whenever an object calls itself. Hailpern and Ossher [8] describe a model with views but it does not permit different versions.

Shilling and Sweeney [23] develop a model that provides views with different method versions for commands. In contrast to our model however, it does not allow different versions for attributes and patterns. In Shilling's und Sweeney's model views may possess their own attributes and may be *multiply activated*. Each activation has its own variables for attributes of the view but may also share variables with other activations. Views therefore do not model aspects but rather different *roles* an object may *play* in a given context. The relationship between the object and the activations of its views is very similar to that between a class and its instances. We believe that aspects and roles are orthogonal concepts and thus should be catered to by separate linguistic elements. Richardson and Schwarz [21] model roles as well, despite calling the linguistic elements *aspects*. Basically, aspects are objects with a pointer to a *base object* the components not implemented by the aspect are forwarded to. The aspect only supports those components of the base object that are explicitly exported, which is a shortened form of using the components by means of the base pointer. Pernici [20] describes a similar model for the specification of objects in the area of office information systems which is primarily aimed at supporting object reuse.

Wieringa, de Jonge, and Spruit [28] distinguish between aspects and roles of an object, like we do. In their model, different aspects of an object are described by means of *dynamic subclasses*. In contrast to conventional or *static* subclasses an object may change its membership to a dynamic subclass over time while its identity remains the same. However, an application may not select a *current* dynamic subclass as it may with views. This is only possible with roles which are described by *role classes*. An object may play a role as given by one role class several times. As with representing roles by instances of patterns of the object in our model, the identity of the object may be pushed to the background in favour of the identities of the roles.

Harrison and Ossher [9] argue that by looking at objects from different aspects the notion of object gets a distributed character. It is their goal to develop a model with the following two features. First, it should make possible the development of applications depending on different aspects of an object separately while at the same time allowing for their cooperation. In particular, it should facilitate applications initially not provided for, without rendering already existing objects and applications useless or subjects to modification and recompilation. Second, each application should be able to utilize separately encapsulation, polymorphism, and inheritance. Particularly, it should enable all applications to classify independently objects according to the corresponding aspects. Harrison and Ossher propose several heuristics to establish automatically the relationships among classes describing different aspects of the same object, that are necessary for different applications to interact with each other. In our opinion this approach has a serious disadvantage. For all aspects of a single object to cooperate, the programmer of an application, and thus of a certain aspect, has to either anticipate other possible aspects of the object to allow for later cooperation by defining appropriate components, or announce modifications to other applications for the appropriate change of corresponding classes. It seems to be unfeasible to separate different aspects to the extent intended by the authors. We have consciously decided to describe different aspects by views inside a single object description. Nevertheless, ARISTARCH/L allows to list several versions of implementation for a component corresponding to several cooperating aspects in a view mapping, thus achieving a degree of separation among aspects that depends on the given situation.

FLAVORS [19], COMMONLOOPS [4], and the COMMON LISP OBJECT SYSTEM (CLOS) [5] try to avoid multiple execution of the same method in the face of multiple inheritance by means of *method combinations*. CLOS, for instance, offers a *standard method combination* which distinguishes between *primary methods* and *auxiliary methods*. *Auxiliary methods* in turn are split up into `:before`, `:after`, and `:around` methods. Whenever a command, or *generic function*, is called on an object, first of all the nested `:around` methods are called which in turn call the `:before` methods, the *primary methods*, and finally the `:after` methods. The sequence of execution is determined by topologically sorting the inheritance graph. Unfortunately, the standard method combination is insufficient, for instance, if one wants a certain method in any case to be executed before all others. To this end, CLOS supports the definition of customized method combinations. It has turned out, however, that this feature is used seldom even by experienced programmers because of its high complexity (Winston and Horn [29]). We restrict ourselves to an approach that corresponds to *primary methods*.

6.2 Delegation and Inheritance

Delegation is described with extensive examples by Lieberman [11]. Lieberman also explains the philosophical background of delegation and claims that delegation is more expressive than inheritance. Many of his examples are picked up in later papers by other researchers to describe problems with delegation and argue for alternative models.

Such an alternative model is presented by Stein [24]. Stein shows that delegation and inheritance have the same expressiveness, and thus Lieberman's claim is wrong, because inheritance is delegation on the level of classes. Our model differs insofar as we refuse delegation both on the level of objects and as inheritance on the level of classes. Specialization takes place by changing clones and deriving patterns. The proposal to reduce the exact guarantee of structure by a class to a minimal guarantee, that is to describe additional behaviour for an abstractly categorized object, is also by Stein.

In the *Treaty of Orlando* [12, 25] Lieberman, Stein, and Ungar, one of the developers of SELF, agree on the fact that a model for sharing of common behaviour should allow for static as well as dynamic and implicit as well as explicit sharing while applying to both single objects and groups of objects. In contrast to our model, their classification scheme is oriented to the mechanical features rather than the purpose of the model.

Ungar and Smith [27] describe the prototype-based language SELF. SELF uses delegation for abstract categorization by factorizing common components of objects into *trait objects* and solving the problem of independent object states by cloning single objects. We use cloning of several objects at the same time for concrete categorization and patterns for abstract categorization. We regard the combination of trait objects and delegation as an optimization by the language system.

Other researchers try to solve the problem of unconstrained generality of delegation by using a rule-based approach. Minsky and Rozenshtein [17] describe their notion of *law-governed object-oriented systems*. In such a system messages between objects may be modified, blocked, or delivered to a different target object by means of rules. It does not support delegation directly but may emulate it by appropriate rules. Minsky and Rozenshtein [18] show how their approach may be employed to constrain the use of delegation. A similar approach is taken by Almarode [2] with *rule-based delegation*. But like Minsky and Rozenshtein, Almarode uses delegation in various ways that are incompatible with the notion of prototype-based programming. For instance, class-based systems are modelled by delegation and appropriate rules. Almarode uses delegation even to forward messages in a *part-of* hierarchy. In this case the *extended self* is unnecessary which is a sure sign that this use of delegation is not adequate. We believe that rule-based approaches are not appropriate for general use because they are too complicated to apply. ARISTARCH/L tries to be straightforward to use by restricting itself to a concrete model of sharing. On the other hand, rule-based approaches surely are suitable for experimenting with different models.

The proposal of *composition filters* by Akşit, Bergmans, and Vural [1] is similar to *law-governed object-oriented systems*. A set of filters accepts messages on behalf of an object and under conditions given by *filter elements* passes them on, for instance to the object itself or to one of its *interface objects*. Interface objects are encapsulated inside the object or given by reference. Different aspects of an object may be modelled by a composition filter with one filter element for each aspect. It is not possible, however, to relate to the current view whenever the object calls itself. By means of the pseudo variable `server` which refers to the used object, delegation may be modelled with interface objects given by reference, that is it is possible to alternatively represent views by delegating objects. Therefore, our arguments against delegation as a linguistic element by itself as well as rule-based approaches are also valid in the case of composition filters.

Dony, Malenfant, and Cointe [6] try to extract features for a language most suitable for prototype-based programming by means of a taxonomy of existing prototype-based languages. They describe different problems of delegation, among them the problem of independent object states and the lack of support for *split objects*. Further, they discover that the description of a guaranteed common component structure of a set of objects, as it is possible with the aid of classes, can be achieved neither by cloning nor by delegation. We support split objects by views and by implicit access to components of a class by its instances. The necessity of independent objects as well as structural guarantee leads us to offer both cloning and patterns in ARISTARCH/L. Delegation is not supported as we believe it to be suitable as a basis for implementing some of the linguistic elements of a model of sharing but not as such an element by itself.

7 Conclusion

We have presented an object model which meets the requirements of a system with a uniform object space. The model permits the description of objects without classes using object expressions, as well as the modification of existing objects to preserve information. Different aspects of objects can be described independently by employing different views and different versions of implementation for components. The model supports concrete and abstract categorization as well as the extension of abstractly categorized objects by cloning, patterns, and object expressions which may refer to patterns, respectively. Classes with different states but instances sharing the same behaviour pattern are expressable by applying nested patterns. Through these features, our model supports new ways of sharing common behaviour and behaviour patterns among objects without using delegation at the language level, either on the level of objects or as inheritance on the level of classes.

References

1. M. AKŞIT, L. BERGMANS, AND S. VURAL. An object-oriented language-database integration model: The composition-filters approach. In: Madsen [13], pp. 372–395.
2. J. ALMARODE. Rule-based delegation for prototypes. In: Meyrowitz [16], pp. 363–370.
3. A. P. BLACK, N. C. HUTCHINSON, E. JUL, H. M. LEVY, AND L. CARTER. Distribution and abstract types in EMERALD. *IEEE Transactions on Software Engineering*, **SE-13**(1):65–76, January 1987.
4. D. G. BOBROW, K. KAHN, G. KICZALES, L. MASINTER, M. STEFIK, AND F. ZDYBEL. COMMONLOOPS: Merging LISP and object-oriented programming. In: Meyrowitz [14], pp. 17–29.
5. L. G. DEMICHIEL AND R. P. GABRIEL. The COMMON LISP OBJECT SYSTEM: An overview. In: J. Bézivin, J.-M. Hullot, P. Cointe, and H. Lieberman, eds., *Proceedings of the European Conference on Object-Oriented Programming* (Paris, France, June 15–17, 1987), vol. 276 of *Lecture Notes in Computer Science*, pp. 151–170. Springer-Verlag, Berlin, 1987.
6. C. DONY, J. MALENFANT, AND P. COINTE. Prototype-based languages: From a new taxonomy to constructive proposals and their validation. In: A. Paepcke, ed., *Proceedings of Object-Oriented Programming Systems, Languages, and Applications* (Vancouver, British Columbia, Canada, October 18–22, 1992), *ACM SIGPLAN Notices*, **27**(10):201–217, October 1992. ACM.
7. B. HAILPERN AND V. NGUYEN. A model for object-based inheritance. In: B. Shriver and P. Wegner, eds., *Research Directions in Object-Oriented Programming*, Series in Computer Systems, pp. 147–164. MIT Press, Cambridge, Massachusetts, 1987.
8. B. HAILPERN AND H. OSSHER. Extending objects to support multiple interfaces and access control. *IEEE Transactions on Software Engineering*, **16**(11):1247–1257, November 1990.
9. W. HARRISON AND H. OSSHER. Subject-oriented programming (a critique of pure objects). In: A. Paepcke, ed., *Proceedings of Object-Oriented Programming Systems, Languages, and Applications* (Washington, Washington, D.C., September 26–October 1, 1993), *ACM SIGPLAN Notices*, **28**(10):411–428, October 1993. ACM.
10. W. R. LALONDE, D. A. THOMAS, AND J. R. PUGH. An exemplar based SMALLTALK. In: Meyrowitz [14], pp. 322–330.
11. H. LIEBERMAN. Using prototypical objects to implement shared behaviour in object-oriented systems. In: Meyrowitz [14], pp. 214–223.
12. H. LIEBERMAN, L. A. STEIN, AND D. M. UNGAR. Of types and prototypes: The treaty of Orlando. In: L. Power and Z. Weiss, eds., *Addendum to the Proceedings of Object-Oriented Programming Systems, Languages, and Applications* (Orlando,

Florida, October 4–8, 1987), *ACM SIGPLAN Notices*, **23**(5):43–44, May 1988. ACM.

13. O. L. MADSEN, ED. *Proceedings of the European Conference on Object-Oriented Programming* (Utrecht, Netherlands, June 29–July 3, 1992), vol. 615 of *Lecture Notes in Computer Science*. Springer-Verlag, Berlin, 1992.
14. N. MEYROWITZ, ED. *Proceedings of Object-Oriented Programming Systems, Languages, and Applications* (Portland, Oregon, September 29–October 2, 1986), *ACM SIGPLAN Notices*, **21**(11), November 1986. ACM.
15. N. MEYROWITZ, ED. *Proceedings of Object-Oriented Programming Systems, Languages, and Applications* (Orlando, Florida, October 4–8, 1987), *ACM SIGPLAN Notices*, **22**(12), December 1987. ACM.
16. N. MEYROWITZ, ED. *Proceedings of Object-Oriented Programming Systems, Languages, and Applications* (New Orleans, Louisiana, October 1–6, 1989), *ACM SIGPLAN Notices*, **24**(10), October 1989. ACM.
17. N. H. MINSKY AND D. ROZENSHTEIN. A law-based approach to object-oriented programming. In: Meyrowitz [15], pp. 482–493.
18. N. H. MINSKY AND D. ROZENSHTEIN. Controllable delegation: An exercise in law-governed systems. In: Meyrowitz [16], pp. 371–380.
19. D. A. MOON. Object-oriented programming with FLAVORS. In: Meyrowitz [14], pp. 1–8.
20. B. PERNICI. Objects with roles. In: F. H. Lochovsky and R. B. Allen, eds., *Proceedings of the Conference on Office Information Systems* (Cambridge, Massachusetts, April 25–27, 1990), *ACM SIGOIS Bulletin*, **11**(2/3):205–215, April/July 1990. ACM.
21. J. RICHARDSON AND P. SCHWARZ. Aspects: Extending objects to support multiple, independent roles. In: J. Clifford and R. King, eds., *Proceedings of the International Conference on Management of Data* (Denver, Colorado, May 29–31, 1991), *ACM SIGMOD Record*, **20**(2):298–307, June 1991. ACM.
22. C. SCHAFFERT, T. COOPER, B. BULLIS, M. KILIAN, AND C. WILPOLT. An introduction to TRELLIS/OWL. In: Meyrowitz [14], pp. 9–16.
23. J. J. SHILLING AND P. F. SWEENEY. Three steps to views: Extending the object-oriented paradigm. In: Meyrowitz [16], pp. 353–361.
24. L. A. STEIN. Delegation is inheritance. In: Meyrowitz [15], pp. 138–146.
25. L. A. STEIN, H. LIEBERMAN, AND D. M. UNGAR. A shared view of sharing: The treaty of Orlando. In: W. Kim and F. H. Lochovsky, eds., *Object-Oriented Concepts, Databases, and Applications*, ACM Press Frontier Series, pp. 31–48. Addison-Wesley, Reading, Massachusetts, 1989.
26. C. A. SZYPERSKI. Import is not inheritance – why we need both: Modules and classes. In: Madsen [13], pp. 19–32.
27. D. M. UNGAR AND R. B. SMITH. SELF: The power of simplicity. In: Meyrowitz [15], pp. 227–242.
28. R. WIERINGA, W. D. JONGE, AND P. SPRUIT. Roles and dynamic subclasses: A modal logic approach. In: M. Tokoro and R. Pareschi, eds., *Proceedings of the European Conference on Object-Oriented Programming* (Bologna, Italy, July 4–8, 1994), vol. 821 of *Lecture Notes in Computer Science*, pp. 32–59. Springer-Verlag, Berlin, 1994.
29. P. H. WINSTON AND B. K. P. HORN. LISP, p. 509. Addison-Wesley, Reading, Massachusetts, third edition, 1989.

ChyPro* : A Hypermedia Programming Environment for Smalltalk-80

Maurice AMSELLEM

Laboratoire d'Intelligence Artificielle, Université Paris 8,
2, rue de la Liberté, 93526 Saint-Denis.
ams@harald.ai.univ-paris8.fr.

Abstract. Smalltalk-80 has introduced the use of interactive programming tools such as browsers, inspectors and debuggers which brought a major improvement on conventional text files based programming environments. However, they still heavily depend on character string representations of code and data and, as such, inherit all the known limitations of text. In this paper, we describe new versions of the Smalltalk-80 programming tools that transcend these limits, based on hypermedia techniques such as outlines, links, annotations and graphics and on direct manipulation interfaces. Particularly, the new tools allow :

◊ browsing simultaneously scattered pieces of software through multiple points of view,

◊ interleaving graphical and textual representations of Smalltalk code, documentation and data,

◊ structuring, organizing and linking heterogeneous or distant pieces of code or documentation.

1 Introduction

Conventional programming languages such as Pascal or C favour a modal programming style : programs are created and modified in editors, then compiled and linked with compilers and then executed and debugged with run-time debuggers. The editor, the compiler, the debugger and the processed programs are independent and communicate via files. This isolation is not deliberate but is a result of the underlying operating system's lack of integration.

In contrast, everything in Smalltalk, from the programming tools to the libraries, the programs and the operating system, is uniformly represented by objects sending themselves messages. Moreover, the user interface of all these tools consists of a short number of powerful adaptable interface components. While the simplicity and the elegance of Smalltalk's implementation and interface contributes greatly to the integration and homogeneity of this environment, it can become a nuisance to its usability, if it is established as the only directing rule.

In the following, we will first focus on the limitations of the Smalltalk's programming tools (the browsers, the debuggers and the inspectors). Then we will present the

* ChyPro stands for Computed **Hy**permedia **Pro**gramming.

ChyPro versions of Smalltalk's programming tools which intend to go beyond these limitations without sacrificing any of the valuable characteristics of the standard tools.

2 Limitations of the Smalltalk-80 Standard Tools

We assume the reader is familiar with Smalltalk's syntax, with the browsers, inspectors and debuggers[1]. We will therefore focus directly on their limitations.
Despite the fact that Smalltalk-80 is a highly graphical environment and provides a complete library of graphical classes, Smalltalk's tools still heavily depend on textual representations of the objects manipulated. Actually, most of Smalltalk's user interface is based on textual pluggable[2] interface components such as list views, text views, labelled switches and menus. For this reason, the Smalltalk tools are restrained by the inherent limits of character strings[3].

2.1 Limitations of the Browser

◊ The browser can handle only strings of characters. Although the text editor, used in

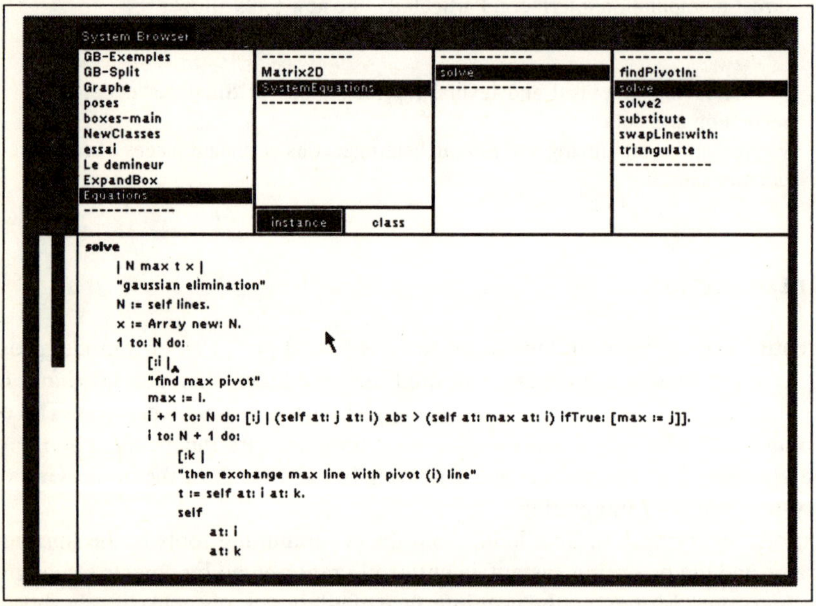

Fig. 1 . A System Browser. The Gaussian elimination algorithm is inspired from [13].

[1] The interested reader will find a thorough description of the language and the environment in [7, 5].
[2] The philosophy of pluggable objects [8] is to avoid the creation of a subclass when an application specific behavior is needed by handling the parametrization of this behavior in the class itself. Examples of pluggable objects are TextView, SelectionInListView and BooleanView.
[3] This issue is so crucial that many recent systems such as Object Explorer [2], Track [3] or MPVC [6] have been built to extend the graphical capabilities of Smalltalk's tools.

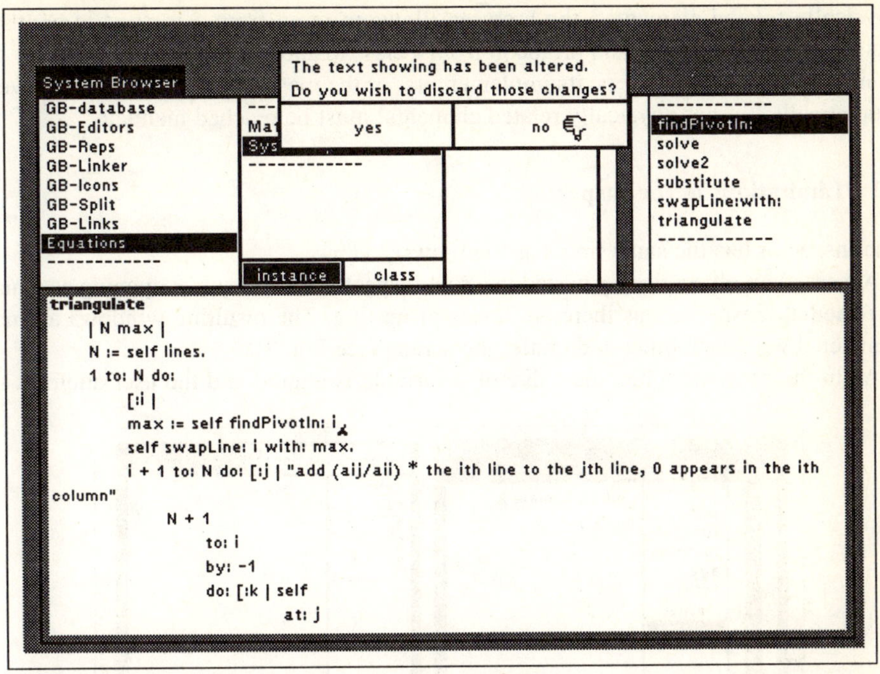

Fig. 2. Browser locking. The programmer instinctively attempted to select the method findPivotIn: to check its content while he was modifying the method triangulate, resulting in a dialogue to prompt him for a validation or cancellation of the modification he did. While this is certainly a good protection against accidental loss of data, it has nothing to do with the user's needs.

all the programming tools, supports multiple fonts and styles, text emphasizes are completely ignored by the compiler and discarded at storage. Thus every other information such as diagrams, software documentation, software organization or graphical annotations of code have to be translated to a string representation so as to be manipulated.

◊ Class and metaclass information are arbitrarily separated and cannot be accessed simultaneously in the browser.

◊ Software elements such as methods' code, class definitions and comments are displayed and manipulated in the browser only one element at a time. Moreover, any modification of the text window's content must be either validated or discarded before the user can make another selection in the browser (cf. Fig. 2).

This limitation is extremely frustrating when methods and classes are still under creation and must be edited all at once or when a large modification that spreads over several methods and classes - and this is often the case - must be performed. It constrains the programmer to open a separate browser window for each modification.

◊ Browsing is limited to 4 levels (categories, classes, protocols and methods[4]) and to

[4] More levels can be simulated with composite names like Collection-Abstract, Collection-Arrayed or private accessing.

physically related elements : the browser allows to jump from a method to another method in the same class and protocol, from a class to another in the same category or from a method to its senders, its implementors or the messages it contains. However, semantically but not physically related elements[5] must be reached manually.

2.2 Limitations of the Inspector

The inspector has the same limits as the browser view:

◊ Access to an object deeply nested in a root inspector view requires opening as many intermediate inspectors as there are levels of nesting. The resulting windows are not connected with each other and clutter the screen (see Fig. 3).

◊ As in the browser, when the value of a variable is altered and the user attempts to

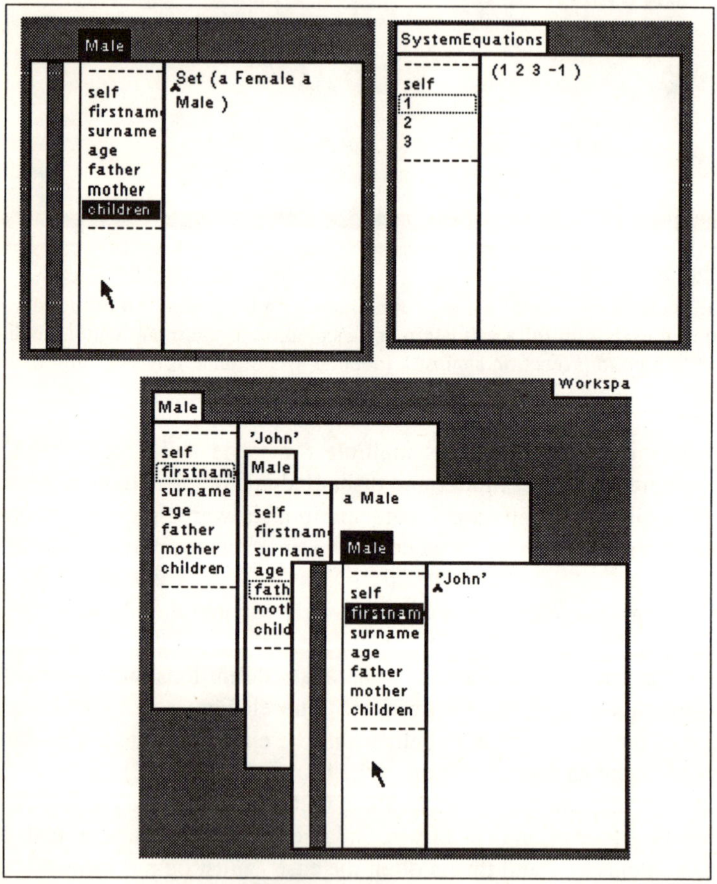

Fig. 3. Inspectors.

[5] For example, the message changed:#text corresponds to some implementation of update: in some class, depending on the dynamic context: these messages are semantically connected but not physically.

inspect another variable in the same window, he is prompted with a dialogue asking him if he wants to accept or discard the modifications.

◊ The values displayed are limited to character strings. Thus even graphical objects or complex data structures can only be viewed and edited via a textual representation. This is quite perplexing with regard to an environment that emphasises its graphical capabilities.

2.3 Limitations of the Debugger

◊ The debugger can be regarded as an inspector of the stack : we know that debugging is a more complex task than a mere inspection of the stack.

◊ In the debugger, it is impossible to inspect more than one context of the stack at the same time, for example to follow the control flow through the stack.

As a conclusion, the Smalltalk programming tools are not adapted to the programmer's needs because the designers privileged implementation issues. In effect, the implementation is a model of elegance. All the programming tool panes consist of only three classes : SelectionInListView handles menus lists, TextView handles text editing and SwitchView handles the Boolean switches of the browser . The panes are synchronised with a dependency mechanism (further details on the implementation can be found in [8]).

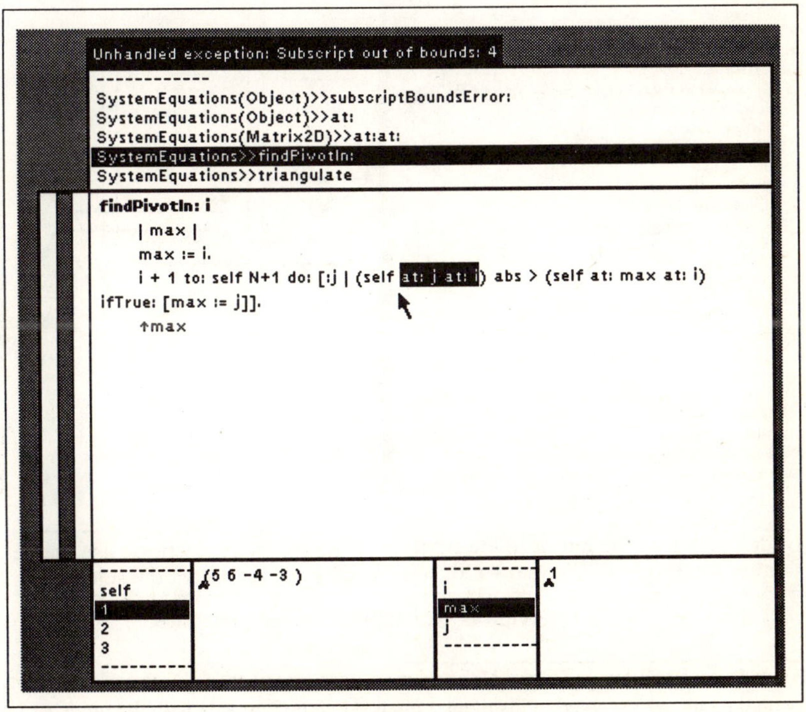

Fig. 4. The debugger.

3 ChyPro: a Hypermedia Programming Environment for Smalltalk

We will now describe the ChyPro versions of the Smalltalk-80 programming tools. We have built new versions of the browser, the inspector and the debugger.
We carefully designed the user interface, implementing direct manipulation interfaces[6] and using abundant visual clues such as animation effects, icons and cursor shapes.

3.1 A Browser Based on Hypermedia

The new browser consists of a three-paned window: a text outline pane, a graphical

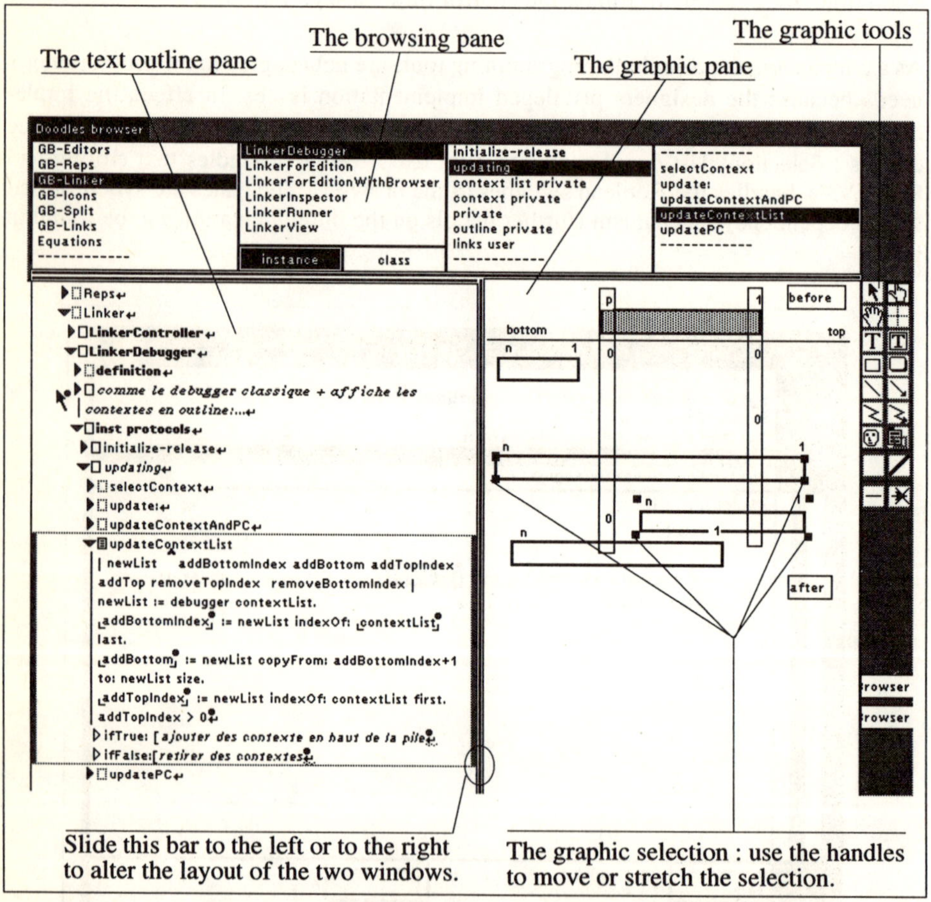

Fig. 5. Overview of the outline browser's interface.

[6] A system is said to have a *Direct Manipulation* user interface if the user feels he is acting directly on the entities involved in his mental plans when he interacts with the objects of the system [10, 12].

pane and a browsing pane (cf. Fig. 5). Depending on the context, each pane can be resized or even collapsed.

Graphics and Text. Programmers think both textually and graphically about their software, so we have included a textual editor and a graphical editor which are available at any time. Some word processors interleave graphics and text but we rejected this solution because we believe that textual and graphical information do not share the same spatial properties[7]. We preferred to juxtapose text editor and graphical editor. The graphical editor handles both pixel maps and geometrical objects such as rectangles, lines, polygons, arrows and blocks of text. The text editor is an extension of Smalltalk's standard text editor. In our system, graphical information can be linked explicitely to text through graphical annotations (see the paragraph on annotations below) or implicitely through computed graphical representations of the semantics associated to the text.

Hierarchical Links. Hierarchical links help in organizing and structuring software objects.
We use *outlines* to implement hierarchical relationships in text.
An outline is a textual representation of a tree structure. Each node of the tree is repre-

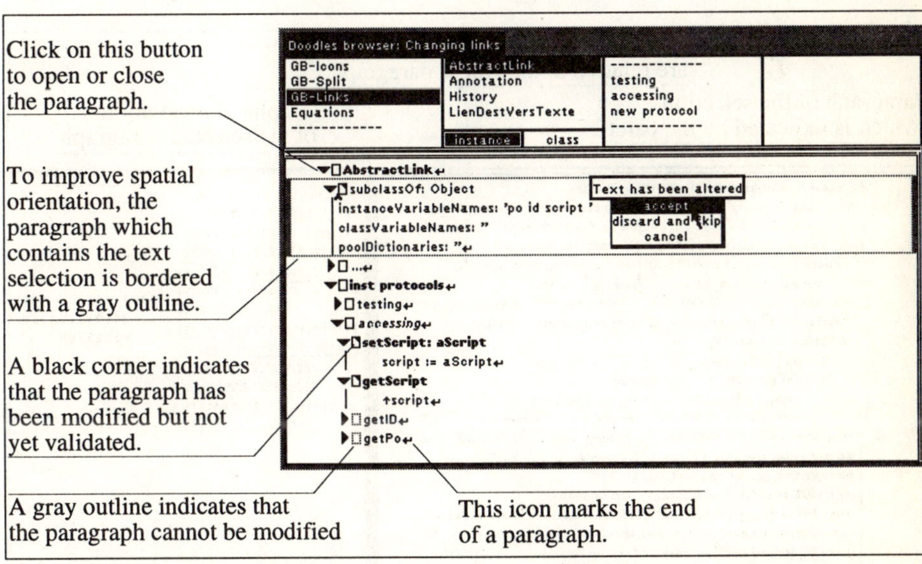

Fig. 6. Modification check. The user has clicked on the button of the first paragraph (AbstractLink) to close it. Since this paragraph contains other paragraphs which have not been validated, the user is prompted with a menu asking him whether he wants to validate the paragraph, discard the modification and skip to the next modification or to abort the checking operation.

[7] Precisely, text is one-dimensional (1.5 in the case of outline) and graphics are two-dimensional (2.5 if we consider graphical layers). Furthermore, graphics take more screen space than text and disturb the flow of text.

sented by a paragraph of text. The level of nesting is indicated by the indentation of the paragraph in a left-to-right ordering.
The user can add new paragraphs, change the indentation of existing ones and open or close paragraphs by simple mouse or keyboard operations (see Fig. 6).

◊ Outlines can be used on a local level to structure long and complex methods by splitting them in paragraphs. Adding a comment at the first line of each paragraph and then collapsing the paragraphs to show only these comments reveals the method's underlying structure. The same can be done to handle long documentation (see Fig. 7).

◊ On a global level, the programmer can use the outlining feature to build a tailored view of his software by opening in one pane the paragraphs of the classes and methods that are of interest for him and closing the others.

◊ Software organization is not limited to 4 levels (categories, classes, protocols and methods) as in the standard browser : the standard classification serves as a basis upon which intermediate arbitrarily nested classifications can be added using the outline feature.

◊ Different methods and classes can be arbitrarily opened and modified on the same window. The editor memorizes all the paragraphs that have been modified but not validated so that no modification will be lost . For example, when the programmer *accepts* a paragraph, the system searches for sub-paragraphs within this paragraph that have

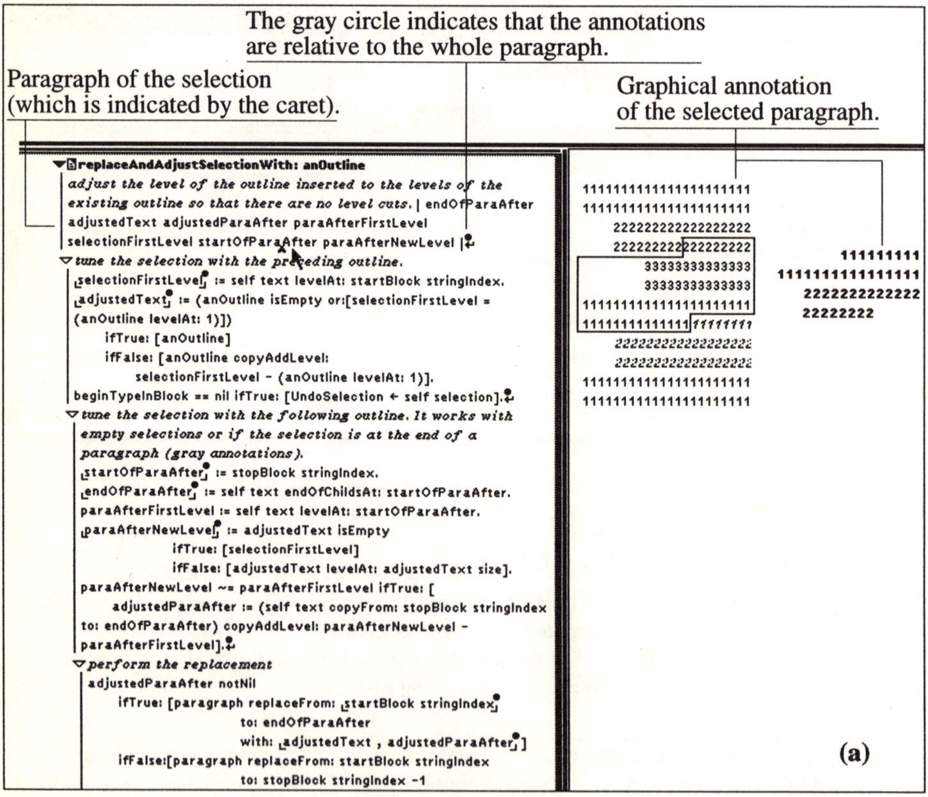

Fig. 7. Annotations.

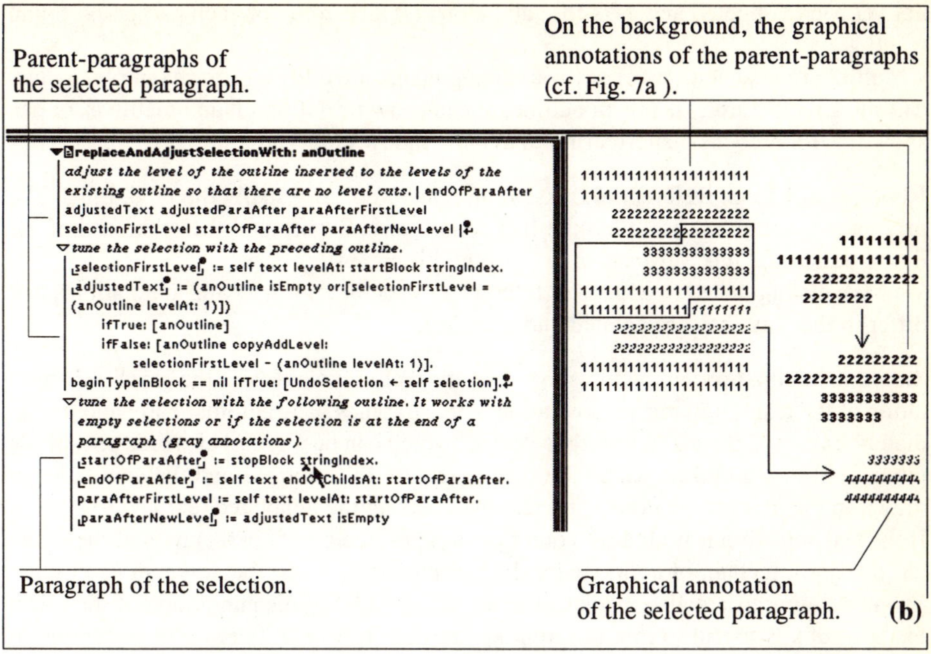

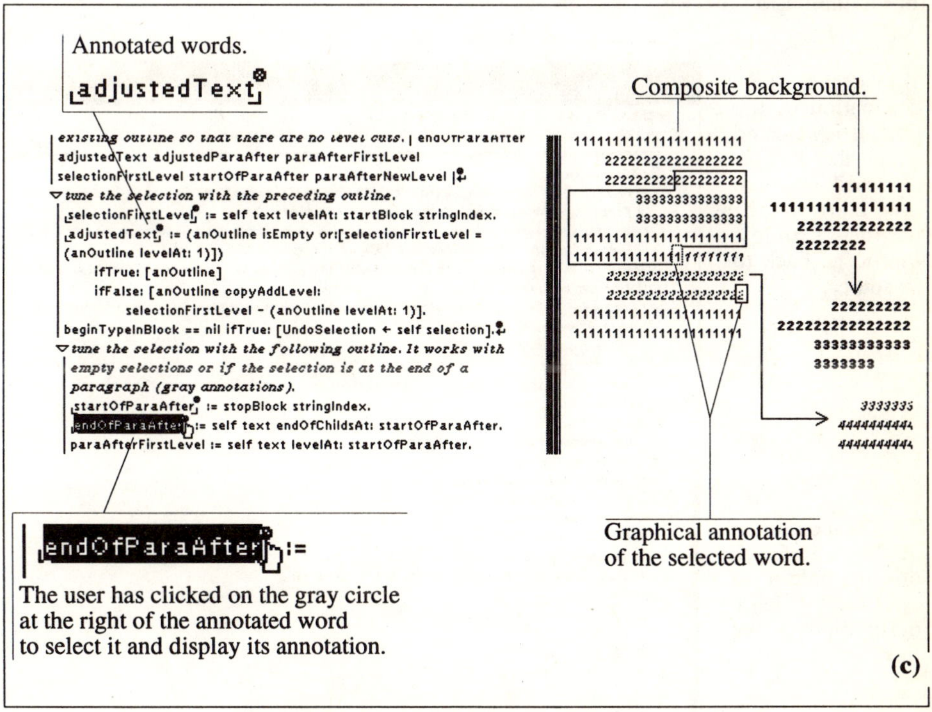

Fig. 7 b and c. Annotations (continued).

not yet been validated and asks for validation and discarding of each paragraph found (cf. Fig. 6).

◊ Multiple representations of software components are allowed : for example, a class can show its hierarchy using an outline, or can show its definition and methods, or can show itself merely as a short string to avoid window cluttering.

Referential Links. Referential links are non hierarchical, usually directed, links. The origination of the link is called the link *source* or *reference* and the other end of the link is called the link *destination* or *referent.* [4, pp. 34].
We have distinguished two kinds of referential links: button-links and annotations, that differ in the way they are created and accessed.

Annotations link text and pictures together: the picture is said to be the graphical annotation of the text. Drawing an annotation in the graphics pane automatically and immediately links it to the text currently selected (which can be a group of words or a whole paragraph) in the outline pane. The link is accessed thereafter - and the annotation is drawn in the graphics window - merely by selecting the annotated text.
If the text selection is nested into other paragraphs, the parent paragraphs of the selected text form a chain of contexts for this selected text. Thus, the annotations of these parent paragraphs are also displayed in the background of the annotation of the selected text: this is useful to mix different annotations or to build graphical backgrounds for an annotation (cf. Fig. 7a, b and c).

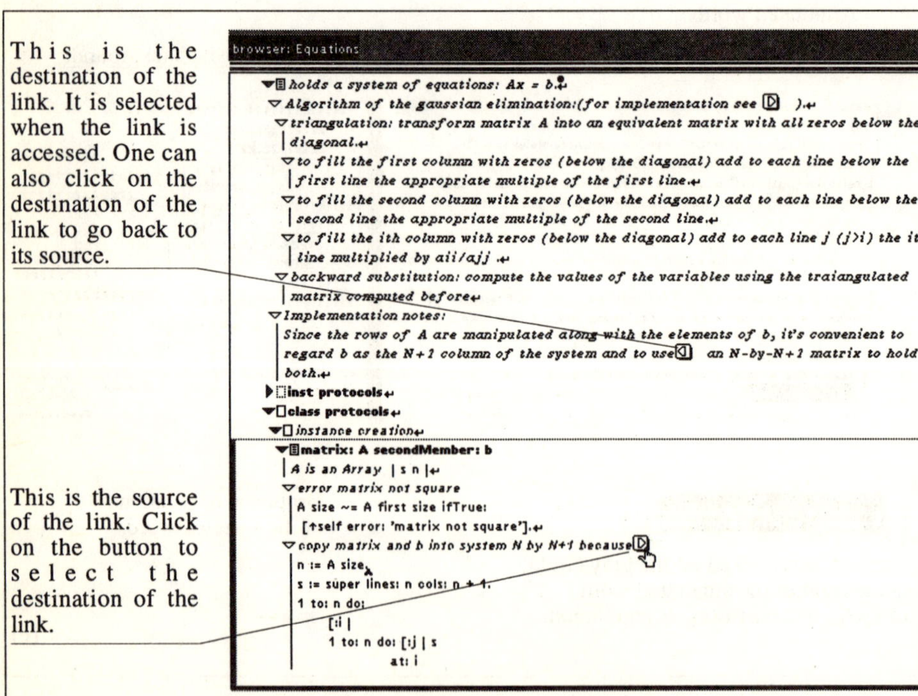

Fig. 8. Browsing buttons-links.

Annotations can be used to add graphical explanations to the code or to link graphical documentation with text. Graphical annotations are extremely useful to help understanding programs. Dynamic composition of annotations renders them even more powerful (see Fig. 5 and 7a, b, c for examples of annotations).

Button-links are used to link together two pieces of text or two pictures. They can be used to handle the connections between components of the software, for example, to connect the code of the methods with their corresponding informal specification in the classes documentation or to connect two pieces of code which are semantically but not physically connected. Button links can be used in the graphical editor to draw road maps or architectural diagrams of the software.
The source of the link is represented as a small button and the destination of the link is accessed by clicking on the button (cf. Fig. 8).
To avoid unnecessary opening of windows, the editor searches for the destination of the link first in the window containing the source link, then in the other opened windows and as a last resort, it spawns a new window to show the destination of the link.

Text Layers. Often Programmers add to their program pieces of text or code which are not involved in the computation. This text or code can be debugging statements, statements to display an animation of the program or to print values of expressions, or merely comments explaining the purpose of some statements. They are all intended to help understanding the program's operations and are usually deleted afterwards, only to be needed six months later.
To handle this issue, we have introduced *text layers*. To affect a layer to a piece of text

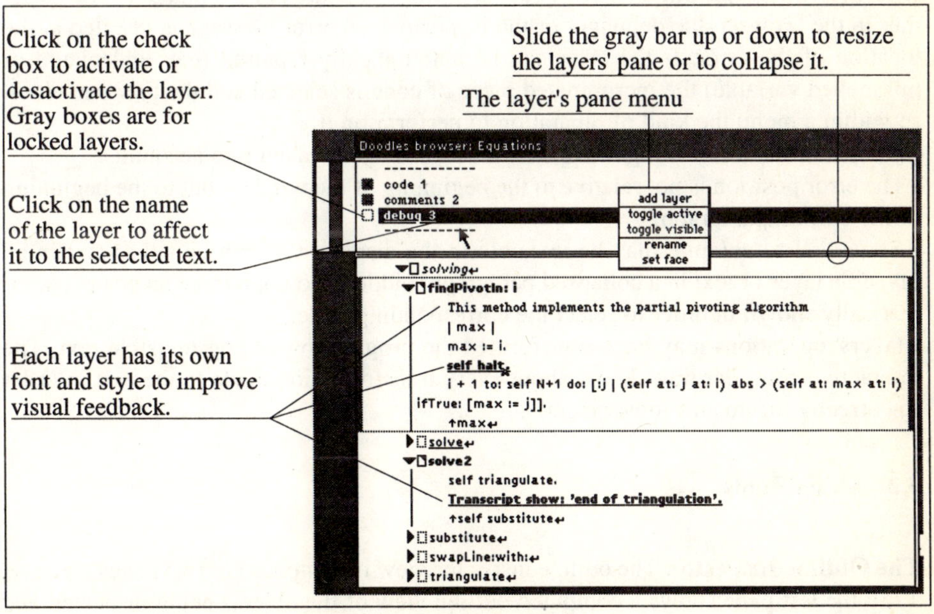

Fig. 9. Text layers.

one first selects the text to alter and then chooses a layer in the layers menu (cf. Fig. 9). Each layer has its own font to recognize it and can be made visible or invisible (this is useful to mask cluttering layers). In addition, each layer has an operation associated to it and a number of flags to interactively parametrize this operation. For example, a debugging layer has an activity flag. When it is inactive, all the statements that are included in the debugging layer are not executed. Thus, debugging statements are virtually added or deleted with the click of a mouse (cf. Fig.9) and without recompilation.
The operation associated to a layer is invoked before the compilation: this operation takes some text and transforms it into another text. For example, the comments layer merely encloses the text into quotes (this way, comments do not need to be enclosed in quotes if they are in the comments layers). An activable layer transforms the code into: (Layer code: N) isActive ifTrue:[CODE], where N is the unique identifier of the layer and CODE the initial code.

Coping with Disorientation. A common problem with hypermedia systems is what Conklin calls *disorientation* [4, pp.38]. Since there is a lot of information displayed in a window, the user is likely to feel *lost in space.*
To cope with this problem, we have included the standard browser pane at the top of the window and are currently experimenting with a mechanism for memorizing previously accessed links.
The browser pane operates exactly as in the standard Smalltalk browser and is synchronised with the outline editor (cf. Fig. 10 a, b and c). Furthermore, it does not have the limitation of the standard browser described in Fig. 2 (compare it with Fig. 11).

Interactive Compiling. If an error occurs during evaluation of a Smalltalk code (whether in the browser, the debugger or the inspector), an error message is inserted at the location of the error. If the error can be automatically repaired (e.g. undeclared or misspelled variable) the incriminated piece of code is selected and the user can choose within a menu the kind of reparation to perform on it.
In our browser, a few things have changed and must be taken into account:
- The error position is not relative to the beginning of the window but to the beginning of the current paragraph.
- Some text to compile may be invisible in the display: this can be either text in an invisible layer or text in a collapsed paragraph: hidden text containing an error is automatically shown in order to select the corresponding code.
- layers' operations may have transformed the program by adding invisible text. The interactive compiler must know about every transformation made to the text in order to correctly locate and show errors.

3.3 Other Tools

The Outline Inspector. The outline inspector view is composed of two panes (see Fig. 12a): the left pane shows a computed outline view of the objects being inspected and the right view a computed graphical representation of these objects. These representa-

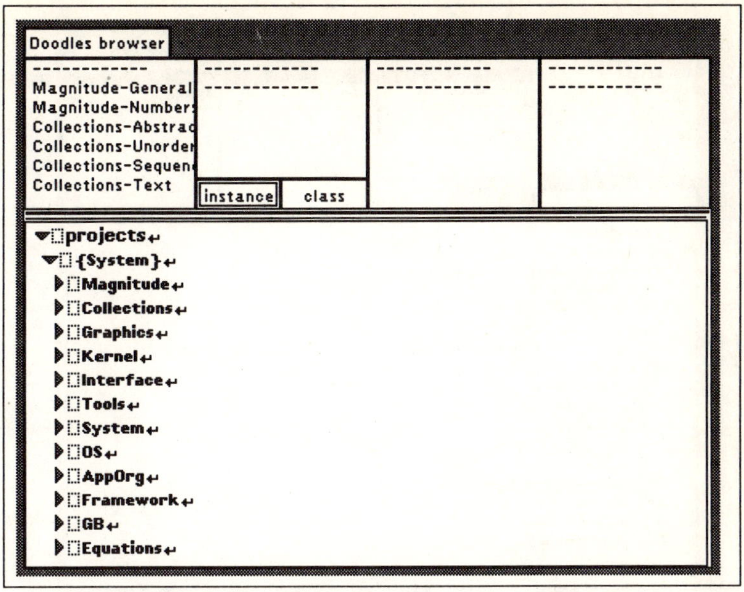

(a)

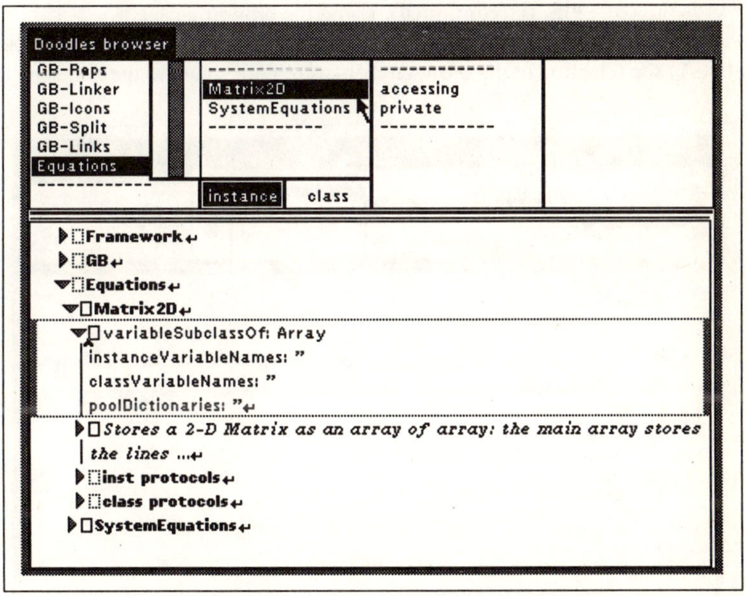

(b)

Fig. 10. Using the browsing pane.
(a) At start-up, the outline pane shows an outline of the whole class library.
(b) If the users makes a selection in the browser pane (for example, if he selects the class Matrix2D), nested outline paragraphs are automatically opened until the paragraph defining the class appears.

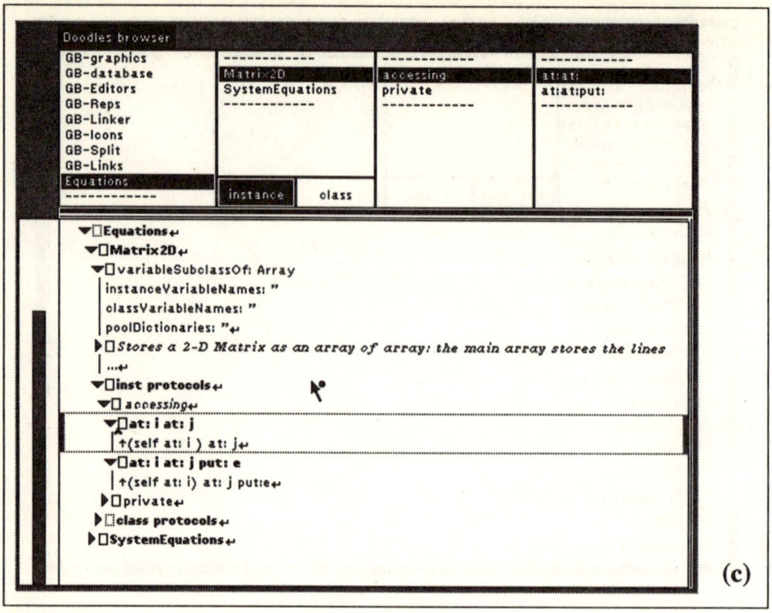

Fig. 10 (continued). Using the browsing pane.
(c) Inversely, if the user manually opens paragraphs in the outline editor (here, the method at:at:) , the selection in the browser changes to correspond to the text selection.

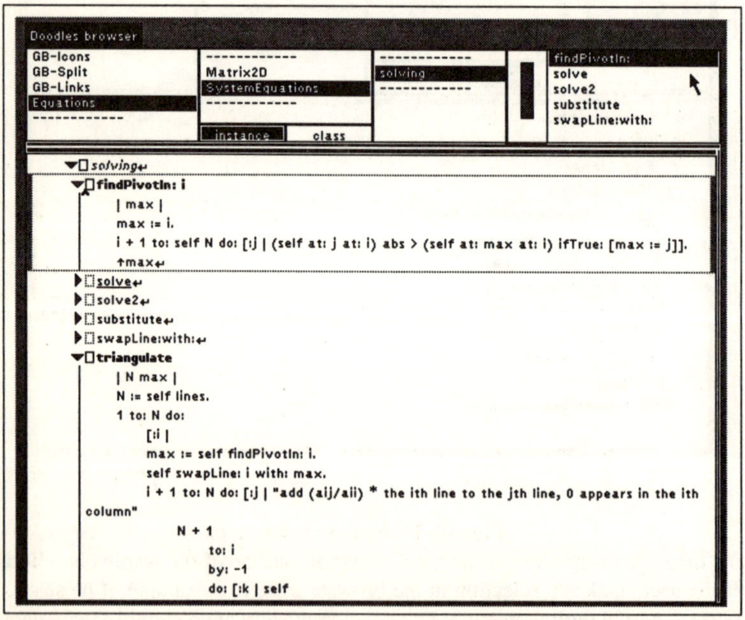

Fig. 11. Multiple browsing. This Figure is the counterpart of Fig. 2. If the user selects the method findPivotIn: while the method triangulate is opened, the paragraph corresponding to the newly selected method is opened, leaving the previous paragraph untouched.

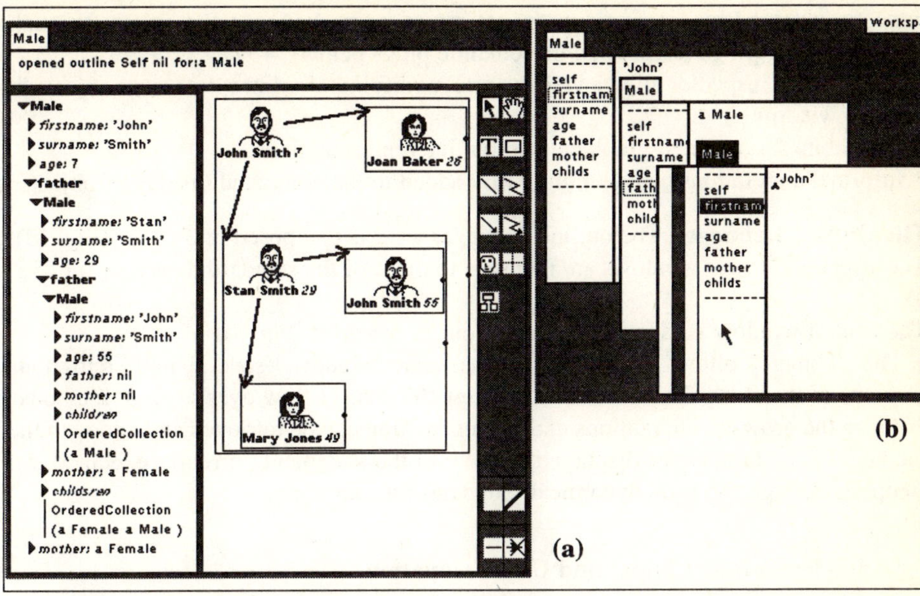

Fig. 12 a and b. Comparing the inspectors. These Figures show how a specific inspecting problem can be addressed by each version of the inspector: We would like to check if a child and his grandfather share the same first name 'John'.
The outline inspector (at the left side) handles the inspection with a single window. Moreover, it shows all the 3 persons' data both as an outline and as a (computed) diagram. The old inspector (at the right side) needs 3 overlapping windows which show only 2 informations and the underlying structure disappears once the windows are moved.

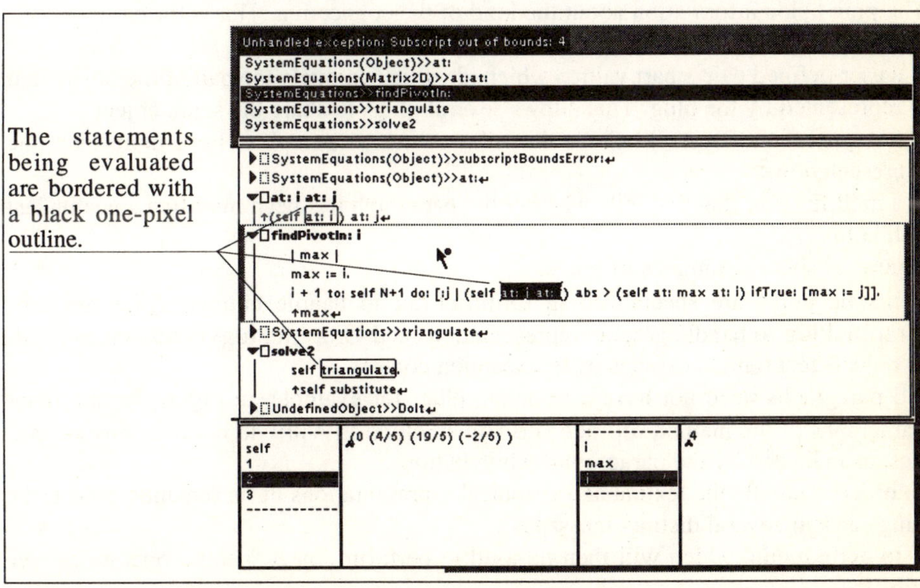

Fig.13. the outline debugger - this Figure and Figure 4 handle the same debugging issue.

tions are obtained by sending appropriate messages to the inspected objects through their semantics plugs (cf. section on semantic plugs below).
◊ The ChyPro inspector allows viewing and modifying of arbitrarily nested objects in a single window.
◊ It combines computed graphical and outline representations.
◊ Informal annotations can be temporarily added to the computed display of objects.

The Outline Debugger. The outline debugger view is composed of 3 panes (Fig. 13): The upper and lower windows are identical to those of the standard debugger (cf. Fig. 4).
The central window is identical to that of our browser (cf. Fig. 5).
◊ The debugger allows to browse in the same window several non-contiguous contexts of the stack. This is useful to follow the control flow over several methods.
◊ As in the browser, annotations and documentation can be retrieved and added to the methods. Annotations are displayed relative to the statement currently executed. So stepping through the code dynamically updates the annotations.

3.4 Implementation Issues and User Evaluation

Semantic Plugs. In the standard browser, the code view holds a computed textual representation of some Smalltalk object, depending on the selection in the browser's lists. In our browser, each paragraph in the outline view is equivalent to the standard browser's code view. Thus, each paragraph must be connected to the object it represents. To implement this connection, we use an intermediate object called a semantic plug : the plug is said to be the semantic of the paragraph.
The plug holds information about the kind of the connection. This information is:
◊ a pointer to a Smalltalk object.
◊ a user-defined pair <part,value> which identifies uniquely the part of the object that is represented by the plug. This allows several plugs to share the same object.
◊ the type of the representation : this allows each paragraph to have more than one representation.
◊ a modification flag that tells whether the paragraph has been modified since its last validation.
Figure 14 shows examples of plugs.
Semantic plugs are specialized in OutlinePlug to handle outline representations, GraphicPlug to handle graphic representations and GraphicPlugWithStack to handle objects receiving messages in an execution context.
All paragraphs need not have a semantic plug: for example, in Figure 7a, the inner paragraphs of the method replaceAndAdjustSelectionWith: do not have any semantics, as indicated by the paragraphs' white buttons.
In order to handle the textual and graphical representations of its semantic object, the plug sends it several distinct messages
◊ to get a menu, which will then be used to perform object specific operations (see Fig. 15).

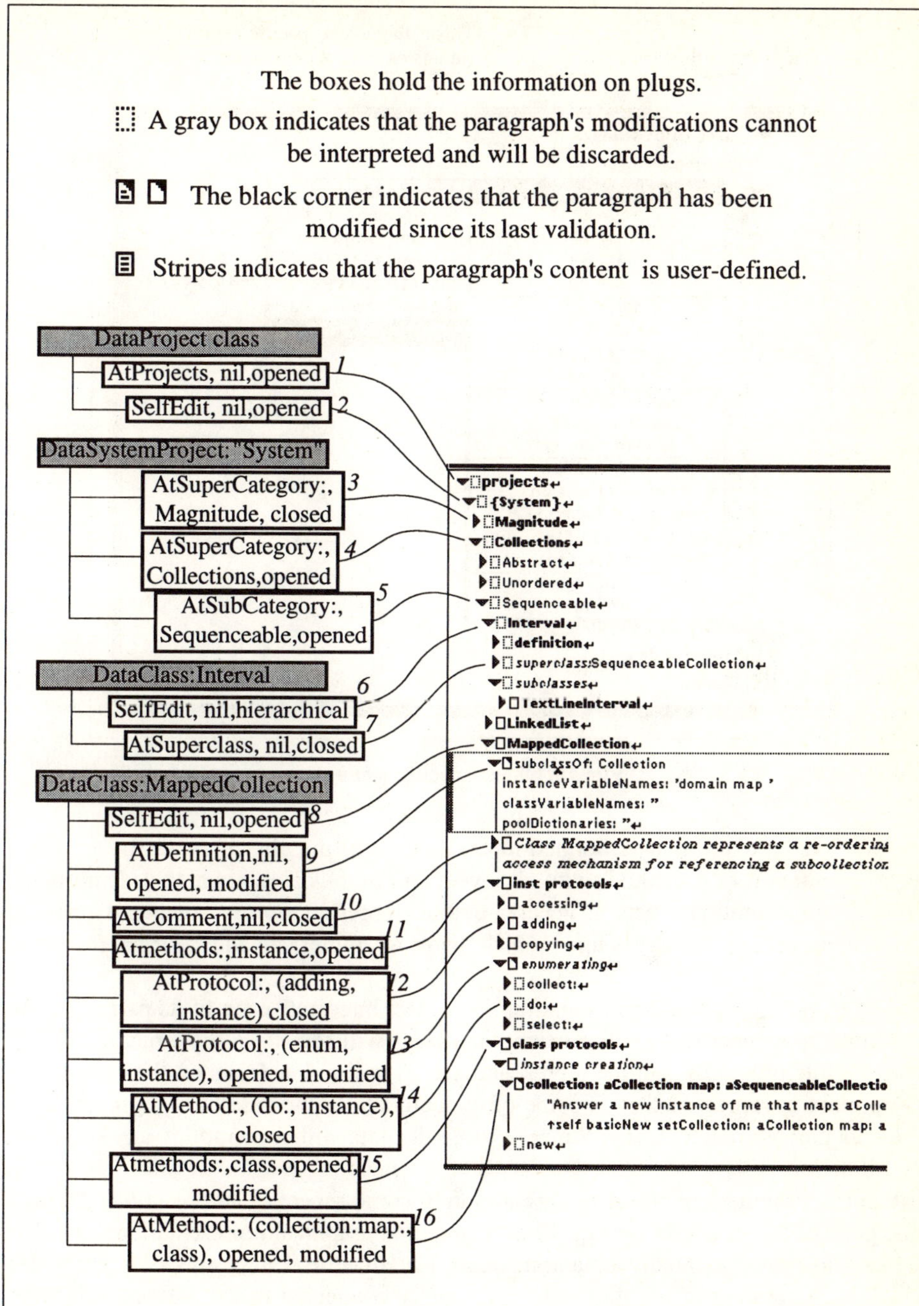

Fig. 14. Plugs and outline mapping. The plugs are in numbered white boxes and the semantic objects are in gray boxes. Each plug is represented by a triplet <part, value, type>. Unlike Smalltalk's standard browser, instance and class methods are plugged to the same object. Thus, we identify a method by an array #(message classOrInstance).

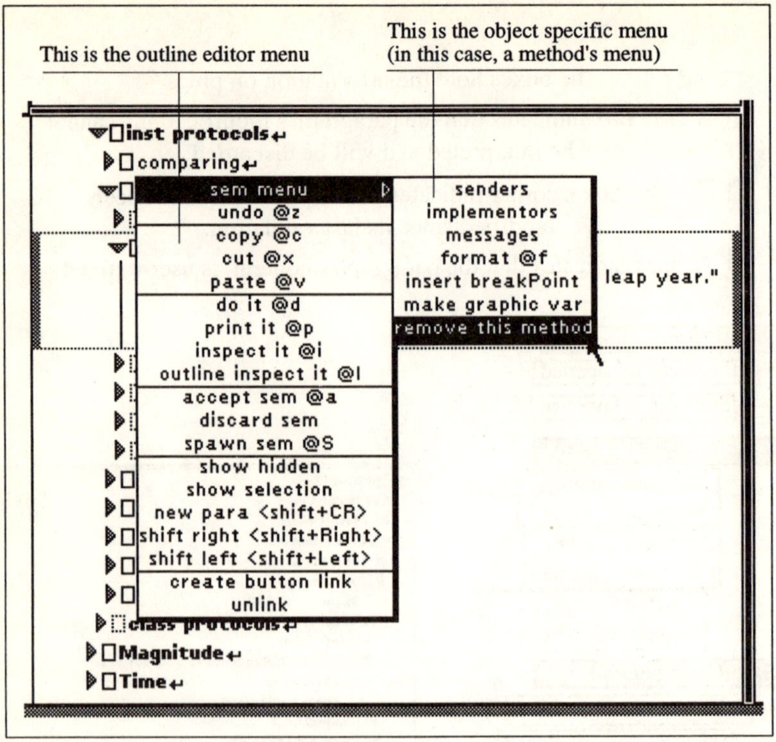

Fig. 15. Object specific menus.

◊ to retrieve an external user-defined representation of the object (typically, an outline representation of a method, with all layers and graphical annotations). If no user-defined representation exists, a generic outline representation is computed instead, which then serves as a canvas upon which the programmer can add informal information.

◊ to interpret the outline representation : an object interprets each of its partial representations in a specific way. For example, a class will focus on the structural information of its protocols outline representations. It will rather focus on the code when interpreting a representation of some of its methods. In the case of a representation of its documentation, a class will merely store the data without tempting any semantic interpretation.

◊ to get a computed graphical representation of some aspect of an object (cf. the graphic pane of the inspector on Fig. 12a). Computed graphical representations can also be used to draw (manually or automatically) architectural diagrams of a software, which each element of the diagram semantically connected to the software object it represents.

◊ we intend to add other messages to handle direct manipulations of graphical objects (i.e. click, move, delete, drag-and-drop and so on), or even semantic interpretation of graphical diagrams.

The messages to be sent, called *representation handling messages,* are computed depending on the plug's type and the operation to perform. For example, The plug #16 <AtMethod:, (collection:map:, class), opened> on Figure 14 will send to the DataClass MappedCollection the message openedOutlineAtMethod:#(#collection:map: #class) In: requestor to get the outline representation of the method, the message openedMenuAtMethod:#(#collection:map: #class) to get the semantic menu, the message accept: someRep openedOutlineAtMethod:#(#collection:map: #class) In: requestor to interpret the representation, or the message openedGraphicAtMethod: #(#collection:map: #class) In: requestor At: aPoint to get a graphical representation of the method.

Chypro's Architecture. ChyPro classes (see Fig. 16) can be grouped in two categories: hypermedia and programming.
The hypermedia classes implement the graphics and outline data structures, the user interface, the links and annotations and the semantic plugs. The graphical and textual classes are symmetrical with respect to the central class LinkerAbstract and its specializations. This class coordinates the outline and the graphic editors and serves as a mediator between the editors, the plugs and the programming environment.
The programming classes implement the representation handling messages for classes, projects, basic Smalltalk classes and object specific methods. Representation handling messages also handle the external storage of outlines and graphics using Smalltalk's 2.5 Binary Object Streaming Service (BOSS) [1].

User Evaluation. The ChyPro tools have an acceptable response time, not much slower than the standard tools on a 68040-based computer.
We have tested it with experienced Smalltalk programmers, so that they can compare the new tools with the standard ones:
• The interface seems confusing at first, but after the user gets adaptated to it, the simultaneous browsing capabilities appear very useful for creating new classes and methods.
• Although adding annotations is quite exciting, users should avoid to graphically annotate every piece of code and restrict annotations to complex methods.
• Text layers are helpful for debugging and exploring implementation alternatives. We are trying to extend text layers to handle versioning.
• Although the debugger updates its display incrementally, it is still slower than the Smalltak debugger on step-by-step execution. We are currently working on a combined debugging, inspection and animation tool with powerful tracing and animation capabilities that should reduce the need for stepping through a program.

[8] The current implementation takes 500k of code and about 75 classes (plus 500k of hypermedia data).

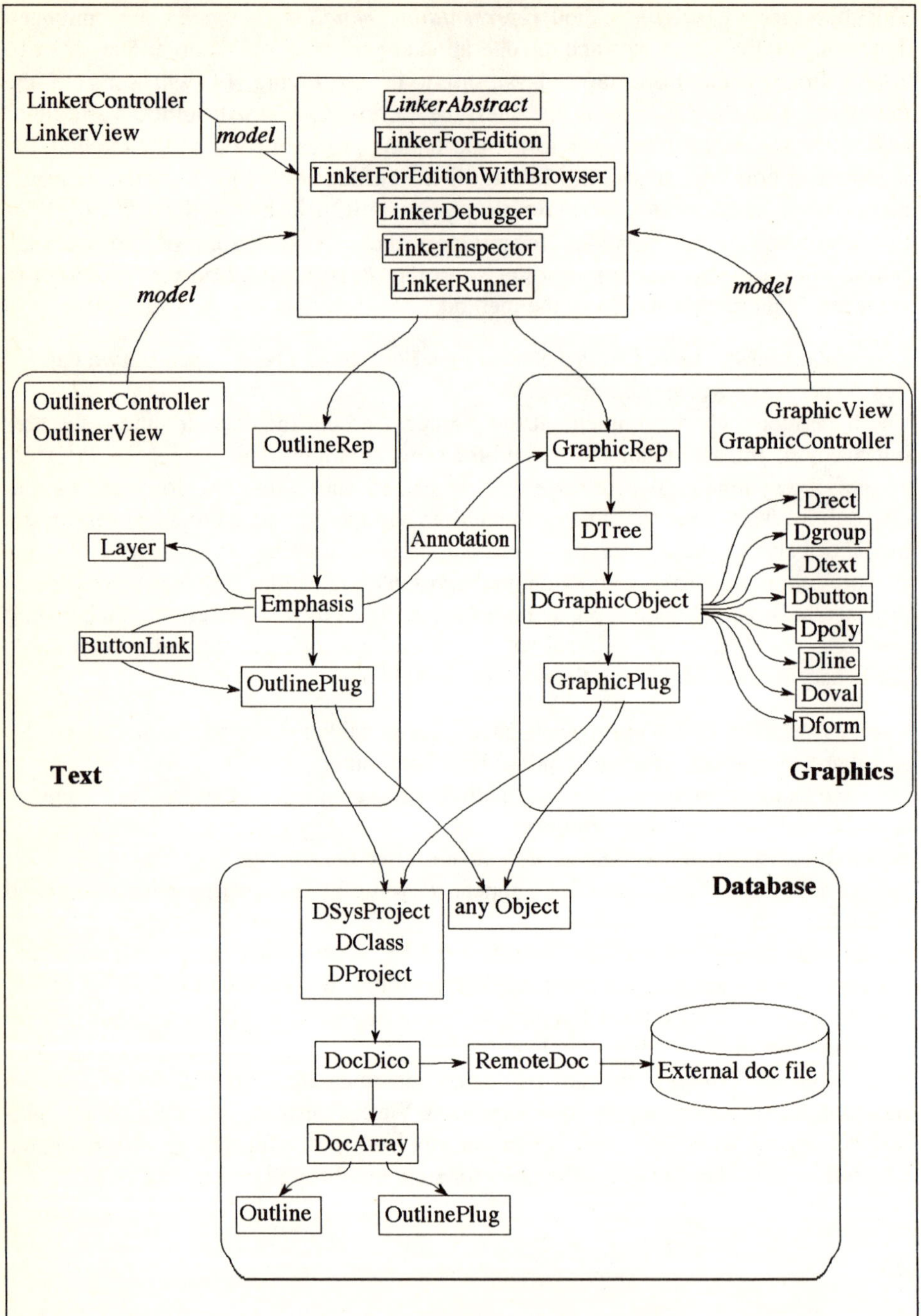

Fig. 16. The ChyPro classes organization. Several classes in the same box are alternatives depending on the tools and the context. Find the symmetry of graphical and outline classes.

4 Conclusion and Perspectives

We have shown how hypermedia techniques can be used to improve the Smalltalk programming environment. Yet, a few important issues remain open :
◊ We started writing ChyPro with Smalltalk-80, release 2.3. We then switched to Smalltalk 2.5 to use the Binary Object Streaming Service. We will soon switch to VisualWorks. Thus we will have to rewrite all the user interface, which represents about half of the code's size.
◊ We have designed ChyPro so that it can handle large scale software. So far, we have used it to write in their entirety small but relevant programs such as the Gaussian elimination. We have also used it to manage several complex issues in the design of a big program such as ChyPro itself[8]. We intend now to experiment it with other experienced programmers in their daily work.
◊ As the power of computers grows, new programming systems using complex techniques such as 3D graphics [9] have appeared. Programming systems based on visual displays and interaction and perhaps virtual reality will certainly manage to break Winograd's *barrier of complexity* [14]. Although virtues of pictorial representations are incontestable, we believe that verbal expression is a necessary part of human reasoning in such complex problems as mathematics, engineering and programming. We believe with Georg Raeder [11] that the programming systems of the future will use appropriate combinations of textual and pictorial representations to handle software. Our proposal for a new Smalltalk environment is a first step in this direction.

References

1. D. Bay & al. : Smalltalk 80 version 2.5, Reference Guide and Advanced User's Guide. Parcplace 1989.
2. S.C. Bilow : Object Explorer for Visualworks. Journal of Object Oriented Programming, Vol. 7, #3, June 1994.
3. H.D. Böcker, J. Herczeg : Browsing Through Program Execution. In: D. Diaper & al. (Eds.) : Proceedings of Interact'90. Elsevier Science Publishing 1990.
4. J. Conklin : Hypertext, an Introductory and Survey. I.E.E.E. Computer, September 1987.
5. A. Goldberg : Smalltalk-80, the Interactive Programming Environment. Addison Wesley, 1984.
6. P. Krief : M.P.V.C, un Système Interactif de Construction d'Environnements de Prototypage de Multiples Outils d'Interprétation de Modèles de Représentation. Technical Report, Université Paris 8, 1990.
7. W.R. Lalonde, J.R. Pugh : Inside Smalltalk vol. I. Prentice-Hall, 1990.
8. W.R. Lalonde, J.R. Pugh : Inside Smalltalk vol. II, Prentice-Hall, 1991.

9. H. Lieberman : a Three-Dimensionnal Representation for Program Execution. In: New Paradigms for Software Development , IEEE Computer Society, 1986.

10. J. Nanard : la Manipultation Directe en Interface Homme-Machine. Université de Montpellier II, Doctorate Thesis, December 1990.

11. G. Raeder : A Survey of Current Graphical Programming Techniques. IEEE Computer, August 85.

12. B. Schneiderman : Designing the User Interface. Addison-Wesley 1992

13. R. Sedgewick : Algorithms. Addison-Wesley, 1984.

14. T. Winograd : Breaking the Complexity Barrier (Again). In D.R. Barstow & al. (Eds) : Interactive Programming Environments. McGraw-Hill 1984.

Author Index

Lecture Notes in Computer Science

For information about Vols. 1–886

please contact your bookseller or Springer-Verlag

Vol. 887: M. Toussaint (Ed.), Ada in Europe. Proceedings, 1994. XII, 521 pages. 1994.

Vol. 888: S. A. Andersson (Ed.), Analysis of Dynamical and Cognitive Systems. Proceedings, 1993. VII, 260 pages. 1995.

Vol. 889: H. P. Lubich, Towards a CSCW Framework for Scientific Cooperation in Europe. X, 268 pages. 1995.

Vol. 890: M. J. Wooldridge, N. R. Jennings (Eds.), Intelligent Agents. Proceedings, 1994. VIII, 407 pages. 1995. (Subseries LNAI).

Vol. 891: C. Lewerentz, T. Lindner (Eds.), Formal Development of Reactive Systems. XI, 394 pages. 1995.

Vol. 892: K. Pingali, U. Banerjee, D. Gelernter, A. Nicolau, D. Padua (Eds.), Languages and Compilers for Parallel Computing. Proceedings, 1994. XI, 496 pages. 1995.

Vol. 893: G. Gottlob, M. Y. Vardi (Eds.), Database Theory – ICDT '95. Proceedings, 1995. XI, 454 pages. 1995.

Vol. 894: R. Tamassia, I. G. Tollis (Eds.), Graph Drawing. Proceedings, 1994. X, 471 pages. 1995.

Vol. 895: R. L. Ibrahim (Ed.), Software Engineering Education. Proceedings, 1995. XII, 449 pages. 1995.

Vol. 896: R. N. Taylor, J. Coutaz (Eds.), Software Engineering and Human-Computer Interaction. Proceedings, 1994. X, 281 pages. 1995.

Vol. 897: M. Fisher, R. Owens (Eds.), Executable Modal and Temporal Logics. Proceedings, 1993. VII, 180 pages. 1995. (Subseries LNAI).

Vol. 898: P. Steffens (Ed.), Machine Translation and the Lexicon. Proceedings, 1993. X, 251 pages. 1995. (Subseries LNAI).

Vol. 899: W. Banzhaf, F. H. Eeckman (Eds.), Evolution and Biocomputation. VII, 277 pages. 1995.

Vol. 900: E. W. Mayr, C. Puech (Eds.), STACS 95. Proceedings, 1995. XIII, 654 pages. 1995.

Vol. 901: R. Kumar, T. Kropf (Eds.), Theorem Provers in Circuit Design. Proceedings, 1994. VIII, 303 pages. 1995.

Vol. 902: M. Dezani-Ciancaglini, G. Plotkin (Eds.), Typed Lambda Calculi and Applications. Proceedings, 1995. VIII, 443 pages. 1995.

Vol. 903: E. W. Mayr, G. Schmidt, G. Tinhofer (Eds.), Graph-Theoretic Concepts in Computer Science. Proceedings, 1994. IX, 414 pages. 1995.

Vol. 904: P. Vitányi (Ed.), Computational Learning Theory. EuroCOLT'95. Proceedings, 1995. XVII, 415 pages. 1995. (Subseries LNAI).

Vol. 905: N. Ayache (Ed.), Computer Vision, Virtual Reality and Robotics in Medicine. Proceedings, 1995. XIV,

Vol. 906: E. Astesiano, G. Reggio, A. Tarlecki (Eds.), Recent Trends in Data Type Specification. Proceedings, 1995. VIII, 523 pages. 1995.

Vol. 907: T. Ito, A. Yonezawa (Eds.), Theory and Practice of Parallel Programming. Proceedings, 1995. VIII, 485 pages. 1995.

Vol. 908: J. R. Rao Extensions of the UNITY Methodology: Compositionality, Fairness and Probability in Parallelism. XI, 178 pages. 1995.

Vol. 909: H. Comon, J.-P. Jouannaud (Eds.), Term Rewriting. Proceedings, 1993. VIII, 221 pages. 1995.

Vol. 910: A. Podelski (Ed.), Constraint Programming: Basics and Trends. Proceedings, 1995. XI, 315 pages. 1995.

Vol. 911: R. Baeza-Yates, E. Goles, P. V. Poblete (Eds.), LATIN '95: Theoretical Informatics. Proceedings, 1995. IX, 525 pages. 1995.

Vol. 912: N. Lavrac, S. Wrobel (Eds.), Machine Learning: ECML – 95. Proceedings, 1995. XI, 370 pages. 1995. (Subseries LNAI).

Vol. 913: W. Schäfer (Ed.), Software Process Technology. Proceedings, 1995. IX, 261 pages. 1995.

Vol. 914: J. Hsiang (Ed.), Rewriting Techniques and Applications. Proceedings, 1995. XII, 473 pages. 1995.

Vol. 915: P. D. Mosses, M. Nielsen, M. I. Schwartzbach (Eds.), TAPSOFT '95: Theory and Practice of Software Development. Proceedings, 1995. XV, 810 pages. 1995.

Vol. 916: N. R. Adam, B. K. Bhargava, Y. Yesha (Eds.), Digital Libraries. Proceedings, 1994. XIII, 321 pages. 1995.

Vol. 917: J. Pieprzyk, R. Safavi-Naini (Eds.), Advances in Cryptology - ASIACRYPT '94. Proceedings, 1994. XII, 431 pages. 1995.

Vol. 918: P. Baumgartner, R. Hähnle, J. Posegga (Eds.), Theorem Proving with Analytic Tableaux and Related Methods. Proceedings, 1995. X, 352 pages. 1995. (Subseries LNAI).

Vol. 919: B. Hertzberger, G. Serazzi (Eds.), High-Performance Computing and Networking. Proceedings, 1995. XXIV, 957 pages. 1995.

Vol. 920: E. Balas, J. Clausen (Eds.), Integer Programming and Combinatorial Optimization. Proceedings, 1995. IX, 436 pages. 1995.

Vol. 921: L. C. Guillou, J.-J. Quisquater (Eds.), Advances in Cryptology – EUROCRYPT '95. Proceedings, 1995. XIV, 417 pages. 1995.